Contents

Part V: Skills development and lifelong learning

Part VI: Learning environments

Part VII: Supporting learners

Part VIII: Institutional strategies

Part IX: Departmental strategies

Part X: Staff development strategies

Part XI: Scholarship of teaching

Part XII: Theories of learning and teaching

Part XIII: Symposia

Preface

The 12th Improving Student Symposium, held at the Jury's Inn Hotel, Birmingham, England in September 2004, attracted over 130 delegates from over 10 different countries.

The major aim of the symposium is to provide a forum which brings together those who are primarily researchers into learning in higher education and those who are primarily practitioners concerned more pragmatically with improving their practice, but from whichever starting point, papers are only accepted if they take a sufficiently scholarly, research-based approach.

Given the UK Government's agenda of social inclusion, its commitment to widening participation in higher education, and changes in rights legislation regarding disability, race, gender, religion and belief, and sexual orientation, as well as the commercial pressure to recruit ever more international students, the title for this symposium, "Diversity and Inclusivity", was considered to be timely.

Papers which addressed these concerns were invited under the following eleven themes:

1. Course and programme design
2. Learning and teaching methods
3. Assessment
4. Skills development and lifelong learning
5. Use of C&IT
6. Learning environments
7. Supporting learners
8. Implementing and managing change and innovation
9. Institutional strategies
10. Departmental strategies
11. Staff development strategies

The symposium also included three keynote addresses, which each raised interesting and challenging questions for participants, which constantly resonated and recurred within the other sessions. In the first keynote, Christine Asmar considered questions such as: "Does it help students from minority cultures to make cultural differences 'invisible' (through notions of good teaching focusing on the similarities of learners)?" And "Do we focus too much on the needs of international students, while ignoring the diverse needs of home students from diverse backgrounds?" She also raised the issue of staff diversity and the negative experiences of minority academic staff.

Louise Archer asked some fundamental and thought-provoking questions about equality, and the significant differences between equality of opportunity, equality of outcome, and equality of participation both in terms of meaning and the subsequent implications for policy and practice. This seriously confronted the symposium with issues of politics, morality and values, which seem to feature all too rarely now in current pedagogic debate.

Mantz Yorke, in the final keynote, considered issues of retention and completion rates and raised further ethical and political questions by suggesting that tackling the 'retention problem' risks mistaking symptom for cause, and confusing the needs of the institution with the needs of the student.

All three of these keynotes are reproduced in these proceedings.

Finally, I would like to use this opportunity once again to publicly acknowledge the invaluable work of the OCSLD/ISL team – Fiona Smith, Roy Grant, and Marje Bolton – in making the Symposium a success, and Elizabeth Lovegrove for the final production of these proceedings.

Chris Rust

Oxford Centre for Staff and Learning Development, Oxford Brookes University

July, 2005

Cultural difference in western universities: intercultural and internationalised responses to a changing world

Christine Asmar

University of Sydney

[Please note that in this keynote address I attempted to model a largely interactive approach, so that this 'paper' is not a formal one. Much of the substance of the presentation will be found in a forthcoming article to be published in *Studies in Higher Education* (in press) under the title of 'Internationalising Students: Reassessing diasporic and local student difference'.]

Thank you for inviting me to speak to you here in Birmingham. I know other speakers will be addressing issues of access and equity, so some of the other questions I hope to raise today are:

- Once we get access and equity right, what comes next in terms of actually integrating our new groups of students into the academic community?

- Do we consider the situation of *staff* who are associated with difference?

- Are we giving as much attention to our local students from diverse backgrounds as we are to the international students upon whose course fees many institutions have come to depend?

- Finally, what are we doing to prepare our students – from whatever background – to take their place in a globalised and multicultural world?

I would like to suggest today that institutions may need a more holistic approach to difference, involving not just support services and facilities for students but changes to curriculum. Should indigenous knowledges, for example, be informing the curriculum in 'mainstream' disciplines such as environmental studies and human geography?

We also need a demonstrated commitment from senior management to consider changes to traditional campus culture. For example, should a historical commitment to secular education get in the way of universities providing Muslims with a space for their daily prayer? The whole issue of what Nash (2001) terms 'religious pluralism in the academy' is one of many new challenges for universities.

Next, I would like to extend the term 'holistic' to consider the needs of staff as well as students. For example, is it fair that indigenous staff, like other minority staff, often have to support and mentor students from their community, teach rising numbers of local and international students, be available as 'cultural consultants' for the whole university, give guest lectures at short notice, meet their obligations to their communities, and can't get promoted because their pedagogy and research remains unrecognised?

I will draw on some of my own research with two groups which are relatively new to western academia – Muslim students (both local and international), and indigenous staff. In the case of Muslims, I think it is fair to say that in the current climate they are probably associated with more deficits and stereotypes than many other groups. And indigenous staff in places like Australia, Canada and New Zealand are still chronically under-represented in the tertiary system. This is despite the fact that we know students from cultural minorities need a critical mass of academics from similar backgrounds to act as mentors and role models. In choosing these two examples I want to be clear that I am not claiming any exceptionalism for them, but I hope you will be able to draw some parallels relevant to your own contexts.

In terms of definitions, the aspects of difference I will be looking at include only linguistic, ethnic, cultural and religious aspects. Also, although I don't like the term non-English speaking background (NESB) because it defines people by what they cannot do, I may use it occasionally for the sake of brevity.

Before I go any further, let's look at exactly what we know about cultural, including religious, diversity here in the UK, in relation to the communities from which so many students now come. [Here I gave out a quiz on religious diversity in the UK]. Note that this is self-reported, so that the data relates only to how people choose to identify themselves.

What's the point of an exercise like this?

- In a conference on improving student learning we should at least *try* to model good teaching practice, so I am attempting to show that large lectures can have an element of interactivity. You might want to try a similar exercise with your own students.

- I am also attempting to be inclusive towards what I assume is a majority of UK participants here. I don't have a lot of expertise about diversity issues in the UK but I have tried to choose at least some material that I think will be relevant for you

A quiz like this provides an opportunity for both teachers and students to think critically about:

- the fact that we all hold preconceptions about the many-cultured world we live in
- whether those assumptions are justified by the facts
- what factors might be influencing those assumptions

■ whether our preconceptions might influence how we interact with others (student-student or staff-staff)

When I have done this exercise in the past with Australian and US academic audiences, people have overestimated the numbers of Muslims in their respective countries (one person suggested that Australia was 30% Muslim). Upon further reflection, they suggested that negative media coverage of Muslim issues might be one factor leading to perceptions of threat on the part of non-Muslims, especially in large cities with visible concentrations of migrant populations. Muslim students, on the other hand, also tend to overestimate their own numbers, but for quite different reasons – one American Muslim student suggested it was because 'we are optimistic'.

To return to the point I was making before, this exercise suggests that apart from the need for a more *holistic* approach to difference, we might also need a more *positive* approach to difference. Western institutions are increasingly dependent on foreign students to supplement their income. In Australia, for example:

■ 12.5% of all students in Australian tertiary institutions are now from overseas

■ This easily exceeds the OECD mean of 4.9% (Gallagher, 2002)

■ Total overseas enrolments grew by 15.5% in 2003 alone, and

■ Overseas enrolments contributed over $AU4 billion to the Australian economy (*Campus Review* 15-21 October 2003).

These trends, which are similar in many western institutions, are not always seen as good news. A tension exists between institutional needs for revenue and the fact that the arrival of those students is seen as a threat to traditional institutional values and practices. A 'leading don' at Cambridge was recently quoted as saying that foreign students are 'corrupting' UK universities. You do wonder if anyone thinks about the fact that those same students actually read our newspapers, or that the media in their home countries are also alert to such pronouncements. Outside the universities things can get even tougher. One Muslim student I interviewed in Australia reported:

> *Some people look at you as invaders, coming to take their country. Someone said to me once, 'You are not supposed to be here'. I said, 'You white people are not supposed to be here either.'*

Returning to academia, the 'soft marking' controversy – that western teachers are far more lenient to fee-paying international students than they are to local students – has been around for a while. But figures I have seen for student pass rates in certain Australian universities suggest that the reverse is also true – namely, that international students are often significantly more likely to *fail* some courses than local students are. Not surprisingly, these data are rarely made public, but are beginning to be much discussed by pro-vice-chancellors and deputy-vice-chancellors in what some of us refer to as 'hyphenated corridor'. I will return to the issue of how international and local students, respectively, may be experiencing their courses a little later.

The view that students from different cultural backgrounds are likely to either have, or to cause problems is often termed the 'deficit' approach. In Australia this approach is often applied to students known as 'Asian'. By this we mean students from East and SE Asia, not (as in the UK) students from the Indian sub-continent. The teachers of these Asian students sometimes have perceptions that these students bring with them questionable academic practices such as rote-learning, unwillingness to reference properly, and annoying habits of silence in class (presumably as opposed to annoying habits of talking in class?).

One academic from my part of the world was talking to me a while ago about the difficulty of getting students to participate in class, commenting that she had – and I quote – 'a dead patch of Asians' in the middle of her lecture. Robert Harris in his book on overseas students in the UK seems to share the deficit view when he refers to students from Pacific Rim countries 'whose educational cultures characteristically... place considerable emphasis on rote learning'.

An alternative view is suggested by John Biggs, who urges that rather than blaming the student we should probably look to the teaching. In his view, inclusive teaching is based on three propositions:

- 'Problems' are likely to lie not in the student but in the teaching
- Focus should be on similarities between students, not differences
- Needs of certain groups should be addressed in the whole teaching system, not separately

A number of important studies, many in Hong Kong and Australia, have actually demolished the validity of negative stereotypes about what some people call the 'Asian learner', 'Confucian Heritage Cultures'(CFCs), or even 'chopstick cultures' (Kember, 2000; Biggs, 1999; Chalmers & Volet, 1997) But the perceptions persist. Is this because most university teachers have little awareness of the higher education literature? And if so, does this mean that the academic developers (of whom I am one) have simply failed to get the message out there? John Biggs (1999), who has played a leading role in research which counteracts such stereotypes, has pointed out that 'deficit approaches to teaching cannot be justified empirically or in principle'. But he also notes that blaming the student remains particularly common among those teaching international students.

I now want to spend a brief minute on some other aspects of the literature relating to these issues. It is interesting that scholars writing about globalisation and internationalisation in the context of higher education rarely refer to students. They seem much more concerned with how academics experience these changes. Fazal Rizvi's important study (2000) of Malaysian students is a notable exception. Inayatullah and Gidley admit in their (2000) book on *The University in Transformation*, involving nineteen contributors, that: 'The perspective of students has only been addressed second hand by academics and this is indeed an oversight'.

On the other hand, what do we find when we turn to the phenomenographic or 'student learning' literature, which certainly *does* focus on students? Here we find that phenomenographic studies, according to a recent personal communication from Michael Prosser, 'have generally overlooked cultural difference as an issue in the variation between students'.

The lack of focus on issues of culture, including gender, has been critiqued by Webb (1997) and by Hazel et al (1997). Elizabeth Hazel and her colleagues call for the inclusion of perspectives of those 'whose relation to the world is different from that of the majority or the dominant groups'. Michael Prosser and Keith Trigwell (1999) acknowledge in *Understanding Learning and Teaching* that they do not specifically address the issue of cultural diversity in their study, but maintain that teaching with an awareness of cultural diversity is simply good teaching. Put another way, the implication is that if you teach well, cultural difference takes care of itself.

There is certainly *some* truth to this assertion. I am reminded of a study we did at the University of Sydney a couple of years ago on diversity and inclusive teaching. In our study we found an interesting disjunction between the views of staff and students. While staff tended to focus on what they perceived as linguistic and cultural barriers to the learning of their international and NESB students, the students themselves simply asked for better teaching.

But it is not so simple. Biggs has carefully analysed some of the educational issues surrounding international students. He is adamant that teaching strategies which merely 'accommodate' diversity are inadequate. He advocates, instead, teaching which focuses on the *similarities* between students, and which minimises the effects of difference. He calls this 'teaching as educating'.

Now, while this approach is certainly an improvement on deficit perspectives, it raises a much bigger question. That question is this: is it really in the overall interests of our student body to try to make difference invisible? Our graduates will, after all, go forth into a globalised and multicultural world – a fact increasingly recognised by university policies on graduate attributes such as global citizenship.

Moreover, while 'minority' students certainly reject negative stereotyping, or unwelcome 'spotlighting' in class, those students themselves do not necessarily want to be treated as if they were invisible. So yes, it is good for us to focus on student similarities rather than differences, as long as we remember that some students wish to be valued for precisely what makes them different. Muslim students in my survey made this very clear, as the following quotes illustrate:

> *We need professors in areas like social psychology, who can get discussions to include other people's perspectives. (Female, USA)*

> *I'm really sick of feeling like the lowest common denominator in this society, especially when we have so much to offer. (Female convert, Melbourne)*

So what I am suggesting here is that we need not just to avoid overt stereotyping – and to prevent it occurring in our classes – and for us not just to be accommodating and inclusive. Rather, we need to find a way for difference to become part of our core business as teachers – for the educational benefit of all our students.

For those of us who face the considerable challenge of convincing our colleagues in the disciplines that there are pedagogical benefits to diversity, there is good news. The good news is that there is some excellent research on the rationale for this, much of it from the United States. Smith & Schonfeld's (2000) overview of several hundred US studies on diversity reported that:

> *Studies on cognitive development show that critical thinking, problem-solving capacities, and cognitive complexity increase for all students exposed to diversity on the campus and in the classroom.*

Similarly, Antonio et al (2004), reporting on a study of small group discussions involving black and white US students found:

> *Generally positive effects on integrative complexity were found when the groups had racial... minority members and when members reported having racially diverse friends and classmates.*

So where I see some of these issues in relation to the literature is this:

1. The literature on globalisation and internationalisation in higher education has tended to overlook *students*

2. The literature on student learning (phenomenography) has tended to overlook *culture*

3. Those of us working on issues of cultural difference in the 'British' higher education system/tradition sometimes overlook the considerable United States literature on *diversity* and its relation to student learning (and the reverse is probably also true).

Given what I suggested earlier about the absence of the student voice, Toshie Habu's (2000) study of female Japanese students in the UK provides some thoughtful insights. She shows that students associated with difference may feel their presence is merely tolerated, rather than positively valued for their scholarly contributions. She notes that for Japanese women, globalisation provides opportunities to break free from conservative social norms at home and seek educational opportunities abroad. But she also notes a rather sad irony. The irony is that the educational advantages of cross-cultural contact between all students are reduced if international students feel they are seen merely as a source of revenue.

Echoing this view, scholars in Southeast Asia – such as Allan Luke – have called on Australian universities to 'take Asian students as intellectual resources rather than cash cows' (Luke, 2003).

So much for 'Asian' international students. I have spent some time on them because of the amount of research available on them in my region. But I want to talk a little now about Muslim students, a group of students about whom not much is known internationally, although important studies have been done here in the UK by scholars such as Anita Pickerden (2002), Julia Preece (1999) and Fauzia Ahmad (2001).

I am returning to an issue I raised at the outset, namely, whether local and international students experience their courses in the same way. Deficit models and stereotypes might suggest that international students would have more problems. Muslim students, who already carry a fairly heavy load of negative expectations, might be expected to report particularly negative experiences. However, my research showed that in many cases it is the opposite:

- ■ Muslim students as a whole are academically committed and satisfied (although less happy with services and support)

- ■ Local Muslim students are significantly less satisfied than international students, on all counts.

The reasons for this disparity may lie in the increasing numbers, confidence and articulateness of local students. In nearly every Australian and American institution where I interviewed, the Muslim students reported that their numbers were rising each year, often reflecting the growth of local Muslim communities. Local Muslims were starting to outnumber the international ones, to take over the Muslim Students Association, and to be increasingly assertive in articulating their needs to the university. The students felt that all this was positive, but that universities were sometimes slow to accommodate both their needs for facilities such as a space for prayer, and even slower in changing teaching practices towards a more inclusive curriculum.

However, these students know they are here to stay, they know their numbers are increasing, and in their view it is only a matter of time until the universities recognise the need to make changes. Those changes could include the inclusion of Islamic accounting practices into business curricula, or introducing new courses in Islamic Studies, or giving Islam a more prominent place in courses on comparative religion.

A word about 9/11. My interviews last year in the United States – which I am still analysing – suggest two things: one, that Muslim students have had and continue to have some very difficult experiences, mostly off-campus but sometimes in class. However, other developments have been positive: first, since 9/11, Muslims report a greater interest in Islam on the part of non-Muslim students and staff; and secondly, shared opposition to the war on Iraq has brought Muslims closer to other student groups such as peace activists and other religious groups with whom they now increasingly collaborate. So similarities can outweigh differences, after all.

I want to turn now to indigenous issues, which I know is a less familiar subject for many of you. Let's first establish the level of prior knowledge on this subject. [Here I gave out another quiz, on indigenous populations in Canada, Australia and New Zealand.] Are we looking here at another kind of deficit view, namely that indigenous peoples are in decline?

Again, from a pedagogical point of view, why have I chosen this particular exercise?

- In addition to the points I made earlier, and in contrast to the previous quiz, where I chose material relevant to the majority of the audience, this attempts to acknowledge and engage groups which are likely to be under-represented at a UK higher education conference – Australians, Canadians and New Zealanders;

- It also acknowledges that there may well be indigenous people here who do not fall into the category known in Canada as 'visible minority', and I want to speak to them and their issues;

- Again, I wanted to model an exercise that could be used with students. It is likely that minority students may be better able to answer such questions than their majority-culture peers, which would be empowering for them;

- The fact that the data invites international comparisons and analysis enriches opportunities for learning, and for critical thinking. We could ask students to find out, for example, whether the reasons for the increase are the same in all three countries.

I am currently doing some research with an Aboriginal colleague (Susan Page) on Aboriginal academics' roles and experiences in Australian universities. We are finding among other things that negative expectations and stereotypes in relation to indigenous people as a whole can affect both students and staff in terms of their sense of efficacy and academic confidence. This mirrors other research in relation to minorities elsewhere.

There is also some interesting work being done in the United States (Harlow, 2003) on the extra 'emotional labour' black teachers have to put into their work in the classroom because of the negative stereotypes their white students bring to that encounter. Aboriginal academics interviewed in our study (Page & Asmar, 2004) reported the same experiences. Clearly, in many parts of the western world there is still a way to go in developing an open and inclusive campus culture.

I want to make it clear that indigenous academics we have interviewed do *not* focus on their own victimhood. But they do express frustration at being blocked off from making a full contribution to the academic mission of their institutions. Here are two Aboriginal academics eloquently outlining some of the issues:

> *The development of an interface for how Aboriginal people and communities could engage with Western knowledge and make that productive, hasn't really come about. We're still stymied by the Western ontological view of the Orientalist... Orientalisation of Aboriginality continues to be what it's very much about. My students still come into my class expecting me to teach them how to make a didgeridoo and a boomerang so it's still the objectification of Aboriginality in universities.*

So we've kind of taken on the mantra that getting global is first getting local and getting local is to get in contact. How can we talk about Australian culture when you have overseas students being the high-ended earner for the university sector, wanting to come over here, not only doing an Australian degree but having meant to have an Australian experience in teaching and learning, if they haven't got any content of indigenous people here? I heard that from an international student... So it's still a white bread university system in any case.

(Please note that these two quotes are from our ongoing research project, most findings from which are still unpublished. The quotes may therefore not be reproduced)

Now I know that indigenous issues probably have limited relevance for many of you, so just before I conclude I want to return to the issue of students and staff from non-English speaking backgrounds, as this probably has greater resonance in many internationalising universities. This is a complex and multi-faceted challenge. International students may find it hard at first to manage the linguistic challenges of their new environment, and may receive negative responses both from teaching staff and from their fellow students, particularly in the context of group work.

English-speaking students may also be hostile to teaching staff for whom English is not their first language. When mainstream students' negative evaluations come to the attention of the head of department, staff members can find themselves in trouble. The solution for both NESB groups – students and staff – is often a 'remedial' one, based on an overall deficit approach – send them away to student support services or to language skills programmes to be 'fixed'.

I would like to propose to academic developers in particular that there must be a better, more inclusive way. A colleague of mine at the University of Sydney, Daniel Sze, has been working on this issue with me. We have come up with the idea that in our orientation programmes for new academic staff, we could include a session or programme called something like 'Teaching and learning across cultures'. Handled in the right way, such a programme could be as beneficial to staff with large classes of NESB students, as to NESB staff facing large classes of English-speaking students.

The emphasis would not be on the 'deficits' of either teacher or student, but rather on how to develop enhanced communication skills on both sides, including non-verbal communication, plus an enhanced awareness of what skills and understandings are required to communicate across cultures. And all of this would be linked explicitly to developing in our students the attributes desirable for a citizen of the world.

On the practical side, here are some suggested strategies for, and characteristics of a holistic approach to difference – all suggested by students I have interviewed:

General characteristics for any institution with a culturally diverse student body

(with special reference to religious considerations):

■ teachers who welcome diverse perspectives in class discussions but do not 'spotlight' individual students

■ teachers who encourage all students to engage in critical thinking about their own cultural biases and values

■ staff skilled in inclusive teaching and learning strategies to pre-empt conflict or discrimination in classrooms

■ assessment tasks where students can negotiate topics relevant to their cultural backgrounds and future careers

■ teachers who are flexible about assessment deadlines that clash with religious obligations (prayer, fasting, feast days)

■ university calendars which include non-Christian religious holidays

■ a culturally diverse staff to act as role models and mentors

Specific characteristics for an institution with Muslim students

(in addition to all the above):

■ a dedicated space for daily prayer with ablution facilities for both men and women

■ a timetable free of classes between 12 and 2 on Friday (the day of congregational prayer)

■ Halal food in the cafeteria

■ alcohol-free zones at orientation programmes and welcomes for local and international students (and for staff)

■ a chaplain or counsellor who is Muslim or has an understanding of Islam

■ interfaith events on campus where all major religions cooperate

■ scholarly courses in Arabic and Islamic Studies

■ awareness by staff of Muslim sensitivities regarding cross-gender contact (eg in partnering students for lab work)

■ strong signals by senior management that all students will be protected in the event of a crisis

Conclusion

In conclusion, I have tried to make the following points:

■ to engage with difference we need to reflect on our own assumptions and help our students to do the same

■ a holistic approach to difference involves services, curriculum and institutional culture; and it involves staff as well as students

■ a positive approach to difference rejects the deficit model in favour of valuing new knowledges

■ difference is not foreign, it is already part of us

I have tried to show that there are members of our academic community who, rather than just being treated the same as everyone else, want to be valued for what makes them different, be they Japanese students in the UK, Muslim students in the United States; or indigenous teachers in Australia. For a final reflection on internationalised and intercultural learning I bring you quotes from two exchange students enrolled in an Aboriginal Studies course in Australia:

The course has impacted significantly on my life. It has been inspiring and shocking and made me completely re-think the way I see myself and my nationality.

I view the world in a different light now, not being so ignorant about other histories to Western ones. I have also become more aware of the Native American 'problem' in the USA.

Here I think we have examples of the truly transformative power of encounters with difference.

Selected references

Ahmad, F (2001) Modern Traditions? British Muslim Women and Academic Achievement, *Gender and Education*, 13, 137-152.

Antonio, L, Chang, M, Hakuta, K, Kenny, D, Levin, S and Milem, J (2004) Effects of Racial Diversity on Complex Thinking in College Students. *Psychological Science* 15, 8 (August), 507-510.

Asmar, C (2001) A Community on Campus: Muslim students in Australian Universities, in: A. Saeed and S. Akbarzadeh (Eds) *Muslim Communities in Australia* (Kensington, UNSW Press), 138-160.

Asmar, C (in press) Internationalising Students: Reassessing diasporic and local student difference. *Studies in Higher Education*.

Asmar, C, Proude, E and Inge, L (2004) 'Unwelcome sisters'? An analysis of findings from a study of how Muslim women (and Muslim men) experience university. *Australian Journal of Education* 48,1, 47-63.

Biggs, J (1999) Teaching for Quality Learning at University (Buckingham, SRHE and Open University Press).

Chalmers, D and Volet, S (1997) Common Misconceptions about Students from South-East Asia Studying in Australia, *Higher Education Research and Development*, 16, 87-98.

Habu, T (2000) The irony of globalization: The experience of Japanese women in British higher education, *Higher Education* 39, 43-66.

Harris, R (1995) Overseas students in the United Kingdom university system, *Higher Education* 29, 77-92.

Hazel, E Conrad, L and Martin, E (1997) Exploring Gender and Phenomenography, *Higher Education Research and Development* 16, 213-226.

Inayatullah, S and Gidley, J (Eds) (2000) *The University in Transformation: Global Perspectives on the Futures of the University* (Westport, Bergin and Garvey).

Kember, D (2000) Misconceptions about the learning approaches, motivation and study practices of Asian students, *Higher Education*, 40, 99-121.

Luke, A (2003) The New Asian Education and its Implications for Australian Universities: The View from Outside. Presentation at Vice-Chancellor's Teaching and Learning Showcase of Scholarly Reflection and Inquiry. University of Sydney (6 November). http://www.itl.usyd.edu.au/showcase2003/luke_pres.pdf

Marginson, S and Considine, M (2000) *The Enterprise University: Power, Governance and Reinvention in Australia.* (Cambridge, Cambridge University Press).

Page, S and Asmar, C (2004) indigenous Academic Voices: Stories from the tertiary education frontline. *HERDSA News* 26, 1 3-15.

Pickerden, A (2002) Muslim women in higher education: new sites of lifelong learning, *International Journal of Lifelong Education* 21, 137-43.

Preece, J (1999) Families into Higher Education Project: An Awareness Raising Action Research Project with Schools and Parents. *Higher Education Quarterly* 53, 3 (July) 197-210.

Prosser, M, and Trigwell, K (1999) *Understanding learning and teaching: the experience in higher education.* (Buckingham, Open University Press).

Rizvi, F (2000) International Education and the Production of Global Imagination, in Burbules, N and Torres, C (Eds) *Globalization and Education: Critical Perspectives.* (New York, Routledge), 205-225.

Smith, D and Schonfeld, N (2000) The Benefits of Diversity: What the Research Tells Us. *About Campus* (November-December),16-23.

Diversity, inclusion and equality: revisiting critical issues for the widening participation agenda

Louise Archer

London Metropolitan University

Abstract

The terminology of 'diversity' and 'inclusion' permeates governmental approaches to higher education and the widening participation agenda. This paper interrogates some of the assumptions that underpin popular notions of 'diversity', 'inclusion' and 'equality' – critically addressing issues and implications surrounding 'diversity' in terms of both students *and* higher education institutions.

The paper begins by outlining the government's main HE agenda, as reflected in the vision of HE detailed in the 1999 and 2003 white papers and enforced through the Higher Education Bill (2004). It then moves on to challenge dominant conceptualisations of 'diversity', 'inclusion' and 'equality', reflecting upon the implications for widening participation. For example, issues are raised regarding what is meant by 'diversity' and 'inclusion' – of whom, to where and with regard to what? How do different approaches to diversity impact on widening participation policy and practice? And what might be gained by distinguishing between equality of opportunity, equality of outcome or equality of participation? Arguments are illustrated with evidence from empirical research. The paper concludes by raising questions about the likely impact and success of existing approaches and suggests potential ways forward.

Introduction

The UK government's widening participation agenda – and the target of achieving 50% participation of all 18-30 year olds by 2010 – is well known. Indeed, the goal of widening university participation is shared and reproduced across the majority of European and OECD countries (OECD 2001). In the UK (as elsewhere), this widening participation agenda has been driven forward through two key discourses, namely the economic rationale and the social inclusion agenda (Archer & Hutchings 2000; Archer 2003).

The *economic* discourse remains by far the more powerful and influential of the two discourses. This economic rationale argues that increased participation in HE is a key component within the 'knowledge economy'. The 'knowledge economy' discourse has filtered through from European policy and proposes that the development of higher level skills among greater numbers of graduates will enable and facilitate the nation state's economic global competitiveness. In addition, increased and widened participation is regarded as providing a route towards neighbourhood regeneration and increasing individuals' earning power.

In contrast, the *social inclusion* rationale justifies widening participation as a means to promote social inclusion and work towards 'the learning society' – in which all individuals will become engaged in lifelong learning to achieve their own potential through education and training. This latter discourse draws in particular on notions of widening participation as a means to promote equality and diversity within society. Socially excluded groups are 'included' via their participation in education, which the learning society discourse emphasises as a process of lifelong retraining and 'up-skilling' which increases employability and hence encourages social cohesion.

As middle class university participation rates reach saturation point and almost all young people from professional backgrounds now go on to study at university (Archer et al, 2003), the main targets of widening participation policy are the working classes and some minority ethnic groups. For example less than 13% of 18 year olds in Hackney currently progress into HE (Evening Standard, 31 August 2004). Within the economic and social rationales, these groups are positioned as an untapped pool of wasted (economic) potential and as socially disadvantaged (ie problematic) groups who need to be 'included' for the good of society.

Within policy texts, these social and economic discourses are often presented as complementary. However, as various critics have argued, they are often enacted in ways that are conflicting and contradictory. In particular I would suggest that the dominant economic rationale often invalidates or compromises the social rationale for widening participation, rendering WP more a tool for social control than social justice.

Within both the economic and the social inclusion agendas, themes of diversity, equality and inclusion are central components that are used to bolt together conflicting and contrasting motivations and interests. In this paper I therefore hope to engage in a detailed deconstruction and investigation of how these central themes are employed, deployed, subverted and reconfigured within widening participation policy and practice.

The widening participation 'net'

Whilst the topic of widening participation appears in the first instance to be predominantly an HE issue, its reach and influence extends across all sectors of educational policy. As Ainley (2003) notes, an integral aspect of the government's widening participation strategy (as espoused in the 1999 white paper), involves the creation and fostering of a 'seamless web' of interconnecting educational provision for

14-19 year olds, in order to ease and encourage their transition into post-compulsory and higher education. This 'web' is designed to act as a net, to snare those who are needed to make up the 50% target, as well as attempting to draw in, or retain, as many of the 'missing' 50% as possible.

The 14-19 web is a highly complex and multifaceted construction, comprising rafts of overlapping initiatives all aiming to raise achievement and increase post-compulsory participation. For example, young working class people are targeted by *Aim Higher* whereas minority ethnic groups are addressed by *Aiming High*. These initiatives seek to increase the target young people's levels of academic achievement and to 'raise' their aspirations. These functions are supported not only within the projects themselves but through wider policies and initiatives. Additional support and resources are provided through the Education Maintenance Allowance, the Connexions service and from numerous university, FE and community-based schemes and projects (eg summer schools, compacts, outreach work). The web/net also stretches beyond the 14-19 age range and can be traced through from Early Years (eg Sure Start) to post-retirement (eg University of the 3rd Age/Life Long Learning).

Most current government-sponsored approaches are also entrenched within assumptions of rational individualism (Ball et al,2000). WP policy focuses on the individual student or pupil and attempts to inspire or motivate them to 'want more' or make 'better choices' by providing information about HE, experiences of university and students, and making them aware of the economic benefits to be derived from gaining a degree. These 'motivational' approaches have been underpinned by changes to the financial system, including the creation of new financial incentives (eg the Education Maintenance Allowance) and the withdrawal of alternatives (eg right to claim income support), thus combining both 'carrot and stick' encouragement for poorer young people to remain in post-compulsory education. However, as will also be detailed below, this focus upon changing/luring individual learners has been accompanied by new managerial (eg Trow 1994) relations with the education sector, and the assertion of ever-greater degrees of surveillance and control over initiatives, providers and institutions through technicist forms of audit and accountability. Furthermore, as I am now going to suggest, some of the most pernicious developments have been dressed up and hidden within the value-laden language of diversity, equality and inclusion.

The rhetoric of 'diversity' within widening participation policy

The ideology of 'diversity' permeates widening participation policy. Diversity is used in three key, overlapping, ways: it is cited as a reason to engage in widening participation (to increase the diversity of students); as a desired outcome (a diverse and differentiated sector) and a means in itself through which to achieve WP (creating further differences between institutions in order to attract more diverse students). The term is used in a variety of often confused and conflicting ways, being subject to differing interpretations and meanings. And, as detailed below, these contradictory notions of diversity are applied to both institutions and students.

In terms of *institutions*, the government regards diversity within the sector as highly desirable. For example, the white paper states:

> *There is already a great deal of diversity within the sector. But it needs to be acknowledged and celebrated, with institutions both openly identifying and playing to their strengths* (2003: 1.38)

Charles Clarke goes on to outline his vision of a diverse HE sector that is differentiated in terms of HEIs' remits and funding[1]. For example, institutions will be encouraged to focus on either research, teaching or serving the local economy. Funding will also be diversified, with centralised money being targeted according to institutions' differing remits – eg research funding will not be for all, but will be concentrated in only a few 'elite' centres. Universities will also be able to charge variable fees that change across subjects within and between institutions, contributing to a variety of course costs and provision. In this way, diversity of funding is proposed as a means of addressing the HE 'funding crisis' and the need for 'sustainability' (Johnson 2004). The nature of learning and qualifications is also to be differentiated (eg the introduction of foundation degrees, e-learning) and the site of HE learning will be broadened to encompass HE learning in FE (and vice versa).

The value of institutional diversity has been justified through appeals to increasing excellence (by targeting resources and increasing competition between HEIs), meeting differential needs within the HE market (dressed up in the terminology of specialisation), and increasing 'consumer choice' (to encourage more potential applicants and to maintain/improve standards). Diversity is envisaged as to be both achieved and delivered via the market – payments (fees, top up fees, loans) are assumed to make students more engaged and demanding 'customers', which in turn should force HEIs to respond and improve. Notions of diversity are therefore integrally interwoven within a market forces discourse that promotes increased competition between institutions as a means for fostering improvement and change. Notions of diversity are also embedded within a discourse of individualisation, as 'new audiences' are assumed to require 'tailor-made' provision to meet their 'specific needs'.

Diversity is also a central tenet of the government's vision of the *student body*. The widening participation agenda is geared towards delivering students from a wider range of backgrounds, particularly those from under-represented groups such as working class groups and some minority ethnic/gender groups (notably African Caribbean men, and Pakistani and Bangladeshi men and women). As previously detailed, the value of increasing student diversity is framed through both economic and social inclusion rationales as a desirable goal. To help achieve this desired diversity among students, the

---

[1] 1999 White paper: learning to succeed; 14-19: Extending opportunities, raising standard, Green Paper 2002; DfES 2003 HE white paper 'The Future of Higher Education'

government has created the new Access Regulator (Office for Fair Access, Offa) in order to surveil, audit (and potentially reward or punish) institutions in this mission.

There are, as I would now like to discuss, a number of key *problems* within these dominant conceptualisations of 'diversity'. The language of institutional diversity glosses over inequalities and injustices by ignoring the role of power. The hierarchy of UK universities is already entrenched, as is the FE/HE divide and the use of market forces will never enable the dream of 'different but equal' institutions.

Ainley (2003)[2] outlines the new tertiary tripartism emerging as a result of the government's institutional diversity agenda, with its clear divisions in terms of power, resourcing and prestige. He relates these distinctions to the old tripartite school system of grammar schools, secondary moderns and technical colleges.

	Gold	Silver	Bronze
HE	International	National	Local
	'great research'	'outstanding teaching'	serving regional economies
FE	6thFC	Centres of Vocational Excellence	General FE
Schools	Beacon	Specialist	'bog standard' comprehensives

The association of geographical remits with types of HE provision (international; national; local) also indicates the considerable power and status inequalities that will be further reinforced by such a system. Excellence at the *gold* standard of HE provision is accorded an international importance (internationally recognised research and reputation, and international competitiveness). In other words, these universities are envisaged as playing a key role in promoting the 'knowledge economy' –developing cutting edge knowledge and research and producing a highly trained graduate workforce who will enable the nation state to compete in the global economic market. The *silver* tranch invokes a national remit in delivering 'outstanding teaching', attracting students from across the country. *Bronze*, however is distinctly immobile, tied only to the 'Learning Society' agenda (fostering social inclusion of disadvantaged groups, reskilling workers to meet the changing demands of a modern workplace). The *bronze* sector is encouraged to look only towards serving the 'local' area (for which we can read working class, poorer areas). Middle class students are, however, accorded mobility and choice at a national level. I would argue that the forms of distinction (Bourdieu 1986) enacted and proposed within these policies are geared towards the protection/defence and increase of the middle classes' privileged access to educational excellence. As Bev Skeggs (2004) argues, mobility and immobility are central to the reproduction of class inequalities: the working classes are rendered immobile and fixed to less powerful places from which

[2]Ainley's (2003) analysis draws on Mackney (2002), in the case of FE and Charles Clarke (2002) in relation to HE

they lack the resources to become mobile. The middle classes also mobilise discourses, resources and policies through which they keep the working classes fixed and tied to these positions, whilst simultaneously fostering their own mobility.

Working class non-participants whom I interviewed for the HE and Social Class study (Archer et al, 2003) also talked about the potential value of a degree for enabling mobility and offering a chance "not to be stuck" (Steve, age 24, builder) and to "move on" (Carmelle, age 16, black Caribbean FE student). However, many also recognised that for working class people like themselves, the (economic) value of a degree in the workplace is mitigated by the hierarchy of institutions – and this was cited as a potential reason *not* to participate. Whilst many recognised that participation has been widened at one level, access to the elite, 'best' universities remains closed – which *limits the 'real' choices* that working class students can exercise (Reay et al, 2001) and reduces the value of Other degrees in the graduate labour market. As one respondent in our study put it:

> *Because anyone can get into [name of university], it's an inner-city polytechnic for God's sake. Like you don't have to be academically elite to get into [University] – because that is why I'm here. Because I live locally and I am stupid, basically* (Neil, 31, white male HE student).

The government's commitment to the differential location of 'excellence' across the sector renders the local HE ('bronze') category fixed and disempowered, whilst also liberating the 'silver' and 'gold' categories from the economic and social responsibilities of engaging in widening participation within the sector. The remit of bronze-level institutions is reduced to the performance of less prestigious social/economic functions – they are not meant to compete for the money, status and power that is associated with working to a 'knowledge economy' remit. Rustin and Rex (1997) note that post-fordist education is characterised by consumer choice, mobility and risk-management. And yet the government's policies concerning the financing of students and HEIs (and the subsequent accentuation of institutional hierarchies), ensures that working class students endure higher risks with little or no choice or mobility, whereas middle class students enjoy lower risks, high choice and high mobility.

Of course policy does not operate in a uniform, unchallenged manner – institutions, students and non-participants all generate multiple forms of *resistance* as well as compliance. Furthermore, the distinctions within the sector are not fixed – as recognised indeed by government ministers, who point towards 'a blurring of institutional boundaries' (Hodge, cited in Ainley 2003:393) particularly between FE and HE (and already there is provision of FE in HE and vice versa). However, I would suggest that the discourse of distinctions within the sector will further encourage institutions to resist, challenge and defend access to the 'best' gradings and positions.

In relation to the issue of increasing student diversity, as Mirza (2003) insightfully notes, the framing of diversity issues within business and economic terms is theoretically and politically problematic and works against social justice goals. The 'economics of diversity' that operate at the level of widening student diversity is dependent upon the reification of diversity. Forms of social difference (such as social class and ethnicity) are dissociated from notions of inequality and injustice. For example, non-traditional identities are pathologised as the 'causes' of unequal patterns of participation and thus the solutions are assumed to reside in changing the ideas, achievement and aspirations of the 'victims'. For example the Aim Higher initiative is fundamentally concerned with raising aspirations and its website positions the prospective 'liminal' (non)participant as unsure, unconfident and directionless ("I don't know what sort of person I am really (what others think of me [or] what really matters to me"). Such approaches to diversity also rely on the essentialisation of identities, as social class, race/ethnicity and gender are all treated as simplistic, distinct and taken-for-granted categories, rather than being recognised as complex, shifting and contested, interlinking indices.

Inclusion

The notion of 'social inclusion' is prevalent within much education and higher education policy discourse, but it is predominantly used in an uncritical manner. The importance of 'inclusion' filters down from European policy discourse, especially from the rhetoric of the learning society, which positions (all forms of) education as a potential means through which the 'socially excluded' can become 'included'. Inclusion of greater numbers of people from under-represented groups into HE is thus understood to be a socially desirable goal.

But we might usefully question what we do we mean by inclusion? *Inclusion of whom, how and to what?*

The question of 'who' should be included into HE seems relatively straightforward. As noted earlier, WP policy is clearly geared towards attracting the 'under-represented' social groups such as working class and some minority ethnic learners. However, a tension arises when we consider the differentiated HE sector into which the 'socially excluded' are supposed to be 'included'. For example, some British minority ethnic groups are proportionally 'over-represented' in HE, but the majority of BME students remain clustered into lower status institutions and subject areas (Modood 1993; 2004). Similarly, when working class students become 'included', they are overwhelmingly to be found within the local/urban, less prestigious, post-1992 sector. Social hierarchies are not just mirrored, but are re/produced and maintained by academic hierarchies. If we do not question what might constitute 'real' (or 'fair') inclusion then these issues can become conveniently relegated to the responsibility (or 'mission') of non-elite universities. Indeed, the exacerbation of the hierarchy of HE institutions has provided the means through which the middle classes are able to ensure the protection of privilege within an age of increased 'inclusion'. As Giddens (1973) put it, the point is not what you study but *where* you study.

We might also usefully question what constitutes inclusion and at what point might we agree that an individual has been 'included' into HE? The 50% target concentrates on inclusion at the point of access/entry as opposed, for example, to participation or graduation rates. But 'non-traditional' entrants appear disproportionately susceptible to non-completion (House of Commons 2001; Thompson & Corver 2001) and – as I will discuss further in the next section – there is currently little equality of participation between social classes nor is there an equality of outcomes on graduation between different social groups.

Research also indicates that even when 'included' (ie participating in HE), some non-traditional students may continue to feel socially excluded from the universities that they attend. In particular, working class, female, mature and minority ethnic students can feel alienated from the dominant/mainstream academic culture which assumes the normative student to be the young, male, white, middle class independent learner (see Read et al, 2003). Indeed, many respondents in our study felt that whilst they could access HE, they felt little sense of entitlement or belonging. Furthermore, these issues of cultural and social inclusion/exclusion are not just issues for students but remain painfully pertinent for many 'included' working class and minority ethnic staff who work within the academy (see eg Mahony & Zmroczek 1997; Hey 2003). So how can enrolment figures, or even graduation rates be unproblematically equated with any comprehensive notion of social inclusion?

The social inclusion agenda seems to also rely upon the premise that inclusion is an undeniably good goal for everyone. But this assumption reflects a particular, dominant perspective – what if not everyone wants to be included? For example, I have been involved in a number of research studies working with working class young people who are not at university (and who do not plan to go to university) in which respondents voice strong resistance to the value of inclusion through HE participation (eg Archer & Yamashita 2003a, 2003b; Archer 2004). For example, in an ongoing study of young people who 'drop out' and drift away from education, 'Jordan' explains her resistance to HE participation in terms of her performance of a desirable form of working class femininity[3]:

> *I don't see that as the path for me... I like to have new Nike trainers and new Nike tops and a new Nike chain every month*

Many respondents in these studies also described the WP agenda as part of the government/universities' 'money-making schemes' which aim to put 'bums on seats' and that are consequently not in the respondents' own interests. In the Social Class and HE study, we also found that few non-participants regarded doing a degree as a way to develop higher-level skills – degrees were seen in either instrumental terms (as a kind of economic passport, a 'bit of paper' or a 'foot in the door') or as conveying a social value (eg 'to make my mum proud'). Many non-participants felt that degrees were intrinsically

---

[3]The importance of 'branding' and being able to invest in the 'right' (most desirable) symbols of femininity/youth style was incredibly important to the inner-city young people in this study- it was more than just fashion, it was tied in to a deep sense of self (some even described themselves as 'I'm a Nike person') which was also classed (indeed, some young people defined social class identities by associating them with different brands). In the case of Jordan and a number of other girls, branding was experienced as enabling a girl to perform an authentic identity, to be 'herself' ('to be me').

less valuable than 'experience' and 'common sense'. There were also instances of clear resistance to the rhetoric of personal development through learning and education:

> *[Education]'s boring. No one sits in here telling us that… it's going to be thrilling, it's going to be a buzz, it's going to be like a drug where you're going to want more and more and more. I don't get that impression at all* (Jodie, 27, unemployed white woman)

I've written with colleagues elsewhere about how we theorise and understand the reasons underpinning these forms of resistance (eg Archer & Leathwood 2003; Archer et al, 2001). But I would like to emphasise here that the views of young people like Jodie and Jordan raise important challenges to the dominant culture and assumptions of (H)E policy and practice, namely: Are they 'wrong', misguided or do they have a point? Who should change – them or the system (that has failed them to date)?

If we employ the conceptual device of a social justice utopian vision of an inclusive HE system, what would it look like? My own vision would be an un-differentiated and un-diverse sector in many respects, as it would contain no elitism and no entrenched forms of hierarchy. The market, however, cannot deliver such a vision of equality of inclusion. It offers only unequal forms of inclusion, whereby people from different backgrounds are included into unequal, different forms of HE on the basis of social privilege/disadvantage.

Equality

I suggest that one potentially useful way to think through the issues outlined is to consciously inject notions of justice and equality into the debate. In particular, it may prove fruitful to focus attention on equality issues across three key areas: equality of access, equality of participation and equality of outcomes.

Equality of access

In an ideal, socially just world everyone would have an equal chance of getting into any institution. In the real (imperfect) world, however, students approach higher education from a variety of very different, highly unequal starting positions – there is no level playing field upon which choices about HE are made. For instance, many of the African Caribbean women in our *HE and Social Class* study (Archer et al, 2003) were additionally battling against racism, unlike their white counterparts. Furthermore, the unequal distribution and possession of cultural and economic capital across social groups meant that working class students did not have the same sorts of 'choice' of university as their middle class counterparts (eg see Archer et al, 2003; Ball et al, 2002; Reay et al, 2001). Indeed, for many working class young people, HE may not constitute a 'thinkable' option or choice – it is more of a 'non-choice', something that may never enter in any real or meaningful way onto their horizons of choice (Archer & Yamashita 2003). And having decided on participation, 'choices' of institution are shaped by differential possession of cultural, economic and social capital, which are all inherently classed (Reay et al, 2001). Furthermore, students approach HE from a variety of routes and the 'choices' of many working class students are constrained by the historical (and continued) channelling of working class students into less prestigious vocational routes. These 'alternative' entry routes do not command an equal exchange value (Skeggs 2004) to A levels and hence act to channel working class learners into less prestigious educational routes and pathways (Leathwood & Hutchings 2003).

Research illustrates how patterns of inequality between social groups are being created and reinforced by educational policy, such as through the emphasis being given to league tables and the school 'choice' agenda (eg Gewirtz 2000; Ball, 1994). Broadly speaking, working class and middle class students have differential resources with which to access 'the best' schooling and hence have a different likelihood of achieving the desired qualifications for entry to the most prestigious HE spaces. Working class young people also report feeling resentful that they are steered towards lower level examinations (eg Archer et al, 2003) and can only access 'rubbish' schools (eg Reay & Lucey 2000) and 'crap' universities (Archer 2003; Archer & Hutchings 2000; Reay et al, 2001).

The risks, costs and benefits of trying to access HE are also experienced unequally between different social groups – and the question of whether HE is seen to be a 'good choice' is influenced more by a person's social location than their individual preference. As I've argued with colleagues elsewhere, the risks and costs of going to university are unequally experienced between working class and middle class groups (Archer et al, 2003; Archer & Hutchings 2000). As Beck (1991) suggests, risks adhere inversely to the class structure: 'wealth accumulates at the top, risks at the bottom... Poverty attracts an unfortunate abundance of risks. By contrast the wealthy (in income, power or education) can purchase safety and freedom from risk' (Beck 1991: 35). Additionally, I would add, risks are not only classed – they are also racialised and gendered (Archer & Francis, 2005). One implication of the abolition of grants and introduction of loans and top-up fees is that working class students will be disproportionately obliged to base their HE decisions on economic factors – they will be increasingly obliged to choose the 'best economic package' with the 'safest' rates of return (Wilkinson 2004). The 'choices' of poorer students will be constrained by even greater risks and costs and may render particular subjects, courses or institutions 'unaffordable'in social, economic or practical terms (see also Archer et al, 2003).

And yet this fundamental issue is not recognised within current educational policies – as the notion of 'choice' becomes ever more central to governmental policy. For example, Charles Clarke's 5 year plan for education centralises the principle of choice of school. HE policy has also framed the diversification of HE in terms of the benefits of increasing consumer/student 'choice'.

Equality of participation

Equality issues do not end at the point of enrolment at university. Students from different backgrounds continue to experience differential risks, costs and benefits of HE *participation* and I would suggest that currently working class students in particular do not generally experience an equal 'quality' of HE experience. The introduction of loans and fees has increased the burden of student debt, which is differentially experienced across social class. For example, evidence shows that working class students are obliged to undertake far higher amounts of term-time employment in order to support themselves because they lack the financial safety-nets of their more affluent peers (Leathwood & O'Connell 2003; Callender 2001; Callender & Kemp 2000).

The dominant academic culture of higher education is also biased towards white, middle class, male values and practices (Harding 1990; Leathwood 2001; Wolffensperger 1993) and working class students can be unequally equipped with dominant forms of cultural capital that would enable them best to play the 'academic game'. 'Non-traditional' students are also faced with a restricted set of 'choices' of institution if they want to be able to feel that they 'belong': for example, minority ethnic and mature students in the Social Class and HE study described how they chose an inner-city, post-1992 university because they did not want to be the only 'speck' (as one student, called Fela, put it) or older person in a predominantly white/young institution. In contrast, young, middle class white students will enjoy a wider choice of institutions where they will feel the potential to feel that they might 'belong' (eg Reay et al, 2001; Read et al, 2003).

From an institutional point of view, it might also be noted that not all universities participate in the HE sector in an equal manner. Just as is the case with individual students, institutions can be advantaged or disadvantaged by their differential possession of/access to economic and cultural capital. The costs of educating students are not spread evenly across the sector – WP students can be more 'expensive' and these additional costs are not currently fully met/recognised.

Equality of outcomes

The current market value of a degree is conveyed less by its grade/level than by its institution of issue or its subject of issue. Whilst the Bologna declaration aims to bring greater coherence to the value of degrees across the European HE area, the intense variability within UK HE remains striking and intractable. Indeed, our research found that the perceived risk of becoming 'overqualified' in an 'overcrowded' graduate job market constituted a common source of resistance to HE participation among many working class respondents. Respondents in our study were aware that whilst access had been widened, the elite institutions remain mostly closed for working class (and many minority ethnic) groups and this reduces the value of their degrees in the graduate labour market (Archer 2003:128). And whilst the economic value of a degree is only one potential outcome, it is a key consideration and continued unequal patterns of graduate earnings across social, ethnic and gender groups remains an important concern.

The subversion of equality

I would suggest that a note of caution also needs to be sounded when discussing equality discourses. There seem to be ever more attempts to colonise and subvert equality discourses, as encapsulated by the rhetorical cry 'But what about the middle classes?' For example, in a recent debate about the HE Bill (2004), Alan Johnson employed a backlash argument to argue against fee remission for poorer students, saying it would be 'unfair' for two different future graduates to be repaying different amounts based on their previous family incomes. This form of backlash is not new – it has been mobilised in relation to a range of struggles across various social and historical contexts, such as in relation to gender equality and race equality movements and initiatives both in the UK and abroad. It is instigated when dominant groups hijack and invert equality discourses in order to argue against practices or values that are designed to reapportion resources and/or power to underprivileged groups. The status quo is defended as 'natural' or 'right', and the attempts of less powerful groups to achieve equality is framed as 'unfairly' impacting on the rights of the dominant group.

So will government approaches 'work'?

I think that the answer to this question depends on how we are defining 'success': the 50% target is almost attained, but this goal can be met almost exclusively through the expansion of middle class participation, without relying on increasing working class levels of participation. Thus achieving the target will not necessarily widen participation nor will there necessarily become a great social revolution in terms of upsetting patterns of privilege or social disadvantage as a result. Current government policy and practice will not have any substantial impacts on social inequalities because it relies on the market – and the market does not deliver equality/social justice. New managerialist regimes cannot be employed to deliver equality outcomes in any meaningful sense because the underlying rationales are so opposed (see Davies 2003). Thus the proposal to improve HE by increasing the diversity of institutions and encouraging customer choice among students will only benefit the elite middle classes and will disadvantage working class groups.

The 'seamless web' may indeed operate as a powerful means for snaring/dragging in the 'disaffected' – but will they be *engaged*? Furlong & Cartmel (1997) warn about the creation of an army of 'reluctant recruits' to post-compulsory education and my own research reinforces this view. Policy and practice need to get away from the model of the rational individual and must start to understand the powerful psychic, cultural and emotional factors that produce resistance to education among under-represented groups. This will also require looking at how distinctions and differences are defended and maintained by more powerful groups. It is unlikely that we will achieve an 'engaged' learning society because the government does not understand why people may resist and because it is not reflexive about its own role in this process.

Furthermore, it is difficult to judge 'success' when core meanings and terms are always under erasure and constantly changing: eg shifting definitions of what constitutes access, participation and outcomes. We are also witnessing changing patterns in terms of modes of study (eg the collapse of the full-time/part-time distinction, shifting modes of study; different forms of HE delivery – in FE, abroad etc). The definition of a degree is also being challenged (eg through foundation degrees).

A question also arises regarding whether WP is sustainable – or even necessary – or whether there will there be a 'graduate glut' – such issues remain under debate. The CIHE argues that it is sustainable and necessary whereas the British Chambers of Commerce report and a recent book by Brown & Hesketh (2004) argues to the contrary. Certainly – irrespective of the 'truth' of such arguments – they are having a real effect. In our research we found that a substantial proportion of non-participants argued that they would not want to risk going to university for fear of being 'over-qualified in an over-crowded' graduate job market in which working classs and minority ethnic graduates suffer the greatest disadvantages.

As I have argued previously, social justice aims will not be achieved until proper recognition and attention is given to the role played by the elite and middle classes in the reproduction of educational inequalities. Privileged groups can be ruthless in the pursuit and maintenance of their privilege – if access to particular qualifications or institutions is widened then they will defend (and find ever new ways of keeping) particular (valued) channels as restricted for themselves (eg see Ball 2003).

I do, of course, welcome the emphasis that is now placed on widening participation in HE (and fully support it as a principle). The introduction of the language of social justice into educational policy documents is also to be welcomed. But I still feel pessimistic for achievement of social justice goals in the face of New Labour's vision of a market-based, differentiated ('diverse') HE system in which variable fees can be charged (across subjects, institutions).

Some ideas for ways forward

Focus on identities, inequalities and injustices

I would advocate shifting the focus of research and policy to address the complexity of social inequalities and *injustices*, as opposed to maintaining a depoliticised social inclusion agenda. This may necessitate reflecting on a more radical vision of the purposes and value of (higher) education: eg for personal and social transformation, as opposed to increasing employability or re-skilling.

Reframe differentiation

Differentiation is not diversity: HEIs positioning themselves to focus on 'what they do best' not only ignores differences and inequalities in status, power and resources, but also plays a role in actively maintaining and reproducing unequal distinctions within the sector.

Equitable funding

WP is a costly exercise, which deserves to be properly funded. Those institutions which take more 'non-traditional' students require substantially more funding in order to meet the needs of, and to support, such students. Additional resources would also enable such institutions to offer forms of higher education that are more comparable with the elite sector (eg smaller class sizes). WP students also need to be additionally funded in order to participate on an equal footing with their middle class counterparts. From an idealistic perspective, this funding would be derived from grants – however given that loans appear to be well entrenched, I would argue that working class students report finding the current amounts inadequate for covering their expenses.

Recognition and redistribution

There is scope for challenging the prevalence of pathologising discourses in current policy (eg notions of 'poverty of aspirations', 'the disadvantaged' etc). Instead, I would like to see a discursive shift towards talking about 'injustices' and consideration given to how a politics of redistribution might be enacted (Fraser & Honneth 2003).

Finally, my idealist vision would involve the dismantling of educational markets and programmes of investment undertaken to enable 'real' choices for all. One step towards this utopian dream would involve doing away with all forms of educational league tables. Another major step would be to challenge the policy of allowing HEIs to charge top-up fees – or, failing that, to at least ensure that caps are not removed in forthcoming years.

Whilst many of the ideas and suggestions outlined are undeniably ambitious, and could be accused of being over-idealistic, I feel that it is important to keep sight of the 'big issues' at stake. If not, we risk losing the potential for HE and WP to make any sort of positive impact on social inequalities.

Increasing the chances of student success

Mantz Yorke, Liverpool John Moores University

Abstract

The widening of participation in UK higher education has increased the pressure on institutions to find ways of increasing the chances of their students' success. Traditional indicators of institutional success include retention and completion rates. However, to tackle the 'retention problem' risks mistaking symptom for cause, and the needs of the institution for those of the student.

This paper considers retention and completion in the context of widening participation. This leads into a discussion of some theoretical and empirical resources that may help the student experience to be made optimally effective in a time of constrained resourcing of higher education. Although this paper emphasises circumstances prevailing in the UK, many of the points have transfer-value elsewhere.

The 'retention problem'

Retention and completion are issues of significance across the world, and are of particular importance where students are disadvantaged by their educational, economic and social background. This is seen particularly vividly in South Africa, where poverty makes persistence within a programme a severe challenge (Bunting 2004). A similar – if not so extreme – inference can be made from the statistics from institutions in the US (Astin and Oseguera 2002) and UK (HEFCE 2003a), in which it is clear that institutions serving disadvantaged areas have lower rates of retention and completion than those serving the comparatively advantaged.

Data from HEFCE (2003a), relating to the UK, illustrate the point. Figure 1 shows an obvious correlation between the proportion of students from socio-economic groups [SEGs] IIIm to V (loosely, working class students) and non-continuation of young entrants after one year of full-time study[1]. Table 1 shows that, in general, the 'old universities'[2] have proportionately fewer students from SEGs IIIm to V, and lower non-completion rates than the 'new universities'[3] and general colleges of higher education[4].

[1]Correlation, however, does not imply causation.

[2]These were designated as universities no later than the 1960s.

[3]mainly former polytechnics, were designated as universities in 1992.

[4]Some specialist colleges of higher education buck this trend, perhaps because of the stringency of their admissions systems.

Not shown in Table 1 is the old universities' greater tendency to enrol young entrants with relatively strong performances in the A-level examinations.

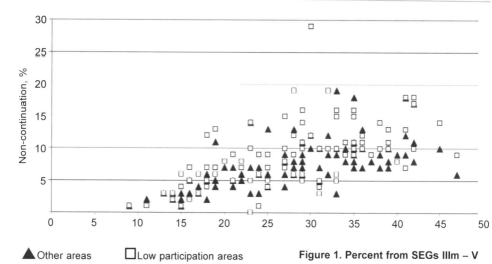

▲ Other areas   ☐ Low participation areas   **Figure 1. Percent from SEGs IIIm – V**

HEI type	Low participation areas	Other areas	% SEG IIIm-V
Old university	6.2	4.9	20.8
New university	10.6	9.3	33.9
General college	12.1	9.4	31.8

Table 1: Non-continuation of young entrants to full-time study in English higher education. Source: HEFCE (2003a)

The comparatively high levels of projected non-completion for some institutions have prompted some commentators to question the governmental aim for 50% of young people in England to have engaged in higher education by the year 2010 – in some instances, using rather intemperate language[5]. The greater the restriction on entry to higher education, the greater the risk that students of potential (but whose actual qualifications do not show this) will be excluded. Nothing is heard, though, about the 'false positives' – those who enter higher education on the basis of adequate qualifications (perhaps gained through strenuous coaching in private schools) but who subsequently find it hard to achieve in a system that expects students to work on a largely self-managed basis[6].

[5] See Yorke (2003) for an account of the treatment of the issue by the UK national press.

[6] Evidence for weak performance of entrants from private schools other than the most selective can be found in HEFCE (2003b). Unpublished work by the Student Assessment and Classification Working Group [SACWG] showed that, across a range of subjects in one new university, such students tended to underperform compared with those from other backgrounds.

In the UK, the 'retention problem' arises primarily as a result of the level of state funding for higher education. The state, reasonably enough, wants to see this funding turned to good account – not least because of the need to ensure that the workforce is equipped to serve national economic needs (NCIHE 1997; DfES 2003). From the state's perspective, non-completion appears as a waste of resources. Economics enters into institutions' calculations as well, in that they lose income from the state if their enrolled numbers decline. There is also the institution's reputation to consider – an institution with high levels of non-completion is singled out in the press for adverse comment, which could be detrimental to recruitment.

Away from the institutional balance-sheet, an institution needs to satisfy student expectations and to be perceived by employers as sending out graduates who are well equipped for the work environment. Students, in general, also seek success in employment (and, more broadly, to fulfil other personal goals) at an affordable cost. However – and particularly in a period of economic buoyancy – the gaining of a worthwhile job may be seen as more important than the completion of a programme of study. During the 'dot-com boom', a number of students studying in the field of computing were snapped up by companies before completing their studies because they had already acquired the capabilities that were needed. The more that students face debt from financing their time in higher education, the more likely it is that they will leave higher education with an interim award or set of credits: they may return in due course, but in some cases this will be after a gap that is too wide to be acknowledged in the official institutional performance measures. Weko (2004) notes a difference of perspective between the UK and the US regarding interim achievement. In the US, 'something is better than nothing' (basing the judgement on the economic return to an individual from engagement in higher education), whereas in the UK 'nothing is better than something': put another way, the US values credit accumulation, whereas in the UK an interim achievement is typically construed in terms of failure to achieve the intended qualification. If changes to student funding in the UK result in a more distributed engagement by students in higher education, the US perspective may gain greater sway.

A focus on retention and completion, then, addresses the concerns of policy makers and institutional managers more than it does those of students. The HEFCE performance indicator methodology is implicitly based on the model of the three or four year full-time programme, and therefore undervalues student success at interim phases of the programme unless they continue to completion. The HEFCE methodology copes less well with student engagement that is discontinuous than it does with that which is essentially continuous: this is likely to affect adversely the statistics of those institutions that enrol students from relatively disadvantaged backgrounds. The power of contemporary data management systems should enable the success of the partnership between student and institution to be indexed at the level of the study unit (module), thus eliminating some of the causes of discontinuation that are not attributable to institutional behaviour: this would be fairer to institutions[7].

---

[7]This approach is discussed, in the light of an empirical study, in Yorke (1999).

Institutions can influence student retention in some respects, but not others. Where they can exert influence, poor retention and continuation are quite possibly symptoms of aspects of provision that can be improved. At the institutional level, sorting out the 'retention problem' involves looking deeply into the ways in which the institution turns its commitments on paper (eg validated programme documents and publicity material) into practical action.

Why do students discontinue?

Two studies in England (Yorke 1999; Davies and Elias 2003) suggest broadly similar normative reasons for student discontinuation, though individuals naturally vary as regards the precipitating cause(s). Accident, illness, and so on influence a few students, but are not frequent enough to appear in normative statistics. The 'broad brush' picture is summarised in table 2. Davies and Elias did not ask their students specifically about the student experience, so no inference can be drawn from its absence from their findings.

For present purposes, the choice of programme and institution made by the student, financial difficulty, personal problems, and dislike of the institutional environment are merely acknowledged: more attention is given to them in Yorke and Longden (2004). From the perspective of improving student learning, the quality of the student experience and – to some extent – the academic difficulties found by students are the most germane.

Yorke (1999)	Davies and Elias (2003)
Wrong choice of field of study	Wrong choice of course
Academic difficulties	Financial problems
Financial problems	Personal problems
Poor quality of the student experience	Academic difficulties
Unhappiness with the social environment	Wrong choice of institution
Dissatisfaction with institutional provision	

Table 2 Influences on full-time and sandwich students' early departure from their programmes.

Qualitative evidence from some students indicates that the learning environment can be inimical to learning, even if the students grit their teeth and persist to the end. Seymour and Hewitt's (1997) study of some 400 students in science, engineering and mathematics, for example, raised serious questions about the treatment of some students in the US system. One of their respondents, a male student who switched out of a science programme, said:

> *I think that in sociology and the humanities, the quality of the teachers was better. They were more interested in teaching you. They seemed more interested if you*

learned something, rather than the grade you got. The biology teachers were just interested in telling you what they had learned, and you'd better learn it too.

Seymour and Hewitt (1997, p148)

The research undertaken by Yorke and colleagues in six institutions in the north-west of England showed that, as far as the student experience went, there were differences between subject areas as regards the influences on student discontinuation[8]. This more quantitative study did not, however, get to the level of detail that Seymour and Hewitt achieved, and so the explanation for the differences remains a matter of conjecture.

Theory and its limitations

There are a number of theoretical models of student discontinuation in the literature, which suggest areas of institutional provision that might be worthy of investigation by an institution seeking to improve its provision, and by extension the retention of its students. Yorke and Longden (2004), in discussing these theories and models, are somewhat sceptical about them. Rather than providing usable causal models, they see the considerable range of available theories as offering multiple lenses through which student behaviour can be understood (and even to some extent anticipated), and hence as providing pointers towards institutional actions in respect of the student experience. The theoretical and empirical resources inform professional judgement regarding the most appropriate ways of supporting student success.

The model that has demonstrated the greatest staying power is Tinto's (1993) model of student departure. Tinto flags the importance of, inter alia, academic and social integration, but the looseness with which these constructs have been treated renders problematic the cumulation of empirical evidence[9]. Braxton and Hirschy (2004) show that the evidence for social integration is stronger than that for academic integration – but it should be noted that social integration can be difficult for commuter and part-time students. Bourdieu's (1973) concept of 'cultural capital' has found adherents in recent studies in both the US and the UK, not least because those from disadvantaged backgrounds are likely to have a lower level of cultural capital than the relatively advantaged. The level of cultural capital is held to have an influence on student engagement in higher education, and this can be inferred to some extent from student comments about the extent to which they feel 'at home' in an institution or department.

The earlier modelling appeared more sociological than psychological, though in Tinto's model there is a strong thread of psychology. Bean and Eaton (2000) emphasise the significance of individual psychology for retention and discontinuation, arguing that the sociological approach exemplified by Tinto's work undervalues the extent to which the individual determines their course of action. Whilst sociological considerations probably

---

[8]The original analyses in Yorke (1999) were repeated at a more disaggregated subject level in Yorke (2000b).

[9]Tinto's model is discussed in Yorke and Longden (2004, p78ff).

weigh quite heavily in the discontinuation of some students, the most potent determinants are likely to be found in the psychological domain.

Towards student success

If an institution focuses attention on student success, the chances are that this will be reflected in statistics relating to retention and completion. Hence there is the possibility of a 'win, win, win' outcome – student successes, good institutional statistics, and a satisfied state. The task of the educator is to bend the odds in favour of student success, through programme design and implementation; through the provision of accessible support services; and so on. The ways in which educators go about their tasks affect student achievement – sometimes crucially, as is implied in the following two quotations:

> *The course was taught very loosely, the tutors were never around to help, and when they were, they were very unhelpful. They were critical of your work to the point of being rude, not constructive criticism, if your work was not the best, average, then you were ignored in favour of the best students*

> *... the way one tutor spoke to me... has put me off higher education and [I] will take a long time considering ever going back.*

> *Student reading art and design, from Yorke (1999, p18)*

> *My personal gain from the FD programme has been a major confidence boost. In the area of ITC I have discovered a self discipline and the ability to work towards a deadline and enjoy it, I did not know I had. The FD has driven me forwards, my self-esteem has expanded. My horizons expanded. My goals are being achieved. I enjoy the lectures delivered by articulate people who are expert in their field. Their encouragement fuels me.*

> *Older female student taking a part-time foundation degree in education*

Both of these quotations point to the importance of the personal dimension of learning – something whose significance may have been backgrounded in programmes that do not explicitly incorporate it (for example, it is strongly present in counselling; social work; and education). The apparent disregard of the personal may have arisen as a consequence of the curricular stress on outcomes rather than on process, and of the relatively limited contact possible between academics and students in modular schemes.

The USEM account of employability (Knight and Yorke 2004), which emphasises the alignment between employability and good learning, connects

- Understanding of the subject discipline and of broader situations
- Skilful practices in the subject discipline, employment and life in general
- Efficacy beliefs and personal qualities and

■   Metacognition

whilst making the point that personal qualities are pervasively important to learning.

Aspects of 'the personal' that are relevant to student success include the following.

■   Motivation to learn and achieve, though not necessarily if the desire to 'perform' overshadows the desire to learn[10].

■   The capacity to learn from misfortune, error and criticism.

■   Belief in the 'developability' of intelligence and other aspects of the self. Dweck (1999) points to the limiting effect of believing that aspects of the self are immutable.

■   Belief that one can, in probabilistic terms, 'make a difference' to situations. This brings together self-efficacy (Bandura 1997), 'learned optimism' (Seligman 1998), and the possession of an internal, rather than an external, locus of control (Rotter 1966).

■   The connection between emotion and cognition (Boekaerts 2003).

■   Emotional intelligence (Salovey and Mayer 1990; Goleman 1996)

■   Practical intelligence (Sternberg 1997).

Regarding the last of these, Marcel Berlins observed, with reference to the proposal by eight 'top' universities in the UK to devise an entry examination to complement A-level,

> *Very many successful lawyers… are not all that bright. Some of our best judges do not shine intellectually. Becoming a good lawyer requires a mixture of talents, of which the intelligence revealed by the proposed [university entry] tests is only one. Equally, many bright people have proved to be rubbish lawyers.*

Berlins (2004, p17)

In the quotation, Berlins directs attention towards the use of skilful practices in context, which Sternberg (1997) would see as a manifestation of practical intelligence. Indeed, one might construct a matrix relating understanding to the exercise of skilful practices in context (Figure 2). Obviously the person with a high level of understanding and capable of exercising skilful practices is likely to be successful, and equally obviously the person relatively low in both respects is unlikely to prosper. Berlins is suggesting that, in the world of law (and, by implication, other milieux), understanding not of top-notch character may be more than compensated by the ability to demonstrate skilful practice, and that a high level of understanding without skilful practice may not yield much by way of personal profit.

The last of the four USEM components, metacognition includes, inter alia, the awareness of how one tackles tasks and learns from the outcomes (reflective practice) and the

---

[10]Dweck (1999) differentiates between learning goals and 'performance goals'. The latter refer to avoiding being shown up in front of peers, or to showing up well in front of them. Pintrich (2000) showed that the latter might not be detrimental to learning.

drawing on accumulated experience for self-regulation – both capabilities that are valued highly by employers.

Whilst understanding (in the senses listed above) and skilful practices in various contexts would probably be seen by academics as a natural focus of their pedagogy, metacognition and the self-system are less likely to be seen in that light – perhaps because their significance has relatively recently entered pedagogic practice. Their importance is indicated by meta-analyses conducted by Marzano (1998) who found statistical size-effects on learning of 0.74 in respect of interventions targeted at the self-system, and of 0.72 in respect of metacognition. Most of the studies reviewed by Marzano, it has to be said, were conducted in school environments, although some applied to post-compulsory education. For this reason, Marzano's findings have to be treated as suggestive for higher education, rather than conclusive.

Understanding

		Lower	Higher
Skilful practices in context	Higher	+	++
	Lower	--	-

Figure 2

Optimising the return on pedagogy

Thomas et al (2001) investigated why a few institutions in England, which enrolled relatively large numbers of students from disadvantaged backgrounds, had been able to produce retention and completion data that were better than the benchmark levels calculated for them by the HEFCE statisticians. Whilst the institutions' natures and student characteristics varied, there was evidence that the following might have been influential in one or more instances.

- A 'friendly' and welcoming institutional climate.

- Support for students, both leading up to and during the critically important first year of study.

- An emphasis on formative assessment in the early phase of programmes.

- Disproportionation of resources in favour of the first year (in the belief that early encouragement of students to be autonomous learners would repay the investment later on).

- Paying attention to the social dimension in learning activities, not least because contemporary students were less able than those from earlier generations to partake in the social opportunities available through the institution.

- A preparedness to acknowledge that the pattern of students' engagement in higher education was changing, and to respond constructively to this in various ways.

Whilst this study focused on institutions which appeared to be particularly successful despite the demographic odds, a follow-up study (Layer et al 2002) showed that others with challenging student demographics were adopting similar practices. These practices would seem to have a still broader applicability. Emphasis is given to formative assessment, since this is of key importance to student success and because it is perhaps the area of pedagogy in the UK that stands in greatest need of improvement.

Formative assessment

Formative assessment, tautologically, is assessment that is intended to enhance – or, better, actually enhances – student achievement[11]. A central purpose is the facilitation of student autonomy. Hence the technical criteria that have to be met in summative assessment (validity, reliability, and so on) can be treated in a more relaxed manner. Validity and reliability need to be construed in terms not only of the nature of the feedback but also of the capacity of that feedback to prompt student development. Formative assessment is 'conversational' (Laurillard 2001), and 'final language' (Boud 1995) is too judgemental when student development is the primary purpose of feedback.

A range of reviews conducted in UK institutions by the Quality Assurance Agency for Higher Education point to the need for improvement in formative assessment. The following two quotations convey the essence of the reviews' findings:

> *In 49 per cent of cases, marking systems could be improved particularly in respect of feedback to students. This sometimes lacked a critical edge, gave few helpful comments and failed to indicate to students ways in which improvement could be made.*
>
> *QAA (2001, para 28: Subject overview report, Education)*
>
> *Students of about one-half of the programmes experience some variation in the quality of written formative feedback. It is not always clear to students how their assessed work could be improved. In five cases review teams highlight this as a serious problem.*
>
> *QAA (2003, para 56: Review of 33 Foundation Degrees)*

Students need to come to terms with the demands of higher education fairly quickly, if they are to succeed. Entrants from school have to learn quickly to take charge of their own learning, instead of having their studies organised for them. Those entering higher education after a break have to develop their appreciation of what studying at this level means. Students without a familial background of higher education are disadvantaged, since they have had relatively little opportunity to gain an understanding of what is involved. The consequence is that formative assessment – especially early formative assessment – is critically important, since it can point to ways of improving (say) a

---

[11]Whilst the term is commonly used in respect of academics' commenting on student performances (the aspect discussed in this paper), it should not be forgotten that formative assessment can be provided from peers, workplace mentors and others, and via computerised testing.

submitted assignment and also to ways of addressing future work: feedback and feed forward.

If formative assessment is provided relatively late in a study unit, then the student has no way of knowing whether they are on the right track – a point captured in the following:

> *I found having large blocks of work without assessment difficult – you don't know if you are grasping it or not until exam time! Assignments weekly would be better from my point of view.*
>
> *[Female in her 30s, pursuing a science-based foundation degree programme]*

Bandura (1997) sees the importance of feedback to the development of capabilities, and that this is even more important when the person may doubt their ability to succeed in higher education, as is most probable in the case of students from disadvantaged backgrounds[12]:

> *The less individuals believe in themselves, the more they need explicit, proximal, and frequent feedback of progress that provides repeated affirmations of their growing capabilities.*
>
> *Bandura (1997, p217)*

The manner in which the feedback is conveyed is also important – another point at which the connection between the cognitive and the emotional comes to the fore. Mentkowski and Associates (2000) summarise findings from research on student achievement over a quarter of a century at Alverno College in the US, where the emphasis is put on formative assessment[13]:

> *Students observed that feedback was given in such a way that they did not feel it was rejecting or discouraging... [and] that feedback procedures assisted them in forming accurate perceptions of their abilities and establishing internal standards with which to evaluate their own work.*
>
> *Mentkowski and Associates (2000, p82)*

Note the emphasis in the quotation on the development of students' metacognitive capacity, and the strong implication of the development of their autonomy as learners.

Levels of engagement

Conditions for student success can be approached at three levels within an institution[14]: the levels of

---

[12]Though some from relatively privileged backgrounds may also benefit from frequent formative feedback, even if they have yet to come to doubt their capacity to succeed (see note 6).

[13]And summative gradings are eschewed.

[14]Further disaggregation is possible, for those who wish to do this.

- the institution itself;

- the department or programme team; and

- the individual or group responsible for the teaching of a particular study unit.

They can also be subdivided with reference to operational considerations, which is the way in which the following paragraphs are organised.

Resource allocation

The allocation of resources preferentially to the first year (or level) of higher education is based on the argument that, if students are encouraged from the outset to become autonomous learners, the supervisory need will be lessened for later years. Sheffield Hallam University has adopted this approach for a number of years and, judging by completion statistics, with some success. This runs counter to much practice in higher education, where final year studies are resourced more favourably than early years through the use of smaller teaching groups and tutoring for projects and dissertations.

Academic culture

An academic culture supportive of student learning hardly needs to be asserted as a condition for student success. However, there is direct evidence (Seymour and Hewitt 1997) and indirect evidence (Yorke 1999) that the academic culture can be unsupportive of student learning. The pressures on staff to undertake research, generate income, liaise with employers and educational institutions, and contribute administratively are distractions from the support of students.

A culture of learning challenges the narrow instrumentalist approach sometimes alleged in respect of student behaviour, and helps to discourage the taking of short cuts, such as plagiarism. It also implicitly encourages metacognitive activity – in particular, self-regulation. It may be necessary to spell out to students what is implied by a culture of learning, perhaps without going as far as expecting students to sign up to a code of honour, as happens in some institutions in the US.

A culture of learning needs to be supported by other aspects of institutional functioning. Programmes that require frequent summative assessments put pressure on students, many of whom will have other life-commitments, to take the easier way of gaining the relevant credit. If the world places more weight on outcomes such as the degree classification or grade-point average than such 'measures' can bear, then again the pressure on students insidiously encourages them to prioritise the getting of grades over learning.

Academic culture is important at all three levels. The institution as a whole sets the context (in the UK, through the promulgation of an institutional learning and teaching strategy); the department or programme team gives this a disciplinary colouring; and the culture is sustained through the efforts of individual academics and teams of academics. One does not need statistical performance measures to infer the presence of a student-focused academic culture. The smiles and friendly exchanges between the head of department reading out the names at a degree ceremony and the graduands approaching the lectern can be testimony enough.

Making expectations clear

Students need to appreciate what is expected of them in higher education: this is one of the corollaries of making a commitment to an academic culture. The cramming and regurgitation not unknown in A-level studies provide a poor base for work in higher education, and this may account for some indifferent performances (including the relatively weak performance of some students who enter higher education from private schools). Many students initially do not appreciate the importance of properly citing the sources on which they draw in their work, leaving them vulnerable to charges of plagiarism. Induction – and even pre-induction in summer schools – can help to inform students of expectations.

Programme structure

Many contemporary students, particularly the less well off, need to intersperse their studies with paid employment. For some, this means that the notion of full-time attendance is unattainable, and various 'workarounds' are employed. With part-time students in the UK being disadvantaged compared to their full-time peers as regards the equity of entitlement of students to loans and grants, there is pressure to maintain the fiction of full-time study even if the student engagement does not warrant it. This does the student, the institution and the state no favours, but is a matter beyond the power of an individual institution to rectify[15].

Institutions do, however, have control over the structure of their programmes. Of particular importance is the scheduling of assessments and feedback. Modular schemes were introduced into many UK institutions in the late 1980s for two main reasons – more effective use of institutional resources and greater potential for students to gain credits from more than a single institution. Neither reason has been justified to the extent originally envisaged. Collaterally, the modular flexibility led to summative assessments taking place in each semester of full-time study rather than typically being at the end of a year. With it being logical to have summative assessments towards the ends of semesters, the feedback from the grading process was often too slow to be of use to the making of module choices by students, and it arrived when students were turning their attention to other things. Consequently, the potential of feedback for learning fell some way short of realisation. If student learning is the primary aim of a programme of study, then institutional imagination is needed to find ways of responding to the challenges thrown up by modularity.

Modular schemes are potentially at risk from the fragmentation of the student experience. Many seek to avert this by designating routes or pathways designed to give coherence to the students' study programmes. If students engage on a part-time basis, then even

[15]Funding support for students is a matter for government policy.

schemes with routes will find it difficult to give coherence to study programmes. In the UK, the expectation that all undergraduate programmes will embody personal development planning [PDP] offers a way round the problem, provided that it is granted sufficient status by both programme designers and students. The 'capability envelope' proposed by Stephenson and Yorke (1998) could be adapted to suit part-time and full-time programmes. In essence, at specified intervals during the programme the student could – as appropriate – review achievements to date, determine needs, and plan accordingly. An ongoing activity during the programme would be tutor-supported reflection on progress in the various strands of the programme, the extent to which achievements are inter-relating, and so on. The capability envelope, modified for part-time study, is schematically represented in figure 3. The student's achievements and reflections could be built up into a portfolio that could act as a resource for career development. This approach, however, sits rather uncomfortably with grade-based certifications of attainment, and would probably need to be developed within a certification framework that valued qualitative evidence as well as the quantitative.

A further issue is that, where grades are progressively accumulated and the assessment system is unforgiving, there is an implicit pressure on students not to get a poor result. Risk-taking in learning is thereby minimised: students play safe. However, learning is a risky business, as Rogers (2000) points out. Interim failure may be a condition of successful learning in the longer term. Should not assessment regulations allow for the possibility of learning from failure?

Programmes blend longer-term intended learning outcomes with shorter-term ones. Heavily unitised programmes risk an over-emphasis on the latter, because assessments –

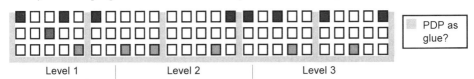

Subject areas represented by rows; chosen modules shaded

Figure 3

those powerful drivers of student activity – are related to units rather than the programme as a whole. The exception, in such programmes, may be a project or dissertation module in which there is a deliberate attempt to encourage students to integrate what they have learned across the programme. A challenge for programme designers is to find ways to place appropriate value on those outcomes that are achieved across the programme as a whole, such as a number of those relating to employability, which are the product of what Claxton (1998) describes as 'slow learning'.

Teaching approaches

Students are more likely to be successful in higher education if they are properly engaged in studying. If the emotional and the cognitive are as closely connected as Boekaerts

(2003) suggests, the relative impersonality of lectures and web-based learning may be insufficient to nurture student engagement, especially at the start. The increasing availability of provision that can be claimed to be resource-efficient (though whose resource-effectiveness is more problematic) does offer institutions the possibility of seriously rethinking the ways in which academics' (expensive) time is deployed. The opportunity exists, perhaps more now than in earlier times, to use freed-up academics' time to construct learning situations that fall under the umbrella term of 'active learning'[16]– for example, investigative activities; problem-solving (perhaps in small groups); and preparing presentations.

For many students, the social component of higher education is important. Whereas in yesteryear they could participate in the variety of social activities attached to an institution, today the demands of part-time employment and other commitments militate against this. The chances of student isolation are thus increased. Hence learning activities that bring students together to work actively on tasks will mitigate the risk of isolation and hence help to generate a level of mutual support sufficient to sustain them when they come up against difficulties.

A third important aspect of teaching is the provision of formative feedback that is simultaneously critical and encouraging, and that is also timely. The importance of formative assessment is now being properly appreciated, but it is still probably a more complex undertaking than is widely appreciated (Knight and Yorke 2003). Formal feedback is teacher-controlled, but does not necessarily have to come from the teacher (with all the costs that this implies). Gibbs (1999) describes how engineering students were required, as part of a series of teaching sessions, to provide feedback on the work of their peers. The effect of this was a marked increase in marks in the subsequent examination.

Student engagement

All that might be done in terms of curriculum design and implementation is of little consequence unless the students play their proper part in the partnership between themselves and the institution. Above all, it means that they have to have an internal motivation to *learn*, rather than merely get the grades. Students who lack such motivation would be better advised to defer entry until such time as they are ready to make the commitment necessary to succeed. For school leavers, particularly, this might mean taking up employment of one kind or another (with the potential collateral benefit of accruing some capital to help fund themselves through their chosen programme), or widening their experience of the world through voluntary work or travel. Evidence from Yorke (1999) and Davies and Elias (2003) indicated that a number of students who discontinued their studies did not have a strong commitment to them, often because they had entered higher education on the basis of expectations expressed by others, such as family members or schools.

---

[16]Relatively little learning can be said to be truly passive.

A student commitment to learning has as concomitants the rejection of both regurgitation and plagiarism. It also implies taking advantage of formal and informal formative assessments. Here the culture of the academic unit to which they are attached has a vital part to play.

For some students, moderate early grades come as a shock after relatively highly graded performances at school. A low grade can be a stimulus for learning, provided that it is accompanied by feedback that helps the student to improve, within a supportive academic climate – and also provided that it is redeemable within the assessment regulations.

Why are we here?

The primary task of most academics is the facilitation of student learning and development. Yet the bureaucratic requirements that wrap around teaching and learning can be a distraction. Assuring quality sometimes seems to have a higher priority than ensuring quality; the regulatory framework sometimes seems more like a cage than something one can climb up; under pressures of various kinds, it is easier to be compliant than to hunt for 'workarounds' that might serve the students better. Then there is the risk that the current orthodoxies will become ossifications (Kuhn, 1970, could no doubt have commented on this), and the risk that successful heterodoxies will be accepted as the new orthodoxy without proper critical analysis of the determinants of their successes and the potential transfer-value of the successes to different contexts.

Yet the picture is not all bleak. First, the development of the scholarship of teaching and learning carries with it the potential for transfer both within and across the disciplines. Second, the contribution that educational development can make to student learning is increasingly being recognised[17]. Third, pedagogic research seems to be on the threshold of a recognition hitherto denied by a bizarre logic that has seen research by higher education into its own practices as implicitly inferior to research into the practices of any other profession and into the subject matter of disciplines and disciplinary areas other than higher education[18]. The improvement of student learning should be strengthened by developments such as these.

Whilst much can be done at institutional and departmental levels, it is the commitment of individual teachers to their students that is critical to student success. That commitment is manifested not in a set of ticks against a list of desired practices, nor in a show of performative pyrotechnics whose glow quickly fades, but in the way that teachers inspire their students to achieve – perhaps beyond their imagining. The last word, perhaps, should be left to the foundation degree student, quoted earlier: 'Their encouragement fuels me'.

---

[17]See for example various papers in Eggins and Macdonald (2003).

[18]This is discussed in Yorke (2000a)

References

Astin, AW and Oseguera, L (2002) *Degree attainment rates at American colleges and universities.* Los Angeles, CA: Higher Education Research Institute, University of California.

Bandura, A (1997) *Self-efficacy: the exercise of control.* New York. Freeman.

Bean, JP and Eaton, SB (2000) A psychological model of college student retention. In Braxton, JM (ed) *Reworking the departure puzzle,* Nashville: Vanderbilt University Press, pp48-61.

Berlins, M (2004) Janet Jackson's right breast could hurt millions – in the pocket, if nowhere else. *The Guardian G2,* 10 February, p17.

Black, P and Wiliam, D (1998) Assessment and classroom learning. *Assessment in Education* 5(1), pp7-74.

Boekaerts, M (2003) Towards a model that integrates motivation, affect and learning. In Smith, L, Rogers, C and Tomlinson, P (eds) *Development and motivation: joint perspectives.* Leicester: British Psychological Society, pp173-189.

Boud, D (1995) Assessment and learning: contradictory or complementary? In Knight, P (ed) *Assessment for learning in higher education.* London: Kogan Page, pp35-48.

Bourdieu, P (1973) Cultural reproduction and social reproduction. In Brown, R (ed) *Knowledge, education and cultural change,* London: Tavistock, pp487-510.

Braxton, JM and Hirschy, AS (2004) Reconceptualizing antecedents of social integration in student departure. In Yorke, M and Longden, B *Retention and student success in higher education.* Maidenhead: SRHE and Open University Press, pp89-102.

Bunting, IA (2004) Student retention: a macro perspective from South Africa. In Yorke, M and Longden, B *Retention and student success in higher education.* Maidenhead: SRHE and Open University Press, pp16-31.

Claxton, G (1998) *Hare brain, tortoise mind.* London: Fourth Estate.

Davies, R and Elias, P (2003) *Dropping out: a study of early leavers from higher education [Research Report RR386].* London: Department for Education and Skills.

DfES (2003) The future of higher education. London: HMSO.

Dweck, CS (1999) *Self-theories: their role in motivation, personality, and development.* Philadelphia, PA: The Psychology Press.

Eggins, H and Macdonald, R (eds), (2003) *The scholarship of academic development.* Maidenhead: SRHE and Open University Press.

Gibbs. G (1999) Using assessment strategically to change the way students learn. In Brown, S and Glasner, A (eds) *Assessment matters in higher education: choosing and using diverse approaches.* Buckingham: SRHE and Open University Press, pp41-53.

Goleman, D (1996) *Emotional intelligence: why it can matter more than IQ.* London: Bloomsbury.

HEFCE (2003a) *Performance indicators in higher education 2000-01 and 2001-02*. Available at www.hefce.ac.uk/learning/perfind/2003/ . (Accessed 27 July 2004.)

HEFCE (2003b) Schooling effects on higher education achievement [Report 2003/32]. Bristol: Higher Education Funding Council for England.

Knight, PT and Yorke, M (2003) *Assessment, learning and employability*. Maidenhead: SRHE and Open University Press.

Knight, PT and Yorke, M (2004) *Learning, curriculum and employability in higher education*. London: RoutledgeFalmer.

Kuhn, TS (1970) *The structure of scientific revolutions* (2nd ed). Chicago: Chicago University Press.

Laurillard, D (2001) *Rethinking university teaching: a conversational framework for the effective use of learning technologies* (2nd ed). London: RoutledgeFalmer.

Layer, G, Srivastava, A, Thomas, L and Yorke, M (2002) Student success: building for change. In Action on Access (2003) *Student success in higher education*. Bradford: Action on Access, pp73-136.

Marzano, RJ (1998) *A theory-based meta-analysis of research on instruction*. Aurora, CO: Mid-continent Regional Educational Laboratory.

Mentkowski, M and Associates, (2000) *Learning that lasts: integrating learning development and performance in college and beyond*. San Fancisco: Jossey-Bass.

NCIHE (1997) *Higher education in the learning society, Report of the National Committee of Inquiry into Higher Education [The Dearing Report]*. Norwich: HMSO.

Pintrich, PR (2000) The role of goal orientation in self-regulated learning. In Boekaerts, M, Pintrich, P and Zeidner, M (eds) *Handbook of self-regulation*. New York: Academic Press, pp451-502.

Rogers, C (2002) Developing a positive approach to failure, in Peelo, M and Wareham, T (eds) *Failing students in higher education*. Buckingham: SRHE and the Open University Press, pp113-123.

Rotter, JB (1966) Generalized expectancies for internal versus external control of reinforcement, *Psychological Monographs* 80, pp1-28.

Salovey, P and Mayer, JD (1990) Emotional intelligence, *Imagination, Cognition, and Personality* 9, pp185-211.

Seligman, M (1998) *Learned optimism*. New York: Pocket Books.

Seymour, E and Hewitt, NM (1997) *Talking about leaving: why undergraduates leave the sciences*. Oxford: Westview Press.

Stephenson, J and Yorke, M (1998) Creating the conditions for the development of capability. In Stephenson, J and Yorke, M (eds), *Capability and quality in higher education*. London: Kogan Page, pp193-225.

Sternberg, RJ (1997) *Successful intelligence: how practical and creative intelligence determine success in life*. New York: Plume.

Tinto, V (1993) *Leaving college: rethinking the causes and cures of student attrition* (2nd ed), Chicago: University of Chicago Press.

Thomas, L, Woodrow, M and Yorke, M (2001) Access and retention. In Action on Access (2003) *Student success in higher education*. Bradford: Action on Access, pp35-72.

Weko, T (2004) New dogs and old tricks: what can the UK teach the US about university education? Paper prepared during an Atlantic Fellowship in Public Policy and presented at the British Council, London, 30 March.

Yorke, M (1999) *Leaving early: undergraduate non-completion in Higher Education*. London: Falmer.

Yorke, M (2000a) A cloistered virtue? Pedagogical research and policy in UK higher education. *Higher Education Quarterly* 54 (2), pp106-126.

Yorke, M (2000b) The rear-view mirror tells a story: subject area differences in undergraduate education and their implications for the improvement of learning in higher education. In Rust, C (ed) *Improving student learning through the disciplines*. Oxford: OCSLD, pp398-409.

Yorke, M (2003) The prejudicial papers? Press treatment of UK higher education performance indicators, 1999-2001. In Tight, M (ed) *Access and exclusion [International perspectives on higher education research, Volume 2]*. Oxford: Elsevier Science, pp159-184.

Yorke, M and Longden, B (2004) *Retention and student success in higher education*. Maidenhead: SRHE and Open University Press.

Threshold concepts and troublesome knowledge (3)*: implications for course design and evaluation

Ray Land (Coventry University), Glynis Cousin (Warwick University), Jan H F Meyer (Durham University) & Peter Davies (Staffordshire University)

1.0 Introduction

It has long been a matter of concern to teachers in higher education why certain students 'get stuck' at particular points in the curriculum whilst others grasp concepts with comparative ease. What might account for this variation in student performance and, more importantly, what might teachers do in relation to the design and teaching of their courses that might help students overcome such barriers to their learning? As students from a much wider range of educational backgrounds now enter higher education these issues are becoming of increasing importance across all disciplines. A further and related concern is why certain concepts within disciplinary fields appear particularly 'troublesome' to students. What makes particular areas of knowledge more troublesome than others, and how might we make such areas less so?

This paper discusses these concerns from the new perspective of 'threshold concepts'. Within all subject areas there seem to be particular concepts that can be considered as akin to a portal, opening up a new and previously inaccessible way of thinking about something. A threshold concept represents a transformed way of understanding, or interpreting, or viewing something without which the learner cannot progress. As a consequence of comprehending a threshold concept there may thus be a transformed internal view of subject matter, subject landscape, or even world view, and the student can move on. In attempting to characterise such conceptual gateways it was suggested in a paper presented at an earlier ISL conference that they are *transformative* (occasioning a significant shift in the perception of a subject), *irreversible* (unlikely to be forgotten, or unlearned only through considerable effort), and *integrative* (exposing the previously hidden interrelatedness of something). They also entail a shift in learner subjectivity and an extended use of discourse.

---

* Please note that this chapter constitutes the third in a series on this topic. The two earlier pieces are listed in the references below under Meyer JHF and Land R (2003 and 2005).

2.0 Threshold concepts

In order to make clear our aims in this paper we begin with an explanation of the meaning and derivation of the term 'threshold concept'. The idea of a threshold concept has been developed by Meyer and Land (2003) in the context of the ETL project. Threshold concepts are defined as concepts that bind a subject together, being fundamental to ways of thinking and practising in that discipline. They have attracted particular interest from economics communities in the UK (Davies, 2003) and Australia (Shanahan and Meyer, 2003). Once a student has internalised a threshold concept they are more able to integrate different aspects of a subject in their analysis of problems. Students who have not yet internalised a threshold concept have little option but to attempt to learn new ideas in a more fragmented fashion. On acquiring a threshold concept a student is able to transform their use of the ideas of a subject because they are now able to integrate them in their thinking.

The integrative aspect of a threshold concept presents distinctive problems for learners who are studying a subject (such as economics) as part of their degree. Students who do not think of themselves as 'learners of economics' are likely to face particular difficulties in grasping concepts that bind together aspects of a subject that may seem quite disparate to a novice. This problem arises because the acquisition of such concepts (eg opportunity cost, price and value, equilibrium) is intrinsic to grasping the ways in which economists 'think' and practice.

3.0 Troublesome knowledge

Such integration and subsequent transformation, though necessary for progress within the subject, may prove *troublesome* to certain learners for a variety of reasons, not the least of which is that such transformation entails a letting go of earlier, comfortable positions and encountering less familiar and sometimes disconcerting new territory. Threshold concepts are inherently problematic for learners because they demand an integration of ideas and this requires the student to accept a transformation of their own understanding.

An accountancy lecturer discusses the problematic nature of the concept of depreciation both for her students, and for her own attempts to get them to engage with the concept:

> *And why I think depreciation is a threshold concept, is that because what it draws in to an understanding of depreciation is a particular way of viewing business events or transactions which demand students to see these within a very particular framework. ie an accounting framework rather than what might be termed a commonsense or intuitive framework… it isn't a particularly natural process and actually the more you look at it the more contrived it gets, because it isn't just a straightforward alternative framework. Actually, within the framework, there are lots of compromises. And it is based, in part, on the intuitive framework. In fact the more I think about it now, I am changing my mind about the students misunderstanding it.*

The transformation mentioned earlier can also entail a shift in the learner's identity. The result may be that students remain stuck in an 'in-between' state in which they oscillate between earlier, less sophisticated understandings, and the fuller appreciation of a concept that their tutors require from them. This in-between state we have termed a state of 'liminality', from the Latin meaning 'within the threshold'. One outcome is that students present a partial, limited or superficial understanding of the concept to be learned which we have characterised as a form of 'mimicry'. A more serious outcome is that students become frustrated, lose confidence and give up that particular course. It is the hope of the authors of this paper that within our various subject areas we can devise ways of helping students to overcome such 'epistemological obstacles' (Brousseau 1983). We would seek to create supportive liminal environments to help students through such difficulty – what might be characterised as a kind of conceptual peristalsis – that they might move on and succeed.

Sometimes the troublesome nature of knowledge stems from its being tacit – that which remains mainly personal and implicit (Polanyi, 1958) at a level of 'practical consciousness' (Giddens, 1984) though its emergent but unexamined understandings are often shared within a specific community of practice (Wenger, 1998). In other instances the troublesomeness is linked to language. Specific discourses have developed within disciplines to represent (and simultaneously privilege) particular understandings and ways of seeing and thinking. Such discourses distinguish individual communities of practice and are necessarily less familiar to new entrants to such discursive communities or participants who are peripheral to them.

> *Now if you think about the word 'cost', really all it means is, it is a value, an acquisition value. So instead of using the word 'cost' you could say this acquisition value, and it would mean the same thing wouldn't it? But the words 'value' and 'cost' are quite troublesome, literally, in accounting (and in economics), because 'cost' can mean very different things depending on who the user is, and for what purpose you are calculating the 'cost'. So, you know, in accounting you might have three or four very different understandings of what 'cost' means.*

4.0 Threshold *conceptions*

To complicate matters further, in some instances students may grasp concepts but the barrier to their learning appears to lie at a deeper level of understanding, where the student finds difficulty in appreciating what Perkins (2005) has termed 'the underlying game', or a threshold *conception*. Like the characters in Buñuel's (1962) film, *The Exterminating Angel*, who cannot leave the house in which they have attended a dinner, but are unable to account for their immobility, the students similarly are unaccountably unable to move on. An example would be where students of electrical engineering can cope with the required concepts from physics but do not have a working understanding of the highly unpredictable and surprising ways in which complex circuits might behave. In computer programming, similarly, students may grasp the concepts of class, objects, tables, arrays, and recursion, but they may not appreciate the threshold conception, the underlying game, of the interaction of all these elements in a process of ever-increasing complexity. Such instances present teachers with particularly difficult challenges in class to assist their students in coming to understand the underlying conceptions of such phenomena.

Savin-Baden's work (2005) on the notion of 'disjunction' in problem-based learning (PBL) would seem to point to something similar to this notion of a threshold conception.

> *'Disjunction' refers to the idea of becoming 'stuck' in learning and I have suggested elsewhere (Savin-Baden, 2000) that disjunction can be both enabling and disabling in terms of its impact on learning. Disjunction, then, can be seen as the kind of place that students might reach after they have encountered a threshold concept that they have not managed to breach. Many staff and students have described disjunction as being a little like hitting a brick wall in learning and they have used various strategies to try to deal with it. These include retreating from the difficulty and opting out of any further learning, using strategies to avoid it, temporising and waiting for an event or stimulus that will help them to move on or engaging with it directly in an attempt to relieve their discomfort (Savin-Baden 2005: in press)*

If the portal appears 'bricked up' then clearly the threshold of new transformative understanding is not visible to the student. Savin-Baden argues that, although disjunction occurs in many forms and in diverse ways in different disciplines, it seems to be particularly evident in curricula where problem-based learning has been implemented. She suggests that this may be because PBL programmes prompt students to critique and contest knowledge early on in the curriculum and thus they encounter knowledge as being troublesome earlier than students in more traditional programmes. However, she goes on:

> *it might also be that problem-based learning encourages students to shift away from linear and fact finding problem-solving. Instead they move towards forms of problem management that demand the use of procedural and personal knowledge as students are asked to engage with strategy or moral dilemma problems. Thus it might be that disjunction is not only a form of troublesome knowledge but also a 'space' or 'position' reached through the realisation that the knowledge is troublesome. Disjunction might therefore be seen as a 'troublesome learning space' that emerges when forms of active learning (such as problem-based learning) are used that prompt students to engage with procedural and personal knowledge*

5.0 Considerations for course design and evaluation

The idea of a threshold concept presents important challenges for curriculum design and for learning and teaching. At a general level we would argue that programmes should be designed and systematically reviewed according to:

a)   the sequence of content;

b)   the processes through which learners are made ready for, approach, recognise, and internalise threshold concepts. We would argue that this process of the student's learning, their encounter with threshold concepts in a given subject, might be considered as akin to a journey or excursion. Such an *excursive* account of the learning experience would see these processes as a framework of engagements, designed to assist students to cope with threshold concepts. (This notion of excursive learning will be discussed further in 5.6 below).

c)   the ways in which learners and teachers recognise when threshold concepts have been internalised – in effect what would constitute appropriate assessment for the attainment of threshold concepts.

More specifically we would draw attention to nine considerations that we feel are important in the design and subsequent evaluation of curricula in higher education.

5.1   Jewels in the curriculum

Threshold concepts can be used to define potentially powerful transformative points in the student's learning experience. In this sense they may be viewed as the 'jewels in the curriculum' inasmuch as they can serve to identify crucial points in the framework of engagement that teachers may wish to construct in order to provide opportunities for students to gain important conceptual understandings and hence gain richer and more complex insights into aspects of the subjects they are studying. They may also serve a helpful diagnostic purpose in alerting tutors to areas of the curriculum where students are likely to encounter troublesome knowledge and experience conceptual difficulty – the 'stuck places' to which Ellsworth refers (1997:71).

5.2   The importance of engagement

There is already a considerable existing literature in relation to how tutors might help students to develop genuine understanding of a troublesome concept. Many of these studies point to the need for active student engagement with, and manipulation of, the conceptual material. For example it is recommended that tutors ask students to explain it, to represent it in new ways, to apply it in new situations and to connect it to their lives. The emphasis is equally strong that they should not simply recall the concept in the form in which it was presented (Colby et al, 2003: 263). We would wish to appropriate these emphases and, with Wenger, think about constructing a *framework of engagement* within the course that might enable students to experience and gain understandings of the ways of thinking and practising (WTP) that are expected of practitioners within a given community of practice, be this the recognition of the importance of contestability amongst historians, or the appreciation of the fluidity of double curvature surfacing in automotive design. We will wish our students not only to understand 'how historians think', but to begin to 'think like a historian'. But within this framework, as a course design question, what will be the specific *forms of engagement* which will be most appropriate to bring about these particular *transformative* understandings at various points in the curriculum and which will assist students to acquire the threshold concepts that are necessary to ensure satisfactory progression through the course? Lather has spoken of the kinds of engagement or praxis 'where the effort is to... provoke something else into happening – something other than the return of the same' (1998: 492). As course designers what 'provocations' might we be seeking through these forms of engagement to bring about the transformations in understanding that we would wish?

5.3 Listening for understanding

However, teaching for understanding of threshold concepts needs to be preceded by listening for understanding. In terms of what we will refer to below as 'pre-liminal variation' in the ways in which students approach, or come to terms with, a threshold concept, we can't second guess where students are coming from or what their uncertainties are. It is difficult for teachers, experienced and expert within the discipline, who long since travelled similar ground in their own disciplinary excursions, to gaze backwards across thresholds and understand the conceptual difficulty or obstacles that a student is currently experiencing. This requires 'cultivating a third ear that listens not for what a student knows (discrete packages of knowledge) but for the terms that shape a student's knowledge, her not knowing, her forgetting, her circles of stuck places and resistances' (Ellsworth1997:71).

5.4 Reconstitution of self

Grasping a threshold concept is never just a cognitive shift; it might also involve a repositioning of self in relation to the subject. This means, from the viewpoint of curriculum design, that some attention has to be paid on the part of course designers to the discomforts of troublesome knowledge. Knowledge may be troublesome because it has become ritualised, or inert, because it is conceptually difficult or alien, because it is tacit and perhaps requires awareness of an 'underlying game' imperceptible to the student (see below), or because of the discourse that has to be acquired for the concept to become meaningful (Meyer and Land 2003; Perkins 1999).

> *as students acquire threshold concepts, and extend their use of language in relation to these concepts, there occurs also a shift in the learner's subjectivity, a repositioning of the self... What is being emphasised here is the inter-relatedness of the learner's identity with thinking and language. Threshold concepts lead not only to transformed thought but to a transfiguration of identity and adoption of an extended discourse (Meyer and Land 2005: in press).*

This transfiguration and extension of the subjectivity of the learner might be exhilarating but might incur a sense of disquietude or even loss on the part of the learner as they let go the security of a previously held conceptual stance to enter less certain terrain. Again we return to the notion of the appropriate forms of engagement within which such transformations might take place and the need for the teacher to provide what Winnicott (1971) used to term a 'holding environment' or nurturing space. We prefer to call this a supportive liminal environment, feeling that Winnicott's term suggests a somewhat static, even inhibitive space, rather than the peristaltic process discussed earlier. Given, too, that the process of acquiring new knowledge tends to involve what Bonamy et al (2001) would call 'provisional stabilities', this means that over the course of an entire programme such periods of letting-go and reconstitution will be repeated and call for metacognitive skills on the part of the learner to cope with such transformation and to tolerate uncertainty.

5.5 Tolerating uncertainty

Learners tend to discover that what is not clear initially often becomes clear over time. One of our respondents, a first year student in media studies, came close to abandoning her course and dropping out halfway through the first year because she found the programme too conceptually difficult. She commented, however, that had she known, at the time of her encountering this troublesomeness in her understanding, that eventually she would come to cope with the programme (and the threshold concepts it involved), the transition would have been easier. The next time she faced such troublesome knowledge, she asserted, she would 'hang in there' with greater confidence because now she knew she would eventually find a way of coming to understand. So, in such a situation, there is a metacognitive issue for the student of self-regulation within what we have called the 'liminal state'. Efklides (2005) has emphasised the indispensable role of metacognition in the learning process 'both directly by activating control processes and indirectly by influencing the self-regulation process that determines whether the student will get engaged in threshold concepts or not.'

> *What distinguishes metacognitive feelings is their cognitive and affective nature. Metacognitive feelings take the form of feeling of knowing, of familiarity, of difficulty, of confidence, and of satisfaction, whereas metacognitive judgments or estimates can take the form of judgment of learning, of where, when, and how we acquire a piece of information, of time and effort spent on a task. Metacognitive experiences serve the* monitoring *and* control *of the learning process and at the same time provide an intrinsic context within which learning processes take place. This intrinsic context is to a large extent affective and determined by self processes, individual difference factors as well as task factors, including task difficulty, task instructions, and feedback used. The intrinsic context influences students' strategies in problem solving, but also their emotions, causal attributions, and self-concept. In this way, metacognitive experiences affect both online task processing and future motivation towards learning. (Efklides 2005:in press)*

5.6 Recursiveness and excursiveness

Given the often troublesome nature of threshold concepts it is likely that many learners will need to adopt a recursive approach to what has to be learned, attempting different 'takes' on the conceptual material until the necessary integration and connection discussed earlier begins to take place. The need for the learner to grasp threshold concepts in recursive movements means that they cannot be tackled in a simplistic 'learning outcomes' model where sentences like 'by the end of the course the learner will be able to…' undermine, and perhaps do not even explicitly recognise the complexities of the transformation a learner undergoes. It is likely that any course requiring student engagement with threshold concepts and troublesome knowledge will entail considerable variation in the conceptual stances and outcomes that are reached by members of the cohort – what we might term *post*-liminal variation. Consideration of threshold concepts to some extent 'rattles the cage' of a linear approach to curriculum design that assumes standard and homogenised outcomes. Lather (1998:492) offers a counter-narrative rejecting 'the rhetorical position of "the one who knows"' in favour of 'a praxis of not being so sure'. A 'praxis of stuck places' might tolerate 'discrepancies, repetitions, hesitations, and uncertainties, always beginning again' (491). What it refuses is 'the privileging of containment over excess, thought over affect, structure over speed, linear causality over complexity, and intention over aggregate capacities' (497). We would argue, similarly, for the notion of learning as *excursive*, as a journey or excursion which will have intended direction and outcome but will also acknowledge (and indeed desire) that there will be deviation and unexpected outcome within the excursion; there will be digression and revisiting (recursion) and possible further points of departure and revised direction. The eventual destination may be reached, or it may be revised. It may be a surprise. It will certainly be the point of embarkation for further excursion.

5.7 Pre-liminal variation

An abiding question for educators, and for course designers in particular, is why some students productively negotiate the liminal space of understanding we have discussed earlier and others find difficulty in doing so. Does such variation explain how the threshold will be, or can be, or can only be approached (or turned away from) as it 'comes into view'? And how does it 'come into view' for individual students? We need to know more about the pre-liminal variation in the constitution of student cohort, given the obvious implications this would seem to have for subsequent student retention and progression (Meyer and Shanahan 2003). To this end a three-year funded study on threshold concepts within a given discipline is currently getting under way (see section 6.0 below) to investigate systematically, amongst other phenomena, the issue of pre-liminal variation and its implications for the sequencing, structure and forms of engagement that a course will contain.

5.8 Unintended consequences of generic 'good pedagogy'

There is emerging indicative evidence from research into threshold concepts (eg Meyer and Shanahan 2003; Lucas 2000) that what has traditionally been considered 'good pedagogy' may, on occasion, break down or prove dysfunctional in relation to the acquisition of threshold concepts. For example, the conventional practical wisdom of simplifying concepts in order to render them more accessible seemed to prove dysfunctional in the case of teaching the threshold concept of opportunity cost in economics in a South Australian context.

one implication of the argument presented thus far is that 'first impressions matter'. Efforts to make threshold concepts 'easier' by simplifying their initial expression and application may, in fact, set students onto a path of 'ritualised' knowledge that actually creates a barrier that results in some students being prevented from crossing the 'threshold' of a concept (Meyer and Shanahan, 2003, p15)

The simplified interpretation of the concept, intended to some extent as a proxy for the fuller, more sophisticated understanding which it was intended to lead on to, was found to operate more frequently as a false proxy, leading students to settle for the naïve version, and entering into a form of ritualised learning or mimicry. Such findings may prove useful as future keys to understanding the pre-liminal variation in student approach discussed earlier.

In a similar fashion the often-advocated form of engagement of relating concepts to everyday phenomena, or to the personal experience of students, was found to be ineffective in a first year introductory accounting course which sought to help students grasp the threshold concept of 'depreciation'. In this case it was the absence of any significant budgetary or financial experience in the students' experience which rendered the approach ineffective. It would seem salutary, therefore, periodically to cast a cold reviewer's eye over tried and tested 'good pedagogy'.

5.9 The underlying game

Finally, in the light of our earlier discussion of threshold *conceptions*, it would seem advisable for course designers to query whether, in addition to the forms of engagement they may have designed to assist students to cope with identified threshold concepts in a programme, there might remain what Perkins calls 'an underlying game' or threshold conception, which, if not recognised and understood by students, might still render their learning troublesome and lead to further frustration or confusion in their studies. Lucas (2000), for example, provides an example of such an underlying conception that Accountancy students are not always aware of. She distinguishes between 'authorised' and 'alternative' understandings of threshold concepts. 'Authorised' understandings are those endorsed and maintained by the disciplinary community and within textbooks. 'Alternative' understandings of events and transactions are independent of authorised versions, and arise from intuitive or everyday (common sense) understandings of a concept such as 'depreciation' or 'profit'. 'Alternative' understandings might on occasion be substituted for, or provide an alternative to, the authorised versions. Often, where students hold these alternative understandings, they do not recognise that these conceptions are in *opposition* to the authorised (and perhaps counter-intuitive or troublesome) versions promulgated within the course. Thus a particularly important (or higher level of) *threshold conception* may be required to recognise the difference between authorised and alternative understandings of threshold concepts.

6.0 Case study – developing first year undergraduates' acquisition of threshold concepts in economics

As a way of testing and implementing these considerations, and furthering our understanding of the issues of student variation in their acquisition of threshold concepts, we are now embarking upon an empirical study of the experience of first year students in a given disciplinary context. A three year national project, funded by the HEFCE FDTL5 programme, is currently getting under way as a collaborative venture led by Staffordshire University and involving the Universities of Coventry, Durham, and the West of England. By focusing curriculum development on threshold concepts in first year economics in the four universities this project provides an opportunity to re-evaluate the key binding ideas of the subject that should be introduced in level one, and what it means for students to understand these ideas in a deep-level transformative way. We aim to develop methods of assessing variation in the acquisition of threshold concepts. These methods will help students as well as lecturers to recognise levels of understanding. Students' acquisition of threshold concepts will depend on their prior experience and learning, and the way they are therefore likely to initially approach their studies. The project will aim to develop ways in which teaching can respond to the variation in which students engage and acquire these concepts. We anticipate that careful evaluation of the process and outcomes of the project will be useful for other colleagues wanting to pursue these issues in economics and in other subjects. The emphasis on teaching strategies that can respond to variation in ways in which students engage with and acquire threshold concepts provides the rationale for self- and teacher assessment that seeks to identify whether students have understood these concepts and this in turn will provide information that will identify 'at risk' students. Shanahan and Meyer (2003) have shown how recognition of failure to acquire threshold concepts can form part of the process of identifying 'at risk' students and that remedial measures can improve retention. We hope similarly to be able to support students through developing responses best suited to the needs of students on different named awards. Based on previous work on threshold concepts in economics (Davies, 2003; Shanahan and Meyer, 2003; Reimann and Jackson, 2003) the initial focus will be upon students' understanding of opportunity cost, price and value, equilibrium and gains from trade. These concepts feature frequently in standard first-year courses. On the basis of dialogue between colleagues in partner institutions and the economics Subject Centre in the UK we anticipate further threshold concepts in economics. The concepts of cumulative causation, externalities and rent-seeking behaviour have been suggested.

7.0 Conclusion

The task for course developers and designers here is to identify, through constructive (and constructivist) feedback, the source of these epistemological barriers, and subsequently to free up the blocked spaces by, for example, redesigning activities and sequences, through scaffolding, through provision of support materials and technologies or new conceptual tools, through mentoring or peer collaboration, to provide the necessary shift in perspective that might permit further personal development. The way in which chess players talk of 'developing' a piece involves the removal of other pieces (obstacles) so as to free up various (multiple) ways in which the piece might now be empowered to move. The significance of the framework provided by threshold concepts lies, we feel, in its explanatory potential to locate troublesome aspects of disciplinary knowledge within transitions across conceptual thresholds and hence to assist teachers in identifying appropriate ways of modifying or redesigning curricula to enable their students to negotiate such transitions more successfully.

References

Bonamy, J, Charlier, B and Saunders, M (2001) 'Bridging Tools' for change: evaluating a collaborative learning network. *Journal of Computer Assisted Learning* Vol 17, no 3 pp295-305

Brousseau, G (1983) 'Les obstacles epistemologiques et les problèmes en mathématiques'. *Recherches en didactique des mathematiques*, Vol 4 no 2 pp165-198.

Colby, A, Ehrlich, T, Beaumont, E and Stephens, J (2003) *Educating Citizens: Preparing America's Undergraduates for Lives of Moral and Civic Responsibility*. Jossey-Bass, San Francisco

Cousin, G (2003) *Threshold Concepts, Troublesome Knowledge and Learning about Others*, 10th Conference of the European Association for Research on Learning and Instruction (EARLI), Padua, Italy, August 26-30.

Davies P (2003) *Threshold Concepts: How can we recognise them?* Paper presented at the Biennial Conference of the European Association for Research into Learning and Instruction (EARLI) Padua, September 2003

Efklides, A (2005) *Metacognition, affect and conceptual difficulty*, in Meyer, J.H.F and Land, R. (eds) *Overcoming Barriers to Student Understanding: Threshold Concepts and Troublesome Knowledge* (forthcoming).

Ellsworth, E (1997) *Teaching Positions: Difference Pedagogy and the Power of Address*, Teachers College Press, New York.

Lather, P (1998) 'Critical Pedagogy and Its Complicities: A Praxis of Stuck Places', *Educational Theory*, Fall 1998, Volume 48, Number 4, 487-498.

Lucas, U (2000) Worlds apart: students' experiences of learning introductory accounting. *Critical Perspectives on Accounting*, 11, 479-504.

Meyer JHF and Land R (2003) 'Threshold Concepts and Troublesome Knowledge (1) – Linkages to Ways of Thinking and Practising' in *Improving Student Learning – Ten Years On*. Rust, C (ed), OCSLD, Oxford

Meyer JHF and Land R (2005) 'Threshold Concepts and Troublesome Knowledge (2) – Epistemological Considerations and a Conceptual Framework for Teaching and Learning' *Higher Education*, May issue (in press).

Meyer, JHF and Shanahan, M (2003) *The Troublesome Nature of a Threshold Concept in Economics*, Paper presented to the 10th Conference of the European Association for Research on Learning and Instruction (EARLI), Padua, Italy, August 26-30.

Perkins, D (1999) The Many Faces of Constructivism, *Educational Leadership*, Volume 57, Number 3, November

Perkins, D (2005) The underlying game: troublesome knowledge and threshold conceptions, in Meyer, J.H.F and Land, R. (eds) *Overcoming Barriers to Student Understanding: Threshold Concepts and Troublesome Knowledge* (forthcoming).

Reimann, N and Jackson, I (2003) *Threshold Concepts in Economics: a Case Study* Paper presented to the 10th Conference of the European Association for Research on Learning and Instruction (EARLI), Padua, Italy, August 26-30.

Savin-Baden, M (2005) Disjunction as a form of troublesome knowledge in problem-based learning, in Meyer, JHF and Land, R (eds) *Overcoming Barriers to Student Understanding: Threshold Concepts and Troublesome Knowledge*. London: Routledge Falmer.

Wenger, E (1998) *Communities of Practice: Learning, Meaning and Identity*. Cambridge: Cambridge University Press.

Winnicott, DH (1971) *Playing and Reality*. New York: Basic Books.

How lecturers experience student-centred approaches to teaching

Norrie Brown, Napier University

Introduction

The current study was conducted at a time of great change in higher education generally and within nurse education in particular. In recent years there have been external pressures on the UK higher education sector with the publication of the National Committee of Inquiry into Higher Education (Dearing, 1997). In this summary report the committee recommended that all institutions of higher education should give higher priority to teaching and learning strategies that promoted student learning. Additional pressures in the field of nursing education come from a review of the preparation and training of nurses and midwives from the United Kingdom Central Council – now the Nursing and Midwifery Council (N&MC) (UKCC, 1999: the Peach Report). The Peach Report called for a review of the teaching methods that were seen to be teacher-centred and a move towards the use of more student-centred and facilitative methods – mainly Problem-Based Learning (PBL). The focus on changing teaching methods as a way of making nurse lecturers more student-centred is not an uncommon view expressed in the literature, particularly the argument for encouraging more student activity in their learning. However, focusing on student activity in learning, or indeed student active teaching/learning methods, is not as unproblematic as it may seem and may not, as the results of my study suggest, lead to lecturers adopting student-focused (or student-centred) approaches to teaching.

Appeal of student-centred, humanistic education for educators

Student-centred teaching is not a new phenomenon to many nurse educators and neither are the humanistic philosophies that are considered to underpin its use. See for example the writing of Rogers, Knowles and Freire. Humanistic education prioritises the need to develop relationships with students and for lecturers to provide teaching/learning opportunities that involve:

■　Fostering the acquisition of self-directed, self-initiated skills that have long-term benefits to the student, the nursing profession and clients (Richardson, 1988)

Changing the asymmetrical power relationship between students and their teachers that is considered poor role-modelling for empathic nurse-client interactions (Sweeney, 1986)

■ Mirroring the need for a more contemporary identification with the ethos of nursing practice away from behavioural models to one that emphasises the humanistic and emancipatory philosophy (MacLean, 1992)

However, and despite the rhetoric contained in much of the literature on student-centredness in teaching and learning and its link to nursing practice, there is little or no research into how student-centred teaching is experienced by nurse lecturers (see for example Jinks (1997) on nurse lecturers' attitudes to student-centred teaching and nurse educators' views that being student-centred in teaching is about teaching methods). Despite the huge amount of literature in support of student-centred teaching and learning there is a dearth of research into such an important area. This latter point may be understood when we become aware of the debate and confusion about some of the main concepts being used. For example:

■ What is meant by 'self-directed learning' in nursing education (Nolan & Nolan, 1997)

■ Student-centredness is a multi-faceted concept that means different things to different people (D'A Slevin and Lavery, 1991; Jinks et al, 1998)

■ Problems promoting a student-centred, adult orientation into nursing curricula due to the multi-dimensional nature of these concepts (Jinks, 1999)

■ The characteristics of self-directed learning logically require no teaching at all (Iwasiw, 1987);

In this latter sense, this research and the approach adopted is a departure from previous work in this area for the following reasons:

■ Previous research into effectiveness of various teaching methods is inconclusive and contradictory

■ Limited research into student-centred teaching in nursing (1 study)

■ Research from other higher education disciplines has focused on *teaching* and researchers' interpretation of teacher-centred/student-centred dichotomy (conceptual change approach)

■ No research into lecturers' experience of student-centred teaching (conceptions or approaches to student-centred teaching)

Research method

Phenomenography is a qualitative research approach that aims to describe the key aspects of the variation of the experience of a phenomenon as opposed to the richness of individual experiences (Trigwell, 1999), and was considered to be an approach that was fit for the purpose of exploring the variation in lecturers' experience of student-centred teaching. I therefore adopted a phenomenographic approach to interviewing and analysis of interview transcripts to look for variation in the ways in which lecturers experienced student-centred teaching, namely:

- Approaches to student-centred teaching
- Conceptions of student-centred teaching
- Relationship between conceptions and approaches

The sample in this study was selected in order to maximise the variation that may exist within a group of nurse lecturers who claimed to adopt student-centred methods in their teaching practice. Interviews focused on specific aspects of lecturers' actual teaching practice/events identified by them.

Interviews with 23 lecturers from a variety of disciplines within Napier University (Adult Nursing $n = 9$; Mental Health $n = 7$; Child Health $n = 5$, and Learning Disabilities $n = 2$).

Results pertaining to data on student-centred approaches to teaching

The analysis revealed five relational (strategies and intentions) categories of description related to these lecturers' experience of student-centred approaches to teaching. The five approaches to student-centred teaching formed an inclusive hierarchy:

- **Approach A:** Student-active teacher-focused strategy with the intention of the students actively reproducing expert knowledge and skills
- **Approach B:** Student-active teacher-focused strategy with the intention of students actively acquiring and applying nursing concepts and skills
- **Approach C:** Student-active student-focused strategy with the intention of the students using their experience to develop personally meaningful conceptions of nursing
- **Approach D:** Student-active student-focused strategy aimed at the students changing their conceptions and skills with a view to improving their practice
- **Approach E:** Student-active student-focused strategy aimed at the students developing their professional attitudes and values (affective components)

This study has demonstrated that there is a qualitative variation between each of the approaches to student-centred teaching. The variation, as constituted in this study, exists in the qualitative differences between the approaches, the teaching strategies and their related intentions. Approach A is considered to be more limited, or less sophisticated, than subsequent categories. Approach E is seen to be the most complex, most sophisticated, and more inclusive of the range of strategies and intentions. Approach E includes Approaches A, B, C and D. Approach A, on the other hand, does not contain or include any of the subsequent categories.

The main characteristics of each approach are as follows:

Approach A: Student-active teacher-focused strategy with the intention of the students actively reproducing expert knowledge and skills.

Teachers adopting this approach prepare teaching and learning events that are highly structured with the intention of transmitting the teacher's knowledge and skills.

Students are active in the sense that they:

- Comply with the teachers' requests to actively engage with the learning activities
- Actively reproduce the teacher's knowledge and skills
- Actively challenge and check each others' understanding of the concepts and skills, but with the intention that the outcomes of their learning are in line with the teacher's conceptions and skills to ensure safe nursing practice
- The knowledge and skills to be reproduced are the teachers' and the students do not need to consult textbooks or other resources
- The knowledge and skills are external to the students and no account is taken of students' prior knowledge, skills or experience
- The students are not engaged in the construction of their own knowledge or skills

Approach B: Student-active teacher-focused strategy with the intention of students actively acquiring and applying nursing concepts and skills.

Similar strategy to approach A and the outcome is safe nursing practice. However, unlike approach A:

- Student prior experience is considered as being useful, but not essential, in the development of and application of both teacher and disciplinary knowledge and skills
- As with approach A, the knowledge and skills are seen to be external to the student but this knowledge can be acquired from the teacher, journal articles, demonstrations and other resources
- The knowledge and skills to be acquired are also seen as being external to the student
- The students are not engaged in the construction of their own knowledge or skills

Approach C: Student-active student-focused strategy with the intention of the students using their experience to develop personally meaningful conceptions of nursing.

As with approaches A and B both students and teachers are active in the teaching/learning process. But unlike teachers adopting approaches A and B:

Teachers utilise students' prior knowledge and experience in order to help the students to develop their understanding of the disciplinary knowledge and skills for *informed or meaningful practice*

■ The knowledge and skills development are seen as a relationship between the student and their experiences and the disciplinary knowledge and skills they are being exposed to, and are considered to increase student confidence and motivation and to aid the transfer of new knowledge and skills to other situations

■ Focusing on student prior knowledge and experience prepares the way for students to change or adapt their understanding, practice and learning

■ The students are engaged in the construction of their own knowledge and skills

Approach D: Student-active student-focused strategy aimed at the students changing their conceptions and skills with a view to improving their practice.

As with approaches A, B and C, both students and teachers are active in the teaching/learning process. Teachers are aware of the need for students to practice in a safe and informed way. But unlike teachers adopting Approach C:

■ Teachers see it as being important for students to develop personally meaningful conceptions and skills for informed practice, but dealing with people and their needs in clinical practice is much more complex and demanding than the possession of personally meaningful conceptions and skills allows for

■ Students are encouraged to adopt a more critical view of the conceptions and skills they are exposed to in order to develop 'deeper' understanding and to provide *effective nursing practice*

■ Adopting this approach is considered to reduce the theory-practice gap

■ The students are engaged in the construction and further development of their own knowledge and skills by being encouraged to consider a range of perspectives, including the client's perspective

Approach E: Student-active student-focused strategy aimed at the students developing their professional attitudes and values (affective components).

As with Approaches A, B, C and D both students and teachers are active in the teaching/learning process. Teachers are aware of the need for students to practice in a safe, informed and effective way. Teachers adopting this approach have an awareness of the positive benefits of facilitating the students' development of their own conceptions and skills of nursing (Approach C) and the need to change their own conceptions of disciplinary knowledge and skills (Approach D). However, and unlike Approach D:

■ More meaningful learning in a nursing context comes about as a result of and change to their disciplinary conceptions and skills in conjunction with the development of appropriate attitudes in order to provide *effective and holistic care*

■ If the students develop a positive attitude to their practice and learning, they are more likely to view clients as unique individuals with unique problems and concerns and to be able to deliver more person-centred care and to be more positively disposed to continued professional development

■ The development of the affective component is not something that can be transmitted or acquired from the teacher, it is something that students need to develop and change by themselves and not have imposed on them by others

Illustrative examples

Student-centred approaches to teaching – categories with illustrative quotations from lecturers.

Approach A: Student-active teacher-focused strategy with the intention of the students actively reproducing expert knowledge and skills:

"They get and work as fast as they can to solve their problem, the thing that they've been set to do. And they can rationalise it until they're blue in the face but ultimately we will, if we have to, counter argue and give them the professional viewpoint of who goes where… Safety in practice… We are people who are smack up to date and pride ourselves in being smack up to date because these are specialist areas of practice. We know what's current. We know the changes that are happening in practice in these areas. And without making sure these are discussed we couldn't be sure that the wrong impression had gone out with the student on the day. So, we want them to be as safe as they can be theoretically before they meet it head-on in reality, from simulation to reality. So, and we have a duty to do that, I believe so. That's what I mean by safely. Without that structure again I don't think you could be sure that conversation would happen that made sure that everyone was clear on what they thought, the real rationale for practice is… and that they've been able to remember bits without picking their books up after those sessions, and that they really feel that it is real. That it is up to date and they've never come back to us after placements in the real A&E settings for example saying, 'It doesn't happen like that in reality'… It's exactly the same session no matter who we put it on for."

Approach B: Student-active teacher-focused strategy with the intention of students actively acquiring and applying nursing concepts and skills:

"Well, we discuss. I mean it's not just a workshop where the students do the work and the teacher has no contact. What tends to happen is that, particularly with elimination skills, is that they're encouraged to explore the information with worksheets, articles, discussion amongst themselves, but the teacher is present. And tends to pick up on areas that particularly they know that they might have difficulty with [Approach B] and also encourages along a certain train of thought. So, I mean, the worksheet's going to do that anyway but the teacher, as a facilitator, is going to make sure that they come out of the session with some form of understanding which he or she wants them to have. Particularly about… I think issues related to practice. About things like catheters, bladder lavage things like that [Approach A]."

"Because the students are controlling more what they're doing. They're actually exploring the information and they're, they're active in their learning"

Approach C: Student-active student-focused strategy with the intention of the students using their experience to develop personally meaningful conceptions of nursing:

"Well, I think it's about the diversity of maybe, opinions, I mean I don't, I suppose when you're in the lecturer role, students maybe view you as the expert, if you like, and to some extent yes you are, but, again, I view myself subject expert in some areas but I view myself more as a manager of the teaching and learning experience and I think that's where my expertise lies. So, for example, we're talking about feeding a baby, now I've never breast fed a baby. Now the chances are there are some women in that group who have, and they will give a completely different perspective on that than me standing up there and saying, 'Well, this is what happens. This is the physiology of breast-feeding. These are the problems that can take place and this is the kind of nursing interventions that we can make' [Approaches A and B]. That might all be very interesting. I might think that I'mquite an expert on that, but in the small group where you may have a woman sitting there and she's saying, 'Well, I'll tell you what, cracked nipples, you know, it's just the end of the world and it would have put me off completely feeding my baby' or whatever. And that, I think, coming from somebody who has experienced that I think will stick better [Approach C] than reading it in a book or having somebody standing up there saying it [Approaches A and B]."

Approach D: Student-active student-focused strategy aimed at the students changing their conceptions and skills with a view to improving their practice:

"…it's about getting them to engage in the material at a deep level rather than sitting listening to me talking about it. And I think what made it really useful was that the scenarios or the motions that I'd identified, they were actually able to relate to. So, they say, 'Well, that actually did happen and I never thought about x, y and z. Because we've never sat down and looked at it from both sides and so on, and that was really useful… I want my students to engage in that deep level of thinking because I want my students to have a deep approach to nursing. Now, and this might be a little controversial than a deep approach, well, it's not more controversial because I suppose it's what is being encouraged now, but essentially what I would want my students, at the end of the course and even during the course to some extent, is to take a deep approach to the practice that they're undertaking so that they aren't doing things by custom and practice. They're not just learning at a surface level how to do something [Approaches A and B]. Because, in the main, in learning disability nursing anyway, most people that you take off the street would be able to go and work in a learning disability environment, and they would be able to practice the same as the staff that are practising there by copying them. But what I want the students to be able to do is not learn by custom and practice, but to look at that in a deeper way and actually underpin their practice with thinking, reading, analysis and really multiple perspectives [Approach D], because there's the danger that they'll become, in the future, like the people I worked with in the past, or that in some services are still around now. That really don't understand why they're doing things and, for example, may work with somebody with a challenging behaviour for ten years and say, 'I can't understand why he's still like that?' or, 'I can't…' and when you look at their practices it's inevitable that the person's just going to get worse and worse [Approach C]. And that's why I want a deep approach because I want to lead to a deep approach to thinking about nursing and underpinning their practice like that [Approach D].

Approach E: Student-active student-focused strategy aimed at the students developing their professional attitudes and values (affective components):

'I think it's recognising that, I suppose part of it is kind of breaking down the barriers between sort of people with mental health problems and ordinary people like they're different species [Approach E] and trying to get people to understand that they're not different species and they're the same [Approach D]. But also valuing what the students bring in terms of previous work experience, previous life experience, you know, just all of them [Approach C]. Although I've got to say that while its also kind of valuing it, it's also getting it out in the air. And it might also be challenging it too [Approach D]."

"Well, what their values, what their attitudes are because it may not just, I think it's not just the case of, 'What's your value and attitude? Yeah, great we all respect them,' because we are trying to promote a philosophy. So sometimes it's about hearing it [Approach C] and encouraging challenge of it. It sounds a bit like brainwashing; it's not how it's kind of intended. It's about, I suppose, getting people's assumptions out on the table and creating a climate where everybody can sort of challenge them. They can look at the evidence for the assumptions that they're holding. Re-frame them I suppose, that's what learning's about I think [Approach D]… it's back to kind of values that I was saying we want to espouse. That it's about valuing people, valuing each other. But, it's also about being active in their learning right from the start. I mean it's not just about the affective part about mental health nursing, I suppose, it's about the affective part of the course [Approach E]. And at least what I would be hoping on the course which is participative and increasingly autonomous, talking in class, because they're going into a profession as well that's all about relationships, interpersonal skills, working together with other people, you know, so its that sort of transferable stuff out of the learning too that's, as well as the mental health specific stuff that they're going to have to be able to do. I also think that's quite important in terms of maybe student support and student experience. You know, that I think if they're used to starting to work in groups together, to relate to each other, to have some humour in class, to have light-heartedness, have kind of some relaxation, but also consider serious issues. I think… that I'm hoping students go away from the session having felt that it was useful but felt good, you know, having enjoyed it [Approach E]. Because my fantasy is that their experience in other modules will be very different. They'll be sitting in a huge lecture theatre with several overheads, writing lots and lots of factual information down. Although I've got to say that I recognise that that's got a role too. And that perhaps if in every module they were experiencing learning in the same way as they're doing in the module I'm talking about, not everybody would like it. Yes, that some people, and maybe some of them are sitting there thinking, 'God, when are they going to actually give us some facts?' or, 'When are we going to get an overhead?' [Approaches A and B]."

Discussion and conclusion

The results from this research indicate that student-centred approaches to teaching are made up of two main categories of description (or groups): group 1 – student-active teacher-focused strategies and group 2 – student-active student-focused strategies, with each category related to two or three intentions respectively. In the first group, teachers adopting this strategy have the teacher as the main focus of their strategy and their intentions are, respectively, for students to actively reproduce expert knowledge and skills or to acquire disciplinary conceptions and skills. The student-active teacher-focused strategy with the intention of the students actively reproducing expert knowledge and skills is the most limiting, or least complex, approach. Teachers adopting approaches A and B, respectively, see student-centred teaching, in this context, as being about skills and knowledge reproduction and skills and knowledge acquisition for safe practice. Teachers in this category have a common strategy but two qualitatively different intentions.

In the second group, student-active student-focused strategy (C, D and E), teachers have a common strategy but with three qualitatively different intentions. Teachers adopting the student-active student-focused strategy focus on the students and their intentions are for students to develop their own conceptions, change their conceptions and to develop their attitudes and values to learning and professional practice in order to promote informed, effective and holistic care respectively. In essence, students are being helped to develop their own knowledge, skills and professional attitudes for learning and practice. This is unlike approaches A and B where the teachers are passing on knowledge and skills. Approach E is suggested as being the most complete, complex, or sophisticated approach to student-centred teaching that subsumes approaches A, B, C and D.

Approaching teaching from the first group may have the impact of limiting student understanding and the development of professional attitudes and values for holistic learning and nursing practice. The focus is upon the teacher and what the teacher is doing, but the students are active in their learning. Learning how to apply teachers' knowledge and skills may lead to students adopting and acquiring expert procedural knowledge and skills that demonstrate safe nursing practice; however, teaching and learning in this way will not result in more effective student learning and practice. Teachers adopting student-active student-focused approaches have strategies and intentions that actively involve the students in their learning but with the related intentions for students to develop their own conceptions and skills, to change their conceptions and for the students to develop professional attitudes and values. The focus in these latter approaches is on the students and what the students are doing. Teachers adopting the most complete approach have an awareness of the preceding strategies and intentions but approach their teaching in a qualitatively different way that is thought to promote holistic student learning and practice.

These findings suggest that being student-centred in their approaches to teaching is not limited to one student-centred teaching method. Being student-centred in their approaches to teaching is seen as involving a relationship between the strategies employed and the teaching intentions and, whilst method is part of this relationship, the teaching method alone is not the sole determinant of whether approaches to teaching are student-centred or not.

Teachers adopting approaches A and B need to change their practice to incorporate more student-active student-focused approaches in their teaching and in order to do so they will have to focus upon the teaching strategies they employ in their practice in conjunction with their motivation, or intentions, for employing these strategies. This also has implications for staff development and teacher training programmes aimed at developing and enhancing student-centred approaches to teaching. Failure to change approaches to teaching in this way may result in students being less likely to adopt deep approaches to their learning (and presumably nursing practice) as has been found from research into teaching and learning in other areas of higher education (Trigwell et al, 1999; Gow and Kember, 1993).

References

D'A Slevin, O and Lavery, C (1991) 'Self directed learning and student supervision'. *Nurse Education Today*, 11: 368–353.

Dearing, R (1997) *Higher Education in the Learning Society: Report of the National Committee*. Norwich, HMSO.

Gow, L and Kember, D (1993) 'Conceptions of teaching and their relationship to student learning'. *British Journal of Educational Psychology*, 63: 20–33.

Iwasiw, CL (1987) 'The role of the teacher in self-directed learning'. *Nurse Education Today*, 7: 222–227.

Jinks, AM (1997) *Caring for Patients, Caring for Student Nurses*. Aldershot, Ashgate Publishing Ltd.

Jinks, AM (1999) 'Applying Education Theory to Nursing Curricula: nurse teachers' definitions of student-centred andragogical teaching and learning concepts'. *Journal of Further and Higher Education*, 23(2): 221–230.

Jinks, AM, Boreham, NC, and Webb, C (1998) 'A Study of the Attitudes to Student-centred Learning and Teaching, and Concepts of Andragogy in Senior Nurse Educationalists in England'. *Journal of Vocational Education and Training*, 50(3): 375–386.

MacLean, BL (1992) 'Technical curriculum models: are they appropriate for the nursing profession?' *Journal of Advanced Nursing*, 17: 871–876.

Nolan, J and Nolan, M (1997) 'Self-directed and student-centred learning in nurse education: 1'. *British Journal of Nursing*, 6(1): 51–55.

Richardson, M (1988) 'Innovating andragogy in a basic nursing course: an evaluation of the self directed independent study contract with basic nursing students'. *Nurse Education Today*, 8: 315–324.

Sweeney, JF (1986) 'Nurse education: learner-centred or teacher-centred?' *Nurse Education Today*, 6: 257–262.

Trigwell, K (1999) ISL Conference Proceedings.

Trigwell, K, Prosser, M and Waterhouse, F (1999) 'Relations between teachers' approaches to teaching and students' approaches to learning'. *Higher Education*, 37: 57–70.

UKCC (1999) *Fitness for Practice: A Report by the Commission for the Future Education of Nurses and Midwifes*. London, UKCC.

Variation in approaches to learning and teaching in disciplinary contexts: how to accommodate diversity?

Linda Drew, Chelsea College of Art & Design, University Of the Arts London

Abstract

This chapter examines the proposition that some disciplinary contexts are more likely to provide an environment which enhances student learning, accommodating individual students' approaches and responding to student diversity.

Commencing with a review of studies of disciplinary variation in teaching to highlight relations between approaches to teaching, academic leadership and disciplinary differences. Conceptual Change/Student-focused approaches are contrasted with Information Transmission/Teacher-focused approaches in the ways in which they relate to the outcomes of student learning and student activity or interactions.

The chapter seeks evidence to explore the proposition by focusing on an examination of studies of disciplinary differences pursued through epistemological characteristics such as structures for knowledge validation and responses to changes in the context. These differences are further explored in a review of studies related to the disciplines and teaching. Studies of particular contexts are also examined to understand the situated nature of disciplinary cultures.

The main discussion in this chapter concerns how these arguments help us to understand why some disciplinary learning and teaching contexts appear to be more successful at accommodating student diversity and variation in student approaches by being more student-focused.

Introduction

Drew (2004) reported five qualitatively different conceptions of teaching which are described as ranging from the teacher as offering something to students, through to the teaching as helping to change students' conceptions to teaching as helping students to change as a person. This pattern of variation in conceptions of teaching relates closely to the patterns of variation found in teaching more generally and gives some insight into an aspect of the qualitative variation in creative practice teachers' approaches to teaching.

Studies conducted on university teachers' approaches to teaching in other disciplines show that in some contexts, some teachers describe their approach as mainly student-focused, and they aim to help their students change their worldviews or conceptions of the phenomena they are studying. Students are seen by these teachers to have to construct their own knowledge, and their role as teachers is to help them achieve this end. While these teachers may use transmission methods among others, they appreciate that alone, transmission methods are unlikely to achieve the intended aims. This approach has been described as a Conceptual Change/Student-focused (CCSF) approach (Prosser and Trigwell, 1999).

In other contexts, other teachers, and some of the same teachers, describe an approach essentially limited to the information transmission elements of the description in the paragraph above, with the strategy being based largely on what the teacher does, rather than with a focus on what the student does. This approach has been described as an Information Transmission/Teacher-focused (ITTF) approach to teaching (Prosser and Trigwell, 1999).

The variations described above are significant as qualitatively different approaches to teaching have been found to relate to students' qualitatively different approaches to learning (Trigwell, Prosser and Waterhouse, 1999) and in turn, these learning approaches have been found to relate the quality of the outcome of student learning (Marton and Säljö, 1997).

Most of the studies that have led to the descriptions of the relations between teaching and learning have been conducted with teachers from the more traditional disciplines. And they have been conducted using an inventory developed from studies of university science teaching. The teaching of creative practice subjects, such as design for example, or other practice subjects, such as nursing or even business studies are often described in ways that are quite different to descriptions of teaching in more traditional subject areas such as science. Less use is made of lecturing and lecture notes, the activities that are employed tend to be more context specific or project-based, and involve smaller groups of students than in the more traditional areas.

Learning to practice

Studies which embrace the sociocultural perspective on practice particularly emphasise learning to practice in various settings. Learning to practice, whether in the workplace or simulated settings is seen as a move towards full participation in a community of practice (Lave and Wenger, 1991; Lave, 1993). That move to full participation takes place by engaging in 'legitimate peripheral participation' which is taking part in the authentic activities of the practice, albeit with guidance, and at the edges of the community. These views emphasise social practice as a premise for learning and that 'knowing in practice' arises from participation in that social practice (Billett, 1998).

Learning that results from participation in social practices means that the participants appropriate ways of seeing the world inherent in those practices. These situational and social factors are a key part of learning to practice (Billett, 2001). Billett argues that a non-dualist view of learning is becoming more accepted, based on the concept that there is an inseparable relationship between an individual's knowing and their social life-world (Rogoff, 1990). Many would argue that preparing learners for life as a creative practitioner, be that as an artist or a photographer, is essentially preparing them for solitary work. Rogoff (1990) suggests that cultural practices and norms shape even the most apparently solitary activities. This is further confirmed by Billett (2001):

> *An artist working in the isolation of his studio reported shaping his practice to account for situational factors determining the kinds and purposes of his work that included physical environments and consideration of the market (p444)*

Jean Lave describes the social participatory perspective on learning as individuals developing and changing their identities, "...people are becoming kinds of persons" (Lave, 1996, p157). Lave's study of the apprenticeship of tailors in Liberia during the seventies identifies how the tailors were primarily making ready-to-wear trousers, but the apprentices also learned other important contextual factors about being a tailor:

> *... they were learning relations among the major social identities and divisions in Liberian society which they were in the business of dressing. They were learning to make a life, to make a living, to make clothes, to grow old enough, and mature enough to become master tailors, and to see the truth of the respect due to a master of their trade. (Lave, 1996, p159)*

These tailors lived in the master tailors' houses in a district full of those houses and also tailoring workshops. In the workshops the apprentices received direct and indirect guidance from participation in the tailoring practices, working with other tailors and other tailors' apprentices. These apprentices were effectively immersed in tailoring practice and this environment helped them to fully participate in tailoring and learn the trade. The community of practice is most certainly about "becoming kinds of persons", and about developing ways of seeing the world through practice.

The cornerstone of these issues for professional learning can be summarised as learning to practice or becoming inducted into a community of practice (Wenger, 1998). Wenger further defines the role of participation in a practice in its relationship with the reification of artifacts or processes particular to the practice. Wenger regards participation as 'the social experience of living in the world' (1998, p55) which involves acting, thinking and feeling as a whole personal experience. It is from participation, Wenger argues, that an *identity of participation* is constituted through the relations formed in participation itself.

Studies of experience, expertise and competence further demonstrate that learning to practice is not just about participation, but also about an experience of meaning which is constructed over time in engaging at the community level in order to build a repertoire of practice. Earlier studies of competence define a linear hierarchy of competence acquisition from novice to expert (Dreyfus and Dreyfus, 1986; Benner, 1984) which do not take account of social factors but do define aspects of competence as context dependent. Schön (1983) criticised the technical rational epistemology by elaborating on what he called an 'epistemology of practice'. His study closely examined the professional work and learning of architects, engineers, psychotherapists, planners and managers. From this study he further determined two different types of human competence, knowing-in-action and reflection-in-action. Knowing-in-action illustrates the context-dependent nature of competence. The professional workers' reflection-in-action further demonstrates and clarifies the context-dependent nature of competence.

Wenger (1998, pp137-139) explains that learning in practice is possible if an experience of meaning interacts with a regime of competence. He also distinguishes between experience and competence, they do not determine each other but they may be out of alignment in the practice learning experience. Developing competence in the skills of a practice does not in itself build experience as the practice has many socially situated elements the meaning of which has to be negotiated within the community of practice. Billett (2001) has produced an authoritative study of knowing in practice and vocational expertise which uses accounts of Australian hairdressers learning to practice. He acknowledges both the social and the situational in the process of coming to know and in developing expertise:

> *Expertise needs to be considered situationally, being related to the circumstances of the enactment of the vocational practice. This does not mean that the individual's capacity to perform is welded to one setting. Rather, it recognises that expertise can only be understood within particular domains of knowledge and action (social practice), thus embedding it in particular social circumstances. (Billett, 2001, p441)*

These studies confirm that although building competence in skills is a crucial part of learning to practice, those skills are not enough on their own. There has to be recognition of the socially situated contexts of the practice of which skills development is part of practice learning. Ideally competence in skills should be integrated into practice learning contexts so that learners construct an experience of meaning. Although there is much in the literature on practice learning there is very little which demonstrates how teachers in practice settings can engage with these concepts. In this chapter I propose that the epistemology of practice learning brings about conditions for accommodating individual students' approaches and responding to student diversity.

The Approaches to Teaching Inventory (ATI) has been used to measure variation in approach to teaching in design teaching contexts (Trigwell, 2002). In that study it was found that, as in other teaching contexts, there is significant variation in descriptions of how teaching is approached in design subjects, and that overall, the approaches adopted by design teachers are described as being more student-focused than in most other areas of higher education teaching. The results also suggest that when those teachers describe their approaches as student-focused they are more likely to say they learn more during the teaching of their subjects and are more likely to give students the opportunity to explore their own creative ideas, than when the teaching is described in terms of teacher-focused information transmission.

Disciplinary differences

Disciplines can be defined in many different ways, including epistemologically, by their practices, their narratives of belonging and by identification. Epistemologically they are defined by their distinctive set of concepts, the structure of propositions, truth criteria by which those propositions are reviewed and the methodology used to arrive at those propositions (Donald, 1986; 1995). Donald (1995) explores those disciplinary differences in knowledge validation and makes distinctions between scientific method and interpretive methods used in disciplines such as the social sciences. Scientific method assumes that there is an objective truth which can be found through processes of deduction. The social science model relies on observations, interpretations and perceptions to make claims for knowledge. The best known description of how disciplines demonstrate these differences is characterised by the hard/soft and applied/pure typology first posited by Biglan (1973) and further elaborated with empirical study by Becher (1989) and revisited in Becher and Trowler (2001). The Becher (1989) concept of academic tribes has been widely adopted as shorthand for categorisation of both academic knowledge and academics. The Becher and Trowler (2001) edition further complements this study with a categorisation of the social features of those disciplinary communities between convergent, tightly knit and divergent, loosely knit disciplinary configurations. Both of these studies also focused on research activity (and not teaching) as an aspect of the disciplinary variation found. A recent study (Cooper and Trowler, 2002) further develops some of the themes relating to disciplinary variation and identities in interaction, recurrent practices and implicit theories of learning and teaching. The notion of disciplinary communities and their teaching and learning regimes (TLRs) proposes a socially constructed notion of how groups of teachers come to know through the practice of teaching and of learning to teach. Cooper and Trowler's main argument is that academic staff bring sets of assumptions and practices rooted in TLRs to their experience of teaching and educational development programmes. In their study examples are given which draw out, through a vignette approach, aspects of the regimes. These aspects can be characterised using the following as a structure for the vignette:

■ Tacit assumptions

■ Implicit theories of learning and teaching

■ Recurrent practices

■ Rules of appropriateness

■ Codes of signification

■ Discursive repertoire

■ Identities in interaction

■ Power relations

Disciplinary differences in teaching and teaching scholarship

Studies of disciplinary variation in teaching or teaching scholarship have received limited attention. A collection of studies edited by Hativa and Marincovitch (1995) is one of the first to gather cases from different disciplines with respect to implications for learning and teaching. Within that collection, Murray and Renaud (1995) examine disciplinary differences in teaching and their relationship to student feedback and ratings of instruction. In their study, arts and humanities teachers scored higher than social science and natural science teachers on six out of ten teaching behaviour dimensions. This finding implies that 'arts and humanities teachers tend to exhibit a wider range of teaching behaviours that contribute positively to student instructional ratings than social science or natural science teachers do' (p38). Further case studies and disciplinary variation in improving student learning was the subject of the seventh International Improving Student Learning Symposium in 1999 (Rust, 2000). In these proceedings, Trigwell, Prosser, Martin and Ramsden (2000) studied relations between approaches to teaching, academic leadership and disciplinary differences. It was noted that arts/business teachers perceived a leadership environment which was supportive of good teaching as they adopt a more Conceptual Change/Student-focused approach. This finding deserves further investigation in relation to the development of teachers and departmental heads in arts departments.

More recently however there have been some studies which connect disciplinary culture to the nature of teaching and learning processes and learning outcomes (Neumann, 2001; Neumann, Parry and Becher, 2002). Neumann (2001) provides an overview of studies of disciplinary difference and further applies this to the nature of teaching, teaching practices and approaches. More importantly, she makes connections between these approaches, disciplinary differences and student learning. This study does also conclude that further systematic study of this area needs to be conducted to further explore the links between teachers' conceptions founded in disciplinary identity and the implications for the improvement of student learning. Neumann, Parry and Becher (2002) have commenced that further study and come to some important conclusions which are well illustrated with disciplinary examples.

> *...hard applied subject fields, where the emphasis, in both curriculum and assessment, on problem solving and practical skills is expected to manifest itself as an important product of a degree course. Here a strong value is placed on the integration and application of existing knowledge... It is commonly observed that the vocational nature of most applied programmes leads to a clear expectation of their subsequent employment opportunities: the claim is rarely made for the development of widely transferable skills.*

> *...soft applied programmes, not unexpectedly, share this vocational slant, and the skills they develop are also practice related, their knowledge base tends to be more*

> *eclectic, and their implicit emphasis – shared with soft pure knowledge – is on the enhancement of personal growth and intellectual breadth. (p410)*

Studies of teaching scholarship have also highlighted disciplinary variation although it is not always clearly demonstrated. Huber and Morrealle (2002) situate this area in an orienting essay as a preface to their edited collection on disciplinary styles in the scholarship of teaching and learning. Their claim is that 'disciplinary styles empower the scholarship of teaching by guiding scholars to choose certain problems, use certain methods, and present their work in certain ways' (p4). In other words, those scholars' findings can be presented in contextually contingent ways. Differences are therefore presented in this collection, but only at the level of the personalised accounts. It should be noted that this is, in effect, work in progress from the outcomes of the ongoing work of the Carnegie Academy for the Scholarship of Teaching and Learning (CASTL). Approaches to teaching have, however, been shown to relate to approaches to teaching scholarship in the disciplines (Leuddeke, 2003). Leuddeke confirms his working hypothesis that staff teaching hard/pure or applied subjects were more likely to adopt an Information Transmission/Teacher-focused approach to their teaching, while those teaching soft/pure and applied subjects generally take a more Conceptual Change/Student-focused approach. He also concludes that this has implications for teacher development and development of teaching scholarship in the disciplines citing both the LTSN (Learning and Teaching Support Network) and CASTL as organisations which can support such disciplinary driven development.

By contrast, the QAA Subject Overview Reports and the QAA Subject Benchmark Statements dominate the contemporary policy literature. However, these reports are useful in situating the current state of these disciplines in terms of learning, teaching and assessment as well as their wider aspirations which are well articulated in the Subject Benchmark Statements (QAA, 2002).

Discussion

There is a widely held view in university-level teaching that a student-focused or student-centred approach helps students to develop as individuals. That they are also associated with approaches to learning, which can lead to higher quality learning outcomes, was confirmed in recent studies by Trigwell, Prosser and Waterhouse (1999). From further application of the ATI in design and creative practice subjects (Drew, 2003; Drew and Trigwell, 2003) it can be added that in the teaching of creative practices the student-focused approach also aligns with an approach in which teachers encourage their students to learn through authentic practices ("real world" projects).

When teachers describe their approach as being more student-focused, they spend more of their teaching time on "real world" and practitioner-related problems. On the other hand, when teachers describe their approach as being more teacher-focused, they report adopting a focus mainly on skills development. It should be emphasised here that most or all of the teachers in this study do develop skills with their students, but those with a student-focused approach focus more on inducting students into the community of practice by using "real world" projects and studio- or practice-based approaches. If teachers of these subjects value the induction of their students into the community of their practice then it also follows that they should develop a student-focused approach and a related practice focus to their teaching.

This confirms the views held by both Wenger (1998) and Billett (2001) that a skills based approach to learning to practice is simply not enough on its own. There also is evidence in that investigation that a skills-based approach corresponds with an Information Transmission/Teacher-focused approach to teaching. Those teachers who do integrate skills into "real world" projects and studio- or practice-based approaches, help learners develop competence in those skills so that they can construct an experience of meaning. This has significance for the development of teachers in these subjects if high-level student learning outcomes in practice-based courses are a desired aim for the teaching.

In one of those studies of approaches (Drew and Trigwell, 2003) a statistically significant positive correlation was also found between teachers' Conceptual Change/Student-focused approaches to teaching a subject and their satisfaction in teaching that subject, and a statistically significant negative correlation between teachers' Information Transmission/Teacher-focused approaches to teaching a subject and their satisfaction in teaching that subject. There is a general consensus in higher education that the idea of transmission is an impoverished view of university teaching. That view is generally expressed in relation to the quality of student learning associated with it, but the word impoverished might also be used in this case to refer to the quality of the experience of the teacher. When, for whatever reason, these teachers report using approaches that have more characteristics of Information Transmission/Teacher-focused approaches, they express lower levels of satisfaction. Components of a teacher-focused approach include a focus on helping students to pass examinations, helping students to get a reliable record of the key issues, presenting the facts so that students know what they have to learn, and feeling that questions asked by students should be answerable by the teacher. Teachers aim to achieve these ends using transmission-based strategies, with the focus being on the content being taught. This approach is synonymous with Biggs' (2001) Level 2 theory of teaching, where the focus is on what the teacher does. From this perspective the teacher accepts responsibility for the success of the action undertaken. With this responsibility, in combination with the nature of the strategies employed it is not difficult to see why this approach is likely to be more stress-inducing, less enjoyable and less satisfying.

The approaches to teaching scores obtained in that study, as with the previous study (Trigwell, 2002), show high levels of adoption of student-focused approaches. These teachers are describing their approaches in terms of using time to question students' ideas, of using difficult or undefined examples to provoke debate, of engaging in discussions with students, and of assessing students in ways that get at their changing conceptual understandings. The teachers that report making more use of conversations with students about the topics they are learning; who are more encouraging of students to restructure their existing knowledge; and who are more likely to create more time for discussions between students, are also the teachers who are more satisfied in their teaching.

Finally, this chapter proposes that systematic study of links between disciplines and approaches to teaching and learning need to be conducted to further explore the links between teachers' conceptions founded in disciplinary identities and the implications for the improvement of student learning.

References

Benner, RN (1984). *From novice to expert. Excellence and power in clinical nursing practice*. San Francisco: Addison-Wesley.

Becher, T (1989) *Academic Tribes and Territories*. Buckingham: Open University Press/SRHE

Becher, T and Trowler, P (2001) *Academic Tribes and Territories: intellectual enquiry and the cultures of disciplines* (2nd edition). Buckingham: Open University Press/SRHE

Biggs, J (2001). The reflective institution: Assuring and enhancing the quality of teaching and learning. *Higher Education*, 41, 221–238.

Biglan, A (1973) Relationships between subject matter characteristics and the structure and output of university departments, *Journal of Applied Psychology*, 57, 195–203.

Billett, S (1998). Situation, social systems and learning. *Journal of Education and Work*, 11, 255–274.

Billett, S (2001). Knowing in practice: re-conceptualising vocational expertise. *Learning and Instruction*, 11, 431–452.

Cooper, A and Trowler, P (2002) Teaching and learning regimes: implicit theories and recurrent practices in the enhancement of teaching and learning through educational development programmes. *Higher Education Research and Development*, 21(3), 221–220.

Donald, J (1986) Knowledge and the university curriculum. *Higher Education*, 15 (3) 267–282.

Donald, J (1995) Disciplinary differences in knowledge validation. In Hativa, N and Marincovitch, M (Eds) *Disciplinary Differences in Teaching and Learning: Implications for Practice*. San Francisco: Jossey-Bass.

Drew, L (2004) *The experience of teaching creative practices: conceptions and approaches to teaching in the community of practice dimension*. Paper presented at the cltad 2nd International Conference, Enhancing the curricula: Towards the Scholarship of Teaching in Art, Design and Communication. Barcelona, Spain

Drew, L (2003) *Approaches to teaching: extending 'theory' in the context of art, design and communication*. Paper presented at the 11th International Improving Student Learning Symposium 2003. Improving Student Learning: Theory, Research and Scholarship. Hinckley, Leicestershire, UK

Drew, L and Trigwell, K (2003) Qualitative differences in approaches to teaching, teacher satisfaction and communities of practice in art, design and communication courses. Paper presented at the 10th Biennial EARLI (European Association for Learning and Instruction) conference 2003. Padova, Italy.

Dreyfus, HL and Dreyfus, SE (1986). *Mind over machine. The power of human intuition and expertise in the era of the computer*. New York: Free Press.

Hativa, N and Marincovitch, M (Eds) (1995) Disciplinary Differences in Teaching and Learning: Implications for Practice. San Francisco: Jossey-Bass.

Huber, MT and Morrealle, SP (Eds) (2002) *Disciplinary Styles in the scholarship of teaching and learning: Exploring common ground.* Washington, DC: American Association for Higher Education and the Carnegie Foundation for the Advancement of Teaching.

Lave, J (1993). The practice of learning. In S Chaiklin and J Lave (Eds) *Understanding Practice*, Cambridge: Cambridge University Press, pp 3–32.

Lave, J (1996). Teaching, as learning, in practice. *Mind, Culture and Activity*, 3, 149–164.

Lave, J and Wenger, E (1991). *Situated learning: Legitimate peripheral participation*. Cambridge: Cambridge University Press.

Leuddeke, G (2003) Professionalising teaching practice in Higher Education: a study of disciplinary variation and 'teaching-scholarship'. *Studies in Higher Education*, 28 (2), 213–228

Marton, F and Säljö, R (1997) Approaches to Learning. In Marton, F, Hounsell, D and Entwistle, NJ (Eds) *The Experience of Learning: Implications for Teaching and Studying in Higher Education*. (2nd edition). Edinburgh, Scottish Academic Press, 39–58.

Murray, HG and Renaud, RD (1995) Disciplinary differences in classroom teaching behaviors. In Hativa, N and Marincovitch, M (Eds) (1995) *Disciplinary Differences in Teaching and Learning: Implications for Practice*. San Francisco: Jossey-Bass, pp31–39.

Neumann, R (2001) Disciplinary differences and university teaching. *Studies in Higher Education*, 26 (2), 135–146.

Neumann, R, Parry, S, and Becher, T (2002) Teaching and learning in their disciplinary contexts. *Studies in Higher Education*, 27 (4), 405–417.

Prosser, M and Trigwell, K (1999). *Understanding Learning and Teaching: The experience in higher education*. Buckingham: Open University Press/SRHE

QAA (2002). Quality Assurance Agency Benchmark Statements and review reports. Viewed 27th August 2004 at http://www.qaa.ac.uk/crntwork/benchmark/index.htm

Rogoff, B (1990). *Apprenticeship in thinking – cognitive development in social context*. New York: Oxford University Press.

Schön, DA (1983). *The Reflective Practitioner: How Professionals Think in Action*. New York: Basic Books.

Trigwell, K (2002). Approaches to teaching design subjects: a quantitative analysis. *Art, Design and Communication in Higher Education*, 1, 69–80.

Trigwell, K, Prosser, M, Martin, E, and Ramsden, P (2000) Discipline differences in relations between learning, teaching and ways of leading teaching departments. In Rust, C (Ed) *Improving Student Learning Through The Disciplines*. Oxford: Oxford Brookes University, Oxford Centre for Staff and Learning Development.

Trigwell, K, Prosser, M and Waterhouse, F (1999). Relations between teachers' approaches to teaching and students' approaches to learning. *Higher Education*, 37, 57–70.

Wenger, E (1998). Communities of Practice: Learning, meaning and identity. Cambridge: Cambridge University Press.

The Reflections on Teaching Inventory (1): initial item trialling and an exploratory conceptual domain

Jan HF Meyer, University of Durham

Malcolm G Eley, Monash University

Ursula Lucas, University of the West of England

Abstract

Deriving in part from criticism that the *Approaches to Teaching Inventory* is flawed in its development, the present project revisits the task of constructing an inventory of teaching practices. Applying an empirically driven approach to item generation and scale development, the expected outcome is a multidimensional model and inventory, capable of useful differentiation, which can serve as both a research and diagnostic instrument.

In the first stage of the project reported here, interviews of university teachers on their teaching practices, and their related thinking, formed the basis for initial item stem generation. Those stems were phrased as descriptions of specific teaching practices and experiences. This initial pool was trialled on separate samples of undergraduate teachers in Australia and Britain. The responses from this trialling enabled items to be selected for further scale development, based entirely on their empirical distributional characteristics. The importance, in inventory development, of applying processes that are open and not pre-judged, is discussed.

Introduction

The general context for the work reported here is a concern to describe the ways in which university teachers' practices might vary. The outcome is expected to be a multidimensional model of teaching couched as an inventory, with scales reflecting those dimensions. Implicit in the work is an assumption that teaching practices are an important part of the educational context within which students learn and, as such, those practices have the potential to influence students' learning approaches and learning outcomes.

Implicit also is an assumption that the practices reported by teachers using inventory instruments can validly reflect the ways in which those teachers actually operate in their teaching. Note however that recent work (Kane, Sandretto and Heath, 2002; Eley, in press) has indicated that expressions of belief about teaching, or of general approaches or conceptions of teaching, might *not* be functionally related to the actuality of teaching practices. Such findings suggest that, in developing inventory items, phrasings that describe observations or experiences more concretely or contextually should be favoured. Such findings also signal that the ability of any model of teaching to predict or reflect actual teaching practices is itself an empirical claim that requires testing.

There are some basic elements that underpin the general research approach taken here. First, beginning with an expectation that any eventual model of teaching will be multidimensional means that throughout the project any methodological practice that might artificially constrain the range of dimensions that could ultimately be manifested must be avoided. Second, potential item stems should be sourced in variation of teaching practice. As a source, such variation can certainly be found from interviews with teachers in which they describe or report actual practice. Such variation of practice may also be reflected in research findings. Third, the selection of item stems to be included in any eventual inventory should substantively be driven by a visible empirical process. The prime focus here, in the absence of imposing conceptual constraints or preconceived dimensional structure, should be on selecting items *that capture variation*.

More specifically, the work reported in the present paper arises out of a recent critique of the *Approaches to Teaching Inventory* (ATI), an instrument developed by Prosser and Trigwell (1999) to 'measure the ways teachers approach their teaching' (p176). That critique (Meyer and Eley, 2003) considered the history of the initial development and trialling processes that resulted in the ATI, and concluded that the validity and reliability of that instrument had been compromised. In particular, it was observed that the samples of teachers used in successive developmental triallings of the ATI overlapped in membership and were thus not truly independent, those samples were small compared to what might be considered normal for scale development purposes, and their membership was exclusively restricted to the physical sciences. Perhaps more critical, the pool of item stems from which the ATI eventually evolved were actually and subjectively selected *a priori* to fit with a particular preconceived theoretical model of teaching approaches. The conclusion of the critique was that the ATI is constrained by its development methodology in the range of variability, and in the sources of that variability, that it is capable of exhibiting. There were also serious perceived flaws in the psychometric methodology of the ATI development. In short, the ATI is capable of indicating only the extent to which any given teacher-respondent varies within a simple two-dimensional model of teaching behaviours and approaches. The point of departure here is the observation that the ATI is simply not capable of more comprehensively measuring 'the ways teachers approach their teaching' (Prosser and Trigwell, op cit).

Although the work by Meyer and Eley (2003) appears to be the first to critique the ATI explicitly in terms of its empirical dimensionality and its development methodology, it is not the first expression of some of the concerns raised. Kember (1997) reviewed thirteen studies of university teachers' conceptions of teaching, including two parallel studies (Prosser, Trigwell & Taylor, 1994; Trigwell, Prosser & Taylor, 1994) based on the same set of interviews of 24 teachers of undergraduate physical sciences, that were the beginnings of the ATI's development. It is quite remarkable that from the one set of interview data these two parallel phenomenographic studies yielded a total of 16 categories of description. Of his reviewed studies, Kember noted that 'a significant proportion of the authors specify their methodology as phenomenography' (Kember, 1997, p263), and further that 'If a researcher sets out to discover categories of description, it must come as no surprise that the results appear as categories of description' (ibid). The point here is that, in developing *inventories* from phenomenographic categories, the 'pre-ordaining' effect on dimensionality that can occur from categories that themselves are created from a constrained data set is self-evident.

In subsequent work specifically looking at approaches to teaching, Kember and Kwan (2000) found that a six-dimensional model was necessary in order to capture the range of variation that existed in their subjects' reported approaches. These six dimensions included motivation, instructional practices, instructional focus, assessment forms, acknowledgement of student characteristics, and the sourcing of experiential links or illustrations. Moreover, each of these dimensions was conceived as a continuous dimension, rather than as a binary set of 'endpoint' categories. Without engaging in any sort of evaluation of Kember's findings, it is interesting here to note how the application of less constrained methodologies can result in interpretations of teaching that are more differentiated than those implicit in the ATI.

Aims of the present study

The present study sets out to approach afresh the challenge of developing an inventory to capture variation in university teaching practice and, in doing so, to adhere as strictly as possible to an empirical, data-driven approach. The intention is to develop initial item stems to reflect as broad a range of potential sources of variability as possible, avoiding any particular extant theoretical position and the privileged selection of items congruent with it. Those items that are subsequently found to capture variation amongst teachers are those that are then retained for further exploratory purposes. It is generally anticipated that retained items will, depending on their psychometric properties singly and in combination, eventually contribute or not to the definition of psychometrically underpinned dimensions of variability. These dimensions, and their interrelationships, will *de facto* constitute an empirically grounded model of teaching within which individual teachers can be conceptually located in varying degrees.

While the present project is couched as the development of inventory scales, its real result will be the development of a model of teaching that will underlie those scales. In that this model will have come from atheoretical *methodological* processes, it will constitute a test of previous theoretical interpretations, including the ATI's two-dimensional underpinnings. The key distinction between this present project's approach and that which resulted in the ATI is that here the model evolves out of the data. It is not predetermined in any way. The procedure is one of isolating and then psychometrically refining sources of variation. It is not a matter of defining scales to reflect *a priori* theoretically predetermined 'sources'.

In the construction of inventories generally, a critical task is the development of an initial pool of item stems and this is a process that needs to be as visible as possible. It is important to guard against the possibility that sources of variation might be prematurely precluded. The general approach needs to be one of erring on the side of inclusion. The yardstick needs to be the empirical test; if in doubt about an item stem, include it in trialling and see whether response variation occurs, in which case the item is retained.

In the present project, the deliberate adoption of this data driven approach led early to the realisation that item generation, and thus scale development, would need to be seen as an iterative process. At any stage in the eventual inventory's development it might be recognised that there existed a further potential source of variation that had to date been untapped in terms of possible items. There would need to be a continuing openness to the possibility that some further scale might be developed, which would reflect a genuine dimension of variation in teachers' practices.

Speculative sources of variation

Probably the first actual work on the present project was an unfettered and far ranging discussion of the perceived dimensional insensitivity of the ATI. The intention here was not pretentiously to lay out a blueprint of scales to be thus developed and, in doing so, propose some notional implicit model of teaching as a starting point for the present work. The intention in considering the conclusions of relevant research studies (see for example Kember, 1997), and the published (see for example Ballantyne, Bain and Packer, 1997), as well as unpublished (as in teaching portfolios) accounts of reflective academic practice, was rather to speculate on dimensions of variation, as opposed to dimensions of conformity, that *might* emerge as candidates for empirical testing at some future point.

In similar vein, in curriculum planning (Stark, 2002), there could be variation in the extent to which teachers consider things like communication skills, thinking skills, or metacognition, as explicit parts of a syllabus. There could be variation in considering a curriculum as an organised body of knowledge, as phenomena explored in common by scholars in the field, or as a set of skills to be mastered. There could be variation in the prominence given to content selection versus objectives definition versus student characteristics. The expert teacher literature (Dunkin, 2002; Kane, Sandretto and Heath, 2004; Ballantyne, Bain and Packer, 1999; Hativa, Barak and Simhi, 2001) suggests, furthermore, that potential dimensions might include the importance given to a well-developed and detailed subject knowledge, and the presence of a rich repertoire of well practised, highly discriminative and specific pedagogical skills, which are evoked in recognised teaching contexts.

In the early stages of the present work there was thus an initial process of becoming more sensitive to possible *signs* of sources of variation as a guard against presumptive exclusion. Some of these signs are illustrated in the following scenarios: Disciplines might differ in the extent to which 'publicly agreed' structures exist, which might then show up as varied emphases given to sequence within curricular organisation, or to the order in which students 'must' meet topics, or even to the content at particular curricular levels. At a more detailed level of consideration, in some fields there might be quite defined and specific forms of prior learning that are seen to function as necessary 'anchor points' for subsequently learning equally defined and specific material, whereas in other fields it might be a looser notion of simply finding some forms of prior learning or experiences that 'will do'. Disciplines might vary in the extent to which they have 'preferred' ways of explaining or developing particular topics, which might then relate to the importance attributed to developing clear, coherent, expositions and frameworks. Across disciplines there might be a variation between a 'guiding towards a particular form of conceptualising' and a more open 'prompting associations or connections that are fundamentally student determined', which might manifest as varying degrees of monitoring and guidance. Some teachers might try to experience vicariously the 'way finding' that their students experience during an exposition in class, concurrently with those students; perhaps suggesting something beyond the simplistic polarisation of teacher- versus student-centredness, namely 'togetherness'.

The preceding considerations give rise to speculation that in some fields it might well be entirely sensible that a teacher could be very 'student-centred' in terms of focusing on what is happening in the student's mind, and in recognising absolutely that learning is something 'constructed' by the student, but *at the same time* be very concerned about 'informational presentation' and the acquisition by the student of 'definitional knowledge'. This tension then throws up a range of qualifications that might need to be applied in how we *define* conceptualisations of teaching in different disciplines. As an example, Linder (1992; 1993) points out that in many areas of science, especially physics, learning is not so much a matter of changing students' conceptions as it is a matter of students accumulating a range of conceptions. We do not want students to change from a wave model of light to a particle model to a photon model. Rather we want them to acquire an understanding of all models. But we also want them to be capable of accurately discriminating amongst the different contexts in which each model might be uniquely applicable. This suggests that in science teaching, the 'highest' level approach to teaching might be seen not as focusing on conceptual change, but more on conceptual accumulation allied with the learning of discriminative context signals. Such an argument must call into question the privileged status within a posited conceptual hierarchy, as was the case with the development of the ATI, of a (sub) dimension of 'conceptual change'.

Development of an initial pool of items

The preceding discussion clearly indicates that there exist many potential dimensions along which teachers might meaningfully vary in ways genuinely relevant to their disciplinary teaching practices. In the present work it was imperative then to begin the process of item generation and development in as inclusive a manner as possible.

The starting point was a set of interview records from research in which teachers of undergraduates had been asked to think aloud while preparing to teach (Eley, 2003). A limitation in using these interview records is immediately acknowledged. The teachers in question were operating in real time within a constrained context of preparing an immediate class on a defined topic. This context could well have lessened the probability that they would 'mention' broader teaching issues, like curriculum, assessment, grading, supervision and consultation. Insofar as this was the case, any pool of resultant item stems would be similarly contextually constrained. It is therefore emphasised that this initial first stage of item generation, as reported here, is *not* the end of the process of item generation. There is available a further corpus of interview data which might allow the generation of more 'broadly focused' item stems. Beyond that, there is the possibility of reviewing literatures on broader teaching issues and practices, with findings suggesting item stems, or of engaging in other targeted empirical item generation exercises.

The 37 teachers who participated in the interviews were from a range of disciplines. They had been given no preliminary rationale or theoretical orientation. They had been asked simply to select an introductory level topic from a list provided, and then to plan an imagined class, thinking aloud while they did so. The records of these interviews were read through as a source of item stems; the approach was to look for things that these teachers said, that seemed to describe or indicate discrete teaching practices. Furthermore teachers' phrasings were used directly, or as a direct basis for generating initial item stems. And there is an immediate recognition that, in this process, there is the possibility for also admitting authentic and *different* ways in which 'teaching approaches' are conceptualised *in student learning* terms within and across disciplines in resonance with what McCune and Hounsell (2005) refer to as 'ways of thinking and practising'.

In that teachers' statements were being selected on a criterion of whether they described some teaching practice evoked by the interviewee, there were certainly judgments being made. But importantly for the present project, these statements were not explicitly *judged* in terms of whether they reflected any particular practice, or ideology, or rationale, or extant model of teaching. The intention in this beginning process was to give no consideration to notions of the quality of the item stem, or to whether that stem related to some previously noted dimension of variation, or to whether similar items had been generated from teacher statements read earlier. While the present authors do not claim pristine objectivity, the process consciously applied by them was one of non-evaluatively allowing teachers' voices to inform the generation of item stems.

The process as outlined generated 438 initial item stems. The next phase was to review the generated items. First, they were classified and sorted. Items that seemed to be similar in meaning were grouped together, and categories were generated that seemed to describe those groupings. This process was performed by two of the authors, and an independent research assistant. Next, the classified items were reviewed within their groupings to find any exact equivalents, allowing redundant items to be discarded. The surviving item stems were then submitted to an editing process in which any obvious reference to a particular discipline field was removed by rephrasing (note however, that it is still possible that some described practices might yet be found empirically to align with particular fields). Finally, all items were rephrased to conform to a 'standard syntax' of a first person description of something that a teacher 'does or experiences'. The resultant pool contained 234 item stems. Examples of initially generated stems, together with their eventual forms, are shown in Table 1 below.

The response scale chosen for the pool items comprised an ordinal five options ranging from 'You recognize the statement as being immediately or very consistently true of you, or as something that you always or almost always do or experience', through to '…only very rarely true of you, or as something that you never or almost never do or experience at all'. The choice of item response scale derives from earlier work indicating that more observationally couched items, with frequency or observationally defined response options, tend to result in greater response reliability, especially in comparison to the strictly attitudinally oriented Likert *agree/disagree* format (see Eley and Stecher, 1997, and Eley, 2001). This choice of item response scale in part dictated the syntactical form of the item stems.

Stems as originally generated	Phrasings as eventually trialled.
I will present counter examples to get the students thinking. Sometimes in running a class discussion, I will deliberately play a 'devil's advocate' role. Sometimes I'll deliberately get students to take another look at material, but from a different perspective. I try to present my students with information or evidence that I know will be contrary to what they have picked up in other contexts.	I use examples or information that I know is contrary to what the students have considered so far.
I decide between different explanation possibilities by imagining what sorts of connections the students might make. I check on an explanation or presentation by imagining myself in the student's place, and then thinking about what I am planning to do. I decide on how to present something by pretending that I'm a student listening to myself, to test whether I would understand it. I put myself in the student's mind, and think what is it that they are going to find difficult if they don't know the material.	I imagine myself as a student who doesn't know the material, and I think about what might be difficult about a presentation or explanation that I'm planning. I decide how to present something by testing whether I would understand it were I a student listening to myself.

Table 1. Examples of items, as originally generated from interview records, and as rephrased for trialling.

The trialling of the first pool of items

The purpose of this first trialling was simply to determine which items attracted a relatively broad distribution of responses. In developing inventory *scales*, the purpose of which is to detect variation amongst individuals, it is necessary to begin with individual *item* responses that themselves exhibit variation. This first trialling was therefore a preliminary step towards scale development work.

The pool of 234 initial items was subdivided into manageable groups for this first trialling. Given the impracticality of administering all 234 items in a single trial inventory, the items were randomly selected and then randomly allocated into six groups of 39 items each. This process ensured that each 39-item group contained items representing a variety of meanings and practices. Also, once each group had been established, the internal sequence of the 39 items within each group was decided by further randomisation. These six groups of items then respectively formed the basis of six trial inventories. That no single respondent to a particular one of the six inventories could see all the items in the other five inventories is not an issue at this stage. The task here was simply to invite responses to items, and to examine the patterns of variation in resultant data at an item level. At this stage there was no concern to explore underlying empirical structure within responses to each of the six inventories.

For each separate trial inventory, respondents were requested to select some major teaching commitment that they had to an undergraduate class. That commitment might range from responsibility for topic teaching over a period of weeks, through to teaching and examination for an entire semester. Respondents were to read each item statement from the perspective of that chosen commitment, and indicate the extent to which the description was true of their personal practices or experiences. It is thus true that responses were solicited in terms of a particular context, but it was a self-selected context, and not one externally imposed. Each item also offered a sixth 'not applicable' response option, which was to be chosen in the case of a statement not making sense in the respondent's context.

The first trialling occurred during July-August 2004, which is summer recess in the northern hemisphere and mid-year in the southern. Two of the trialling inventories were distributed electronically to academics known to the two UK-based authors. The other four were distributed to academics known to the Australia-based author. In all, 118 responses were obtained, with samples for any single trialling inventory ranging between 15 and 30. The Australian respondents were all people known through contact with teaching development activities. The two UK samples were respectively enrollees in a PGCert programme in higher education, and members of a discipline oriented teaching network group. It is likely that all three samples comprised people who were already sympathetic and positive towards teaching.

There is thus a possibility that this first trialling may be conservative in yielding a set of items exhibiting a spread of responses. If it is assumed that respondents in all likelihood were 'good' rather than 'poor' teachers, then items exhibiting skewed response distributions might simply be reflecting things that 'good' teachers tend to do, perhaps with relative consistency. Were teachers who were more heterogeneous in terms of teaching commitment and ability sampled, these same items might have exhibited more dispersed distributions. This first trialling might thus have yielded fewer variation-sensitive items than might otherwise have been the case. But in an overall sense this possibly conservative bias may also be an advantage; the items that prove sensitive here to variation exhibited by a 'teaching biased' set of respondents can be confidently expected to also be sensitive to variation exhibited by a more heterogeneous set of respondents.

Findings from the first trialling

Response frequency distributions were calculated for each of the 234 trialled items. The task was to detect items on which a broad range of the sampled teachers did actually respond differently. Items on which responses show little variation would be of little use in subsequent scale development.

A simple, *empirically based decision rule* was used to select items that were clearly candidates for future scale development work. First, response distributions were inspected to find all those items for which all five possible response options had been used. Next, any of those items for which fifty percent or more of the respondents had indicated the 'not applicable' response option, were excluded. Finally, any items for which fifty percent of the responses were at one of the extreme response options were also excluded. This left some 91 items exhibiting non-extreme dispersions of responses across all response possibilities. Distributions that seemed bi-modal were not used to exclude items, since simple dispersion was judged more important for discriminative scale development purposes.

A second decision rule was used to further determine items that would be excluded, even at this initial stage. Any item whose distribution showed all or all but one of its responses at either the two positive extremes, or the two negative extremes, was excluded. In essence these were items reflecting practices that everyone reported doing, or nobody reported doing. Sixteen items were thus excluded on the grounds that they were capturing conformity rather than variation.

The simple outcome of this first trialling exercise then was a group of 91 items clearly included for further scale development, 16 clearly excluded, and some 127 that were ambiguous. The next immediate stage in the project will employ at least the 91 item set in scaling trials. A new set of respondents will be asked to respond to the full set of 91 items, and in sufficient number to permit exploration of underlying empirical structure. This exploration using common factor analysis, coupled with scale reliability analysis, typically identifies discrete and non overlapping groups of items that present themselves as candidates for further psychometric refinement. This process is iterative, proceeding through successive cycles of trialling and analysis until the scales present in a conceptually interpretable stable form.

The 127 'ambiguous' items will be inspected to determine potential for rephrasing and retrialling. It is possible that their initial phrasings might have proved unclear, and that revision might both tighten an item's meaning and yield a broader distribution of responses. Any of these items so re-phrased would be subjected to a further 'initial' trialling, with any that subsequently exhibit good distributional characteristics becoming part of the scale development pool.

Concluding discussion

It is emphasised that the process of analysing response distributions, and selecting items for inclusion in scale development or not, has thus far been entirely empirical. No consideration has been given at any point in the 'included' or 'excluded' item selection process to the phrasings or meanings of individual items. The possibility that items with particular meanings might receive 'privileged' treatment in inclusion/exclusion decisions has thus been carefully avoided.

Having reached this point however, there is nevertheless a curiosity as to the discriminatory power of the empirical process in terms of the *possible* broader meaning of what has thus far been excluded and included. A brief description is thus provided, but not in any sense in a form intended to prejudice at this early stage the conceptual domain that may be finally be reflected in the Reflections on Teaching Inventory.

A conceptual analysis of the excluded items suggests a theme in terms of a focus on main ideas or points that students need to learn (two items), with sub themes in terms of students' prior knowledge (three items), an internal structural focus (two items), student 'centredness' (four items), specific aspects of teaching behaviour (five items). The *excluded* set of 16 items is thus exhausted.

In similar vein a conceptual interpretation of the included item set is suggested in terms of structure and sequence (four items), an unstructured approach (five items), various aspects of students' prior knowledge (six items), preparation and teaching strategies (nine items), teaching intentions (five items), teaching behaviours or techniques (nineteen items), use of 'troublesome knowledge' (five items), simplification of difficult material (two items), 'about me' the teacher (seven items), teacher 'in control' (two items), non-centredness or 'togetherness' (two items), coverage (three items), metacognition (one item), students' motivation (one item), conformity (two items), responding to variation in students' learning (four items), clarification of important issues (two items), active learning (seven items), the importance of the (probably discipline-specific) historical perspective (five items). The included set of 91 items is thus exhausted and some examples from this set are presented in table 2 opposite.

There is a rich potential of variation sources suggested by the included items. There is furthermore every indication here that the 'ways of teaching' reflected in these included

I build an explanation by imagining that the students have never seen anything like the idea before.

I make my students aware that how they learn new things is influenced by what they currently think and understand.

When choosing an analogy, I check whether it might introduce something that could instead mislead the students.

I develop alternative ways to present a topic, before I then choose what I will actually do.

To make things simple to begin with, I might deliberately present an oversimplification of a topic.

I imagine myself as a student who doesn't know the material, and I think about what might be difficult about a presentation or explanation that I'm planning.

I decide what comes next in a lecture by fitting with what the students are likely to think next.

When an approach to a topic has been well established over time as the accepted way of treating that topic, I will conform to that approach.

I will describe the historical context within which an idea originally developed, to assist the students' fuller understanding of it.

I spend time in my classes considering the field itself, how it is structured, how it has developed over time.

I work on having students understand an idea intuitively, before I treat it more theoretically.

I have students describe explicitly the steps in their thinking that led to some conclusion or decision.

Table 2. Illustrative items from the 'Clearly in' selections.

items are indeed multidimensional – at least for the moment in conceptual terms – in an obvious celebration of the diversity of practice that subsumes, and perhaps even trivialises, the more simplistic notion of teacher- versus student-centredness that is at the base of the ATI. The expectation is that in the next stage of the work this diversity will be more formally captured in terms of empirical structure.

References

Ballantyne, R, Bain, J and Packer, J (1997) *Reflecting on university teaching: Academics' stories*. The Australian Government Publishing Service, Canberra.

Ballantyne, R, Bain, JD and Packer, J (1999) Researching university teaching in Australia: Themes and issues in academics' reflections'. *Studies in Higher Education*, 24, 237-257.

Dunkin, MJ (2002) Novice and award-winning teachers' concepts and beliefs about teaching in higher education. In Hativa, N and Goodyear, P (eds), *Teaching thinking beliefs and knowledge in higher education*. Dordrecht: Kluwer. pp41-57.

Eley, MG (2001) The Course Experience Questionnaire: Altering question for phrasing could improve the CEQ's effectiveness. *Higher Education Research Development*, 20, 293-312.

Eley, MG (2003) Teacher thinking during detailed planning, and a possible need to re-define the role of higher level constructs like conceptions of teaching. Paper presented at the 10th Biennial Conference of the European Association for Research on Learning and Instruction, 26-30 August, 2003, Padua, Italy.

Eley, MG (in press) Teachers' conceptions of teaching, and the making of specific decisions in planning to teach *Higher Education*.

Eley, MG and Stecher, EJ (1997) A comparison of two response scale formats used in teaching evaluation questionnaires. *Assessment and Evaluation in Higher Education*, 22, 65-79.

Hativa, N, Barak, R and Simhi, E (2001) Exemplary university teachers: Knowledge and beliefs regarding effective teaching dimensions and strategies. *Journal of Higher Education*, 72, 699-729.

Kane, R, Sandretto, S and Heath, C (2002) Telling half the story: A critical review of research on the teaching beliefs and practices of university academics. *Review of Educational Research*, 72, 177-228.

Kane, R, Sandretto, S and Heath, C (2004) An investigation into excellent tertiary teaching: Emphasising reflective practice. *Higher Education, 47, 283-310.*

Kember, D (1997) A reconceptualisation of the research into university academics' conceptions of teaching. *Learning and Instruction*, 7, 255-275.

Kember, D and Kwan, KP (2000) Lecturers' approaches to teaching and their relationship to conceptions of good teaching. *Instructional Science*, 28, 469-490.

Linder, CJ (1992) Is teacher reflected epistemology a source of conceptual difficulty in physics? *International Journal of Science Education*, 14, 111-121.

Linder, CJ (1993) A challenge to conceptual change. *Science Education*, 77, 293-300.

McCune, V and Hounsell, D (2005) The development of students' ways of thinking and practising in three final-year biology courses. *Higher Education*.

Meyer, JHF and Eley, MG (2003) A factor analysis of the Approaches to Teaching Inventory. Paper presented at the 10th Biennial Conference of the European Association for Research on Learning and Instruction, 26-30 August, 2003, Padua, Italy.

Prosser, M and Trigwell, K (1999) *Understanding learning and teaching*. SRHE and Open University Press, Buckingham

Prosser, M, Trigwell, K and Taylor, P (1994) A phenomenographic study of academics' conceptions of science learning and teaching. *Learning and Instruction*, 4, 217-231.

Stark, JS (2002) Planning introductory college courses. In Hativa, N and Goodyear, P (eds), *Teaching thinking, beliefs and knowledge in higher education*. Dordrecht: Kluwer. Pp. 127-150.

Trigwell, K, Prosser, M and Taylor, P (1994) Qualitative differences in approaches to teaching first year university science. *Higher Education*, 27, 75-84.

Note-making as active learning

Charlotte Mbali, University of KwaZulu-Natal

This research started with an invitation to give a lecture on note-taking during orientation week of February 2003. This was an opportunity to do a quick survey of how students entering tertiary education (first week, first term, before getting any lectures in their chosen programmes) conceive the purpose of note-taking. It was an opportunity, indeed, to awaken their awareness of meta-learning, of helping them see the links between purpose and technique. From a perspective of active or "deep" learning (Marton 1976; Marton 1976; Marton 1984; Ramsden 1992), it seemed better to call the activity note-*making* rather than note-taking (Brown,1978)

In the first few minutes of the lecture, students were asked to note down three reasons why they make notes. Then the lecture proceeded to discuss in turn each purpose as in the list below, which was shown step by step on the OHP, and at each stage students were asked to raise their hands if a purpose they had written corresponded to that purpose on the OHP. There were 2 groups (one from humanities/business studies and one from science/agric) each of about 600 students. The results below indicate the hand-counts.

As can be seen above the general trend of the responses is that the students use notes for *passive* learning. These results should not be interpreted as a strict quantitative exercise. There seems to be some noticeable differences between humanities and science (the former using lecture notes more for assignments, and the latter slightly more keen on books and web-sites) but not too much weight should be put on this as it is likely that some students turned up at the wrong time. Also the numbers show that not every student in the room joined in the exercise.

The lecture itself seemed to go well, as for each step on the OHP, there was further explanation of the activities that might go with that purpose: something about research into memorising for purpose one, something about signals for key ideas for purpose two; about mind-mapping for purpose four and so on.

	Humanities/ Business	Science/ Agriculture
To revise for tests and exams	194	128
To take down key ideas from lectures	170	197
To record key ideas from books/texts	35	39
To help me see patterns in ideas/facts	20	13
To use when I do assignments	137	37
To help me decide what I think of ideas	11	22
To discuss with my fellow students	26	42
To make an action list of things to do	3	1
To note details of books and web-sites to follow up	6	28

The exercise of asking for three statements of purpose for note-making has since been repeated with other groups:

- Chinese graduates coming to British universities for post-graduate study
- Conference participants at a conference on academic development in South Africa
- Lecturers enrolled for an introductory course in higher education practice

As might be expected, all these groups showed a pattern of response closer to active learning (more answers corresponding to the lower half of the list) than the mainly passive learners of the orientation lecture.

For example, the lecturers' responses can be grouped into nine categories:

1. Recall

   "To remember things later"

2. Regurgitate

   "to enable me to accurately use the information given in the lecture in my assignments" (lecturer in taxation)

3. Salience

   "remind myself of key issues"

   "to highlight what I consider to be very important"

4. Summarise

   "to simplify information"

5. Structure

   "to see pattern of argument" "have a clear picture"

6. Analyse

   "categorise information"

7. Integrate

   "create links between sections" (lecturer in anatomy)

8. Follow-up

   "to read up on topics further later"

9. Reflection

   "building blocks for my reflective notes for my portfolio"

It is worth drawing attention to the lecturer's discipline (in two cases above) as the type of knowledge that is involved is likely to influence the type of note-making. Taxation being about regulations and procedures puts high value on accuracy, so notes are required for accurate recall. Anatomy is a discipline which has a high memory demand, for itemised analytic labelling of the parts of the body, but this lecturer values the ability to *make* links between the different parts of this learning. This need to be aware of discipline differences has also been studied by Neumann (2001) and McKnight (2001).

Tony Buzan (Buzan and Dunn 1990), of mind-mapping fame, declares there are four functions of notes:

- Mnemnonic
- Analytic
- Creative
- Conversational

The mnemonic has the purpose of recall; the analytic identifies the underlying structure, the creative is using notes as a springboard for further thoughts, and the conversational is "spontaneous thoughts that arise in your mind while listening to the lecture or reading the book". Bearing in mind the reply from the anatomy lecturer, it seems that identifying the underlying structure is just as likely to be integrative as analytic. The mnemonic and the creative can also be subtly linked through evocation, as is so well expressed by de la Garandine (1991):

> *Memorising adds to the act of attention the pattern of an imaginary future surrounding the thing to be remembered and actively used to recall it.*
>
> *The source of creative imagination lies in the relationship with the world of perception. We need to look at the world, listen to it with the intention of evoking whatever riches it may have which are waiting to be discovered or invented.*

If we are to be creative with knowledge, we are not just reproducing what the lecturer or the book gave us, we are also activating what mental processes were evoked by our perceptions.

Buzan and Dunn (1990) too, are clear that the notes are not just reproduction:

> *Note-taking is receiving other people's ideas from speeches, books and other media, and organising them into a structure that reflects their original thought or enables you to re-organise it to suit your needs. Note-taking should be supplemented with the note-taker's own thoughts.*

As I explored further how note-taking is taught, I have become concerned that there is too much of tips for techniques that are aimed at reproduction, and not enough that are designed for the "evocative", "creative" and "conversational" purposes of active learning.

I attended a session on note-taking which forms part of the study skills programme arranged by student counselling service. What was presented was a neat technique for optimal revision and recall by using one word summaries of sections of notes in margins, the plan being that then by glancing at the one word summaries, the recall for the rest of the notes would be activated. Apart from the problem of the serial arrangement (so different from the flexibility of mind-mapping), my reaction to this presentation was to recognise that this type of "study skills" prescription is yet again re-enforcing passive learning, and not encouraging the learner to think beyond recall of the lecture. It seems to be derived from the type of learning inculcated in big classes of Psychology 101 (so many of the studies done on note-taking also utilise psychology students!)

I have also looked at the EASEL software produced by a team at Warwick University to assist international students with comprehending lecturers at British universities. The units are arranged sequentially, with lots of voiced examples from a variety of disciplines and dialects, to cover such things as lecture introduction, clues to the lecture's structures, signals for attitude, and closure. It serves its purpose well in providing structured learning for international students who may otherwise struggle with comprehending their lectures at first. But again, it does not encourage the student to think beyond and around the lecture.

With regard to note-making while reading, Fairbairn and Fairbairn (2001) begin their part six with a consideration of different *purposes* for note-making while reading. These include:

> *to link new knowledge to what you already know*
>
> *to help you to understand what an author is saying*
>
> *to make a record of points that you might want to use in an essay (p98)*

which suggests a before and after mental life for the activity of note-making. In discussing both the whys and the hows of note-making in the same section, this book encourages students (it is sub-titled "a guide for students) in meta-learning about a major activity in university life. It warns against the dangers of mindless note-taking:

> *Reading actively, always attempting to relate what you read to what you know, will help you to avoid the possibility of becoming a mindless note-taker (p99)*

In quest of more rigorous research that might have been done into the mental processes involved in note-taking, I followed up Tony Buzan's references in the Journal of Educational Psychology, most of them studies from the early 1970s. One significant finding (Aiken, Thomas et al 1975) concerned whether students should take notes while listening ("parallel") or in pauses during a lecture ("spaced"):

> *Newman-Keuls contrast tests on the note-taking variable indicated that spaced note-taking was superior both to parallel note-taking and to no notes, but that the condition did not differ reliably from no notes*

The article cites a study (Peters 1972) that found that taking notes during lectures was inferior to no notes. However, when Aiken et al explored the finding

> *it was approximately twice as likely that lecture material noted would be recalled than if it was not noted*

Apparently the superior recall in the spaced condition was reflected primarily in memory for those parts of the lecture perceived as important enough to deserve a note, with little spill-over on to the non-noted material

What is commendable about this article by Aiken et al is scepticism with regard to the methodology, as they point out that it could be queried on the ground that other factors could have affected the scores obtained on the post-test such as:

- Use or non-use of study notes before the test
- Other behaviour between the tested events, such as reading a summary
- Asking questions
- Covert rehearsing

My own scepticism grew as I scanned down the titles of these 1970s exercises in psychometric testing:

Effect of Question Production and Answering on Prose Recall (Frase and Schwartz 1975)

Prose recall? Yes, but at what level of difficulty?

Effect of type of objective level of test questions and the judged importance of tested material upon post-test performance (Duell 1974)

My main problem is that these psychometric methods used multi-choice tests but mostly they do not seem to be aware of how the validity of the tests could be undermined by language considerations. Some tried to control for language level by using some acceptable method of grading the text or lecture to be remembered, such as Flesch (1949) but none seem to have tried to scrutinise the actual wording of the tests for language difficulties in the cue-stems. They state what the material was about – mostly biographic material or a psychology lecture – which provokes further questions, as to whether different disciplines or genres might throw up different results. There is a danger of quoting these findings of the psychologists as worthy of generalisation across the whole gamut of learning in higher education without consideration of how this psychometric method of ignoring what might be significant factors in the "experiments". Here I am in agreement with McKnight (2001), who expressed worries about decontextualised teaching of note-taking.

As it happens, I (Mbali 1975) was also doing experiments with texts and recall via multi-choice pre- and post-tests during the 1970s, when I was involved in a project for graded reading cards in Botswana. The experiment involved a pre-test which was supposed to ascertain whether the test respondents either had prior knowledge or interest in a particular topic, then they read the graded reading passage, and then answered the multi-choice questions. To test "learning" there was then a post-test for recall a month or so later. This study could be criticised for the same reasons that Aikens et al mention: a recall test such as this has no control over the other variable or other activities that the learner might be doing in between the pre- and post-test. However, the merit of this study is the focus on prior knowledge and interest, an aspect usually neglected by those seeking to give tips for note-making. Yet some of the psychological articles cited above found that what is noted is what is regarded as important, and this is what is recalled. The decision about whether something is important is shaped by, of course, prior knowledge and interest .

Following this line of thought, I have now started doing listening exercises with the current intake of international students (Chinese) by telling them *not* to take full notes, but just to listen and then answer these four questions (one sentence each):

1. What did you already know about this?
2. What was the most interesting thing you learnt?
3. What was the most surprising?
4. What question do you still have?

This was after a lecture about Durban (the city where I live) given as a demonstration of how they were to give presentations about their own home cities. When I scanned through their responses the most surprising thing is the diversity of responses. Although nearly all of them are post-graduates from China coming to do business-related studies, the range of their interests and questions is striking. Of course, the lecture was a one-off, and they are not yet harnessed to a formal programme. Would the same apply, I wonder, if these four questions were asked within their formal taught programme, where the learning is more lock-stepped, and if the questions were asked in the midst of the learning cycle. But if such research reveals similar variety of responses, this would show the folly of trying to regulate students' note-taking too closely, either by "study skills" sessions or such spoon-feeding as giving OHP notes as hand-outs. These then put too firm a frame-work on the permissible "knowledge" and possibly close down the student's further thoughts – Buzan's "creative" and "conversational" phases.

Another way of encouraging these phases is through the reflective portfolio. In the course for lecturers, on higher education practice, most of the assessment is through a reflective portfolio, and we encourage candidates to write notes after seminars, and then to make later comment on these notes, perhaps after they have done a try-out activity (Mbali 1999), which is what the lecturer above is referring to in comment number nine under reflection above.

It is a pity that some of the Study Skills tipsters have not yet grasped the need for the creative and conversational phase. What is needed is more explicit advice to students to either leave wide margins for their comments and queries on their own notes, or leave spare lines (Brown, 1978).

It must also be realised that the "conversational" is not just with oneself. The questions given to students in two different disciplines (accounting and mechanical engineering) at the local technikon in Durban revealed that a surprising majority of them used their notes to discuss with other students (see appendices 1 and 2). Getting students to ask each other questions was, in fact, the focus of one of the old articles (Frase and Schwartz 1975) cited above where they concluded:

The results suggest that engaging in question production, whether individually or in a tutorial situation, facilitates recall over just studying

Conclusion

It is hard to summarise an article that has ranged over some diverse attempts to gain some insights into note-making. The underlying motivation of this research is the notion that stimulating meta-learning about note-making would improve learning. Nothing has been proved, but then there are too many variables to do conclusive experiments. But some pointers have become more visible for further research:

1. that lecturers need to allow for possible diversity of response

2. that different genres and disciplines may require different methods of note-making and of knowledge-making.

3. That there are activities which could stimulate students to be both "creative" and "conversational" with their notes.

References

Aiken, EG, Thomas, GS, et al (1975). "Memory for a lecture: Effects of notes, lecture rate and information density." *Journal of Educational Psychology* 67(3): 439.

Brown, D (1978) *Lecturing and Explaining*. London: Methuen

Buzan, T and Dunn, B (1990). *The Mindmap Book*, BBC.

Duell, OK (1974). Effect of type of objective level of test questions and the judged importance of tested materials upon post-test performance. *Journal of Educational Psychology* 66: 225-232.

Fairbairn, GJ and Fairbairn, SA (2001) *Reading at University* Buckingham: Open University Press

Flesch, R (1949). *The art of readable writing*. New York: Harper.

Frase, LT and Schwartz, BJ (1975). Effect of Question Production and Answering on Prose Recall *Journal of Educational Psychology* 67(5): 628-635.

de la Garandine, A (1991). Thought Processes in Learning. *Learning to think and thinking to learn*. Maclure, S and Daires, P. Oxford: Pergamon.

Marton, F, Säljö, R (1976). On qualitative differences in learning: 1 Outcome and process. *British Journal of Educational Psychology* 46: 4-11.

Marton, F and Säljö, R (1976). On qualitative differences in learning: 11 Outcome as a function of the learner's conception of the task. British Journal of Educational Psychology 46: 115-126.

Marton, F and Säljö, R (1984). Approaches to learning. The experience of learning. Marton, F and Entwistle, N. Edinburgh: Scottish Academic Press.

Mbali, VC (1975). The effects of prior knowledge or interest on comprehension of topics in graded reading cards. *Distance Education* IEC. Cambridge

Mbali, VC (1999) Using Portfolios to develop reflective Higher Education Practitioners" *South African Journal of Higher Education* 13.2

McKnight, A (2001) 'I taught them, but did they learn?' in Rust, C (Ed), *Improving Student Learning Strategically*, Oxford: OCSLD.

Neumann, R (2001). Disciplinary Differences and University Teaching. *Studies in Higher Education* 26(2): 135-146.

Peters (1972). Journal of Education Psychology 63: 276-280.

Ramsden, P. (1992). *Learning to Teach in Higher Education*. London: Routledge.

Appendix 1 (from Karen Bargate, accounting lecturer)

I had approximately 75 students present at the lecture. The number varied as some left when they realised there was no lecture and others arrived from a colleague's class. The students tend to float between my class and her class. See table below.

1.	To revise for tests and exams	73
2.	To take down key ideas from lectures	75
3.	To record key ideas from books/texts The students commented that they would underline in their textbooks.	36
4.	To help me see patterns in ideas/facts	0
5.	To use when I do assignments	20
6.	To help me decide what I think of ideas	8
7.	To discuss with fellow students	73
8.	To make an action list of things to do	7
9.	To note details of books and web-sites to follow up	5

Comments made by students

One of the students felt it was important what the students did with their notes at the end of the course. The general comments were: give them to friends who are doing the course the following year, throw away or keep.

Two students wanted to write comments and these are their comments:

Notes are very important, because they help when you are preparing a test, exams and assignment. So it is good to take notes in class. Dumisani

To have the section in a summarised form.

For the breakdown of subject.

Appendix 2 from Graham Thurbon, engineering lecturer

Survey of "reasons for taking notes"

Presented the class with a slip of paper onto which they could write their reasons for taking notes. Collected in and then went over the overheads, doing a quick numerical survey of the 10 categories presented, explaining each one as we went through. Results of survey are tabulated below.

Reason	S2	S3	S4
total number surveyed	70	43	23
1 – To revise for tests and exams	27	17	8
2 – To take down key ideas from lectures	15	6	8
3 – To record key ideas from books/texts	2	5	0
4 – To help me see patterns in ideas/texts	0	1	0
5 – To use when I do assignments	2	4	0
6 – To help me decide what I think of ideas	0	2	0
7 – To discuss with fellow students	0	29	0
8 – To make action lists of things to do	0	2	2
9 – To note details of books and web–sites to follow up	0	1	0
10 – Mind maps	0	1	0

The S2 class are totally new to me.

The S3 class were in the S2 level last semester and had therefore been with me for one previous semester.

The S4 class were in the S3 level last semester and had therefore been with me for two previous semesters.

Some of the more unusual reasons (as written):

S2s

To pay more attention in the class. It helps me because they are shorter than the book notes.

Is to get use the habit of writing.

Because I can.

Our brain cannot store everything we want it to store from what we hear.

Cause I said so.

To show my parents that I'm working at tec.

My mom gave me a pen & a book & said must use it.

Make the parents happy.

I hate taking notes. It breaks my concentration.

To look busy.

To save cost since eng: books are costly, yet used in short pr time.

They suck all THE IMPORTANT INFORMATION.

To by pass time.

Lucter must teacher us the real park of test.

They keep me awake in class.

To show the lecturer that I'm busy.

S3s

I don't take notes, I like to listen.

To fill up space in my books.

To see how much work has been covered.

I like working with engine. I like I pass thermo 2.

I can go home and recap, or try to understand what the Hell U were saying. So I didn't fall asleep in the lecture.

Recall what has been done. To study. Haven't got one!

I got short term memory loss. Keep me occupied. Allows me to concentrate.

Force of habit from high school.

To keep awake. To excercise my hand.

To keep myself busy. A persons own handwriting can be interperuted faster.

S4s

Useless varsity geeks, find something better to do...

Diverse student needs: the challenge of teaching international students. A business school case study

Joanne Smailes, Northumbria University

Pat Gannon-Leary, Newcastle University

Keywords

Supporting international learners, assessment, social inclusion

Abstract

The pedagogic environment in which most UK academics work is very different to that of five or so years ago. Successful widening participation strategies have lead to the creation of significant clusters of students with disparate experience. At Newcastle Business School (NBS), Northumbria University, the most significant clusters are international students. In 2003-04, international students account for 26% of the full-time undergraduate cohort with the majority originating from China and the Pacific Rim. Indeed, Northumbria's vice chancellor believes that Northumbria has the highest number of students originating from China in the UK HE sector

The increased influx of international students, although a recent development in the UK, has been the norm for some time in Australia and has produced a plethora of academic research into the challenges they have faced. The main issues are neatly summarised by Cronin (1995) and include:

- Unfamiliarity with skills such as critical thinking, decision-making and independent thought.

- Adjusting to new ways of thinking and presenting material.

- Becoming confident in speaking up, participating and asking questions in class.

- Wanting to uphold Confucian traditions such as respect for teachers.

Following a staff survey at Northumbria University in May 2003 many of these issues were reiterated by NBS staff who concluded that the increased number of international students had either a highly or fairly significant impact on their teaching.

In the light of this information a number of studies initiated within the university have been drawn upon to examine the international student experience at Northumbria. These have included questionnaires and focus groups conducted on a pre-sessional English course (ELAN) prior to NBS entry, followed up by questionnaires, group feedback analysis, and observation involving all NBS students.

This paper draws upon the findings of these research instruments and constructs a snapshot of international students within one UK HE institution. Examination of the data has revealed that the perceptions highlighted by the research literature (Ballard & Clanchy (1997), De Vita (2002) Watkins & Biggs (2001)) and Northumbria's academic staff is not necessarily mirrored within the international student response.

The paper goes on to consider, by utilising Newcastle Business School as a case study, how academic staff may be assisted to prepare an appropriate learning environment to support, enhance and draw upon the strengths of the diverse student population.

Introduction

Successful widening participation strategies in both HE and FE have led to the creation of significant clusters of students with disparate experience. International students in particular bring into the classroom a differing educational background and cultural knowledge from those in the UK. At Northumbria University international students originating from China and the Pacific Rim are the most significant cluster of students. Between 1999 and 2003, students originating from this region have increased from 4% of the total student cohort to 11% of the total cohort. Indeed, figures suggest Northumbria has the highest number of students originating from China in the UK HE sector. The majority of these students are located in Newcastle Business School (NBS) and account for 26% of the full-time undergraduate cohort in 2003.

International students are an important source of income and as such should merit academic investment, in order not to be viewed as 'cash cows' (Ackers, 1997; Wisker, 2000). Northumbria University wishes to provide a learning environment which recognises, and is responsive to, the needs of international students. Therefore in 2003 a project was initiated to identify and disseminate best pedagogical practice to support diverse student needs.

The aims of this project are:

- To examine the implications of teaching culturally diverse groups of undergraduates within the context of increasing student numbers.

- To examine the problem of 'participation in learning' from the perspective of the international student within a large group.

- To examine the adjustment issues and communication difficulties encountered by international undergraduates.

In order to fulfil these aims the project was intended to develop an understanding of the learning/teaching issues facing a group of NBS students from their initial application to the university, through their participation on the pre-sessional English language (ELAN) course, and through the first year of their main undergraduate programme.

The issues

The increased influx of international students, although a recent development in the UK, has been the norm for some time in Australia and has produced a plethora of academic research into the challenges they have faced. The main issues are neatly summarised by Cronin (1995) and include:

- Unfamiliarity with skills such as critical thinking, decision making and independent thought.

- Adjusting to new ways of thinking and presenting material.

- Becoming confident in speaking up, participating and asking questions in class.

- Wanting to uphold Confucian traditions such as respect for teachers.

Following a staff survey in May 2003 many of these issues were reiterated by NBS staff who concluded that the increased number of international students had either a highly or fairly significant impact on their teaching.

Methodologies

Three questionnaires were used in the collation of observations within this paper. The first survey instrument comprised a large number of statements on aspects of learning and teaching, derived from extensive reading of the literature on international students. This was distributed in either English or Chinese, according to preference, to students on Northumbria University's ELAN programme.

Later in the academic year a second student survey instrument, containing all statements in the ELAN survey, plus others, was administered to a wider group of NBS students, including UK and international undergraduates. The third, a short questionnaire focusing on assessment, was distributed late in the academic year.

For each survey instrument a Likert scale (strongly agree to strongly disagree) was used. For qualitative purposes a number of techniques were employed including focus groups, group feedback analysis and observation. However, poor participation rates were encountered.

Data gathered allowed comparisons to be made between international students' experience on ELAN and as an NBS undergraduate, and between the UK and international students on NBS programmes.

Findings

Relationships

In this era of globalisation, international students can enrich academic life and thinking by sharing their culture with academics, support staff and domestic students alike. Domestic students also benefit from interaction with international students, as they will develop the intercultural skills that are becoming increasingly valued by employers (Ryan, 2000; Wisker, 2000).

Chinese teachers traditionally enjoy status and authority because of their age, life experience and knowledge. Mullins, Quintrell and Hancock (1995), in discussing problems experienced by international students and the academic staff teaching them, highlight the move from an academic culture of respect for, rather than critique of, texts and teachers. McRobie and Barbera (2002) similarly comment that international students commonly conclude that the more 'casual' atmosphere in a Western classroom equates with less respect for the authority figure (ie the lecturer). This was addressed in the survey by the statement 'You have to respect your teachers'. As expected, a significant proportion (73%) of the NBS undergraduate international students agreed with the statement. However, a similar proportion (76%) of UK students also agreed.

Beaven, Caldensi and Tantral (1998) discuss how academic staff speak faster than the international students can a) comprehend and b) take notes. McSwiney (1995) points out that it is not only speed of delivery that can make cross-cultural communication difficult, but also regional accents, choice of words, colloquial expressions and use of jargon. As Cammish (1997) indicates, teachers of English as a second language (ESL) make a conscious effort to restrict vocabulary and control the structures used.

Two statements addressed this: 'teachers talk too quickly' and 'teachers' accents are difficult to understand'. For both, only small proportion of respondents on the ELAN programme (15%) agreed with the statements. On the follow-up undergraduate questionnaire this figure doubled to 30% ($p<0.05$) for the former statement, with the latter statement showing a slight, but insignificant, increase to 19%. While this is a favourable result for lecturers in general, it could indicate that ELAN teachers have developed specialised skills, which others may benefit from.

Chapple (1998) discusses the dependent student-tutor interactive patterns in which international students seem to expect that the tutor 'knows the answer' and will impart the required knowledge fully and clearly. Macrae (1997) contrasts lecturer and international student expectations in this respect, with the former presenting key issues and expecting students to develop their own ideas via independent learning while the latter may be expecting the 'right' answer for future regurgitation in essays and exams. Mullins, Quintrell and Hancock (1995) discuss problems experienced by international students and the academic staff teaching them, including the move from an academic culture of respect for knowledge and teachers, rather than critique of texts and teachers.

To investigate this, students were asked in two separate statements whether they liked to discover knowledge rather than being told everything by the teacher and whether they felt comfortable expressing disagreement with a teacher.

In both cases, as illustrated by figures one and two, responses to those statements radically differed according to the study situation. During the ELAN course students

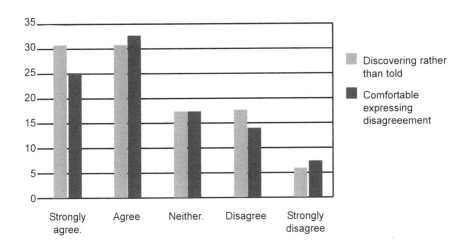

Figure 1: ELAN reponses to statements 'I like discovering rather than being told everything by the teacher' and ' I feel comfortable expressing disagreement with the teacher'

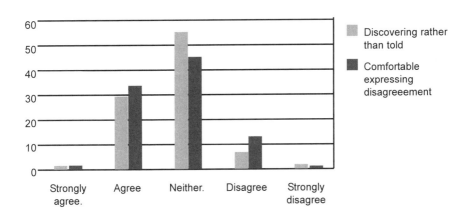

Figure 2: NBS undergraduate responses to statements 'I like discovering rather than being told everything by the teacher' and 'I feel comfortable expressing disagreement with the teacher'

appear to contradict many of the previous academic findings with, in each case, over 60% agreeing or strongly agreeing with the statements.

However, whilst on an NBS undergraduate programme, even though, for each statement the majority are unsure, students appear to tend towards more tutor reliant and overly respectful tendencies. Is this subject- or environment-related? This is an area meriting further investigation.

Rifkin et al (1996), Romm, Patterson and Hill (1994) and Pe Pua (1995) report that international and local students do not mix readily either in class or socially. This was initially investigated by posing the statement 'I like being in a classroom with a cultural mix of students'. Table one illustrates the responses from the international students when studying their ELAN course, results from the same question once the UG programme was underway and the responses from the UK students to the same question.

%	Strongly agree	Agree	Neither	Disagree	Strongly disagree
ELAN	69	20	10	2	0
NBS International	28	48	20	3	0
NBS UK	9	30	41	13	6

Table 1: Responses to 'I like being in a classroom with a cultural mix of students'

Although international students respond positively to this statement, there is a marked shift in opinion from the strongly agree category to the agree category between ELAN and NBS. UK students exhibit a more mixed response to the statement. Ledwith (1997) found international students working in groups with UK students perceived them as exclusive, unfriendly and unwelcoming, either ignoring or excluding from group processes students with poor English language skills. In a previous study conducted at Northumbria University, Montgomery and Thom (2000) discuss how students had expected to be able to make friends with British students and fit into British cultural life. Several reported feeling that British students were 'cold' and 'close'. During observations, this gulf is also evident, in many cases international students literally sit on the opposite side of the room from UK students. In consequence, currently, any classroom-based group activity militates against the formation of groups with a cultural mix.

Classroom experience

There is some research evidence that note taking during lectures is problematic. Dunkel and Davy's (1989) study revealed that significant differences existed between the perceptions of Western and international students concerning the usefulness of note-taking while listening to lectures, methods employed and the adequacy of their note-taking skills. Beaven, Caldensi and Tantral (1998) agree that their South East Asian (SEA) students were unable to simultaneously listen and take notes, finding that they could make little or no sense of those notes they had managed to make when they referred to them after class.

The statement 'It is hard to listen to a lecture and take notes at the same time' was posed to students.

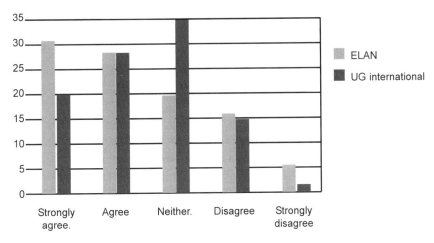

Figure 3: Response to statement 'It is hard to listen to a lecture and take notes at the same time'

As can be seen in figure three, there was a distinct difference between responses from international students from the ELAN programme and those on NBS undergraduate programmes. During ELAN 59% believed it was difficult to listen and take notes at the same time. This reduced to 48% for NBS programmes. In NBS courses, handouts and the use of the Blackboard VLE is common, whereas in ELAN handouts and set texts are regularly used but little use is made of the VLE. When questioned about this practice 80% of respondents agreed making materials available via the VLE helped their study, with international students having a higher appreciation rate for all visual aids as compared with UK students ($p < 0.05$).

A lack of mixing, and associated feelings of not fitting in the local culture, according to Rifkin et al (1996), frustrates academic staff's efforts to get international students to 'speak up' in class. The statement 'I participate in class discussions only when someone asks me a direct question' addressed this. Whilst participating in the ELAN course a healthy 80% of respondents disagreed with the statement. Response to the same statement for the international undergraduate programmes reduced dramatically to 30% in disagreement. This is likely to be due to a lack of self confidence related to language ability. In the undergraduate survey three statements relating to this were posed.

In each case, UK students exhibited more confidence than their international peers. This appears to indicate that, once international students enter a mixed group, there are more inhibitions in relation to speaking up. Does this also affect confidence within group work?

Statement	International Students (%)	UK Students (%)
I know what I what to say but find it difficult to put into words	45	34
I can express ideas clearly when speaking*	21	42
I feel comfortable expressing my own opinions	27	39

(* p <0.01)

Table 2: Proportionate levels of agreement on statements relating to language fluency

Jones (1994) reports that international students were rarely observed participating in group planning sessions, being content to leave things to local students to arrange, and never volunteering to act as spokesperson. Barnett (1994) identified the chief problem, in respect of tutorials, as being the fact that dominant speakers were at an advantage making it difficult for ESL students to participate either fully or actively. Some students in her survey expressed a desire to have a tutorial group expressly for international students to counteract this perceived disadvantage. In group study Wang (2002) reports he found that the ESL student is often the one listening to the others and then being told what to do. The questionnaire addressed some of these issues by asking whether students volunteered to act as a spokesperson in group activities.

It can be seen from figure four that, although a healthy percentage agree with the statement on both the ELAN and NBS courses, there is a categorical shift in responses between the two situations, once again indicating some loss of confidence on encountering a mixed group.

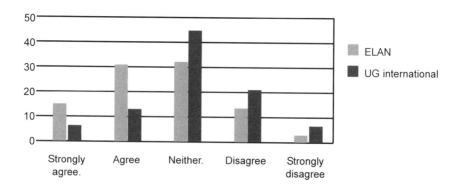

Figure 4: Reponses to statement 'I volunteer to act as spokesperson in group activities'

Reading and writing

SEA students interviewed by O'Donoghue (1996) recognised that, when adapting to western HE, their learning styles and writing practices had to change and that it was necessary to do more independent reading prior to lectures. This was certainly the case in the Northumbria undergraduate study. 86% (49% strongly) agreed that in the UK students are encouraged to be more independent with 79% also stating that different study skills were required for UK study. Additionally, 31% of international students indicated they carried out preparatory reading before seminars, significantly higher ($p<0.01$) than UK students, only 17% of whom did preparatory reading. This is actually quite pleasing as a number of academic staff complain about the general lack of seminar preparation.

Flowerdew and Miller (1992) point out that, in addition to struggling with a new vocabulary, international students also experienced difficulty with new terminology and concepts necessitated by the nature of the subject matter of some courses. Beaven, Caldensi and Tantral (1998) report that SEA students find topics such as accounting particularly difficult since they involve learning concepts and specialised language simultaneously. They also report that journal articles use abstract vocabularies and complicated linguistic structures and therefore take SEA students an inordinate amount of time to read. In a study conducted by Burke and Wyatt-Smith (1996) international students reported problems comprehending what they read in English during their first semester. Unfamiliar, discipline-specific, terminology meant that they read considerably more slowly than their peers, making excessive use of dictionaries whilst reading and spending overmuch time re-reading texts.

These issues were examined by a series of statements, the first of which addressed whether they could read English academic texts with understanding. Whilst, on ELAN, 77% agreed with the statement, this reduced significantly ($p<0.05$) to 51% for NBS undergraduate study. This was probed further by asking whether they felt they encountered too much specialised language and too many unfamiliar concepts during reading. Around half of the respondents felt that they did indeed come across specialised language with a slightly lower percentage (41%) reporting they came across many unfamiliar concepts.

Wang's (2002) study found that Chinese graduate students had difficulties in writing, even though those who obtained high English language TESL scores. Writing was perceived by almost all of Burke and Wyatt-Smith's (1996) study participants to be their greatest difficulty.

This issue of writing was addressed through three statements:

- 'It is difficult to write essays.'
- 'I can write summaries of academic texts.'
- 'I can express my ideas clearly in writing.'

In the case of the first statement, for both the ELAN and NBS programmes, around half of the international cohort agreed that they found it difficult to write essays. When the same question was posed to UK students this number was much less at around 30% (p<0.05).

However, discrepancies between ELAN and NBS study appeared in response to the latter two statements.

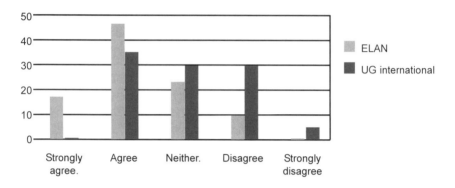

Figure 5: Responses to the statement 'I can write summaries of academic texts'

Figure five illustrates that, although during the ELAN course they generally felt comfortable in summarising information, international students' confidence plummets (p<0.01) once they embark on their subject-based programme. Similar differences were recorded in respect of the final statement. During ELAN 63% of students felt they could clearly express their ideas in writing but only 31% agreed with this statement in relation to their NBS undergraduate course (p<0.01). These data may be indicative of a compounded difficulty between the specialised language and unfamiliar concepts encountered by students when reading.

Assessment

Bliss (1999) reports how SEA students are familiar with end of year examinations as the main assessment method. Yet, research conducted by De Vita (2002) and Beaven et al (1998) indicated international students, due to language difficulties, might be disadvantaged by examinations. Indeed, De Vita stressed that coursework is more "culturally fair" than examinations. To address this students were asked whether they felt they learnt more from non-examination based assessments, 67% of international students agreed that this was the case. However, no significant difference was found between international and UK students' response, of whom 63% also preferred other assessment methods.

Bliss (1999) also noted that ESL students might need to make considerable adjustments to a HE system that commonly assesses more often. Beaven et al (1998) found that SEA students "appreciated frequent quizzes or exams" in order to be given the opportunity to learn material well, indeed, 85% of international students agreed that they would prefer hand in dates for in-course assessments to be more regularly spaced across the year, significantly more than UK students (p<0.05), although the majority 68% would also prefer more regular assessments.

Over the last few years, plagiarism is an issue with which staff have become increasingly concerned. Unfortunately, this coincides with increased international intakes onto courses. However, Introna et al (2003) point out that the assertion that international students are more likely to plagiarise than their host peers raises an issue of potential discrimination since detection of plagiarism may be easier in respect of their work than in that of a 'home' student. In consequence the identification of a higher percentage of plagiarised texts among international students may lead to the possibly flawed conclusion that plagiarism is more common among this group.

Within the questionnaire concentrating on assessment, students were asked whether each assessment must make it clear what constitutes plagiarism. A large majority of students (77%) agreed that this should be the case; interestingly, significantly more (p<0.01) UK students: 82%, compared with 63% of international students.

A high rate of plagiarism, or neglect of referencing, among international students is frequently a reflection of other cultures' differing academic practices. Some of the basic issues surrounding citation were addressed within the student questionnaires. Students were asked whether they understood the need to use referencing and quotation marks and the need to explain authors' ideas in their own words.

It is clear from figure six that international students are aware of the main basic issues of citation and collaboration, with over three quarters of respondents agreeing with both statements, similar levels of awareness to those of UK students where 82% and 77%, respectively, agreed with the above statements.

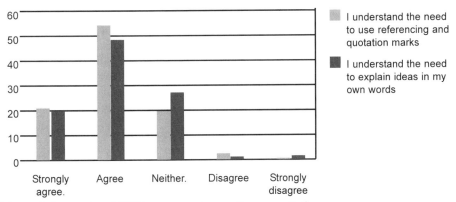

Figure 6: International NBS responses to questions on citation

In some cultures, knowledge is considered to be in the public domain (Bell, 1999) and other cultures believe, according to Ladd and Ruby (1999), that alteration of an authority's original words is disrespectful. These possible cultural differences, for author respect, were addressed through three questionnaire statements (table three):

Statement	International Students (%)		UK Students (%)	
	Agree	Disagree	Agree	Disagree
A Understanding a topic demands that, first of all, the student should thoroughly master the thoughts of important writers on that topic. Only then is it right for the student to hold his own view of the topic.[2]	49	3	45	12
B Sometimes the textbooks express the subject in a way which can't be improved. It is right to repeat their words when asked an essay question on a topic on which they have spoken[1,2]	45	11	18	41
C I feel uncomfortable about rewriting important authors' statements in my own words, because I believe they are the experts.[2]	48	28	26	36

([1] indicates $p < 0.01$, for agree; [2] indicates $p < 0.01$ for disagree)

Table 3: Proportionate levels of agreement/disagreement on statements relating to author respect.

When comparing international responses to those of UK students a clear picture substantiating the findings of potential cultural differences emerges.

For statement A, dealing with topic mastery, although both groups similarly agree, it is notable that four times as many UK to international students disagreed with the statement.

For statement B, concerning repetition of authors' words, significant differences were found between both numbers of international and UK students agreeing and disagreeing with the statement. This goes some way in explaining a general observation, by NBS staff in the May 2003 survey, that international students tend to "over quote" academic works.

A similar trend also continued in respect of the unease of rewriting authors' ideas, statement C, where almost half of international students expressed some discomfort as opposed to just over a quarter of UK students.

It would appear that, even though international students have a good understanding of the issues surrounding plagiarism, the respect for the experts generates a great deal of unease in their ability, or right, to change the way in which academic findings are expressed.

Conclusion

Confucian traditions are manifested by Chinese and Pacific Rim students' unease in UK education's approach to published research. Students recognise that, within the UK, work must be seen to be an individual's own, but problems arise with the implicit expectation that this work must be informed by, but in no way repeat, more respected authors within a particular topic. These misunderstandings can lead, in the eyes of UK lecturers, to a serious act, ie plagiarism. Lecturers could perhaps help international students adjust to UK practices by providing short exemplar paragraphs illustrating the ways in which academic writing can be paraphrased appropriately.

Further, minor adjustments can be made in didactic teaching practice to help international students adjust to a new study environment. Wherever possible lecturers should be encouraged to use a restricted vocabulary, reduce or explain jargon within a glossary and regularly review concepts which may be unfamiliar. Ideally these should be provided in a written format and made available on a VLE.

Other Confucian traditions such as respect for lecturers and inhibition to debate are apparent, but perhaps not to the extent currently assumed. Results indicate these emerge more within their relationship with UK peers. Sheer numbers of international students signify that it is often easier to adhere to their own cultural cohorts. The perceived lack of approachability of UK students only encourages this. A matrix approach to group formation may be more suitable than the imposition of a cultural mix. In plenary situations, a simple adjustment by requesting and addressing an individual by name could encourage equality in contribution.

Induction processes could also be utilised to aid cultural communication. For example, Hall and Toll (1999) review some of the ways in which modern language students gain intercultural awareness in preparation for residence abroad. Seminar activities such as a "sociogram" (Coleman, 1999) and "barnga" (Thiagarajan and Steinwachs,1990) would lend themselves to adaptation for use with students in disciplines with culturally mixed groups. Steps could be taken at a school or institutional level for "buddy" support schemes such as Peer Assisted Learning, where mature UK students, reported as being more 'friendly' and 'open' (Montgomery and Thom, 2000), and successfully integrated international students may provide a cooperative and collaborative learning support mechanism.

By taking a few of the steps suggested, a varied and rich learning environment which supports, enhances and draws upon the strengths of the diverse student population may be created within the classroom. This can only serve to benefit all students.

Acknowledgements

The authors wish to acknowledge the contribution made by Julian Given and Brenda Greene who assisted in the data collection processes.

References

Ackers (1997) *Evaluating UK Courses: The Perspective of the Overseas Student*, in McNamara, D and Harris, R (eds) (1997) *Overseas Students in Higher Education: Issues in Teaching and Learning*, Routledge

Barnett, J (1994) Learning experiences among second language students In: Barnett, J (ed) *Working with student diversity: contexts, issues and strategies in the University of South Australia*. CUTL Inclusive Curriculum Research Project. University of South Australia: Centre for University Teaching and Learning. p63-94.

Beaven, M, Calderisi, M and Tantral, P (1998) Barriers to Learning Experienced by Asian Students in American Accounting Classes. Paper Presented at *American Accounting Association Mid-Atlantic Regional Meeting*, p64-71. http://www.vmaps.net/barriers.html [accessed September 2003]

Bell, K (1999) *Plagiarism: highway robbery in the classroom*. Cambridge Language Consultants http://www.camlang.com/sp005print.htm [accessed October 2003]

Bliss, A (1999) Diversity and Language: ESL Students in the University Classroom *University of Colorado, Boulder, Faculty Teaching Excellence Program. Teaching and Learning Series on Diversity* http://www.colorado.edu/ftep/diversity/div11.html [accessed April 2003]

Burke, E and Wyatt-Smith, C (1996) Academic and Non-academic Difficulties: Perceptions of Graduate Non-English Speaking Background Students *TESL-ej* 2 (1) March. http://www-writing.berkeley.edu/TESL-EJ/ej05/a1.html [accessed September 2003]

Cammish, NK (1997) Through a glass darkly: problems of studying at advanced level through the medium of English In: McNamara, D and Harris, R (eds.) *Overseas Students in Higher Education: Issues in teaching and Learning*, Routledge p143-155.

Chapple, S (1998) How do you foster enthusiasm and participation in tutorials particularly by international students? *Teaching and Learning Forum Proceedings, HERDSA Conference*, 4-5 February, UWA, Perth WA, p61-65. http://216.239.33.100/cobrand_univ?q=cache:u4yi-X2PzY4J:cea.curtin.edu.au/tlf/tlf1998/chapple.html+Chappleandhl=enandie=UTF-8 [accessed June 2003]

Coleman, JA (1999) "Sociogram" one of a series of four lesson plans available from the Department of Area Studies, University of Portsmouth.

Cronin, M (1995) Considering the cultural context in teaching and learning for Korean tertiary students by western teachers. In: Summers, L (ed), *A Focus on Learning, Proceedings of the 4th Annual Teaching Learning Forum*, Edith Cowan University,

February. Perth: Edith Cowan University. p53-56
http://cea.curtin.edu.au/tlf/tlf1995/cronin.html [accessed June 2003]

De Vita, G (2003) Rethinking the Internationalisation Agenda in UK Higher Education, *Journal of Further and Higher Education* 27(4) pp383-398

Dunkel, P and Davy, S (1989) The heuristic of lecture notetaking: Perceptions of American and international students regarding the value and practice of notetaking *English for Specific Purposes*, 8 (1), p33-50 available from: http://www.sciencedirect.com [accessed July 2003]

Flowerdew, J and Miller, L (1992) Student perceptions, problems and strategies in second language lecture comprehension. *Regional English Language Centre Journal*, 23(2), p60-80. http://teaching.polyu.edu.hk/t2/t2e3.asp?topic=2andsubtopic=5 [accessed June 2003]

Hall, S and Toll, S (1999) Raising Intercultural awareness in preparation for periods of residence abroad – a review of current practice in UKHE. *Sub-Project report, The Interculture Project.* http://www.lancs.ac.uk/users/interculture/docs/ria.rtf [accessed December 2003]

Introna, L et al (2003) *Cultural attitudes towards plagiarism: developing better understanding of the needs of students from diverse cultural backgrounds relating to issues of plagiarism.* Lancaster University http://online.northumbria.ac.uk/faculties/art/information_studies/Imri/Jiscpas/docs/external/lancsplagiarismreport.pdf

Jones, R (1994) Encouraging classroom participation of overseas MBA students. *Overview*, 2 (1), np. http://cedir.uow.edu.au/CEDIR/overview/overviewv2n1/RJ.html [accessed June 2003]

Ladd, P, and Ruby, R (1999). Learning Style and Adjustment Issues of International Students. *Journal of Education for Business*. Jul/Aug, 74 (6) 363-368

Ledwith, S et al (1997) *Multi-culturalism, student group work and assessment.* Oxford Brookes University.

Macrae, M (1997) The induction of international students to academic life in the United Kingdom. In: McNamara, D and Harris, R (eds) *Overseas Students in Higher Education: Issues in teaching and Learning*, Routledge p127-142

McRobie, KF and Barbera, N (2002) The challenge of class participation in the international classroom or: what they don't tell you can hurt them! *Business, Education and Technology Journal*, 4(1), Spring p6-10. http://www.ggu.edu/schools/techandind/betj/sp2002/betsp02.pdf [accessed September 2003]

McSwiney, C (1995) *Essential understandings: International students, learning, libraries.* Adelaide: Auslib Press.

Montgomery, C and Thom, V (2000). International students – a case for widening participation? *UKCOSA Worldviews*, 4, UKCOSA.

Mullins, G, Quintrell, N and Hancock, L (1995) The experiences of international and local students at three Australian universities. *Higher Education Research and Development*, 14 (2), p201-231.

O'Donaghue T, (1996), Malaysian Chinese Students' perceptions of what is necessary for their academic success in Australia: a case study at one University, *Journal of Further and Higher Education*, 20 (2), p67-80

Pe Pua, R (1995) *Being an Asian on Campus: A Look into Cross-Cultural Experiences of Overseas Students*, Centre for Multicultural Studies, University of Wollongong.

Rifkin, W, Hellmundt, S, Fox, C and Romm, C (1996) Getting international students to speak up Overview, 4 (2), np. Http://cedir.uow.edu.au/CEDIR/overview/overviewv4n2/rifkin.html [accessed June 2003]

Romm, C, Patterson, P, and Hill, C.(1994) Overseas Students in Australia: a retrospective longitudinal study of pre-purchase expectations and post-purchase satisfaction, *Journal of Marketing for Higher Education*, 5 (2) p31-52.

Ryan, J (2000) *A Guide to Teaching International Students*, The Oxford Centre for Staff and Learning Development

Thiagarajan, S and Steinwachs, B (1990) *Barnga: a simulation game on cultural clashes* Yarmouth, ME: Intercultural Press

Wang, Y (2002) The contextual knowledge of language and culture in education: Exploring the American university experiences of Chinese graduate students PhD Thesis University of Southern Mississippi. http://wwwlib.umi.com/dissertations/fullcit/3067255 [accessed June 2003]

Wisker, G (ed) (2000) *Good Practice Working with International Students*, SEDA

Ethnic minority students: diversity and the practicalities of assessment regulations

Raj Dhimar[1] and Peter Ashworth[2]

1. Learning and Teaching Institute, Sheffield Hallam University

2. Faculty of Society and Development, Sheffield Hallam University

Abstract

Analysis of one university's 2000/2001 data on student academic appeals indicated disparities in the proportion of students of Asian origin who had appealed against the decisions of Award Assessment Boards. A snap interpretation of these disparities was that they might indicate evidence of racial discrimination in particular schools of the university. But it soon became obvious that no unequivocal interpretation of the data was possible. We were asked by the university authorities to re-interrogate those 2000/2001 data, considering both the statistics and the individual appeal submissions. We also analysed the data for 2002-2003. Additionally, we conducted a small number of in-depth interviews with students and staff. We were particularly concerned to uncover any incompatibility between the cultural practices of ethnic minority students (especially members of communities holding the Islamic faith) and the taken-for-granted assumptions underlying university assessment procedures. The findings indicate that there may be insufficient knowledge and understanding of cultural beliefs, practices and lifestyle of Asian students amongst those who design assessment processes, extenuating circumstances rules, and appeals regulations.

1 Introduction

Student academic appeals statistics of one university for the year 2000-2001 indicated disparities in the proportion of students of Asian origin who had appealed against the decisions of Award Assessment Boards in comparison with non-ethnic-minority students. Indeed, ethnic minority students were not only submitting proportionately more appeals, but were also apparently being disproportionately rejected by the Appeals Panel. It was thought possible that anecdotal evidence of the experience of staff in certain schools might be related to these observations, raising the question of racial discrimination in particular schools. However, the data were not susceptible to this sole interpretation, and the project on which we are reporting here was driven by the need to come to some clear understanding of the actual meaning of the statistics.

We re-interrogated the existing 2000/2001 student academic appeals, paying attention both to the statistical data and to the written cases which the students had submitted. We similarly investigated data regarding the appeals submitted in 2002/2003, again paying particular attention to the *grounds* of the appeals. Finally, we undertook very small-scale qualitative research interviewing with six students from a range of disciplines and levels and seven members of staff. The purpose of the interviews was to get a rich understanding of a (necessarily) few people's situations so as to give a grounding in reality to the interpretations we made.

Therefore, the stages of the research were as follows

- Consideration of appeals statistics 2000/2001, together with a close reading of the cases which students made to support their appeals

- Consideration of appeals statistics 2002/2003, again with careful reading of the cases made

- Interviews with members of staff and ethnic minority students

We report on the findings of all the appeals and interview data, followed by a summary of the overall implications of the research, with recommendations.

2 The Data and their analysis

2.1 Appeals cases 2000/2001

The target group for detailed analysis was the eighteen students of Asian origin who (a) had presented appeal cases with valid grounds for appeal within categories 3 and 4 (that is, they claimed extenuating circumstances), but (b) these were in the end not accepted by the Assessment Regulations Panel. The grounds for appeal which are regarded as valid by the appeals panel – that is, they are allowed to go forward for consideration and judgement – are as follows:

- Ground 1 – there was error or irregularity in the assessment process.

- Ground 2 – the Award Board decision was not in accordance with the regulations.

- If both 1 and 2 were cited, 2 is recorded below.

- Ground 3 – extenuating circumstances were not [properly] submitted, but that this was for good reason and the extenuating circumstances should now be considered.

- Ground 4 – extenuating circumstances were insufficiently recognised by Award Board and should now be given proper consideration.

- Grounds 3 and 4 are combined below; the student reasoning appeared comparable on analysis.

- "None" below means that the Appeals Panel did not consider that the statement of appeal fell into the accepted categories of valid appeal.

■   *Not tabulated below* are cases on file which were incomplete, withdrawn, out of time, or in some other way inadmissible as data. There were 37 such cases.

Of the target group of 18 students, eleven cases were available on file (the remainder were out of the office being dealt with at Academic Board level).

Ethnicity	Ground 1		Ground 2		Grounds 3 & 4		None
	Accepted	Rejected	Accepted	Rejected	Accepted	Rejected	
White n = 80	5	3	1	0	18	20	33
Black n = 7	0	0	0	0	1	2	4
Asian n = 40	1	2	3	0	9	**18**	**7**
Chinese n = 2	0	0	0	0	0	0	2

Table 1 Number of student appeals 2000/2001 by ethnicity

The data in table 1 indicate that only seven out of 40 appeals by students of Asian origin were deemed by the Appeals Panel to fall outside the grounds regarded as valid according to the Regulations, whereas 33 out of 80 white students' appeals were *a priori* invalid. The outcomes of the decisions, however, were "back in proportion"; 24/80 (one third) of appeals by white students in this sample were accepted, and 13/40 (just over one-third) of the appeals of students of Asian origin were accepted. This finding is partly a consequence of the fact that there are a disproportionate number of claims of extenuating circumstances from students of Asian origin which are not allowed by the Appeals Panel (almost exactly two-thirds, compared to half of the claims of white students).

There does on the face of it appear to be a disproportionate tendency for students of Asian origin to appeal. Possibly this arises from the course cultures of Law (41 cases) and of Business Studies (31 cases), from which many of these appeals may come. It does seem that appeals are made on grounds which are valid (ie which claim grounds which are within the regulations), but a larger proportion of these are not, in the end, accepted. In this context, two processes must be distinguished: a) a student demonstrating or claiming grounds to submit an appeal, and b) the process which investigates whether grounds claimed and any other information and supporting documentation from the appeal and its investigation shows whether the grounds claimed (or anything else) adversely affected the student's *assessment*. This may help explain why there may be good reasons for students who claim grounds for appeal might not have the appeals accepted.

The important issue here is whether the rejection of appeals for ethnic minority students might have been because specific kinds of extenuating circumstances (involving cultural factors) were not deemed sufficiently strong or were felt not to have impacted on assessment. The further question arises concerning whether the interpretation of such cultural factors shows sufficient understanding, either in the regulations or in the interpretation of the Appeals Panel and other officials. The interview research reported later was designed to help us to a view on these issues.

2.2 Appeals Cases 2002/2003

An analysis of the 2002/2003 student academic appeals was undertaken to discover what the initial investigation into the 2000/2001 appeals statistics meant in terms of possible incompatibility between cultural practices of ethnic minority students and the taken-for-granted assumptions of university assessment procedures. A similar investigatory approach was taken with the 2002/2003 appeals as for the 2000/2001 appeals. Twenty-four academic appeals cases submitted by ethnic minority students were investigated, paying particular attention to the details of claims about extenuating circumstances.

Table 2 below summarises the 2002/2003 ethnic minority appeals investigated. The differences between this table and the one for 2000/2001 show how dangerous it can be to use one year's statistics as the basis for analysis and decision making. It is also important to note that new regulations governing the assessment process were introduced between the times covered by these tables, though we do not believe these affected the meaning of the appeals. The important question remains, whether ethnic minority students' appeals could have been rejected on occasion because the extenuating circumstances which formed the basis of the appeals involved cultural issues which are not sufficiently reflected in the regulations as currently formulated.

The target group for detailed analysis was the 16 students of Asian origin who had presented cases with valid grounds for appeal within categories 3 and 4 (that is, they

Ethnicity	Ground 1		Ground 2		Ground 3&4		None
	Accepted	Rejected	Accepted	Rejected	Accepted	Rejected	
White n=98	4	3	0	0	5	34	52
Black n= 2	0	0	0	0	1	1	0
Asian n= 24	2	0	0	0	0	**16**	**6**
Chinese n= 3	0	0	0	0	0	1	2

Table 2: Number of student appeals 2002/2003 by ethnicity

claimed extenuating circumstances), but the appeals were in the end not accepted. Again, the issue to be investigated was whether cultural practices were implicated in the rejection of the appeals.

Only six out of 24 appeals by students of Asian origin were deemed to fall outside the grounds regarded as valid according to the Regulations, whereas 52 out of 98 white students' appeals were *a priori* invalid. 12/98 of white appeals in this sample were accepted. 2/24 of the appeals of Asian students were accepted.

2.3 Student and staff interviews

The interview process explored staff and students' understanding of the appeals process as well as looking in more depth at ethnic minority students' approaches and responses to assessment, and the meaning for them of extenuating circumstances regulations and procedures. One-to-one interviews were conducted with six ethnic minority students and seven staff members from a variety of backgrounds and disciplines to investigate these issues. Broader ethnic minority issues emerged as a consequence of the open nature of the interviews covering aspects and influences of university life personal to the student experience, including academic life, social life, religious and cultural life and the influence of family. Plainly the small number of interviews means that general claims cannot be made, but it is certainly the case that the in-depth nature of the interviews provided an insight into the realities which lay behind some of the cases which students had put forward in their appeals.

The analysis of the transcripts of the interviews focused on themes and concerns related to the purposes of the research, and we paid attention to the variety and complexity of these across the student sample. The transcripts of interviews with students were coded to reflect the following critical questions relevant to this study:

■ The extenuating circumstances put forward ú especially by members of ethnic minority students ú and their meaning.

■ Assessment from an ethnic minority viewpoint

■ The meaning of the findings for inequality of esteem and treatment ú possible discrimination

■ Considerations about regulations and procedures regarding extenuating circumstances

3. Key themes from the interviews and appeals cases

The majority of students interviewed had no personal experience of the appeals process, although they generally did know of someone else who had. Despite the original narrow interview framework, concentrating on extenuating circumstances and appeals, all students interviewed were very open and provided rich perceptions of their overall university experiences. They also had strong views on self-motivation, identity, familial influences, role models, learning and teaching, student support and relationships with staff. What follows is a representative selection of what students have said in the interviews and appeals cases about the meaning of ethnicity and their understanding of higher education as an ethnic minority student.

3.1 Family and the meaning of university

The family *community* played an important role in the life of the students. It became apparent that the definition of 'family' differed between students. For some, 'family' is a closed set of partner and children, while for others it is a wider community which extends to aunts, uncles, grandparents and cousins who may live in the same house, or in another country. Families can be both problematic and extremely supportive. For some students there was a strong pressure from family to succeed academically:

> *Yeah. Well, family because they want me to do, want me to do well. Um, me brother, me older brother, he went to university as well, so it was like kind of expected of me. And, friends, like, all my friends are at university, like, we all left A-levels, and we're all at uni now, so you just want to be in the same place as them really.*

One student talked about the pressures which his parents had exerted on him to become an engineer, and the effect of going against their wishes:

> *Yeah, I have. Engineering was one. Cos my uncle's an engineer, you know, they class engineering as a good career. I've had them pressures, but I don't want to do it. That's why I left... after three months because I started civil engineering and I thought, what do I want to civil engineering for? I'm not even enjoying it. So that's why I took time out, came back to Sheffield and did construction management.*

The strong family bond exists though the student is away at university. This is possibly significant in the choices made by the student to move away from home (which might not be entirely their own decision) when contemplating doing a course at a HE institution:

> *But I know that a lot of, like, Asian friends and stuff, or even my mixed race friends, they spend a lot time at home, some of them. Most of my friends live at home who are studying, and I do as well, and like, if you live at home I think you've got other responsibilities you know, like, just family stuff. You've got to do stuff like that and... I don't know, I think it's you spend more time doing different things.*

This student also had the added pressure of his home community (by this we mean his own family and the close networks of people in the area where he lives).

> *You just get it when you come home man. So what does your son do? Oh, my brother's an optician. The sun shines out of his arse man. You get what I mean, I'm a construction worker and no one wants to know you.*

The majority of staff interviewed felt that some ethnic minority groups experience cultural and familial expectations and pressures that other students do not. These pressures can often 'conflict' with the educational demands placed on students, for example, making it very difficult for students to attend and have sufficient time to achieve their full potential. For example one staff member explained:

> *I think some students that come here are incredibly courageous because they are stepping outside of their family norms and they are becoming independent and sometime that results in conflict.*

The majority of ethnic minority student and staff interviews and appeals demonstrated the importance and significance of the immediate and internationally extended family, affecting student progress to a greater extent than for non-ethnic-minority students. These issues were all linked with family or personal circumstances, often in addition to circumstances which non-ethnic-minority students may face. These are not currently recognised in extenuating circumstances criteria.

3.2 Lifestyle clash

Immersion in a culture, 'way of life' and personal circumstances seem inevitably to clash with the lifestyle requirements of academic life. In some cases, the home culture is such as to make demands of time and space which render normal attendance and/or performance at university, or private study, impossible. To appreciate such influences, we now record some of the issues raised in student comments from the appeals cases.

One student talks about the experiences of having severe financial problems due to delays in receiving his student loan, pressure from his parents who wanted him to get married and obtain a suitable degree or else move to Pakistan and work on the family farm. This caused him to turn to drink and attend lectures when far from sober. He had less than suitable living conditions during part of the year, which made study difficult. He wrote:

> *If I didn't get married they said the alternative would be to move to Pakistan and work on the family farm. This really placed immense pressure on me and I am ashamed to say that I turned to drink (for the first time ever in my life) to help me cope. This living situation was certainly not conducive to studying and led me to become tired, lack concentration and my self-esteem was extremely low… I have been at the lowest I could ever be, homeless, eating left-overs, wearing other people's clothes. I thought life was unbearable… Your positive decision [reference to the Appeals Panel] would mark the turning point for the rest of my life… I am very close to my family and do not wish to retaliate against anything they say, however I do not think I will be able to survive over there.*

Despite the severity of this case, the appeal made by this student was rejected by the Panel.

On the whole, students put forward appeals which are valid within the regulations, but a large proportion of these were not, in the end, accepted. It is possible that among these cases there were instances where students put forward extenuating circumstances which a panel would find difficult to interpret.

3.3 Student support

Where students were unable to put forward in interviews guidance or support that they had personally received, they were instead given scenarios ú hypothetical situations ú and asked what they would do. These included stories of racism, discrimination, harassment, or religious or cultural issues that an ethnic minority student may well come across during their time at university. The responses indicated that none of them (in an admittedly small sample) had used nor were aware of services such as the Multifaith Chaplaincy, Multicultural Office, Counselling, Student Service Centre or Guidance. However, they did identify the need for students to use their own initiative in seeking support:

> *I should really know this because I'm student rep. We did some training, and a lot of the stuff's on the home website isn't it? I think it's just a case of going and looking for it really ú getting up to date on the stuff, but I'm not really sure, I don't really know.*

A majority of staff identified support as instrumental in retaining ethnic minority students. Some schools within the university have an 'open door' system where students are encouraged to 'drop in', whereas in other schools academic staff are located in private closed offices, which means students have to telephone or email lecturers and/or arrange specific times through an appointments system to speak to them. Students reported feeling most supported in those systems where the member of staff was known to the student, and where there had been plenty of opportunity for a relationship to develop between the student and member of staff concerned. The significance of the proximity of tutors to students may also be reflected in the fact that the majority of students said they would approach their tutor to talk about their problems. But some students said they would not choose to speak to their personal tutor about ethnicity, culture or religious related issues because, as one student said "I would not be able to talk to someone that I know would not understand or want to understand where I was coming from".

Where there are systems with designated staff who are responsible for personal support of students, there will be staff who do not have this designated responsibility who may view the personal concerns of students to be outside of their role. For example one member of staff said:

> *Well, no doubt that is the case that some staff are purely interested in the individual's academic performance rather than their family and other circumstances. You're only seeing student from an academic point of view. You don't knowing anything about their background; you don't know them individually very well at all.*

Some staff were conscious of the fact they were unfamiliar with some of the ethnic minority cultural/religious practices:

> *Yes, I think it's ignorance on our part and they probably know just how ignorant we are... although perhaps we're getting better and perhaps students may not think they can come to us because it's not part of our values that they would expect us to understand how an arranged marriage works. So it's only when more and more students come and talk that you realise what they're up against.*

Indeed, some students who had approached tutors to inform them that their personal and family circumstances were affecting their academic performance had commented that some tutors are uninterested and unsympathetic towards them. For example, one student said: "It's just hard luck if your tutor isn't going to listen". For another student, having tried confiding in her tutor in the first year with little support, this affected her wanting to approach the tutor again:

> *Having had the experience of the first year, and how much sort of red tape and stuff it was, I think it could be quite off-putting, you know, to go and talk to a tutor about things.*

For other students, lecturing staff responded to student's cultural needs in ways that ensure they do not negatively impact on their learning experiences.

> *Because it could really, couldn't it, cos we've had reading week this week, but like I'll be fasting, and then it's Eid [religious festival] next week, so I'll have be having time off, and I could miss an important lecture or something and, then it will be hard to get the work done. It's not easy, but I'll catch up. But my lecturers are good like that. They understand and let me have time off.*

It seems therefore, that although there are different systems of supporting students in the university, students view their tutors as the first person they would approach with any problems they were having. Hence the response a student receives from their tutor may be pivotal in how the student perceives the course or the university to be willing to listen to the views and cultural and religious needs of students from minority ethnic groups.

What became apparent in the interviews were the difficulties that students have in seeking/asking for support when facing personal predicaments. The majority of students were unaware of the more formal support mechanisms made available by the institution, such as the Student Service Centre, Multifaith Chaplaincy or Counselling Service. This is of course dependent on the background of the student, their previous experiences and what they deem acceptable and appropriate in light of their own moral understandings, their own values and norms. However, this could be further exasperating for young ethnic minority students as they may feel uncomfortable in approaching and asking for support.

3.4 Extenuating circumstances

One student who had been through the appeals process talked of her negative experience with relation to the death of her grandmother:

> *When, I handed in my form they wanted to see the death certificate, and I thought that was quite bad... I just thought, 'Oh my God!' and I went home and I like said to my mum, oh, we've got to like, see the death certificate, and my mum was like, well, I don't think that's like a good idea, because it was on my dad's side, and my auntie who sort of dealt with all the funeral and stuff, she was quite upset at the time, and I didn't want to like say, oh, can I have the death certificate please, so I went to my doctor's instead and got like a doctor's note to say what had happened.*

It can be identified that some ethnic minority students need an increased level of support and advice in the submission of extenuating circumstances:

> *I don't know, I think there were some other people who did submit extenuating circumstances forms, but they were for, like, a lot of different reasons compared to mine I think, I'm not quite sure what they were exactly, but, I think most of them got like referred, so I don't know what or how they judge it or anything. I mean I don't know exactly how they do it. I just sort of handed in the form and sort of hoped for the best.*

However, different staff reported responding to expressions of personal difficulties in different ways when dealing with complaints or issues within a cultural context, including:

- Strictly adhering to university assessment regulations
- Viewing each student's case individually before granting permission for an extension etc
- Viewing the 'personal' to be of little concern and as falling outside their academic 'role' (as previously shown)
- Ignorance of other cultures

Of the staff interviewed there was a view that students fitting with the main or dominant culture of the university will experience an easier transition into higher education. The transition to university for students who do not share in the dominant culture in terms of ethnicity and religion is much more complex. It is therefore important for the university to be explicitly proactive in finding a common base-line of what a student can reasonably be expected to cope with during their university life and when it is acceptable and advisable for students to seek help. This help needs to be sensitively embedded into the teaching and learning within a student's course, yet the importance of independent and more informal supportive mechanisms must not be underestimated.

4 Conclusions

A complex picture of ethnic minority students' academic appeals has emerged. On the whole, the research suggests the following recommendations to be considered (subject to consideration of the impact and monitoring of the revised assessment regulations and procedures).

Support

■ The responsibility of lecturers/tutors is sometimes taken as being purely academic; there is a need for academic staff to understand their role to entail some personal awareness. And this means that they should have an understanding of the broader cultural contexts of the student experience. Guidance to staff in this matter is required. It is important that staff understand the significance of major religious occasions and how observance of them might affect student attendance or performance.

■ If a student wants to appeal, they need to be given the appropriate support. Although mentioned in assessment regulations and procedures on the student intranet, there needs to be more explicit reviewing of the processes for referring students to Student Services Centre. Students also need to be made aware that they can directly access the services provided by Student Services Centre, and that access is not only via lecturing staff.

■ Some students from ethnic minority backgrounds would benefit from the services of someone from a similar cultural group/background, who could represent them, for instance, in the case of appeals where there was personal information which would be hard to disclose unless the hearer could be expected to understand.

Evidence of extenuating circumstances

■ The research highlights developments which may be needed in the rules for the submission of evidence of extenuating circumstances, and particularly in the submission of personal and/or confidential circumstances relating to the student's cultural practices. There may be inconsistency in the understanding of extenuating circumstances amongst decision makers, especially where cultural and religious practices are concerned. The current regulations on extenuating circumstances may be inappropriate for culturally diverse practices, for example mourning rituals. The rule which links life events to the timing of assessment may assume that mourning is a relatively brief matter.

■ The understanding of the meaning of domestic/personal circumstances needs to be more culturally sensitive.

Cultural awareness

■ The findings from the study indicate that there may be insufficient knowledge and understanding of cultural beliefs, practices and lifestyles of Asian students amongst those who design assessment processes, extenuating circumstances rules, and appeals regulations. The interpretation of the meaning of extenuating circumstances events, and the effects they have on students, need to be more clearly defined for staff and students. There are varying understandings of assessment procedures among Asian students, possibly for cultural reasons.

Ethnic minorities and the majority culture

■ From the analysis of appeals it is difficult to exclude the possibility that some of the issues may be equally applicable to white students, though our feeling is that the details will differ (for example, the calls of elderly members of extended families versus the requirements of the children of single parents).

■ The direct applicability of some findings is hampered by the broad issue of whether the aim of policy in this area should be to seek *consistency* (as QAA guidelines would suggest), or to seek *equity* – in which case it might not be that students of different ethnicities would be treated the same, but rather they would be treated appropriately given their known cultural circumstances.

■ One solution would be to follow the path of setting aside the requirement for extenuating circumstances, and instead opening up assessment so that there would be an element of student choice in the timing of assessment for a given module. The arguments for and against this suggestion go beyond the scope of this report.

How valid are group marks as a proxy for the individual learning that comes from group assignment and project work?

Malcolm G Eley[1], Paul Lajbcygier[2], Christine Spratt[3]

1. Centre for Learning and Teaching Support, Monash University, Australia

2. School of Business Systems, Monash University, Australia

3. Tasmanian School of Nursing, University of Tasmania, Australia

Abstract

In assessing group assignments, common practice is either to attribute a collective project mark unaltered to group members individually, or to moderate that collective mark dependent upon judged individual contributions to the group's activities. Such marking practices seem to assume first, that overall project outcomes reflect some aggregate of the group members' individual learning, and second, that individuals' contributions to group activities are sensitive to variation in that learning. The present study measured individual students' contributions to group processes, individual students' influence on their peers' topic understanding, and the influence of the overall group experience on personal learning. As well, the learning objectives underlying the project work were tested individually as part of the final examination. Findings suggested that neither of the above assumptions were supported. Rather, group outcomes seem better interpreted as reflecting the effectiveness of a group's operation, than of its members' individual learning.

Having students work together in small groups on some common assignment task is part of most fields in university teaching (eg Lejk, Wyvill and Farrow, 1997). Claims in support of using group work have ranged across such providing for practice in group skills, preparation for professional life, the fostering of learning-related interaction, and even the reduction of teachers' marking loads (eg Bourner, Hughes and Bourner, 2001; Goldfinch, Laybourn, MacLeod and Stewart, 1999). Such activities can involve groups from three or four students up to larger teams of perhaps a dozen students. The work undertaken by those groups can range from some small defined task that could take only days, through to large-scale multi-faceted projects that might take an entire semester, and consume the bulk of the study time that a student has available within a single enrolment unit.

The use of group work unavoidably raises some very real assessment issues. How should the learning that has hopefully resulted from the group work experience be best assessed? How can measures of that learning be translated into individual marks, which in turn contribute to individual grades? One very common response to these issues is to use the group work's outcome as a proxy for the learning attained by the individual group members (Conway, Kember, Sivan and Wu, 1993; Goldfinch, 1994; Godfinch and Raeside, 1990; Lejk, Wyvill and Farrow, 1996). The group's product is marked as a single entity, and the resulting mark is then translated into marks attributed to the individual group members. In the simplest case, the product mark becomes the individual group member's mark, unaltered. When within-group variations are made, the most common approach is to moderate the product mark to reflect an individual's rated contribution to the group and that group product.

There are at least two assumptions implicit in such approaches to marking group work. First, higher levels of individual learning are assumed to manifest as higher quality products or outcomes. This assumption allows the single mark for the group product to be taken as an indicator of the 'centroid' of the members' individual attainments. Second, higher levels of participation in the group's work are assumed to result in higher levels of learning by the participating individual. This assumption allows a single member's rated contribution to be taken as an indicator of that member's relative learning from the group work experience.

But what if these assumptions are false? The primary role of educational assessment is the determination of students' attainment of course or unit learning objectives. From this perspective, a mark is intended to be an indicator of the extent of those learning objectives' attainment. But if contributions to group activity do not necessarily relate to individuals' learning, and product quality does not relate strongly to the aggregate of members' learning levels, then our common practice of using moderated product marks as individuals' marks could well constitute an unrecognised shift in the fundamental meanings of marks and grades.

Work by Lejk and Wyvill has demonstrated that when such contribution ratings are used to moderate group marks, the resulting individual marks can vary considerably dependent upon how those ratings are generated. When those ratings are made against separate aspects of contribution, rather than judged holistically, then individual marks are more likely to vary from the overall product mark, and to spread more evenly over a mark range (Lejk and Wyvill, 2001a; 2002). When contribution ratings result from a pooling of individual judgments made in private, rather than from consensus judgments made in public by the group, then the resulting individual marks tend to spread wider (Lejk and Wyvill, 2001b). In summary, a psychometrically desirable greater differentiation amongst group members would be encouraged by nominating specific aspects of contribution to be considered, and by having students rate their peers in private. But this will not guarantee that any resultant contribution ratings will yet relate to individual learning attainments; it simply increases the chance that such a relationship will evidence, should it exist.

Other work by Lejk and his colleagues has demonstrated that group work outcomes might relate only loosely to individual learning (Lejk, Wyvill and Farrow, 1999). Groups arrived at consensus solutions to discrete computing tasks; separately, students were tested individually on task-related material. The quality of group solutions related strongly to the mean test performances of group members only for groups that were homogeneous with respect to those test performances. For more heterogeneous groups, group solution quality was essentially independent of mean test performances. It seemed more that group outcomes were a function of the simple presence of higher capability students, than that individual learning was a function of the quality of group activities. Indeed there were some indications that mixed group membership might even have had a levelling effect on the learning of the individually more capable.

The starting point for the present study then was a concern to test whether group marks based on the quality of group products do reflect the learning attainments of the group members, or knowledge and skills directly relevant to performing the group activity. If independent and individual measures can be found for those learnings, can they be shown to relate positively to group work outcomes? But further, the present study sought to test some alternative approaches to deriving individual marks, based on ratings other than contribution to group functioning. If we define group work as first and foremost a learning experience, and not as an assessment exercise, then perhaps we could rate individuals' performances as facilitators of their peers' learning. Might ratings based on perceptions of peer tutoring effectiveness be a better basis for deriving individual marks from product marks? Might more direct measures of individual students' involvement in learning-related discussion be better indicators of those students' learnings as attained from the group experience? Relationships amongst these measures were expected to test the assumptions outlined previously relating to the use of group outcome marks, and group contribution ratings as mark modifiers.

Subjects

The subjects were the 66 students enrolled in a Business Systems unit in financial computing, versions of which are taken at final year undergraduate or as part of a coursework masters degree. All 66 eventually received a mark for their major group project work, although at the time of the present analyses only 64 had sat the final examination. Some 52 completed the various rating instruments that provided data for the present analyses.

The group project

Working in five groups of ten students, one of nine, and one of seven, all students completed a major project activity. Groups made virtual investments across five market sectors, with the aim of maximising their returns over the period of the project. Each group met at least once per week to review its portfolio, and to decide on any investment changes. The learning objectives associated with the project involved the use of various information sources in the making of investment decisions. These sources included company balance sheets, financial news media, technical price action reports, and macroeconomic indices. The intent was for students to recognise that investment decisions are not uniquely determined by the range of information available.

Work on the project began in week four of the semester, and continued through to week twelve, when groups made class presentations and submitted their final project reports. Group marks for the project were decided predominantly on the bases of these final reports. The semester comprised 13 weeks of class activities, followed by a four week period in which examinations were taken. The mark received by an individual student for the group project contributed ten percent of the final grade in the unit.

The ratings measures

Three paper-and-pencil instruments were developed, with which students could rate their group project experiences. On the first, students separately rated each of their group peers on contribution to the functioning of the group. In forming their judgments, students were explicitly prompted to think about a peer's contribution to decisions on investment sector weightings and on specific firms, to providing extra information from media sources, to debate and discussion of issues, to fulfilling group coordination and allocated responsibilities. A five-point response scale was defined by descriptors at the extreme and mid-scale points; *'participated consistently and reliably ... usually cooperative ... typically showed genuine interest and enthusiasm', 'participated satisfactorily ... at least sufficient that the group's work could proceed adequately'*, and *'participated negligibly ... either rarely contributing or simply absent'*. Point values of five through one were ascribed to the most participative scale response through to the least.

The second instrument also required separate ratings of individual peers, but this time on contribution to a student's present understanding of the project's related topic material. Students were explicitly reminded of the main topic areas and learning objectives underlying the project. They were prompted to judge how interaction with a peer might have contributed to topic understanding. A five-point response scale was again defined by descriptors at extreme and mid-scale points; *'... frequently led directly to me learning new things ... having topic learning clarified ... discovering and correcting errors ... had strong influence on my topic understanding', '... had an influence on my topic understanding, but overall not strong or frequent or crucial'*, and *'... rarely had any direct influence on my learning of the topic material ... my understanding predominantly from my own study, or from other members'*. Point values of five through one were ascribed to the most influential scale response through to the least.

The final instrument required students to make a relative judgment of the influence of the group experience *per se* on their topic learning. Again, students were explicitly reminded of those topic areas and learning objectives. They were asked to decide whether the discussions and meetings with the group contributed to their present topic understanding, more or less than their own reading and study. Extreme and mid-scale descriptors defined a five-point response scale; '*... discussion with the group often led directly to me learning new things, or to correcting inaccuracies ... learning of the project content was strongly influenced by project oriented discussion and interaction*', '*...learning of project content was influenced in roughly equivalent proportions by project discussions as by my own personal study and reading*', and '*... project discussion rarely resulted in understanding beyond that from my personal study and reading ... my learning of project content only minimally influenced by project oriented discussion and interaction*'. Point values of five through one were ascribed to the most influential scale response through to the least.

In the summer prior to the semester in which the present study was conducted, the present unit was taught to a summer enrolment cohort. Earlier drafts of these three instruments were used then, in a pilot trialling of their structure, and of their administration to the students. The versions used here were developed out of that piloting.

Procedure

For the bulk of the semester, the financial computing unit ran as it would have done were no empirical investigation being conducted. In week 12, students completed their group projects, and submitted their reports for marking. In week 13, after submissions but before marking and examinations, the three instruments were distributed to students within a normal scheduled lecture class. The purposes of the study were explained as being to consider alternative ways in which project marks might be derived. Students were told that their responses to the three instruments would be used to compare different approaches to modifying the marks that individual students might receive for group project work. However, students were assured that for the purposes of their actual marks in the unit, the present study was 'hypothetical'. They would receive marks for their project work in exactly the way that was described in their original unit outlines; that being that all members in a group would receive the mark that the group report and presentation earned.

Students were invited to complete the instruments there and then, privately. They were promised that their individual responses would not be made known to any of their classmates. The instrument forms used were individually customised to simplify the practicalities of responding; they were labeled with the respondent student's name, and for the two peer rating versions, the names of the 'other' group members were already entered.

During the four-week examination period that followed week 13, students sat a two-hour examination on the unit. That examination comprised 28 true-false questions scored one or zero, 38 multiple choice questions scored three or zero, and 12 extended multiple choice questions scored five or zero. Nine of the three-mark multiple choice questions targeted the learning objectives associated with the group project. Performance on those project-related questions thus contributed 27 of the 202 raw marks possible on the examination. The examination contributed 60% of the final grade; thus the project-related questions contributed 8% of the final grade. In unit outline materials provided to students, the structure and content of the final examination had been advised.

Results

In the first analysis the performances of individual group members on the nine project-related examination questions were compared to the project marks attained by their groups. A simple perusal of table 1 indicates no obvious relationship between project outcome quality, as indicated by project marks, and the individual attainment of those learning objectives directly related to the project work, as indicated by performance on related examination questions. There would seem to be considerable spread in individual achievement within each of the groups, except perhaps for the fourth in the table. The simple correlation of group marks against mean number of questions correct was 0.198; but at $df=5$, this correlation would need to have exceeded 0.75 to be treated as significant at $p<0.05$, 2-tailed. The present findings then provide no basis for concluding that group marks in any systematic way reflect the learning of individuals from the group experience. If the marks allocated to an individual should reflect the learning demonstrated by that individual, then awarding the mark for a group outcome to the individual group members would seem invalid as an assessment practice.

If overall group product marks do not then reflect the relevant learning of group members, at least in some 'averaging' sense, it can still be asked whether those group

Group project mark	Number of examination questions correct							Mean number of questions correct
	3	4	5	6	7	8	9	
7.0	1	2	1	2	4			5.6
7.0	1	1	3	2		3		5.8
7.5		1	3	2	3			5.8
7.5				5	4	1		6.6
8.5	1	1	1	4	2			5.6
8.5			1	1		4	1	7.4
9.3	1		2	4	1	1		5.8

Table 1. Numbers of group members performing at different levels on project-related examination questions, compared to group mark for the project.

marks could yet be modified to reflect learning variations amongst group members. That is, can the way in which we transform single group product marks into individual marks be such as to ensure that those individual marks yet reflect learning variations within a group? Within each group, the ratings for contribution to group functioning that any single student received separately from each of his or her group peers were averaged to yield a single 'derived' contribution rating for that student. Likewise, the separate ratings that a student received from each of his or her peers for influence on those peers' topic understanding were averaged to yield a single 'derived' learning influence rating.

As a preliminary, quartile values were calculated for both of these derived rating variables, across the available class enrolment as a single pooled group. Further, frequencies of ratings of the influence of the overall group experience on personal topic learning were calculated. It can be seen from Table 2 that all three measures spread widely. For the overall group experience rating, responses spread across all possible scale points (lower panel, table 2). For the two derived rating measures, values spread almost across the possible range of one through 5 (upper panel, table 2). Given that individual values for both derived ratings represent means, this is quite exceptional, and indicates that students were minimally 'defaulting to the mid-scale'. It seems reasonable that the scale point definitions for all three measures effectively represented variation in perceived experiences, and that students genuinely differentiated when making their respective rating judgments.

	Minimum	1st quartile	Median	3rd quartile	Maximum
Contribution to group functioning	1.25	2.38	3.06	3.67	4.67
Influence on peers' topic understanding	1.38	3.09	3.87	4.43	5.00
Influence of overall group experience on topic understanding	Point value 1 (weak)	Point value 2	Point value 3	Point value 4	Point value 5 (strong)
Count (%)	7 (13.5)	3 (5.8)	20 (38.5)	13 (25.0)	9 (17.3)

Table 2: Distributions of point values derived from the three rating measures, across all groups

Pearson correlations were calculated using the entire data as a single pooled set, amongst the derived contribution rating, the derived influence on peer understanding rating, the influence of the overall group experience rating, the project mark, the number of related examination questions correct, and total raw score on the final examination (see table 3). The correlation between individual performances on project-related examination questions and project marks is effectively zero (at 0.067), corroborating that the two measures can be treated as independent. Further, project marks correlated minimally and non-significantly with examination total raw scores (at 0.173), indicating that project outcomes seem also not to relate to student learning in an overall aggregate sense.

Contribution to group functioning		peers'	overall	mark	questions
Influence on peers' topic understanding (peers')	**0.832** (66)				
Influence of overall group experience on topic understanding (overall)	0.015 (52)	-0.100 (52)			
Mark for group project (mark)	**0.348** (66)	**0.375** (66)	*0.290* (52)		
Number of related questions correct (questions)	-0.022 (64)	0.056 (64)	0.173 (51)	0.067 (64)	
Examination total raw score	**0.368** (64)	**0.441** (64)	-0.126 (51)	0.173 (64)	**0.370** (64)

Table 3. Correlations amongst rating measures, project mark, and examination scores.

Top figure is correlation, lower figure is number of data pairs.

Bold indicates significant at 0.01, 2-tailed; italics indicates significant at 0.05, 2-tailed.

The correlation between students' contributions to group functioning, as perceived by their group peers, and those students' performances on project-related questions was effectively zero (at -0.022). The correlation between students' influences on the project-related topic understanding of their group peers, as judged by those peers, and performances on project-related questions was effectively zero (at 0.056). Finally, the correlation between students' own perceptions of the influence of the overall group experience on their project-related topic understanding, and their subsequent performances on project-related questions was positive, but only minimally so, and not significant statistically (at 0.173). The present findings thus suggest that using contribution ratings to moderate project marks would not yield individual marks that reflected project-related learning, but neither would 'learning facilitator' ratings nor self-perceptions of the influence of the overall group experience, that is if the benchmark is that individual marks should in some fashion reflect on individual's learning on relevant learning objectives.

If group project marks do not necessarily reflect the learning of group members on project-related topics, might the present findings suggest an interpretation of how project groups operate, and thus what such group marks do reflect? The correlations of each of the contribution and learning influence ratings with project marks proved moderately positive and significant (at 0.348 and 0.375). Project groups that include students whom their peers rate as having contributed well to group functioning, and as having had a positive influence on those peers' related topic learning, tend to achieve better marks for their project outcomes. The correlation of judged influence from the overall group experience and project marks also proved positive and significant, albeit slightly less so (at 0.290). Students who rate the overall group experience as having positively influenced their own related topic learning tend to have belonged to groups that achieved better project marks. The correlation between the two derived ratings measures, contribution and learning influence, was high, positive, and clearly significant (at 0.832). Students rated well by their peers for contributing to group functioning, and for influencing those peers' topic learning, seem largely to be the same individuals. Finally, the correlations of each of the derived ratings measures with examination raw scores were moderately positive and significant (at 0.368 and 0.441). Students rated well for contributing to group functioning, and for influencing peer learning, tend also to be higher achieving students, at least in overall examination result terms.

What is a possible picture of group functioning that emerges? The group project mark, or rather the quality of the group project outcome, might be seen as primarily a function of the effectiveness with which a group operates in pursuing the project aims. That effectiveness might be defined by group members who 'work well together', which in more specific terms might include cooperating, collaborating, sharing duties and responsibilities, assisting each other in overcoming confusions and misconceptions. In the present study's terms, group effectiveness could be seen as a function of the presence of students who are good contributors, and good 'learning facilitators', and who are perhaps also above some threshold in terms of their basic academic learning capabilities.

And none of this need have any necessary predictive relationship to the learning attained by individual group members, specifically as a result of the group experience. The group outcome is determined by how well the group operates as a group, in pursuit of the group's goal of completing the project task. So long as the group ensures that its tasks are properly completed, by whomever, then a higher quality outcome is more likely. But that outcome quality need not depend directly on all or most of the group members achieving a higher level of understanding of the group project and its composite tasks and understandings. To use a sporting analogy, a 'champion team' is not necessarily a 'team of champions'.

One might speculate that in group functioning, a 'critical mass' model might apply. That is, if some minimum proportion of a group's members are good 'group operators', then the group can function effectively. Until the membership passes that hypothetical

Mark for group project	Proportion members above 'collaborative' cut-off	Mean rating for contribution to group functioning	Mean rating for influencing peer learning
9.3	0.60	3.57	3.93
8.5	0.78	3.54	4.48
8.5	0.57	2.96	3.91
7.5	0.50	2.84	3.79
7.5	0.10	2.26	3.27
7.0	0.50	3.21	3.51
7.0	0.30	2.71	3.04

Table 4. Comparison of group marks against proportions of members judged 'collaborative'.

proportion, it will remain dysfunctional. As a rough test, the simple multiplication of each student's contribution rating with his or her learning influence rating was calculated. The possible scale range for each of these derived rating measures is one through five, with a mid-scale three. A somewhat arbitrary cut-off of 12 was selected for this multiplication, in that 12 would require a product of a 'mid-scale' with a 'point above mid-scale'. This cut-off of 12 was intended to represent a 'minimally but clearly collaborative' group member. To re-state, this is a rough test. But from table 4 it can be seen that the three best performing groups, in terms of project mark, had the three highest proportions of members above this arbitrary definition of 'collaborator'.

Discussion and conclusions

The purpose of the present study was to test two assumptions that underlie the common practice of using project outcome marks as the basis for ascribing marks to individual students, with ratings of contribution to group functioning moderating any differentiation amongst those individual marks. Neither assumption was found to hold. Project outcome marks did not reflect an aggregate of within-group individual attainment. Contributions to group functioning did not relate to within-group variation in individual attainment. The present study also tested two possible alternative bases for mark moderation, namely individual students' ratings for influence on their peers' learning, and individual students' personal perceptions of the influence of the group experience on their related topic learning. Neither was found to relate to individual learning.

What the present findings did suggest instead was that group outcomes might be better interpreted as reflecting the effectiveness of a group's operation, which in turn might be a function of some threshold presence of group members who are both 'good group operators' and generally good academically. Such an interpretation is perhaps supported by recent findings that while group project marks can relate strongly to changes in a group's group functioning skills, there can yet be considerable variability on both group skills and marks within groups. (Laybourn, Goldfinch, Graham, MacLeod and Stewart, 2001).

How could it be that a group operates effectively, produces a high quality outcome, and yet not all group members benefit in terms of personal learning and understanding? If the mark that individual group members receive for group work is the project mark, or some function of it, then it is to each member's advantage that that the group outcome be of the highest quality possible. This will be true regardless of how individual marks might be moderated. We might expect then that groups will tend to operate in whatever fashion efficiently maximises the probabilities of such higher quality outcomes.

We might speculate that high quality outcomes will result when groups align whatever relevant expertise they might possess with the tasks and activities required by their projects. This might mean members singly undertaking particular tasks for which they are well suited. It might mean varying combinations of members working on different activities. It would require expertise at group organisation and functioning, somewhere in the group. It would require some minimum of content expertise somewhere, to enable substantive critiquing of project work. But none of this would necessarily require that all members develop high or even equivalent levels of content understanding. Such an operational picture of student project groups might not fit with an image of cooperative interaction in which group members support and develop their lesser peers, and we might lament that. But such a picture could be seen as the simple result of contingencies inherent in a project-based marking regime. And in hindsight, this picture is probably not too different from how project teams in a commercial, 'non-educational' environment might operate.

In conclusion, we should perhaps return to what is probably the central issue, how we assess the learning that occurs in group project work? If project outcomes cannot be trusted to reflect individual learning, and a variety of group process measures cannot be trusted as learning sensitive moderation indices, how can we validly assess that learning? The present findings suggest that in the final analysis individual learning should be assessed individually. We caution that the present study is just one within a particular instructional context. But if the findings here prove generalisable, then maybe we should redefine group projects to be not assessment opportunities, but a form of learning experience (see Lejk, Wyvill and Farrow, 1999). Given the possible influence of contingencies discussed above, we might need to find ways to structure them to ensure that students commit and participate. This might mean not modeling group projects on workplace project teams, but rather deliberately designing them to encourage the student learning behaviours that we desire. But the simple conclusion here is that we cannot assume that individual assessments necessarily or directly derive from project outcomes. Perhaps this was an unfounded expectation in the first place.

References

Bourner, J, Hughes, M and Bourner, T (2001) First-year undergraduate experiences of group project work. *Assessment and Evaluation in Higher Education*, 26, 19–39.

Conway, R, Kember, D, Sivan, A and Wu, M (1993) Peer assessment of an individual's contribution to a group project. *Assessment and Evaluation in Higher Education*, 18, 45–56.

Goldfinch, J (1994) Further developments in peer assessment of group projects. *Assessment and Evaluation in Higher Education*, 19, 29–35.

Goldfinch, J, Laybourn, P, MacLeod, L and Stewart, S (1999) Improving group working skills in undergraduates through employer involvement. *Assessment and Evaluation in Higher Education*, 24, 41–49.

Goldfinch, J and Raeside, R (1990) Development of a peer assessment technique for obtaining individual marks on a group project. *Assessment and Evaluation in Higher Education*, 15, 210–231.

Laybourn, P, Goldfinch, J, Graham, J, MacLeod, L and Stewart. (2001) Measuring changes in group working skills in undergraduate students after employer involvement in group skill development. *Assessment and Evaluation in Higher Education*, 26, 364–380.

Lejk, M and Wyvill, M (2001) Peer assessment of contributions to a group project: A comparison of holistic and category-based approaches. *Assessment and Evaluation in Higher Education*, 26, 61–72. (a)

Lejk, M and Wyvill, M (2001) The effect of the inclusion of self-assessment with peer assessment of contributions to a group project: A quantitative study of secret and agreed assessments. *Assessment and Evaluation in Higher Education*, 26, 552–561. (b)

Lejk, M and Wyvill, M (2002) Peer assessment of contributions to a group project: Student attitudes to holistic and category-based approaches. *Assessment and Evaluation in Higher Education*, 27, 569–577.

Lejk, M, Wyvill, M and Farrow, S (1996) A survey of methods of deriving individual grades from group assessments. *Assessment and Evaluation in Higher Education*, 21, 267–280.

Lejk, M, Wyvill, M and Farrow, S (1997) Group learning and group assessment on undergraduate computing courses in higher education in the UK: Results of a survey. *Assessment and Evaluation in Higher Education*, 22, 81–91.

Lejk, M, Wyvill, M and Farrow, S (1999) Group assessment in systems analysis and design: A comparison of the performance of streamed and mixed ability groups. *Assessment and Evaluation in Higher Education*, 24, 5–14.

Negotiating academic assignments: the experiences of widening participation and traditional students

Liz McDowell and Kay Sambell

Northumbria University

Introduction

In 2000 the UK Labour government set a target for fifty per cent of the under-30s population to have participated in higher education by 2010. This has accelerated the trend towards 'massification' (Scott, 1995; Altbach, 1999) of UK higher education. In addition to increasing overall student numbers, universities are admitting students from groups who have been 'under-represented' (Medway et al, 2003). These widening participation or 'non traditional' students include, for example, mature students (over the age of 25), those drawn from the first generation in their families to enter higher education, students from manual, semi-skilled, unskilled, unemployed and unwaged parental backgrounds and those with non-traditional entry qualifications. The terminology of 'non-traditional' implies that these students are different. In this paper we challenge current conceptions of this difference, in relation to students' experiences of learning at university.

A discourse of difference

There is a growing professional discourse focusing on the perceived differences between so-called 'traditional' (or 'conventional') and 'non-traditional' (or 'new' students). A number of universities are rapidly developing new support services, curricula and pedagogies to meet the needs of non-traditional entrants. Such developments are strongly promoted by policy-makers and national agencies (National Audit Office, 2002; UCAS, 2002) and there is a growing body of research highlighting a number of inter-related barriers faced by many non-traditional students in higher education (Leathwood & O'Connell, 2003; Reay et al, 2002). Whilst some of the barriers identified are economic (eg financial hardship, poor living conditions, demands of paid employment) or social (eg managing study alongside domestic responsibilities, health problems, lack of family or peer encouragement), in many cases the key differences highlighted relate to non-traditional students' lack of what Gibbs and Simpson (2002) call 'academic preparedness'. This encompasses lack of preparation in terms of knowledge background, study skills and appropriate conceptions of learning. The National Audit Office (2002: p15) for example suggests that non-traditional students are less well equipped with 'individual or self-learning skills', and that an inability to cope is a main reason offered by those withdrawing from university. This includes not being prepared for independent study, lacking understanding of what is required to pass the course, not having adequate study skills or appropriate cognitive styles. A study of socio-economically disadvantaged school pupils' views of learning in our own region (Miller, 2002) revealed high levels of dependence on teachers. The school students that Miller interviewed expected teachers to make all the decisions about what they should learn and had achieved, rather than expecting to play any part themselves in regulating their own learning. These attitudes and beliefs run counter to the levels of self-direction expected at university.

Unfamiliar academic writing conventions and disciplinary practices can act as major barriers to non-traditional students according to Warren (2002). This can mean that the 'aspirations of students to participate and feel valued within the university are being hindered by their perceptions that they are struggling to achieve accepted conventions of writing' (Rai, 2004, p155). In other words, many students soon find there is a difference between the ways in which they write and what is deemed 'acceptable' when they enter university, but they are not sure how to achieve the new goal. To compound the issue, students do not always understand the feedback they receive on their academic writing, so find themselves unable to adjust their approach (Lea & Street, 1998; Wotjas, 1998; Chanock, 2000). Moreover, such students may well lack the confidence to approach lecturers, worry about how to approach essays and be overly-anxious about appearing to be less able than their peers. Leathwood and O'Connell (2003) suggest that low self-esteem can result in non-traditional students labelling themselves as inherent 'failures', who are somehow less worthy. Rather than viewing learning as a process within which they can exercise some control, they may attribute failure to an intrinsically fixed attribute, such as intelligence (Knight & Yorke, 2003).

There is a danger that the current discourses concerning barriers to learning pathologise non-traditional students, whilst appearing to be supportive and aimed at promoting students' success at university, by making the case for support such as targeted study skills provision. Differences which can be attributed to the individual and/or their immediate social and family context are being foregrounded rather than economic, structural and broader social issues. Furthermore, there is a somewhat uncritical acceptance in much of the literature that the experiences of non-traditional students are *qualitatively* different with respect to approaches to learning, coping with academic work and interpreting study requirements, when compared with the experiences of traditional students. Whilst traditional and non-traditional students differ in some respects, by definition, our research leaves us unconvinced that they experience learning at university in fundamentally different ways. This paper examines students' experiences of academic assignments, a crucial nexus within which students' experiences of learning can be illuminated, and questions the validity and utility of making categorical distinctions between traditional and non-traditional students in relation to their experiences of the study context.

Method

The research reported here is comparative, being based on two separate studies undertaken within the same research group at Northumbria University. In methodological terms, comparative analysis can have a range of meanings (Evans, 2002). Our comparative analysis derived from discussions concerning the interpretations made and inferences drawn from two separate empirical studies which led to a re-analysis of sections of the two data sets. The analysis led us to identify significant commonalities in students' experiences and in the implications for pedagogic strategies. The first study was designed to examine the barriers and difficulties faced by non-traditional students in relation to academic assignments and their progressive development as autonomous learners, in a new university where non-traditional students were in the majority (Sambell & Hubbard, 2004). The second study examined learning and learner autonomy, including a significant element focusing on students' experiences of assignments. The research was conducted in two old universities and the sample of students included some who might, with some justification, be termed not merely 'traditional' but 'elite'. An integral part of this study concerned the difficulties or problems which students faced. This provided the opportunity to look comparatively at the two studies in relation to the barriers and problems identified.

Context	Subject and module	Sample
Study 1 New university	Combined/modular social science Module: Writing at university	36/112
Study 2: Old university A	Biological sciences Module: Plant physiology	8/47
Study 2: Old university B	Combined social science Module: Area studies	6/14

Table 1: Data sources

Both studies gathered data chiefly from students, using semi-structured interview schedules to support reflective phenomenographic interviewing strategies (Marton & Booth, 1997). In the non-traditional student study, students were interviewed in small groups at different stages throughout the semester. Volunteers were recruited in tutorial groups, which had been allocated administratively, on the basis of alphabetical registers. Three groups of students were interviewed, with initial interviews, focusing on students' expectations of studying at university, conducted in the first three weeks, and the second interviews, exploring students' experiences of the module, in the final week of the course. In the old university research study, students on specific modules were studied, chiefly through individual interviews at two points in the semester, and this data was complemented by observational data, documentary analysis and interviews with academic staff.

Results: the challenges of academic assignments

When the data from non-traditional and traditional students were examined and compared, similar variations in experiences of academic assignments emerged. Of key interest are the associated challenges and barriers faced by students, since these revealed that there was much in common across the supposedly distinct student groups.

Uncertainty and lack of confidence in the academic context

A non-traditional student in Study 1 said:

> *"Writing an essay at university is so different!... At first I was lost, I'd no idea. I didn't know what they expected of me."*

However, other students also talked about their uncertainties about academic requirements, in terms of what was expected and the standard they needed to achieve in their assignments.

A student in Study 2 admitted, when talking about an essay:

> *"I don't know what she [the lecturer] is after, or what any lecturer is after"*

Another 'traditional' student said that he hoped his essays were "coherent and good" but he could not really judge that himself: "that's for the lecturers [to decide]"

Lack of confidence that they understood requirements and standards left many students feeling out of control at times, so that they placed their trust on being lucky or on putting in a lot of effort:

> *"I'm not sure what mark it'll get [but] in terms of my working hard... I worked very hard" (Study 2)*

This sense of a lack of control might lead *any* student to doubt their own abilities, at least for a time, but some students had developed, perhaps from earlier or current educational experiences a somewhat fixed belief that they were not capable of doing well. This was found even amongst some students who would be regarded as 'traditional':

> *"... even if I spent hours I could not get the same mark [as some others on my course] because they are just a better writer" (Study 2)*

Lack of support

Students can feel that they are very much 'on their own' in large student groups with little opportunity to get specific personal help and advice from lecturers. A student in Study 1 talked about what he had anticipated at university:

"I imagined sitting in class, not knowing what was going on, and getting no chance to ask if I wasn't sure."

A biology student in Study 2 had very similar comments about her course which was, in her second year, including 'small' group seminars (around 30 students) for the first time:

"in large lectures... the lecturer wouldn't even recognise you, but in seminars they notice... which I find is a lot easier because then you get to know the lecturer as a person and find it easier to talk to them about things [you are studying]. "

Whilst many lecturers try to make themselves available (for example through publicising office hours), students may be unwilling to take up what is on offer as shown by another biology student:

"I find them – I don't know, not patronising, but professors are a bit scary, aren't they?"

The nature of academic knowledge and learning

Students, especially those who have undertaken vocational rather than academic courses prior to university may struggle with the nature of academic knowledge expecting 'right answers' and a definitive formula that will produce a good assignment and a good mark. One student in Study 1 described her college experience in this way and was concerned that it was not the same at university:

"At college, you're given all the criteria... you really can't go wrong. You know all you have to do is put in the things they tell you. If that goes in, then really, you're going to pass."

This is also found amongst other students. A biology student (Study 2) was strongly in favour of lectures as a teaching method because it gave her 'on a plate' all she needed to know:

"you know exactly what you're being taught. You're given something that you know that you need to know, because obviously everything boils down to the exam at the end of the day and you know what's going to be in that exam, whereas if you were given a chapter in a book to read you don't know which points are the most important"

Whilst a social science student in Study 2 talked about assignments as:

"like regurgitating – sort of – bringing all the books together and putting it into your own words, but it's not really your own words"

A social science lecturer in Study 2 made this comment about his traditional/elite students:

"our biggest problem, especially with a certain kind of student that we get... the privately educated, bright enough student... is that they come believing there's a

> *right answer and they come believing that your job is to teach them the right answer"*

Students in both studies who came to realise that university was 'different' and that it was not just a matter of learning the right answers often talked about 'argument', 'interpretation' or having "your own perspective on it" but knowing that an argument was needed did not mean that there were no difficulties in putting this awareness into practice:

> *"I usually try and get one strand of thought and develop that and put other people's thoughts into it and counter argue it with that... it can end up a bit woolly" (Study 2; social science)*

Another student on the same degree course said that she knew all the lecturers' comments such as "argument not cogent", "use suitable evidence", "conclusion not adequate", but that she never knew what was going to apply to a piece she was writing.

Autonomy in learning

A number of the statements made about non-traditional students relate broadly to a lack of capability to work independently or autonomously. This is a complex area. There is an important distinction to be made between managing one's studies and being an independent handler of subject knowledge. The first of these which might be termed procedural autonomy (Ecclestone, 2002) refers to matters such as organising your time, meeting deadlines, paying attention to requirements and following guidance and instructions. Subject-matter or epistemological autonomy (Candy, 1991) is the ability to make sense of subject matter, use evidence and theories, and experience some feelings of control and ownership of subject knowledge.

Procedural autonomy is a challenge for many students:

> *"This year it's been, you do the work [in class] and then you perhaps go and find more information and write up about it... There isn't enough time to do all my work... it got quite stressful. And then you've got other commitments and other worries that have not got to do with your degree... So you've got quite a lot of things going on around and so it can be quite hard to set the time to do the biology, the actual degree." (Study 2; Biology)*

Another student said that whether he completed his assignments properly or met deadlines was variable. Sometimes he admitted to:

> *"messing about, playing sports, socialising, rather than doing work... it's quite hard to be able to do everything at an even par." (Study 2 social science)*

Subject-matter autonomy presents other challenges even to students who can manage their studies effectively, as in the case of this student of biology:

> *"We are really encouraged to write what we think, not just regurgitate what we're told... but if I did have an idea I don't think I'd be that confident in putting it in*

because the way I see it is the people that I'm learning from obviously know more than I do and I think I might look a bit stupid if I wrote the wrong thing."

Students may be too pre-occupied with what the lecturers really want to even consider what their own view might be. When asked about her essay conclusion one social science student said:

"Well, I stated that this was a perspective [from the literature]... I don't know whether I answered the question so I wasn't too sure... I think different lecturers want different things... it's difficult" (Study 2, Social Science)

Out of place at university

For many students the university, with its many demands on them, can be a stressful and frightening place.

"It has been very stressful and not being able to sleep at night thinking I have got so much to do tomorrow" (Study 2: Biology)

"It's terrifying, but the only way you can do [assignments] is by trial and error" (Study 1)

This student was prepared to keep trying, adding "I know I haven't got it, yet, but I feel like I'm really on the ladder to learning", but it is suggested that many non-traditional students are particularly hindered by feeling 'out of place' at university. Again we can illustrate that they are not the only ones. A number of students in Study 2 voiced similar feelings based on a variety of reasons. One biology student who had not quite achieved the A level grades she had been asked for but who was still admitted to the course said "I shouldn't really be here you know", whilst a social science student said "I didn't really want to be a student because of what you associate it with... [such as] going out and getting drunk". Activities which are quite 'routine' can cause real anxiety for students:

"for the first two terms I was scared to go [into the library] because it's such a nightmare to actually use those things [computers] if you haven't been shown."

Discussion

Many of the specific barriers and difficulties that have been identified in relation to non-traditional students are found to affect other students too. What have been identified as specific problems in the early or transition phase of non-traditional students into university, may simply reflect that this is an early stage in students' development. There are well-known developmental models of university students (Baxter Magolda, 1992; Perry, 1999) which illustrate changes in concepts of learning and knowledge, and in the personal capabilities to cope with and make sense of academic learning over time at university. With respect to autonomy in learning, all students need to work out what is required in a new context. This may be particularly difficult if the new context is very different from prior experience. Biggs (1999) warns, in relation to international students at Western universities, that many people have assumed that inherent and cultural differences cause their 'difficulties' however such supposed differences tend to disappear when students are able to adapt to the new context. If we consider autonomy in relation to subject matter Candy (1991) identifies that anyone moving into a new subject area, or perhaps being required to look differently at a subject as they move into university from school or college, looks for and needs support and guidance. Autonomy in relation to subject matter needs to develop over time. Some of the difficulties identified as pertaining to non-traditional students can be related to 'inappropriate' conceptions of learning or the adoption surface approaches to study. Since approaches to learning research over many years has identified similar conceptions and behaviour amongst many university students, these cannot be regarded as specific to non-traditional students.

In the new university context where Study 1 was conducted, changes were made to teaching and learning to better support non-traditional students. Specifically, time was set aside in some course modules to assist students to understand academic expectations by working actively with the criteria applied to judging academic work, and seeing examples. Formative assessment which is vital to learning (Black & Wiliam, 1998; Gibbs & Simpson, 2002) was implemented through practice tasks, and the provision of feedback from lecturers, but increasingly through group activities. Collaborative assignments and sharing their work helped students to gain confidence by working with others before having to strike out on their own. They frequently expanded their own ideas by seeing how fellow students approached and dealt with academic tasks:

> *'Although it's a bit funny other people seeing your work, I've got used to it… you feel OK about saying – I did it this way, how did you do yours? – then you get the opinions of the whole group, not just your own ideas so that's got to be better than doing it on your own and you learn from your mistakes'*

The changes made to the course were later viewed as promoting the kind of supportive environment which would benefit *all* students (Entwistle, McCune & Hounsell, 2002). Good teaching and study support services can help students in general to adjust to university and to learn more effectively by helping them to understand what is required and review their own needs, learning and progress.

Conclusion

We contend that non-traditional students do not have a distinctive qualitatively different experience of university learning, as shown by our comparative study. However, we did not investigate whether there were some differences of a quantitative nature or some combinations of personal, social and economic circumstances which place non-traditional students more 'at risk' than some other groups of students. For example, considering quantitative differences, it is possible that, perhaps due to prior educational experiences, non-traditional students may be more likely than their better-prepared peers to adopt surface approaches to learning at university. However this proposition remains to be fully tested. The developmental pathways followed by non-traditional students as they move towards autonomy in learning and adopt critical and relativistic thinking may have some distinctive features. Baxter Magolda (1992) showed gender-related patterns in the ways that students develop, although the end-points did not differ significantly between males and females. It seems likely that we might also find different patterns of development related to variables such as socio-economic class and this would be worthy of further investigation on a longitudinal basis.

Often obvious problems which occur amongst non-traditional student groups, such as higher than average drop-out rates, are used as evidence of their failure to learn appropriately in the university context. It may be that they are not especially bad at learning but that a combination of factors outside the educational context such as finance, housing conditions or lack of effective family and peer support result in 'normal' learning difficulties becoming insurmountable. Research does show that, with particular reference to drop out, normally a cluster of factors are at work (Yorke, 1999). Whilst supportive pedagogical approaches and university support systems can assist non-traditional students to learn more effectively, they may not be able to resolve all of the problems which these students face. If we wish to help students to succeed at university we may also need to address the broader contexts and structures within which their learning is situated.

References

Altbach, P (1999) 'Patterns in Higher Education Development' in Altbach, P, Berdahl, R Gumport, P (eds) *American Higher Education in the Twenty-first Century*. Baltimore: John Hopkins University Press.

Baxter Magolda, MB (1992) *Knowing and reasoning in college: gender-related patterns in students' intellectual development*. San Fransisco: Jossey-Bass

Biggs, J. (1999) *Teaching for quality learning at university*. Buckingham: SRHE & Open University Press

Black, P and Wiliam, D (1998) Assessment and classroom learning. *Assessment in Education*, 5(1), pp7-74

Candy, PC (1991) *Self-direction for lifelong learning* San Fransisco: Jossey-Bass

Chanock, K (2000). 'Comments on Essays: do students understand what tutors write?' in *Teaching in Higher Education*, 5 (1): 95-105.

Ecclestone, K (2002) *Learning autonomy in post-16 education*. London: RoutledgeFalmer

Entwistle, N, McCune, V and Hounsell, J (2002) *Approaches to studying and perceptions of university teaching-learning environments; concepts, measures and preliminary findings*. Enhancing teaching-learning environments Project Occasional Report 1. Edinburgh: School of Education, University of Edinburgh (www.ed.ac.uk/etl)

Evans, L (2002) *Reflective practice in educational research*. London: Continuum

Gibbs, G and Simpson, C (2002) 'How assessment influences student learning – a literature review.' Unpublished paper, Milton Keynes: Centre for Higher Education Practice, The Open University

Knight, PT and Yorke, M (2003) *Assessment, Learning and Employability*. Buckingham: Society for Research into Higher Education/Open University Press.

Lea, MR and Street, B (1998) 'Student Writing in Higher Education: an academic literacies approach' in *Studies in Higher Education* 23(2): 157-172.

Leathwood, C and O'Connell, P (2003) '"It's a struggle': the construction of the 'new student' in higher education" in *Journal of Education Policy*, 18 (6): 597-615.

Marton, F and Booth, S (1997) *Learning and awareness*. Marwah, NJ: Lawrence Erlbaum Associates Inc

Medway, P, Rhodes, V, Macrae, S, Maguire, M and Gewirtz, S (2003) *Widening Participation through Supporting Undergraduates: what is being done and what can be done to support student progression at King's?* London: Department of Education and Professional Studies, King's College.

Miller, K (2002) *Widening Participation and Social Class: A Study of Young People's Perceptions of Schooling and Higher Education in the North East of England*. Unpublished report, Northumbria University.

National Audit Office (2002) *Improving Student Achievement in English Higher Education: Executive Summary. Report by the Comptroller and Auditor General, HC 486 Session, 2001-2002*, 18 January. London: Her Majesty's Stationery Office, NAO.

Perry, WG (1999) *Forms of intellectual and ethical development in the college years: a scheme*. San Fransisco: Jossey Bass

Rai, L (2004) Exploring Literacy in Social Work Education: A Social Practices Approach to Student Writing *Social Work Education* 23(2): 149–162.

Reay, D, Ball, S, and David, M (2002). 'It's taking me a long time but I'll get there in the end': mature students on access courses and higher education choice *British Education Research Journal*, 28 (1): 5-19.

Sambell, K and Hubbard, A (2004) The Role of Formative 'Low-stakes' Assessment in Supporting Non-traditional Students' Retention and Progression in Higher Education: Student Perspectives *Widening Participation and Lifelong Learning*, 6 (2) pp25-36

Scott, P (1995) *The Meanings of Mass Higher Education*. Buckingham: Open University Press.

UCAS (2002) *Paving the Way Project Report: Informing change in higher education and progression partnerships with the voice of the under-represented*. Cheltenham: UCAS.

Warren, D (2002) Curriculum Design in a Context of Widening Participation in Higher Education *Arts and Humanities in Higher Education*, 1(1): 85–99

Wotjas, O (1998). 'Feedback? No, just give us the answers' *Times Higher Education Supplement*. Sep 25 1998.

Yorke, M (1999) *Leaving early: undergraduate non-completion in higher education*. London: Falmer Press

Supporting students to improve their essay writing through assessment criteria focused workshops

Lin Norton[1], Katherine Harrington[2], James Elander[2], Sandra Sinfield[2], Jo Lusher[2], Peter Reddy[3], Olaojo Aiyegbayo[1] and Edd Pitt[1]

[1]Liverpool Hope University College

[2]London Metropolitan University

[3]Aston University

Keywords

assessment, essays, assessment criteria, workshops, literacy, supporting students

Overview

Students from diverse backgrounds and with differing abilities need help in writing academic essays. This paper reports on the efficacy of a workshop programme specifically designed to help students understand what we have described as core assessment criteria. The programme, which is part of a HEFCE funded FDTL4 psychology project (www.assessmentplus.net), was delivered at three institutions in the UK. At two of the institutions, workshops were offered as an optional support system for first year psychology students. At the third, the programme was embedded into the delivery of a third year module on health psychology. In addition, some of the workshop activities were incorporated in a generic study and academic skills programme offered to all students (undergraduate and postgraduate) from any discipline as well as in a workshop delivered within a postgraduate business course. Student evaluations of the workshop programme were positive and measures of their performance in exams and in essays indicated some beneficial effects of attending workshops. The picture that emerges from this research is that of students actively trying to make sense of the essay writing task.

Theoretical background

Research has shown that students do not have the same understandings of assessment criteria as their tutors (Pain & Mowl, 1996; Merry, Orsmond & Reiling, 1998, 2000; Higgins, Hartley & Skelton, 2002; Elander, 2003). The work described here draws theoretically on the work of O'Donovan, Price and Rust, 2001; Price & Rust, 1999; Price, Rust & O'Donovan, 2003; Rust, 2002, who have led the field in making assessment criteria explicit to their students. However our work is substantially different in its focus on what we have called 'core criteria' which we link to taking a deep approach to studying and complex learning (Elander, Harrington, Norton, Robinson, Reddy & Stevens, 2004).

The overall Assessment Plus research is a multi-faceted investigation exploring ways in which using core assessment criteria can support student learning, mainly but not exclusively, in the subject of psychology. The area we focus on here is a workshop programme built on identifying core assessment criteria. The workshop programme was designed with an awareness of the need to be inclusive, to pay heed to diversity and to enhance not only retention but success for our students. It was foregrounded in some relevant findings from an interview study with psychology lecturers (Norton, Robinson, Reddy, Elander & Harrrington, 2004) and comments from focus groups with psychology students.

The interview study with psychology lecturers

One to one interviews were carried out with 22 psychology lecturers from two institutions. Of many themes that emerged from these interviews two were of particular relevance when designing the workshop programme. The first theme was that staff were generally doubtful about whether students understood the assessment criteria. Seventeen of the lecturers felt that most students did not even read the criteria but eight of them thought students have problems with the terminology of the assessment criteria and applying the criteria in their own work. There was also a consensus that students tended to improve as they went through their degree and became more practised in the art of essay writing:

> *"I think in some respects they must [understand the criteria] because their essays improve… they must perhaps have picked up what we mean."*

Part of the rationale for the workshop programme was, therefore, to help students to 'pick up what we mean' more quickly in the aims of inclusivity. At the same time we were acutely aware of the need to avoid a strategic approach that focusing on assessment criteria can potentially have (Norton, 2004).

The second theme was a wide variability in how lecturers made use of assessment criteria in marking. When asked to describe what they believed made a 'good essay' there was no clear cut consensus:

"Evidence of having read around the core texts, some sort of independent research, mentioning studies or theories that haven't been mentioned in the course..."

"I'm heavily influenced by the quality of written English; I suspect a good essay is a well-written essay,"

"If a student can arrange material and find the problems and use the material to explain why they're problems, and I don't mean the first-year text book."

This variability is a particular concern for students and was one of the issues talked about in the focus groups.

The focus groups study with psychology students:

These were carried out at two institutions by two different researchers. At institution C three focus groups consisting of first, second and third years were facilitated by the project manager. At institution B the focus groups were carried out by the research assistant, supplemented by some one to one interviews. They consisted of students from all undergraduate years and a postgraduate student. Those issues which relate specifically to workshop provision were:

1. Students' understanding of the importance of assessment criteria – this was very shaky in some cases.

2. Actively trying to make sense of the assessment task by paying attention to feedback – one second year focus group at institution C formed a self help group to compare comments on feedback on their psychology projects.

3. Difficulties in interpreting tutors' comments – many students commented on this and expressed frustration.

4. Variability between tutors – students were keenly aware of differences between lecturers, but at least one focus group in institution C had a sophisticated and mature understanding of the complexities involved in marking their work

5. Views on workshops – where students had attended these, they were seen to be a helpful resource

Conclusions

Overall, what emerges from reading all the transcripts is a general picture of students who on the whole are trying valiantly to do their best in what sometimes appears to be an elaborate guessing game. This is consistent with Higgins, Hartley and Skelton's (2002) view of the student as a 'conscientious consumer' rather than one who is motivated only by marks and does not take account of feedback comments. Another theme that came clearly out of the focus groups overall, is how students tend to come up with their own ideas of what works and then generalise from just one experience. One of the principles underlying all workshops is the sharing of experiences and why this can be useful in a workshop environment.

These themes confirm what we had suspected anecdotally and through our own lecturing experience that students need more guidance and support in writing psychology essays and this is particularly important in our three institutions where widening participation is an important and valued feature of what we are achieving. The Assessment Plus workshop programme was designed to help students to find their way more readily through the assessment maze by spending time on exploring each of the six core assessment criteria.

Description of the Assessment Plus workshop programme

This programme is available to download and adapt for readers' own needs at www.assessmentplus.net, however a brief description is presented here. The full version of the programme consisted of five workshops:

- Workshop 1. 'What are assessment criteria?'

- Workshop 2. 'Addressing the question and structure.'

- Workshop 3. 'Showing understanding and developing an argument.'

- Workshop 4. 'Use of evidence and evaluation.'

- Workshop 5. 'Applying the criteria to your own work.'

The full version was delivered on an optional basis to first year psychology students at institution A where the sessions were run once a week in the lunch hour, by a senior psychology lecturer with an interest in essay writing, for five weeks at the beginning of semester two. A total of 33 students attended though numbers at each workshop ranged from 14 to 20. At institution B the same programme was run during weeks seven to 11 of semester one for first year students as an optional follow-up to six compulsory seminars. These were led by a number of postgraduate psychology students. About 40 first years attended to begin with but attendance declined in the last two weeks of delivery.

At Institution C the programme was adapted for use for two very different student groups. The first of these was a cohort of 111 third year health psychology students as part of their taught course, the aim of which was to increase students' understanding of the subject by focusing on the assessment criteria. The workshops were renamed 'study groups' and were run by four postgraduate psychology students who had been trained by the course leader who designed the study group activities. The main strategy was to help students by reviewing material that had been covered in lectures and looking at how it could be used to construct essay-style examination answers. The sessions covered essay writing, academic argument, critical evaluation, integration and revision, all in the context of health psychology theory and research. 80% of the students attended one or more study group sessions but only 19% attended all four.

In the second application, two versions were delivered by the study skills expert who adapted some of the workshop materials. In the first, generic, version a two hour workshop was run as part of the open-door (drop-in) study and academic skills programme and included material from the Assessment Plus workshops. In addition, the study skills expert also integrated an activity of her own called 'The paragraph as dialogue'. 18 students attended at least part of this workshop, including students from all undergraduate years and postgraduate; subjects included business-related courses, politics, maths, dietetics and arts. In the second version which was devised for delivery within the MBA (strategic management) programme, two workshops were run by the study skills expert with a colleague who was the learning support strategist for business. Each workshop lasted one and a half hours. Seventeen students attended the first workshop and 15 students attended the second workshop; all were postgraduates. Various activities from the Assessment Plus programme were integrated together with more subject specific exercises.

Evaluation of the workshop programme.

A number of different methods of evaluation were carried out in this research to capture as fully as possible the richness and variation in student and staff responses. Thus psychology students were asked at institution A to evaluate each workshop separately as well as an overall programme evaluation. The drop-in students and MBA students at institution C were also asked about specific workshop objectives. These provided qualitative and quantitative data. In institutions B and C staff and students were invited to comment on the overall programme. A summary of the main findings will now be presented.

Objectives related to:	Range of positive evaluations
Workshop 1 (N = 20) 'The key to improving your grades'	
Understanding the role of assessment criteria	85% – 100%
Understanding what makes a good psychology essay	75% – 80%
Workshop 2 (N = 20) 'Where to begin'	
Addressing the question	60% – 95%
Structuring the answer	70% –100%
Workshop 3 (N = 17) 'How to show you know what you're talking about'	
Developing understanding	77% – 100%
Developing argument	88% – 94%
Workshop 4 (N = 14) 'Looking for the evidence'	
Use of evidence	71% – 93%
Evaluation	29% – 50%

Table 1. Summary of positive responses to workshop objectives delivered at institution A

Individual workshop evaluation

The first four workshops were evaluated separately using objectives for each session . and are briefly summarised in table 1 on the previous page.

As can be seen here, the students' responses were mainly positive for all the objectives with the exception of those related to evaluation. Close inspection of these responses showed that students felt unsure not only about how to evaluate the quality of their sources but also of the information contained within those sources. This is a clear indicator that more effort and attention needs to be devoted to this area in any future workshops with an emphasis on giving students hands on practice and feedback.

Students were also asked several open-ended questions to which their responses have been grouped into broad themes:

- Usefulness of discussion and working in a group – "Knowing what the tutors look for in your essays when marking. Participation with other students. Discussing ideas. Handouts for future reference."

- Understanding the importance of assessment criteria – "Learning order of importance for psychology marking assessment."

- Understanding how to structure an essay – "Getting an introduction and conclusion to an essay, which shows good and bad points. It can help me structure my next essay better."

- Provision of examples and handouts – "Looking through examples given. I have never had opportunity to look through other essays to see different styles and techniques…"

- Examples/specimen essays – "Being able to see other text and understand their understanding of the subject they are writing about."

- Argument strategies – "Discussion about arguments for and against looking at several books and journals to access real data." "The part where we were told how to dissect what we are reading." "Ensure I have a balance of pros and cons of essay." "To be able to evaluate both sides of an argument and also how to present an argument or critical account."

- Referencing – "I am very weak in referencing, so this has helped immensely." *"It will help me reference more appropriately." "To back up evidence used plus reference." "Have always fallen down in referencing – so this has greatly helped." "I will be able to use evidence better in my essays plus I have a better understanding of plagiarism."*

- Reassurance – "Re-assurance that I am definitely on right lines here"

- Workshops should be longer – "More time, slow workshop down more, focus on essay techniques rather than content of examples."

■ Greater understanding of what is required – "It will help me essay writing because it gives a better understanding of what the tutor is looking for."

■ Writing appropriately – "It will enable me to flush out my preconceived notions of essay writing and develop university level skills." "Deciding what style I might wish to use and how to lessen any 'risk' attached to it." "Structuring my essay but most importantly, make sure I understand what the question title is asking."

Such evaluations give us useful clues as to where particular difficulties lie and in what ways future workshops need to be adapted to better support our students, particularly in the first year when some of them may feel unsure and vulnerable.

At institution C, the generic and MBA workshops were evaluated individually but the questions were different as can be seen in table 2. The less positive responses to the item about strategies echoes the findings with the first year psychology students at institution A where they felt confident about understanding the criteria but less sure about how to turn this knowledge into actual writing strategies. This suggests students need and want practice at essay writing before they are assessed.

Again students were also asked a series of open-ended questions, of which some illuminating responses have been selected.

Item	Generic (N = 12)	MBA (N = 17)	MBA (N = 15)
I understand the difference between writing to address an essay title and writing everything I know about a topic	58%	88%	80%
I understand the importance of structure and argument when responding to the essay title	92%	94%	93%
I have a clear idea of strategies I can use to stay focussed on the essay title	75%	53%	20%

Table 2. Summary of positive responses to workshop objectives delivered at institution C

Which were the most helpful aspects of this workshop?

"The actual workshop 'worked' examples and our own applications/views; then the comparison with other members within the group to see other sides of the argument/other examples" (Generic workshop)

"Showing lecturers' ranking on assessment criteria. Showing use of various sources" (MBA workshop 1)

"Helped clear up my mind as it was getting very confusing as every teacher had their own demands and I was not knowing how to respond exactly." (MBA workshop 2)

How could the workshop be improved?

> *"I feel there wasn't enough time to explore different strategies to help me to write better essays" (Generic workshop)*

> *"Present some example and explain what is good or bad of the essay" (MBA workshop 1)*

> *"If it is given at the beginning of the course and re-visited at regular intervals during the course" (MBA workshop 2)*

How will what you have learned help you with your essay writing?

> *"As a 'former' get-to-the-subject type of person, this workshop will assist me in breaking down the relevant parts of a question, brainstorming and formulating a well-structured essay" (Generic workshop)*

> *"I will be able to do structures, will enjoy more about my study" (Generic workshop)*

> *"I will use drop in sessions, as I am convinced they are useful now" (MBA workshop 1)*

> *"To use these techniques when writing, to improve quality of the paper. To avoid mistakes that commonly happen because of not knowing the tips and style of proper writing" (MBA workshop 2)*

The interesting point about these evaluations shows that even postgraduate students feel unsure about writing academically. Many of their concerns and comments are similar to those of the first year psychology students.

End of programme student evaluations

Another form of evaluation carried out with the psychology-based workshops was an overall end of programme evaluation which gave quantitative as well as qualitative responses. The quantitative results are presented in table 3 opposite.

What is interesting to pick out of this table is that while most of the items received very positive responses, there were some that students clearly felt more uncertain about. For example, the items about generalisability of what had been learned to writing outside university were low across all three institutions (the previous item was negatively scored therefore low percentages here indicated most students thought they *were* useful outside university). The contradiction between these two items may be an artefact of the phrasing. The other item where scores were less positive was the item about most of what was learned was new where only 45% of the first year students thought this was the case. Perhaps workshops then serve the purpose of reinforcement and reassurance. Looking at the comparison across the institutions, it is not surprising that the responses from the third year health psychology students were generally lower than the first year

Item	Institution A First year psychology (N=11)	Institution B First year psychology (N=11)	Institution C Third year psychology (N=50)
Helped me to understand assessment criteria	100	100	61
Helped me to prepare for exams	N/A	N/A	63
Helped me to understand what makes a good essay	91	91	75
Did not confuse me about what makes a good essay	73	73	77
Helped me to understand my subject	73	64	48
Helped me to prepare for the module assessment	91	27	N/A
Will help me write better essays	100	82	55
Will help me to achieve a better grade in future essays	100	82	45
Will help me to make better use of feedback from tutors	100	60	36
Helped me to study more effectively	64	70	30
*Were useful only for university writing	27	36	27
Were useful for writing outside university	45	55	16
The discussion about assessment criteria was useful (workshop 1)	100	100	77
The specimen essays were useful	N/A	N/A	80
The exercise to mark the essays based on criteria was useful	N/A	N/A	68
Exercise on answering questions was useful (workshop 2)	100	82	N/A
Exercise on structuring was useful (workshop 2)	90	82	N/A
Exercise on showing understanding was useful (workshop 3)	100	73	N/A
Exercise on spotting plagiarism was useful (workshop 3)	100	82	N/A
Exercise on developing argument was useful (workshop 3)	91	100	N/A
Exercise on using evidence was useful (workshop 4)	89	75	N/A
Exercise on citation errors was useful (workshop 4)	100	50	N/A
Exercise on detecting bias was useful (workshop 4)	89	38	N/A
Exercise with essay feedback checklist was useful (workshop 5)	91	57	N/A
Helped me to understand how to 'critically evaluate'	100	82	N/A
Helped me to understand how to 'use evidence'	100	82	N/A
Helped me to understand how to 'develop an argument'	82	100	N/A
Helped me to understand how to 'structure'	91	91	N/A
Helped me to understand how to 'address the question'	100	91	N/A
Helped me to understand how to 'demonstrate understanding'	91	82	N/A
Helped me to understand how to use language	100	73	N/A
Helped me to identify strengths and weaknesses	91	55	N/A
Helped me feel more confident about writing	100	55	N/A
*Made me feel anxious about writing	55	27	N/A
Most of what was learned was new	45	45	N/A

*Items that are negatively scored where low percentage indicates a higher positive response

Table 3 Comparison of the three institutions on percentages of positive responses

students, but it was disappointing that few of them thought it would help them study the subject more effectively or help them write better essays. This may of course be a reflection of the fact that this course was assessed by examination essays, not coursework essays. The large differences between responses from the first year students in institutions A and B may have come about due to differences in delivery – at institution A by a senior psychology lecturer, at institution B by several postgraduate psychology students.

Open-ended questions to the health psychology students and to the first year psychology students at institution B gave a wealth of data that is summarised below; again a selection of illustrative responses is presented.

First thoughts on hearing about the workshops:

> *"Slightly surprised, a little apprehensive. Curious to see how useful they would be. Thought that they were a good idea"* [health psychology]

> *"Good what there is added learning time but worried I might miss out on something if I can't go to some of them"* [health psychology]

> *"Thought it would be a good chance to learn about assessment criteria "* [psychology first year]

What was good about the study groups?

> *"A sense of belonging, heading towards a clear goal, ideas from other students and their approaches, all quality"* [health psychology]

> *"Specimen essays, though I think more of specimen essays would have been very useful"* [health psychology]

> *"The first study group, we were all provided with the assessment criteria for exams and essays, this reminded us and encouraged us that we can perform better in exams"* [health psychology]

> *"Gave insight to psychology and aspects of psychology"* [psychology first year]

> *"Helped me to start writing at uni level"* [psychology first year]

What would you say to a student who was considering these workshops?

> *"Go. They may not be 100% useful, but the one that you miss will probably be the one that was most useful"* [health psychology]

> *"Highly recommend especially for getting a better understanding how to structure and argue in essays"* [health psychology]

> *"They are useful to your understanding of the field"* [health psychology]

"A lot of group discussion involved, can only really understand if you participate" [health psychology]

"It's good and it will help you to develop skills and understand what is expected of you." [psychology first year]

"Makes transition to university life from sixth form" [psychology first year]

"Why not make the most of any help your uni are going to give you." [psychology first year]

"Go along as some areas of psychology writing are different to say a normal English essay" [psychology first year]

"They are especially helpful for students who haven't studies (sic) psychology before." [psychology first year]

Taken together, what emerges from both first and third years was a general feeling that the workshops were useful, but sometimes hampered by lack of participation from other students and sometimes by poor organisation. Some of the comments from the first years indicated an appreciation of any support to help them adjust to the demands of university. Comments from staff involved in delivering the workshops added a further perspective:

"I thought the rationale behind the content of the study groups was excellent and the format 'user friendly'." [health psychology postgraduate tutor]

"They felt the need for more, instead of the action learning groups, when they were meant to revise as a group-but without a seminar leader. They wanted a leader in these groups. They really enjoyed the essay task, they found it very helpful and useful." [health psychology postgraduate tutor]

"For the core few that attended regularly they were overall very pleased with the workshops – as these were students who were very concerned/anxious with taking degree level psychology and how to go about writing in psychology. Typically these students had either taken a few years out, or had never done A-level/year 0 psychology. I found that the students who only attended one or two sessions did not see the benefits, but perhaps it was because the majority of these students had come straight from A-level/year 0 and had previously studied psychology." [First year psychology postgraduate tutor]

Conclusions

Student evaluations are vital; they give us understanding about their perceptions of what we offer and their difficulties. Starting from where the learner is has to be one of the hallmarks of good teaching. However, evaluations only give us one side of the story; they do not tell us whether or not attending the workshops had any measurable effect on students' performance in their written work, which leads us to our final analyses.

Performance

Performance measures were only available from institutions A (coursework essays) and C (exam marks).

Institution A

Seventeen students had essay scores for both before and after the workshops so a Wilcoxon signed ranks test was carried out to see if there was any improvement on the second essay. This showed a modest but significant improvement, $Z = 1.73$, $p<0.05$, $N=17$. Of course it is hard to prove that this was due to the effect of the workshops, particularly since a spearman correlation showed no significant relationship between the number of essay workshops attended and the second essay score, $(r = 0.11, N= 17, NS)$ so the students who had not attended workshops were also subjected to the same analysis. Out of 190 students who had submitted both essays, a Wilcoxon signed ranks test also showed a much larger significant improvement, $Z = 4.63$, $p< 0.00001$. On first glance then it might not appear that the workshops had any particular effect but a closer analysis paints a more accurate picture.

Students	Essay 1		Essay 2	
	Mean	Std dev	Mean	Std dev
Workshop attenders (N =17)	60.5	9.6	62.9	11.5
Non-attenders (N = 190)	54.2	9.1	57.6	9.8

Table 4. Comparison of essay performance between workshop attenders and non-attenders

Firstly, a comparison of the means as shown in table 4 shows that the students who attended the workshops were scoring better on essay one than students who did not attend, so these students were not only better at writing essays but also had less room for improvement. A Mann Whitney U test gives us a Z score of 2.67 which is significant for a two tailed test at $p<0.01$. The question then is, do the attenders maintain this superior essay performance in their second essay? A further Mann Whitney test confirms they do; $Z =2.18$, $p< 0.05$.

Secondly, when comparison of the percentages for groups who improved, worsened or stayed the same was made as shown in Figure 1 opposite, it can be seen that while the improvements were almost exactly the same, this was not the case for the percentage who did worse second time around; 54% of the non workshop attenders as opposed to only 18% of the workshop attenders.

Conclusions

The evidence then seems to suggest that workshops tend to attract better performing and perhaps more conscientious students but also they maintain the superior performance

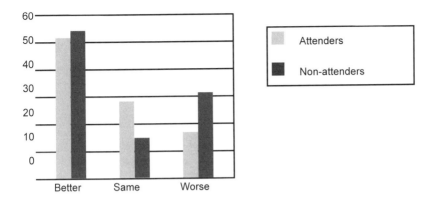

Figure 1 Bar chart showing percentage comparison of change from essay 1 to essay 2

overall. Furthermore, fewer proportionately do worse on their second essays as compared to their non-attending peers.

Institution C

As explained above, the workshops were called study groups and the performance measures were different at this institution as the students concerned were third year health psychology students who were assessed by examination only. In order to see if attending the study groups had had any effect, the mean examination performance scores (ranging from 0 to 70%, with a mean grade of 51%) were correlated with the number of study groups attended which revealed a significant relationship ($r = 0.254$, N= 111, $p<0.01$). Table 5, below, and figure 2, overleaf, illustrates that generally, students who attended more study groups achieved higher grades in the examination and students who attended two or four groups obtained higher than average exam scores (Lusher, 2004).

Number of study groups attended	N	Mean examination grade (%)	Standard deviation
0	22	46.6	20.0
1	20	45.3	20.1
2	18	52. 9	4. 6
3	30	50.1	18.7
4	21	59.9	5.3
Total	111	50.9	16.5

Table 5. A comparison of the number of study groups attended and examination performance (from Lusher, 2004).

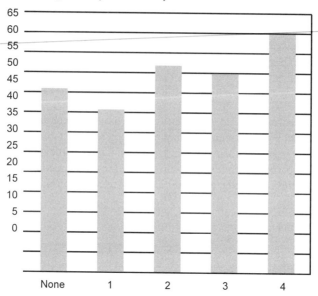

Figure 2 showing exam performance against number of study groups attended (adapted from Lusher 2004)

Conclusions

Here it can be seen that attending workshops does appear to have a direct beneficial relationship on the overall mean examination percentage mark obtained, with students attending all four gaining the most benefit. Of course correlation does not imply causation and it might be that the more able students attended the workshops (as the data from institution A would indicate) but this was tested out using a multiple regression analysis where it was found that performance did not independently predict attendance.

Implications for inclusivity and diversity

In this research, we have shown that there are a number of issues that are important when considering how we can best support students who come to university from different backgrounds and with different abilities.

Our main findings suggest that staff and students have different perceptions of the assessment process. Staff tend to believe that students tend not to bother with assessment criteria nor do they pay attention to the feedback they are given. The focus groups and workshop comments in our research show a different picture with students acting more like 'conscientious consumers', the term coined by Higgins et al (2002). The problem seems to be that students feel unclear about expectations of university writing; they comment on the variability between tutors and the difficulty of interpreting feedback which is often quite general and vague. Many of the more positive comments about the workshops showed their appreciation of clarification and reassurance. At the same time there was a strong request for more tutor guidance and more hands-on practice at developing their essay writing strategies, such as how to actually go about evaluating evidence from other sources. Another main finding was that it tended to be the better, more conscientious students who attended voluntary workshops so maybe lecturers should consider incorporating them into the subject curriculum.

The implications of this research are that students need to have much more directive guidance and support in what traditionally may have been regarded as outside the remit of a university lecturer's job. Academic literacy is fundamental to most university courses and widening participation means we need to offer more practical and supportive opportunities for students to develop and practice the necessary writing skills.

References

Elander, J (2003) A discipline-based undergraduate skills module, *Psychology Learning and Teaching*, 3(1), 48–55.

Elander, J, Harrington, K, Norton, L, Robinson, H, Reddy, P and Stevens, D (2004). Core assessment criteria for student writing and their implications for supporting student learning. In Rust, C (ed), *Improving Student Learning 11. Theory, Research and Scholarship* (pp 200-212). Oxford: OCSLD

Higgins, R, Hartley, P and Skelton, A (2002) The conscientious consumer: reconsidering the role of assessment feedback in student learning. *Studies in Higher Education*, 27 (1), 53-64.

Lusher, J (2004). How study groups can help examination performance. Unpublished report, London Metropolitan University.

Merry, S, Orsmond, P and Reiling, K (1998) Biology students' and tutors' understanding of 'a good essay', in: Rust, C (ed) *Improving student learning. Improving students as learners*. Oxford: OCSLD.

Merry, S, Orsmond, P and Reiling, K (2000) Biological essays: how do students use feedback? in: C. Rust (Ed.) *Improving student learning through the disciplines* Oxford: OCSLD.

Norton, LS Using assessment criteria as learning criteria. A case study using psychology Applied Learning Scenarios (PALS). *Assessment and Evaluation in Higher Education*. Vol 29(6) 687-702.

Norton, LS, Robinson, HL Reddy, PA, Elander, J and Harrington, K (2004) Exploring psychology lecturers' view on assessment criteria. Paper given at psychology Learning and Teaching Conference, University of Strathclyde, 5-7 April, 2004

O'Donovan, B, Price, M and Rust, C (2001) The student experience of criterion-referenced assessment through the use of a common criteria assessment grid, *Innovations on Learning and Teaching International*, 38(1), 74–85.

Pain, R and Mowl, G (1996). Improving geography essay writing using innovative assessment, *Journal of Geography in Higher Education*, 20(1), 19–31.

Price, M and Rust, C (1999) The experience of introducing a common criteria assessment grid across an academic department, *Quality in Higher Education*, 5,2, 133-144.

Price, M, Rust, C and O'Donovan, B (2003). Improving students' learning by developing their understanding of assessment criteria and processes, *Assessment and Evaluation in Higher Education*, 28, 147–164.

Rust, C (2002) The impact of assessment on student learning. *Active Learning in Higher Education*, 3, 2, 145-158.

Transparent opacity: assessment in the inclusive academy

Susan Orr, York St John College

In this paper we identify and critique the techno-rationalism inherent in aspects of contemporary assessment discourse and research. Locating assessment as a social practice, we argue that non-traditional students are not automatically empowered by the current focus on transparency which, particularly in relation to the widening participation agenda, has promised, but not delivered, equitable assessment.

Techno-rationalism characterises assessment as a procedure or a technique that can be objective and unbiased. Techno-rationalism arguably is the dominant paradigm in today's HE assessment literature (Filer 2000). Broadfoot and Black (2004 p19) believe that this 'extreme rationalism' reached a high point in the last ten years. Our difficulty with a techno-rationalist approach is that within it, assessment becomes socially decontextualised (Broadfoot and Black 2004). By acknowledging social context, we work from the perspective that assessment is 'an art as much as a science' (ibid p8). Assessment is 'a human encounter' (Rowntree 1987 p4) and imbued with culture, values and attitudes (Lillis 2001, Higgins 2000). Power relationships underpin this social context and permeate the practice of assessment (Layder 1997, Higgins 2000). The current emphasis on assessment as a technology has drawn focus away from the power relations inherent in the act of assessment (Allen 1998, Filer 2000, Delanshere 2001). Very little research explores how lecturers actually make judgements and how these judgements are affected by social context (Yorke et al 2000, Wolf 2000). A key technology of a techno-rationalist approach is the concept of transparency.

Transparency as a powerful idea in education

Transparency has come to have a significant hold in the academy, identified by Strathern (2000a) as the 'tyranny of transparency'. We argue that transparency is a discourse regime of power (Foucault 1994). It is impossible to be against transparency. Being transparent and open to examination has become normalised (Foucault 1995). It is one of the few ideas, albeit for different reasons, that is held both by those who position themselves primarily as committed lecturers and those with a managerialist perspective.

Why lecturers like it

For many academics transparency is seen as the antithesis of the inequitable hidden curriculum, an idea associated with the reproduction of structural inequalities aided by the absence of formal institutional structures (Margolis and Romero 1998). Strathern (2000b) argues that:

> *transparency of operation is everywhere endorsed as the outward sign of integrity (p2).*

It is about 'fairness' to students. Transparency is sought after in course information; academics work hard to make what they see as improvements in the clarity of course handbooks. Similarly with assessment's rules and regulations, feedback to students, learning outcomes and assessment and grading criteria, lecturers generally feel that students are entitled to know the rules of judgement and perceive this mainly as an issue of clarity.

Transparency as a means to combat the hidden curriculum is important to those of us with a commitment to widening participation. Notions of cultural capital (Bourdieu 1997) foreground the disadvantage faced by students who do not arrive already able to grasp the tacit side of the academy, and who have few family resources to help. Ecclestone (1999) questions the basis of outcome based assessment (OBA) that promised 'publicly available criteria' aiming to 'democratise assessment' (p35) in opposition to elitism and mystery. She points out that OBA research is permeated with humanist language and the notions of fairness. Transparency also seems to offer a lecturers' shared language which enhances pedagogic discussion. The assumption is that learning outcomes such as 'demonstrate efficient self-management, independent and collaborative working methodologies' or 'evaluate research material and apply analytical skills and judgement' give us a shared position against which to measure students fairly.

Why managers like it

Transparency also has its attractions for institutional management. It makes the curriculum transportable between staff. If a module is described in detail then someone other than the author can deliver it. Becher and Trowler (2001) argue that when higher education becomes:

> *a 'thing' capable of being bought and delivered in module sized chunks, with learning outcomes being the unit of currency (p10).*

They then point out how attractive this model is from a managerialist perspective. Teachers become interchangeable; expensive full-time academics can be replaced by graduate students or hourly paid lecturers. This model makes transparent institutional expectations of students thus contributing to the power base of the university by offering protection for the institution when faced with appeals by students challenging academic judgements.

Why transparency is seen to improve quality

'Clear' and 'clarity' are favourite terms of the QAA, the UK quality audit agency. The model of pedagogy favoured by QAA has a focus on explicitness and transparency.

Whilst it is simplistic to characterise HE teaching and learning theory as having a single voice, within current pedagogy:

There is a focal awareness of the learner and the learner's world

(Marton and Booth 1997 p23).

Linked to this, there has been a 'world wide paradigm shift towards student-centred outcomes-based approaches to assessment' (Rust 2002 p145). Lecturers view outcome-based approaches as student-centered (Ecclestone 1999). Of particular relevance is 'Approaches to Learning' literature which has become the 'normative paradigm' in higher education pedagogic research (Haggis 2003 p94). Working within this paradigm, Biggs (1996, 2002, 2003) describes a model of constructive alignment that has informed UK approaches to teacher training and staff development. Biggs (2002, 2003) challenges lecturers to write clear learning outcomes that encapsulate the intended learning. Setting learning outcomes is now the prevailing approach to assessment in higher education. Race (1995 p67) states that 'assessment needs to be transparent to students, staff and employers'. Thus, the specification of learning outcomes has largely replaced the identification of content (Brown and Glasner 1999).

At policy level, the specification of learning outcomes and the use of criterion referencing is promulgated by the QAA (for example QAAHE 1997, QAA 2000) reflecting the political need to make HE accountable and transparent to its stakeholders. As Subject Review (the recent form of Teaching Quality Assessment) with its preparations and aftermath, swept through the sector, the power of transparency increased particularly for assessment processes (Henkel 2000). If assessment was criticised in a Subject Review report then increased transparency, whether in learning outcomes, or feedback to students, became an institutional goal. The last twenty years has been a period of increased accountability in higher education. O'Neill (2002) argues that accountability arises from a 'crisis in trust' (Reith Lecture 1) and trying to prevent abuse of trust. Responding to demands for increased transparency becomes a key form of accountability. Consequently assessment becomes more prescriptive thus more transparent to the stakeholders of 'students, examiners, employers, admissions tutors' (Ecclestone 1999 p33). The transparency agenda has led QAA to explicitly set out that institutions must describe assessment in terms of learning outcomes (QAAHE 1997). University education becomes auditable, an important government response since audit is also perceived as a response to consciousness of the production of risk in post-industrial society (Beck 1992, Power 1994). A key technology of accountability is transparency.

Contesting transparency

1 .Can mask as well as reveal

Transparency is a more complex and contested concept than is often acknowledged. Strathern (2000a) argues that the notion of transparency can mask as well as reveal.

> *What does the quest for transparency conceal… what does visibility conceal?*
> *(p310)*

Arguably much information given to students is only surface level (eg length and format requirements). Additionally, volume of information can obfuscate and there are opportunity costs. Many students regard themselves (quite rightly we might argue) as swamped with information. The sheer volume of apparently transparent information can become a fog, questioning the whole notion of information as transparency (O'Neill 2002). Vast amounts of individual and institutional energy go into the creation of this information. Staff have less time to talk to students because they are writing the course handbook or working out detailed learning outcomes. For staff who are unwilling to devote so much time to these activities transparency can become simply compliance and illusion.

The regime of transparency also fails to recognise the multifactorial nature of pedagogic relationships including the tacit, implicit, invisible which makes such relationships difficult to analyse (Haggis 2002). Additionally, transparency produces a 'within-student model' which identifies difficulties over communication in the assessment relationship as mainly being a student problem. It often fails to recognise the relational nature of learning including power relations (Webb 1996), and in doing so, if it does not blame the student then it responsibilises the teacher. It assumes a 'what works' philosophy. The quest for transparency has drawn the focus away from the tacit practice that is a strong element in assessment.

2 . Tacit practice

All lecturers have intuitive ideas and beliefs about assessing from personal experience of being assessed. This helps to establish how to do the job before the lecturer actually does it (Rowntree 1987, Yung 2001). It forms part of lecturers' 'general academic folk knowledge' (Strathern 2000a p318). Samuelowicz and Bain (2002) explored lecturers' beliefs about how the nature and function of assessment can impact on the approach they adopt. They note that these beliefs and attitudes are generally hidden from view. Research in other sectors of education suggest a range of biases. Gender and ethnic biases have been revealed, as has the fact that knowledge about a student lifts the marks they are assigned (Bradley 1984). Wolf (2000) argues that this is because assessors have internalised models that lead them to make allowances when assessing. This implicit approach may contradict the explicit requirements. The vast majority of assessors are not consciously biased when they mark a student's assignment. Instead, the belief systems or 'subtexts of assessment' inform practice at a tacit level (Sambell and McDowell 1998 p394). As Rowntree points out:

> *we often pursue assessment constructs we are unaware of, sometimes at the expense of those we think we are pursuing' (p85).*

This results in assessment having its own hidden curriculum (Sambell and McDowell 1998, Wolf 2000) which could be described as the 'shadowy, ill-defined and amorphous nature of that which is implicit' (Sambell and Mc Dowell 1998 p391). The role of tacit practice limits transparency claims (Knight 2002).

Strathern (2000a) argues that there is a widely held assumption that the more that is written the more that is clear but in the field of assessment:

> *such practices cannot be made fully transparent simply because there is no substitute for the kind of experimental and implicit knowledge crucial to expertise (p313).*

However, more positively, the significance of tacit knowledge in relation to assessment has been explored by O'Donovan, Price and Rust (2004) who suggest a number of successful strategies to share tacit and explicit assessment information with students.

3 . Language

Higgins (2000 p3) argues that the quest for transparency assumes that language is a conduit that delivers messages from giver to recipient in a process involving a simple transfer of information. Strathern (2000a), Lillis (2001) and Hussey and Smith (2002) contest this notion and the concept of transparency. They argue that language does not simply reflect or conduct meaning, instead, it actually *constructs* meaning. Thus meaning comes into being between participants (Lillis 2001). Hussey and Smith (2002) reject the idea that knowledge can be made totally explicit. Wolf (2000) argues that learning outcomes are not, nor can they be, precise or transparent. Individuals and communities construct meaning so learning outcomes will be understood differently by different people.

Transparency seems predicated on a positivist view of communication with no recognition of the way meaning is mediated. The assumption is that if something is stated 'clearly', a favourite QAA word, then students will understand it in the meaning intended by the author. Chanock (2000) challenges this assumption by showing that there was no common understanding between students and staff of phrases like 'too descriptive, not enough analysis' (p97). Learning outcomes may be viewed as a central tenet of transparent assessment, but Wolf (2000) and Ecclestone (1999) argue that learning outcomes end up being transparent only for the groups of people who create and write them. This is confirmed by O'Donovan, Price and Rust (2000) who found that even when they wrote what they considered to be clear learning outcomes, students interpreted them in a variety of different ways.

Hussey and Smith (2002) state:

> *The claim that [learning outcomes] can be made precise by being written with a prescribed vocabulary of special descriptors so as to serve as objective, measurable devices for measuring performance is fundamentally mistaken. (p220)*

Examination of the outcomes based model of pedagogy reveals assumptions of rationalist, consistent human behaviour, including communication, (Malcolm and Zukas

2001) which fail to recognise 'the paradoxical power of address' and 'the space between.' (Ellsworth 1997).

4 . Transparency as a technology of commodification

Hussey and Smith (2002) argue that the concept of learning outcomes has been explicitly designed, not to meet the needs of students, but to commodify learning to meet the needs of a managerial environment that seeks to make lecturers' work highly accountable. We argued above that this is one reason why the concept is so attractive to institutional management. Noble (2002) quotes from one of his respondents: 'the syllabus and lecture notes are not an education, an education is what you do with these materials' (p10). Transparency can be a process of objectification which turns performance into objects, a point illustrated by the role of course handbooks, learning outcomes, assessment criteria and feedback to students. In contrast, when Rowntree (1987) defines assessment, the dialogic, social nature is emphasised:

> *Assessment in education can be thought of as occurring whenever one person, in some kind of interaction, direct or indirect, with another, is conscious of obtaining and interpreting information about the knowledge and understanding, or abilities, and attitudes of that other person (p4).*

5. Accountability

Commodification and accountability work together. Commodification of knowledge makes accountability easier. Accountability in the form of audit constructs as well as describes (Power 1994; Ranson et al 1987). It is a response to risk and can lead to a culture of compliance (Power 1994). But, for O'Neill (2002), accountability, rather than rebuilding trust, leads to back-covering, and 'compromise and evasions' (Lecture 3), particularly when faced with conflicting aims. Transparency makes trust retreat and production of too much information can lead to deception (Lecture 4). As argued above the process of objectification or reification constructed by this form of accountability also has opportunity costs and moves valuable academic time and energy from the real university to the parallel documented university where the textual form of reality is more important than the real world of student learning.

6 . Contesting that transparency aids widening participation

Ecclestone (2004 p3) argues that 'assessment regimes codify cultural and social capital' thus, although tutors are working within a 'discourse of transparency' (Lillis and Turner 2001 p61) power and privilege still operate to disadvantage certain groups. In contemporary HE, the emphasis is on assessment of merit regardless of status in society, but differential achievement between social groups persists (Delanshere 2001). Bourdieu (1989) in Delanshere (2001) argues that society supports a position where assessment reproduces (instead of redistributing more fairly) cultural capital. Thus assessment practices can reproduce unconsciously the values and priorities of the society in which the assessment is carried out (Bourdieu 1989). In the words of Knight (2002) 'high stakes assessments are marked by unequal power relations between assessor and assessed' (p277). An emphasis on transparency and the explication of learning outcomes masks disadvantage/power inequality and role of 'inside knowledge' (Ecclestone 2004 p35). Non traditional students may feel that they do not always know the conventions of what constitutes knowledge in the academy. Guidance can raise more questions than answers because they are 'embedded socio-rhetorical norms' that were not explained. (Lillis and Turner p65).

There is an implicit assumption that all students are able to use learning outcomes and the specification of standards to improve their work. However, different students can have different ideas about what constitutes good work (Adams and King cited in Tan and Prosser 2004 p279). They do not all share an idea of what to aim for to get high marks. Ecclestone and Swan (1999) identified students who felt that no amount of transparency would stop them getting low grades and argue that these students would need to address issues of identity and self-esteem if they were to use written guidance and learning outcomes to develop their work. Morias (1996) researched making assessment criteria more explicit to students to encourage a greater understanding of the assessment process. She found that middle class students were better able to utilise teachers' guidance for clarification about learning outcomes. We need to acknowledge the differential knowledge and skills bases that students bring to HE (Maclellan 2004).

Case study

The case study conducted by one of the authors explored the socially situated practice of assessment within the art and design department of a small HEI. Lecturers were interviewed and asked to report on their assessment approaches. Being conscious that the interview data offered retrospective accounts of practice, groups of lecturers conducting group moderation meetings were also observed. This methodology is an adaptation of an approach adopted by Orrell (2003). Orrell sought to explore congruence and disjunction between lecturers' espoused beliefs about assessment and their assessment behaviour. This version of her dual methodology was used because we wanted to build up an understanding about how lecturers thought they went about assessment and to compare and contrast this to assessment practice as it manifested itself in a group moderation context. This research focused on the dialogic aspects of assessment because we are of the view that assessors have:

> *Co-constructive roles in subjectively making and transforming meaning (Higgins 2000 p5)*

This case study is contextualised by the arguments developed above because the findings indicate that assessors operationalised the written learning outcomes in complex ways that were not fully available for public scrutiny. Learning outcomes were referred to as useful signposts, but were, in some cases, seen as a mechanistic checklist and were just one component in the act of assessment:

> *Learning outcomes are useful, but the assessment process is looking holistically. (Respondent a)*

No respondents said that they were able rely solely on learning outcomes to set standards and marks. When making judgments about marks, other factors were called upon. These factors were identified as being elusive by their very nature. Each of the lecturers interviewed said that they drew on their experience to help them make judgements.

> *You have all this unconscious expertise built up over years of experience, you don't even know that you know it. It is the layers of experience that you use to help you and enable you to make judgments. It sits on your shoulder. (Respondent c)*

The limitations of learning outcomes were pointed out:

> *[Learning outcomes are] identified in a list format so students understand, but they are quite general in the way that they are written. (Respondent d)*

The conduit model of language was questioned:

> *As soon as language is involved language is never clear. (Respondent a)*

When respondents referred to transparency in the interviews they mentioned the written guidance that is given to students. For these respondents, transparency was located in text. In addition, transparency was linked to notions of accountability:

> *What you do now is more open to scrutiny by your peers and colleagues. (Respondent c)*

In contrast when they talked about the act of assessment they referred to the tacit dimension, referred to by one respondent as 'your inner sense of fairness'. Respondents did not explore the fact that transparency and tacit practice may be in conflict with each other because tacit practice is not open to public scrutiny (Torff 1999, Sternberg and Horvath 1999).

Thankfully no evidence was found of conscious bias operating against certain student groups, but the case study did suggest that assessment was not 'transparent' and that written guidance for students (in the form of learning outcomes) was used differentially by lecturers. This suggests that lecturers are assessing students' work in more complex ways than current HE assessment literature would suggest. Orrell (2003) observed that assessment is a 'largely private, unscrutinised aspect of academic work' and research is needed to enable 'academics to reflect critically on their practice and to increase their professional literacy about assessment' (p17).

The way forward: a pragmatic approach

We recognise that, in spite of the difficulties noted above, lecturers do have to assign grades to students' work on a daily basis, and whilst those decisions may be complex, and they may draw on a range of conscious and hidden criteria, the work is an essential part of the academy as it is currently constructed, so there is no alternative to the act of human judgement. We now explore a range of strategies to enhance assessment practice by focusing on the act of judgement. In this context the term *enhance* means that assessors are more likely to award the same marks, be aware of their biases and preferences and be part of an assessment community with a team approach through discussion.

Within HE there is an assumption that new lecturers know how to assess without any training (Race 1995). Staff development could address this (Sadler 1987, Hawe 2000) but focus less on technical aspects of assessment and offer opportunities for lecturers to explore and discuss hidden criteria (Sambell and McDowell 1998). Assessors and students need opportunities to open up dialogues to construct assessment communities. This sounds uncontentious and obvious but stands in apparent opposition to the dominant monologic view that argues that what assessors and students need is clear written guidance.

Moderation and internal verification should offer staff development opportunities, rather than technical box ticking to meet the needs of external audit (Hawe 2003), thus helping lecturers benchmark and establish reference points for their assessment practices (Dunn et al 2004). In this way assessors can 'domesticate' assessment and make it their own (Yung 2001). Assessors need to exploit the *process* of agreeing standards. Contemporary focus is only on the learning outcomes *produced* by such deliberation but the *process* of writing and agreeing learning outcomes can contribute to the formation of an assessment community. This maximises dialogic opportunities and is referred to as a 'process tool' (O'Donovan et al 2000) that can be used to 'facilitate shared understanding' (p83).

We are not calling for a return to the mysterious assessment practices of former eras. Equally we are not arguing against attempts to make things clearer to students but rather that we need to avoid an over-simplistic model (Meadmore 1998). We are encouraged by O'Donovan et al's research (2004) that explores ways to share the tacit elements of assessment with students. A reflexive approach to assessment practice opens up opportunities to explore and confront issues of social inequality. As Stowell (2004) points out 'unfairness may arise from treating unequals equally as much as from treating equals unequally' (p497). In the context of assessment it may be unfair to assume that all students benefit from transparency.

Higher education is not a level playing field.

References

Adams, C and King, K (1995) Towards a framework for student self assessment, *Innovations in Education and Training International*. Volume 32 (4) p3336-343 cited in Tan, K and Prosser, M (2004). "Qualitatively different ways of differentiating student achievement: a phenomenographic study of academics' conceptions of grade descriptors." *Assessment and Evaluation in Higher Education* 29(3) p268-281.

Allen, G (1998). "Risk and Uncertainty in Assessment: Exploring the contribution of economics to identifying and analysing the social dynamic in grading." *Assessment and Evaluation in Higher Education* 23(3) p241-258.

Becher, T and Trowler, PR (2001) *Academic Tribes and Territories: Intellectual Enquiry and the Cultural of Disciplines* (2nd ed). Buckingham: SRHE/OUP.

Beck, U (1992) *Risk Society: Towards a New Modernity.* London: Sage.

Biggs, J (1996) Enhancing Teaching through Constructive Alignment. *Higher Education* 32 p347-364

Biggs, J (2002). *Teaching For Quality Learning at University.* Buckingham: Open University Press.

Biggs, J (2003). *Aligning teaching for constructing learning*, ILTHE http://www.ilt.ac.uk/portal/showarticle.asp?-article=3609and-topicid=4and-section=1and-.2003.

Bradley, C (1984). "Sex Bias in the Evaluation of Students." *British Journal of Social Psychology* 23 p147-153.

Bourdieu, P (1989) *La Noblesse d'etat* (Paris, Ed de Minuit) cited in Delandshere, G (2001). "Implicit theories, Unexamined Assumptions and the Status Quo of Educational Assessment." *Assessment in Education* 8(2) p113-132.

Bourdieu, P (1997) The Forms of Capital. In Halsey, AH and Lauder, H and Brown, P and Wells, A (Eds), Education: Culture, Economy and Society. Oxford: Oxford University Press.

Broadfoot, P and Black, P (2004). "Redefining assessment? The first ten years of Assessment in Education." *Assessment in Education* 11(1) p7-27.

Brown, S and Glasner (1999). *Assessment Matters in Higher Education.* Buckingham: SRHE and OU Press.

Chanock, K (2000) Comments on Essays: Do students understand what tutors write? *Teaching in Higher Education* 5(1) p95-105

Delandshere, G (2001). "Implicit theories, Unexamined Assumptions and the Status Quo of Educational Assessment." *Assessment in Education* 8(2) p113-132.

Dunn, L, Morgan, C, et al (2004). *The Student Assesment Handbook.* London, RoutledgeFalmer.

Ecclestone, K (2004). "Learning in a comfort zone: cultural and social capital inside an outcome-based assessment regime." *Assessment in Education* 11(1) p29-47.

Ecclestone, K (1999). "Empowering or Ensnaring?: The Implications of Outcome-based Assessment in Higher Education." *Higher Education Quarterly* 53(1) p29-48.

Ecclestone, K and Swann, J (1999). "Litigation and Learning: tensions in improving university lecturers' assessment practice." *Assessment in Education* 6(3) p377-389.

Ellsworth, E (1997) *Teaching Positions.* New York: Teachers College Press.

Filer, A (2000). *Assessment: Social Practice and Social Product.* London, RoutledgeFalmer.

Foucault, M (1994) Truth and Power. In Faubion, J (Ed), *Michel Foucault: Power: essential works of Foucault 1954-1984 Vol 3*. London: Penguin.

Foucault, M (1995) *Discipline and Punish*. New York: Vintage.

Haggis, T (2002) Exploring the 'Black Box' of Process: a comparison of theoretical motions of the 'adult learner' with accounts of postgraduate learning experience. *Studies in Higher Education* 27 p207-220

Haggis, T (2003) Constructing Images of Ourselves. *British Educational Research Journal* 29(1) p89-104

Hawe, E (2003). "'It's Pretty Difficult to Fail': The reluctance of lecturers to award a failing grade." *Assessment and Evaluation in Higher Education* 28(4) p371-382.

Henkel, M (2000) *Academic Identities and Policy Change in Higher Education*. London: Jessica Kingsley.

Higgins, RA (2000). *"59% Excellent!": Making Sense of Assessment Feedback*, www.ilt.ac.uk/archives/itac2000-resources/Higgins/default.htm. 2001.

Hussey, T and Smith, P (2002). "The Trouble with Learning Outcomes." *Active Learning in Higher Education* 3(3): 220-233.

Knight, P (2002). "Summative Assessment in Higher Education: practices in disarray." *Studies in Higher Education* 27(3) p275-286.

Layder, D (1997). *Modern Social Theory: Key Debates and New Directions*. London, UCL Press.

Lillis, T (2001). *Student Writing: Access Regulation and Desire*. London UK, Routledge.

Lillis, T and Turner, J (2001) Student Writing in Higher Education: contemporary confusion, traditional concerns. *Teaching in Higher Education* 6(1) 57-68

Maclellan, E (2004). "How convincing is alternative assessment for use in higher education?" *Assessment and Evaluation in Higher Education* 29(3) p311-321.

Malcolm, J and Zukas, M (2001) Bridging Pedagogic Gaps: conceptual discontinuities in higher education. *Teaching in Higher Education* 6(1) p33-42

Margolis, E and Romero, M (1998) "The Department is Very Male, Very White, Very Old": The Functioning of the Hidden Curriculum in Graduate Sociology Departments. *Harvard Educational Review* 68(1) p1-32

Marton, F and Booth, SA (1997). The learner's experience of learning. *The Handbook of Education and Human Development: New Models of Learning, Teaching and Schooling*. Olsen, DR and Torrance, N. Oxford: Blackwell.

Meadmore, D (1998) Changing the Culture: the governance of the Australian pre-millennial university. *International Studies in Sociology of Education*. 8(1) p27-45

Morias, AM (1996). "Understanding Teacher's Evaluation Criteria: A Condition for Success in Science Classes." *Journal of Research in Science Teaching* 33(6) p601-624.

Noble, D (2002) Technology and the Commodification of Higher Education. *Monthly Review* March

O'Donovan, B, Price, M, and Rust, C (2000). "The Student Experience of Criterion-Referenced Assessment (through the Introduction of a Common Criteria Assessment Grid)." *Innovations in Education and Teaching International* 38(1) p74-85.

O'Donovan, B, Price, M, and Rust, C (2004). "Know what I mean? Enhancing student understanding of assessment standards and criteria." *Teaching in Higher Education* 9(3) p325-335.

O'Neill, O (2002). A Question of Trust, *Reith Lectures*: BBC.

Orrell, J (2003). "Congruence and disjunctions between academics' thinking when assessing and their beliefs about assessment practice." Paper delivered at 11th Improving Student Learning: Research and Scholarship conference p1-19.

Power, M (1994) *The Audit Explosion*. London: Demos.

QAA (2000). *Code of Practice for the Assurance of Academic Quality and Standards in Higher Education*: Assessment of Students, Quality Assurance Agency. 2000.

QAAHE (1997). *Subject Review Handbook*, October 1998-2000. Bristol, QAA.

Race, P (1995). What Has Assessment Done For Us – And To Us? *Assessment for Learning in Higher Education*. Knight, P. London: Kogan Page Limited.

Ranson, S, Hannon, V and Gray, J (1987) Citizens or Consumers? Policies for School Accountability. In Walker, S and Barton, L (Eds), *Changing Policies, Changing Teachers*. Milton Keynes: Open University Press.

Rowntree, D (1987). *Assessing Students: How shall we know them?* London, Kogan Page Limited.

Rust, C (2002). "The Impact of Assessment on Student Learning: how can the research literature practically help to inform the development of departmental assessment strategies and learner centred assessment practices." *Active Learning in Higher Education* 3(2).

Sadler, R (1987). "Specifying and Promulgating Achievement Standards." *Oxford Review of Education* 13(2) p191-209.

Sambell, K and McDowell, L (1998). "The Construction of the Hidden Curriculum: Messages and Meanings in the Assessment of Student Learning." *Assessment and Evaluation in Higher Education 23(4) p391-401.*

Samuelowicz, K and Bain, J (2002). "Identifying academics' orientation to assessment practice." *Higher Education* 43 p173-201.

Sternberg, RJ and Horvath, JA (1999). *Tacit Knowledge in Professional Practice*. Mahwah NJ, Lawrence Erlbaum Associates Inc.

Stowell, M (2004). "Equity, justice and standards: assessment decision making in higher education." *Assessment and Evaluation in Higher Education* 29(4) p495-510.

Strathern, M (2000a) The Tyranny of Transparency. *British Educational Research Journal* 26(3) p309-321

Strathern, M (2000b) Introduction: new accountabilities. In Strathern, M (Ed), *Audit Cultures: Anthropological studies in accountabilty, ethics and the academy*. London: Routledge.

Torff, B (1999). Tacit Knowledge in Teaching: Folk Pedagogy and Teacher Education. *Tacit Knowledge in Professional Practice*. Sternberg, RJ and Horvath, JA. Mahwah NJ: Lawrence Erlbaum Associates.

Webb, G (1996) *Understanding Staff Development*. Buckingham: SRHE/Open University Press.

Wolf, A (2000). *Competence-Based Assessment*. Buckingham, Open University Press.

Yorke, M, Bridges, P and Woolf, H. (2000). "Mark distributions and marking practices in UK higher education." *Active Learning in Higher Education* 1(1) p7-27.

Yung, B (2001). "Examiner, Policeman or Students' Companion: Teachers' perceptions of their role in an assessment reform." *Educational Review* 53(1) p251-260.

Diversity in high places: variation in highly achieving students' experiences of course work assignments

Nicola Parker

University of Technology, Sydney, Australia

Themes addressed

Assessment; skills development and lifelong learning; supporting learners.

Abstract

Student diversity often exists where we least expect it. This paper presents findings from a phenomenographic study of postgraduate students' ways of experiencing aspects of their course work assignments. The research is illustrated with examples from a series of conversational interviews with six postgraduate coursework students. A variety of goals and aspirations of *personal significance* which form part of their intrinsic motivation were emphasised by these highly achieving students. The students experienced *assignment information processes* in six qualitatively different ways that are hierarchically related. They also described five qualitatively different experiences of *enough* for different purposes in the context of doing the assignment. Other interesting discoveries are that not only is a wide range of variation apparent within this group of students, but also *micro contextual variation*: that is, students oscillate between experiences at different points in the process.

Introduction

Student diversity in higher education is an ever-increasing challenge for teachers interested in optimising student learning. Diversity often exists invisibly and where we least expect it. Highly achieving students may seem alike and in need of minimal support to succeed in traditional assignments that continue to dominate assessment regimes in many faculties (Elton and Johnston, 2002).

This paper will firstly describe a doctoral project in progress that is exploring links between information and learning processes in the discipline of information and knowledge management (IKM). Using both phenomenographic and case study methods the focus is on how students learn subject content through information interactions. Secondly, elements of highly achieving postgraduate coursework students' experiences of aspects of their assignments are outlined using examples from the research in three parts:

- Themes of *personal significance* emphasised by the students

- Students' experiences of the *assignment information process* (*AIP*) and

- Students' experiences of deciding what *enough* is (for their purposes) in the context of doing an assignment.

Considerable diversity is evident amongst these students in all these areas during one assignment. The paper closes with a summary of the implications for approaches to learning, supporting all learners and the role of traditional assessment.

The project

This research set out to explore students' learning through their interactions with information in an Australian university. Research questions focused on patterns of 'variation' that might be seen in students' experiences of learning (Marton & Booth 1997) and information during a single report assignment.

To investigate these questions 18 phenomenographic interviews were conducted with six volunteer full-time and part-time postgraduate coursework students in a compulsory introductory subject of a postgraduate IKM course. This course is a professional qualification for information and knowledge management careers in both traditional library and information management and a variety of emerging roles.

The participants were students from classes I tutored or coordinated (grading was done by the head of department) and this was an important factor in the conduct of the interviews and during analysis. For example, the interviews were very conversational in style (Kvale, 1996; Dortins, 2002), and were used by the students to clarify their task. The interviews took place at a time and place of each student's choosing and focused on 'what was important for the student' at each of the three interviews (before, during and after the assignment). The assignment required students to research, analyse and write a report of 3,000 words on an industry area of interest. Interviews were tape recorded, transcribed verbatim and minimally edited as written speech, rather than standardised text, to preserve as far as possible their meaning and emphasis. All the participants achieved high grades in both the assignment and the subject overall.

Analysis of the variation in experiences of *AIP* and *enough* followed broad phenomenographic methods (Bowden & Walsh 2000; Marton & Booth 1997). An extensive initial phase used the audio tapes to focus on what the students were emphasising. Whole transcripts were also used to mark the significant fragments that emerged from this procedure: information seeking; knowing when they had *enough* and what doing the assignment meant for them as individuals.

Individual case studies are being developed to see how the highly dynamic nature of the variation in the phenomena comes together in an individual's experience over the course of the task. The next section outlines some features of the *personal significance* elements of these students' experiences.

Personal significance

All of the students talked frequently about the professional and personal significance of their activities as they completed their assessment work. Prior and ongoing personal and professional goals and aspirations were particularly apparent in their early comments about how they came to be doing the course and why they had chosen this particular programme and again when reflecting back on what the assignment had left them with. These students variously described:

1. Finding stimulation and interest to enhance a job that has become stale and lacks challenge, by engaging in structured chunks of research and learning

2. Learning how to develop as a professional and to work at that level in a recently chosen field

3. Expanding their knowledge of a field they had worked in for many years

4. Learning more about their chosen field and particular aspects of it, and understand the work of their associates

5. Learning how to operate in their job more effectively by really understanding the links between information and management

6. Wanting to know how information works in the world in more depth and breadth in order to work out how they wanted to position themselves in that world.

The expected links for postgraduate students in a professional course with job aspirations, upgrading skills and qualifications went beyond simply retraining or qualifying for a professional role and were highly personalised and developmentally oriented. Personally significant goals and aspirations formed part of the rationale or intrinsic motivation for these students to undertake the assessment task and the subject itself. These personal elements are also part of their reason for postgraduate study at this point in their lives. They are an important part of the relationship between the students and the context, or situation (Prosser & Trigwell 1999, p. 18), and may contribute to the *micro contextual variation* in these students' experiences which will be discussed later in the paper. The following section will describe student experiences of *AIP* using an example of each category of description to indicate the range of variation in experiences.

Students' experiences of assignment information processes

One of the key parts of an assignment for all students is the many information intensive processes they must successfully engage in to complete the task. Labelled *AIP* these include information seeking, using the information they find and writing. Highly achieving students' experiences of *AIP* when completing assignments varied in quite distinctive ways, in relation to how they go about this assignment and the intentions they are seeking to realise as they do so.

The categories describing the variation in postgraduate students' ways of experiencing *AIP* are hierarchically related through the variation in meaning of each category. They are also related in their changing structure or focus across the categories. This focus expands in scope from a task with a blueprint in category one, to a change in the way the students see themselves and the topic in relation to the world in category six.

The six different ways that postgraduate students experienced *AIP* are:

Category 1. Shaping a task: AIP as completing a substantial but straightforward task by using strategies to shape and manage the task

In this category the students describe a straightforward, familiar and unproblematic task and they focus on the task itself. Students repeatedly describe a predictable process of movement using a variety of flexible and creative strategies to complete a personalised version of the specific task. They continually develop patterns of working and apply their considerable knowledge, skills and judgement to 'make it their own'. Structuring the task and product is critical and clear definitions are repeatedly sought and reconfirmed in order to anchor and interpret the task. To do this students regularly come back to the assignment outline (and their interpretation of this) to check the pertinence of their production efforts. Note taking, reading and collecting are also described as clear cut and there is a strong focus on streamlining the task and keeping on track. For example:

I: *Right so, when you're doing, making those notes you've already stopped looking for anything else…?*

D: *I do, I do my first read and highlighting. I do my notes from the readings, then it's in there, then it just comes out in an argument and I go back to the reference material to check on material… or to get a citation… I am really, really focused. I've got all my call numbers down and I know exactly where I am going. I don't stuff around.*

This way of experiencing *AIP* is focused on completion of the assessment task, but becomes inherently absorbing despite the task, information and knowledge being 'objectified'. This is part of the movement to the following category.

Category 2. Finding out: AIP as a way of finding out something they want to know

This way of experiencing *AIP* is as a quest for information not just a task to manage. It is an instrumental process that is no longer principally about the task (ie completing the assignment) but has expanded to include wanting or needing to know about something in particular to move forward in life. To accomplish this, multiple strategies and patterns of working are implemented as in category 1. In the context of this research, in a subject leading to professional accreditation and an assignment based on the profession, the 'finding out' is career or job related. For example, a student talks about the need to 'find out' about job possibilities as particularly pressing:

A: *The other issue is that... I suspect that the research for this project is going to be meshed with my job seeking process over the next month or so (laughs).*

I: *Right. Oh well, in a way that's good it makes it more useful, does it?*

A: *It does but it also uhh... trammels it up with umm... a more emotional side...*

I: *And what effect does that have?*

A: *Umm so, so that process of ummm problem solving that is going to occur throughout the research process isn't just going to be problem solving for an essay but actually problem solving to try and find a way of making a buck as well and so I'm concerned. (laughs)*

I: *So does that make it more complex?*

A: *...Yes and more useful, ultimately.*

This expansion has made *AIP* more taxing, but also more useful and meaningful, because potentially personally important answers are sought.

Category 3. Voyaging: AIP as a journey to discover and understand interesting things by hunting leads and reflection

In this category the focus on finding out something quite specific in category 2 has expanded to become finding out for its own sake. This experience of *AIP* is as a process of discovery. Learning about whatever they find interesting along the way is now their focus. The students become engrossed in 'hunting down leads' and 'following the threads' they are discovering despite the considerable time and commitment required to do this. Time and space to think, reflect and immerse themselves is emphasised because the process has become more important than an end product or an answer. Finding new information and discovery keeps life interesting and generates new challenges in the following example.

D: *I love researching, it doesn't matter what it is as long as it changes fairly regularly. I get bored doing the same thing over and over again...*

I: *Oh good and what, do you know why you like really doing research or...?*

D: *Umm...I like finding out about things. It doesn't matter really what it is. But I just, I like discovering new information.*

The enjoyment and 'mental challenge' of this way of experiencing AIP means that it is intrinsically worthwhile.

Category 4. Self awareness: AIP as a growing awareness of different facets of oneself through activity and thought

Students have moved beyond the joy of discovery in this category, to an experience of clarification and a new awareness of themselves as a result of *AIP*. In this way of experiencing *AIP* students emphasise discovering and clarifying how and what they think and do: a process of learning about themselves. For example, the process of using information from an article is described as:

I: *...I'm just trying to get, sort of get an idea of how it gets from... just flesh out that, the way it gets from the article here... into the finished form in your, in your, report.*

H: *...it's very much, at that stage, it's for me. It's, it's the first time I'm probably really, really um...making everything very clear. I'm sort of, I'm, it's the first time I'm really... It's the first time I'm explaining my logic to myself. Because I actually use the PC... to make my logic visible to me. That's what it is! So just, just as, just as this, this stage is making the logic of the report clear to me. Whenever I start down, writing this and this, I'm explaining the logic of each part, to myself.*

This focus on self and skills and its inherent challenges also includes some painful self doubts and negativity (feeling they 'should know how' to do things or they have inadequate information-seeking skills). This contrasts sharply with the pleasure of discovery found in the previous category.

Category 5. Self expansion: AIP as a means of growing by expanding ideas and skills through communication, reflection and action while investigating a topic

In this category students go beyond learning about themselves to experience *AIP* as a process of changing the way they think and act. Their skills are honed through 'doing' and reflection, so they constantly seek ways to improve their information techniques and better ways of doing things. These include: integration of computer technology into their information processes; consciously building a personal store of tools (eg text structures) to draw upon as required, and enhancing knowledge and skills. In this professionally oriented IKM subject, skills are also enhanced through the content they encounter. For example:

B: *And I'm also learning through reading about um, Mary Ellen Bates (sic) has a lovely description of a day in her life. Have you read that? On her web site... It's*

193

fascinating um, talking about work of information professionals, that's the whole thing.

I: *No, no. Oh well that'll be great, well that'll be a good one to, you know, you could use that?*

B: *...And it's funny because it's actually through a relationship with the content of what I'm looking at... and through learning about, researching the work of information professionals I'm taking on that stuff... It's exactly what I've done.*

IKM strategies are used to expand ideas and skills through communication with texts, activity and self reflection. This experience is of growth while focusing on a topic and doing an assignment.

Category 6. Changing views: AIP as changing their way of seeing the world and personal values through sustained engagement with part of that world

In this most complex category students experience *AIP* as bringing about a radical shift to their thinking. This change in their relationship to the world can be to an extent that a shift in personal values occurs. This is a result of moving through a focused engagement with a topic during the assignment information seeking, finding and generating processes. A reversal of previous understandings and important personal values is articulated in this example:

I: *Can you just sort of, explain for you why that was building a new knowledge base?*

H: *...I had to read outside the... Library and Information Science literature. And I had to change my viewpoint. I had to change, um... Yea, I did. I had to change my sort of, this sort of, firmly held and untested belief in information for the public good... So there was a fundamental shift going on in there [laughs] you know.*

I: *Ohhh! Why did you, when you said you had to... change why did you have to change... what made you change?*

H: *Um because... because I had to acknowledge that um... you know my research had certainly confirmed that information, the creation and storing and gathering of information requires, financial resources...*

I: *And this, these other things they were... the opposite of what you'd thought or...?*

H: *Um, they challenged my belief. Yea, they challenged my values? Uh, I was, it seems strange, I was sort of calling that a new knowledge base but um... maybe it's a new values base?*

The end result of this way of experiencing AIP is (and part of the world) a completely different perspective on the world and a shift in personal values.

Summary

Considerable variation is apparent even in highly achieving students' experiences of *AIP*. Their experiences also varied dynamically at different points in the process, depending on what was important to them at that point (for example, time and deadlines). This *micro contextual variation* goes beyond contextual or situational variation and is also apparent in students' experiences of having *enough* for the assignment which will be described in the next section.

Students' experiences of enough

enough is an everyday concept that is a phenomenon of study in many fields and an important issue in these times of 'information overload'. It is a key concept for the discipline of IKM (Kuhlthau 1998), an important part of *AIP* and learning and turned out to be extremely important in this study. As students complete an assignment they have to negotiate what *enough* is for different purposes in the context of doing an assignment. This decision making in terms of information and a range of other criteria is necessary in order to successfully move through and complete the task. Interestingly, highly achieving students experienced *enough* during the assignment in five qualitatively different ways:

Category 1. Enough is experienced as the right amount of essential elements of acceptable standard in place to get the task done and avoid disaster

This category is characterised by experiencing *enough* as just what is necessary to get the assignment done. Aiming to properly complete the requirements to their own minimum standards (which are quite high) and accommodating prevailing academic requirements, to avoid personal embarrassment, *enough* is experienced as a risk avoidance strategy. In order to control and produce what is required for the assessment and to meet the deadline, a focus on quantification of assignment components, construction and composition is required. Students strongly emphasise physical elements. They make the task concrete by:

- breaking the assignment down into bits
- quickly structuring sections under headings
- managing information primarily to complete the structure
- filling in dot points, putting 'stuff' in
- filling knowledge gaps

For example:

K: *I could, could... I mean, I could be... writing... a whole thesis even... So I think that is another thing with the assignment, you tend to... like you can get a bit lost in your research and then you feel...*

I: *So how do you stop yourself doing that?*

K: *Well I keep having to come back and look at well what, what are the key headings?...Yeah it usually happens (laughs) and I'm really worried I'll do it again (laughing) that it's going to happen so... (laughing)... And I thought 'Well okay. I'll just stick to these otherwise I could get too out of control'.*

Enough is used to anchor and limit students' information seeking and writing activities and gauging their own accomplishment in the final product. This conception enables 'stopping judgements' and is linked to feeling organised and in control. The intention is to cope with overload, pressure and uncertainty. This category represents how the students experience *enough* when it seems straightforward, or they need to make it so at the end of *AIP*, when overloaded with other assignments or matters.

Category 2. Enough is experienced as what enables optimal physical production in order get it right and create a good report

In this way of experiencing *enough* is focused on being effective, in order to create a coherent piece of work that will satisfy external and personal criteria. As in the previous category the emphasis is on the product, but now incorporates qualitative dimensions: the optimal production of a quality thing (report) without wasting time. In this category there is a concern with making sense which is not a major priority in category 1. For example:

G: *I craft as I go. My first draft is probably one of two. I do my draft! And it's, it's... probably it takes me about three days to do that.*

I: *So you're very economical?*

G: *Very economical. I cannot write, I can't write crap! [both laugh] You know, I can't write reams and reams of what I consider crap. It, I'd look at it and say this doesn't make sense to me. You know, I literally craft each paragraph. I've got my – my opening paragraph. Then I – I try to make sure that within each paragraph I have made, you know, it sort of sensible. It's logic, it is flow.*

The emphasis in this category on optimisation of the process and the product makes it a key mechanism for highly achieving students' successful assignment outcomes.

Category 3. Enough is experienced as qualitative engagement with a process of 'working out' in order to understand and successfully produce

In this category *enough* is experienced as engagement and interest in the content and process of learning. This conception focuses on the quality of the process and interest rather than the product and on whatever it takes to enjoy that process. This can include: understanding; finding out; clarifying and learning more about an area; enhancing skills and learning more about oneself. The explicit focus on what is *enough* for a useful and enjoyable learning process is illustrated by:

A: *I think at this, perhaps this post graduate level the work that we're doing is about, a learning process rather than, a product in the end – yeah, yeah and what I find with the, I guess, first four assignments was that I'm really not happy with the quality of the products, but I am very happy with the quality of the learning that's gone on in producing these things.*

This interest can be part of the impetus for the topic choice, or part of a process of engagement that emerges during the assignment and is also linked to avoiding boredom. The pursuit of personal understanding is paramount.

Category 4. Enough is experienced as an internal qualitative sense of completeness and coverage in order to satisfy curiosity and make sense to oneself

Although this category is similar to category 3 in that *enough* is strongly focused on what is needed for learning, in this category it has changed to a state or feeling of satisfaction, rather than a dynamic part of *AIP*. By making sense and coming to know what, why or how, students satisfy their innate curiosity and experience an internal sense of feeling complete. There is unsurprisingly more evidence of this meaning of *enough* at the closing stages of *AIP* when it has all come together. One example of satisfaction is described as follows:

P: *I suppose especially with report type assignments, it felt like when I found material that… it felt to me, was, satisfying the criteria or meeting it to a certain level then and I could use it, and I'd written a section that I felt answered – the question, then I was, like, that feels complete… that does feel as such… yes!*

This is the most satisfying but least frequent way of experiencing *enough* for highly achieving students. This sense of closure and feeling of completion is absent in all of the other conceptions.

Category 5. Enough is experienced as a generative driver of the content vision and development in order to discover and create something unique

The experience of *enough* in this category is distinctly different from all the previous categories because an aesthetic requirement has emerged. This conception goes far beyond production, engagement and satisfaction and includes a creative need. This experience incorporates an idealised vision of something intrinsically worthwhile, valuable and useful beyond the learning and assessment process. There is willingness at this level to go beyond not only what they know, but also perceived boundaries and to take risks. For example, equating research products with art, using intuition and in doing so taking risks:

C: Well I think – for me the biggest thing about the assignment was deciding to take the risk to use non-traditional-sources... And I felt like I was being pretty radical in doing that [laughs]... but also, it sort of feels like a breakthrough because I went through incredible angst, and, almost like great sort of depression. I think getting sick too helped. But I went through awful angst. Because that was what I wanted to do! I wanted to do it that way. But I felt like it perhaps wasn't appropriate and there was another sort of product that should be coming out the end?

I: Did I, did I ever say that?

C: No never! [laughs]

This conception drives a deep level of exploration and the need to balance multiple sets of criteria is recognised.

Summary

The variation in highly achieving students' experiences of *enough* is interwoven with the six different types of enough (Parker 2004). The criteria that the students use to make decisions alter, depending on which type of enough is being considered at that moment and contribute to the *micro contextual* nature of assignment experiences discussed below.

Discussion and implications

This research into students' experiences in IKM education and assessment has provided a new perspective on the experiences of highly achieving students. Considerable variation exists amongst these students. This variation has implications beyond the links between learning, information and *enough* for an assignment. These are summarised below:

1.   The students' descriptions of highly dynamic individual experiences suggest that these experiences consist of continuous movement between contexts and experiences. Their experiences are not only situational (Prosser & Trigwell 1999) but also *micro contextual*. The fine grained exploration of the variation in approaches to assignments amongst highly achieving postgraduate students in this research opens up another way to understand student diversity in learning and assessment.

2.   An important issue is raised by the fact that each of these highly achieving students moved through the conceptions outlined above, including the least complex, many times. In other words a significant part of their assignment experiences is at a level usually associated with surface learning. At the same time they are engaging with their work in meaningful ways and achieving high marks. Therefore we should probably not assume that when highly achieving students complete a questionnaire, for example, they are always engaged in 'deeper approaches' to learning in a particular context.

3.   The nature of variation itself needs to be considered in light of the diversity in highly achieving students' experiences of one assignment. The variation in this

group in terms of their experiences of *AIP* and *enough* indicates that variation can exist even amongst students who seem quite similar. Exploring this 'variation in variation' has implications for maximising inclusivity for all students.

4. The affective aspects of students' experiences of *AIP* and *enough* (Parker 2002), mean that we cannot assume that any student does not deal with fears and adopt surface approaches during an assignment. Therefore we need to consider how to best support all students with this important aspect of learning and achievement.

5. Although the traditional research report style of assessment investigated here is often considered old-fashioned, the students in this study were highly engaged in the assignment task. This indicates that traditional assignments can still play a useful part in providing complex and enriching learning experiences.

Conclusion

Looking more closely at the *personal significance* of an assignment and the variation in experiences of *AIP* and *enough* for highly achieving students, highlights the extent of the diversity of these experiences in broader student populations. This variation may have implications for assessment achievement and supporting learning in traditional assignment tasks. It also offers alternative perspectives on student experiences as *micro contextual* and, the extent of 'variation within variation' that can exist in a single assignment. These perspectives can help our understanding of how to optimise assessment for all students.

References

Bowden, JA and Walsh, E (2000). *Phenomenography*. Melbourne: RMIT University Press.

Dortins, E (2002). Reflections on phenomenographic process: Interview, transcription and analysis. Proceedings of HERDSA. 25. Milperra, Australia: The Higher Education Research and Development Society of Australasia.

Elton, L and Johnston, B (2002). Assessment in Universities: A Critical Review. York: Learning and Teaching Support Network Generic Centre Website. Available at: http://www.ltsn.ac.uk/genericcentre/index.asp?id=17219.

Kuhlthau, CC (1998). Investigating patterns in information seeking: concepts and contexts. In Wilson, TD and Allen, DK (Eds) *Exploring the contexts of information behaviour: proceedings of the second international conference on research in information needs, seeking and use in different contexts*, 13/15 August 1998, Sheffield, UK. London: Taylor Graham.

Kvale, S (1996). *InterViews: An Introduction to Qualitative Research Interviewing*. Thousand Oaks, USA: Sage Publications, Inc.

Marton, F and Booth, S (1997). *Learning and Awareness*. New Jersey. USA: Lawrence Erlbaum Associates Inc.

Parker, N (2002). Processes and Meaning in Individual Postgraduate Assignments: the Effects of Affect? Proceedings of HERDSA. 26. Milperra, Australia: The Higher Education Research and Development Society of Australasia.

Parker, N (2004). Assignment information processes: what's 'enough' for high achievement? Summary of research note at the ISIC 2004 conference, Dublin, 1-3 September, 2004. Information Research. 10 :1. Summary 3. Available at http://InformationR.net/ir/10-1/abs3.

Prosser, M and Trigwell, K (1999). *Understanding Learning and Teaching: The experience in higher education.* Buckingham: Society for Research into Higher Education and Open University Press.

Acknowledgements

The author gratefully acknowledges the generous feedback and support from supervisors Emeritus Professor Mairead Browne and Doctor Jo McKenzie.

The limitations of difference. Exploring variation in student conceptions of the link between assessment and learning outcomes.

Alison Shreeve, Jonathan Baldwin and Gerald Farraday

University of the Arts London and Brighton University

Abstract

The move towards using learning outcomes to define and structure the learning and assessment of students has been widespread in UK higher education. Much emphasis has been rightly placed on the role of assessment in student learning (eg Biggs, 1996; 2003). The results of the researchers' phenomenographic study into student conceptions of assessment using learning outcomes in the design project (Shreeve, Baldwin, & Farraday, 2003) indicates that within a body of students there will be variation in the way that assessment itself is conceived of in a given situation and such variation can affect the way that students approach learning (Laurillard, 1984).

This paper examines the nature of the variation in conception of the link between learning outcomes and assessment and discusses the implications for improving the quality of learning through assessment. The variation found here may be influenced by tutor orientation (Samuelowitz and Bain, 2002) or by the students' previous experience in assessment (Prosser and Trigwell, 1999). But with an increasingly diverse body of students the range in variation of conception where assessment is concerned is an issue that academics should be addressing.

Assessment is fundamental to the way in which students learn. It places a premium on what is to be learned signalling that academics place value on what is assessed. The form the assessment takes can also dictate the way in which students approach the assessment task; students perceive that certain assessments can afford either a deep approach or a surface approach to learning for the assessment (Laurillard, 1984). The design of the assessment task is then central to the way students learn.

Innovative assessment (McDowell and Sambell, 1999) is thought to produce a more meaningful activity for students in which the design of the assessment relates to understanding and applying knowledge in new or different circumstances and engages the student in the process of assessment, promoting deep approaches to learning (Marton and Säljö, 1976). In design based subjects it is common practice to use project work for assessment which provides a realistic context, with an expectation that the individual will find their own response to the brief. This would fulfil McDowell and Sambell's definition of innovative assessment. However, in a study to investigate how students conceived of assessment using learning outcomes in design project work it was found that students conceived of assessment in at least three qualitatively distinct and different ways (Shreeve et al. 2003).

Underlying conceptions are linked to the actions or approaches which academics and students will adopt (eg Kember, 1997, Prosser and Trigwell, 1999). Where conceptions do not extend to the highest or broadest category of conception the approaches adopted will be limited. Students who only conceive of assessment as being something which is done to them for purposes of correction will be unable to see their role in assessment as a partnership to develop their understanding of the project task. With the focus of awareness on the quantity of work and the grades, students showing a correction conception are not likely to understand the importance of the quality of their work or the evaluations that academic staff will be making in order to award a high grade. Their conception of assessment is limited to producing lots of work and energy spent in this direction rather than trying to understand the underlying reasons for the assessment task. Students who conceive of assessment as a partnership in which they are working with tutors to improve their own performance and understanding with a view to their future career are potentially more likely to gain understanding and therefore students do not start with the same opportunities for achieving success. If the factors influencing conceptions of assessment could be identified it might be possible to change the conceptions of students to create more equitable opportunities for learning. The three conceptions of assessment construed in the original research are summarised in table 1.

	Focus on:	Tutor controlled	Tutor informed	Tutor guided
Correction conception Assessment is done to me	Quantity Products Grades/marks	A		
Developmental conception Assessment is done for me	Quality Progress Performance		B	
Self-knowledge conception Assessment is done with me	Quality Career Understanding			C

Table 1. Categories of student conceptions of assessment in the design project

The students interviewed were all part of a large foundation degree in design, which has five pathways with different specialist areas. The students were unknown to the interviewers and when they responded they were asked to situate their answers within one project which had been assessed so that the whole assessment process was the context of the experience they described. The semi-structured interview questions were designed to elicit their views about assessment, learning outcomes and the link between the two. The student conceptions of learning outcomes has been described elsewhere (Shreeve et al, 2004). In brief, three categories of conceptions for learning outcomes were construed from the interview transcriptions. Within the college, learning outcomes are central to the alignment of the curriculum (Biggs, 1996), are written on the project brief given to all students and form the basis of assessment, being written again on the feedback forms returned to students after assessment. It is perhaps surprising that there is significant variation in how learning outcomes are conceived of by the students. The differences are summed up in table 2.

Category of conception	Focus on	Products	Progress	Learning
Product conception	Products and lists	A		
Personal development conception	Knowing and doing Feedback		B	B
Relational development Conception	Myself and the world			C

Table 2. Categories of student conceptions of learning outcomes in the design project.

The significant qualitative differences are that students who conceive of products as the learning outcomes, that is the things that are made for the assessment, whether written, drawn or constructed, understand these to be the learning outcomes and the focus of their experience. Students demonstrating this conception do not understand the learning, which is embedded or represented in the products as the outcome of the learning process, and cannot therefore separate or abstract qualitative standards or achievements from the physical products. For these students it appears to be the product alone that is graded, not the learning or the skills embodied within the process and the products submitted for assessment. Other categories of conception of learning outcomes relate to personal progress and how personal development has significance with the world beyond the student. Both of these conceptions have a common focus on learning.

The transcripts were revisited to investigate the responses to questions about the relationship of learning outcomes to assessment. Out of the original 23 transcripts three were not included in the analysis due to insufficiently probing questions in this area and inconclusive statements made. Ostensibly the link between assessment and the learning outcomes for the unit studied is a fairly obvious one, as this is stated on the project brief: 'Assessment will be based on attainment of the learning outcomes for the unit'. However, there were three distinctly different categories of conception construed by the researchers after analysing the transcripts again. The three categories are best described using quotations to explore the conceptions held by students, of the link between learning outcomes and assessment.

Category A: a material/product link between assessment and learning outcomes.

In their responses to interview questions, students demonstrating this conception foreground (Marton and Booth, 1997) the items made and designed throughout the project. The underlying emphasis is on fulfilling the physical requirements of the project. The basis of the conceived link or relationship between learning outcomes and assessment is a material, physical one. In the following extract the overriding focus in the replies is the work, or doing the material and physical, the lists of evidence required for the assessment. *I* denotes the interviewer and *S* the student in the quotations from the transcripts which were all numbered and anonymous.

I   How do learning outcomes link to assessment?

S   Learning outcomes is like on the brief they always give out learning outcomes at the end of this project this is what you should have included in your – at the end of this brief this is what you should have included in your project. So the way the learning outcomes... Sorry what was the...?

I   How does it link to assessment?

S   Obviously there's – me personally – I think there's quite a bit of link because if you've completed the learning outcomes then you're going to have a good assessment because then the tutor is going to see that you've filled the criteria and you've done the specification that was required but sometimes I think that the learning outcomes does not always go in with the assessments.

I   Can you explain that?

S   In the way that you're required – in the learning outcomes this is what you're required to do, but you end up doing something totally different but keeping that sort of – how can I put it? Sort of like theme but not completing – because with the Hewlett Packard project like I said, I was really baffled so I think half the learning outcomes I didn't even do, but the tutor got the message that what I was trying to do was the same sort of thing, but in just like different words. (Transcript 6)

The student struggles to find words to explain what she means and finally uses the analogy of spoken communication where artefacts would be produced. Although terminology such as criteria and specification are used the sense resides in the things that she does or makes for the project. In referring to the Hewlett Packard project her conception of the link produces the misunderstanding. If she were unable to produce 'half the learning outcomes' she would not have been able to pass. If she had only produced half the material evidence required it is possible that she could demonstrate the learning outcomes to a basic standard. Learning outcomes are listed at the start of project briefs and the requirements (eg sketchbooks, learning journals, and practical work) at the end. For this student the link between assessment and learning outcomes is the fact that you have done the physical requirements and can tick the box (or not!) to complete the work required. It is also evident here that by conceiving of the link between learning outcomes and assessment as material products, a 'good assessment' is dependent on only doing the material requirements. This will limit the way in which any potential understanding of quality can be developed and thus limiting the approach taken to the assessment.

Category B: a personal development link

For students demonstrating this conception of the link between learning outcomes and assessment the relationship is very tenuous. There is a vague sense that the link is somehow about their own personal development, that if they perform better than in previous assessments they will be rewarded accordingly.

I   So how do learning outcomes link to assessment?

S   I think they want to see like – in assessment as well they want to see like your progression stages. So obviously the way they've assessed before they've looked at the marks and obviously if you're doing better and they're seeing your sewing techniques and all the pattern cutting is obviously getting better then obviously they're seeing that you're learning from it and obviously... That's it. (Transcript 7)

Another student describes the link as demonstrating her own development:

S   They want to see that you've progressed from the previous term. They want to see that you've taken what they've said on board and you've evidence of that and you've gone a step further. (Transcript 12)

The link between the learning outcomes and the assessment is conceived of as a personal progression. This resides solely within the student and there is no sense of external criteria or evaluation in relationship to having achieved a specified learning outcome, something that has been set out as a goal to aim towards.

Conception C: an aligned link

This category of description demonstrates that students conceive a very clear link founded on learning. For students demonstrating this conception of the relationship between learning outcomes and assessment the focus of awareness is on the goals and aims of the project and having to achieve or demonstrate specific learning outcomes. They describe the relationship as one of having to demonstrate that you have learned what was explained on the project brief and that it formed the purpose and function of the project's activities. It is this learning which is assessed. There is a clear conception that learning underpins the assessment process and it is explicitly stated.

I   How do learning outcomes link to assessment?

S   *They can – I suppose when tutors are assessing they can only really – the only way they can actually assess our work, because ~~everybody's work is quite different~~, is by ~~actually~~ – hang on a minute, I know what I'm trying to say. Learning outcomes are the things that you've learnt throughout the project and, for instance, if you're doing a project based on a retail market then you're learning about how to fit the project to a retail market. So that would be your learning outcome and that's what they're assessing you on. (Transcript 1)*

Another student explains her view of assessment with the same underlying concept of a link founded on what you are supposed to have learned:

I   *So how would [a learning outcome] link to assessment?*

S   *Well it's their way of seeing what you've learnt and you learn. You do your work for assessment so you just have to use everything you've learnt for that assessment and then you'll be assessed on how well you've used that, what you've learnt.*

I   *So how might that happen? How might a tutor do that?*

S   *Well they've got specific things that they'll expect you to have done and they'll look for that in your work. (Transcript 9)*

It is interesting to note here the student appears to conceive of learning as being embodied within the products (work) required to be submitted for assessment, unlike the earlier category A. With this conception there is potential for abstraction or perhaps detachment from the manufacture or production of the artefact. The actual work or production is not the link between the learning outcome and the assessment of the outcome, but it is the embodied learning, which is represented within the artefact. With a conception of a link that aligns the project work with learning and assessment, a student may also encompass aspects of personal development and the product focus in their responses. Students who demonstrate only conceptions A or B cannot hold conceptions of the link which is aligned in this way. The conceptions are qualitatively different and are hierarchical.

These three different categories of conception between learning outcomes and assessment and the relationship between them are summarised in table 3.

Category of conception	Focus on	Product	Development	Learning
A Material/product link	Evidence	A		
B Personal development link	My development		B	
C Aligned link	Achieving the specified learning outcomes			C

Table 3. Categories of student conceptions of the link between learning outcomes and assessment

Providing an explicitly worded explanation of the link between learning outcomes and assessment on the project brief is obviously insufficient to enable all students to perceive this link as an aligned conception. In order to promote greater clarity in the assessment process for all students it could be beneficial to look at ways in which conceptions can be formed or influenced and ways in which the more limited conceptions could be developed.

The different conceptions of the relationship between learning outcomes and assessment within a group of students at the same stage of the same course is evidence that the quality of learning achieved is likely to be variable. Although this study did not identify a grade achieved and thus missed an opportunity to relate conceptions to achievement, the way in which aspects of assessment vary is likely to limit or influence the approaches to study adopted by these students. Previous research has demonstrated a link between conceptions and also between approaches and the quality of the learned outcome (Prosser and Trigwell, 1999).

One of the factors Biggs (1996) cites as essential for quality outcomes in learning is the alignment of the curriculum, that is what you set out to achieve in the curriculum is the focus for constructing the learning activities and for assessment. For students demonstrating a conception of the link between learning outcomes and assessment as aligned, as in category C, the design of the assessment and project work would appear to be providing the clear goals that students see as part of good teaching. However, only 11 of the 20 transcripts analysed demonstrated this conception. For nearly half of the students sampled learning outcomes do not appear to be fulfilling the function of clear goals. Their conceptions demonstrate that the forefront of their awareness is filled with either a vague sense that assessment is linked to improving their performance, which is desirable in itself, but does not seem to provide external goals and criteria, or through evidence and material outcomes, which provide physical goals, but not necessarily qualitatively successful and meaningful learning outcomes by the end of the project. Students demonstrating conception C may in fact be using strategic approaches to learning, seeing the learning outcomes as cues for successful assessment rather than providing a context to develop deep approaches. Further research between conceptions of the link between assessment and learning outcomes and the actual grade or result of assessment is needed in order to detect a correlation between conceptions and achievement.

Other factors influencing these students' conceptions of the relationship between learning outcomes and assessment might be through previous experiences. Though they had completed over one and a half years of their programme when they were interviewed it is possible that they still held conceptions that were formed on previous courses. Where particular strategies may have been successful in the past, such as producing lots of work, putting in effort or producing a particular kind of artefact without understanding why or what is represented, students may hold a conception at odds with practices in higher education. These students may not perceive the current learning environment in a different way to their previous one in which their product-focused conceptions were appropriate or successful.

One of the influential factors in the learning environment could be tutor conceptions or orientations to assessment and to learning, which can affect the way in which students respond. This is suggested by an exchange in one of the transcripts. The student describes being aware that the learning outcomes are listed on the project brief, but she doesn't really read them and they are usually forgotten, certainly not in the forefront of awareness (Marton and Booth, 1999). They have little meaning or significance for her. She demonstrates a material/product conception of assessment in this context, but what is also interesting in the following quote is a possible transmission conception of learning, actually being in class and doing what is asked of you means that learning will take place. It is similar to a teacher focused transmission orientation to learning, (eg Kember and Gow, 1994, Trigwell et al, 1999) or a concept of filling up empty vessels. In a practical and skills based subject, the emphasis on product is perhaps not surprising, but it is also limiting. If learning is perceived as simply being present to learn through passively engaging in what you are told to do there seems little scope to develop autonomy, independence or originality, ideas which are central to the creative subjects being studied.

I *Why don't you read the learning outcomes? Why don't they matter to you?*

S *I just read what – it says like evidence, what you have to have and that's what I really base my thing on and then – yeah – because I think in my learning outcomes I'm going to learn it. If I turn up for my lesson, I'm going to learn it, so I don't need to read what I'm going to learn. I might give it a quick read through but I don't pay too much attention because if I turn up then I'll get what I'm supposed to get.*

I *So what's most important to you there then in doing the project?*

S *You mean what I like best kind of thing?*

I *Yes.*

S *I like making the actual product. (Transcript 2)*

And another student also appears to believe in a similar way, that being there means that you will learn,

> *Keep coming to the lectures and classes and I think you'll be fine. (Transcript 15)*

But as Trigwell and Prosser (1999) point out, the same learning context is populated by students who perceive the learning environment in different ways and who can perceive the same context as affording different approaches to study.

Perhaps the best way to promote the broadest conceptions of both learning and assessment is to engage students in discussions or activities which are targeted at raising their awareness of the highest conceptions of learning within their subject. Closely linked to this must be activities aimed at raising their awareness of assessment and its function in developing meaningful approaches to learning in practical subject areas. In order to do this, tutors must first be engaged in developing their own concepts of learning and of their subjects, supported by an awareness of research into their own students' learning in the context in which it occurs.

Further research is being developed to investigate tutor's conceptions of assessment using learning outcomes in the design project. There are distinct differences and relationships between what tutors believe about teaching and the assessment strategies they use across a range of subject areas, (Samuelowitz. and Bain 2002), but no work has yet been carried out in the specific area cited here. It is possible that there is a relationship between tutor concepts of teaching, learning and assessment and student concepts. It could shed further light on ways to improve the broader conceptions of assessment so that students in creative assessment situations will have more opportunities to understand the clear goals provided by actually understanding the relationship between learning outcomes and assessment as an alignment of specified learning outcomes embodied within the evidence produced through project work.

Further research is needed to fully explore the differences in conception in design project work and assessment, particularly in relation to the quality of the learning outcome. Where practical work forms the basis of portfolio assessment greater emphasis may need to be placed by tutors on the more abstract qualities of attaining the desired outcomes. This will need to be done by developing a common set of understandings between both students and tutors who work together on projects, though often in isolation across sites, rooms and through the part time engagement of specialist practitioners. Exploring through discussion and showing of examples, through the kinds of activities described by Price et al (2003), which can increase understanding of assessment, become harder to implement as student numbers and pressure on academics' time increases. Innovative ways to engage in developing meaning and understanding in order to change conceptions of assessment and learning outcomes will need to be sustained and long term. Quick fixes to complex sociological learning environments are not calculated to bring about changes to conceptions and practices in academics (eg Ho et al, 2001). They are also unlikely to help in developing students' conceptions of assessment in order to promote the highest categories of conception of the link between learning outcomes and assessment.

To exploit the power of assessment to the benefit of all students it is important to develop the highest categories of understanding. Where differences in products, portfolios and designs is positively encouraged and welcome, the differences in conception of assessment, learning outcomes and the links between the two have the potential to limit the ways in which students approach their project work and also in what they are capable of achieving.

Acknowledgements

This research project was funded by a Pedagogic Research Fund grant from the Art Design And Communication subject centre in the Learning and Teaching Support Network in the UK (ADC-LTSN), now part of the HE Academy. We would like to thank the subject centre staff for their support and encouragement throughout the project, in particular, Linda Drew, who was the Subject Centre Co-Director at the time of formulating the research and collecting data. The project was assigned a mentor, Keith Trigwell, who has provided invaluable experience and help at key points of the research.

References

Biggs, J (1996) Enhancing teaching through constructive alignment *Higher Education* Vol 32, pp347-364, Netherlands, Kluwer Academic Publishers.

Biggs, J (2003) *Teaching for Quality Learning at University*. Buckingham: SRHE and Open University Press.

Drew, L, Bailey, S and Shreeve, A (2002) Fashion Variations: student approaches to learning in fashion design In *Enhancing Curricula: Exploring effective curricula practices in art, design and communication in Higher Education*. Centre for Learning and Teaching in Art and Design, Proceedings of 1st international conference, 2002 London pp179-198

Ho, A, Watkins, D and Kelly, M (2001) The conceptual change approach to improving teaching and learning: An evaluation of a Hong Kong staff development programme. *Higher Education*. Vol.42, pp143–169 Netherlands, Kluwer Academic Publishers

Kember, D (1997) Teaching beliefs and their impact on students' approaches to learning. In: Dart, B and Boulton-Lewis, G (eds), *Teaching and learning in Higher Education*. Camberwell, Vic: ACER Press.

Kember, D and and Gow, L (1994) Orientations to teaching and their effect on the quality of student learning. *Journal of Higher Education* Vol 65, pp59-74 Netherlands, Kluwer Academic Publishers

Laurillard, D (1984) Styles and approaches in problem solving. In. Marton, Hounsell and Entwhistle (eds) *The Experience Of Learning: Implications For Teaching And Studying In Higher Education*. Edinburgh, Scottish Academic Press

Marton, F and Booth, S (1997) *Learning and awareness*. Mahwah: NJ, Lawrence Erlbaum.

McDoewll, L and Sambell, K (1999) The experience of innovative assessment: student perspectives pp71-82 In Brown, S and Glasner, A (Eds) *Assessment Matters in Higher Education*. Buckingham, SRHE/Open University Press.

Price, M, O'Donovan, B and Rust, C (2003). Improving students' learning by developing their understanding of assessment criteria and processes. In Rust, C (Ed) *Improving Student Learning: Theory and Practice – 10 years on*. Oxford Brookes University, Oxford Centre for Staff and Learning Development

Prosser, M and Trigwell, K (1999) *Understanding learning and teaching.* Buckingham: SRHE and Open University Press.

Samuelowitz, K and Bain, J (2002) Identifying academics' orientations to assessment practice *Higher Education* Vol.43 pp 173-201 Netherlands, Kluwer Academic Publishers

Shreeve, A, Baldwin, J and Farraday, G (in press) Variation in Student Conceptions of Assessment. In: Rust, C (ed) *Improving Student Learning: Theory Research and Scholarship.* Oxford: Oxford Brookes University, Oxford Centre for Staff and Learning Development.

Shreeve, A, Baldwin, J and Farraday, G (in press) *Variation in student conceptions of learning outcomes in the design project.* In proceedings of the second CLTAD International Conference, Enhancing Curricula: The Scholarship of Learning and teaching in Art and Design Barcelona, April 2004.

Trigwell, K, Prosser, M and Waterhouse, F (1999) Relations between teachers' approaches to teaching and students' approaches to learning, *Higher Education*, Vol 37, pp57–70 Netherlands, Kluwer Academic Publishers

Information literacy in the curriculum: selected findings from a phenomenographic study of UK conceptions of, and pedagogy for, information literacy

Sheila Webber, University of Sheffield

Bill Johnston, University of Strathclyde

Abstract

This paper reports on a phenomenographic study investigating UK marketing academics' conceptions of pedagogy for information literacy, part of a larger project, funded by the Arts and Humanities Research Board. Existing definitions and models of information literacy are identified. Previous relevant studies of conceptions of teaching are reviewed briefly, and the phenomenographic research approach is outlined. After discussion of sample and methods, five qualitatively different categories of pedagogy for information literacy are described. The paper concludes by noting some similarities and differences between previous research into conceptions of teaching and this study, and by suggesting implications for academics in an information society.

Keywords

Phenomenography, information literacy, marketing, UK, conceptions of pedagogy

Introduction

We report on a phenomenographic study investigating UK marketing academics' conceptions of pedagogy for information literacy. This is part of a larger project, studying academics in four disciplines, funded by the Arts and Humanities Research Board (see http://dis.shef.ac.uk/literacy/project/).

The key research questions we are addressing in our project are:

1.   What conceptions of information literacy are held by UK academics?

2.   What are academics' conceptions and reported practice in educating students for information literacy?

3.   Do differences in conception correspond to differences in discipline?

Literature on information literacy is discussed briefly in the next section. Our own conception of information literacy is "the adoption of appropriate information behaviour to obtain, through whatever channel or medium, information well fitted to information needs, together with critical awareness of the importance of wise and ethical use of information in society". (Johnston and Webber, 2003)

The first stage of the project consists of a phenomenographic study of the conceptions of pedagogy for information literacy held by 20 academics in each of four disciplines; marketing, civil engineering, chemistry and english. The second phase, which will take place in the final year of the project, will draw on the data collected in the first phase in order to draw up a questionnaire tailored to academics in each discipline. The questionnaires, which again will focus on conceptions of, and pedagogy for, information literacy, will be distributed to a larger sample of the population of UK academics in each discipline.

The following sections provide the rationale and context for the research in terms of the focus on academics' conceptions of information literacy and their conceptions of teaching. The paper goes on to describe our methodology and the phenomenographic categories of description that have emerged from our analysis of the marketing transcripts.

Rationale and background for research into information literacy

Information literacy has been a major focus of attention from library and information professionals, and has increasingly received wider recognition. For example, Candy et al (1994), in their report on Australian higher education, identify information literacy as one of the five key elements in the profile of a lifelong learner. A UNESCO-sponsored meeting in 2003 produced the Prague Declaration "Towards an information literate society", which asserts that:

> *Information literacy encompasses knowledge of one's information concerns and needs, and the ability to identify, locate, evaluate, organize and effectively create, use and communicate information to address issues or problems at hand; it is a prerequisite for participating effectively in the Information Society, and is part of the basic human right of lifelong learning. (Information Literacy Meeting of Experts, 2003)*

Models such as the Society of College, National and University Libraries' seven pillars (SCONUL Task Force on Information Skills,1999) have been produced by library and information science (LIS) professionals as definitions and as proposed frameworks for teaching information literacy. Although existing research has been considered when drawing them up, the models themselves were not developed through application of a specific research method and they reflect LIS professionals' conceptions. Johnston and Webber (2003) have identified that, although librarians are increasingly engaging with their pedagogic role, there are still problems, for example, lack of meaningful assessment of student learning.

The key role of academics in producing information literate students has been identified by librarians (eg by the British SCONUL Task Force (1999; para 6) and by the American ACRL IS Research and Scholarship Committee (2003; p485.) However, librarians comment on the difficulty of collaborating with academics and Julien and Given (2003) have found that librarians' attitudes towards academics may also be problematic.

Whilst the librarians' voices and their views on information literacy are well represented in the literature, academics' own conceptions have received comparatively little attention. There have been a small number of research studies focusing on academics' perceptions of information literacy outside the UK. These include Bruce's (1997) phenomenographic study of educators in Australian universities, a Canadian survey of information literacy perceptions and activities amongst science and engineering faculty (Leckie and Fullerton, 1999) and McGuiness' phenomenographic investigation into Irish academics' conceptions of information literacy (early findings are reported in McGuiness, 2003).

In Bruce's (1997) study the core participants were 16 interviewees from Australian universities. The sample included academics, librarians, staff developers and learning counsellors. She identified seven qualitatively different conceptions of information literacy ("7 Faces"). Each has a different aspect of information literacy in focal awareness, for example: information technology conception: using IT for information retrieval and communication; wisdom conception; using information wisely and ethically for the benefit of others.

Conceptions of teaching

A growing body of research investigates academics' conceptions of teaching. A number of these studies use the phenomenographic approach. We have not identified any studies of marketing academics (the focus of this article). Martin et al (2000) included business and social science lecturers in their phenomenographic study of how teachers intended to teach a subject or topic. They also observed the lecturers' practice, to compare intention with practice. In describing the lecturers' approaches to teaching, Martin et al developed categories which drew on an earlier phenomenographic study (Trigwell et al, 1994) of university science teachers. Martin et al (2000) identified six categories. The first three focus on information transmission, the next two categories are focused on conceptual development and the final category focuses on conceptual change.

Samuelowicz and Bain (2001) note that there are "many points of calibration between the descriptive categories [for approaches to teaching] that have been used in the literature" (p300) and organise the categories into three groups: knowledge conveying categories (which would, for example, include Martin et al's "information transmission" categories), facilitation of learning categories (including conceptual development and change categories) and (between these two) intermediate categories (which, for example, focus on student-teacher interaction).

Martin et al (2000) put forward the importance of considering the "object of study" that teachers construct for their students (the "what" as opposed to the "how" of the act of teaching). They note a study of teaching creative writing by Martin and Ramsden which suggested that students learned what their teachers presented as learning: for example if creative writing were taught as a set of skills, then students were more likely to see creative writing as consisting primarily of skills development. Martin et al (2000) conclude their paper by suggesting that "the object of study", more than anything else, will determine the quality of teaching and probably the quality of learning outcome as well." (p411) Our own study explicitly illuminates the "object of study" ie information literacy, as part of our analysis.

The research approach: phenomenography

Phenomenography "aims to reveal the qualitatively different ways of experiencing various phenomena". (Marton and Booth, 1997, 136). Trigwell (2000) has identified distinguishing aspects of the phenomenographic approach, in particular that the approach aims to identify variation in experience of a phenomenon and that phenomenography takes a second-order perspective.

Marton and Booth (1997) characterise the phenomenographic approach as one which does not recognise a dividing line between the inner world and the outer world. The individual and the phenomena he or she experiences are bound together: the world is "constituted as an internal relation between them. There is only one world, but it is a world that we experience, a world in which we live, a world that is ours" (13). Phenomenography is a means of opening up these individual worlds, to form a picture of all the different ways in which the same phenomena might be seen: "by learning about how the world appears to others, we will learn what the world is like, and what the world could be like" (13).

Samples for a phenomenographic study are normally purposive, seeking to cover variations of experience in population being covered and the preferred method of data collection is a semi-structured interview, with questions which aim to encourage the interviewee to focus on describing their experience of the phenomenon. The individual questions circle around and illuminate this central question. During the interview, it is important that the interviewer does not let his or her own conception of the phenomenon colour the interview (Ashworth and Lucas, 2000).

The interviews are transcribed verbatim, and the researcher(s) familiarise themselves with the data through repeated readings. The interview transcripts are pooled, since the focus is not on one interviewee's conception, but the variety of conceptions held between all interviewees. Each variation in conception which is expressed is held as valid. The researchers seek to identify concepts upon which the interviewees focus (looking for indicators such as repetition or emphasis). The result of the analysis process is a description of categories of variation in experience, and an "outcome space" which includes articulation of the ways in which these experiences are internally related. Diagrammatic representation may be used in addition to textual description. Quotations are an integral part of the descriptions (Entwistle, N and Marton, F (1984) 226).

Methodology

In this section we describe the methods we have adopted for sampling, data collection and analysis. In selecting our sample, of 20 academics in each of the four disciplines, we aimed for a varied population within our target group. The following factors were considered in selecting our sample:

- Institution: interviewees come from 26 universities in England, Scotland and Wales.
- Sex: 39% of our sample are female.
- Post-1992 and pre-1992 universities: 69% are from pre-1992 universities
- Departmental rating in the Research Assessment Exercise (RAE)
- Departmental rating in the latest teaching quality assessment for that country/subject.

We surveyed other characteristics, such as age, through a brief factual questionnaire administered as part of the interview. The characteristics of the sample of 20 marketing academics were as follows:

- 12 male and 8 female, with 15 of UK nationality
- Age ranges from 21-30 and those in between to 51-60
- Years of teaching in ranges from 0-5 and those in between to 26-30. A few academics were members of the Academy
- All taught undergraduates, 18 taught masters students, eight taught PhD students
- 10 were course or programme coordinators
- They came from 12 different universities: four post-1992 and eight pre-1992
- Research Assessment Exercise ratings ranged from 2 to 5*
- Teaching quality grades ranged from satisfactory to excellent

We contacted interviewees either by emailing individual academics directly or via librarians. The large number of interviewees who said that they had not heard of the term "information literacy", and the variation in conception that we are discovering, lead us to contend that we did not just interview those already interested in information literacy.

The research team (Webber, Johnston and the research assistant Stuart Boon) drafted interview questions, and the semi-structured interview was piloted with three lecturers. The key questions were:

1. What is your conception of information literacy? Supplementary questions included asking how the academic personally engaged with information literacy, for example in their research.

2. How do you engage your students in information literacy? Supplementary questions included asking about the desired outcomes; challenges; collaboration with librarians; and whether information literacy was assessed.

3. What is your conception of an information literate university? Supplementary questions included goals and outcomes; challenges; and who would be affected by change.

The questions provided a good progression within the interview, moving it from current personal experience and practical teaching experience to organisational context. Each of the questions helped to develop the picture of how the interviewees experience information literacy.

The interviews for the whole project were carried out and transcribed by Boon. Each interview lasted approximately 45 minutes. Initial analysis began once the first few interviews (from a mixture of the four disciplines) were transcribed. We have taken a collaborative approach to analysis. Each team member read the transcripts and presented their reflections at the team meeting. A pattern was established of holding team meetings roughly every six weeks. Marked-up transcripts, concise minutes and in some cases other media (eg flip charts) recorded discussion and decisions.

Once all the interviews were transcribed, the key analysis phase began, with concentration focusing on one discipline at a time, beginning with the marketing transcripts. In addition to the work already done in highlighting key quotations and flagging up key themes and potential categories the data was loaded into Atlas/ti text analysis software. Codes were developed through an iterative process and the coded data was output in the form of lists of numeric occurrences of the codes, charts derived from numeric data about the codes, and sets of quotations coded to different themes and categories. External presentations on the project also stimulated separate analysis of subsets of the data. Through an iterative process, moving between analysis and readings of the data, the categories described in the following sections were identified. Firstly, categories of description for conceptions of information literacy were identified. These categories then contributed to the categories of description of the academics' conceptions of pedagogy for information literacy.

UK marketing academics' conceptions of pedagogy for information literacy

1. Someone else's job

2. Upgrading students' information toolbox at an appropriate point

3. Facilitating access to a variety of resources

4.   Showing students how and when to use information skills

5.   Helping students understand how information literacy is critical to them, for marketing and life

The key dimensions of variation are:

i.   Pedagogic focus on: (in combination) the subject (marketing), the course of study, self, assumptions about students, student expectations (of the course or lecturer), student understanding.

ii.   Conceptions of information literacy. These were analysed into the following phenomenographic categories:

1. *Accessing information quickly and easily to be aware of what's going on*: The focus is on being able to get access to a wide variety of information quickly and easily. The key purpose is keeping in touch with, and drawing on, what is going on in the outside world.

2. *Using IT to work with information*: The focus here is on using information technology (software applications and networks) efficiently and effectively to work with information. Both textual and numeric information is explicitly mentioned.

3. *Possessing a set of information skills and applying them to the task in hand*: The focus is on developing a set of information skills and being able to apply the relevant skills to a particular task (eg writing an article, producing an assignment).

4. *Using information literacy to solve real-world problems*: focuses on understanding a problem and understanding how information can be used to solve the problem. It is qualitatively different from conception three, in that the central focus is on the problem, rather than on skills.

5. *Becoming critical thinkers*: The central focus is on becoming a critical thinker. Most important to this development are higher order information skills such as understanding and interpreting information.

6. *Becoming a confident, independent practitioner*: The focus is on the use of information literacy as an important part of becoming a confident practitioner. Thus there is a focus on personal development to become this practitioner, which will happen in a real world context.

Category 1. Someone else's job

The subject (marketing) is in focal awareness; the role of teaching information literacy may be explicitly rejected.

> *It's my job in a two hour lecture to lecture to them on the subject area for two hours. Uh, when I go to a lecture I teach in a lecture. I don't teach them how to use the library. I don't teach them how to use the internet. I don't teach them how to do electronic searches. (Interviewee 13)*

	1. Someone else's job	2. Upgrading students' information toolbox	3. Facilitating access to a variety of resources	4. Showing students how and when to use information skills	5. Helping students understand how information literacy is critical to them
Conception of information literacy	Toolbox Accessing information	Toolbox	Accessing information Using IT	Accessing information Using IT	Problem solving Critical thinker Independent practitioner
Focus of pedagogy	The subject (marketing) plus assumptions about students	The course of study plus assumptions about students	Self plus student expectations	The course of study plus student expectations	Student understanding

Table 1: Outcome space for UK marketing academics' pedagogy for information literacy

Insofar as the teacher is involved in information literacy education, it is in providing reading lists and handouts, or directing students to resources at appropriate points. Information literacy is seen as relevant to the students, but it is just not the lecturer's responsibility to develop them. The conception of information literacy is one or three. Assumptions are made about the students and the skills and knowledge they may or may not possess.

Um, my students are third years so I am making the generally, probably wholesome, assumption that over the previous two years they probably have learned these skills to some degree, and if they haven't then… again because it is such a short semester, I don't really have time to go into things like how to go to the library, how to find information, um, I give them a reading list, and I try to make it explicit which library they need to go to. (Interviewee 08)

Category 2. Upgrading students' information toolbox at an appropriate point

The focal awareness is on the interaction between a toolbox of information skills and a given course of study. The conception of information literacy is *possessing a set of information skills and applying them to the task in hand.*

Pedagogy for information literacy is experienced as giving teaching or classes to meet the course requirements, driven by their expectations of what students need at that point.

Well, it means having a, uh, a kind of toolbox of skills that I can show the students how to use. But I should point out that I don't teach a lot of information literacy, not as it would be called information literacy, but there are important bits or specific tools that I do bring out for different classes. (Interviewee 14)

Their expectations of students are that they will arrive at university with deficiencies in specific areas of information literacy. Students learn by being exposed to teaching at an appropriate point in the course of study.

T: *Evaluation is important, but I do it for them until second year.*

I: *Why is that?*

T: *There isn't a lot of call for evaluation in first year. And I don't think they possess those skills until we cover them." (Interviewee 05)*

Where the manner in which teaching and learning takes place is elaborated, reference is made to showing and demonstration, with mention of PowerPoints and handouts in particular.

Category 3. Facilitating access to a variety of resources

In this conception the focus is on the lecturer's role in facilitating access to information. There is a focus on being aware of what the students' expectations are, and tailoring the pedagogic approach to those expectations.

The conception of information literacy is of *accessing information quickly and easily to be aware of what's going on* or (where there is a particular concern with numerical data) *Using IT to work with information efficiently and effectively* (access to information and using IT tools effectively are part of the internal horizon for both these conceptions). The focal awareness is on the lecturer making information accessible at a point that fits in with his or her own teaching, and on the students being able to access the information.

> *As an educator, I suppose it would mean, um, well, if we are talking about education, then I suppose it [information literacy] would mean – because my first answer was based on research – I suppose this would mean more about using it in teaching and teaching other people where to get information from, and what exists out there, and how to get a hold of it. (Interviewee 18)*

Students are perceived as having expectations about course delivery and there is a desire to meet the perceived expectations.

> *Full-time MBAs and executive MBAs are expecting guru-like experiences, so that's the… the way to approach that is to be up to date with the latest stuff, adding your own research, and having consultancy experience, building on the field work. (Interviewee 07)*

These information sources include the lecturers' own material, the library, the students themselves, and books, and also the systems the students use to access the sources. Verbs such as "post", "give", "show", "send [the student to…]" are used in this context.

Category 4. Showing students how and when to use information skills

The focus for those with this conception is on introducing information literacy skills when the students need them. There is similarity to the conception *upgrading students' information skills at an appropriate point* in that the requirements of the course are important. The key qualitative differences from the latter conception are that

1) When talking about changes in teaching, academics often talk about adapting to student expectations and preferences, or reacting to observations of student behaviour. eg

> *I asked them [the librarians] last year to come in and to present a session with students to show them how to use different databases like EBSCO and ABI Inform and things like that, because the students were professing that they didn't know how to do that... (Interviewee 03)*

2) The academics talk about how they aim to persuade students that the skills will also be useful in their lifecourse, as well as during the course itself.

> *Aside from all the stuff they have to learn about what this topic is, I like them to learn, um, how to find things out to use for essays and the resources that are available on the computer and in the library. I like them to learn, um, a more practical side of things like communication and discussion and things like that, but I don't know if you'd class that as information skills or not. But I think that the learning experience is about, um, can you go out and work at the end of the degree and not just can you recite who wrote this particular journal article in 1978? (Interviewee 03)*

There are two variations, depending on whether the conception of information literacy is one or two, and the emphasis in what is done in the classroom will vary accordingly. For example, variation one with information literacy conception one (accessing information quickly and easily) focuses particularly on students learning about finding resources and his/her own role as a provider of information. However, this is qualitatively different from the *facilitating access to a variety of resources* conception, in that this is combined with an awareness of developing learning through a course of study.

When describing teaching practice, there is an emphasis on demonstration, provision and student activities (searching, using information systems etc).

Category 5. Helping students understand how information literacy is critical to them, for marketing and life

The focus is on students' understanding of the role and importance of information literacy in the discipline of marketing and/or in students' life outside formal education.

> *The MBA is all about learning to swim in information and to make heads or tails of where you are and where you need to go. (Interviewee 01)*

T: *People really know how important it is and how increasingly important those skills are in terms of doing things in the real world, whether they are going to be academics or practitioners, it doesn't matter. You know, the world is about information and we are breeding a generation of knowledge workers. The better they are when they leave us.*

I: *So that is something you are trying to instill in the students as well?*

T: *Oh, I think, I think that it is something that comes with everything they do."* *(Interviewee 10)*

Thinking and reflection very important

> *Students want to rush off to Yahoo and get started. They want everything to be waiting for them. They want it now, now, now! A lot of what I tell them is to slow down. 'Slow down,' I say. 'Think about what you're doing.' So I tell them to start by looking at the problem. Really have a good look at it. [Pause] You've got to try to get your hands on it. Try to work out how to go at it, like, uh, how you want to approach it. (Interviewee 12)*

The intention is that student understanding comes about variously through participation, questioning, problem solving, case study work etc as well as demonstration and facilitating access to resources;

> *I want them to think about information. I want them to feel like they can really participate. I put a lot of pressure on the students to get interactive, to go out and to learn. I want them to see that information is essential and that it doesn't have to be boring. Information acquisition can be driven by a high level of creativity, or idea creation, and a lot of these things can be taken straight from everyday things. My own methods for teaching in this way is to make things kind of sexy or funky. (Interviewee 20)*

Discussion and conclusions

We will confine our discussion to two points. Firstly, it was noted in a previous section that there appear to be "many points of callibration" (Samuelowicz and Bain, 2001) between the various categories produced by investigations of conceptions of teaching. Our study is similar in that it reveals both knowledge conveying (our categories two and three) and facilitation (our category five) approaches to teaching. Our study is different in that it has produced a category "someone else's job" that has not appeared in previous studies. Note that the "object of study" (information literacy) *was* experienced, and conceived as having value for students, but the teaching of the "object of study" was not seen as the lecturer's job.

This shows that it is worth distinguishing between investigation into teaching "your subject" and investigation into teaching those skills or knowledge outside "your subject". Teaching other skills and knowledge (in this case information literacy, but other examples would be team working and learning to learn) are increasingly framed as part of a UK academic's job. It cannot be assumed that because a university teacher has a certain approach to learning and teaching of their core subject area, that they will take the same approach to teaching and learning of subjects such as "key skills". This has been an under-researched area.

Secondly, we would contend that development of IL within the curriculum might be seen as one form of a nascent response to the *information society*. The idea of an information society has gathered pace as a description of the growth and impact of information services, products and systems as key features of economy and communication. Academic institutions are implicated in this wider social development as the scale of relevant information services, particularly online services, has grown, and impacted the research and teaching practices of academics and students. Some of the interviewees acknowledge the existence of an "information society" in which IL is important or even essential "You know, the world is about information and we are breeding a generation of knowledge workers" (marketing 10). However, despite recognising the value of information literacy, this recognition did not always mean that information literacy was taught. The extent to which academics engage with information literacy may illuminate the ways in which notions of an information society are being translated into pedagogical practice.

References

ACRL (Association of College and Research Libraries) IS Research and Scholarship Committee (2003). ACRL Research agenda: research agenda for library instruction and information literacy. *Library and information science research*, 25, 479-487.

Ashworth, P and Lucas, U (2000) Achieving empathy and engagement: a practical approach to the design, conduct and reporting of phenomenographic research. *Studies in Higher Education*, 25 (3), 295-308.

Bruce, C (1997) *The seven faces of information literacy*. Adelaide: Auslib Press.

Candy, PC, Crebert, G and O'Leary, J (1994) *Developing Lifelong Learners through Undergraduate Education*. National Board of Employment, Education and Training Report; 28. Canberra: Australian Government Publishing Service.

Entwistle, N and Marton, F (1984) Changing conceptions of learning and research. In Marton, F, Hounsell, D, and Entwistle, N *The experience of learning*. (pp211-228) Edinburgh: Scottish Academic Press.

Information Literacy Meeting of Experts. (2003) *The Prague declaration: Towards an information literate society*. National Commission on Library and Information Science; National Forum on Information Literacy and UNESCO. http://www.nclis.gov/libinter/infolitconfandmeet/post-infolitconfandmeet/post-infolitconfandmeet.html

Johnston, B and Webber, S (2003) Information literacy in higher education: a review and case study. *Studies in Higher Education*, 28 (3), 335-352.

Julien, H, and Given, L (2003) Faculty-Librarian Relationships in the Information Literacy Context: A Content Analysis of Librarians' Expressed Attitudes and Experiences. *Canadian Journal of Information and Library Science*, 27(3), 65-87.

Leckie, G and Fullerton, A (1999) Information literacy in science and engineering undergraduate education: faculty attitudes and pedagogical practices. *College and Research Libraries*, 60 (1), 9-29.

McGuiness, C (2003) Attitudes of academics to the library's role in information literacy education. In: Martin, A and Rader, H (Eds) *Information and IT literacy: enabling learning in the 21st Century*. (pp244-254). London: Facet.

Martin, E et al (2000) What university teachers teach and how they teach it. *Instructional science*, 28, 387-412.

Marton, F and Booth, S (1997) *Learning and awareness*. Mahwah: Lawrence Erlbaum.

Samuelowicz, K and Bain, JD (2001) Revisiting academics' beliefs about teaching and learning. *Higher education*, 41, 299-325.

SCONUL Task Force on Information Skills. (1999) *Information Skills in Higher Education*. London: Society of College, National and University Libraries.

Trigwell, K (2000) *Phenomenography: variation and discernment*. In: Improving student learning: Proceedings 1999 7th International Symposium. Oxford. 75-85.

Trigwell, K, Prosser, M and Taylor, P (1994) Qualitative differences in approaches to teaching first year university science. *Higher Education*, 27, 75-84.

Influencing inclusive practice: the role of VLEs

Barbara Newland, Bournemouth University

Juliette Pavey, University of Durham

Victoria Boyd, University of Durham

Abstract

The use of Virtual Learning Environments (VLEs) within education has experienced a rapid increase internationally. Consequently there is a massive potential for them to have a positive or negative influence on encouraging inclusive practice in learning and teaching.

The Accessibility in Learning Environments and Related Technologies (ALERT) project examines the use of VLEs by disabled students. It focuses on the attainment of pedagogical objectives rather than the technical implications of VLE use by evaluating the implementation of a range of e-tivities such as online discussion, virtual chat and role play. ALERT aims to establish whether the use of a VLE makes learning easier for disabled students or whether it creates a further barrier. The project identifies ways of supporting students with a wide range of disabilities and is producing guidelines that have pedagogical, practical and strategic recommendations.

Introduction

VLEs provide students with easy access to an integrated set of learning resources including access to communication, assessment and group work tools. Access to these facilities is offered through a personalised portal, whereby students are presented with the courses that are relevant to them. This environment supports both flexible learning and an inclusive approach. Collis (2001) defines flexible learning as 'learner choice in different aspects of learning' and an inclusive approach is characterised by making sufficient provision so as to enable all students to have productive access to resources, regardless of their individual needs. This combination of flexibility and inclusivity has the potential to have great impact on students' experience, particularly disabled students (Pearson and Koppi, 2003, Grimaldi and Goette,1999).

Such flexibility enables self-paced learning, and the opportunity to adapt digital materials allows disabled students to customise resources to suit their learning needs. Learning through a VLE is a form of online learning, which is defined by Boettcher as 'an educational philosophy for designing interactive, responsive, and valid information and learning opportunities to be delivered to learners at a time, place, and in appropriate forms convenient to the learners' (Boettcher, 2004). Online learning can remove physical barriers to learning and encourage many forms of participation (Salmon, 2000).

Most commercial VLEs are technically accessible for disabled students. Commercial companies, such as Blackboard and WebCT, have a strong commitment to making sure their products are compliant with international legislation, such as Section 508 in the US and the Special Educational Needs and Disability Act 2001 (SENDA) in the UK. Much of this commitment is driven by the WAI (Web Accessibility Initiative), part of the WWW Consortium (W3C), which provides specifications and guidelines for the creation and interoperability of web-based materials.

Some disabled students use VLEs in conjunction with assistive technologies, such as voice recognition software, screen readers and alternative input devices. Many recent studies have considered the ways in which the experience of disabled students' use of a VLE may be supported and improved, focusing in particular on the technological aspects of software compliance with legislation and assistive technologies (Cowork, 2002, Stiles, 2001, Evans, 2003).

Richardson, Barnes and Fleming's research with hearing-impaired students and their approaches to study used a specially adapted Course Experience Questionnaire (CEQ) and Approaches to Study Inventory (ASI). They concluded that the disability does not have a significant effect on perception of academic quality and is not instrumental in the establishment of an approach to study (Richardson, Barnes and Fleming, 2004). However, it is plausible that the use of a VLE may impact on the learning approach adopted by the student, as the way in which it is used may encourage a surface, strategic or deep approach, as defined by the extensive work of Entwhistle and Ramsden (1983) and Biggs (1987). The differences in the way the VLE is used can be particularly problematic for students with additional needs, exemplified in Whitlock's support of Skinner's claim that 'failure to provide for differences among students is perhaps the greatest single source of inefficiency in education' (Whitlock, 2001).

Marton and Booth's analysis of approaches to learning suggests that students have distinctly different ways of understanding what learning is, and adopt an approach in accordance with a specific task (Marton and Booth, 1997). Again, in considering the experience of disabled students, the range of tasks that may be provided within a VLE may help them to adopt an approach that will enhance their learning.

The constructivist school of thought purports that education itself is a product of past and present influences on a learner and requires the amendment of schemata in order to induce learning (Fry, Ketteridge and Marshall, 2003). If a student's experience and environment are vital factors in the creation of a successful learning experience, then it follows that consideration must be given to learners with diverse educational needs, in order that adaptation of the learning environment (as a broad definition of the holistic educational experience) produces robust methods of active construction of knowledge (Biggs and Moore, 1993). Students and academics believe that the use of a VLE enhances their learning and teaching (Newland, 2003). However, it is vital that the VLE provides an inclusive curriculum.

According to the 2003 UCISA (Universities and Colleges Information Systems Association) report, 86% of all Higher Education Institutions (HEIs) in the UK now have a VLE in place (UCISA, 2003). The VLE market is also booming internationally, with commercial software forerunners Blackboard and WebCT citing partnerships in over 50 and 70 countries worldwide respectively (Blackboard, 2004, WebCT, 2004).

ALERT

ALERT is a Higher Education Funding Council for England (HEFCE) funded project being run between the University of Durham and Bournemouth University over a two year period. It is run in conjunction with the NDT (National Disability Team) within HEFCE's Strand 2 initiative for 'Improving provision for disabled students'.

Fourteen case studies have been undertaken across various departments and throughout all year groups where the impact of the VLE on individual and collaborative learning was assessed through a series of interviews. The study aims to facilitate a clearer understanding of the issues faced by disabled students with online learning. In addition, the participation of members of academic staff in providing information based on their own experience investigates how institution-wide support and staff development can be improved.

The outcomes give examples and provide guidelines as well as points for reflection and discussion. They are designed for use by academics and academic support staff such as learning technologists, staff developers and disability support staff. A database-driven web site and a series of themed leaflets are being produced from the outcomes.

Methodology

The ALERT project aims to provide guidelines for the development of inclusive practice in the use of VLEs. The guidelines are developed from this series of case studies with disabled students and academic staff. The case studies included a range of academic disciplines, disabilities and e-tivities. Salmon defines e-tivities as 'frameworks for online active and interactive learning' (Salmon, 2004). Details of the case studies are provided in the table overleaf.

The contributing students took part in two semi-structured interviews centred on their use of the VLE, levels of confidence in using computers and learning and teaching issues including their personal approaches to learning. All students were aged between 17 and 25 and were full time students at the University of Durham. Seventy per cent of those interviewed had been using a computer for more than ten years with the remainder varying between one and ten years, and 80% said that they were either confident or very confident computer users. By virtue of having used computers for such a long time, and

Academic discipline	Disability	E-tivity
Anthropology	Cerebral palsy	Animation
Computing science	Dyslexia	General usage
Economics	Dyspraxia	Online discussion
Geography	Hearing impairment	Online quizzes
Geology	ME	Role play
Law	Spinal problems	Use of media
Mathematics	Visual impairment	
Medicine	Wrist problems	
Sociology		

Table 1: Distribution of ALERT case studies according to subject, disability and focus

considering the age band of the participants, many of them are unable to remember a time when they did not use them as an integrated part of their education.

Interviews with academic staff were largely focused on their individual and departmental use of the VLE in teaching, and their observations of any effect the use of digital materials had on students' learning. Staff also spoke about their experience of supporting disabled students, and the role that they perceived the VLE played in the extended educational experience of students with a wide diversity of needs.

Both staff and student interviews provided a wealth of data from which themes emerged. However, the limited size of the sample means that it is inappropriate to make generalised conclusions.

Emerging themes

Despite the often varying needs of the students who took part in the interviews, as well as the nature of the academic discipline, particular aspects of the use of the VLE were mentioned consistently throughout the course of the case studies. These provide the focus for the guidelines that are being produced in the following areas:

- Provision of lecture support materials
- Use of synchronous discussion tools
- Use of asynchronous discussion tools
- Use of online assessment
- Consistency of use of the VLE
- Technical aspects
- Training needs

Each of these themes is considered from a pedagogical, practical and strategic point of view.

Pedagogical aspects of each theme are those that have an immediate impact on the direct learning experience of the students, such as the provision of lecture notes in advance of a lecture. Those classed as practical have a dimension that can be governed by staff intervention, for example, ensuring that lecture support materials are delivered in a usable and readable format. Strategic issues include liaison between members of academic staff in order to ensure a consistency in use of the VLE, in terms of content, appearance or navigation.

This paper focuses on the pedagogical, practical and strategic issues relating to the delivery of lecture support materials.

Provision of lecture support materials

One of the strongest and most permeating issues to arise has been that of the provision of lecture support materials through a VLE. Without exception, each of the student and staff participants had an opinion on this aspect of online course delivery, with all students stating that being given access to lecture notes had helped their learning.

Pedagogical issues

Independence

ALERT and Durham's annual evaluation (Newland et al, 2003) of the VLE have highlighted the value placed on the enhanced notes that come from annotation of the materials made available prior to the lecture. Students are then able to customise the materials themselves in order to make them more personally meaningful to develop their understanding.

Having lecture materials online also empowers some students who are unable to take their own notes. Rather than having to rely on classmates either taking or copying notes, students with, for example, wrist or handwriting problems are able to spend more time annotating the generic notes given to the class and thus attach their own interpretation. By learning from someone else's notes, students not only have the threat of 'secondary learning' as the transcribed data has already been interpreted by another student, but they also have a potential dependency and reliance on other classmates which may result in feelings of inequality in terms of the quality of the learning experience.

> *"I felt I just had to rely on friends who I didn't really know – cos I'd only been here for, like, a week – to copy their notes or photocopy them, and often their shorthand or their writing or their notes to themselves didn't make sense to me."* ALERT Student

Support

Along with students being able to familiarise themselves with material that will be presented in a lecture, having lecture notes available also allows students repeat access to potentially complex terminology and vocabulary. The availability of spellings of words helps with cognition and acts as a point of reference for students later on in a module. Furthermore, having information such as reading lists or links to web pages within the VLE allows students with cognitive disabilities to be able to work with a more focused and relevant array of materials. This also benefits students with mobility impairments, who are able to visit a library with a more specific list of the resources they seek, rather than being forced to spend longer looking for and physically carrying irrelevant resources. An advantage of the VLE is that it enables the student to benefit from the interoperability of digital resources.

> *"...you get the references and you can put them straight on to the online journal search thing and find the articles and get them there and then, and so it's really useful."* ALERT Student

Revision

Having printed and structured notes as a retrospective of the development of a module essentially provides students with a ready-made revision plan. At exam time, rather than having lecture notes that may be of a varying standard, and in some cases from different sources, students can refer back to an ordered and developmental collection of notes, which they have annotated with their own observations and interpretations. This structuring is also invaluable for students who have concentration or memory problems.

> *"...when you read back through my notes you can tell which lecture notes came up before and which ones didn't because the other ones are so much more disorganised compared to the ones which have been done beforehand."* ALERT Student

Practical issues

Timing

The provision of lecture notes before a lecture is often a controversial issue. Staff are concerned that students may no longer attend lectures. However, research into this has shown that only 1% of students feel that being given access to lecture materials in the VLE would result in their non-attendance to lectures (Newland et al, 2003).

Students stated that not only was it helpful to have lecture support materials available online before the lecture, but that having this resource available at least a day in advance allowed them to print the materials and familiarise themselves with concepts, terminology or complex diagrams before the face to face session. For students with slow reading and writing speeds and those with cognitive impairments such as dyslexia or dyspraxia, having advance knowledge of the content of the lecture enables them to listen more, without rushing to copy text.

> *"...it's a bit frustrating when they'll put (the lecture notes) on at kind of 10 o'clock in the morning when you've got a lecture 11 and you've had a lecture at 9 so you couldn't actually print it beforehand..." ALERT Student*

Format

The format of how lecture support materials might be delivered also has ramifications in terms of usability. Though the very nature of digital media enables students to customise materials to their own preferences, for students with concentration or memory problems, or for those with dexterity problems, this can be a laborious task.

> *"Some of the lecturers put stuff up in Word and that's kind of slide size, so it's like, point 18 or something, so that's quite time consuming to go through it all, change the size and re-shuffle it on the pages so it fits." ALERT Student*

Strategic issues

Consistency

The consistency of use of a VLE includes both navigational and content issues. An advantage of a VLE is that it can provide consistent navigation across a whole range of web pages, so that disabled students do not have to become familiar with different structures.

Student expectations are a significant factor in the planning and delivery of learning support materials through a VLE. As a result of this, consistency of use is a highly significant factor in the way online modules are used. Whether this pertains to the way information is organised, the visual appearance of the different modules or the navigation system, where staff work together to take a strategic and holistic approach to how their modules are delivered, students show a greater satisfaction with the learning experience. Additionally, some disabled students with cognitive impairments find significant changes in navigation confusing as their slow reading speed means that they must rely on memory to find certain documents or content areas.

> *"...I think continuity of layout of the different course pages is definitely (a problem)... and continuity of the way they're used as well...also clarity... and these aren't necessarily things which are lacking in my experience, but other people's experience, I see how they could be." ALERT Student*

Conclusions

The use of a VLE has many potential benefits for supporting the learning of disabled students. In order to maximise these benefits it is vital that staff take a pedagogical, practical and a strategic approach to their use of the VLE. Recommendations from the guidelines produced from the ALERT project will raise awareness on issues that disabled students face in their use of the VLE, and how use by academic and student support staff can be adapted to make the learning experience more inclusive.

Imperative to meeting student requirements is liaison between staff members; Finding out where extra support might be needed and collaboration between members of academic staff with those with a more technical focus and also disability support staff is key to ensuring the adoption of a more consistent approach. This pooling of specialised knowledge, and the shared responsibility in the decision-making process creates a solid foundation for a prescient and strategic use for the VLE, and ultimately, creates the potential for a more holistically inclusive environment.

By adopting a strategic and communally agreed approach, a number of benefits will be apparent through more consistent use of the VLE. These benefits, based on decisions relating to timing and format of the delivery of lecture support materials as well as on the appearance and architecture of the courses within the VLE, have the potential to impact considerably on the learning experience of not just disabled students, but all groups across the student population. By revising considerations into those that have pedagogical, practical and strategic implications, ALERT hopes to assist staff in taking a more considered approach to inclusive provision of materials through a VLE.

References

Blackboard (2004) www.blackboard.com/about/index.htm, accessed Nov 04

Biggs, J (1987) *Student approaches to learning and studying*, Australian Council for Educational Research, Hawthorn, Victoria

Biggs, J and Moore, P (1993) *The process of learning*, Prentice Hall, London,

Boettcher, JV (2004) *Teaching and learning online*, CSU Sacramento, http://www.csus.edu/uccs/training/online/overview/define.htm, accessed Nov 04

Collis, B and Moonen, J (2001) *Flexible learning in a digital world*, Kogan Page, London

Cowork (2002) http://techdis.ac.uk/archive/cowork/development/materials, accessed Nov 04 @note:broken link

Entwhistle, N and Ramsden, P (1983) *Understanding student learning*, Croom Helm, London

Evans, S, RNCB Hereford, Sutherland, A, TechDis and RNC Task Force, RNCB Hereford (2003) Virtual Learning Environment User Testing Project www.techdis.ac.uk/resources/VLE002.html, accessed Nov 04

Fry, H, Ketteridge, S and Marshall, S (2003) *A handbook for teaching and learning in higher education* 2nd Edition, Kogan Page, London

Grimaldi, C and Goette, T (1999) 'The internet and the independence of individuals with disabilities,' *Internet research: Electronic networking applications and policy*, Vol 9, No 4

Marton, F and Booth, S (1997) *Learning and awareness*, Lawrence Erlbaum Associates, New Jersey

Newland, B (2003) 'Evaluating the impact of a VLE on learning and teaching', Proceedings of EDMEDIA World Conference on Educational Multimedia, Hypermedia and Telecommunications, USA

Newland, B, Newton, A, Pavey, J, Murray, M and Boardman, K (2004) *VLE Longitudinal Report*, duo (Durham University Online) 2001–2003, IBSN 1-85899-185-4,

Pearson, E and Koppi, A (2003) 'Developing inclusive practices: Evaluation of a staff development course in accessibility'. *Australian Journal of Educational Technology*, 19(3), 275-292. http://www.ascilite.org.au/ajet/ajet19/pearson.html, accessed Nov 04

Richardson, JTE, Barnes, L and Fleming, J (2004) 'Approaches to studying and perceptions of academic quality in deaf and hearing students in higher education', *Deafness and Education International*, Vol 6, No 2

Salmon, G (2000) *E-moderating: the key to teaching and learning online*, Kogan Page, London

Salmon, G (2002) *E-tivities: the key to active online learning*, Kogan Page, London

Salmon, G (2004) www.atimod.co.uk/e-tivities/intro.shtml, accessed Nov 04

Stiles, MJ (2001) www.techdis.ac.uk/resources/stiles01.html, accessed Nov 04

UCISA (2003) www.ucisa.ac.uk/groups/tlig/vle/vle2003.doc, accessed Nov 04

WebCT (2004) www.webct.com/success, accessed Nov 04

Whitlock, Q (2001) 'Course design for online learning - what's gone wrong?', in Stephenson, J (Ed) *Teaching and learning online, pedagogies for new technologies*, Kogan Page, London

Student involvement and learning outcome in professional education in Norway

Anton Havnes and Per O Aamodt

Oslo University College

Abstract

The main purpose of this paper is to test how learning outcome among students in professional education is affected by the background of the students or characteristics of the learning environment of the institution. The analyses are based on a survey among students in their final year of professional education. The effects of students' family background are very weak. This is surprising, since school marks, which usually explain a considerable part of study results, strongly correlate with family background. The study effort, measured by average study hours per week, explains very little, but interactive and autonomous study strategies seem to lead to positive learning outcomes. Also teaching quality and social climate have an impact on learning outcome.

Introduction

The aim of this paper is to examine the impact of social background and study strategies on learning outcome among students in professional education. The topic addressed by the paper is one of general interest in education, psychology and educational sociology, but its starting point is local.

In Norwegian higher education a reform, The Quality Reform, has been implemented. It is both structural and pedagogical. Important changes are:

- a degree reform according to the Bologna declaration

- increased focus on teaching and the supervision of students

- changes in the assessment system away from final examinations towards coursework and portfolio assessment

A core aim is to improve the quality and efficiency in higher education, and the goal is formulated that "students should succeed in their studies". One of the main agendas for Norwegian higher education, as in many other countries, is that students are expected to work more and better, and the institutions are expected to implement structures and practices that work to reach these aims.

There are some basic assumptions underlying reforms in higher education. One is that there are some ways of studying that are of higher quality than other ways of studying. Institutional changes are expected to result in improved practice. Reforms are based on some assumptions about what makes a difference. But how certain are we about the outcomes of the changes that are implemented? Are there good reasons for the educational optimism that educational reforms are based on? How do the students learn? Are the resources for learning inside or outside of the higher education institutions? Are they internal or external to the didactic structure of the higher education institutions? There are different views on these questions. Among researchers different perspectives and disciplinary orientation create different views on the same issues. In this paper we will particularly look at the impact of background and contextual variables and the role of agency on study behaviour and finally on learning outcome. The approach has similarities with Biggs' (1989, 1993) model of classroom learning with presage, process and product as core components. Our model is different particularly in that it addresses social background and gender rather than students' preparedness for studying as individual traits.

The study is based on survey data from Oslo University College, the largest institution for professional education in fields like teacher training, social work, health sciences and engineering.

What makes a difference?

Sociology – societal reproduction

One view, mainly based on sociological theory is that the most influential sources for student learning are external to the educational context. Education tends to reproduce inequality and maintain existing social structures in society, and the individual students' preferences are related to the social class he/she comes from. Some students face cultural barriers, unfamiliar values etc when they enter higher education and will have more problems succeeding than others (Boudon 1974, Bourdieu and Passeron 1992). To explain how the social reproduction takes its form within education, sociological reproduction theories can be combined with typological psychological theories that focus on individual differences that students bring into higher education. Students act in congruence with their social background and with results accordingly. Social patterns manifest themselves in individuals as relative permanent personality traits resulting in preferences that are socio-culturally derived. From such perspectives we can expect students from higher social classes to be more involved and to place a higher value on learning activities that go beyond the minimum requirements than students with another social background.

On the other hand, new sociological theories tend to have less emphasis on the significance of social background and stress that young people are concerned about realising themselves and their own potentials (Maccoby 1989, Inglehart 1990). Focusing on future opportunities might compensate for the impact of socio-cultural background on student behaviour.

Pedagogy – facilitating learning

From a pedagogical or educational perspective, the different aspects of the educational setting and the pedagogical programme are attributed significance, rather than factors external to the institutional context. The point is to identify mechanisms within the educational context that support learning. Among educational perspectives we find a broad spectrum of such contextual dimensions that can facilitate student learning.

One approach has transmission of knowledge in focus and emphasises learning as a result of instruction and the aligning of the components of the learning material, skills and competences.

Another approach focuses on the individual student as an active agent. Students' conceptions of learning, their approaches to learning, and their learning strategies are viewed as primary mechanisms influencing the outcome of higher education. Learning is construction of knowledge based on the relationship between previous knowledge and skills. The activity of the individual is crucial for learning. Reviewing nearly 3,000 studies on the effect of university on students, Pascarella and Terenzini (1991 p610-611) concludes that

> *...the most inescapable and unequivocal conclusion we can make is that the impact of college is largely determined by the individuals' quality of effort and level of involvement in both academic and non-academic activities.*

> *Such a conclusion suggests that the impact of college is not simply the result of what a college does for or to a student. Rather, the impact is a result of the extent to which an individual student exploits the people, programs, facilities, opportunities, and experiences that the college makes available... it is the individual student who perhaps most determines the extent to which college makes a difference.*

Learning and agency

The current state of affairs in the area of research on student learning in pedagogical perspective is that the focus particularly is on the significance of the learning practices of individual agents in solitude or in collaboration with teachers and peer students. The emphasis is on the opportunities that students have to influence their own learning and how students appropriate them. But there is also an expansion from individually oriented approaches toward the more socially oriented ones. Biggs' (1993) systemic approach integrates students' activities with the activities of teachers as well as cultural and structural aspects of education. This does not represent a move back to learning being dependent on external factors. It is rather a move from learning as an independent and individual process, to learning as an interdependent and social process.

There are different views on the character of agency in learning. It can be attributed to the individual agent or viewed as an aspect of the relationship between the agent and his or her ambient environment. Winne (1995) argues for intensifying research on learning processes when students study mainly by themselves in chosen or forced solitude. "Learners should develop and have the will to exercise effective means for self-directing their learning…" Winne (ibid, p174). Vincent Tinto (1997), on the other hand, conceptualises colleges as communities of learners and emphasises that for most students, learning is enhanced when they find themselves in learning settings which require them to share the experience of learning and become connected learners.

Across the different views on agency and about the impact of individual work and interaction on learning, there is general agreement about the significance of student involvement.

Analytical approaches

This study takes an inter-paradigmatic approach. Its starting point is a continuum of factors to which researchers attribute influence on students' learning. In one end of the continuum we find a mainly structuralist approach focusing on how wider social structures underlie individual students' learning and socialisation. In this perspective, embedded in a mainly sociological research paradigm but linked to a psychological individualistic paradigm, the individual, and even the educational system, has little real influence on the students' development. Education sustains social reproduction.

Against this rather deterministic approach there is a scope of approaches that are more clearly pedagogically grounded. On the one hand we have the transmission or teaching-learning approach that attributes influence to the didactic programme and to teachers and teaching (Tyler 1950). The quality of the teaching and the didactic structures – or, more generally, characteristics of the institutional context – determines student learning practice and outcome.

Student agency in learning can be seen as the counter piece of instruction and predetermined social structures. But there is a diversity of notions of agency. The individual approach particularly focuses on the influence of the individual learner and his or her way of meeting the task of learning (Winne 1995, Bandura 1986, Zimmerman 1990). Others emphasise social interaction and cultural integration in communities of learners as basis for learning and attribute learning to the learning cultures in the ambient educational context, rather than to the individual as solitary actor (Tinto 1997, Lave and Wenger 1991, Engeström 1987, Sä ljö 2001). Peer-student interaction is highly regarded. This latter position focuses on learning as contextually situated practice. Agency is viewed as much as a response to what the educational context affords or demands as attributes of the individual. To understand human practice we have to study the context of action and interaction.

Taking an inter-paradigmatic position this study tries to investigate the relevance of various explanatory models. What impacts on student learning? We do not intend to answer this question in depth. Our main intention is to question the assumptions underlying educational reforms that we raised earlier.

Data and method

The paper is based on "StudData", a panel survey following student cohorts from entering higher education to two and four years after graduation. The present data set is based on those who completed their studies in spring 2001. The data was collected at the end of the students' final term, before their final exams. The data covers all professional programmes at this institution, some other state university colleges, and medical students at the University of Oslo. 3,067 questionnaires were distributed, and the total response rate was 70%, varying between 61% and 95% between programmes.

Data was distributed to, and completed by, students during their lectures. This means that students who do not attend classes regularly are underrepresented. So far, the analyses based on this dataset support our impression that there are not serious biases and that the representativeness could be considered satisfactory.

Clarification of variables

Background variables are of two kinds: gender and parents' education. Structural variables are the specific educational (professional) programme, as a set of six items measuring the teaching quality and two items measuring the social climate among the students. Study behaviour is defined through a factor analysis based on a set of questions about how students approach their studies.

One of our main challenges has been how to measure learning outcomes. Our survey data do not contain any examination marks or other "objective" measures. However, information about marks would probably not have helped us much, both since many modules of professional programmes are rated only as "passed" or "not passed", and since the assessment system and grading practice may vary considerably between programmes. We rely on the students' own self-reporting, and look for process indicators which may represent relevant measurements of student gains. Kuh, Pace and Vesper (1997) have assessed indicators to estimate student gains associated with good practice in undergraduate education, and their findings are particularly relevant for our paper. They conclude that students' assessment of experienced gain, or learning outcome, is a valid measure of academic achievement. Cassidy and Eachus (2000, p319) similarly found "self-reported proficiency within an academic field to be a positive predictor of academic achievement within that field". Another aspect is that low-achieving students tend to overestimate their achievement. High-achieving students, on the other hand, tend to underestimate their achievements (Boud and Falchikov 1989, Mowl and Pain 1995, Orsmorn et al 1997, Dochy et al 1999).

Learning outcome is measured by student assessment along a five point scale of what competencies they have gained from their study on 18 items:

- Broad, general knowledge

- Profession-specific knowledge

- Knowledge about planning and organisation

- Understanding on rules and regulations

- Ability to critically reflect and assess own work

- Ability to work under pressure

- Practical skills

- Ability to work independently

- Ability to collaborate

- Ability to take initiatives

- Personal engagement

- Oral communication skills

- Written communication skills

- Tolerance, ability to value others' opinions

- Leadership ability

- Ability take responsibility and to make decisions

- Ethical skills

- Empathy

These items differ somewhat from the instruments developed by Kuh and Pace, the College Student Experience Questionnaire (CSEQ), but the principle is the same.

The items were selected from a larger battery implemented by a large European study on the transition from higher education to work. The items are specially aimed at measuring competencies that are valued both in the work context and in education.

Results

According to our analytical approach, we will present the results in a stepwise way. We will shortly describe findings concerning students' study effort. Next, we will try to identify the dimensions of study strategies and how study strategies are affected by background factors, contextual factors and study effort, and finally, we will analyse how individual background, contextual factors, study effort and study strategies affect learning outcome.

Study effort

Previous studies (Wiers-Jenssen & Aamodt 2002, Aamodt 2003) found that the average number of hours studied per week was about 30. Also in the present data the average numbers of study hours is about 30 per week.

Study strategies

Study strategy could be defined in several ways, either as a one-dimensional index, or along different aspects or components. In the questionnaire, the students were asked if they agreed or not on a set of nine statements concerning their way of studying. The responses were given on a 7-point Likert scale. Based on the responses to these statements, we have conducted a factor analysis to identify the dimensions of study behaviour, and from the results of the factor analysis we have constructed indices to measure these dimensions.

		Factor 1	Factor 2	Factor 3	Communality
1	I try to take a critical attitude towards my subject	0.07	0.07	**0.66**	0.45
2	I prepare before classes	-0.18	0.16	**0.56**	0.37
3	I am usually present on campus only during classes	**0.58**	-0.32	0.36	0.57
4	I find it useful to discuss with other students	0.07	**0.70**	0.18	0.52
5	I raise questions to teachers about my study	-0.08	**0.56**	0.21	0.36
6	My studying is predominantly doing obligatory work	**0.77**	-0.05	-0.12	0.62
7	I prioritise what is expected of me at exams	**0.74**	0.05	-0.30	0.64
8	I often participate in student-initiated group work	-0.13	**0.75**	-0.08	0.58
9	I often read subject-matter that is not part of the syllabus	-0.39	0.11	**0.59**	0.51
	Eigenvalue	2,22	1,25	1,15	
	Accumulated explained variance	18,1	35,5	51,3	

Table 1: Study strategies: Factor analysis (principal components, varimax)

The three highest factor loadings on each factor are marked in bold.

The first factor identified has the three highest loadings on the statements 3, 6 and 7. We have described this study strategy as minimalist, in the sense that students do what they think is expected from them and not more. The notion of a minimalist strategy probably covers two meanings. One refers to time spent on studies; students spend the minimum time they think needed to reach their goals. The other refers to the tendency to focus only on the content that is minimally required by the system, eg problems, literature, exercises and assignments. Data that we are not including here also document that students with relatively low study effort tend to fall into the minimalist group. The second factor has the highest loadings on statements 4, 5 and 8. We have named this factor interactive, in the sense that it characterises a "social" study strategy where students participate actively in the learning environment, collaborate with other students and interact with teachers. The third factor has high factor loadings on items 1, 2 and 9. We have named this study behaviour autonomous, indicating that these students have an independent strategy and have preferences for working individually.

At this stage, we have not made any assessment on whether these three study strategies are "good" or "bad". In principle, at least at this stage in the analysis, all strategies may be favourable for achieving positive learning outcomes. But the minimalist strategy can be seen as being in contrast to high quality learning, which is often associated with independent learning, involvement in learning activities, "deep" learning and critical thinking.

Table 2 shows that the autonomous study strategy appears less often than the interactive or minimalist study strategy.

	Mean	Standard deviation	N
Minimalist	4.69	1.48	2,383
Interactive	4.49	1.28	2,381
Autonomous	3.90	1.16	2,384

Table 2: Mean scores on study strategies

Female students had a slightly more interactive study strategy than men; there were no gender differences on autonomous behaviour. Female students also reported a significantly stronger score on minimalist study strategy. Students with parents having higher education had a less minimalist study strategy, and a slightly stronger interactive strategy, while we found no effect of social background on autonomous study strategy.

The differences between study programmes are visualised in figure 1 (overleaf) for five programmes: teacher education, nursing, social work, engineering and medicine.

The profiles follow the same pattern across programmes, but nursing students had stronger predominant minimalist study behaviour than students in teacher education, social work and medicine. There were no significant differences between nursing and engineering. Engineering and medicine scored lowest on autonomous strategy, while an interactive strategy is most visible among engineering students. One explanation of the latter result could be engineering students spending much time in laboratories being guided by instructors and discussing with other students and they are often involved in project work.

Medicine is a university study, highly research-based and one of the most selective and prestigious study programmes; these are the only postgraduate students included in the survey. We could, therefore, expect medical students to show less minimalist and a stronger autonomous study strategy than state college students. This assumption is not supported by the results. If the autonomous-minimalist dimension characterises degree of

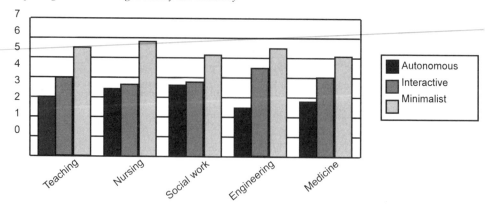

Figure 1: Study strategies in five study programmes[1]

'academic' study behaviour, medicine, according to this criteria, is not significantly more academic than the state college programmes.

Learning outcome

How is students' learning outcome affected by (1) background factors, (2) the study context, (3) study effort and (4) study strategies? Table 3 below shows the result and an analysis of learning outcome in relation to

	B	Std. Error
(Constant)	2.454	0.091
Gender (females=ref)	-0.207	0.024
Parents' education (ref=only basic school)		
Upper secondary level	-0.017	0.029
Higher education < 5 years	-0.023	0.029
Higher education 5+	-0.062	0.035
Study hours per week	0.002	0.001
Study behaviour:		
Minimalist	-0.016	0.008
Interactive	0.044	0.009
Autonomous	0.049	0.010
Teaching quality	0.118	0.010
Social climate among students	0.063	0.008
Adjusted R2:	0.188	

Table 3: Effects on learning outcome. Results of linear regression analysis.

[1]Estimated by linear regression.

- background variables (gender and parents' education)
- contextual variables (teaching quality and social climate)
- study behaviour (study effort and study strategy)

Male students report lower learning outcome than females. But we found no effect of parents' education. This is surprising, especially since there is a quite strong interrelation between social background and previous school achievement. In our data, we do not have information about school marks from secondary education, but Aamodt (2004 in a study based on another set of StudData) found that neither school marks nor parents' education had any effect on learning outcome, as it is operationalised here.

The impact of study strategy is more important than the impact of study effort. There is a significant, but rather small, positive effect on learning outcome of study effort. There is a slightly negative effect of minimalist study strategy, and positive effects of both interactive and autonomous study strategies.

Students' evaluation of both the quality of teaching and the social climate have positive effects; teaching quality in particular seems to be important.

In the next analysis, we want to compare whether the effects of study behaviour on learning outcome vary between study programmes. For these analyses, we have only included the largest programmes: teacher education, nursing, social work, engineering and medicine.

Since the number of observations for each study programme is rather small, we expect to "lose" some of the significant effects that we had in our analysis for all programmes together.

In these separate analyses, we find a negative learning outcome among male students compared to female students in teacher education. There is still no relationship between social background and learning outcome in our sample.

The effect of study effort is only persisting in social work and medicine, and there is no effect of a minimalist study strategy in any study programme. In engineering, which had the most interactive study strategy, this strategy also seems to have the strongest effect, an effect also found among students in teacher education. An autonomous study strategy had a slight effect only in teacher education.

Students' assessment of teaching quality has an important effect on learning outcome in all study programmes, while social climate had an effect in teacher education, social work and medicine, but not in nursing and engineering.

Our general impression is that there are some significant differences in how learning outcome is affected by the various variables in our models. Nursing deviates from the other study programmes by being affected only by teaching quality, no other factors. The explained variance is also much lower in nursing, which means that our analytical model

	Teacher education	Nursing	Social work	Engineering	Medicine
(Constant)	**2.306**	**2.849**	**2.112**	**1.806**	**1.633**
Gender	**-0.144**	-0.078	-0.144	-0.018	-0.056
Parents education (ref=only basic school)					
Upper secondary level	0.102	-0.077	0.049	-0.042	-0.201
Higher education < 5 years	0.062	-0.095	0.045	0.106	-0.252
Higher education 5+	-0.056	-0.005	0.169	0.115	-0.241
Study hours per week	-0.001	0.002	*0.006*	0.001	*0.006*
Study behaviour:					
Minimalist	-0.002	-0.013	0.005	0.041	-0.025
Interactive	**0.061**	0.025	0.044	**0.120**	0.069
Autonomous	*0.040*	0.020	0.034	0.027	-0.018
Teaching quality	**0.095**	**0.137**	**0.134**	**0.152**	**0.210**
Social climate among students	**0.091**	0.026	**0.079**	-0.012	**0.134**
R2 adjusted	0.165	0.082	0.197	0.179	0.275

Table 4: Programme-specific effects on learning outcome. Results of five separate linear regression analyses

explains less, and other unobserved factors more, among nursing students than the other programmes.

Discussion

In this paper we have tried to answer a series of questions concerning student involvement and learning outcome in professional education. Our primary intention was to investigate the explanatory power of a background variable against context variables and agency in learning.

Social background

Most striking is the result regarding the connection between social background and learning outcome. Earlier research has shown that there is a rather strong correlation between social background and school marks in upper secondary education, and also between school marks and learning outcome. Our data do not contain school marks, but we expected to find an effect of parents' education on learning outcome. We did not find any effect at all, which is quite surprising. This means that the social reproduction theory, which is regarded as important to explain educational preferences and choices, is not valid for explaining learning outcome, at least in professional education. A possible explanation could be that the graduating students have been selected during previous stages in the educational career, or that professional education favours a broader range of qualifications which are less affected by social background than traditional academic achievement.

We did find an impact in that students having parents with higher education are less inclined to study according to a minimalist, and have a slightly more interactive study strategy. To conclude, the effect of social background, as measured by the level of parents' education, is minor.

The background factor that turned out to have explanatory power is gender. Female students report a significantly higher learning outcome than male students. Female students also have higher study effort and a stronger interactive study strategy, but at the same time also a more minimalist study strategy.

College affects

Compared to the effects of individual background, we conclude that the effects of the study context, that is the specific characteristics of study programmes, are more dominant than background variables.

Our findings show that learning outcome, as students report, is significantly affected by the educational programme and the quality of teaching and the social climate. We find both direct effects of the study context (programme and teaching quality) on learning outcome, as well as indirect effects where the study programme affects the study effort and the study strategies of the students. Another important finding is that the social climate among peers seems to affect the learning outcome. Learning is hence not entirely promoted by the students' interaction with the teachers, but also in collaboration with other students.

We find the most significant differences between educational programmes. There are dramatic differences in how much time students spend on their studies between different programmes, from an average of 44 hour per week in arts and design to less than 27 hours in library. Similarly, there are significant differences between students' study strategies in different programmes. We do not know what aspects of the programmes created these differences. Some of the findings are surprising, eg that in a "hard fact" programme like engineering, students show preference for an interactive study strategy while students in social work do not. In this respect engineering students differ from students in economics and administration, which could also be regarded as more "hard facts" programmes.

These results indicate that the structure of the educational programme has an impact on how students work and the outcomes of their studies. One of our main findings is that the study context, that is field of study, teaching quality etc, has great impact both on the study behaviour and the learning outcome of students. Students' learning is not predominantly determined by their background. Pedagogical research paradigm seems to have stronger explanatory power than sociological explanations, with few exceptions.

Agency

Agency refers to the impact of study behaviour on learning outcomes. Our study show that study strategy impacts on learning outcome. A minimalist study strategy is combined with lower learning outcome than an interactive and autonomous strategy.

The study documents that interactive and autonomous study strategies are more favourable than a minimalist strategy. These findings support the principle for good teaching and learning discussed by Chickering and Gamson (1987). This is also in line with eg Tinto (1987) who emphasises the importance of academic and social integration (both formal and informal) for succeeding in higher education.

In this study it is clear that student agency in learning is an intermediate variable. It impacts on learning outcomes, but it is itself an effect of the educational programme. Different programmes seem to promote different study strategies. But the situation is more complex, because we find more than one strategy to be significant in several programmes. For example, the two categories female students and engineering students both have a combination of a minimalist and an interactive strategy. These two strategies might not exclude each other. Minimalism in the meaning of focusing on what is (minimally) required can go together with an interactive strategy. Students can have preference for discussing the (minimally) required. Similarly, the autonomy strategy is not in conflict with an interactive, but we have found no such link in our material. The combination of an autonomous and a minimalist strategy, that we find eg in teacher education and in medicine, seems more problematic. While the combinations minimalist/interactive and autonomous/interactive seem possible, the minimalist and autonomous strategies seem to exclude each other as individual study strategies. But a programme can afford, even actively initiate, strategies that are exclusive to each other by being contradictory in its requirements to students. Another, more friendly, explanation is that a programme has an open form and open up for, even support, different ways of learning.

Final comments

Coming back to the questions we posed in the beginning, our study gives support to the educational optimism that underlies educational reforms. Changes in the learning context will have impact on students' learning practice and the learning outcomes. The main mechanisms influencing the quality of learning are internal to the educational context. The study does not point to what factors internal to the educational programme have impact and what changes should be made to increase the quality of studies. To come to terms with such questions we would need another, and probably more qualitative, research design.

Bibliography

Aamodt, PO (2003) Tidsbruk og studieinnsats. I Aamodt, PO and Terum LI (eds): Hvordan, hvor mye og hvorfor studerer studentene? HiO-rapport 2003 nr. 8

Aamodt, PO (2004): Studiestrategier og studieutbytte. I Abrahamsen, B and Smeby J-C (eds): Sykepleierstudenten – Rekruttering, studietilfredshet og studieutbytte. HiO-rapport 2004 nr 7

Bandura, A (1986). From thought to action: Mechanisms of personal agency. New Zealand Journal of Psychology, 15, pp1-17.

Biggs, JB (1993): From theory to practice: A cognitive systems approach, Higher Education Research and Development, 1/93.

Biggs, JB (1989). Approaches to the enhancement of tertiary teaching. Higher Education Research and Development, 8(1), 7-25.

Boud, D and Falchikov, N (1989) Quantitative studies of student self assessment in higher education: a critical analysis of findings, Higher Education, 18, pp529–549.

Boudon, Raymond (1974): Education, Opportunity, and Social Inequality. New York:

Bourdieu, P and Passeron, J-C (1992). Reproduction in education, society, and culture (2nd edition), translated by Lois Wacquant. London and Newbury Park, Calif.: Sage.

Cassidy, S and Eachus, P (2000) Learning style, academic belief systems, self-report student proficiency and academic achievement in higher education. Educational Psychology, Vol. 20, No. 3, pp307-322.

Chickering, AW and Gamson, ZF (1987) Seven principles for good practice in undergraduate eduation. Wingspread Journal, 9(2), special insert.

Dochy, F, Segers, M and Sluijsmans, D (1999) The use of self-, peer and co-assessment in higher education: a review. Studies in Higher Education, Vol. 24, No. 3, pp331-350.

Dæhlen and Havnes (2003) Å studere eller gå på skole. Studiestrategier i profesjonsutdanningene [Studying or going to school. Study strategies in professional education]. HiO-rapport no. 8, 2003.

Engeström, Y (1987). Learning by expanding. Helsinki: Orienta-Konsultit Oy.

Inglehart, R (1990): Culture shift in advanced industrial society. Princeton, NJ: Princeton University Press.

Kuh, GD, Pace CR and Vesper, R (1997) The development of process indicators to estimate student gains associated with good practices in undergraduate education. Research in Higher Education, 38(4), pp435-454

Lave, J and Wenger. E (1991). Situated Learning. Legitimate Peripheral Participation. Cambridge: Cambridge University Press.

Maccoby, M (1989): Hvorfor jobber vi? Om motivasjon og nye generasjoners verdivalg og krav til arbeidsmarkedet. Oslo: Dagens Næringsliv Forlag.

Mowl, G and Pain, R (1995) Using self and peer assessment to improve students' essay writing: a case study from geography, Innovations in Education and Training International, 32(4), pp324-335.

Orsmorn, P, Merry, S and Reiling, K, (1997) A study in self-assessment: Tutor and students' perceptions of performance criteria, Assessment and Evaluation in Higher Education, Vol. 22, 4.

Pascarella, ET and Terenzini PT (1991). How college affects students. San Francisco: Jossey-Bass

Sä ljö, R (2001) Lä rande i praktiken. Ett sociokulturellt perspektiv. Stockholm, Prisma.

Tinto, V (1987): Leaving college: rethinking the causes and cures of student attrition. Chicago: The University of Chicago Press.

Tinto, V (1997). Classrooms as communities: Exploring the educational character of student persistence. Journal of Higher Education, 68, pp599-623.

Tyler R (1949) Basic principles of curriculum and instruction. Chicago, Chicago University Press.

Wiers-Jenssen, J and Aamodt PO (2002): Trivsel og innsats. Studenters tilfredshet med lærested og tid brukt til studier. Resultater fra "Stud.mag."- undersø kelsene. Rapport 1/2002. Oslo: Norsk institutt for studier av forskning og utdanning.

Winne, PH (1995). Inherent details in self-regulated learning, Educational Psychologist 4/97, pp173-87.

Zimmerman, BJ (1990). Self-regulated learning and academic achievement: An overview, Educational Psychologist 1/9, pp3-17.

The dynamics of motivation, life experience and conceptions of knowing of students from non-standard academic backgrounds

Jenny Morris, Colchester Institute, UK

Abstract

This exploratory, longitudinal, qualitative study investigated the experiences and perceptions of students from non-standard academic backgrounds as they progressed through a part-time undergraduate vocational degree programme. Up to seventeen students were interviewed on five occasions on a number of topics relevant to their learning experiences. Phenomenographic analysis was undertaken on the data relating to motivation, the influence of their life experience, their conceptions of 'learning' and 'understanding' and the relationships between understanding and memorisation. A rich, positive picture emerged which reinforces the place of such students in higher education.

Introduction

It has been recognised that so-called 'non-standard' university students present with a number of characteristics which differ from the standard school leaver eg mature age, different academic backgrounds. Widespread debate has considered whether such students are 'suitable' for university education and/or whether university education is appropriate for them without a need to dumb down or alter its fundamental purpose and nature (Richardson, 1994). The large increase in students from non-standard backgrounds in higher education in the UK is likely to have had an effect and it is important to monitor and evaluate the impact of higher education on these students in addition to their influence on higher education. Richardson's (1994) assertion still holds true that much of the research so far relating to this student group has focused on their academic outcomes per se with limited consideration of their actual learning experiences in higher education. This study aims to go some way towards addressing this imbalance.

The study

The subjects were students on a four year part-time undergraduate physiotherapy programme which had been specifically designed to offer employees in the health sector an opportunity to qualify as physiotherapists. Although a number of part-time physiotherapy programmes are now available in the UK, at the time the study began in 2001 the programme was unique in physiotherapy education, as were the students in terms of their backgrounds. In recognition of these unique features, a broad ranging longitudinal qualitative investigation was undertaken in order to explore the experiences of the students while on the programme in order to identify and evaluate the influence of a number of intrinsic and extrinsic variables on their learning.

In addition to a philosophy of widening access, the programme design follows an ethos of a coherent model of learning based on established educational research evidence. The learning experiences offered to students aim to facilitate achievement of optimal quality of learning and enable them to continue their professional development as self-directed learners after graduation. Strategies include learning of relevant, integrated material, active participation of students in the learning process and overt recognition and use of students' life experience (Ramsden, 1992; Wilss et al, 1999).

The scope of content of the study was determined by established research into a number of factors which have been demonstrated to influence students' learning outcomes. These were motivational factors (Biggs, 2003) and student's conceptions of the nature of 'learning' (Prosser and Trigwell, 1999) and 'understanding' (Entwistle and Entwistle, 2001) and the relationship they perceive between understanding and memorisation (Meyer, 2000). The meaning of the word 'understanding' in the study is that used by Entwistle and Entwistle (2001) as comprehension or 'grasping the overall meaning'. In addition, the students' experiences of the different learning and assessment formats used on the programme were explored. Finally, the impact of their past and continuing clinical experiences on their learning (Wilss et al, 1999) was also investigated.

Sample

The students in the cohort under consideration were employed either as physiotherapy or rehabilitation assistants and continued in this employment when not attending college or undertaking clinical placement learning. Some subjects were under 21 years of age at commencement of the programme, but the majority were of mature age. They had a variety of academic entry qualifications ranging from A levels through access courses and first degrees. Although possession of A levels or a degree may raise questions as to their 'non-standard' status, the levels of attainment, in almost all cases, would not have reached the minimum entry requirements for standard full-time physiotherapy programmes. Their continuing employment in the area of their study was definitely not the norm.

Seventeen of the 23 students in the 2000 cohort took part in the study. Sampling was purposive overall, as the experiences of students with a wide range of background characteristics were sought, in order to obtain as full a picture as possible. Volunteers were first identified and then others approached directly. No lower limit had been set on the number of participants. However, a proportionally large number was needed to account for possible wastage owing to the longitudinal nature of the study. As part of obtaining ethically sound informed consent, the status of the investigator as one of their tutors was taken into account and addressed.

Data collection

Five sets of semi-structured interviews were undertaken as students progressed through the course. These took place before Easter in year 1, before Christmas in year 2, at the end of year 2, before Easter in year 3 and around the Easter vacation in year 4. This timetable allowed for consideration of the whole learning experience of the students.

The interview questions addressed a number of relevant topic areas, including the following, which are presented in this paper: motivational issues relevant at that stage of the programme, the influence of past clinical experience on clinical placement learning and the conceptions held by students at the time of each interview around learning, understanding and memorisation. These conceptions were explored at each interview in order to identify any change for the group and for individuals over time. Most studies have only investigated these cross-sectionally and not longitudinally.

All the interviews were undertaken by the same interviewer and lasted around 45 minutes each. They were tape recorded and then transcribed, using anonymous numbering, for analysis (transcriptions for Interview 5 were incomplete at the time of writing this paper).

Data analysis

A phenomenographic approach was followed throughout, with hierarchical relationships sought among identified categories of description. The anonymously labelled transcriptions for the first four sets of interviews were read and coded manually while the tape recordings for Interview 5 were coded directly from the recordings.

The phenomenographic staged process of analysis described by Marton, (1988), Entwistle and Entwistle (1992) and Trigwell (1997) was followed. Firstly, a manual coding system was used to identify all relevant responses to each of the questions on each transcript or tape. In identifying responses, the importance emphasised by Marton (1988) of the responses being considered in relation to their context and not just to the words themselves was borne in mind. For each set of interviews, categories of description which encapsulated the content of the identified responses were then provisionally named. Interviewee numbers were also recorded in order to allow for easy referral back to the transcripts or tapes.

The second stage of analysis involved reviewing and sorting the provisional categories and identifying groups of similar responses. The resultant categories were then reviewed, with reference to the transcripts or tapes, when necessary, until all the responses had been included and the full range of clearly defined categories of description had been identified. The transcriptions were then revisited to record quotations for each category of description which were representative of the range of responses represented by each category (no quotations are available for Interview 5). Doing this at this stage, rather than extracting quotations during the grouping process, allowed for further review of the accuracy of category allocation, as responses were again read in context. Completion of this process ended the iterative process (Marton, 1981; Booth, 1997). The wording of each category was reviewed to ensure that it was succinct and true to the meaning it was presenting and also to ensure that each category was unique and independent of the others.

Finally, the content of the outcome space for each topic addressed was studied in order to identify whether a hierarchical relationship existed among the categories of description. This process was undertaken because such internal relationships among categories of description have been argued to be a feature of the results of phenomenographic research (Booth, 1997; Trigwell, 1999).

Results

All 17 subjects completed Interviews 1 and 3, 16 undertook Interview 2, 15 completed Interview 4 and 13 undertook Interview 5. Fourteen interviewees were female and three male. Two of the females were under 21 at the start of the programme. The age range on first registration was 19–51 years (mean age 29 years). Academic entry qualifications included A levels, access, NVQ Level III, BTech National Diploma, ITEC diploma and undergraduate degrees.

Two summary tables are presented for each topic area. The first identifies the categories of description which resulted from the analysis while the second provides representative quotations for each of the categories of description which formed the final outcome space. The first table also identifies the categories of description which arose during each of the five sets of interviews. The numbers identify the total number of students at each stage who had responses which informed each category. The inclusion of numbers in addition to the categories of description themselves is different from the usual way of presenting the findings in the phenomenographic approach, but these have been included in order to identify the frequency of responses within each category. This allows for both comparison across the interviews, but also provides useful information on the number of responses within each category, information which identification of the categories alone does not provide.

Motivational factors

Table 1 opposite summarises the motivational factors identified at each set of interviews and table 2, overleaf, contains the quotations which represent the range of responses which are included within each category. No hierarchical relationship was found among the categories of description. As a means of recognising apparent groupings among the categories, these were initially grouped as either positive or negative in nature and then each group further subdivided into 'intrinsic' or 'extrinsic' sub-headings, if present

A number of approaches to classifying motivational factors exist which could have been followed. This two group system was followed as it represented the motivational factors identified in the literature relevant to university students from non-standard backgrounds well. Pintrich and Schunk's (1996) definitions were used when grouping the categories.

Categories of description	Interview 1 (17)	Interview 2 (16)	Interview 3 (17)	Interview. 4 (15)	Interview. 5 (13)
Positive					
Intrinsic					
Interest in nature and practice of physiotherapy	15			1	4
Want to be a physiotherapist	8				10
Still want to do it		9	10	7	
Learning achieved		5	5		5
Extrinsic					
Career/academic development aspirations	9				
External support and expectations	7	3	1		6
Progress made/can see the end		6	14	13	
Placement experiences			5		3
Familiarity with course requirements				1	
Negative					
Extrinsic					
High workload		5	2		4
Less practical work on course			1		2
Less clinical learning				2	
Increasing amount of self-directed study				1	
Poor placement experiences			2		
Long way to go		1			
External pressures			1		5

Table 1 Motivational factors – summary table

Categories of description	Representative quotations
Positive *intrinsic*	
Interest in nature and practice of physiotherapy	'...it's the subject... this is what I'm interested in.' (I1 S17) 'Because I'm interested in it and the sort of thinking and using your initiative involved.' (I1 S7)
Want to be a physiotherapist	'I always wanted to do it.' (I1 S2) '...just working as an assistant and working with the physios and seeing how you can, what you can achieve as a physio and I thought 'Yes'.' (I1 S16)
Still want to do it	'It's still what I want to do...' (I3 S12) 'I'm still motivated to finish the course... and get qualified.' (I4 S1)
Learning achieved	'...the more we've learned the more interesting I've found it.' (I2 S13) 'I feel a bit more confident (having passed earlier assessment)' (I3 S14)
Positive *extrinsic*	
Career/academic development aspirations	'It's further learning that appeals really, to learn, to know a lot about something...' (I1 S5) 'I wanted to better myself really. I'd like to have a degree' (I1 S10)
External support and expectations	'It's for my family as well.' (I1 S11) 'my Mum and Dad keep going 'Oh it's only two more years...'.' (I3 S15)
Progress made/can see the end	'You see that there is light at the end of the tunnel' (I2 S10) '...you sort of count the years down...and that kind of keeps the motivation going...' (I4 S12)
Placement experiences	'...the last placement I found very interesting and I thought, once again I realised that that is what I want to do...' (I3 S7)
Familiarity with course requirements	'...we've become a lot more familiar with the ways of studying and the ways you like us to work, so that really helped...' (I4 S14)
Negative *extrinsic*	
High workload	'The amount of work we've got to do I think has actually decreased my motivation' (I2 S4)
Less practical work on course	'...the practical things in college are going to stop...the things that really motivate me for coming will start to stop...' (I3 S17)
Less clinical learning	'I've lost a lot of motivation... because we're doing less clinical stuff...' (I4 S5)
Increasing amount of self-directed study	'...we've been doing a lot of self-study... so you've really had to work on your own...so it's been quite hard to motivate yourself...' (I4 S1)
Poor placement experiences	'I think the de-motivation has a lot to do with my clinical placement.' (I3 S6)
Long way to go	'Sometimes you think, oh dear, it's such a long way off.' (I2 S6)
External pressures	'It (motivation) did take a bit of a nosedive... but I think was mainly because of personal issues' (I3 S9)

They define intrinsic motivation as 'motivation to engage in an activity for its own sake' and extrinsic motivation as 'motivation to engage in an activity as a means to an end' in which individuals work on tasks 'because they believe that participation will result in desirable outcomes'.

It is important to note that there were some differences in the question asked at different stages of the study. For Interview 1 students were asked why they had decided to take on the programme, for Interviews 2 – 4 the questions were around how their motivation felt at that stage of the course and the responses for Interview 5 reflect an overview of positive and negative influences on their motivation across the course as a whole.

Influence of assistant experience on learning during clinical placements

The categories of description and representative quotations are presented in tables 3 and 4. This topic was not addressed in Interview 1 as the students had not yet undertaken a clinical placement. In Interviews 2 – 4 the question related to placements which had been

Categories of description	Int. 2 (16)	Int. 3 (17)	Int. 4 (15)	Int. 5 (13)
Positive				
Experience and skills				
Have experience and skills				2
Communication skills	13	6	9	10
Familiar with environment	11	3	6	2
Professional behaviour established			1	
Influences on learning				
More confident	3			
More relaxed	1		1	1
Learning easier	4			
Quicker progress and greater responsibility	10	1	2	6
Able to use initiative more			2	
Felt able to question clinicians	1			
Others				
Treated as a student	7			10
Able to learn while at work	1			
Support from work colleagues			1	
Maturity the advantage	1			
Negative				
Stayed/kept in assistant role	8	2		1
Educators' expectations high	5			
Difficulty delegating to assistants	3			

Table 3 Influence of assistant experience on clinical placement learning – summary table

Opposite: table 2 Motivational factors – quotations.

Categories of description	Quotations
Positive *experience and skills*	
Have experience and skills	(from Interview 5)
Communication skills	'it... did make it a lot easier for me because having just the experience of being able to communicate with people...' (I2 S12) '...the way we spoke to patients, we already had that slight edge because we'd worked with patients for so long.' (I3 S13)
Familiar with environment	'You more or less know how things work, how things are run.' (I2 S6) '...you know almost where to find something, you have a clue of where they might be.' (I3 S17)
Professional behaviour established	'...your professionalism is there...' (I4 S10)
Positive *influences on learning*	
More confident	'They're (clinical educators) happy to let you go off on your own a lot earlier purely because you are obviously more confident.' (I2 S15) '...it (experience) made me feel more confident...' (I2 S14)
More relaxed	'You're more relaxed...' (I2 S9) '...you can... almost relax into things a lot quickly than maybe if you don't have that other experience.' (I4 S12)
Learning easier	'I'd probably be more out of my depth if I hadn't had some experience.' (I2 S2) 'It made if a lot easier for... me to pick up things.' (I2 S12)
Quicker progress and greater responsibility	'...you quite often get the impression that the educators are happy to let you go off and see a patient on your own...' (I3 S5) 'once I got a caseload then I was really able to work' (I4 S16)
Able to use initiative more	'you're just more used to using your initiative a bit more' (I4 S1)
Felt able to question clinicians	'...like we got into a few debates with the physios on why we do this and why we do that.' (I2 S14)
Positive *others*	
Treated as a student	'I was treated like how a normal student would have been.' (I2 S1) 'I wasn't treated as an assistant at all.' (I2 S7)
Able to learn while at work	'...analysing your physios (at work), watching your physios, how they work is really really helpful.' (2 S11)
Support from work colleagues	'...the staff (at work) are very supportive... and I feel that that's helped me when I go on placements.' (I4 S2)
Maturity the advantage	'I don't know if being an assistant, you know, I think that being a more mature student helps.' (I2 S11)
Negative	
Stayed/kept in assistant role	J: 'Do you feel that at any time you were being used as an assistant rather than treated like a student?' S: 'To a certain extent I would say 'Yes...'.' (I2 S8) 'I tend to start off taking the role of the assistant still.' (I3 S5)
Educators' expectations high	'Sometimes I think they expected too much.' (I2 S4) 'I think you are expected to be more familiar with certain things.' (I2 S6)
Difficulty delegating to assistants	'I find it really hard to ask someone who is at the same level as me to do something for me.' (I2 S4)

Table 4 Influence of assistant experience on clinical placement learning.

undertaken in the time period since the previous interview. As with the motivational factors, the question in Interview 5 asked students to give an overview of their placements throughout the programme.

The responses fell into groups of either positive or negative influences and these are used in the tables. Within the positive group, some categories of description formed natural sub-groupings and the outcome space has been presented under these sub-headings. The only area in which hierarchical relationships were found was in the 'Influences on learning' sub-group among the positive categories and these categories of description have been presented in hierarchical order.

Conceptions of learning

The question asked at each interview was 'How do you know when you've learned something?' In order to optimise the likelihood of obtaining useful longitudinal data, in Interviews 2 – 5 the students were asked to give their perceptions at that time and not to try to remember what their responses had been during earlier interviews.

Although familiar, the research literature on conceptions of learning by Säljö (1979) and Marton et al (1993) was not used as a guidance framework during identification of the categories of description. It was used, however, when seeking hierarchical relationships among the identified categories in order to use the same approach to deciding the basis for accepting the presence of a hierarchy. For those categories which match those identified by Säljö and Marton et al the relevant number is given in brackets after the category title. The order in which the categories of description are presented in tables 5 and 6 may or may not be hierarchical. This and related issues will be addressed in the discussion.

Categories of description	Interview 1 (17)	Interview 2 (16)	Interview 3 (17)	Interview 4 (15)	Interview 5 (13)
Knowledge accessible/able to recall (2)	12	6	10	7	3
Able to use/apply learning (effectively) (3)	5	5	6	7	4
Able to tell/explain to others (effectively)	6	5	8	6	9
Know you know it	1	2		1	
Understand it/it makes sense (4)	2	4	4	2	1
Able to process/discuss learning		8	4	2	
Able to reason/modify behaviour/actions			3		
Look at things differently (6)		1			

Table 5 Conceptions of learning – summary table

Categories of description	Quotations
Knowledge accessible/able to recall (2)	'because you don't have to think about it.' (I1 S1) '...when I recall things without any prompting.' (I1 S15) '...and I know what I've learned...' (I3 S15)
Able to use/apply learning (effectively) (3)	'...you're able to use the information you've got.' (I3 S16) '...if I know how to implement knowledge practically on a patient.' (I2 S4) '...when you're able to apply it and you're getting the results you expect.' (I4 S8)
Able to tell/explain to others (effectively)	'...I can describe it to someone, explain it...' (I3 S16) 'When you can explain it to somebody else and they understand what you're saying' (I1 S9) '...I should be able to teach someone else how to do it and they should be able to do that and get something out of it.' (I2 S17)
Know you know it	'I know whether I know it or don't.' (I2 S7) '...knowing that you know it...' (I1 S16)
Understand it/it makes sense (4)	'When I've understood it...' (I1 S7) '...everything then kind of fits into place.' (I2 S14) 'It just clicks all of a sudden... it's like the lights have been switched on.' (I4 S3)
Able to process/ discuss learning	'Because you are able to see where it links in...' (I2 S2) 'You know how to talk about it afterwards' (I2 S10) '...having a debate and stuff and you know what you're actually talking about...' (I3 S14) '...when I can go away and think about it and sort of think about the implications of it...' (I4 S5)
Able to reason/modify behaviour/ actions	'Because you know you can apply it and see your outcomes and adapt them if you know they're not right and know what to adapt them to.' (I3 S2) '...because when I'm at work I try to think about why people are treating patients like that, or why the patient is why they are and what's causing the problem, trying to apply that knowledge' (I3 S5)
Look at things differently (6)	'...if you see something and you start, you sort of, the way you're thinking and looking at things is different.' (I2 S12)

Table 6 Conceptions of learning – representative quotations

Conceptions of understanding

The question 'How do you know when you've understood what you've learned?' was asked after the question on conceptions of learning. Again, students' perceptions at the time of the interview were sought.

The categories of description were first identified directly from the interview transcripts and then compared with those which have been identified in the literature. Less work has been undertaken on this concept than on conceptions of learning and the Entwistle and Entwistle (1992) study of final year students' thinking round understanding was the main source of comparison. As for conceptions of learning, a hierarchical relationship was sought. The outcome space is presented in tables 7 and 8 (overleaf). Those categories of description which are the same as those found by Entwistle and Entwistle (1992) are marked with an asterisk (*).

Categories of description	Interview 1 (17)	Interview 2 (16)	Interview 3 (17)	Interview 4 (15)	Interview 5 (13)
Knowledge accessible/able to recall	2	1	3	1	
Learning retained over time	1	1			
Able to use/apply learning	4	3	3	4	5
Able to tell/explain to others (effectively)*	7	8	11	8	7
Feedback from outcomes			4		
Know you know it /it makes sense*	10	4	4	2	2
Understand what others are saying		2			
Able to process/discuss learning	1	3	1	3	2
Able to transfer learning in different contexts*		3	4		
Able to relate/link learning	2				

Table 7 Conceptions of understanding

Relationship between understanding and memorisation

This question was the final one asked in this section of the interviews and followed the one on conceptions of understanding. The wording varied, but essentially asked students to identify how they felt understanding and memorisation related to each other. In order to avoid directing responses, the order in which 'understanding' and 'memorisation' were included in the questions was varied among interviews at one stage and at different stages.

As for the other conceptions, influence of the literature on the relationship between memorisation and understanding on identifying the categories of description was avoided. This appropriate approach raised some interesting differences between the

Categories of description	Quotations
Knowledge accessible/ able to recall	'Once I can come up with an answer almost before someone else.' (I1 S13) '...if I have it in my head after you've learned something ...you can see it in front of you, then you know you understand it.' (I3 S7) 'If I don't understand I won't be able to remember it.' (I4 S17)
Learning retained over time	'...if I learn something and I remember that next year.' (I2 S4) 'If you understand something that knowledge is always going to be there.' (I1 S16)
Able to use/apply learning	'...I know how to use my knowledge and put that into practice.' (I4 S4) 'I think if you can apply it to something... then you know you've understood it.' (I3 S8) 'Because I know what I'm doing.' (I2 S14)
Able to tell/explain to others (effectively)*	'...when I'm able to tell someone else about it...' (I1 S7) 'You can explain it to other people.' (I3 S15) '...if I can put across what I perceive it to be... and they say 'Yes that's right'.' (I2 S12)
Know you know it/it makes sense*	'I just know when I've understood it.' (I3 S6) '...you know in your own mind and can link it to other things...' (I3 S15) '...all the pieces of the jigsaw fit together really...' (I1 S10) 'When I make sense out of it.' (I2 S7)
Understand what others are saying	'...if somebody else will say something and I think 'Oh yes, I knew that' then I think 'Yes, maybe I have understood it' (I2 S12) '...I go away and start reading it then I think 'Oh yes' and it kind of triggers it to come back and then I know that I have actually understood it.' (I2 S13)
Able to process/discuss learning	'It's being able to sort of reason round it and sort of justify your choices...' (I3 S2) 'When I can have a conversation with people and talk about it and think 'Well that's not right...' (I1 S14)
Able to transfer learning in different contexts *	'Understanding is when you can take it across.' (I2 S8) '...I can apply it to something else, not just to the one thing...' (I3 S12)
Able to relate/link learning	'When you can fit it into a bigger picture.' (I1 S17) '...able to relate it to something else in life' (I1 S6)

Table 8 Conceptions of understanding – representative quotations.

nature of content of the identified categories identified in the study and those identified in the literature. These will be considered in the discussion.

In tables 9 and 10, those categories of description which have the word 'understanding' before 'memorisation' have been presented first. This arrangement reflects the evidence in the literature that this order generally represents more desirable perceptions in terms of student learning (Meyer, 1999). Hierarchical relationships among categories of description on this topic area have not been identified in the literature. As part of the phenomenographic approach being used, however, the categories found in this study were scrutinised. The only possible hierarchy was identified between the first two categories listed in the tables.

Categories of description	Interview 1 (17)	Interview 2 (16)	Interview 3 (17)	Interview 4 (15)	Interview 5 (13)
Understanding before memorisation	11	10	7	8	8
Understanding aids/facilitates/required for memorisation	10	11	10	6	3
Understanding and memorisation concurrent			8	6	2
Memorisation before understanding	1				1
Repetition after memorisation facilitates understanding	2				
Memorisation aids understanding					1

Table 9 Memorisation/understanding relationship

Categories of description	Quotations
Understanding before memorisation	'I think understanding comes first...' (I4 S2) 'I personally would try to always understand things before memorising it.' (I3 S7)
Understanding aids/facilitates/required for memorisation	'I don't really think you can remember something that well before you understand it.' (I2 S1) 'I think the only way that you can memorise things is... to understand them.' (I3 S10) '...I have to understand it in order to memorise it.' (I4 S12)
Understanding and memorisation concurrent	'...stuff that I understand I actually remember anyway.' (I3 S15) 'they happen at the same time... by understanding it you just automatically remember it.' (I4 S1)
Memorisation before understanding	'I suppose memory comes first because you can remember something and then give it a lot of thought and understand it' (I1 S6)
Repetition after memorisation facilitates understanding	'If it's difficult, I will memorise it first and the more I say it over and over again and think about it, the picture becomes clearer.' (I1 S7) '...sometimes by going over something over and over and over again, trying to memorise that particular thing, suddenly it will just, I'll understand it.' (I1 S12)
Memorisation aids understanding	(Interview 5)

Table 10 Memorisation/understanding relationship – representative quotations

Discussion

Motivational factors

It is encouraging that, despite the presence of some negative influences on students' motivation, there were many more positive factors. Also, many more students identified the positive influences than the negative ones.

Many of the factors identified in this study agree with those found in other research into the motivations of students from non-standard backgrounds. The intrinsic motivation of interest was also identified by Woodley et al (1987), Wilson (1997) and Olaussen and Braten (2001) while the desire for personal and professional advancement was also found by Woodley et al (1987), Wilss et al (1999) and Boulton-Lewis et al (2001). The influences of external factors like family and friends were found to be both positive in terms of support, but negative in terms of time pressures and demands. In fact, external pressures and their effects were the main negative factors found in this study. This apparently contradictory pattern is not new. While Shanahan (2000) and Olaussen and Braten (2001) found that the support of others like friends and family had a positive effect on motivation, Shanahan and other researchers (Woodley et al, 1987; Young, 1990) also found that students' motivation was challenged by external demands and pressures on their time. This situation is understandable when one considers that mature students are more likely to have ongoing responsibilities to others, which younger students are less likely to experience. However, as Young (1990) found among mature physiotherapy students, such negative influences did not deter them from obtaining the qualification, an outcome which was the same in this study.

There were some motivational factors found in this study which reflect the longitudinal nature of the study, for example the positive effect of making progress through the programme. Also, the impact of specific elements of the programme were important to some students, for example experiences on clinical placement and the content being covered on the course at different times. Such factors are also likely to have influenced the motivation of students in other studies. However, the cross-sectional nature of these studies might not have facilitated responses of this type.

Influence of assistant experience on clinical placement learning

The central importance of prior experiences of learning on student learning is well established in educational research and associated models (Prosser and Trigwell, 1999; Biggs, 2003). Work around prior experiences does recognise the influence of prior knowledge gained in experiential, rather than formal learning settings. However, research on this area of influence on learning has tended to focus on the influences of formal study and learning.

Wilss et al (1999) describe learning from life experience as informal learning in contrast to the formal learning associated with dedicated learning experiences. The obvious link between students' work experiences and their learning experience on the programme made inclusion of this area in this study an imperative. The interaction between informal and formal learning experiences identified by Wilss et al served to strengthen the need to investigate this relationship in the study.

Research has identified the importance of life experience on learning among students from non-school-leaver backgrounds. One of the themes that emerged in Shanahan's study (2000) on the learning experiences of mature aged occupational therapy students was the positive effects which previous employment and life experience was perceived to have in several areas of learning, including clinical placements. In a study of an earlier cohort of physiotherapy students on the same programme as the current study (Jackson, 2003), the students also identified advantages arising from their clinical experience for their learning when on clinical placements. The findings from these studies confirm the strong influences of students' prior and ongoing experiences in the work setting on their learning.

In this study, in all four sets of interviews which addressed this topic, several students identified the positive influences of their familiarity with clinical environments and established communication skills with patients, staff and others on their learning while on placements. These are obviously advantages which students without such experience do not share. Students who have been employed in the past would be likely to find that experience of some assistance when they were undertaking placement learning. However, this would only be a shadow of that experienced by students with both past and ongoing experience in similar settings. These findings were thus not surprising. Although also not unexpected, the additional findings that students perceived that this experience enabled them to learn and function at a higher level when they were on placement is gratifying. As Wilss et all (1999) state, it is the interaction between informal and formal learning which is important, not their mere co-existence. It is clear from table 3 that the majority of responses relating to this interaction were given at Interview 2 which took place soon after the students' first placement. Its low level of presence in Interviews 3 and 4 could suggest that this strength did not persist. However, the proportionally large number of students who identified that their experience enabled them to make faster and greater progress in Interview 5 suggests that this advantage did continue throughout the programme.

Some students also perceived that their experiential learning made them feel more relaxed and confident, able to use initiative more and question their educators. Jackson (2003) found a similar theme of increased confidence, present mainly when on clinical placements, associated with the students' prior experiential learning. These findings also agree with those of Boulton-Lewis et al (2000) that the insights which students gained by relating their formal to their informal learning enabled them to question and challenge their teachers. These findings support the general assertion made by Richardson (1994) that students with experience undergo learning processes which are integrative and informed rather than largely acquisitive and one-sided. The ability and willingness of some students in this study to question people in positions of power within their educational milieu posits that the learning which is occurring is more likely to be of a desirable qualitative, transformative nature than a quantitative, accumulative one.

Parallels were also present between other categories of description found in this study and those identified by Jackson (2003). These included clinical educator's expectations sometimes being too high and the opportunity to continue learning while at work. Although the focus and method used by Jackson was not identical to that used in this study, the similarity in findings regarding the influences of students' past clinical experience and their learning while on placement suggests that these influences are consistent and not unique to one group of students.

The literature and most of the findings in this study identified positive influence of informal learning. However, some negative factors were also found. One identified by some students was the difficulty they found in delegating work to assistants when on placement. This is an understandable finding when their ongoing role as an assistant when not in college is taken into account. Although those who raised it found it a significant challenge, the issue was only identified as a factor during the interview which followed their first placement. This suggests that those who had this difficulty were able to resolve it over time. Jackson's study (2003) did not investigate this issue, so there is no data to identify whether other students on the programme experienced similar difficulties or not.

In early placements, some students also felt that they were either tending to stay in or be limited to their assistant role while on placement. Again, this issue disappeared over time and, by the end of programme, when reviewing their experiences overall in Interview 5, almost all those interviewed stated that they had been treated as a student.

Conceptions of learning

One obvious difference between this study and others which have investigated students' conceptions of learning is the wording of the question asked. The question 'What do you actually mean by learning?' (Säljö, 1979) might have elicited a different set of responses from the question 'How do you know when you've learned something?', which, in this study, was also asked within the specific context of the physiotherapy programme under consideration.

Despite this difference, the fact that some of the Säljö/Marton et al conceptions are also represented in the outcomes space in this study, suggests an alignment between these findings and those of other research into this topic (Säljö, 1979; Marton et al, 1993; Boulton Lewis et al 2001). However, the results of this study do not agree with the conclusions drawn by Säljö and others that conceptions around knowledge acquisition, recall and application are quantitative in nature. The representative quotations in table 6 for the category of recall do identify a quantitative conception. However, this is not true for the category of application. Some of the responses were quantitative and agree with the level of response found by Säljö (1979), but a number of responses related application to effectiveness, which suggests a possibly higher order qualitative conception. These, and similar findings in the category around explanation, suggest that, in this study, unless the responses are sub-divided into additional categories, only the first category of description on recall is purely quantitative in nature. An alternative to expecting that individual categories of description will be either quantitative or qualitative in nature is to accept the argument by Meyer (1995) that, although a number of conceptions of learning exist among learners, these may be neither purely quantitative nor purely qualitative in nature

The data in table 5 do not suggest any noticeable development in the complexity of conceptions in the subjects as a group across the four years of study on a programme whose design and implementation embodies sound educational principles. These findings agree with those of a larger quantitative study of physiotherapy students in England and Wales (Morris and Meyer, 2002) and those of a qualitative study of students from non-standard academic backgrounds by Boulton-Lewis et al (2001). However, they disagree with those of the study by Morgan and Beatty (1997) in which a transition in conceptions of learning from predominantly quantitative towards more qualitative ones occurred in students they interviewed as they progressed through their studies. In light of the findings of Morgan and Beatty and the established position within educational research that lower level conceptions are associated with poorer quality learning, the absence of such a transition in this study could suggest a similar effect. However, these students obtained a much higher number of first class honours degrees than the national average within physiotherapy.

The presence of a hierarchical relationship among the categories of description was sought as part of the phenomenographic analysis. However, the issues already identified around the level of complexity of the scope of some categories and apparent lack of progressive development in thinking among some categories questions the existence of a simple linear relationship. For example, the categories on knowing and understanding were located where they are in the table as Säljö's classification places responses round understanding after those round application. However, if the suggestion made earlier that some of the responses around explanation and application imply understanding in order for the learner to know whether they are being effective or not, this raises questions about the presence of a linear hierarchy among all the categories of description. It is possible that a multi-directional flow diagram may represent the relationships more accurately, if such relationships, in fact, need to be sought. Meyer (1995) also argues that range of conceptions of learning held by students may not be related in a linear or hierarchical way.

Other studies have also found conceptions of learning in addition to those found by Säljö (1979) and Marton et al (1993). Purdie et al (1996) identified nine categories, six of which were very similar in nature to the Säljö/Marton et al ones. None of the remaining three was similar to the additional categories found in the current study. Purdie et al did not discuss the presence or absence of a hierarchical relationship among the categories, possibly because the study did not involve a phenomenographic approach. The findings for the meaning of learning obtained from interviews by Wilss et al (1999) and Boulton-Lewis et al (2001) on students from indigenous backgrounds in Australia were also a mix of some of the Säljö/Marton et al categories of description and others which were different. Although these two studies did use a phenomenogrpahic approach no discussion around hierarchical relationships was included. There appears to be difference of opinion among researchers regarding the necessity for seeking the presence of hierarchical relationships among categories of description. In the study under consideration, the presence of such relationships with regard to conceptions of learning was sought, but do not appear to be consistently present for the whole outcome space.

Overall, the findings from this study identified a number of conceptions of learning, some of which are additional or different from those found by other researchers. While some of the categories of description are linearly related to one another, a more complex picture of inter-relationships has been identified. The absence of a consistent progression in depth of conceptions over time does not appear to have adversely influenced the learning outcomes for the student group.

Conceptions of understanding

Three of the six categories of description identified by Entwistle and Entwistle (1992) were also found in this study. Some aspects of other Entwistle and Entwistle categories were present in others, but either the scope or overall tenor of their representative quotations did not match those in this study closely enough to be considered analogous. As for conceptions of learning, the nature of the question asked in the Entwistle and Entwistle study was different from that asked in this study: 'What is understanding?' versus 'How do you know when you have understood what you have learned?'. It is thus again possible that the disparity in the findings may reflect the difference in the wording and contexts of the questions.

Newton et al (1998) argue that, while learning can be rote, understanding is a dynamic process which requires the active engagement of the learner. The majority of the categories of description found in the study involve such active manipulation of learning at a cognitive and/or application level, a finding which supports this assertion.

A large number of respondents in the first interview in this study held an internal conception of understanding making sense, but across the interviews, the largest number of responses was in the categories of explanation and application. This suggests that these students have a largely pragmatic view of this concept. This is in contrast to the findings for the final year students in Entwistle and Entwistle's study (1992) where the majority of responses were internal and cognitive in nature. This difference may reflect the dissimilarities between the nature of the subjects being studied by the two student groups.

There is a notable resemblance, in this study, between many of the categories of description regarding learning and understanding which suggests that there may be a closer link between the two concepts for some students than studies which have only considered one of these concepts will have identified. The presence of the category 'understand it/it makes sense' in table 5 under conceptions of learning, supports this possibility. Some researchers have also used the two concepts interchangeably. For example, in the Boulton-Lewis et al (2001) investigation, some of the questions asked when investigating conceptions of learning specifically asked about understanding. The findings in the current study suggest a complex relationship between learning and understanding. For some students they are synonymous, while, for others, they may be separate or relate to one another in different ways in different learning contexts.

As for conceptions of learning, although some categories of description for understanding involved more complex levels of cognition than others, a single, inclusive linear hierarchical relationship was not found, with a more complex pattern of association being present.

Another similarity between the pattern of responses for conceptions of learning and understanding was the absence of a notable change in conceptions across the five sets of interviews. No other longitudinal investigation into conceptions of understanding has been found, making it difficult to further interpret these findings.

Relationship between understanding and memorisation

Research has identified a conceptual difference between memorising before understanding and memorising after understanding, with the latter being associated with higher quality learning outcomes (Meyer, 1999). It is thus gratifying that, in this study, with only a handful of exceptions, all responses demonstrated perceptions which prioritised understanding.

Across the five sets of interviews, students consistently asserted that they believe that understanding precedes memorisation, the equivalent of the concept of 'memorisation after understanding' used by other researchers (Meyer, 1999). Additionally, a large number of respondents stated that understanding is an important prerequisite to achieving useful memorisation. This finding adds strength to the subjects' perception that memorisation is preceded by understanding.

The finding that, in the last three sets of interviews, some responses identified that the processes of understanding and memorisation were concurrent is also of interest. This concept has been described in the literature as 'memorisation with understanding' (Marton et al, 1997; Meyer, 2000; Meyer and Shanahan, 2001). It is interesting to note that this concept was originally identified in Eastern students and seen to be different from the processes present in Western students. The findings from the current study confirm those of Meyer and Shanahan (2001) that this conception is less culturally exclusive than some research to date has found (Au and Entwistle, 1999).

In addition, although only identified by a couple of students in the first set of interviews, the presence of a category involving achievement of understanding via repetition after memorisation is also notable. This process was originally found to be present in studies of Easter students (Kember, 1996), but has also subsequently been incorporated into research in Western cultures (Meyer and Shanahan, 2001). The findings from the current study confirm that this category of description is not culturally unique.

Based on previous research around this topic, a hierarchical relationship among the categories of description was not expected, and none was found.

Conclusion

The findings of this exploratory study have identified that students from non-standard academic backgrounds possess a rich range of perceptions across a number of relevant topics, most of which are positive in terms of their influence on the quality of the students' learning. In addition to agreeing with those from other studies on students from both standard and non-standard backgrounds, the findings have identified additional features associated with the students' greater length and depth of life experience which demonstrates that, in addition to being able to benefit from undertaking higher education, they are also able to make a positive contribution to it.

References

Au, C and Entwistle, N (1999) 'Memorisation with understanding' in approaches to studying: cultural variant or response to assessment demands *8th EARLI Conference, Goteborg, Sweden*

Biggs, J (2003) *Teaching for quality learning at university* (second edition) Buckingham: Open University Press

Booth, S (1997) On phenomenography, learning and teaching. *Higher Education Research and Development* 16: 135 – 158

Boulton-Lewis, G, Lewis, D and Wilss, L (2001) Dissonance between the conceptions of learning and ways of learning for Indigenous Australian university students *9th EARLI Conference, Fribourg, Switzerland*

Boulton-Lewis, G, Marton, F, Lewis, DC and Wilss, L (2001) The experience of learning for indigenous Australian university students: conceptions and strategies *9th EARLI Conference, Fribourg, Switzerland*

Boulton-Lewis, G, Wilss, L and Lewis, D (2000) Conceptions of formal learning; changes and developing awareness for indigenous university students *HERDSA Conference, Towoomba*

Entwistle, A and Entwistle, N (1992) Experiences of understanding in revising for degree examinations. *Learning and Instruction* 2: 1 – 22

Entwislte, N and Entwistle, D (2001) The interplay between memorising and understanding in preparing for examinations *9th EARLI Conference, Fribourg, Switzerland*

Jackson, J (2003) The lived experience of part-time in-service physiotherapy students in their final year *Unpublished EdD thesis, University of East Anglia*

Kember, D (1996) The intention to both memorise and understand: another approach to learning? *Higher Education* 31: 341 – 354

Marton, F (1981) Phenomenography – describing conceptions of the world around us. *Instructional Science* 10: 177-200

Marton, F (1988) Phenomenography: exploring different conceptions of reality. In: Fetterman, D (ed) *Qualitative approaches to evaluation in education: the silent scientific revolution* New York: Praeger

Marton, F (1993) Conceptions of learning *International Journal of Educational Research* 19: 277 – 300

Marton, F, Watkins, D and Tang, C (1997) Discontinuities and continuities in the experience of learning: an interview study of high school students in Hong Kong *Learning and Instruction* 7: 21 – 48

Meyer, JHF (1995) A quantitative exploration of conceptions of learning *Research and Development in Higher Education* 18: 545 – 550

Meyer, JHF (1999) Embryonic 'memorising' models of student learning *8th EARLI Conference, Goteborg, Sweden*

Meyer, JHF (2000) Variation in contrasting forms of 'memorising' and associated variables *British Journal of Educational Psychology* 70: 163 - 176

Meyer JHF and Shanahan, M (2001) Dissonant forms of 'meaning' and repetition *9th EARLI Conference, Fribourg, Switzerland*

Morgan, A and Beaty, L (1997) The world of the learner In: Marton, F, Hounsell, D and Entwistle, N *The experience of learning: implications for teaching and studying in higher education* (2nd edition) Edinburgh: Scottish Academic Press

Morris, J and Meyer, JHF (2003) Variation in the conceptions of learning of physiotherapy students in England and Wales: a longitudinal multi-centre study In: Rust, C (ed) *Improving student learning theory and practice – 10 years on* Oxford: OCSLD

Newton, DP , Newton, LD and Oberski, I (1998) Learning and conceptions of understanding in history and science: lecturers and new graduates compared *Studies in Higher Education* 23 (1): 43 – 58

Pintrich, PR and Schunk, DH (1996) *Motivation in education: theory, research and applications* USA, Prentice Hall

Prosser, M and Trigwell, K (1999) *Teaching for learning in higher education* Buckingham, Open University Press

Purdie, N, Hattie, J and Douglas, G (1996) Student conceptions of learning and their use of self-regulated learning strategies: a cross-cultural comparison *Journal of Educational Psychology* 88 (1): 87 – 100

Ramsden, P (1992) *Learning to teach in higher education* London: Routledge

Richardson, JTE (1994) Mature students in higher education: 1 A literature survey on approaches to studying *Studies in Higher Education* 19 (3): 309 – 325

Säljö, R (1979) Learning in the learner's perspective 1; Some common sense perceptions No 76 *Department of Education, University of Goteborg*

Shanahan, M (2000) Being that bit older: mature students' experiences of university and healthcare education *Occupational Therapy International* 7 (3): 153 – 162

Trigwell, K (1997) Phenomenography: an approach to research. In: Higgs, J (ed) *Qualitative research: discourse on methodologies* Sydney: Hampden Press

Trigwell, K (1999) Phenomenography: discernment and variation. In: Rust, C (ed) *Improving student learning through the disciplines* Oxford: OCSLD

Wilson, F (1997) The construction of paradox? One case of mature students in higher education *Higher Education Quarterly* 51 (4): 347 – 366

Wilss, L, Boulton-Lewis, G, Marton, F and Lewis, D (1999) Learning in and out of university: Aboriginal and Torres Strait Islander students' conceptions and strategies used to learn. *HERDSA Conference, Melbourne*

Woodley, A, Wagner, L, Slowery, M, Hamilton, M and Fulton, O (1987) *Choosing to learn: adults in education* Buckingham: Open University Press

Young, J M (1990) Mature students in physiotherapy undergraduate education *Physiotherapy* 76 (3): 127 - 131

Aligning teaching-learning environments with students – a new perspective on constructive alignment in the light of student diversity

Nicola Reimann, University of Durham

Abstract

The data and findings reported in this paper have emerged from the 'Enhancing Teaching-learning Environments in Undergraduate Courses' (ETL) project whose initial thinking about high quality learning was informed by Biggs' notion of *constructive alignment*. It presents a critique of constructive alignment based on interview data in economics which highlighted the challenge of constructively aligning teaching-learning environments with a very diverse student intake. Aspects such as different levels of previous knowledge were perceived by staff and students as having a significant impact on learning and teaching in the economics modules investigated and various strategies were adopted to deal with the situation. Including students as an integral component into the model of a constructively aligned system would provide practitioners with a way of thinking about teaching and learning which resonates much more with their experience of diversity as well as affording a discussion of both the advantages and limitations of alignment strategies.

Keywords

Constructive alignment, higher education, teaching-learning environments, economics

Introduction

This paper proposes a critique and extension of Biggs' concept of constructive alignment, based on data collected and analysed for the 'Enhancing Teaching-Learning Environments in Undergraduate Courses' (ETL) project. ETL aims to increase our understanding of the discipline-specific nature of teaching-learning environments (TLEs) and constructive alignment (CA) is one of the core concepts which informed the ETL Project's initial understanding of high quality TLEs. The data analysed so far have

271

allowed the project team to develop a differentiated understanding of constructively aligned TLEs in the disciplines which will be presented in this paper.

A critique of Biggs' notion of CA

Biggs' concept of CA

Biggs describes CA as a "marriage between a constructivist understanding of the nature of learning, and an aligned design for teaching" (Biggs 2003: 27). In order to be effectively facilitated, high level understanding aims must be aligned with the other components of the TLE, in particular with teaching/learning activities and assessment procedures. Biggs portrays an effective TLE as a *system* in which all components are aligned and mutually supportive to achieve maximum consistency. The main components of the system are identified as:

1.   the curriculum (expressed as objectives),

2.   teaching methods,

3.   assessment procedures,

4.   climate of interactions with students,

5.   institutional climate

(Biggs 2003).

If all these components are aligned with the constructivist aim of supporting the active construction of personal meaning and deep understanding, then students are 'entrapped in a web of consistency' which, according to Biggs, will inescapably lead to high quality learning (Biggs 2003).

Student diversity in Biggs' model

Biggs (1999, 2003) regards diversity as one of the main factors which have significantly affected contemporary university teaching. He argues that in today's university classrooms, lecturers are confronted with a wide range of students of whom some, ie the more 'academic' students, spontaneously use higher order cognitive activities, while others do not. "Good teaching is getting most students to use the higher cognitive level processes that the more academic students use spontaneously" (Biggs 1999: 4). For this purpose he advocates teaching and assessment methods which require students to use a deep approach and discourage a surface approach. Rather than differentiating the approaches taken to teaching and course design in the light of differences in ability, age, experience, socio-economic status and cultural background, Biggs suggests that a constructively aligned TLE will encourage *all* students, regardless of their individual differences and backgrounds, to use high cognitive levels of engagement and understanding, including the less 'academic' students.

Reactions of the academic community to CA

The idea of CA has been eagerly picked up by parts of the HE community. Individual academics and academic staff developers on the one hand (Griffin 2003, Foley and Stead 2002, Hagemeier 2002, Meyers and Nulty 2002, Brown et al 2001) and policy makers and institutional managers on the other (LTSN Generic Centre 2002, Jackson 2002, Houghton 2002), in particular those concerned with quality assurance and enhancement, have bought into the concept and contributed to its dissemination and application to a wide range of contexts. In academic staff development CA mainly appears to have been used to enhance practitioners' thinking about course design and its relationship with student learning. Accounts focus on the application of CA to individual courses or modules and demonstrate that the main benefit of CA lies in the fact that it provides university teachers with an accessible and actionable framework for course planning. One particular strength of CA seems to be that it reminds teachers to consider the multiple dimensions of TLEs (McLoughlin 2001). There are some critical voices, such as Cuthbert (2002) and Webster (2002) who draw attention to the fact that CA does not take account of those aspects which escape rational design and planning. Webster describes constructive alignment as limited, subjective and ultimately unattainable.

Considering the relatively widespread use and acceptance of CA within the HE community, there is a curious absence of literature *not* written from a managerial or individual case study and academic staff development perspective. Literature searches (keyword "constructive alignment") conducted in ERIC on 29 January 2004 and the British and Australian Education Indices, the Web of Science and the Web of Knowledge on 5 February resulted in hardly any conceptual discussion or empirical research other than that described above.

The ETL perspective on CA

The data collected for the ETL project have enabled us to evaluate and develop the concept of CA on the basis of extensive empirical evidence. Within the ETL team Hounsell and McCune (2002) were the first ones to show that when designing constructively aligned TLEs, staff considered important components *in addition* to those originally identified by Biggs[1], namely alignment to students, alignment of learning support, alignment of course organisation and management (Hounsell and McCune 2002: 20) and feedback provided in relation to assessment (McCune and Hounsell 2004). McCune and Hounsell (2004) also draw attention to the various contextual constraints and affordances of course and departmental contexts which impact on the extent to which CA can be achieved. If teaching and learning is regarded as a socio-cultural enterprise, TLEs are also influenced by disciplinary cultures and *ways of thinking and practising* (WTP). Due to the multitude of influences on TLEs, CA can therefore only be conceived as an ideal rather than an achievable reality. McCune and Hounsell also reject the geometrical connotations of the term alignment which imply a 'line of sight', while in reality various configurations are possible. They suggest *congruence* as an alternative.

[1]Jackson, Shaw and Wisdom (2002), Houghton (2002), McLoughlin (2001) have also, implicitly and explicitly, suggested the inclusion of additional components into Biggs' model.

Biggs' perspective on TLEs is that of an instructional designer who deliberately manipulates the components of a complex system in order to obtain optimal results, while the more 'messy', emergent aspects of TLEs are not considered. The data analysed by the ETL Project, however, show that real-world TLEs can only be understood if emergent aspects are taken into account as well, such as those aspects which are called "organised anarchy" by Cuthbert (2002) and "chaos" by Webster (2002).

The role of students within CA

Despite the emphasis on a constructivist theory of learning, Biggs, paradoxically, portrays students as objects of instruction. In his model they are 'entrapped', they 'react' to the teaching system, and learning tasks 'elicit' desired behaviour. If, however, the socio-cultural nature of teaching and learning is emphasised, understanding becomes a co-construction of meaning (Anderson and Day 2004) in which students (as well as lecturers) are attributed a much more central and active role. Within such a conceptualisation of TLEs, CA is a dynamic process rather than a mechanistic manipulation of system components as Biggs' model implies.

ETL interview data suggest that *students* need to be incorporated as a core component of constructively aligned TLEs. One could argue, of course, that the notion of *constructive* alignment automatically includes students as it is based on a theory of learning which places the learner at its centre. However, this is not conveyed explicitly enough in Biggs' representation of CA. The remainder of this paper will therefore be devoted to discussing examples of the way in which *alignment with students* has featured in the ETL interviews in economics.

CA with students: evidence from ETL interviews in economics

Data

In phase 2 of the ETL project, interview, questionnaire and documentary data about individual course units/modules were collected over two academic years from staff and students in a wide range of institutions of higher education across the UK. As the author of this paper was predominantly involved in the economics strand of ETL, the examples used below have been taken from the semi-structured interviews conducted in the context of six economics modules (see table 1 opposite).

Staff and student perspectives on student heterogeneity in economics

When interviewed about the students on the respective modules, staff frequently talked about the way in which the heterogeneity of their students' backgrounds and needs challenged them when trying to provide coherent TLEs which were appropriate for *all* students accommodated within a single module.

Institution	E1		E2		E3	
Type of university	'new' post-1992 university		'new' post-1992 university		'old' university	
Type of students	non-traditional		non-traditional		traditional	
Typical entry level grades for A-levels or Highers	CCD/CDD		CCC		ABB + grade A at GCSE in maths (or higher level maths)	
Module	E1F 1st year	E1L final year	E2F 1st year	E2L final year	E3F 1st year	E3L final year
No of students on module	10-20	20-45	200+	45-55	200+	50-60
Module content	intro micro-economics	applied macro-economics	intro micro and macro-economics	money and finance	intro micro and macro-economics	industrial organisation
No of staff interviews	3	2	9	2	5	2
No of student interviews	11	3	16	14	16	13

Table 1

L: *It [heterogeneity] is the main challenge for our teaching and their learning... It's a real... battle, constantly.*

    (E1F-sta1)

In the economics modules under investigation, heterogeneity came in many guises. The following discussion will focus on aspects which were described by staff and students as having a particular impact on learning and teaching in the modules investigated.

Different levels of previous knowledge and majoring in different disciplines and programmes of study

One aspect which was highlighted both by staff and students as particularly important for student learning on first year modules was *previous knowledge of economics*. To a lesser extent differences in *previous knowledge of mathematics* also featured in the interviews.

L: *The first question to ask is what are these students coming in with in terms of economic knowledge and what they need to go out with. As an introductory core module we have a very wide range of ability in fact, from those people who've done no economics and no maths beyond the age of... 15, 16, whereas others have come in with a fairly high degree of specialisation in economics and maths at A-level. And between those two extremes there is a whole range of different combinations and backgrounds, including some people who are not doing economics as a main degree at all... So there is a very wide ability range, a wide range of motivations and in a lecture hall of 200+ ... you've got to offer something for everyone.*

    (E3F-sta1)

All first year modules comprised differing proportions of students with and without previous knowledge of economics (such as A-level, Scottish Higher, HND). As a consequence, one important aim of both E1F and E3F was to level out the differences between these students before the second year of the programme. As was shown in a previous paper (Reimann 2004), a background in economics made the modules much easier and decreased the workload considerably. Students without previous knowledge were more likely to struggle to understand and had much more work to do in order to keep up.

Getting everybody up to the same standard was particularly important for those students who were going to continue their studies of the subject, especially students majoring in economics. E2F and E3F comprised both *economics majors* and *students majoring in other disciplines* who took economics as a compulsory or elective module. Since E2F was a core module for students across the entire faculty, economics majors were actually in the minority, while in E3F the majority of students were economics majors.

Different entry levels and modes of study

Economics is a subject to which recruitment has decreased over the past few years and this was one reason for E2L being offered in two very distinct incarnations. In the standard *full-time mode* economics majors took E2L during the final year of their programme of study. In addition, people working in financial services and insurance were admitted directly to the final year of the programme since their qualifications were recognised as prerequisites for final year study. For these mature *direct entry* students, E2L was available in *part-time distance mode*. Specific challenges arose from all students having to achieve the same learning outcomes. While the full-time students had had ample opportunity to become acquainted with economic theory in the preceding years of the course, the direct entry students reported a lack of theoretical understanding which made it more difficult for them to apply theory to real-world problems, as required on E2L.

S: *I would be able to get better marks if I could understand the theory behind economics, if I could apply the theory to real life. I think I'd be doing better in the course if I had a fundamental knowledge of economics.*

   (E2L-stu3)

In addition, the direct entry students were less able to cope with the requirements of economic essay-writing as they had not been inducted into the ways of thinking and practising in economics and their application to academic writing over the same length of time as the full-time students.

S: *An interesting point on the assignment was the vagueness of the question... in the sense of what direction we were expected to take it in... The comments that did come back on one of the assignments was that I hadn't been very specific.*

   (E2L-stuA)

276

L: *It's to be more analytical, to look on things and think: if this happens that happens. And also to be more critical of things and also to relate things together: if we have a problem here, what? That has been a problem with the assignments, that some of the ones that have done poorly because they have made it very descriptive and therefore they have failed to pick up… the implied thing that is there at the base of the question.*

(E2L-sta2)

Different life experience and professional backgrounds

Being a part-time student was also said to have advantages as the students on E2L brought with them their professional backgrounds and experiences which helped them to engage with and understand some of the content covered on the module. The advantage which *mature students* have against *school leavers* when studying economics was also highlighted within the context of other modules:

L: *Economics [is] best done by mature people or at least older people, because you can't see how things fit together quite the same if you haven't had that… Mature students that have come in through our access scheme… have always helped bring a more realistic approach generally to the undergraduate student body.*

(E1F-sta1)

Different cultural and linguistic backgrounds

Modules at E1 comprised a considerable proportion of *international students*. These students pointed out the ways in which TLEs which were geared towards UK students could be problematic for non-UK students. Their lack of familiarity with the political and economic culture made engagement with the examples used more difficult.

S: *I think the problem I had, because I am foreign… for example I don't know what happened to Britain ten years ago… Or for the Black Friday, for the assessments. And one of the lecturers used to give this kind of examples, so I couldn't understand.*

(E1L-stu1)

In addition, being non-native speakers of English was perceived by these students as affecting their performance in, for instance, the detailed comprehension of lectures and economic textbooks. The specific difficulties of the language used in economics writing has been described by applied linguists (contributions to Dudley-Evans and Henderson 1990). Research conducted by Meyer and Shannahan (2001) found that having English as a second language had a negative effect on learning outcomes within first year economics in Australia.

Different levels of academic ability and motivation

Finally, several staff interviewees from E1 and E2 commented on the challenges of teaching what were labelled as 'weak' or 'academically less able students' and who, in some instances, were also seen to be *less motivated*. The perceived lack of ability was described as having implications for the quality of economic understanding achieved by these students.

L: *The ability range is quite wide. We have very good students this year… And then we tend to get a fairly large tail of weaker students…We have taken people who perhaps five six years ago we would not have taken.*

   (E1L-sta2)

L: *On the level three, what we found is that the weaker students have difficulty applying economic analysis… The students are less happy grappling with theoretical abstract models than they perhaps were in the past… Obviously if they haven't got a firm grasp of the model, then it becomes difficult when they are asked to apply it.*

   (E1L-sta2)

Strategies for dealing with diversity

The following paragraphs will provide examples of ways in which staff tried to respond to diversity. It will review some of the ways in which the module teams sought to align the TLEs which were investigated with the very different students who they were trying to accommodate.

CA with students and ways of thinking and practising in economics

In E1 changes were made to the economics curricula in order to align the programme with those students who were regarded as 'weaker':

L: *We are trying to do different things with econometrics… We are trying to use it as a tool to look at data… In years gone past perhaps there's [been] more emphasis on the theory of econometrics, statistics and so on. So [now] there is more of an emphasis on the application rather than the theoretical construction.*

   (E1L-sta2)

For E1L more specifically, aligning the TLE with those students who were described as less able to understand economic theory involved making the *assessment* more discursive:

L: *We are going to change the nature of the assessment. We are going to ask them to do fewer questions in the examination and make them more… discursive… play down the analytical theoretical core… give them a bigger field to gallop in rather than making them jump over hurdles. We are going to see if they can see the implications more of what they are doing more than just repeat this bit of analysis or explain this bit of analysis and then say why it's important.*

(E1L-sta2)

E2F is an example of a first year module whose curriculum was radically changed in order to achieve CA with students. The aim was to make economics accessible to non-majors in the subject by largely eliminating technical aspects, concentrating on "clear principles" and using examples which are as close as possible to the student experience.

L: *My idea for an introductory economics is that it's got to be a base for all students... It's not dumbing down. It's to take issues in economics and spend more time on parts of it rather than swamp them with diagrams and equations... Well, last year I took a number of classes... and in three weeks I've used two diagrams. Some of my colleagues would use 200... Instead of talking hypothetically about factories and stuff, the economics we can use for micro-economics is the economics of their everyday life. How do you spend money, use opportunity costs that way rather than saying the factory can produce guns or butter and that the factory produces so much of each. We're actually saying things like: you have a choice of going to the cinema, or you have the choice of staying home and saving money, or work at the pub. That's real economics! It relates it to the students' background. We have other programs where the students only do economics for 1 year so the module is for them as well and to get a basic grasp of principles of economics.*

(E2F-sta2)

Both the examples from E1L and from E2F demonstrate that alignment with students is closely connected to ways of thinking and practising in economics. Economics is a discipline characterised by a widely accepted standard curriculum with a set curricular progression delivered in a relatively uniform manner. It can be assumed that for many economists, theoretical models, diagrams and econometrics lie at the core of the discipline so that putting less emphasis on these aspects would be unacceptable. Different schools of thought and approaches to economics, however, might have contradictory views on this issue (Ormerod 2003, Bartlett and Ferber 1998, Cole 1993). What one economist would regard as a lower level of economic understanding, ie 'dumbing down' as it was referred to in the excerpt above, would be accepted as an equally valid and sophisticated, yet philosophically different approach to economics by another one.

Separating groups of students

A relatively common strategy of constructively aligning TLE with students found within the modules investigated was to *separate different groups of students taking the same module*. E2F, for instance, was offered to students on economics and business-related degrees in semester one, while students from social science, psychology and engineering degrees took the module in semester two. In E2L the provision for full-time and part-time distance students was entirely separate. In E2F tutorial groups were allocated according to students' main programmes of study, whereas in E3F they were allocated according to previous knowledge of economics. A tutor described his approaches to these tutorials as follows:

L: *The tutorials are deliberately designed so that we capture different ability ranges, those with prior knowledge and those without prior knowledge. Those without prior knowledge, they drive the tutorial: 'what do you not understand that you've done in lectures recently, what do you want me to go through?'... The other ones I'm much harder on: 'you should have done this... why don't you know the answer to this... get up there and show me'. In a very light-hearted way, one emphasises the point that you ought to know the basics... I'm much more demanding on one than the other at the beginning.*

      (E3F-sta1)

Alignment with the majority

Aligning the environment with the majority, or with a group that has considerable representation on the module, appears to be another strategy taken to CA with students. E3F, for instance, was predominantly aligned with students majoring in economics. This, however, caused difficulties for non-economics majors.

L: *They've got to leave first year well equipped for... second year single honours economics. So there is a relatively high standard that's got to be achieved. Now that is a problem for those who don't want to go on with economics again because it does require a depth of analysis maybe they'll never ever see again, and some of them actually complain a bit.*

      (E3F-sta1)

Both E1F and E2F were aligned with students who did not have any previous knowledge of economics, while they were less concerned about those students who did. This was why students who had expected to go beyond what they already knew were surprised about the lack of in-depth study required.

L: *I would say 50% of them have A-level Economics recently and 50% approximately do not and perhaps unfortunately for those that have, we start from quite a fundamental level... So I would imagine if you got A-level grade C, you will be particularly au fait with most of what we are doing.*

      (E1F-sta1)

S: *Because I have done economics at A-level, so I am finding the work easier... It's really hard to concentrate in lectures because I know most of the stuff in micro... If you know the stuff as well, [it] makes you feel a bit lazy, [you] don't concentrate on lectures then.*

      (E1F-stuH)

In all three first year modules students with previous knowledge of economics tended to perceive the TLEs as predominantly providing revision, particularly in microeconomics.

This perception might well have a negative impact on engagement and learning since a TLE which is constructively aligned to students *without* previous knowledge may not stimulate those students *with* previous knowledge sufficiently to rethink their existing knowledge and replace potential misconceptions by more sophistcated conceptualisations. At the same time, it is not surprising that most of the students we interviewed were not too concerned about this effect as their previous knowledge allowed them to achieve good grades relatively easily without having to work very hard.

It seems that constructively aligning TLEs with one particular group of students may have implications for the other group(s) with which the TLE is *not* aligned. Recently considerable attention has been devoted to non-traditional students who may struggle with the requirements of traditional academic courses and may lose out because TLEs are not aligned with them. The data discussed above, however, have drawn attention to the needs of *all* students to whom a TLE is not aligned. In the latter example, it was the statements of students *with* previous knowledge of economics which suggested that some of them might be insufficiently challenged and stimulated within an environment which is aligned to students *without* previous knowledge.

Conclusion

The discussion has shown that certain student characteristics had an impact on learning in economics and that staff took account of the differences between students by attempting to constructively align the respective TLEs *with students*. Therefore, incorporating students as an integral component into the model of a constructively aligned system would capture the challenges of contemporary higher education and resonate much more with the actual experience of diversity made by academic staff and students.

Recognising CA *with students* would also afford a discussion of the dilemmas involved in identifying actionable and effective alignment strategies. Each of the strategies described above has its limitations and the variety of the strategies reported confirms McCune and Hounsell's proposition that various configurations of CA are possible and that CA is an ideal rather than an achievable reality (McCune and Hounsell 2004). It may be more useful to focus on the process of align*ing* than on the product of align*ment*.

Explicitly integrating students into the conceptualisation of CA would also draw attention to the fact that TLEs need to contribute to the achievement of high quality learning and understanding by *all* students which a TLE comprises, not just by the majority or the perceived 'average' student. It would reinforce the message that, in the light of diversity, adaptations and changes may have to be made to TLEs in order to make them effective for a wide range of students.

In today's UK universities, staff are increasingly required to accommodate extremely heterogeneous student bodies within single modules. Modularisation, widening participation and the drive to recruit more students have all contributed to this trend which is widely seen by institutions as economically more viable and therefore likely to stay. Thinking about CA *with students* may be one possible way of helping practitioners to deal with this situation.

Acknowledgements

At the time of writing, other members of the ETL Project were Charles Anderson, Adrian Bromage, Kate Day, Noel Entwistle, Dai Hounsell, Jenny Hounsell, Ray Land, Velda McCune, Erik Meyer and Jennifer Nisbet. I am grateful for the comments from Dai Hounsell and Peter Hughes.

References

Anderson, C, and Day, K (2004, in press) 'Purposive environments: engaging students in the values and practices of history'.

Bartlett, RL, and Ferber, MA (1998) 'Humanizing content and pedagogy in economics classrooms'. In Walstad, WB and Saunders, P (eds) *Teaching undergraduate economics. A handbook for instructors*. Boston: McGraw-Hill, 109-125.

Biggs (2003) *Teaching for Quality Learning at University. What the student does*. Second Edition. Maidenhead: Society for Research into Higher Education and Open University Press.

Biggs, J (1999) *Teaching for Quality Learning at University. What the student does*. Buckingham and Philadelphia: Society for Research into Higher Education and Open University Press.

Biggs, J (1996) 'Enhancing teaching through constructive alignment'. *Higher Education* 32, 347-364.

Brown, DA, Sivabalan, P, McKenzie, J, and Booth, P (2001) *An action research approach to improving student learning outcomes using constructive alignment: some evidence and implications for teaching cost accounting*. Faculty of Business Working Paper Series, School of Accounting, Working Paper No. 53, May 2001, University of Technology, Sydney.

Cole, K (1993). 'New directions in teaching economics'. *Economics and Business Education* 1 (2), 79-84.

Cuthbert, R (2002) 'Constructive Alignment in the World of Institutional Management'. Paper presented at the *Constructive Alignment in Action: Imaginative Curriculum Symposium*. 4 November 2002, LTSN Generic Centre. http://www.ltsn.ac.uk/application.asp?app=resources.aspandprocess=full_recordandsectio n=genericandid=170 [last accessed on 30 July, 2004]

Dudley-Evans, T, and Henderson, W (eds) (1990). *The language of economics: the analysis of economics discourse*. ETL Document. No place: Modern English Publications in association with the British Council.

Foley, T, and Steed, A (2002) 'Reflective conversation as a course development method: A case study in legal education'. Paper given at HERDSA Conference , 7-10 July, 2002.

www.ecu.edu.au/conferences/herdsa/main/papers/nonref/pdf/TonyFoley.pdf [last accessed on 30 July, 2004]

Griffin, JD (2003) 'Technology in the teaching of neuroscience: enhanced student learning'. *Advances in Physiology Education* 27(3), 146-155.

Hagemeier, L (2002) *Teaching research competency at the Sociology Foundation level: some thoughts and practices.*
http://www.qut.edu.au/talss/fye/papers02/HagemeierPaper.doc [last accessed on 30 July, 2004]

Houghton, W (2002) 'Promoting constructive alignment through programme specification and subject benchmarks'. Paper presented at the Constructive Alignment in Action: Imaginative Curriculum Symposium. 4 November 2002, LTSN Generic Centre.
http://www.ltsn.ac.uk/application.asp?app=resources.aspandprocess=full_recordandsectio n=genericandid=168 [last accessed on 30 July, 2004]

Hounsell, D, and McCune, V (2002). *Teaching-learning environments in undergraduate biology: initial perspectives and findings.* Universities of Edinburgh, Coventry and Durham: Enhancing Teaching-Learning Environments in Undergraduate Courses (ETL) Project, Occasional Report No. 2. http://www.ed.ac.uk/etl/publications.html [last accessed 21 May 2004].

Jackson, N (2002) 'QAA: Champion for constructive alignment!' Paper presented at the Constructive Alignment in Action: Imaginative Curriculum Symposium. 4 November 2002, LTSN Generic Centre.
http://www.ltsn.ac.uk/application.asp?app=resources.aspandprocess=full_recordandsectio n=genericandid=169 [last accessed on 30 July, 2004]

Jackson, N, Shaw, M, and Wisdom, J (2002) 'Imaginative Curriculum Story: An Experiment in Collaborative Learning'. Paper presented at the Constructive Alignment in Action: Imaginative Curriculum Symposium. 4 November 2002, LTSN Generic Centre.
http://www.ltsn.ac.uk/application.asp?app=resources.aspandprocess=full_recordandsectio n=genericandid=166 [last accessed on 30 July, 2004]

LTSN Generic Centre (2002) 'Constructive Alignment'. Guide for Busy Academics. LTSN Generic Centre.
http://www.ltsn.ac.uk/application.asp?app=resources.aspandprocess=full_recordandsectio n=genericandid=156 [last accessed on 30 July, 2004]

McCune, V, and Hounsell, D (2004, in press) 'The development of students' ways of thinking and practising in three final-year biology courses'.

McLoughlin, C (2001) 'Inclusivity and alignment: Principles of pedagogy, task and assessment design for effective cross-cultural online learning'. *Distance Education* 22(1), 7-29.

Meyer, JHF, and Shanahan, MP (2001) 'A Triangulated Approach to the Modelling of Learning Outcomes in First Year Economics' *Higher Education Research and Development* 20(2), 127-145.

Meyers, NM, and Nulty, D (2002) 'Assessment and student engagement: some principles'. Paper presented at the Learning Communities and Assessment Cultures

Conference organised by the EARLI Special Interest Group on Assessment and Evaluation, University of Northumbria, 28-30 August 2002. htttp.leeds.ac.uk/educol/documents/2240.0000.ht [last accessed on 5 February, 2004]

Ormerod, P (2003) 'Turning the Tide: Bringing Economics Teaching into the Twenty First Century' *International Review of Economics Education* 1(1), 71-79.

Reimann (2004) 'First Year Teaching-Learning Environments in Economics' *International Review of Economics Education* 3.

Webster, C (2002) 'Curricula, Chaos and Constructive Alignment'. Personal perspective posted in response to the *Constructive Alignment in Action: Imaginative Curriculum* Symposium. 4 November 2002, LTSN Generic Centre. http://www.ltsn.ac.uk/application.asp?app=resources.aspandprocess=full_recordandsection=genericandid=181 [last accessed on 30 July, 2004]

Different students, different needs, different times: a retheorisation of tertiary transition

Maureen Burke, Soheil Ahmed

Malcolm McKenzie, University of Queensland

Abstract

Trow's (1974) prediction about the massive shift from elite to mass education has been found to be largely correct. However, the realities – pre-eminently in the form of the postmodern challenges of diversity and the consequent demand for inclusivity – that now face us are far more complex than anyone could have imagined. What does the notion of transition mean in this context? How can we re-theorise it to reflect our existing and emerging realities? What discursive challenges are imminent in such a project? Historically, the term transition has applied to the rites of passage of a specific group of students, those moving from secondary to post-secondary, or tertiary learning institutions. A re-theorised transition, we argue, will have to come to terms with the fact that there are many transitions, not one. However, this narrow conceptualisation excludes other – and we would argue, equally valid – forms of transition that students undergo, for instance, students moving from traditional modes of learning to problem based learning, or digitised online forms of learning or from graduate to postgraduate studies. Although many designated groups (such as mature students, overseas students, single parents, differently-abled students) also undergo transitions, their transitions are often viewed in terms of special circumstances, or more disturbingly as a deviation from the norm. Tinto's (1987) and Viney's (1980) theoretical explorations into transition portray it as a slipzone between an initial and a final state in a student's journey through the university system. But rather than being an existential position, as it were, transition is also a discursive transformation. This is the broader conceptualisation we propose in which students negotiate a number of new discourses – such as their discipline, their academic endeavour, and their role identity – simultaneously. The conventional practice of dealing with students' problems in a predominantly post hoc fashion itself suggests that universities conceptualise transition poorly, if at all. In order to be meaningful, transition has to account on the one hand for difference, and on the other, it has to reposition itself more strategically within the greater discourse of university education. The transition process is characterised by responses to the physical, psychological and social environment encountered by individuals (Huon and Sankey, 2000). Accordingly, we need to recognise that individuals differ in their ability to respond, particularly during the first year of any new university experience. The much-vaunted goal of inclusivity cannot be achieved without 'normalising' this difference. The very notion of transition itself has to undergo the necessary conceptual transformation. Transition occurs not only for one group of students, but for all students entering the university system, albeit differently; it occurs continuously throughout the term of the learning process. As a corollary to reconceptualising transition we must reconceptualise the role of student support services, which can no longer remain ancillary to higher education. If transition occurs continuously, is it not reasonable to suggest that these services become an integral part of the entire learning process? Only then can we ourselves move from the margins to the centre of the discourse.

We may take as our launching point Val D Rust's somewhat lamenting observation that the debates of postmodernism have "almost by passed the comparative education community" (1991 p610). The debates of postmodernity, we might add, have bypassed not only the comparative education community but also the governance structures of the universities, perhaps to the detriment of all. For the most part, the university as a postmodern organisation has not yet arrived; however, the issue has been broached at some length by a number of researchers gathered by Smith and Webster (1997) under the rubric of *The Postmodern University*?

Since the formulations of transition that we are interrogating appear to form a continuum with the same meta-narratives of modernity within which the university itself remains embedded, we become implicated from the outset in a much larger debate – where do we place ourselves in relation to modernity in this inquiry?

The modernity we have come to inherit is the continuation of the project of the Enlightenment. However, the historical specificity has been lost. Apparently because in the considerable time since the Enlightenment that we have been 'officially' modern, many elements of modernity have themselves come to occupy the very position of tradition that they once opposed. One such element is rationalist epistemology. The reason why any opposition to modernity must now be undertaken in a historically unspecific manner is because we want to avoid the confusion of the conventional opposition between tradition and modernity which is no longer tenable because modernity itself has become a form of tradition.

We are not opposed to modernity per se but what Habermas calls "classical modernity" (1981, p4) because of its totalising potentials. In the context of our inquiry into transition, our relation to modernity is not historically specific.

Decidedly, the 'post' in our postmodernity does not signal an 'after' modernity, but a particular attitude to modernity defined by our interrogation of meta-narratives and hierarchies.

Our project of scrutinising the notions of transition – including the many different first year experiences – and how Others are often excluded is indeed a critique of the university as a modernist institution. The broad structural attributes of the university such as its general reliance on functional units to define and locate individuals are the same as those of a modernist organisation. And like all institutions, the university forms us as its subjects, whether as students or as 'workers' within it, through specific rationalist practices. These are discernible in the strictly supervised governance structures, for example. Consider how the ever-widening administrative networks of control penetrate and regulate the minutiae of everyday practices in the university. A comprehensive institutional gaze, it seems, encompasses every aspect of our existence. What we call organisational values and goals are indeed a carefully planned regime of shared meanings.

We become acutely aware of the existence of this system of shared meanings, which Trow (1982) calls the "old consensus" as it is brought into crisis by the transition from elite to mass higher education. The "broad set of shared assumptions" which sustains relations within the elite university becomes "increasingly uncertain" and begins to break down when challenged by diversity. Although in Trow's conceptualisation of the problem the reference is more overtly to the transition of the institution rather than to the transition of the individuals within them, we cannot view one independently of the other.

In fact, Trow himself problematises, albeit somewhat indirectly, the issue of how individuals and institutions shape one another: "The move toward participatory forms of governance often presupposes the survival of the old consensus, or the possibility of its recreation". In this formulation of "participatory forms of governance" and its inextricable relationship with the "old consensus" where does the institution begin? And where does the individual end? Such a lack of clear demarcation has the unmistakeable appearance of a dialectic that evidently governs the relationship between the individual and the institution. Trow's analysis of "the internal governance of higher education institutions" (p70) is penetrating and still largely relevant. However, it stops short of registering how the dynamics of power in the university may have their ultimate basis in the politics of knowledge production.

As producers of knowledge, universities generally favour rationalist – what is called logical positivist – methods of inquiry as reflected in their funding policies. Budgetary and financial forms of control have effectively become tools for translating these rationalist agendas into practice. This is reflected in differential forms of funding and the consequent hierarchisation of the disciplines. Consider, for instance, the valorisation of the sciences at the expense of the humanities, the privileging of quantitative over qualitative forms of research, or the sidelining of conceptual research by the prevailing hegemonies of narrow empiricism. Bloland's study (1995) corroborates this.

The relationship between the disciplines and other services – such as what we call learning assistance – is also shaped largely by institutional imperatives, both stated and unstated. Rationalist management practices thrive on tangibles, while many of the university services (counselling, learning assistance, disability services) deal in intangibles. Such services are positioned eternally outside the discourse because they lack demonstrability in the logical positivist sense. Conceptual consensus on effectiveness may never be reached. But in the ensuing conceptual battle to define and control the meaning of effectiveness, rationalist discourses usually win the battle, often by defining effectiveness in narrowly formulated quantifiable terms. Learning services usually bear the brunt. Thus, as Greville Rumble observes, the difficulties of "demonstrating the service and showing its effect, makes it vulnerable to cuts" (2000, p221).

Essentially, the question is: how do we assess an intangible 'product' which arises through an interaction between two parties, and one in which, to quote Normann, the product "does not exist before purchase" (1991 p15)? In other words, what does the service inhere in?

Rationalist assessments which seem constitutionally incapable of accounting for such ontological predicaments would ignore them.

The general perception of many academics that these services are peripheral to the main functions of the university gives evidence of how institutional discourse determines what is core and what is an ancillary knowledge activity. This is amply demonstrated by Rumble's study (2000). One cannot imagine how the very intellectual processes on which the disciplines depend for their perpetuation and which learning services promote can be ancillary. Learning assistance is intrinsically constituted as the Other in relation to the disciplines.

Clearly, higher education operates as a hierarchy. But the deconstructive 'techniques' inaugurated by Derrida provide us with the wherewithal to delegitimate these hierarchies – without, however, establishing alternative ones. Bloland (1995) demonstrates how "Derrida's powerful attack upon the hierarchies of the modernist world can be used with great effect in challenging higher education's hierarchies and exclusions" (p527).

This relationship between the disciplines and learning assistance may itself be seen as a negotiation between two forms of discourse, one specialist and one more broadly generalist in nature. Learning advisers may be seen as presiding over the practical aspects of academic life that both sustains and is sustained in turn by the specific disciplinary discourses in which students participate.

Owing to its essentially generalist nature, the discourse of everyday academic life (consisting of such practices as building arguments, synthesising information from diverse sources, transforming information into knowledge through interpretive gestures, translating assignment requirements into tangible written outcomes and so forth) tends to be taken for granted within the institution. Academics per se are not to blame for that, but our assumptions about this discourse are. What we take for granted may be specific skills students need to be taught. We cannot assume that students always come equipped with these skills. But we are too ready to gloss over the discrepancy between such expectations and the reality not as a form of discursive difference but as a negation. That is why academics in general take – to borrow Jill Lawrence's phrase – a "deficit view" (2000, p7) of difference.

We have to remember that the practices of academic literacy are often not taught formally and we cannot hope that they will be transmitted automatically in the teaching of the specific disciplines. In making the transition to university, students are also making a discursive transition as Moore et al (2000) demonstrate. Learning advisers mediate this discursive transition and in doing so also provide the very model of the open-ended and genuinely student-centred institutional framework lacking in conventional academic practice for the most part.

If such conventional academic practices, intrinsically "immersed in the dominant 'elite' discourse" of the academia, need to be interrogated, then they are already being interrogated, albeit indirectly, by the practices of learning advisers, because in the end they are the ones who actively seek on behalf of the students they assist "to make explicit the hidden agendas, the covert or hidden curriculum, the implicit expectations as well as the expected (but not stated) behaviours intrinsic to achieving success" (Lawrence 2000, p7).

The delegitimation of the hierarchies can begin with Derrida's suggestion that "the movements of deconstruction do not destroy structures from outside. They are not possible and effective, nor can they take accurate aim, except by inhabiting those structures" (1974, p24).

Postmodern and poststructuralist theories provide both the means and the incentives for renegotiating the relationship between the centre and the periphery, between the Self and the Other, between disciplines and apparent 'non-disciplines' such as learning.

These debates have also been taken up vigorously in the context of organisational studies (Clegg 1990; Parker 1992; Tsoukas 1992). Addressing Parker's delineations of the postmodern organisation Tsoukas warns, "A strong version of postmodernism risks being incoherent and untenable (1992, p645). Tsoukas undercuts the postmodern interrogations of modernity by suggesting that such interrogations fall "well within the Graeco-Western cultural tradition, whether we like it or not" (p647).

Crucially for us, Tsoukas points out that "a 'soft' version of postmodernism is not incompatible with reflexive rationalism" (p648). However, it is the "'hard' version" which is "in danger of descending into solipsism, for it under-estimates the importance of institutions in patterning social life and in making it intelligible via rational enquiry" (p648). In the end, Tsoukas concludes, "reflexive reason has made space for its own interrogation" (p648.).

Does this not sound suspiciously as a form of totalisation? Nothing, it seems, lies outside rationalism. The organisational rationality of universities, moreover, is not reflexive. How else would it be possible for the university to remain unaffected in its operational practices by the discourses of theory developed in its academic departments?

To provide an example of this totalisation and lack of reflexivity we might look at the problem of the student as the subject. Understanding this problem may be crucial to an understanding of the theorisation of transition.

As Linstead and Grafton-Small (explicating Derrida) suggest, "the constitution of the subject is the result of an ideological practice that conceals its own contingency" (1992, p343).

A practical demonstration of this would be how our understanding of students is determined largely by the status bestowed upon them by the institution by virtue of their different circumstances. But what may be an administrative 'convenience' may also become a form of cognitive shorthand, and a notoriously unreliable one which in the end betrays deep seated prejudices.

But it is Tinto who provides us with a particularly good example of this when he notes that "the label *dropout* is one of the more frequently misused terms in our lexicon of educational descriptors. It is used to describe the actions of all school leavers regardless of the reasons or conditions which mark their leaving" (1987, p3) (italics Tinto's).

The formation of the student here follows the general pattern for the formation of the subject delineated so vividly for us by Foucault: the subject is an outcome of institutional practices; the historical circumstances in which the subject is formed recedes far into the background. In *Discipline and Punish* (1979) Foucault illustrates how towards the end of the 18th century we were formed as "juridical subjects" (1979, p13), subjects of the law, by the discourses of the state.

Similarly, the institutional practices (eg admissions policy, administrative procedures) which make such categorisations possible or necessary in the first place recede to the background and may even become invisible altogether. Mature students, for instance, enter the discourse marked, as Jill Lawrence has observed, "by their method of entry to university" (p 2).

What is the ideological practice here and what is the contingency?

The ideological practice here, categorisation according to method of entry, (or departure, if we take Tinto's example) is not an intrinsic attribute of the student but an incidental or contingent outcome of the classificatory system employed by the institution.

And yet our perception of the student can be greatly influenced by the classificatory procedures employed: we cannot see the student for the classification, which in this case also carries many unfortunate ageist connotations. But what is more insidious is that we are likely to see the status of such students as being constituted by an inherent deficiency. We have a tendency to confound difference – or to use the Derridean term, différance (1978) – with "deficit" (Lawrence's word).

Generalisations about mature age students even in the literature reflect an obliviousness to their real needs as Ashar and Skenes (1993) have demonstrated through an analysis of the applicability of Tinto's model of student departure to "nontraditional students"(p91). And for the most part, the "different learning needs" of mature age students receive scant attention. Arguments for a retheorisation of transition are implicit in Ashar and Skenes' assertion that "Tinto's concept of intellectual integration does not fully apply to adult learners" (p92).

Although in delineating the different stages in the necessary rites of passage that mark entry into higher education ("separation, transition, and incorporation" p92), which Tinto bases on Van Gennep's model (1960), he relies heavily on the example of first year students. Nevertheless, it would be less than accurate to suggest, as Ashar and Skenes seem to suggest, that he is not cognisant of the problem. In fact, Tinto does acknowledge why "disadvantaged students, persons of minority origins, older students and the physically handicapped are more likely to experience such problems than are other students" (p97).

Here it is important to ask, what are the conditions under which our knowledge about the student is formed? What is it possible to know about the student? When does it suit the institution to know the student?

Significantly, studies in this area seem to be motivated by economic considerations. The student enters discourse as an economic subject. The very articulation of the problem as one of student retention suggests that it is being perceived primarily from the institutional point of view. As Tinto's analysis suggests, our need to know about the "ability, study skills, social background, educational and occupational goals and commitments, needs and concerns… " (p192) seems to be driven by the imperative "to tell administrators" (p4) how to retain students. Tinto notes how "institutions have come to view the retention of students to degree completion as the only reasonable course of action left to ensure their survival" (p2).

Even though the students' interest are given expression, they are ultimately subordinated to the institutions' interests. Huon and Sankey's study (2000) citing other influential studies in this area (Evans and Peel 1999; McInnis and James 1995; Peel 1999) also identifies "significant cost to the student and to the institution" as a motivation for the study. The professed "needs of the students" (p1) can become a proxy for the needs of institution.

Let us, however, be clear about one thing: we are not interested in highlighting these issues as limitations of these studies but as the conditions of possibility for knowledge. This is indeed a disclosure of the contingencies in the theorisation of transition.

Another issue emerges from this discussion of contingency: classificatory procedures become forms of representations. Jill Lawrence (2000) has corroborated for us that the transition of some groups is represented as being somehow more 'normal' than that of others. Imagine how much more complex the issue becomes in the case of students with disabilities. The notion of the student elides crucial differences as Kantanis (2000) has demonstrated.

But the terrain of transition is not even. For instance, where there is no disability or language or age barrier, there may be other barriers: students moving from conventional to problem based, or digitised online forms of learning, or students moving from graduate to postgraduate courses may equally experience difficulties. But these difficulties which have to do more emphatically with discursive transformations, ie shifts in the nature of institutional practices, may also be represented as deficits.

As Rust reflecting on the prospects of the postmodern for higher education in general suggests, "Postmodernism provides a sense of hope and legitimacy for those Others; it outlines the conditions for resistance in totalizing institutions such as jails, mental institutions, and military organisations and schools, as well as the promise of liberation in more open environments" (1991, p619).

It is in the light of these issues that we are interested in discussing the notion of transition as it is formulated in the discourses of higher education.

In Tinto's description, individuals in transition, the "second stage of passage" (p96), are in "a highly anomic situation in which they are neither strongly bound to the past nor yet firmly tied to the present" (p97). But Tinto's notion of the self is based on a stable reality which, in turn, is guaranteed by the same meta-narratives that have come under attack lately by poststructuralist and postmodern theories.

But at the same time we need to clarify that our project is not a mere deconstruction for its own sake of transition and the modernist discourses in which it has been articulated. After Habermas we would like to say that "instead of giving up modernity and its project as a lost cause, we should learn from the mistakes of those extravagant programs which have tried to negate modernity" (1981, p11).

Neither is our project a simplistic repudiation of modernity. Because postmodernity as Laclau suggests, "cannot be a simple *rejection* of modernity; rather it involves a different modulation of its themes and categories, a greater proliferation of its language games" (1988, p65) (italics Laclau's).

The conditions of possibility for transforming this 'principle' into practice may already be present in the government's policy positions in relation to university governance as articulated by Gallagher (2001): "We also need to value plurality in higher education as an ingredient of a functioning democracy while accepting the fact of rapid and unpredictable shifts in the formation of knowledge across disciplinary and institutional boundaries".

Inscribed into this exhortation to a greater democratisation of the discourses is a subtle acknowledgement that academic institutions control and manage knowledge through established boundaries. But more importantly, this statement underscores a fundamental irony: the very boundaries which seem to sustain the status quo can also hinder it: newer forms of knowledge by definition transcend the classificatory mechanisms of institutional power. Thus the production of knowledge, on which the viability of academic institutions depends, can only be possible through a delegitimation of traditional boundaries, both disciplinary and institutional. Registering the problems of knowledge in this manner also constitutes a pre-emptive move from within the establishment, paving the way for institutions to develop and implement policies which can respond to change effectively.

Crucially Gallagher (2001) urges universities to strike a balance between "intellectual pursuits that may not have apparent application" and a "speedy application of ideas to develop market opportunities," acknowledging perhaps our usual readiness to embrace logical positivist formulations of usefulness as far as knowledge is concerned. But this is by no means a wholesale repudiation of modernist principles either. Rather it is an accommodation of modernist principles with the emerging realities of our contemporary existence. A new paradigm is being created through the negotiation between the imperatives of learning for its own sake and the imperatives of a market economy. At the same time, the simplistic binary useful/useless is being rendered obsolete. Thus what we are witnessing is not an internal contradiction but a breaching of conventional boundaries between the pure and applied forms of knowledge.

However, such breaching of boundaries can be both liberating and challenging as the boundaries of the university themselves shade off into other realms. The main agent driving this change is, of course, technology, which completely changes our relationship with the institution as well as the individuals within it. Information technology is rapidly making inroads into the areas that have been considered the exclusive domain of universities. The monopolistic grip that universities once had on the production and dissemination of knowledge is loosening. As knowledge production moves outside the institution, the authority of universities to preside over matters of knowledge becomes decentred. These are also some of the issues Krishan Kumar (1997) explores broadly: "universities no longer have a monopoly (if ever they had) of the skills and knowledge to be passed on to the new generation" (p27).

If this trend continues, then the very identity of the university may become indistinguishable from that of online service providers:

> *Universities risk losing market share if they are unable to match competitors who can offer programs (7 days/24 hours a day is now international practice) customised to suit individual needs (including options to pay for additions to their core requirements) at reasonable prices and comparable quality (Gallagher 2001).*

The shift from the old to the new ushers a profound shift in our perception of knowledge itself. Understandably, the relationship between the producers of knowledge – the universities – to the knowledge they produce will also change.

This prediction has also been made by Lyotard who pointed out that:

> *The old principle that the acquisition of knowledge is indissociable from the training (*Bildung*) of minds, or even of individuals, is becoming obsolete and will become even more so. The relationship of the suppliers and users of knowledge to the knowledge they supply and use is now tending, and will increasingly tend, to*

> *assume the form already taken by the relationship of commodity producers and the consumers to the commodities they produce and consume – that is, the form of value. Knowledge is and will be produced in order to be sold, it is and will be consumed in order to be valorized in a new production: in both cases, the goal is exchange (1979, p4) (emphasis Lyotard's).*

Lyotard's pronouncements hardly require a reality check. We are now living this reality. However, the pervasiveness of the culture of information far exceeds even Lyotard's predictions as can be seen from the rise of the Internet. Sohail Inayatullah (2000) articulates this for us: "The Web and globalizing will end the monopoly of the university and paradoxically place the university simultaneously at the centre of society" (p232).

What are the prospects of the notion of transition in the light of these contemporary changes? One thing is certain: no more is transition a matter of moving from high school to university. Regardless of how one enters university, the fundamental issue becomes how we negotiate technology or how technology mediates the experience of being human, in the first place. Moreover, there is the prospect of endless transition as technology is in a state of constant flux. The conventional conceptualisations of the problem of transition were predicated ultimately on the notion of a stable reality. But can we rely any more on what seems from our perspective a myth to understand and cope with changes in evidence everywhere? The crux of the matter is that even Trow's (1973) conceptualisation of "permanent education" (p93), or lifelong learning, could not have prepared us for this state of permanent transition.

For sometime now, the problem of transition has been articulated for us by Viney (1980). But Viney's own statement, "different transitional events generate different mediating experiences" (p159), provides the pretext for a revision of the problem.

Decidedly, information technology and the consequent rapid dissemination of information are among the new realities that have to be accounted for in the reformulation of the notion of transition. Our relationship to information has changed irrevocably in the sense that the boundaries of information are being pushed out further every day to encompass not only what we once recognised as knowledge but also the general realm of human experience itself:

> *Many informal aspects of organizations – the ways in which people work around official lines of communication, develop tacit understandings, and trade moral capital – are also methods of processing information.*

> *"Information," in all these contexts, does not just mean data. Qualitative judgements, affiliation, and emotion are all part and parcel of information we exchange, and are inextricably intertwined with the sharing of numbers and facts. Denotation and connotation are fundamentally inseparable. (Evans and Wurster 2000, p11). (emphasis Evans' and Wurster's).*

In this new paradigm the distinctness of knowledge shades off imperceptibly into information. In fact, we might say that conscious existence itself is now being subsumed to the ubiquitous flows and networks of information. In the domain of higher education this means that we are also witnessing the convergence of information literacy and learning, one of the many social consequences of information in general (Smith 1993).

As Lyotard (1979) points out:

> *The nature of knowledge cannot survive unchanged within this context of general transformation. It can fit into the new channels, and become operational, only if learning is translated into quantities of information… Along with the hegemony of computers comes a certain logic, and therefore a certain set of prescriptions determining which statements are accepted as "knowledge" statements. (pp4–5).*

Technology has given birth to a new epistemology altogether, but one which also requires us to examine the potential of technology to both build and undermine community. Just as information technology improves access, it can also distance individuals. Computers and the Internet can become a substitute for social interaction on which much of knowledge production and transfer depends. Human agency and community are still a very important part of our experience. The moot question is: does technology increase these potentials or decrease them? Thus learners could be united as much as divided by technology.

A far more complex issue is how the inherited notions of human subjectivity are brought into a crisis – a productive crisis, one hopes – by the Internet. As Mark Poster (2000) observes,

> *The particular change that occurs in the Internet is that the experience of identity, the experience of one's self-presentation and ones' individuality is structured as constructed, so that there is a referentiality built into the structure of communication. It can be illustrated very simply in such things as having to designate your own name, and designate your own gender in certain kinds of Internet configurations. (p148).*

Entering and exiting chat rooms at will, for instance, we experience a new mode of being or ontology that also makes us aware of the constructed and fluid nature of our identities. We cannot but discover in the process that we have many selves, that even our offline incarnations are fictive, provisional entities cobbled together in response to discursive imperatives. The internet which has become an integral part of our lives now mediates our self-understanding, and therefore makes for new forms of subjectivity.

How we communicate with each other has a profound effect on our relationships and our expectations. And this is no less true of students entering institutions of higher learning who may perceive the university, not without some justification, as an anachronism. To avert the ideological struggle between our student populations immersed in new forms of digital self-construction and the university, the very notion of the university may have to be renegotiated.

Earlier, problematisations of transition, understandably, could not have anticipated our technologised present, which becomes increasingly complicated everyday. Both transition and diversity will be viewed through the prisms of technology and its potential to both complicate and enhance the individual student's relationship with the university and those who work within it.

Tinto (1982) and Trow's (1973) conceptualisations of transition provide useful tools for understanding a vital issue in higher education. Many of Trow's pronouncements are remarkably prescient. However, these pronouncements are made within institutional contexts which themselves no longer hold true. For instance, universities are now becoming increasingly corporatised, giving rise, therefore, to newer forms of accountability. Under the pressures of corporatisation universities have had to reinvent themselves as service organisations. What is the status of learning in such a context? What does it mean to be a student now? How does this affect the relationship between teacher and student? The status of the notion of transition changes inevitability when students become our clients.

These (self-)interrogations also follow the general trajectory described by George Ritzer's McDonaldisation thesis which holds that in a postmodern consumer society students expect the same level of service from universities as they do from "other cutting-edge, exciting and efficient means of consumption such as ATMs, fast food restaurants, mega malls, superstores, theme parks and cyber malls" (1988, p151).

Ritzer's McDonaldisation thesis applied to the university highlights the postmodern condition, that ironic suspension between the "past and the present" (p19) which becomes at once "the continuation of Modernism and its transcendence" (p10) as Jencks (1985) put it. In the end, responding to transitions entails a search for new institutional paradigms, at once transforming and transformed. As Rust (1991) points out: "The major schooling lesson for us is that the factory model of schooling is directly connected with modernity, and it is as obsolete as the factory has become in postmodernity. We must contribute to a new definition of school that is appropriate to the new age (p622). This may be a further project for us.

Our attempt here has not been to discredit conventional conceptualisations of transitions. Rather, we have explored the sorts of complexities that may arise through the encounter between these conceptualisations of transition and postmodern theories. In the best tradition of intellectual inquiry we have tried to raise questions instead of providing convenient answers or prescriptive formulas. Admittedly, such an inquiry raises expectations of possible policy formulations. But we postpone these speculations for the time being.

References

Ashar, H and Skennes, R (1992). Can Tinto's Departure Model Be Applied to Nontraditional Students? *Adult Education Quarterly* 43 (1), 90–100.

Bloland, Harland G (1995). Postmodernism and Higher Education. *The Journal of Higher Education*. 66 (5), 521–559.

Clegg, Stewart R(1990). *Modern Organisations*. Cited Parker (1992).

Derrida, J (1974) *Of Grammatology*. Gayatri Chakravorty Spivak (Trans). Corrected Edn. Baltimore and London: The Johns Hopkins University Press.

Evans, M and Peel, M (1999). Factors and Problems in School and University Transition. Cited Huon and Sankey (2000).

Foucault, M (1979). *Discipline and Punish*. Alan Sheridan (Trans). New York: Vintage.

Habermas, J (1981). Modernity versus Postmodernity. *New German Critique*. Seyla Ban-Habib (Trans.). 22, 3–14.

Huon, GF and Sankey, M (2000). The Transition to University: Understanding Differences in Success. Retrieved 12 December 2003 First Year in Higher Education Database http://www.qut.edu.au.

Inayatullah, S (2000). Corporate Networks of Bliss for All: The Politics of the Futures of the University. In Inayatullah, S and Gidley, J (Eds), *The University in Transformation: Global Perspectives on the Futures of the University*. 221–233. Westport, Connecticut & London: Bergin & Harvey.

Evans, P and Wurster, Thomas S (2000). *Blown to Bits: How the Economics of Information Transforms Strategy*. Boston, Massachusetts: Harvard Business School Press.

Gallagher, M (2001). Modern University Governance – A National Perspective. Paper presented at *The Idea of a University: Enterprise or Academy*. Retrieved 20 Aug 2004 www.dest.gov.au.

Jencks, C (1987) *What is Postmodernism?* London and New York: St. Martin's Press.

Kantanis, T (2000). Same or Different: Issues that Affects Mature Age Undergraduates Students' Transition to University. Retrieved 11 December 2003 from First Year in Education Database.

Laclau, E (1988). Politics and the Limits of Modernity. In Andrew Ross (Ed.) *Universal Abandon?: The Politics of Postmodernism*. 63–82. Minneapolis: University of Minnesota Press.

Lawrence, J (2000). Rethinking Diversity: Re-Theorising Transition as a Process of Engaging, Negotiating and Mastering Discourses and Multiliteracies of an Unfamiliar Culture Rather Than as a Problem of Deficit. Retrieved 11Dec 2003 from First Year in Higher Education Database.

Linstead, S and Grafton-Small, R (1992). On Reading Organizational Culture. *Organization Studies*. 13 (3), 332–355.

Lyotard, J (1979). *The Postmodern Condition: A Report on Knowledge*. Minneapolis: University of Minnesota Press.

McInnis, C and James, R (1995). First Year on Campus: Diversity in the Initial Experiences of Australian Undergraduates. Australian Government Publishing Service, Canberra. Cited Huon and Sankey (2000).

Normann, R (1991). *Service Management: Strategy and Leadership in Service Business.* 2nd edn. Cited Rumble (2000). Chichester: Wiley.

Parker, M (1992). "Post-Modern Organizations or Postmodern Organization Theory?" *Organization Studies* 13 (1), 1–16.

Peel, M (1999). Where to Now? Cited in Huon and Sankey (2000).

Rumble, G (2000). Student Support in Distance Education in the 21st Century: Learning from Service Management. *Distance Education.* 21 (2), 216–235.

Rust, V (1991). Postmodernism and Its Comparative Education Implications. *Comparative Education Review.* 35 (4), 610–626.

Ritzer, G (1998). The McDonaldization Thesis. London & Thousand Oaks & New Delhi: SAGE Publications.

Poster, M (2001). Communication and the Constitution of the Self: An Interview With Mark Poster, 14.8.1995. In *The Information Subject.* Australia & Canada & France: The Gordon and Breach Publishing Group.

Smith, A (1993). *Books to Bytes: Knowledge and Information in the Postmodern Era.* London: British Film Institute.

Smith, A and Webster, F (1997). *The Postmodern University?: Contested Visions of Higher Education in Society.* Buckingham, England & Bristol, USA: SRHE and Open University Press.

Tinto, V (1987). *Leaving College: Rethinking the Causes and Cures of Student Attrition.* Chicago & London: The University of Chicago Press.

Trow, M (1974). Problems in the Transition from Elite to Mass Higher Education. In General Report: Policies for Higher Education. Paris: OECD.

Tsoukas, H (1992). Postmodernism, Reflexive Rationalism and Organizational Studies: Reply to Martin Parker. *Organizational Studies.* 13 (4), 643–649.

Van Gennep. (1960). *The Rites of Passage.* Cited Tinto (1987). Chicago: The University of Chicago Press.

Viney, L (1980). *Transitions.* Melbourne: Cassell Australia Limited.

Chinese students in a UK business school: hearing the student voice in reflective teaching and learning practice

Yvonne Turner, University of Newcastle Upon Tyne

Abstract

This paper presents the outcomes of a 2001/02 study exploring the UK educational experiences of nine Chinese postgraduate business students. The research aimed to explore the evolution of the students' implicit theories of learning during their year of study in the UK. The project was designed to facilitate the researcher's academic reflection. The underlying rationale resided in the importance of ensuring high-quality teaching and learning experiences for all students, irrespective of their country of origin. The methodological context of the project was essentially action-research based, working within the researcher's own professional context. The data collection process was qualitative, involving monthly meetings with the participants throughout the academic year to discuss their learning experiences. The outcomes of the work included a comparison of the student's evolving orientations to learning with established research models. The overall conclusion of the work highlighted the study participants' emotional struggles with UK academic conventions.

Introduction

Universities in Britain have long been multicultural, multiethnic communities. Until recently, however, the international contingent was small and the majority of students and academics remained domestic, mainly white British. Teaching policies and practices in universities, therefore, reflected that constituency (Scott, 1995, Barnett, 1997). Recent changes in UK higher education (HE) have increasingly encouraged universities to increase overseas recruitment, both to generate revenue and to broaden cultural diversity (Humfrey 1999). In this context, Chinese students (PRC) have emerged as a significant group.

While it is clear that full-fee-paying Chinese students have contributed financially to British HE, nonetheless a range of difficult issues potentially influence the quality of their educational experience. Life as an international student in Britain is not always easy (McNay, 1996; Humfrey, 1999). A body of literature has developed, documenting the challenges experienced by international students in Britain, both in the fulfillment of their initial expectations and their ability to succeed academically (McNamara and Harris, 1996; Mortimer, 1997; Turner, 1999, 2000; Devos, 2003). Key within this literature are accounts of the learning implications that stem from a UK-centric pedagogy which is unfamiliar to students from non-Anglo cultures (Earwaker, 1992; Turner and Acker, 2002). In spite of such challenges, however, numbers of students from the PRC have continued to rise (Economist, 2003a, b). Today, they constitute one of the largest international student groups in universities, one whose participation is likely to exert considerable influence on teaching and learning dynamics. Deriving from this environment, this small-scale project investigated the experiences of a group of Chinese postgraduate (PG) students in UK HE. It also facilitated my own professional reflection, as a British academic working with Chinese students in an increasingly internationalised context.

Chinese teaching and learning: a pen portrait

Historically, much of the Chinese education literature has focused on general characterisations of the education system or descriptions of the formalities of teaching and learning dynamics. It provides fewer insights into individual student experiences (for examples see Hayhoe, 1996; Bai, 2000; Chen 1999; Lin, 1993). Nonetheless, an exploration of the literature helps to develop broad insights into Chinese students' previous academic contexts and can generate an initial context of understanding.

The environment described in the literature is formal, disciplined, teacher-centred and didactic (Reed, 1988; Cleverly, 1991; Leung, 1991; Chen, 1999; Cortazzi and Jin, 2001; Turner and Acker, 2002). The approach to a unitarist, factual construction of knowledge is established early – questions and criticisms of knowledge content or methods are not tolerated (Turner and Acker, 2002). Responding to more than fifty-five years of Socialism, education is designed to be socially normative, a cornerstone of the country's economic modernisation policies (Goldman, 1981; Ho, 1986; SEC, 1996; Li, 1994). Political and civic education exert a strong influence on the curriculum, determining which subjects are favoured by students (sciences, not humanities) and how assessment and progression is managed (Turner and Acker, 2002). In spite of high levels of unassessed homework, written examinations comprise most formal assessments, with large set-piece assessments marking educational progression. Student class rankings and class streaming according to ability derive from exam marks. Assessment is predominantly individual.

In spite of classroom formality, teachers and students engage in friendly extramural relationships. The teacher acts as personal mentor as well as educator and disciplinarian (Biggs and Watkins, 2001; Ho, 2001). This construction of the teacher's role correlates not only with Confucian notions of educational relationship hierarchies but also with socialist constructions of education as taking place within local neighbourhoods, facilitating the formation of social and political character alongside cognitive development (Partington, 1988; Lee 1996). Civic and moral education and the governance of personal behaviour are strong themes featuring in the typical Chinese student's education career (Turner and Acker, 2002). Parents are also highly involved in routine discussions about children's education (Ho, 1986; Zhu, 1999; Economist, a, b, 2003). In spite of such high levels of involvement and support from teachers and parents, however, many Chinese students do not regard their schooling positively. Highly competitive classroom dynamics and scarcity of places at 'good' institutions means that the education is highly pressurised – "like stuffing a duck" (Turner and Acker 2002, p110). When confronted with high-school and college entrance examinations, which are extremely competitive, student suicides are not uncommon. The popular view remains, however, that education correlates strongly with future career success and will bring security to both the student and their family (Economist, 2003 a, b).

The pre-Socialist tradition

Within a wider picture of Chinese education, Confucianist views about learning remain influential within contemporary pedagogy. Confucianism strongly equates learning and 'knowledge' – learning functions as the process of factual and tangible knowledge-acquisition, within a cognitive taxonomy (Fu, 1996; Lee, 1996; Allinson, 1989). A strong traditional value is placed upon 'wisdom', characterised as gerontocratic and male (Szalay et al, 1994). Within this value system, education is part of a ritual progress through life, conferring a 'social passport' to adulthood. Confucianist educational constructs, therefore, assert youth, formality, a focus on propositional knowledge, and open-access. Procedural knowledge, where explicit (mainly confined to learning techniques and structures), follows in linear fashion from the propositional, reflecting the didactic learning context (Bruner 1996). Historically, popularly-practised Confucianist ethics have driven a meditative aspect to learning (Biggs and Watkins, 2001), which many 'western' commentators have classified as 'rote' learning (Cleverly, 1991; Ramsden, 1992; Chan and Drover, 1996). In Chinese learning conceptions, however, an important contextual role exists for meditative, repetitive, memory-based approaches as vehicles for achieving deeper learning (Mok et al, 2001). Confucianism also equates effective learning with labour – success derives from hard work and disciplined concentration, irrespective of one's intrinsic intellectual gifts (Zhaowu, 1998). Lack of educational success is constructed as lack of effort rather than an absence of cognitive gifts. Accompanying this specific, incrementalist construction of learning, critique is not privileged. Given the central role of teacher as sage and the concept of wisdom gained step-by-step, critique is reserved as an activity for those who have already completed the learning journey rather than for students embarking on it. Again there is an emphasis on ritual progress through stages of learning, accompanied by stoic labour and contemplation rather than critical engagement with the objects of learning or of those who are teaching. It also highlights the role of contemplative memorisation as a central activity in the process of learning (Mok et al 2001).

The contemporary scene

In the twentieth century, Socialist revolutionaries sought to eradicate every trace of the imperial system, often through violent means. Many of the measures taken, however, did little initially to replace existing pedagogies (Pepper, 1996). Ways of teaching remained in place and notions of learning and assessment were unchanged. Post-revolutionary educational models remained normative, becoming institutionalised. Continuity of practice within the Chinese system has been largely practical, however, the result of scarcity of resources and – because of the continued persecution of intellectuals (Hayhoe, 1989; Pepper, 1996) – a serious shortage of intellectual capital with which to develop alternative pedagogical approaches. Certainly for students in China today, learning tends to focus on knowledge content, remains mainly teacher-centred, is competitive, exam-centred, elitist, and largely male-gendered. Contemporary social progression is secured through education.

Picturing Chinese students

Summarising the preceding discussion, figure one (below) draws out a range of learning characteristics and expectations of a notional Chinese university student.

Employing a range of literature discussing the context of UK HE (including Entwistle, 1988; Barnett, 1990, 1992, 1997; McNay, 1995; Dearlove, 1997; Bauman, 1997; Thorens, 1998; Brockbank and McGill, 1998; Biggs, 1999, Foreman and Johnston, 1999; Ketteridge et al, 1999; Light and Cox, 2001), it is possible to develop a similar archetype of UK students, shown at figure two (opposite), to provide an exploratory comparison and identify potential sources of teaching and learning challenges for Chinese students when studying in the UK.

The gaps between the two models are fairly obvious. Most of them influence student motivations and orientation to work. Practically, a number of potential differences in orientation to learning could inhibit Chinese students' success in UK HE, unless they are able to adapt and work within academic conventions quickly.

The 'model' Chinese student
Young, unmarried, full-time student
Works hard to achieve results – the harder working, the better the student
Passive learner, listens to the teacher and studies privately
Learns mainly by reading and processing knowledge
Responds to teacher direction obediently and adopts both structures and substance of study according to teacher direction
Combines intellectual capability and 'good' moral behaviour – a good citizen
Highly competitive with others in cohort, strives to be the 'best'
Does not question accepted norms and ideas in the classroom
Learns within defined disciplinary rules and boundaries

Figure one: Chinese student archetypes

The 'model' British student
Any age, studying through many patterns
Combines hard work and trained/natural ability
Active learner, asks lots of questions and participates vocally in class
Learns by combining a range of learning skills – an active, problem-solving-based learner
Meets the teacher's suggestions with independent mind and imagination, studies in trained but personalised style
Intellectual and moral behaviour not an inevitable combination – the development of individual ethics
May strive to 'do one's best' against the standard
Takes a critical stance on knowledge and learning
Contextualises learning and relates learning to other aspects of life in a holistic manner

Figure two: British student archetypes

Research themes

The contextual and theoretical frameworks that boundaried the project under discussion are broad, encompassing cultural pedagogies, teaching and learning theories and HE practices. Taking the literature briefly summarised above, however, a coherent set of project themes emerged. First, the broadest question was to explore how participants responded to studying in the UK and how they framed their experiences in relation to their past education. The participants had experienced many years of education in China before coming to Britain. To what extent, therefore, did their experiences reflect the themes suggested by the literature and how far did their struggles reflect the 'gaps' inferred from a notional "UK/China" comparison? The second theme focused on individual and collective resonances in participant accounts: did each student differ in their approach to learning or did their collective accounts coalesce meaningfully around themes in the literature? Third: how did participants construct learning – did this change during their UK studies? Finally: what insights could I gain from the student accounts that might help me work effectively with Chinese students in Britain?

Research schedule

The research took place over the course of one academic year, 2001-02, at a post-1992 university, involving nine students from the PRC enrolled on one-year taught masters degrees in business. Lightly-structured data-collection conversations, which were tape-recorded and supplemented by my reflective journal entries, took place approximately monthly during the academic year.

Discussion

The emphasis in the project was primarily on illumination of the individual accounts. Within this interpretative emphasis, a range of elements in the participants' accounts resonated strikingly with themes in the literature. Firstly, participants struggled to accommodate perceived differences in approaches to teaching and learning in the UK from what they had experienced in their previous education in China. For example, their accounts highlighted a structured, teacher-centred environment in China, focused on propositional knowledge, compared to a discovery-based, procedural emphasis in Britain:

> *In China the teachers always tell the students what to do, when to do, how to do, everything they will tell us!...In university in China, the whole lecture is the teacher saying. (QWY, p3-4)*

Similarly, accounts also highlighted the relatively limited extent of transition and change that the students underwent during their year in the UK and identified that much of their experience was confined to attempting to *learn about how to learn* in the UK rather than *participating in* the implicit cultures of learning that existed:

> *I think the difference is in the teaching style... here the lecturer only point something, the next thing you must do by yourself... they only give the guidance, the rest of the thing you must do by yourself. So you have to worry. If I go in the wrong direction, I totally lost. You learn a lot of things there, but it is no use (LG, p15).*

Their experiences, therefore, largely illustrated the considerable human effort of accommodating two different culturally-articulated notions of education and learning in a relatively short time-period. These themes are further developed in figure three (opposite), which compares the notional models of Chinese and British students and the study participants as revealed in their accounts over the year.

What emerged from the comparison in figure three is that the starting-point for participants aligned closely to the Chinese student archetype. Given the highly normative and uniform structure of education in the PRC, this is relatively unsurprising. Moreover, participants' views, attitudes and recollections of their previous learning correlated closely to other research accounts from Chinese students (Gallagher, 1998; Turner and Acker, 2002). Equally, it was clear that though the majority of participants attempted to move away from their initial position to accommodate the demands of UK study, this proved to be very difficult:

> *I think after we finish the study here, we can't learn more. We are just busy with our coursework each week, I think...Even though we don't take the lecture, maybe we read some books and we can finish the coursework...I think the courses, not the courses, but the course-works are nonsense. (HLG, p16-17)*

> *I have become a bad student here in Britain...I can't get an excellent or good score for my study. In China, I am not top three, but I'm top ten student. But here I'm a bad student... (HLG p25)*

Most participants primarily attempted to shift their orientation to learning and practice by explicitly focusing on knowledge-based techniques for improved learning, especially when struggling with both subject and English-language challenges in assessments. This was consistent with technical-propositional pedagogies which had underpinned their previous education, but proved largely ineffective:

The 'model' Chinese student	The 'model' British student	Participants
Young, unmarried, full-time student	Any age, studying through many patterns	All between 22 and 25; unmarried
Works hard to achieve results – the harder working, the better the student	Combines hard work and trained/natural ability	Focused on hard work – striving to be a 'good' student through hard work; self-recrimination for poor effort; sought emotional reassurance in research interviews
Passive learner, listens to the teacher and studies privately	Active learner, asks lots of questions and participates vocally in class	Frequently embarrassed to ask questions in class; limited participation – an emotional issue; sought reassurance in research interviews
Learns mainly by reading and processing knowledge	Learns by combining a range of learning skills – an active, problem-solving-based learner	Focus on reading and remembering; some took notes – found problem-solving learning challenging
Responds to teacher direction obediently and adopts both structures and substance of study according to teacher direction	Meets the teacher's suggestions with independent mind and imagination, studies in trained but personalised style	Sought guidance from lecturers; adapted own approaches to study where environment was highly unstructured and independent; some put off work where insufficient guidance was given
Combines intellectual capability and 'good' moral behaviour – a good citizen	Intellectual and moral behaviour not an inevitable combination – the development of individual ethics	Somewhat critical of UK students on moral grounds; sought to meet expectations of family by doing consistently well
Highly competitive with others in cohort, strives to be the 'best'	May strive to 'do one's best' against the standard	Highly competitive; disappointed with poor marks; actively benchmarked personal performance against groups in the cohort
Does not question accepted norms and ideas in the classroom	Takes a critical stance on knowledge and learning	Struggled with criticality – most used research interviews to explore conceptions of learning and critique
Learns within defined disciplinary rules and boundaries	Contextualises learning and relates learning to other aspects of life in a holistic manner	Seeking the 'way' to succeed in the UK system – looking for rules; differing levels of independence emerged over the year

Figure three: Model students and real people compared

Although she [the lecturer] tried to explain it to me and she tried her best to explain it, but I still can't get anything. I still can't get any information. I don't think I can connect to the things that she said, connected with the knowledge that I learned before. (CD p13)

The minority who experienced the highest levels of understanding of the UK system (and academic success), also expressed the highest degree of personal emancipation and independence during the year:

> *I think this should be important or good memory…Because before I came to Britain, I haven't lived alone. My parents looked after me. But here, everything you should do yourself, so I think this should improve the life skill, yeah. (PT, p45)*

They were also the oldest in the group, with either previous work experience and/or previous exposure to international companies and people. These factors coalesced to enable a more open response to their new context and an enhanced reflective ability – embracing an implicitly reflexive, pluralistic positions. For the majority, however, both academic success levels and accounts of personal happiness were lower:

> *To be honest, I think it is really hard work! I don't think everyone enjoys studying. They just do things they have to, they just study because they have to. (CD p24)*

For some, this resulted in a rejection of the UK experience and expressions of anger and unhappiness at their treatment by the university, and especially by lecturers whom they felt unfriendly and uncaring towards students and responsible for students' lack of success:

> *I do not think they very care about us. (HLG, p25)*

> *In Chinese [there is] a saying. "There is no bad student, just a bad teacher"…Because every student, every people, they can learn. Why they didn't learn well, maybe is the method of the teacher…the teacher has some problems. They cannot teach the student well. (YMX, p7)*

For one participant, the initial shock of the first semester was sufficiently great to prompt his abrupt departure from the UK in January. Others attempted to adapt to the UK context through relatively simple, instrumental accommodation, with the aim of satisfying the extrinsic objective of obtaining a degree certificate:

> *I study here for more than half a year and to do lots of work just to understand other people's thoughts, just like translate, no just like paraphrase their thoughts in my own words, but basically those thoughts are theirs. It is not difficult. (CD p36)*

The main theme emerging from this aspect of the project-work were accounts of the emotional turbulence accompanying the intercultural transition between educational systems. For all participants, whatever their ultimate academic or personal destination, the UK year involved considerable suffering, and enforced personal reflection in ways that tended to undermine confidence. For some, this inhibited their ability to more forward effectively. Moreover, most participants questioned the academic usefulness of their experiences, though they valued the opportunity to live overseas and acknowledged the usefulness of a master's degree for future employment. While the extrinsic benefits of the experience were clear, therefore, the intrinsic aspects remained more ambiguous.

The pattern of development over the year

One underlying key question for the project was to explore how far the students' attitudes towards learning changed during their year in Britain. Again, figure three illuminates this question. In spite of participants' own assessment of their development, an exploration of the interview data showed a complex pattern of change and stability, of conflict, challenge and resistance as each person was exposed to new experiences. The main focus was in the students' expectations of themselves and how they developed. In this context, the first assessment was an important watershed. Having overcome this developmental hurdle (with differing levels of success), participants were able to reflect on their learning progress and to evaluate how they had responded to the need to develop new skills. As noted above, for some, this facilitated personal reflection and questioning about their underlying approach to learning. For others, the focus was more instrumental, resting on deconstructing explicit aspects of successful assessment techniques. Indeed, unsurprisingly, the main focus of reflection was about the technical areas of academic work – essay-writing, citation etc. This was followed by group-work skills, though participants articulated little enthusiasm for group activities and regarded interpersonal skills development as external to the formal learning process:

I don't like groupwork…I don't think it is useful. (HLG p28)

An interesting issue within this context is the generally low-level of awareness that participants' showed of shifts in their orientation to learning. Their discussions about learning did not acknowledge any concomitant changes in personal world-view. For example, one participant commented that he cited references in essays only because it was a UK academic convention, part of assessment requirements, and not because he believed it had value:

Actually, I like to write article that use my own point of view. I do not like to use other people's point of view instead…But I think most people believe that you have to quote some people from the gurus or there very famous people in this field – you have to quote them. But I think…the people who want to know what you studied, what you learned from your work, they have to see your own idea, not what you quoted from another work. (WS, p26)

These incidences illustrated both a maintenance of the obedient, 'passive-receptive' student persona (Biggs 1999; Gay, 2003) – just doing what's necessary to pass and what the teacher required, not asking questions, keeping opinions to oneself – and was an example of participants' essentially unchanging conceptual framework. What emerged clearly from the accounts attested to the persistence of pre-existing implicit theories of learning. These aspects of the interviews illustrated the difficulties that participants experienced in shifting towards a new mental framework from which to evaluate their learning experiences. Overall, the response typifying attitudes to new behaviours and new styles of classroom interaction was to judge them negatively based on criteria established in China.

It seemed clear that, in terms of cultural interfaces and communication exchanges, participants encountered significant emotional difficulties in accommodating their new cultural environment and integrating their experiences into the context of their existing values. Nonetheless an active sense of self-determination and independence in their broader lives seemed also to stem from the patterning of learning experiences in which they had engaged. To this extent, it was clear that the group's implicit theories both of learning and self had shifted, though not without emotional struggle, as discussed above. Linking this with the simple fact that their previously unitarist conception of learning had been confronted with the playing out of a different epistemology suggested a strongly-present but almost unrealised articulation of a shift in the underlying implicit theory for the students as a group. The brevity of their experiences over a single academic year may account for its relatively unrealised presence and may also account for their inability to articulate its presence other than in general life terms.

Did participants' attitudes to learning change?

Overall, the group revealed a counterintuitive pattern of shifts in implicit theories of learning. On the one hand, participants' self-perceptions acknowledged only superficial change, to acquire new educational skills and knowledge, and maintained that participants were relatively unaffected by their UK experiences. The interview data certainly seemed to underline consistency in their fundamental sense of learning-self. Nonetheless, participants were aware of emotional shifts in how they negotiated their personal lives, related in some way to their learning experiences. In this way, their implicit theories of learning did, indeed, develop. The untested question touches the profundity of these changes. Both the literature and interview accounts support a view of Chinese students as adaptable and flexible to new environments, but in a framework where the learning process remained objectified, not touching the individual deeply. In such a context, it is interesting to consider whether participants retained the emergent sense of independence and self-determination they articulated after their return home or whether it remained somehow emotionally 'boxed' within the cultural dynamics of their UK experiences.

Personal and professional reflections

There is no doubt that this project exerted profound influence on my professional practice. In many ways, this was surprising to me. Having worked with Chinese students and researched Chinese education for some time, in China and the UK, I set out on the project feeling that I could anticipate some of the likely outcomes of the work. I also maintained a professional identity that, I believed, took into account student diversity. From the beginning, however, the project surprised me because of the relatively high levels of personal contact that I experienced with the students in the study group compared to others that I had worked with in the past. What I realised, as I worked through the months of the project, was that my orientation to the students and to my professional position in the university existed within an emotionally-British cultural framework which effectively maintained and protected distance from students. To a large extent, that dualism dissolved as the project progressed. The students came to talk with me about a range of personal issues over the course of their discussions about education and learning. They were also interested in my personal life as well as our professional contact. During interviews, participants treated me as an old friend. It was clear that they both trusted me and enjoyed the contact that we had together. Indeed, some who participated in the study told me that, given the little contact they had with British people, I was their 'only British friend'. I have to say that I found this very sad, though it went some way to explaining the deep sense of hurt and anger they expressed when I asked them to reflect on their experiences at the end of the year.

In terms of specific teaching and learning issues, it became clear that the participants studied differently to the prevailing implicit norms operating in my institution and governing lecturers' working assumptions. It was also apparent that accommodating these UK culturally-implicit norms was difficult for participants and that they needed personal and emotional support to succeed academically. Moreover, a sense of academic success was intrinsic to participants' general sense of well-being and confidence and constituted a virtuous circle. In some cases, the simple provision of a clear pedagogical rationale for a particular educational convention in the UK – which I was able to provide in a matter of minutes – scaffolded their learning development considerably. An ethical question intruded, however, which I have considered deeply since, about how far – in a globally-connected educational world – it is reasonable to articulate academic success in a culturally-normative manner which inherently privileges the domestic cohort. It also encouraged a continuation with the conscious pedagogical experimentation I had embarked upon and a further exploration of the teaching and learning needs of other groups of international students.

In reflecting on professional practice, therefore, the main contribution that project made for me is that it has encouraged me to trust students more with myself. I am also able to see that the combination of personal confidence and learning support are extremely important if students are to be both successful and happy in the course of their studies, especially when they are in the UK for one year. I am willing to take more responsibility for individual and group welfare and see myself much more as advocate, teacher and friend than in the past. Within the construct of my current academic life, this is not an easy combination of roles to maintain. The emphasis in my professional environment is very much focused on scholarly pursuits rather than students. To balance obligations to research activity, teaching and student support is demanding. Nonetheless, striving to do so lets my conscience rest more easily.

An end-point: drawing the threads together

In assessing the outcomes of the project, the most important conclusion attaches to questions about the relationship between implicit theories and practical actions to support student learning. It was clear that participants strove continuously to grapple with UK academic conventions in an attempt to understand and evaluate their learning experiences. It was also clear that their practical efforts to work within UK epistemological and pedagogical frameworks were largely frustrated because of a lack of opportunities to contextualise and discuss these issues within the framework of formal study. Essentially they were left to try and grasp UK academic culture almost piecemeal from such tangible practice-based aspects of life as rules about referencing and plagiarism etc, to which, as students, they not only had access but also were required to master quickly in order to obtain their degree. Throughout the interviews, participants discussed these study techniques and used them both to illustrate and explore UK conceptions of learning. It is no surprise, therefore, that it is in these areas there is evidence of change in the student accounts. Essentially, any more fundamental shifts in conceptions of learning were impossible because those conversations did not take place within the boundaries of their studies and there were few other places to generate them. As a result, participants' underlying cultural ideas and attitudes, values and belief about what constructed learning and education and their practice remained undiscussed and inviolate. Ultimately, in one year, the students did not have the time to do much more than satisfice in their conformity to extrinsic degree standards because there were simply so many things to learn.

References

Allinson, RE (1989), An overview of the Chinese mind in Allinson. RE (Ed): *Understanding the Chinese mind: the philosophical roots*. Oxford University Press

Bai. L (2000), The metamorphosis of China's higher education in the 1990s in Keith Sullivan (Ed) *Education and change in the Pacific Rim*. Oxford University Press.

Barnett, R (1990), *The idea of Higher Education*. Open University/Society for Research into Higher education. Buckingham.

Barnett, R (ed) (1992), *Learning to effect*. Society for Research into Higher Education and the Open University. Buckingham.

Barnett, R (1997), *Higher Education: a critical business*. Buckingham Society for Research into Higher Education/Open University Press. Buckingham

Baumann, Z (1997), Universities: Old, new and different in Smith, A and Webster, F (Eds) *The postmodern university? Contested visions of Higher Education in Society*. Open University/Society for Research into Higher Education. Buckingham.

Beamer, L and Varner, I (2001), *Intercultural communications in the global workplace*. New York. McGraw-Hill Irwin.

Biggs, JB. (1999), *Teaching for quality learning at university: what the student does*. Society for Research into Higher Education and Open University Press. Buckingham.

Biggs, JB and Watkins, DA (2001), The paradox of the Chinese learner and beyond in Biggs, JB and Watkins, DA, (Eds) *Teaching the Chinese learner: psychological and pedagogical perspectives*. Comparative Education research centre, the University of Hong Kong. Hong Kong.

Brockbank, A and McGill, I (1998), *Facilitating reflective learning in Higher Education*. Society for Research into Higher Education and the Open University. Buckingham.

Bruner, J (1996), *The culture of education*. Harvard University press.

Chan, D and Drover, G (1996), Teaching and learning for overseas students: the Hong Kong connection in McNamara, D and Harris, R (Eds) *Overseas students in Higher Education: issues in teaching and learning*. Routledge

Channell, J (1990), The student-tutor relationship in Kinnell, M (ed) *The learning experiences of overseas students*. The Society for Research into Higher Education and Open University press. Buckingham

Chen, Y (1999), Tradition and innovation in the Chinese School curriculum, *Research in Education*, no 61

Cleverly, J (1994), "On the evidence before me…" Putting the case for educational reform in China, *Comparative Education* vol 27, 1

Cortazzi, M and Jin Lixian (2001), Large classes in China: 'good' teachers and Interaction, in Biggs, JB and Watkins, DA (Eds) *Teaching the Chinese learner: psychological and pedagogical perspectives*. Comparative Education Research Centre, the University of Hong Kong. Hong Kong.

Dearlove J (1997), The academic labour process: from collegiality and professionalism to managerialism and proletarianism? *Higher Education Review*, vol 30, no 1.

Denscombe, M (2003), *The good research guide for small-scale social research projects*. Maidenhead. Open University Press.

Denzin, NK, Lincoln. YS (1994), Introduction: entering the field of qualitative research in Denzin, NK, Lincoln, YS (Eds) *Handbook of Qualitative research*. Sage

Devos, A (2003), Academic standards, internationalization, and the discursive construction of "the international student", *Higher Education research and Development*, vol 22, no 2, pp155-191.

Earwaker, J (1992), *Helping and supporting students: rethinking the issues*. The Society for Research into Higher Education and Open University Press. Buckingham

Economist, the (2003a), Chinese students: Western promise, 29 March – 4 April 2003. p33. London

Economist, the (2003b), Education in China: a private matter, 29 March – 4 April 2003. p65-66. London

Ellis, C, Bochner, AP (2000), Autoethnography, personal narrative, reflexivity: researcher as subject in Denzin, NK, Lincoln, YS (Eds) *Handbook of Qualitative research*. Sage

Ellis, C, Bochner, AP (1996) *Composing ethnography*. Altamira press

Entwistle, NJ (1988) *Styles of teaching and learning: an integrated outline of educational psychology for students, teachers and lecturers*, London. Fulton

Flowerdew, J, Miller, L and Li, D (2000), Chinese lecturers' perceptions, problems and strategies in lecturing in English to Chinese-speaking students, *RELC*, vol. 31, no 1.

Fu, W (1996) *Cultural flow between China and the outside world throughout history*. Foreign languages press. Beijing.

Gallagher, T (1998) *In their own words: profiles of today's Chinese students*. China books and periodicals. Beijing.

Gay, G (2003), Culture and communication in the classroom in Samovar, LA and Porter, RE *Intercultural communication: a reader*. Belmont. Thomson Wadsworth.

Goodman, D (1996), The People's Republic of China: the party-state, capitalist revolution and new entrepreneurs in Robinson, R and Goodman, D (eds) *The New rich in Asia: mobile phones, McDonald's and middle-class revolution*. Routledge, London/New York, pp225-243.

Gough, L (1998), *Asia meltdown: the end of the miracle?* Capstone

Hamilton, D (1994), Traditions, preferences and postures in applied qualitative research in Denzin, NK and Lincoln, YS (Eds) *Handbook of Qualitative research*. Sage

Hannum, E (1999), Poverty and Basic-level Schooling in China: equity issues in the 1990s, *Prospects*, vol 29, no 4.

Hantrais, L and Mangen, S (1996), Methods and Management of cross-national research in Hantrais, L and Mangen, S (Eds) *Cross-national research methods in the social sciences*. Pinter. New York

Hayhoe, R (1989) *China's universities and the open door*. Sharpe

Hayhoe, R (1996) *China's universities 1895-1995: a century of conflict*. Garland Publishing

Ho, DYF (1986) Chinese patterns of socialization: a critical review in Bond, M (Ed) *The Psychology of the Chinese people*. Oxford University Press

Ho, IT (2001) Are Chinese teachers authoritarian? in Biggs, JB and Watkins, DA (Eds) *Teaching the Chinese learner: psychological and pedagogical perspectives*. Comparative Education Research Centre, the University of Hong Kong. Hong Kong.

Hodges, L (2001) A cultural revolution for the 21st century, *The Independent*, Thursday 31 May 2001. London.

Humfrey, C (1999) *Managing international students*. Open University press. Buckingham.

Ketteridge, S, Fry, H, Marshal, S (eds) (1999) *A handbook for teaching and learning in higher education: enhancing academic practice*.

Kinnell, M (ed) (1990) *The learning experiences of overseas students*. The Society for Research into Higher Education and Open University Press. Buckingham

Kipnis, A (1997) *Producing Guanxi: sentiment, self, and subculture in a north China village*, Duke University Press, Durham.

Lee, WO (1996) The Cultural Context for Chinese Learners: conceptions of learning in the Confucian tradition in Biggs, JB and Watkins, DA (Eds) *The Chinese learner: cultural, psychological and contextual influences*. Comparative Education Research Centre, the University of Hong Kong. Hong Kong.

Leung. YM (1991) Curriculum development in the People's Republic of China in Marsh C and Morris P (eds), *Curriculum development in East Asia*. Falmer press.

Leung. YM (1995) The People's Republic of China in Morris P and Sweeting A (eds) *Education and development in East Asia*. Garland Publishing inc.

Li Peng (1994) *Report at the National Conference on education*. Department of foreign affairs/State Education Commission, People's Republic of China. Beijing.

Light, G and Cox, R (2001) *Learning and Teaching in Higher Education: the reflective professional*. Paul Chapman publishing. London

Lin Jing (1993) *Education in post-Mao China*. Praeger, 1993

McNamara, D and Harris, R (eds) (1996) *Overseas students in higher education: issues in teaching and learning*. Routledge

McNay. I (1995) From the Collegial academy to corporate enterprise: the changing culture of universities in Schuller, T (Ed) *The changing university?* Society for Research into Higher Education and Open University. Buckingham

Min Jiayin (Ed) (1995) *The chalice and the blade in Chinese culture: Gender relations and social models*. The Chinese partnership research group. Beijing.

Ministry of Education, People's Republic of China, Department of Development and Planning, (2003), *Educational statistics yearbook of China*. People's Education Press. Beijing.

Mok, I, Chik, PM, Ko, PY, Kwan, T, Lo, ML, Marton, F, Ng, DFP, Pang, MF, Runesson, U and Szeto, LH, (2001), Solving the paradox of the Chinese teacher? in Biggs, JB and Watkins, DA (Eds) *Teaching the Chinese learner: psychological and pedagogical perspectives*. Comparative Education Research Centre, the University of Hong Kong. Hong Kong.

Moon. J (1999) *Reflection in learning and professional development: theory and practice*. Kogan Page. London.

Mortimer, K (1997) Recruiting overseas undergraduate students: are their information requirements being satisfied? *Higher Education Quarterly*, vol 51,3, 1997

Partington, G (1988) The concept of progress in Marxist educational theories, *Comparative Education*, vol 24, 1

Pepper, S (1996) *Radicalism and education reform in 20th-Century China: the search for an ideal development model*. Cambridge University Press.

Ramsden, P (1992) *Learning to teach in Higher Education*. Routledge. London.

Reed, LA (1988) *Education in the People's Republic of China and US-China educational exchanges*. National Association for Foreign student affairs. Washington D.C.

Scott, P (1995) *The meanings of mass Higher Education*. Society for Research into Higher Education and Open University Press. Buckingham.

Schwandt, TA (2000) Three epistemological stances for qualitative enquiry: Interpretivism, Hermeneutics, and Social Constructionism in Denzin, NK and Lincoln, YS (Eds) *Handbook of qualitative research (second edition)*. Sage. London

Shotnes, S (1987) *Overseas students – destination UK?* UK Council for Overseas Student Affairs.

State Education Commission of China (1996a) *Basic education in China*. SEC Beijing.

State Education Commission of China (1996b) *5-year plan for education and development towards year 2010*. SEC Beijing.

State Education Commission of China (1996c) *Introduction to education in China*. SEC Beijing.

State Education Commission of China (1996d) *Regular and Higher education in China*. SEC Beijing.

Strauss, Anselm and Corbin, Juliet (1998) *Basics of qualitative research: techniques and procedures for developing grounded theory*. Sage

Szalay, LB, Strohl, JB, Fu, Liu, Lao, Pen-Shui, (1994) *American and Chinese perceptions and belief systems: a People's Republic of China-Taiwanese comparison*. Plenum press New York.

Tierney, WG (2000), Undaunted courage: life history and the postmodern challenge in Denzin, NK and Lincoln, YS (Eds) *Handbook of qualitative research* (second edition). Sage, California

Tsui, AS, Farh, Jiing-Lih, Xin, KR (2000), Guanxi in the Chinese context in Li, JT, Tsui, AS, and Weldon, E (Eds) *Management and organizations in the Chinese context*. Macmillan

Tsui Kai-yuen (1998) Economic reform and attainment in basic education in China, *China Quarterly*

Turner, Y (2000) *When an unstoppable force meets an immovable object: Chinese students in UK universities*. Proceedings of European Learning styles Conference, June 2000.

Turner, Y (2002), Chinese students in Europe: the influence of culture and society in *Chinese students in Ireland: new opportunities, new needs new challenges*. Irish Council for International students.

Turner, Y and Acker, A (2002) *Education in the New China: shaping ideas at work*. Ashgate, Basingstoke.

Winter, R (1989) *Learning from experience: principles and practice in action research (with contributions from Susan Burroughs)*, London. Falmer

World Bank (1997) *China 2020*. World Bank New York.

World Bank (1997) *China: Higher Education reform*. World Bank, New York.

Zhao, Y and Campbell, KP (1995) English in China, *World Englishes*, vol 14, no 3.

Zhaowu, H (1998) *An intellectual history of China*. Foreign languages press, Beijing.

Zhu, M (1999), The views and involvement of Chinese parents in their children's education, *Prospects*, vol 29 (2).

Associations between research students' experiences and learning outcomes

Paul Ginns[1], Paul Ramsden[1] and Linda Conrad[2]

[1]University of Sydney

[2]Griffith University

The research reported in this article was supported by an Australian Research Council grant to the second and third authors.

Abstract

There is considerable evidence that undergraduate students' experiences affect their approaches to study and subsequent outcomes. The effects of research students' experiences and outcomes have not yet been systematically studied. The study aimed to test the generalisability of a structural model of the research student experience, testing the relative importance of supervision and support, clarity of goals and expectations, research climate, and infrastructure, in predicting ratings of skill development and overall satisfaction with degree quality. The sample consisted of 3,137 research students in 15 Australian universities. Students completed surveys of their experiences and estimated frequency of types of supervision. After initial testing for multilevel effects in the outcome variables, structural equation models of the research higher degree (RHD) student experience were developed and tested. These analyses indicated a model separating out effects for Supervision and Intellectual/Social Climate fitted well for humanities and professional studies students, but not for sciences students. Additional analyses investigated correlations between departmental completion rates and departmental aggregate scores on the independent variables investigated in the structural models.

The Australian Commonwealth Government expects that higher education research will "maintain and strengthen Australia's knowledge base and research capabilities, by developing an effective research and research training system, thereby enhancing Australia's economic development, international competitiveness and attainment of social goals" (DEST, 2004). This statement recognises that active researchers are not only responsible for developing the body of knowledge, but must also develop the next generation of researchers through research training, ie PhD and masters (research) programmes. In order to promote quality outcomes in research training, in 2001 the Commonwealth Government developed the Research Training Scheme, in which funding for research training is based on institutional performance on RHD completion rates (50%), research income (40%), and a publications measure (10%). While the Research Training Scheme has been criticised for leading to perverse funding outcomes, and is under review, the goal of improving RHD student completions remains. But what aspects of the RHD experience will achieve this goal? In this paper, we explore results from a large-scale, multi-institution survey of Australian RHD students, testing a model of the RHD experience that draws upon prior research with coursework students.

RHD student attrition and persistence

What do we know about the reasons RHD students complete their degrees? Bair and Haworth (2004) reviewed both qualitative and quantitative research on this issue conducted between 1970 and 1998. Based on 118 studies, they reached the following major conclusions:

a) Attrition and persistence rates vary considerably by fields of study, with the lowest rates of attrition generally being found in the laboratory sciences, and the highest rates occurring in the humanities and social sciences.

b) The quality of relationships between doctoral students on the one hand, and supervisor and faculty on the other, is strongly and positively related to completion. The student/supervisor relationship in particular may be the most important variable in persistence and attrition.

c) Student involvement in structured activities contributes positively to completion. Such activities may be at the departmental level, institution-wide, or associated with professional groups.

d) Student satisfaction with academic programmes is positively associated with completion. Bair and Haworth identified a number of contributors to programme satisfaction from the body of available research, including quality of the programme, communication with other students, fairness of requirements, consistency of student evaluation, concern for students as professionals, and level of guidance.

e) Doctoral students who complete are more likely to have interacted with their academic peers than non-completers.

f) Receiving financial support (research or teaching assistantships, fellowships, or graduate assistantships) is related to completion: students who are offered such support are more likely to complete than those who rely on other funding sources.

g) Difficulty with the dissertation phase (eg topic selection, lack of structure compared to the coursework stage) is related to attrition.

h) Academic achievement and demographic variables are not good predictors of completion (with the exception of Graduate Record Exam Advanced scores).

i) Individual differences, such as level of motivation and commitment, are important predictors of completion. "Although most persisters confessed to having wanted to leave their programmes, they also overwhelmingly stated that it was their unwillingness to experience failure that kept them in school... one persister said he stayed in the programme because 'I really wanted that degree. I really like to face up to a challenge'" (Reamer, 1990, p23; cited in Bair and Howarth, 2004, p507).

j)   Retention rates vary widely between institutions.

k)   ABD (all but dissertation) is not the stage where most doctoral students necessarily depart.

l)   Time-to-degree is positively related to attrition; that is, the longer the time spent in graduate school, the smaller the chance that a student will receive a degree.

m)   Doctoral programmes with smaller entering cohorts have lower times to degree and higher completion rates than programmes with larger entering cohorts.

While Bair and Howarth's review reiterates previous research findings emphasising the importance of the relationship of the RHD student with the supervisor, several of the above broad conclusions move beyond this dyadic relationship to identify the role of contextual variables. These include the supportive role of academics other than the supervisor; participation in structured activities; and degree of interaction with peers. Previous research in coursework settings has also identified the importance to learning of aspects of context other than disciplinary features (eg Crawford, Gordon, Nicholas & Prosser, 1998; Lizzio, Wilson, & Simons, 2002). Together, these findings suggest a stronger focus is needed on the contexts supporting the learning of research higher degree students, as well as students' perceptions of those contexts. Such research should illuminate how learning environment affect postgraduate students' approaches to their research, and how supervision and support might be made more effective.

Measuring the RHD Student Experience

For some years, the Course Experience Questionnaire (Ramsden, 1991; Wilson, Lizzio & Ramsden, 1997) was used by the Australian Commonwealth Government as a performance indicator for the experience of RHD students, but in the late 1990s, the Graduate Careers Council of Australia commissioned the development of an instrument, the Postgraduate Research Experience Questionnaire (PREQ) more appropriate for RHD students; detailed coverage of the PREQ's development and evaluation can be found in ACER (1999). The PREQ has been criticised as inappropriate for benchmarking across universities (Marsh, Rowe, & Martin, 2002), but more recent analyses using an expanded dataset have detected small but reliable institutional differences (GCCA, 2003). Together, these results suggest considerable care must be taken if PREQ results are to be used for institutional benchmarking purposes. However, Marsh et al's confirmatory factor analysis of PREQ items demonstrated the PREQ has very good psychometric qualities for individual-level responses. As such, the PREQ is currently the most developed instrument for assessing both supervisory and contextual influences on the RHD student's experience.

Many investigators have investigated a variety of aspects of the RHD experience, but these investigations have often been limited by a focus on only one or two aspects of the RHD experience (eg supervision), relatively small samples, comparing the experiences of a small number of schools or departments, and/or a small number of fields of study included in the sample (for recent examples see Chiang, 2002; Hollingsworth & Fassinger, 2002; Pearson, Kayrooz & Collins, 2002; Seagram, Gould & Pike, 1998; Weidman & Stein, 2003). The present study aims to investigate the RHD student experience using a large sample, from a large number of departments and fields of study, and with a broad range of quality indicators.

The present project aims to test models of the RHD experience, taking into account the RHD student's experience of both supervisory and contextual variables. The PREQ already makes use of some items and underlying concepts derived from the CEQ. We used the PREQ as a starting point in developing instruments assessing students' and supervisors' perceptions in both groups and added new items as well as additional questions outside the scale structure. Details of the psychometric properties of this expanded PREQ are given in Ramsden, Conrad, Ginns and Prosser (2003).

The goals of the following analyses are as follows. Firstly, we investigate the fit of a structural equation model of the RHD student experience, examining the associations between indicators of supervision, intellectual and social climate and outcomes. Secondly, we investigate the validity of several of the scale scores by examining the correlations between departmental level aggregate scores and departmental completion rates for a prior cohort of students.

Method

Participants

Surveys were sent to 8,528 Australian research higher degree students, and usable responses were received from 3,137 students enrolled in 137 different departments across 16 Australian universities, representing a response rate of 36.8%. 53.4% of respondents were male, and the average age was 34.4 years (SD = 10.5). The majority of respondents (90%) were Australian residents. Most respondents (81.7%) were completing a research PhD; the remainder were completing either a professional doctorate such as a Doctorate of Education (3.0%), a combined coursework and research PhD (1.9%), or a research masters degree (13.3%).

Materials

Participants completed a four-page questionnaire. The first section was comprised of demographic questions, including questions related to type of degree, date of commencement, and enrolment status. The second section collected information related to the student's perceptions of their research degree experience, using 5-point Likert scales (where 1 = strongly disagree and 5 = strongly agree). The third section asked the student about the frequency of different modes of supervision or support, such as face-to-face meetings with supervisors or meeting in a group. For these items, an 8-point Likert scale was used, ranging from 1 = daily to 8 = so far, not at all. For the purposes of analysis these ratings were reversed and recoded to a 5-point scale, so that a higher score indicated a higher frequency of supervision or support.

Ramsden, Conrad, Ginns and Prosser (2003) reported tests of the psychometric properties of scales derived from responses in the second section of the questionnaire. Indicators of the degree context and degree outcomes, as clustered in the hypothesised model, are described below.

1) Indicators of quality of supervision.

Supervision. This scale covers aspects of supervision including: supervision being available when needed; understanding by the supervisor(s) of difficulties; provision of additional information relevant to the thesis topic by the supervisor(s); provision of guidance in topic selection and refinement; provision of helpful feedback on progress; and provision of good guidance in literature search (Cronbach's α = 0.90).

Clarity of goals and expectations. This scale covers perceptions of the clarity of goals and expectations of the degree, including: understanding of the standard of work required; understanding of the required standard for the thesis; and understanding of the requirements of thesis examination (Cronbach's α = 0.83).

Frequency of supervision. This item asked students to rate the frequency of face-to-face individual meetings with the supervisor or supervisors.

2) Indicators of departmental climate.

Climate. This scale covers aspects of the prevailing research climate in a student's school/department, including: opportunities for social contact with other postgraduate students; integration into the school/department community; opportunities to become involved in a broader research culture; perception of other research students as supportive; feelings of isolation within the school/department (reversed); encouragement of interaction with other research students; provision of a good seminar programme; stimulation of personal work by the prevailing research ambience; provision of a supportive work environment; and feeling respected as a fellow researcher (Cronbach's α = 0.90).

Infrastructure. This scale covers aspects of the infrastructure available to research students, including: access to a suitable working space; access to technical support; access to a common room; access to necessary equipment; access to computing facilities and resources; and appropriateness of financial support (Cronbach's α = .79).

Frequency of group discussions. This item asked students to rate the frequency of group discussions on research-related issues between the student, his/her supervisor(s), other students, and/or other academics.

3) Indicators of student outcomes.

Generic skills. This scale reflects the extent to which students perceive their studies to have fostered the development of the generic skills recognised as being a valuable outcome of university education, in addition to discipline specific skills and knowledge. These skills include problem solving; oral and written communication; development of ideas and their written presentation; and analytical skills (Cronbach's α = .76).

Life-long learning. This scale is distinct from the previous scale in that it is future-oriented, less intimately related to the student's current research project and thesis than the "Generic skills" scale, and hence relevant to addressing or solving new or unfamiliar problems or communicating issues in varied and unpredictable situations. These skills include planning; confidence in tackling unfamiliar problems; and ability to learn independently (Cronbach's α = 0.77).

Overall rating. This items asked students to rate the degree to which they were satisfied with the overall quality of their research higher degree experience.

Results

Variance component models of outcome measures

Before testing the hypothesised structural model of the research student experience, it is necessary to test the degree to which the variance in outcome variables is affected by group membership. It is becoming increasingly recognised in educational research that the existence of hierarchies in data structures (eg student within department) is often associated with an intraclass correlation (ICC) that violates the assumption of independence, a cornerstone of general linear models (see Hox, 2002). The ICC can be interpreted as "the expected correlation between two randomly chosen individuals within the same group" (Hox, 2002, p31). However, when conducting multilevel analyses, of greater importance than the ICC is the *design effect* (Kish, 1965) indicating the degree to which standard errors are underestimated. If the design effect (= 1 + [average cluster size – 1] x ICC) is less than 2, using single level analysis on multilevel data should not lead to misleading results (Muthén & Satorra, 1995). The average departmental cluster size for the national student data set is approximately 23; thus, the ICC would have to be greater than 0.045 to warrant multilevel analysis. Calculation of variance component models for the three outcome measures yielded ICCs for the department level of 0.016 (overall satisfaction with degree quality), 0.018 (generic skills), and 0.020 (lifelong learning). The small magnitude of these ICCs suggested standard structural equation modelling techniques should not produce unduly biased results using the current data set.

Structural modelling

The central hypothesis of the present study is that research students' perceptions of key outcomes of their degree (development of generic skills and life-long learning skills, and overall satisfaction with the quality of the degree) are jointly determined by their experiences of supervision and departmental intellectual and social climate. Correlations between the variables used for structural modelling are given in table 1.

	Mean	SD	1	2	3	4	5	6	7	8	9
1. Supervision scale	3.74	0.88	1.00								
2. Clear goals scale	3.78	0.81	0.48	1.00							
3. Frequency of individual supervision	2.98	1.07	0.35	0.14	1.00						
4. Climate scale	3.34	0.86	0.43	0.36	0.23	1.00					
5. Infrastructure scale	3.58	0.82	0.36	0.32	0.28	0.52	1.00				
6. Frequency of group meetings	2.70	1.41	0.17	0.14	0.37	0.32	0.26	1.00			
7. Generic skills scale	4.02	0.67	0.39	0.43	0.18	0.37	0.27	0.18	1.00		
8. Life-long learning scale	3.97	0.71	0.31	0.36	0.16	0.30	0.23	0.13	0.71	1.00	
9. Overall quality rating	3.74	1.00	0.60	0.48	0.24	0.55	0.46	0.20	0.46	0.41	1.00

Table 1: Means, standard deviations and zero-order correlations for research degree student responses (n = 3137).

These relations were expected to hold across fields of study. Structural models were evaluated according to the recommendations of Hu and Bentler (1999), who examined the behaviour of a variety of fit indices, concluding that control of both Type I and Type II error is best achieved through a combination of relative fit indices (eg Tucker-Lewis Index, also known as the Bentler-Bonett non-normed fit index, NNFI, and the Incremental Fit Index, IFI), where model fit is greater than or equal to 0.95, and the standardized root mean square residual, SRMR, with good models > 0.08. Model fit was estimated using robust maximum likelihood estimation, a method less sensitive to violations of the normality assumption than other estimation methods (Boomsma & Hoogland, 2001).

Tests of multivariate normality were conducted using PRELIS 2.54. Results indicated significant multivariate non-normality – multivariate skewness z = 43.46, p<0.001, multivariate kurtosis z = 22.35, p<0.001. Scores were transformed to normal equivalent deviates using PRELIS, a process which maintains the mean, standard deviation, and rank ordering of scores but reduces skewness and kurtosis (Jöreskog, Sörbom, du Toit & du Toit, 2001). Results of further checks of multivariate normality following transformation indicated reduced multivariate non-normality – multivariate skewness z = 19.79, p<0.001, multivariate kurtosis z = 12.15, p<0.001.

The initial model was tested with no correlations between the error terms of indicators. This model did not have good fit to the data, NNFI = 0.84, IFI = 0.89, SRMR = 0.085. Inspection of modification indices indicated fit could be improved substantially by fitting three covariances between indicator error terms that could be justified on substantive grounds. Among the independent variables, the error covariance was freed to be estimated between "frequency of meeting individually with the supervisor(s)", and "frequency of meeting with supervisor(s), other students, and perhaps other academics", on the grounds that the two measures are partially redundant (Byrne, 1998). The error covariance between "frequency of meeting individually with the supervisor(s)", and the Supervision scale score, was also freed, as strength of agreement with the items making up this scale (eg "I am given good guidance on topic selection and refinement"; "My supervisor(s) provide(s) helpful feedback on my progress") would presumably be largely driven through the medium of face-to-face meetings with supervisors. Among the dependent variables, the error covariance between the generic skills and independent learning scale scores was freed, on the grounds that the two scales are distinct yet related constructs, both being desirable skill-based outcomes of the RHD experience. Re-estimation of the model with the above error covariances resulted in substantially better model fit, NNFI = 0.98, IFI = 0.99, SRMR = 0.032. The revised model, showing standardised path coefficients and correlations between latent constructs in plain text, is given in figure 1 opposite.

The next stage of analysis involved follow-up analyses by broad field of study. Inspection of the fields of study given by respondents suggested three broad groupings. The first group (n = 1339) consisted of students from the humanities, arts, social sciences and education (referred to below as the humanities group); the second group (n = 213) consisted of business, administration, economics and law students (referred to below as the professional studies group); and the third group (n = 1585) consisted of students from science, health, engineering and surveying (referred to below as the sciences group). Overall model fit was good for each broad field of study: NNFI = 0.98, IFI = 0.99, SRMR = 0.029 for the humanities group; NNFI = 0.99, IFI = 0.99, SRMR = 0.040 for the professional studies group; and NNFI = 0.98, IFI = 0.99, SRMR = 0.029 for the sciences group.

However, these analyses revealed a major difference in the structural model due to field of study, indicated in Figure 1, where the model's structural paths are given in bold text, italic text, and bold italic text for the humanities, professional studies, and sciences groups respectively. The results for the humanities group and the professional studies group were similar in magnitude, with the latent construct of supervision predicting variation in the Outcomes latent construct more strongly than the climate latent construct, but with both paths statistically significant. For the sciences students, a markedly different pattern of results was found. For these students, the correlation between the latent constructs of supervision and climate was considerably higher (0.88) than for the

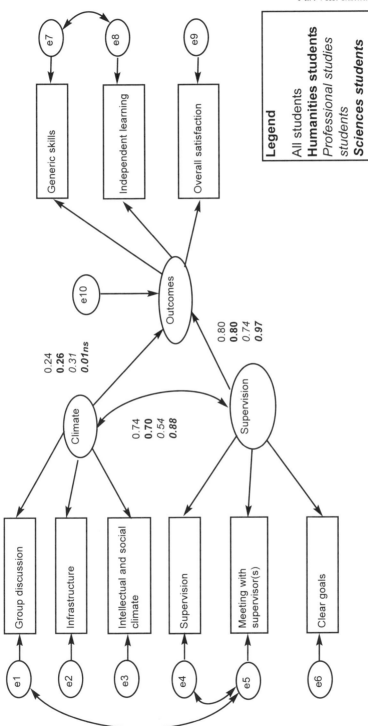

Figure 1: structural model of the RHD experience.

other fields of study (0.70 and 0.54 for the humanities and professional studies groups, respectively). In addition, the path from climate to outcomes was not statistically significant for the sciences students.

The above results suggest the model shown in Figure 1 was not correctly specified for students within the sciences broad field of study. In particular, the high correlation between the hypothesised latent constructs of supervision and climate indicates insufficient evidence of discriminant validity between these constructs. A revised model was tested for the sciences students in which all of the independent observed variables were fixed to load on a single latent construct, entitled "RHD experience". This more parsimonious model had good fit to the sciences group data, NNFI = 0.97, IFI = 0.98, SRMR = 0.034; the standardised path coefficient between the RHD experience latent construct and the outcomes latent construct was 0.95 (t = 20.15). The revised model was tested on the other groups, but did not fit as well as the original model (humanities: NNFI = 0.94, IFI = 0.96, SRMR = 0.045; professional studies: NNFI = 0.91, IFI = 0.94, SRMR = 0.059). Thus, the structural models of RHD student responses suggest humanities and professional studies students distinguish between experiences of supervision and intellectual/social climate, both of which predict these students' experiences of quality RHD outcomes. In contrast, sciences students do not appear to distinguish between supervision and intellectual/social climate. This distinction in students' experiences by broad field of study will be discussed further below.

Completion rates

The above analyses provide evidence for associations between students' perceptions of supervision, intellectual and social climate, and indicators of quality RHD outcomes such as skills development and overall ratings of satisfaction with degree quality. If these variables are relevant indicators of the RHD student experience, we would expect them to correlate with other outcomes, such as completion time or survival. The present study, being cross-sectional rather than longitudinal, was not designed to investigate such hypotheses. However, evidence of the criterion validity of these variables might be collected retrospectively, by examining the completion rates of departments for a cohort other than that examined in the present study. Evidence of validity of this kind has been termed *post-dictive* criterion validity (Netermeyer, Bearden, & Sharma, 2003).

The rationale for such an approach is as follows. For at least some of the variables, we would expect their impact to be experienced at the aggregate level, that is, as an emergent property of student and staff interactions within a department (eg climate), or as a property of overall funding levels to a department (eg infrastructure). Furthermore, such effects could be expected to change only slowly over time. Departmental completion rates for a prior cohort may act as a suitable proxy.

For 67 departments for which data were available, we correlated the aggregate student context scale scores for each department with the average 1997 (masters research and doctorate) departmental completion rate. This completion rate was adjusted using the arcsine transformation, since completion rates are percentages and hence violate the assumption that the underlying distribution is normally distributed. The correlation between predictor and transformed departmental completion rate was not significant for supervision ($r = 0.18$, $p = 0.153$), or clarity of goals ($r = -0.20$, $p = 0.107$), but was significant for climate ($r = 0.25$, $p = 0.042$), infrastructure ($r = 0.33$, $p = 0.007$), frequency of face-to-face meetings with the supervisor(s) ($r = 0.48$, $p < 0.001$) and frequency of group meetings ($r = 0.38$, $p = 0.001$). These aggregate level results provide further evidence of the validity of several of the independent variables used in the structural models reported above, as the completion rates were derived from a cohort that preceded the survey cohort.

Discussion and conclusion

The aim of the present study was to test a model of the RHD student experience, assessing the extent to which students' perceptions of supervision, and the intellectual and social climate of their department, are related to perceptions of quality outcomes, including skill development and overall satisfaction with RHD experience. In addition, we investigated the associations between the independent variables, measured at the aggregate departmental average level, and completion rates for an earlier cohort of RHD students.

The results for the structural models indicate that RHD students' perceptions of quality outcomes are determined not only by perceptions of the quality of supervision, but also by other variates such as the quality of the prevailing intellectual and social climate in the student's department; the quality of available infrastructure in the department; and the frequency with which students meet with their supervisor(s), as well as with other students and/or academic staff. A major finding of the present study, however, was that the structure of these perceptions differed by broad field of study. For humanities and professional studies students, a model in which latent constructs for supervision and climate could be distinguished had a good fit to the model. In contrast, for sciences students, such a model was not as plausible as one in which the various independent variables all loaded on a single latent construct, termed "RHD experience". For these students, it appears that the experience of quality supervision is tightly bound up in the experience of a quality intellectual and social climate. Thus, for students working in a laboratory environment such as is typical in the sciences, supervisory behaviours and processes may occur in an inherently more social milieu than for students from other fields of study; for example, during lab meetings, in which guidance is given by the supervisor, other students, and other academics such as postdoctoral fellows.

While the present study provides evidence of the importance of supervision, climate and infrastructure variables in determining perceptions of a quality RHD experience, and provides additional evidence for the validity of these indicators via associations with departmental completion rates, the cross-sectional design of the study is an inherent limitation. A future longitudinal study could build on these results by investigating the associations between the contextual variables identified in the present study, and outcomes such as time to completion or attrition. A longitudinal study would also benefit by examining indicators of research output quality, such as number and quality of publications.

References

Australian Council for Educational Research. (1999). *Evaluation and validation of the Postgraduate Course Experience Questionnaire.* Camperdown: Australian Council for Educational Research.

Bair, CR, and Haworth, JG (2004). Doctoral Student Attrition and Persistence: A Meta-Synthesis of Research. In Smart, JC (Ed), *Higher education: Handbook of theory and research* (vol. 19). Dordrecht: Kluwer.

Boomsma, A and Hoogland, JJ (2001). The robustness of LISREL modeling revisited. In Cudeck, R, du Toit, S and Sörbom, D (Eds), *Structural equation modeling, present and future: A festschrift in honor of Karl Jöreskog.* Lincolnwood: Scientific Software International.

Byrne, BM (1998). *Structural equation modeling with LISREL, PRELIS and SIMPLIS: Basic concepts, applications and programming.* Mahwah: Sage.

Chiang, KH (2002). Relationship between research and teaching in doctoral education in UK universities. Paper presented at Annual SRHE Conference, Glasgow.

Crawford, K, Gordon, S, Nicholas, J, and Prosser, M (1998). Qualitatively different experiences of learning mathematics at university. *Learning and Instruction*, 4, 331-345.

Department of Education, Science and Technology (2004). Introduction to research in higher education. Retrieved June 15 2004, from www.dest.gov.au/highered/research/index.htm

Graduate Careers Council of Australia (2003). *Postgraduate Research Experience Questionnaire 2002.* Parkville: Graduate Careers Council of Australia.

Hair, JE, Anderson, RE, Tatham, RL, and Black, WC (1998). *Multivariate data analysis.* Upper Saddle River: Prentice-Hall.

Hollingsworth, MA, and Fassinger, RE (2002). The role of faculty mentors in the research training of counseling psychology doctoral students. *Journal of Counseling Psychology*, 49, 324-330.

Hox, J (2002). *Multilevel analysis: Techniques and applications.* Mahwah: Lawrence Erlbaum Associates.

Hu, L and Bentler, PM (1999). Cutoff criteria for fit indexes in covariance structure analysis: conventional criteria versus new alternatives. *Structural Equation Modeling*, 6, 1-55.

Jöreskog, KG, Sörbom, D, du Toit, S, and du Toit, M (2001). *LISREL 8: New statistical features.* Lincolnwood: Scientific Software International.

Kish, L (1965). *Survey sampling.* New York: Wiley.

Lizzio, A, Wilson, K, and Simons, R (2002). University students' perceptions of the learning environment and academic outcomes: implications for theory and practice. *Studies in Higher Education*, 27, 27-51.

Marsh, HW, Rowe, KJ, and Martin, A (2002). PhD students' evaluation of research supervision: issues, complexities, and challenges in a nationwide Australian experiment in benchmarking universities. *Journal of Higher Education*, 73, 313-348.

Muthén, B, and Satorra, A (1995). Complex sample data in structural equation modelling. In Marsden, PV (Ed), *Sociological Methodology*, 1995 (pp267-316). Oxford: Blackwell.

Netermeyer, RG, Bearden, WO, and Sharma, S (2003). *Scaling procedures: Issues and applications*. Thousand Oaks: Sage.

Pearson, M, Kayrooz, C, and Collins, R (2002). Postgraduate student feedback on research supervisory practice. Paper presented at Annual SRHE Conference, Glasgow.

Ramsden, P (1991). A performance indicator of teaching quality in higher education: The Course Experience Questionnaire. *Studies in Higher Education*, 16, 129-50.

Ramsden, P, Conrad, L, Ginns, P, and Prosser, M (2003). Students' and Supervisors' Experiences of the Context for Postgraduate Study. Paper presented at the Tenth European Conference for Research on Learning and Instruction, Padua, Italy, 26 August 2003 to 30 August 2003.

Seagram, BC, Gould, J, and Pike, SW (1998). An investigation of gender and other variables on time to completion of doctoral degrees. *Research in Higher Education*, 39, 319-335.

Weidman, JC, and Stein, EL (2003). Socialization of doctoral students to academic norms. *Research in Higher Education*, 44, 641-656.

Wilson, KL, Lizzio, A, and Ramsden, P (1997). The development, validation and application of the Course Experience Questionnaire. *Studies in Higher Education*, 22, 33-53.

Research and design of programmes that attract and fulfil the needs of Britain's ethnic groups.

Helen Higson, Sushmita Jha and Catherine Foster, Aston Business School, Aston University, Birmingham, UK

Previous research reveals that ethnic minorities as a whole are more than proportionally represented in higher education (HE), compared with the general population. Adia reported that ethnic minorities were over-represented during the application stage to HE (1996, p1). A closer examination indicates, however, that under-representation does exist across some ethnic groups, as well as amongst gender groups within specific ethnic populations. If we have a commitment to encouraging greater participation in HE by these groups, we must then increase our efforts to monitor the learning experience of students from these groups in order to gain an understanding of the complexity of issues surrounding Britain's ethnic minorities in HE.

This paper discusses a small study within a very specific context which was designed to build on previous more large-scale surveys. The study investigated aspects of participation and experiences in HE of ethnic minority (in this instance, non-white-British) students at Aston Business School (ABS). It aimed to enhance our understanding of ethnic minorities in our specific school, in order to devise effective pedagogic policies and intervention strategies to help improve students' learning experiences. The findings are now assisting ABS to support and facilitate practical solutions in order to attract students from under-represented groups, as well as creating a more enriching experience for all students. The paper begins by outlining previous work in this area via a discussion of the published literature. It then describes the methods of investigation used in this study, including a questionnaire survey and student interviews, which were conducted with first year ABS undergraduates. Finally, it discusses the results, draws conclusions and gives some indication of further work now being undertaken.

Literature review

Since the early 90s participation in HE has increased and there have also been increases in participation rates for non-white ethnic groups. Adia has described the full-time undergraduate population in the sector as increasingly multi-ethnic (1996, p71). Connor et al echo this in their report, highlighting that since the 1990s minority ethnic students have been well represented in higher education. In 2002 about 15% of students in UK higher education institutions were from a minority ethnic group; the figure had risen from the 8% in 2001 (2002, p2). Taking a closer look at their data researchers identified that there were disparities in levels of representation of different minority ethnic groups and subgroups (such as gender) (Conner et al 2002, Adia 1996).

Adia illustrates such disparities amongst different ethnic minority groups. In comparing representation in the age 15-24 population, he demonstrates that most ethnic minority groups were over-represented during the application stage, with the exception of the Caribbean group (who accounted for 1.2% of all 15-24 year olds in the population, but only 0.8 % of applicants), and Black Other (0.6% of the 15-25 group but only 0.4% of applicants) (p1). Bailey similarly reports that, in comparison with the general population, non-white ethnic groups appeared to be statistically over-represented in the undergraduate population (2003, p5).

Adia also discusses data which presents gender difference amongst applicants to university via UCAS for 1995 entry. He reports that a higher proportion of females than males applied to university from Caribbean, Black Other, White, and Chinese groups, whereas a higher proportion of males than females applied from all other ethnic groups, including Indian, Pakistani, Bangladeshi and Black African (p2). In reviewing the Dearing report, Preece (1999) concludes that Bangladeshi and Pakistani women and African Caribbean men and women were under-represented (p198).

To understand why rates of participation differ between British-white students and ethnic minority students it is essential to take a deeper look at the pre- and post-application process to highlight what issues affect student learning experiences and performance. The literature highlights a wide range of personal and social attributes, as well as institutional practices, which impact on both retention rates and performance (for example, Thomas 2002, p426). Research reviewing retention of students in the USA and the UK emphasises the significance of the external environment including family and communities. Thomas explains that families or communities with little or no experience of HE may be less supportive of members' participation (Thomas, 2002 p436).

Shiner and Modood (2002) explore the 'apparent' ethnic differences in rates of admission. They reveal that those from ethnic minority communities are more likely to favour institutions in their home region than white applicants, and so limit their choice and possibly compromise their chances of securing a place (p212). Farley (2002), who examines the retention of minority and working-class undergraduates, suggests that ethnic minority and working-class students are more frequently found to attend part-time, to commute and to attend campuses where these were more common (p14).

Farley suggested that ethnic minority students experience discrimination on campus, and both ethnic minority and working-class students experience isolation and a lack of 'belongingness' on many campuses. Furthermore, within their home communities, where they have strong ties, there are many who have no insight into higher education and its requirements and expectations, and present competing expectations and demands on students' time (p.15). Thomas similarly shows that students not living in 'student' accommodation (ie either halls of residence or a shared house in the private sector) were more likely to feel marginalised from their peers (p436).

In reviewing such research it becomes clear that the issue of Britain's ethnic minorities and higher education is a complex one in which rates of participation vary between different ethnic minority groups and types of institutions. For an institution to develop policies and practices to support their growing ethnic minority population it is essential to examine how the issues raised above relate to their population. This brings us to the present research described in this article.

Method

Student survey

A student survey was undertaken in February 2003. The purpose of this questionnaire survey was to enable the investigation, with a proportional sample, of a range of factors which are associated with ethnic minority students' learning experience and to compare their experience with those of white-British students.

Participants

Questionnaires were sent out to all the 412 first-year undergraduates at ABS; there were 86 replies. Seven respondents were late replies and not included in the analysis. Only a total 79 responses were, therefore, analysed in the report. Forty respondents were white-British students and 39 respondents were from ethnic minorities, which reflects the student population at ABS. Further details shown in table 1 below. Participation in the study was voluntary.

Ethnic origin	Gender		Total
	Male	Female	
White—British	19	21	40
Ethnic minority	10	29	39
Asian-British	1	5	6
Bangladeshi	0	2	2
Indian	1	3	4
Pakistani	1	1	2
Chinese	5	10	15
Black-African	1	4	5
Any other ethnic group	1	4	5

Table 1. The participants' background information

Questionnaire design

The instrument used in this study was a semi-structured questionnaire exploring students' learning experience at Aston Business School. A portion of the questionnaire consisted of statements that have been adopted and modified from previous research (Hurtado et al 1998). The survey instrument consisted of a covering letter and an information sheet, as well as the questionnaire itself. This was a paper-based questionnaire and divided into four distinct sections:

- 'Background information about yourself'
- 'Perception of higher education'
- 'Your experience of higher education at ABS'
- 'Learning skills self-assessment'

The participants' basic background information obtained from the instrument included age, gender, year of the study, subject of study, and their first language. Although not all background information was necessarily used for this particular study, gender was used to enable cross-analysis of the results in terms of gender difference and to check the breakdown of the sample. The covering letter with the questionnaire provided a brief research background to the potential participants, and assured confidentiality of the results for each participant. Closed question formats were used for the majority of questions (in which the students simply circled numbers). Six open-ended questions were included to allow students the opportunity to comment on their opinions about their learning experience at ABS.

The first draft of the questionnaire was piloted with six undergraduate students from ABS, to ensure that the content of the survey was a comprehensive representation of the areas being studied and that the questions were clearly and unambiguously worded. The pilot subjects were also asked questions regarding readability and ease of completion. The questionnaires were handed out to subjects by the researcher at the beginning of their lectures, and they were asked to fill them in at their leisure and return them to the researcher through the Undergraduate Programme Office.

Responses to the questionnaire were coded and analysed through the use of the SPSS (Statistical Package for the Social Sciences) v10.0.

Student interviews

Student interviews were conducted in May and June 2003. The aim of the interviews was to investigate further the perceptions and experiences of ethnic minorities at Aston Business School.

The interview schedule was designed to capture students' perception on a variety of issues, which had emerged from the student questionnaire survey. These issues were as follows:

- Family and parents' influences on entering higher education
- Academic preparedness

- Expectations about higher education, institutional expectations and subsequent commitment to the institution

- Career orientation and employability, finance and employment

- Learning/academic experience at Aston Business School (curricula, teaching and learning issues, accessibility of and relationship with staff, flexibility, and academic support)

Participants

Emails were sent to all undergraduate Aston Business School first year students seeking students from ethnic minorities (non-white-British) to participate in the interviews. Participation was on a voluntary basis. A total of 15 students from ethnic minorities participated in the interviews. The basic demographic information on the student sample that took part in the interviews is presented in Table 2.

Ethnic origin	Gender		Total
	Female	Male	
Asian-British	1	0	1
Indian	5	1	6
Pakistani	4	2	6
Black-British	1	0	1
Black-African	1	0	1
Total			15

Table 2 Background information of students participating in student survey.

Interview design

The method of data collection used was a semi-structured interview exploring students' learning experiences at Aston Business School. Questions were developed in the light of findings from the student survey in the first stage of the research.

Background information obtained from the interviews included gender, subject of study and ethnic origin. At the beginning of each interview the researcher provided a brief research background to participants, and assured confidentiality of results for participants. Open question formats were used for the majority of the interview; this was designed to allow students to comment on their opinions about learning experience at Aston Business School.

A pilot was carried out with two independent participants to test whether the interview questions were comprehensible and to ensure questions were clearly and unambiguously worded. During the pilot testing the duration of the interview was timed so that an estimate could be given to students participating in the interviews.

Interviews took place in a quiet room and arrangements were made in order for students to feel comfortable. Ethical issues were addressed by choosing a voluntary sample selection design, informing participants of the option to withdraw if they felt uncomfortable and informing them that by request reports would be available to them.

Findings

Student survey

In this study, 62.5% of white-British students reported that the members of their immediate family had been educated at HE level, compared to only 46.2% of the ethnic minority students (see figure 1), however, the difference between the two groups was not statistically significant due to the small sample size.

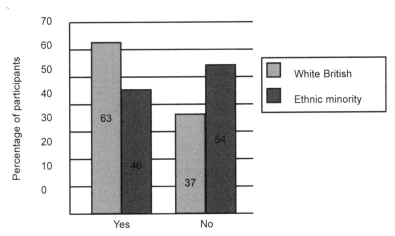

Figure 1. The members of the immediate family have been educated at higher education

Of the ethnic minority students, 82.1% reported that parents/guardians are the most important influence on the decision to enter higher education, while only 55.2% of the white-British students did (see figure 2 overleaf) ($p < 0.05$).

Perceptions of higher education

As can be seen from the results in table 3, overleaf, there is a significant difference between the views of ethnic minority students and white-British students in the following statements; "Higher education is greatly valued by my family", "Higher education is valued in the community I come from", "My parents/guardians wanted all their children to go to university", "In my culture both girls and boys are encouraged to enter higher education". From analysis of the mean scores for these statements, ethnic minority students reported a stronger belief in the above statements except for "In my culture both girls and boys are encouraged to enter higher education".

Table 4, overleaf shows the results from student responses about the reasons that they selected ABS. Both white-British and ethnic minority students reported that 'the academic reputation of the institution' and 'course content' were the important reasons.

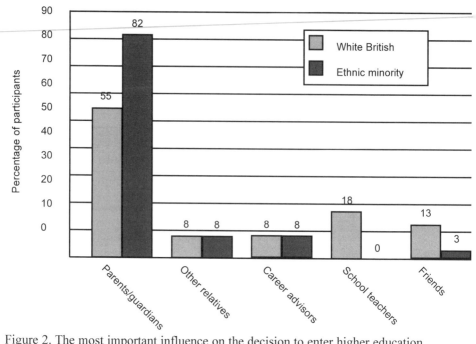

Figure 2. The most important influence on the decision to enter higher education

Statement	White-British Mean (SD)	Ethnic minority Mean (SD)	T-test
Higher education is greatly valued by my family	4.200 (0.8828)	4.641 (0.5843)	P < 0.001
Higher education is valued in the community I come from	3.775 (0.8316)	4.179 (0.7564)	P < 0.05
My parents/guardians wanted all their children to go to university	3.800 (1.0669)	4.487 (0.8230)	P < 0.001
My family takes my education seriously	4.400 (0.7442)	4.538 (0.6426)	NS
My friends take education seriously	3.800 (0.8227)	3.794 (0.8328)	NS
The people close to me take an interest in my studies	3.957 (0.6196)	3.820 (0.8230)	NS
The people close to me encourage me to get my degree	4.200 (0.6868)	4.179 (0.7904)	NS
In my culture both girls and boys are encouraged to enter higher education	4.600 (0.4961)	4.025 (1.180)	P < 0.001

Table 3. Family influence and perceptions of higher education

The reasons that you selected ABS:	White-British Yes (order)	Ethnic minority Yes (order)
The academic reputation of the institution	37 (1)	32 (1)
Distance from home	22 (3)	13 (4)
Know somebody who is studying/has studied at the institution	8 (7)	7 (7)
Cost of living in the locality of the institution	4 (8)	4 (8)
Attractive/informative prospectus	18 (5)	12 (5)
Entry grade requirements	19 (14)	14 (3)
Course content	33 (2)	23 (2)
Good social life or outdoor activities	16 (4)	8 (6)
Higher proportion of ethnic minority students in general	0 (10)	3 (9)
Higher proportion of students from own ethnic group	1 (9)	3 (9)

Table 4. The reasons that you selected ABS

The white-British groups also reported that 'distance from home' is another important reason, while the ethnic minority British groups reported 'entry grade requirements' is one of the important reasons that they chose ABS. In this survey, neither group considered 'higher proportion of students from own ethnic group and higher proportion of ethnic minority students in general' an important factor when they applied to ABS.

Experience of higher education at Aston Business School

In general, both white-British and ethnic minority groups were satisfied with content and design of the degree course at ABS. The white-British group was more likely to agree that they have access to all the learning resources necessary for their course ($p < 0.05$).

Ethnic minority students were found more likely to be unsatisfied with the environment for learning at ABS; for the statement 'My school creates a good environment for learning', the ethnic minority group hold stronger negative attitudes ($p < 0.05$).

The survey found that the ethnic minority students were more likely to disagree with: 'I can discuss most problems I have with my lecturers' than their white-British counterparts; the difference was significant ($p < 0.05$). The white-British students were more likely to 'have support from their friends or there is someone they can turn to' than their non-white-British counterparts ($p < 0.05$).

Student interviews

Factors determining students' choice of university

Interview data gathered from the interview regarding why students selected Aston Business School echoed the findings from the student survey. The responses offered by students to the question were gathered together and content analysed and placed in categories according to common themes. Table 5 below shows the reasons why participants selected Aston Business School.

As shown in table 5 below the most frequent reason why participants selected Aston Business School was the School's reputation, followed by the university's location

Factor	Frequency	Example
Reputation	11	It's a well renowned school – good reputation
Location	10	Able to stay at home
Graduate employment figures	2	Good employment rates/status
Small university/campus	3	Small size so I don't feel so isolated, everything on campus
Course offered	6	Course structure
Pre-entry information	5	Visited Aston and liked it.
Recommendation	6	Cousin came here they told me about it
University ranking	5	Rating of ABS in Times newspaper

Table 5. Frequency of common factors indicating students' reasons for selecting Aston Business School

Family influence and its perception of higher education

Students were asked to provide information about whether parents and other immediate family members had been educated at HE level. Table 6 below shows the number of family members educated at HE level from the interview sample.

Family member	Frequency
Parents	3
Siblings	15
Other family (cousins, aunts, uncles)	12

Table 6: Number of family members educated at HE level

The figures above show that a only a small number of non-white-British students' parents had been educated at higher education level, although there was a higher frequency of siblings and other family members educated at HE level. It is therefore likely that these are first generation ethnic minority students taking advantage of the opportunities available that their parents did not have.

When questioned about their parents' influence, perceptions and aspiration it was interesting to find that students commonly reported that parents had a large influence and a positive perception of HE. Parents' influences are demonstrated below:

> *"My dad had a strong opinion about education as he himself came here and worked in a factory, he worked really hard. He doesn't want us to go down the same route. So even if I don't do this for myself, I'll do it for dad. Family view education highly and so then value highly too."*

These findings lend support to results of the student survey showing that students from ethnic minority groups were more likely to be influenced by their parents on the choice of entering higher education than white students.

Although many of the responses indicated that students faced pressures and restrictions from parents, as many parents had no experience of HE they did not have any particular influence in the choice process. As the following students commented,

> *"Mum was educated up till college in Pakistan, she gave support for education till A Levels then her attitude was you are getting old now so get married. She doesn't see the point of going to university."*

> *"My dad was not particularly bothered; his attitude is if you want it, then go get it."*

Participants' responses show that students were more likely to turn to siblings and cousins for advice on institutions and courses. The main reason for this was likely to be the fact that for students these individuals were the closest source of information. Students' comments suggest that siblings and other family members who had experience of HE were a strong influence, offering advice, sharing experience and possibly acting as a role model. Such influences are clear in students' comments such as:

> *"My brother and cousins have influenced me, I can see that they are doing something with their life other than the usual that Asians generally do."*

> *"My uncle did help me; he went through all the different courses and explained them."*

Was it important to study at university near to home or to move away?

From the fifteen ethnic minority students interviewed eight lived near to home and seven moved away. In exploring students' responses more closely it was found that of the eight participants who lived at home six of them reported that their decision to stay at home was based on parental constraining influence. An example of students' responses is demonstrated below,

> *"I did not have a choice I had to live at home, but it has been good because I'm really attached to my family, especially my mum. I know I could not have lived away."*

Other reasons why students reported it was important to stay near to home was because of financial reasons and not being able to give up home comforts.

> *"Financially it was important to live at home. I've always lived at home and everything is done for you. Did not know anything about university life so it was best to stay close. Parents knew I would not cope away from home."*

Another common theme that emerged from responses was that students who lived at home felt that they were socially disadvantaged, as one participant said,

> *"I had lived away I think I would have been more independent not just going out but learning to mix with other people."*

In contrast, students who lived away from home commonly explained that the most important reasons for studying away from home were for independence and freedom and be at social advantage in terms of making friends. As one participant explained,

> *"Yes it was important to move away. As part of the university experience you do want to be independent and live by yourself. The social aspect and doing things yourself. I've been more sociable, have more time for friends."*

Experience of higher education at ABS

Findings from the student survey revealed that the non-white-British group were generally not very satisfied with the learning environment at Aston Business School. An aim of the interview was to investigate this issue further in order to gain an understanding of why students were unsatisfied with the learning environment. From information collected from the interviews two reasons which may be contributing to this dissatisfaction are problems with the mathematical elements of courses and interaction with teaching staff.

Many students suggested that more information be offered to students during the pre-entry and induction stage about the level of maths skills required, this would give them time to prepare or choose the right course suited to their skills. A further concern is that students reported that their mathematical difficulties were the reason why they perceived they were not meeting the demands of the course.

> *"I have had problems with Financial Accounting module – I didn't understand it too well or like it."*

> *"Financial Accounting was a weak area. I was not aware of the maths side."*

It is important to review what mathematical support is currently provided to students and what initiatives can be introduced to further support them.

Students were asked to comment on their interaction with lecturers and tutors, as well as their accessibility.

A typical finding was the students' comment that they 'did not really know' the lecturers or 'had not really spoken to them'. As the following comments demonstrate,

> *"I don't really know them, just go to the lectures and that is it, I haven't really spoken to them."*

> *"Quite distant really, I think it is because in the ABS people share so many modules, so in the lecture there are so many people."*

It was found, however, that students felt more comfortable with teaching staff in tutorials, using tutorials as an opportunity to voice concerns about modules.

Factors influencing students' experience

Perceptions of self and attitude to learning

The findings of the student survey were mirrored in the student interviews: students typically reported that they were confident they were meeting the demands of the course.

When asked, "are you confident you are meeting the demands of the course?" nine out of fifteen students quite confidently felt they were. Typical responses were:

> *"Yes, it's been about bridging the gap. So I have just been refreshing my memory"*

> *"Yes, I have worked hard and got good results so far."*

Students who were not so confident that they were meeting the demands of their course offered various reasons for their perceptions of self performance. Reasons students offered to explain their lack of confidence included: lack of effort and time invested, adjusting to university life and difficulties with certain modules.

A review of all the student comments show that the majority of the students are enthusiastic about their degree course; typical responses were:

> *"Yes I am currently enjoying the course. I know what I want to go into in the future."*

> *"Yes I wanted to go to university and having the opportunity to be here was motivating.*

A few students were not as positive about their degree course, students made comments such as:

> *"Partly yes, in the business side some of the modules are a bit boring other than that it's ok. I enjoy the education. The lecturers are not very motivating."*

> *"No it's actually boring but I have always wanted to do it so I just do it. The lecturers are encouraging."*

The consistent presence of family influence and pressures was found to be a strong factor again behind students' motivation and support systems. When talking about motivation students discussed how they wanted to live up to parents' expectations, re-pay parents for investing in them and taking the opportunities not available to their parents.

When students were asked who they turn to for support and advice students typically identified they turned to friends or family; interestingly, support from tutors or support services was not found to be a common response among students. Typical responses were:

> *"Family and close friends support me, tutors helped with stats."*

> *"University friends are a great support"*

Financial issues

When asked whether they had faced any financial problems, students generally did not report any major financial worries, as seen in table 7 below

Factors	Frequency
Parents	5
Loans/grants	4
Employment	2
Living at home	2
No comment	5

Table 7. The frequency of different factors students reported as causing financial worries.

Typically participants stated that they were dependent on student loans or the parents for financial support. The following statements show such examples,

> *"I have loans to pay rent and tuition fees"*

> *"I'm dependant on my parents and student loans"*

Other comments given by students with regards to finances were that they worked to cope with financial issues; students also commented that living at home helped deal with financial issues.

Discussion

The findings from the student survey show that the family is one of the most important influencers on decisions made by students, especially ethnic minority students. This supports previous research such as Adia (1996) who suggested that students from ethnic minority backgrounds were in some cases four times more likely to be influenced by their parents on their choice of entering higher education than white pupils. Adia also suggested that much greater proportions of ethnic minority families valued education highly compared to white families. They valued education as an important goal, in itself, as well as a means for obtaining a successful career (Adia, p19). The findings from the student survey also support this view.

It is possible to suggest that students from ethnic minority backgrounds benefit from close knit communities and extended family connections. It is also important however to encourage these students to seek advice from formal student services, such as advice centres at college and college tutors, when applying for HE.

The conclusions drawn from the interview results are similar to those drawn by other researchers who discovered that ethnic minority students are likely to favour institutions close to their home (Shiner and Modood 2002, Farley 2002). It is possible that such students face pressures and demands in terms of time and of competing expectations and commitments. With respect to time, students spend more time travelling or find they have more outside demands on their time (eg looking after siblings); therefore they have less time to study than their peers.

Moreover, Farley suggested further that home-based students face family and peer pressures of a cultural nature (p14). Preece (1999) offered the explanation that many parents worried that they might lose their child if they were left to the influences of a foreign environment. This strongly suggests that students from ethnic minority backgrounds are disadvantaged in terms of choice of institution and possibly courses. It is important therefore to educate parents about HE, for example encouraging them to attend open days.

Competing demands such as these can explain why participants reported being socially disadvantaged as they have less involvement in campus activities. Empirical research such as those investigated by Thomas (2002) and Farley (2002) have reported that those student not living in 'student' accommodation report feelings of isolation and lack of belongingness.

Results indicate that students relate their performance and aspiration to their families' opportunity and experience. By taking up opportunities in education and life available to them students from ethnic minorities believe they are repaying their parents for all the hardship their parent faced. Research investigating students' experience found the majority of participants in their study discussed failure in-terms of actual assessment units, and constructed failure as a very real risk (Archer and Hutchins, 2000). They follow this by explaining that the meaning of failure was a concept perceived of economic, social and personal terms (p561).

This discussion indicates that institutions would benefit in terms of meeting the needs of ethnic students and retention rates by considering issues highlighted above. Suggestions as to how institutions can address such issues include promoting the development of social networks via the induction and teaching process, for example, employing initiatives such as team building activities, group work and social meetings. Saenz et al (1999) proposed that friendship with peers was key to academic integration and student success (p205).

Relationship with university academic and support staff is also important to academic integration. Previous researchers (Farley 2002) agree staff and student relationship is important to course satisfaction and retention.

Clearly it is evident that Aston Business School would benefit from promoting increased interaction of teaching staff and students, this may be achieved through the following initiatives such as social meeting between staff and students, and introduction of administration staff.

It is possible to comment that students did not identify any real financial worries because they were ill informed about financial issues and funding in HE. In their 'Paving the Way' research UCAS found that participants were misinformed and confused about student funding (UCAS (2002), p16). It is important to investigate further how informed students are in regards to finances and how much of a concern this is to them as research has suggested that finance is an issue for retention (UCAS (2002), p16).

Conclusions and further work

This report has presented findings on the research undertaken in student surveys and interviews. From this research, the influence of parents and family has emerged as a strong factor in student's perception of Higher education. Parents of ethnic minority students play a vital role throughout their children's learning experience from the choice of university through to support and motivation to succeed, more so than for white-British students.

More interestingly students reported that parents had a large influence in the choice of university and choice of course, however, findings also show that only a small proportion of students' parents attended higher education (Figure 1).

In response to these findings, ABS has implemented student support facilities in order to provide the appropriate support to ethnic minority students. These include the creation of a Mathematical Support Centre where students can go for additional support from staff as students discussed their concerns for the numerical element of their degree. This facility is available to students throughout the University. In the area of financial assistance – a help guide and poster were created to provide further support to students with regards to their finances and a list of useful contacts. This is distributed to all first year students. In addition, and in response to the key finding of the role of parents/families, Aston Business School has launched the Phase II – Informing and Involving the Family project.

Further work – phase II

The key findings from this project were used to inform the design of Phase II of the project. As discussed, key findings of the first phase are that while groups traditionally well represented in HE consult careers/school advisers before coming to university, those from low participating groups seek advice from their parents and families. Findings from both the student survey, and interviews with ethnic minority students indicated that parents of ethnic minority students are less likely to have been to university or have clear ideas of what to expect.

In response to this, Phase II is being developed to involve and inform the families of ethnic minority students in order to raise awareness and understanding of Higher Education. Focus groups have been conducted with students and parents with a view to inform the design of the programme and to develop a list of key issues to be addressed as an outcome of the programme. The programme when launched in full will consist of visits into the University following a 'masterclass' style of activity. These aim to give parents/family members a taste of University life whilst also addressing any key issues and answering questions. Sessions will also be available within a community setting if required or felt appropriate.

The main aims of Phase II are:

■ To increase the awareness of parents and other close advisers of students from under-represented groups of what going to university entails

■ To bring participants in to the University in a way which will make them familiar with the main features of university advice

■ To draw up a checklist of the main factors which students and their families need to expect when coming to university

In order to provide an experience which encourages and informs parents/family members with accurate and appropriate information, all programmes and activities will be actively monitored throughout the life of phase II. This will take the form of questionnaires and focus groups.

As an additional outcome, a "Family Guide to Higher Education" will be developed to support the programmes of activity for local parents/families and also parents/families of overseas students. The guide will provide information about University Life, facilities and pastoral care available to students on campus as well as broader University issues. The guide will be available for use throughout the University and specifically the Business School. This will ensure that research undertaken in Phase I and Phase II of the project is embedded into working practise within the Business School.

References

Adia E (Roberts D, Allen A, eds) (1996), *Higher Education: The Ethnic Minority Experience*, The Higher Education Information Trust, Leeds

Archer, L. and Hutchinings, M. (2000) 'Bettering Yourself'? Discourse of risk, cost and benefit in ethnically diverse, young working-class non-participants' constructions of higher education. *British Journal of Sociology of Education*, vol 21, no 4: 555-574.

Farley, J.E (2002) Contesting our everyday work lives: The Retention of Minority and Working-Class Sociology Undergraduates. *The Sociological Quarterly*, vol 43, no 1: 1-25.

Hurtado, S., J.F. Milem, A. Clayton-Pedersen, and W.A. Allen (1998) Enhancing Campus Climates for Racial/Ethnic Diversity: Educational Policy and Practice, *Review of Higher Education*, 21(3): 279-302.

Preece, J. (1999) Families into Higher Education Project: An Awareness Raising Action Research Action Research Project with Schools and Parents. *Higher Education Quarterly*, vol 53, no 3: 197-210.

Saenz, T., Marcoulides, G.A., Junn, E., and Young R. (1999) The relationship between college experience and academic performance among minority students, *The International Journal of Educational Management*, vol 13 no 4: 199-207.

Shinner, M. and Modood, T. (2002) Help or Hindrance? Higher Education and the Route to Ethnic Equality. *British Journal of Sociology of Education*, vol 23, no 2: 209-231.

Thomas, L. (2002) Student retention in higher education: the role of institutional habitus. *Journal of Educational Policy*, vol 17, no 4: 423-442.

UCAS (2002) *Paving the Way: Project report informing change in higher education and progression partnerships with the voice of the under-represented* available from http://www.ucas.ac.uk/candq/paving/report.pdf

Complex coherence and the teaching researcher – metaphors of professional life

Elaine Martin, Victoria University, Melbourne, Australia

Gillian Lueckenhausen, La Trobe University, Melbourne, Australia

Michael Prosser and Heather Middleton, University of Sydney, Australia

Introduction

This paper addresses an issue of perennial interest to academics – how their research relates to and informs teaching and student learning.

The paper draws on our previous work that has found a relation between the way academics understand their subject matter and the way they teach (Martin et al, 2001). We argue that this relationship can be extended to include research. We suggest that it is the understanding of subject matter that mediates the way an academic both explores their subject when researching and the way they present, explain and engage with it when they teach.

Some preliminary work has already been presented to support this argument but this has been from a phenomenographic perspective (Trigwell et al, 2003). In the present paper, we explore the relationship between teaching and research through subject matter through an analysis of metaphor.

Background

There is a good deal of conflicting evidence and much debate concerning the relations between teaching and research. Typically, academics assert that there is a positive relation between teaching and research; and that the two aspects of academic practice enrich each other (Jenkins, Blackman, Lindsay and Paton-Saltzberg, 1998; Brew, 1999), but previous studies have found little evidence of this relationship (Ramsden and Moses, 1992; Hattie and Marsh, 1996).

These previous studies, however, have focused on the relationship in terms of student evaluations of teaching, as a measure of teaching and output measures of research. We have explored the connection in a different way. We have begun from a student learning perspective.

The student learning perspective has established that the way in which university teachers approach their teaching is systematically related to how their students approach their learning. University teachers who approach their teaching with an information transfer approach are more likely to encourage surface oriented approaches to learning. University teachers who approach their teaching with conceptual change and student-focused approaches are more likely to encourage deeper approaches and higher quality learning outcomes.

More recent work has extended this student learning research to show how qualitative variation in the way academics experience understanding of their subject matter is also related to their experiences of teaching (Martin, et al, in press). We have found that student-focused perspectives on university teaching – which our earlier work had already established as being associated with higher quality student learning – are linked to more complex and research-based understandings of subject matter. Specifically phenomenographic work showed how understanding of subject matter ranges from one where the subject is seen as a series of facts and/or techniques with little awareness of how that subject matter relates to other aspects of the field of study, to an understanding in which the focus is on underlying theories and conceptions, with a coherent understanding of how the parts fit to form a whole and how that whole relates to the entire field.

Working with metaphor

In this present paper, we build upon this previous work, and argue that the key to the research-teaching connection lies in understanding of subject matter. We suggest there is a relation between the way a university teacher understands his subject, the way he explores that subject when he researches it and the way he explains it when he teaches it and we use an analysis of metaphor to explore this connection.

We have used metaphor to extend and complement our phenomenographic work in previous studies. The argument is that phenomenography explores the variation in the ways in which a phenomenon is understood within a given population. It helps us to see the range of understandings and it also highlights the relationship between the understandings. It is a sort of mapping. Like all mapping, however, it simplifies and focuses on key aspects of the understanding. It has been described as sketching an anatomy of understanding and for those who find meaning in rich descriptions rather than structured maps, it has been thought limited. Another limitation that has been noted is that it is not an appropriate method with which to explore change in an individual's understanding. Phenomenography does not focus on individuals and individual responses; rather it takes a whole data set and looks for variations within the set. Individual responses are decontextualised into categories of response. In consequence, data on the individual is lost.

Metaphor analysis, however, can provide insight into how an individual feels and thinks about a phenomenon or a series of related phenomena. It can do this in a way that is very accessible once articulated but in a way that the individual themself may not be aware of. One way to describe the complementarity of the two methods is to say that phenomenography explores the structure of understanding within a group, whereas metaphor analysis helps us come to know how understanding and feelings are structured within the experience of the individual.

In developing metaphor analysis as a research tool we have built on the work of Lakoff and Johnson, 1982; Munby, 1986 and Lakoff, 1993. Working from this position it is assumed that metaphor is not a purely linguistic phenomenon, it is rather a phenomenon of thought at the heart of every-day thinking and language. It is a way of a making sense of our lived experience, which is often abstract, emotional and complex, in terms of other, more solid phenomenon. It cross-maps our overall abstract and sensory experience of the world to the solid structures that underpin our concrete everyday life. So, we can explore the way a university teacher makes sense of their subject and the way s/he feels about this and their teaching, by attending to their comments. They might describe the subject as a package, or as a complex map, or as an uncharted landscape. They will also tell us about their teaching by revealing if they are 'with' or 'apart from' the students. They will let it be known if the landscape is to be 'explored' or if 'ground has to be covered', whether, for instance, there are 'set routes' and whether students 'find their own routes' or are set 'on track' and if they are sometimes 'left by the wayside' or 'get into deep water'.

What we typically find, however, is that there is not a single metaphor that is relevant across the whole of an individual's interview. Indeed there is a range of cross-mappings between abstract thought and concrete objects. Overall, however, there is some coherence in the ways in which metaphors are used by individuals. A complex, but consistent, picture of how a teacher makes sense of the area in focus and how they work does emerge.

An analysis of metaphor requires the researcher to do more than search the text for obvious and literal use of metaphor. Metaphor is deeply embedded in our everyday language, it is not just a rhetorical flourish. Our ordinary conceptual system is fundamentally metaphorical in nature (Lakoff and Johnson, 1983) and we have to look hard at language to recognise the extent that metaphor is present and structures our thinking and our words. If we focus only on that which is obviously metaphoric we will likely come away with a minimal and false impression. There is the requirement to go into an analysis with something of a suspension of everyday, commonsense understanding. The text has to be read with fresh eyes, with openness and a willingness to attend to possibilities, with particular attention to where the key components are positioned in the text, how they relate to each other and where they and any action take place. Is the teacher with the students in their learning, for instance, or is she more remote, giving instruction from a distance? What and where is knowledge? Where are students and teachers in relation to knowledge?

- We work individually, and then in collaboration with at least one and preferably two other research colleagues. We go into the analysis with openness and with a willingness to shed everyday commonsense understanding. In this way, we enter into a non-judgemental exploration of the lived experience of interviewees as they reflect on their teaching, their subject matter and changes to both. The aim is to be open to metaphors that might suggest insight into deeply held beliefs and emotions relating to the subject and its teaching and learning.

- We begin by highlighting the terms and fragments of the transcript text that appear to signal metaphor and metaphoric thinking.

- Using the highlighted sections of the text we construct lists of repeated and concordant terms and fragments found throughout the transcript. We use these to develop some first impressions of the metaphoric figures and structures found in the texts.

- We then identify and list textually related terms used in conjunction with these metaphors, often recording the frequency with which the terms are used and the contexts in which they were used.

- We maintained an awareness of the variation in metaphors in the transcript but we focus on identifying patterns and linguistic relationships among the terms used in different contexts.

- Through a process of refinement, we develop a collection of metaphors reflecting these patterns and relationships.

- From the results of our analysis we determined any generative metaphors that seem to be central to each teacher's experiences.

This method is presented diagrammatically in figure 1 opposite

Results

In this paper we highlight initial work with four academic staff – Adam and Alan (both from history), Ian (physics), and Tim (astronomy).

Adam (history)

Generic metaphor

History is a story that is written by looking through a particular frame or lens at connections and relations between people and social and cultural institutions. Research is a personal and energetic endeavour. It involves forcing through, into new areas, pushing yourself, making connections, within the new areas and writing the stories. Stories are written about one group of connections, then the researcher pushes himself into new areas, to tell new stories about another group of connections. For Adam, history is a craft involving writing and method. Teaching involves developing the craft in students who are seen as apprentices. They learn by looking at how it is done and they pick up and absorb the method and then write and work themselves from a personal perspective.

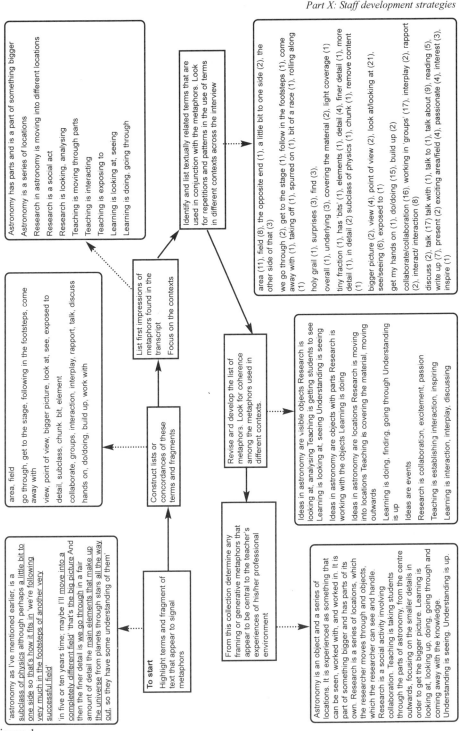

Figure 1

349

When we ask how Adam positions himself in terms of researching the subject matter, there is the feeling that he is *not* a part of it. He is energetic and forceful and pushes to get in and see and write it , but he does not become a part of it. In terms of teaching Adam is also not with the students in their learning, rather he demonstrates as a master and they see and absorb and learn as apprentices.

The subject matter

- History is a story (8 mentions)
- It is a method/ology (9) for making sense of relationships between people and social and cultural institutions.
- It is a strand of endeavour (1) that weaves (1) draws (4) pushes (1) and forces(1) its way into (2) and across (1) a frame within a bigger picture.
- There are a range of frameworks (2) and focuses (5) and lenses (1) through which the story is told.
- It cannot be pigeon-holed (2). It is about making connections (5) rather than drawing (4) boundaries (2)

Research

- Research is writing (33)
- It is pushing (2) forcing (1) your way into an area and making connections (8)
- It is a craft (3) that involves structuring (2) stories (8) and exploring relationships
- It involves looking at things in a new way (1), focusing (5) through different frameworks and lenses (1)

Teaching

- It is about imparting (1) and imbuing (1) and picking up (2)
- Looking at (4)
- Forcing students to think (2) outside of their comfort zones (1)
- It is about making connections (5),
- It is about getting under the subject matter (2)

Learning

- Learning is an apprenticeship (4)
- Seeing and looking (4)
- Linking parts (1)
- It is absorbing materials and method
- Asking pertinent questions

Alan (history)

Generic metaphor

For Alan the subject is a broad canvas with broad tracks of mainstream interpretations. For him the excitement lies in going beyond the mainstream. To go beyond the mainstream, you push at the edges of what is already known and then new ideas and vistas might open. There is also a strong sense of flow and movement, in the transcript. Although Alan moves the boundaries and starts with the small and the quirky, he always connects back to the broader picture. There is a sense that Alan is in the subject, researching from inside. Working inside out to break boundaries.

With teaching also, Alan seems to be with the students in the learning, trying to get them to change. He aims to help them to see differently. He disorientates them, challenges them, constructs a creative tension.

The subject matter

- The subject is a canvas (2) a broader canvas 2, a theatre (2)
- There are mainstream ideas (3) and broad strands (2) and tracks (2)
- History is fitting topics (8) and focuses (2) into the broader contexts (2)
- The mainstream can be push/ed (6) a little bit further (3)
- It can be tweaked (1) and new vistas open (2)
- Tracks can be changed (5) and ideas flow (4)
- You can start at the margins (1) and build (2) and flow (4) out from there
- But all things fit within the broader contexts (2)

Research

- He explores a stereotype (1) He traces it through popular and cultural representations
- He moves (5) beyond (4) accepted interpretations.
- He is push/ing (6) boundaries (4), going beyond (4) taking projects beyond (6)
- Research is tracing through (2) flowing through (4) fitting together (2) building (1)
- It is working with the quirky (1) and the small (2) and going beyond(4) connecting (4) back to the general (1)
- Things are re-thought (2) so they challenge the mainstream (2)
- He is passionate and excited (7) about research

Teaching

- Challenging (2) the students
- Disorientating them (3)

- He takes the accepted and works backwards (2) and outwards (2)

- He creates a constructive tension (1) to drive (3) the students forward and test assumptions (2)

- Gives direction (1) but says it is not a one-way traffic (1)

Learning

- Being disorientated (3)

- Interpreting (3) getting out of boxes (1) going out on a limb (2)

- Pulling apart (1) putting together again (2)

Ian (physics)

Generic metaphor

The subject is an environment, a field, a series of interconnected fields, bounded by an expanding frontier. There are areas of stability and other areas, of activity and development. Research is a journey through the environment, a quest to find the hidden unity. The journey is undertaken by groups of people who build on each other's theories

The subject matter for early undergraduate teaching is a condensed representation of the research field. The rings of theories built during research are transformed into interconnected circles and systems of subject matter. Teaching and learning involve helping students take the steps around the circles and loops that are the fabric of the subject matter as well as seeing the links and relations between them

Subject matter

- The subject matter is an entity, a field

- The field is stable in places but developing and changing and active in others, particularly at the edges

- In the more stable parts are a number of systems, stories, circles

- These are unified by threads, connections and links

- The developed areas are 'compressed' into the stories.

- In the growing and moving areas of research, there are theories, contested theories and puzzles and problems

- There are different camps and battles and controversy

Research

- Research is at the edge of the fields/areas

- These are the research frontiers

- These areas are moving and growing, and it is hard to keep up

- Research in science involves building new theories

- Laying down another 'ring of bricks' which will eventually be transferred into the circles and systems of the subject matter
- Researching is a journey along a path
- There are researchers who set out on a quest
- This is sometimes an army of people, who stand on the shoulders of other researchers
- The quest is a search for links, connections
- There is a firm belief in a hidden unity
- Threads and lines of investigation result in theories unifying broad areas, within, and sometimes across, the field/s

Teaching

- Teaching is telling the stories of physics
- Teaching is a system, a conditioning system that involves challenging and stretching students without overwhelming them
- Teaching produces transferable skills/training in the ways of physics
- Teaching is thinking about what you are putting in front of them, and teaching them to think
- Bringing their noses straight up against the things that puzzle, and helping them see links and relations between theories, probing to clarify and seeking out a rigour of thought
- Being on their side
- It is not teaching the facts but they have to know these

Learning

- Learning is a journey. It is taking steps around circles and closed loops that are the subject matter and involve thinking as physicists. It is climbing
- Learning involves training as a physicist
- It is developing a high level of transferable physics skills, including accuracy and fluency of intellectual skills, being able to employ analogies between situations, and seeing threads and connections
- Learning is not learning about something
- Not collecting facts but looking for interconnections and threads and unifying ideas
- Understanding is up (building metaphors, climbing metaphors, stretching metaphors in all fields)

Tim (astronomy)

Generic metaphor

Astronomy is looking and seeing (through a telescope). It is something that can be seen, worked with, and worked in. It is part of something big, very big. It has parts of its own. The parts are the focus. Research is working in a series of locations, with a series of objects, which the researcher can see and handle. Teaching is taking students through the parts focusing on the smaller details. Learning is looking at, looking up, doing, going through and coming away with.

The subject matter

- Is what can be seen, what can looked at
- Literally the sky, the universe
- The whole has parts, which fit together in certain ways
- The focus is on the parts
- The parts can be added to or removed from the wholes
- It is full of surprises

Research

- Research is moving into fields and areas
- Research areas/fields are also objects that can be worked with
- Research is both (literally and metaphorically) 'looking at' and 'doing'
- It is a social activity – we look at, we collaborate

Teaching

- Teaching is moving through the parts, to get students to see the big picture
- It is covering the material, covering a lot, the whole universe in a semester.
- It is interacting with students (specifically, talking to them)
- It involves getting to know students, the students getting to know him, developing a rapport, interacting with the class
- The focus is on the process

Learning

- Learning is doing, seeing, interacting, finding
- Going through leads to understanding
- Understanding is acquiring, coming away with the knowledge
- Learning is looking at, being exposed to
- Understanding astronomy is seeing the big picture and the detail
- Understanding is up

Metaphor and phenomenography

We now illustrate the way that metaphor analysis and phenomenographic categories of description complement each other. As explained early in this paper, a phenomenographic analysis focuses on the variation in the core aspects of understanding a phenomenon within a population. The consequence is that categories are typically minimalist, because they look only for the essence, what is at the core. Whilst there is little rich description, there is a clear picture of how one category relates to others, that is what is similar and what is different. Nested categories of description are typically developed, with each new category extending the perception of the previous one.

Below we illustrate the parallels between the phenomenographic categories, which have been the focus of another research paper (Trigwell et al, 2003) and the metaphor analysis explored in the paper so far. We look at each of the categories of subject matter, research and teaching.

Subject matter

Categories A and B show one group of academics who experience their subject matter as a series of facts or techniques. It is seen as something fairly atomistic and focused. Tim expresses this idea in metaphor: what can be seen, what can be looked at (both literally and metaphorically). There might be something beyond, some kind of organising theory, but this is not his concern. The elements and detail are the focus of his attention.

People in categories C and D show more awareness of a bigger disciplinary picture when they describe their subject matter. Their focus is on the way in which subject matter is organised. Adam says that history is a story that weaves, draws, pushes and forces its way into and across a frame within a bigger picture. It cannot be pigeonholed. It is about making connections rather than drawing boundaries.

Category E is the focus on the discipline in a holistic sense. Ian talks about his subject matter as an entity. As such it is difficult to atomise. He says that the growing and moving fields of research are 'compressed' into the stories, while Alan wants to push the mainstream, which can be tweaked to open vistas. He starts at the margins and uses them to critique the mainstream. See table 1 overleaf.

Teaching

With teaching, categories A and B are about information transfer to students, whether this is transferring facts, techniques or topics. Tim expresses this as "covering a lot, knowing and seeing by looking, learning as doing and seeing". Adam on the other hand in category D talks about teaching as imparting, imbuing" and learning as "picking up". He also talks about forcing students to think outside of their comfort zone but it is still a fundamentally teacher-focused process, though the object of study is conceptualised as related parts within a larger whole, and on students' acquiring concepts rather than atomised parts.

Category	Name	Metaphor
Category A & B		
A series of facts and/or techniques	Tim	What can be seen, what can be looked at. Parts added to or removed from whole.
Category C & D		
A series of concepts, issues, or procedures which are integral to the formation of a whole with a coherent structure and meaning	Adam	History is a story that weaves, draws, pushes and forces its way into and across a frame within a bigger picture. It cannot be pigeonholed. It is about making connections rather than drawing boundaries.
Category E		
A coherent whole, which is supported by organising theories within one or more broader fields of study.	Ian Alan	The subject matter is an entity. The growing and moving fields of research are 'compressed' into the stories. The mainstream can be pushed a little further. It can be tweaked and new vistas open. You can start at the margins and build and flow out from there.

Table 1

Category	Name	Metaphor
Category A & B		
The act of teaching is teacher-focused with the intention of transferring information to the students.	Tim	Moving through parts Covering material, moving outwards Interacting with students
Category C & D		
The act is teacher-focused, student activity with the intention of students acquiring the concepts of the discipline.	Adam	Imparting, imbuing and picking up Looking at (4) Forcing students to think outside of their comfort zones
Category E & F		
The act is student-focused, student activity with the intention of students developing or changing their conceptions.	Ian Alan	A conditioning system that involves challenging and stretching students without overwhelming them Challenging the students Disorientating them Creating a constructive tension to drive the students forward Getting out of boxes

Table 2

Categories E and F show a student-focused teaching process whose purpose is conceptual development or conceptual change in students. Ian describes this process as "a system, a conditioning system that involves challenging and stretching students without overwhelming them" while Alan wants to both challenge and disorientate the students a bit, creating a constructive tension to drive the students forward and getting them out of their boxes. See table 2 above.

Research

To date, we have defined four different approaches to research.

Category A is classic paid or contract consulting work, and once again it is quite atomised. Category B is the further development of a series of field-of-study based concepts, issues or procedures which are linked and integrated coherently. We have placed both Tim and Adam in this category. For Tim, research is a series of locations, fields, areas that can be worked *in* or *with*. It is both (literally and metaphorically) 'looking at' and 'doing' or moving into fields or areas. For Adam research is pushing and forcing your way into an area and making connections. It is focusing through different frameworks and lenses.

Both Ian and Alan have a more holistic concept of research. For Ian, the research is fields, and areas. At the edge of the fields/areas are research frontiers. The fields are moving and growing, and it is hard to keep up. He is searching for a hidden unity within the field. For Alan it is pushing boundaries, moving beyond. It is also working with the quirky and the small and connecting back to the general. See table 3 below.

Category	Name	Metaphor
Category A		
A series of projects which do not in themselves extend disciplinary knowledge		Not illustrated here
The further development of a series of field-of-study based concepts, issues or procedures which are linked and integrated coherently.	Tim Adam	Research is a series of locations or fields, areas that can be worked in or with. It is (literally and metaphorically) 'looking at', 'doing' or moving into fields or areas. Research is pushing and forcing your way into an area and making connections Focusing through different frameworks and lenses
Category C		
The application or development of theory within the boundaries of the field of study.		Not illustrated here
Category D		
The development and change of understanding about a field – it is open ended and inquiry-focused.	Ian Alan	At the edge of the fields/areas, frontiers Areas moving, growing, hard to keep up with it Quest for hidden unity Pushing boundaries, going beyond Working with the quirky and the small, connecting back to the general

Table 3

Metaphor	Phenomonography						
	Subject matter	A	B	C		D	E
	Teaching	A	B	C	D	E	F
	Research	A	B			C	D
Subject matter is concrete, can be moved through Teaching is guiding students through Research is a series of locations		Tim Adam					
Subject matter is bounded field which can be moved or critiqued from margins Teaching is challenging, unsettling conceptions Research is finding unity, moving beyond						Ian Alan	

Table 4

Table 4 above summarises how metaphor and phenomenography connect across the three domains of investigation

For Tim and Adam (and also for the rest of the subjects in the first set of categories, the subject matter is concrete, and there is a sense of fixedness and locatedness which can be moved through. For Ian and Alan, the focus is on a whole with borders that can be pushed or moved to create a new whole.

Conclusion

We began by asking a question asked often in higher education: how does an academic's research relate to and inform teaching and student learning. We argued that there was a relationship but that this would be mediated through their understanding of subject matter and we used metaphor to explore that relationship. We have found this relationship exists – and whilst it certainly is mediated through understanding of subject matter – it also appears to exists as a direct relationship.

Furthermore, there are metaphors and ways of structuring understanding that clearly apply across disciplines In particular draw attention to the way that Alan (history) and Ian (physics) similarly describe their subject areas as bounded fields or landscapes through which they move and where they work at the margins. Both also see teaching as being with the students and challenging them and research as finding unity and moving beyond present boundaries.

On the other hand Tim (astronomy) and Adam (history) both see the subject matter as a focus on specific parts or locations, with little attention to the interconnection of the parts of locations; both see teaching as leading, giving, and research as a focus on working in a series of specific locations

This work is very much a work in progress and we welcome comments and views.

We wish to acknowledge the support of the Australian Research Council in the funding of this research.

References

Lakoff, G and Johnson, M (1983) *Metaphors We Live By*. Chicago: University of Chicago Press.

Lakoff, G and Johnson, M (1999) *Philosophy in the Flesh: The Embodied Mind and its Challenge to Western Thought*. New York: Basic Books.

Martin, E, Prosser, M, Trigwell, K, Lueckenhausen, G (2003) *Change and development in teachers' understanding of their subject matter: Satisfaction, exhilaration, disturbance and consternation* Paper presented at the Conference of the European Association for Research on Learning and Instruction, Padua, Italy.

Martin, E, Prosser, M, Trigwell, K, Lueckenhausen, G and Ramsden, P (2001). Using Phenomenography and Metaphor to Explore Academics' Understanding of Subject Matter and Teaching. In Rust, C (ed) *Improving Student Learning Strategically*, Oxford: Oxford Centre for Staff and Learning Development, 325-336.

Munby, H (1986) Metaphor in the thinking of teachers: an exploratory study. *Journal of Curriculum Studies*, 18, (2), 197-209.

Ortony, A (1993) *Metaphor and Thought*, New York, Cambridge University Press.

Prosser, M and Trigwell, K (1999) *Understanding Learning and Teaching: The experience in higher education*. Buckingham: Open University Press.

Prosser, M, Trigwell, K and Taylor, P (1994). A phenomenographic study of academics' conceptions of science teaching and learning. *Learning and Instruction*, 4, 217-231.

Trigwell, K, Prosser, M and Taylor, P (1994) Qualitative differences in approaches to teaching first year university science. *Higher Education*, 27, 75-84.

Trigwell, K, Prosser, M, Martin, E and Ramsden, P (2003) Teachers' Experience of Change in their Understanding of the Subject they Have Just Taught, Paper presented at the Conference of the European Association for Research on Learning and Instruction, Padua, Italy.

Closing the gap between educational research and educational development: a model of engagement

JHF Meyer, University of Durham

Abstract

The University of Durham is a medium-sized research-intensive university that is strongly committed to the professionalisation of university teaching and, in particular, to fostering practice that is theoretically underpinned, reflexive, and student-centred. Implicit in its Teaching and Learning Strategy there is a spirit to empower newly appointed university teachers to begin the process of developing a mental model or conceptual framework of not just 'teaching', but of *learning* and teaching, in a form that is *actionable*; that is, in a form that can initially serve, and be further developed, as a basis for professional practice. The capacity to articulate and reflect upon such a mental model as part of one's teaching philosophy is in fact also a criterion that has to be addressed in applications for the Durham Award for Excellence in Teaching and Learning.

One explicit strategy employed (within a PGCert Module) to develop such mental models is to expose university teachers from across the disciplines to a largely self-directed form of *research-based learning*. In essence, participating academic colleagues undertake a major assignment in which they are required to establish how some of their own students engage learning in context, for example, a particular topic that they teach. In terms of process, the assignment requires colleagues to (a) submit (and then receive, and take into account, formative assessment on) a list of interview questions, each underpinned by a rationale grounded in the student learning research literature, (b) conduct the interviews subject to ethically approved protocols, (c) locate and interpret findings within the research literature, (d) reflect on, and consider the implications of, their findings in terms of developing a mental model of learning and teaching that can inform reflexive practice.

The conceptual and 'constructively aligned' framework for this activity (after Biggs, 1999) is that of *research* (as object and basis of learning); essentially defined by the 'student experience of learning' research literature. The threshold concept (after Meyer and Land, 2003) – the transformative gateway to the reconceptualisation of practice – is *variation in student learning*. The aim is for colleagues to reconstitute aspects of generic theory within their own disciplines in terms of some of the classic patterns (of variation) in student learning engagement. In doing so, and in reflecting on their own gathered evidence, the theoretically underpinned focus or mental model of professional practice shifts from that of teaching to that of *learning* and teaching.

An analysis of the experiences and outcomes of this process over a four year period has been used to construct a *model of engagement*; that is, a model that captures (within conceptually discrete dimensions) variation in the engagement of the task and attainment of associated learning outcomes.

The structure of the research assignment and the materials used to support it, as well as the detail of the 'model of engagement' and a consideration of the likely import of an individual location within it on reflexive practice, is presented.

Introduction

> *You need development (*you are deficient in some way*), and we developers (*the mainly self anointed experts*), are here to help you (*the chilling words of promise*)*

The setting for the present paper is that of medium sized research-intensive university committed, in resonance with the recommendations of the Dearing report and its aftermath, to the professionalisation of university teaching. Informed by this report, and by the impetus given to the professionalisation of university teaching through the establishment of the then Institute for Learning and Teaching (now the Higher Education Academy), the University of Durham established a Centre for Learning, Teaching, and Research in Higher Education. From the outset this centre has been an integral component of the Durham Teaching and Learning Strategy. The present author was appointed as the (foundation) director of this centre and took office in December 1999. At the time there was an institutional climate of considerable scepticism about the value of traditional and indulgent forms of academic 'staff development' and their application to the (then emerging) agenda for the accredited professionalisation of university teaching. Views expressed typically reinforced a perception already held by the present author that academic 'staff development' in relation to teaching could easily be viewed as embracing a deficit model, and a patronising 'tips for teachers' mentality that lacked theoretical underpinning and credibility.

Informal discussions at the time with peers from numerous other UK universities further reinforced a view that, despite a considerable and expanding research literature on learning and teaching in higher education, there was (in general) a peculiar history of resistance on the part of academic colleagues to *engage* with that literature as part of their own professional development. A common theme in these discussions was the view that simply attempting to 'teach' this literature and its implications for practice appeared to have little or no observable effect on the manner in which learning and teaching was reconceptualised. Three speculative, but powerful, reasons for this lack of engagement centred on the barriers presented by pedagogical jargon, the credibility of findings emanating from unfamiliar forms of (particularly) qualitative 'research', and a pe-

lack of relevance of generic educational theory to personal disciplinary discourse and practice.

In research-intensive universities there was (and still is) the additional and widely experienced phenomenon of 'research comes first' coupled, in some cases, with a view that good research and good teaching go hand in hand. As an aside, and as put to the present author at the time, there were several variations on the theme of 'we are an RAE Grade 5* department and we have received 24/24 in QAA subject review, so what do we need from you?' A good question, and fairly framed as well in terms of powerful rhetoric. The response to it was usually a genuine expression of surprise and delight at discovering a source of disciplinary teaching practice of such excellence that it was clearly imperative to share it more widely in 'best practice' terms in the strategic interests of the university as a whole. And, as a follow up, and often (unfortunately) terminal, question there was an expression of curiosity as to what sort of theoretical underpinning or craft knowledge was driving this practice, and how it might be articulated and transported to other cognate disciplines.

Two key decisions subsequently contributed to the development of a 'model of engagement' at Durham. First and foremost was a decision to establish a *research-based* postgraduate certificate in learning and teaching in higher education (60 credit units comprising two 30 credit unit modules). Both modules were substantively research-based in that participants were required to *engage in a process of educational research* within their own disciplines. In addition, the first 30 credit 'core module' was research led; its theoretical underpinning appealed to the most current research findings, and key aspects of content were taught by invited eminent researchers. Module-specific research-based learning material was also developed (Meyer, 2004).

Second, successful completion of the first 'core module' became a *probationary requirement* at Durham, and the research component of this module effectively created the landscape of the model of engagement that is the subject of the present paper. (The PGCert has subsequently evolved into a two 15, and one 30, credit unit structure and successful completion of the full 60 credits is now the probationary requirement. The research component of the previous 'core module' is now a self contained 15 credit module entitled 'The Scholarship of Learning and Teaching'.)

The seminal research activity of interest here, as present in the original 'core module' and subsequently refined, is aimed at supporting the development of a theoretical foundation for teaching *as seen from a student learning perspective*. There is an accompanying research assignment in which colleagues are required to interview their own students on their engagement of learning, for example, a particular topic. In essence, and in order to meet the learning outcomes of the module, course participants are required to locate and interpret their findings in the research literature, and then reflect on their findings in relation to the development of their own practice. Apart from the accompanying graded assessment criteria, the research assignment specification is presented in full in Appendix . It is emphasised that the structure of the model emerged from data substantively

theory within their own disciplines in terms of some of the classic patterns (of variation) in student learning engagement. In doing so, and in reflecting on their own gathered evidence, the theoretically underpinned focus or mental model of professional practice shifts from that of teaching to that of *learning* and teaching.

An analysis of the experiences and outcomes of this process over a four year period has been used to construct a *model of engagement*; that is, a model that captures (within conceptually discrete dimensions) variation in the engagement of the task and attainment of associated learning outcomes.

The structure of the research assignment and the materials used to support it, as well as the detail of the 'model of engagement' and a consideration of the likely import of an individual location within it on reflexive practice, is presented.

Introduction

*You need development (*you are deficient in some way*), and we developers (*the mainly self anointed experts*), are here to help you (*the chilling words of promise*)*

The setting for the present paper is that of medium sized research-intensive university committed, in resonance with the recommendations of the Dearing report and its aftermath, to the professionalisation of university teaching. Informed by this report, and by the impetus given to the professionalisation of university teaching through the establishment of the then Institute for Learning and Teaching (now the Higher Education Academy), the University of Durham established a Centre for Learning, Teaching, and Research in Higher Education. From the outset this centre has been an integral component of the Durham Teaching and Learning Strategy. The present author was appointed as the (foundation) director of this centre and took office in December 1999. At the time there was an institutional climate of considerable scepticism about the value of traditional and indulgent forms of academic 'staff development' and their application to the (then emerging) agenda for the accredited professionalisation of university teaching. Views expressed typically reinforced a perception already held by the present author that academic 'staff development' in relation to teaching could easily be viewed as embracing a deficit model, and a patronising 'tips for teachers' mentality that lacked theoretical underpinning and credibility.

Informal discussions at the time with peers from numerous other UK universities further reinforced a view that, despite a considerable and expanding research literature on learning and teaching in higher education, there was (in general) a peculiar history of resistance on the part of academic colleagues to *engage* with that literature as part of their own professional development. A common theme in these discussions was the view that simply attempting to 'teach' this literature and its implications for practice appeared to have little or no observable effect on the manner in which learning and teaching was reconceptualised. Three speculative, but powerful, reasons for this lack of engagement centred on the barriers presented by pedagogical jargon, the credibility of findings emanating from unfamiliar forms of (particularly) qualitative 'research', and a perceived lack of relevance of generic educational theory to personal disciplinary discourse and practice.

In research-intensive universities there was (and still is) the additional and widely experienced phenomenon of 'research comes first' coupled, in some cases, with a view that good research and good teaching go hand in hand. As an aside, and as put to the present author at the time, there were several variations on the theme of 'we are an RAE Grade 5* department and we have received 24/24 in QAA subject review, so what do we need from you?' A good question, and nicely framed as well in terms of powerful rhetoric. The response to it was usually a genuine expression of surprise and delight at discovering a source of disciplinary teaching practice of such excellence that it was clearly imperative to share it more widely in 'best practice' terms in the strategic interests of the university as a whole. And, as a follow up, and often (unfortunately) terminal, question there was an expression of curiosity as to what sort of theoretical underpinning or craft knowledge was driving this practice, and how it might be articulated and transported to other cognate disciplines.

Two key decisions subsequently contributed to the development of a 'model of engagement' at Durham. First and foremost was a decision to establish a *research-based* postgraduate certificate in learning and teaching in higher education (60 credit units comprising two 30 credit unit modules). Both modules were substantively research-based in that participants were required to *engage in a process of educational research* within their own disciplines. In addition, the first 30 credit 'core module' was research led; its theoretical underpinning appealed to the most current research findings, and key aspects of content were taught by invited eminent researchers. Module-specific research-based learning material was also developed (Meyer, 2004).

Second, successful completion of the first 'core module' became a *probationary requirement* at Durham, and the research component of this module effectively created the landscape of the model of engagement that is the subject of the present paper. (The PGCert has subsequently evolved into a two 15, and one 30, credit unit structure and successful completion of the full 60 credits is now the probationary requirement. The research component of the previous 'core module' is now a self contained 15 credit module entitled 'The Scholarship of Learning and Teaching'.)

The seminal research activity of interest here, as present in the original 'core module' and subsequently refined, is aimed at supporting the development of a theoretical foundation for teaching *as seen from a student learning perspective*. There is an accompanying research assignment in which colleagues are required to interview their own students on their engagement of learning, for example, a particular topic. In essence, and in order to meet the learning outcomes of the module, course participants are required to locate and interpret their findings in the research literature, and then reflect on their findings in relation to the development of their own practice. Apart from the accompanying graded assessment criteria, the research assignment specification is presented in full in Appendix 1. It is emphasised that the structure of the model emerged from data substantively gathered in the period *before* the model itself was used as a basis for (what are now) the graded summative assessment criteria.

The Durham 'model of engagement'

> *Theories are never more convincing for a researcher than when previously abstract ideas manifest themselves as immediate and concrete evidence. [The research assignment] provided compelling, and at times alarming, evidence of what had been up to then, for this learner-teacher at least, the largely theoretical notion of 'variation in student learning'. In many cases the transcripts illustrated the research literature examples exactly. For me this produced a sudden and clear understanding of the literature I had read, and I returned enthusiastically to articles I had previously struggled to assimilate. It was quite rewarding to see that many of the conclusions that I have drawn from these interviews were actually backed by research in the field.*

The above set of quotations, and those that appear further on in this section, are literal extracts from participants' written assessed work or evaluative comments, but are composite (multiple voices present in each set) to enhance the anonymity of the single voices. A steadily growing and consistent body of such evidence over the initial three years of the PGCert attested to the fact that participants *varied* in their engagement of the research literature as it applied, or was perceived to apply, to their own practice. An analysis of the accumulated evidence suggested a 'model of engagement' comprising initially four, and later, five conceptually discrete dimensions of variation.

Dimension 1. No initial engagement – the vocabulary, the discourse and its theoretical underpinning, are alien and troublesome.

> *I found this assignment difficult to do, because I did not feel that I had any real command of the concepts. All the theory was boring and irrelevant. Theory is a lot of wind.*

Dimension 2. Descriptive – there is 'semantic infiltration'. There is an adoption of the discourse for essentially descriptive purposes.

> *I am now able to use the appropriate terminology to explain how I approach teaching and learning. The approach to studying is a major explaining factor among the multivariate factors causing variation in the learning outcomes. I found evidence of the 'paradox of the Chinese learner' during my interviews. The influence of context and locus on student learning is very important. The interplay between student and teacher regulation of student learning provided me with inspiration and goals to aim for.*

Dimension 3. Interpretive – concepts embedded in the discourse provide an interpretive framework

My teaching practice has been considerably enriched as a direct result of this [research] assignment, in that it convinced me of the value of 'repetition as a means of encouraging understanding'. I now have a clear sense of the rationale behind certain traditional language teaching methods. I can pick out the precise moment at which my own approach changed from that of a diligent 'surface' learner to that of a 'deep' and 'transformative' learner. How the students learned was the key to understanding what they learned. This course offered information on how to encourage students to adopt an approach that leads to understanding... allowed me to see how students experienced and perceived my teaching.

Dimension 4. Evaluative – discourse informs judgments in context; the first stage of reflexive practice.

As a result of these interviews, I radically rethought my teaching. At the most fundamental level, this exercise has awakened an awareness of the variety of ways in which students learn. My experiences... brought home very clearly what was evident from the literature; different students learn differently. It was evident... that at least two of the students fell into the classical categories of deep... and surface... learners with associated different conceptions of learning... I initially began to reflect without even knowing I was doing it. It is clear... that superficially similar students possess very different conceptions of learning which relate to their motivations, methods and intentions... I now find that I question traditional teaching methods, often, and sometimes unthinkingly, adopted by me in the past... provided me with an invaluable opportunity to reflect on my teaching: to consider how I teach, why I teach that way, why it works and how my teaching could be improved. As a new teacher the results of these interviews give me some cause for concern about the approaches that my students take to learning and lead me to believe that my teaching should change to reflect these concerns.

Dimension 4. Actionable – discourse informs reflexive practice and decision making in context; there is actionable theory underpinning a mental model of learning and teaching.

This exercise has drastically altered my conception of teaching. I have been required to view teaching and learning from the student perspective. Adopting the students' perspective [now] much easier to see how I must change my teaching. I have found evidence that suggests that the modifying strategic element employed by deep learners does not always lead to successful learning outcomes. This reinforces the conclusion... that the way a student approaches a task depends on the perceived rather than actual learning environment... In my consideration, one response would be to attempt to ascertain the students' conceptions of their learning context as the course progresses. While I was aware that different students are likely to differ in their ways of studying, these [research assignment] interviews have given me direct experience of what those differences are. In particular the fact that even a deep learner ... takes a surface approach to exam preparation has prompted me to consider the way in which assessment can be conducted and exam questions structured to try and prevent repetitive answering. In terms of direct implications for the way I teach, I have learnt that the way I set assessed material or exams has a direct impact on the way students approach learning. My belief was that by making the assessment process more transparent, and allowing the students space to self-assess their learning requirements, so their control over the learning situation would increase. I think it [the research assignment] will turn out to be a useful tool in diagnosing how PhD students think, why students may be failing or more generally why their experience or performance may be unsatisfactory. I have become more aware of my responsibility as a university teacher ... am in the process of shifting my focus from my own teaching activity to the perception of the course by the students and the way students actually engage the material. My own learning from this exercise is that I now have access to a conceptual framework which I did not have before. I can apply this in lesson designs, and will be less disposed to adopt a 'deficit model' of student learning needs.

Discussion

The Durham 'model of engagement' is firmly grounded in the experiences of PGCert participants and has evolved over a period of four years. In its present form this model also serves as a basis for the summative assessment for the 'Scholarship of Learning and Teaching Module'. The dimensions of variation captured in the model arose, originally, from an analysis of three years *formatively* assessed work (the student learning assignment: Appendix 1) and has been refined to its present form on the basis of some subsequent *summatively* assessed work over a further one year period.

The research assignment has furthermore consistently reconfirmed the existence of generic aspects (of variation in) student learning across a wide range of disciplinary contexts, and across a wide range of interviewees (level 1 students to PhD students). In some cases new theoretical insights have also been revealed as, for example, in the distinction in students' minds between 'coursework' and 'revision' learning.

While it is not possible for ethical reasons to discuss individual cases, there is in general an observed correspondence between the *level* of engagement within the model and the quality of reflexive practice subsequently exhibited in the portfolios that form the basis of the summatively assessed work in the final (30 credit) module of the PGCert. It is furthermore clear that, at the upper levels of engagement within the model (Dimensions 4 and 5), associated portfolios exhibit reading beyond the core generic texts that are the recommended reading for the research assignment.

Attribution

Although the substance of the present paper has developed within a particular institutional context over a period of some years, the views expressed here are those of the present author writing in an individual capacity and not as a representative of the University of Durham.

References

Biggs, J (1999). *Teaching for quality learning at university: What the student does.* Buckingham: SRHE and Open University Press.

Meyer, JHF (2004). Variation in student learning: *An empirical nested model. Course materials to support PGCert (Learning and Teaching in Higher Education) Module 2: The scholarship of learning and teaching,* University of Durham (unpublished). Electronic copy can be downloaded from my personal website under 'work in progress' section: http://www.dur.ac.uk/j.h.f.meyer

Meyer, JHF and Land, R (2003). *Threshold concepts and troublesome knowledge: linkages to ways of thinking and practising within the disciplines.* In Rust, C (ed) Improving Student Learning Theory and Practice – 10 years on, 412-424. Oxford: OCSLD

Appendix 1

Student Learning Assignment: Postgraduate Certificate in Learning and Teaching in Higher Education module: The Scholarship of Learning and Teaching

This is a 15 UCU level 4 Module

Module leader: Professor JHF. Meyer

Centre for Learning, Teaching and Research in Higher Education, University of Durham

Introduction

This assignment is research-based and introduces you to the fact that students may *vary* in their engagement of both the content of learning (subject matter), and the context of learning (aspects of their perceived course environment). It is only by being aware of such variation, as exhibited by your own students in your own disciplinary context, that you can begin to reflect on its implications for the development of your own 'mental model' of professional practice. Such reflexive practice constitutes a vital part of what is referred to as 'student-centred teaching'[1] insofar as it helps you to develop not simply a mental model of 'teaching', but of *'learning* and teaching'.

The assignment is in two parts; Part 1 is formatively assessed, and Part 2 is summatively assessed according to the graded assessment criteria (not presented here).

The assignment is in two parts; Part 1 is formatively assessed, and Part 2 is summatively assessed according to the graded assessment criteria (not presented here).

For Part 1 you are required to formulate a set of *theoretically grounded* interview questions and the submission deadline for these questions and their rationale is… (date given typically allows six weeks for completion of Part 1, with written formative feedback supplied one week after submission).

For Part 2, and based on your interview questions (as possibly modified in light of the formative assessment received), you are required to conduct interviews with three of your students and write a 2500 word report based on an analysis of your findings. In this report you are required to (a) provide an introductory theoretical framework against which your findings are then presented and interpreted as three independent and *individual cases*. In doing so (b) your findings are required to be explicitly located where possible within the student learning research literature. You are then required to (c) reflect on the implications of your findings for your own professional practice[2]. The submission deadline for this report is… (date given typically allows eight weeks for completion of Part 2, which is summatively assessed).

Prescribed reading for this assignment is:

(a) Chapters 25 in Ramsden, P. (2003). Learning to Teach in Higher Education (2nd Edition). RoutledgeFalmer: London.

(b) Chapters 13 and 9 in Marton, F. et al (1984). The Experience of Learning. Scottish Academic Press: Edinburgh.

(c) Working paper on 'Variation in student learning: An empirical nested model' by Meyer (2004) (which is available electronically). The various empirical models discussed in this paper are intended to serve as a basis for conceptually locating your interview questions and their underpinning rationale.

(d) Given that the threshold pass criterion for Module 2 requires engagement with research literature that is discipline (or cognate discipline) specific, there is a further requirement to access such material as is available within your discipline area (see, for example, the *Supplementary References* at the end of the 'nested model' paper above and the *list of journals* in the Foundations Module Guide).

Length of the report

A cutoff word count is not specified for the Part 2 report as this is likely to vary from one interview context to another, the degree of variation between the cases, and the length of pertinent interview excerpts used as supporting evidence. As a guide, a typical report would be 2500 words in length **excluding references and interview excerpts**.

---

[2]Professional practice cannot simply rely on craft or tacit knowledge about learning and teaching; it needs to be underpinned by a theoretical knowledge base.

Assignment summary – what you need to do

Student interviews[3] form the basis of this assignment which focuses on several important concepts in the student learning research literature; in particular the concept of an 'approach' to learning – essentially the contextually influenced predisposition(s) and states of prior knowledge with which students proceed towards *engaging a learning task in process terms*[4]. In this assignment you are required to interview three students in one of the courses you teach[5], and your interviews are intended to reveal how the students go about their studying in, for example, motivational, intentional and process terms. In particular you should therefore form, in respect of each student, an impression of:

- How they perceive a specific learning task (or topic) in context[6] rather than simply generally

- What they think 'learning' means (their conception of learning) in this same context

- How they 'approach' the learning task.

In thus carrying out this assignment you are specifically required to:

1. Carry out the prescribed reading. This reading establishes the *conceptual framework* within which you will need to **locate and interpret** your findings.

2. Construct a set of *interview questions* (submitted initially for formative assessment, then returned to you, then resubmitted with possible modifications as an integral part of the Part 2 report). Given that the aim of the assignment is to explore relationships between various sources of explanatory variation (conceptions, intentions, motives, process, and so on) you need to provide a *rationale* for your questions. Specifically, for example, in terms of what you think they might reveal, the degree to which they sample aspects of the various nested models of student learning that have been considered, and why you might have decided to foreground particular issues in relation to the subject/topic context of the questions. In short your rationale establishes at a conceptual level what you are trying to access (as sources of explanatory variation) and how the questions are to be viewed in terms of sampling the domain of one or more models of student learning[7].

---

[3]Being able to talk supportively to students about how they approach learning, and what difficulties they may be experiencing in doing so, is an important aspect of professional development.

[4]In common sense terms drawn from everyday experience, 'an approach' to a task is shaped by a perception of what is required ('reading the signals'), what is known already about how to do it, and the strategic or tactical choice of the means to accomplish it.

[5]This activity requires formal ethical approval and you must assume that this will be granted.

[6]Context determined eg by level, module, course and further differentiated by eg learning taught coursework, revising for examinations, preparing for seminars, carrying out laboratory experiments, and so on.

[7]Please note that the models put forward as a basis for this exercise are essentially empirically grounded in both qualitative and quantitative studies of student learning across the disciplines.

3. Conduct and transcribe three interviews (excerpts from these interviews are required to support the categorisations of the cases). Structure the interview to focus initially on a particular course, and then focus in on a single topic or section within that course. Within this focused context try to find out what students think 'learning' means. Be alert to the opportunity to distinguish in learning terms between how a particular topic has been approached in two response contexts; for example, attending lectures and revising for examinations.

4. Write an introductory conceptual framework (about 500 words). Against this framework, categorise students' contextualised approaches. (What is being categorised here in terms of a more sophisticated concept than 'approach' are students' *study orchestrations*[8]). As a guide:

(a) Present each case (in about 500 words in each case, excluding excerpts) in terms of an overall interpretation; that is, in student learning terms, present a summary of each 'student in context' as encapsulated in the interview. To do this you clearly have to read the transcript (or listen to the interview) as a whole *and interpret it within* the student learning literature available to you. As one colleague (2001) put it: 'The aim is to produce a descriptive analysis of the relationship between students' conceptions of learning and their approaches to studying.' This is *not* the same as simply presenting the extracts of the interview transcript.

(b) Justify where possible any key features of your case interpretations with concise supportive evidence (transcript excerpts). Seek, where possible, to locate 'classic' quotations in the literature *by means of explicit referencing*. For example, if a student says '… you understand the actual meaning rather than just the words themselves', then you have an almost literal expression of (a defining feature of) of a deep approach.

5. Finally, in about 500 words reflect on your findings, and background reading, in relation to their implications for your own teaching practice.

General advice on conducting the interviews and completing the assignment

You should begin by briefly explaining to the students why you want to talk to them about their learning experiences without using any technical terminology or explaining exactly what you are after. You need to emphasise to students that their participation is **voluntary**, confirm that they are willing to be interviewed (there is a **consent form** they have to sign), emphasise that there is **nothing invasive** about this ethically approved process, and that there will be **no recording of their names or any other form of personal identification**.

It is suggested that you use a cassette tape recorder and conduct your interviews in a quiet location where you will not be disturbed for 15–20 minutes.

---

[8] After the work of Meyer (1991).

Interview one student at a time and tape record the entire interview. Listen carefully to the interview afterwards before proceeding to the next one because it is likely that you will pick up missed opportunities, examples of what seemed to work well/not well in terms of specific questions and follow up, and so on.

The key to good interviewing is keeping quiet for most of the time! Ask only one question at a time, and *wait* for a response before rephrasing or moving on. Ask simple questions and let the students answer in their own way. Only interrupt to avoid time wasting digressions.

Do not ask leading questions, eg Does learning help you to see things differently? Do you have a heavy workload in this course/subject? Do you memorise your notes?

Do not ask questions in terms of presenting a choice between predetermined answers, eg Do you see the topics you have learned as being isolated from one another or do you see them as being related in some way?

Do not respond to statements in an evaluative manner eg Well that's not a good way of going about things now is it?

Instead, ask questions like:

> *In this course/subject/topic can you comment reflectively on any effect that learning has had on you?*
>
> *How are you experiencing the workload here?*
>
> *How do you make use of your notes after lectures/during revision?*
>
> *How do you go about learning/revising topic x in this course?*

If you are unclear as to the meaning of what a student says, then seek clarification and elaboration. You may, for example, ask:

> *Can you expand on that point a bit further?*
>
> *Can you tell me anything... more about what you just said?*
>
> *When you said you were doing x, what did you have in mind?*
>
> *When you say x, what exactly do you mean?*
>
> *Can you give me an example of what you have just described?*
>
> *Do you always do things like that?*
>
> *Can you give me a contrary example?*

Students' recollections about learning in process terms – recollections about *how* something was learned rather that *what* was learned – can be difficult to externalise and interpret if they are not specifically tied to a response context that is relevant for the purpose(s) of the interview. There is also often a sharp distinction in process between what students may describe as coursework learning as opposed to learning or revising for examinations. It helps to ask about recent and specific experiences, and preferably in terms of having 'learned' something new in the course. For example:

Please describe what you were thinking during the lecture[9] on topic x. Can you tell me what you did during the lecture, and in the days that followed, on that particular topic? You've mentioned that you took notes during that lecture. How did you decide what to write down? What did you subsequently do with your notes? Can you explain the rationale behind what you have just said? How did you develop this technique? How does it work for you?

'X' is a topic that we recently dealt with in class. Can you tell me how you went about learning it? Did you know anything about this topic beforehand? You've mentioned reading some more about it. What role has reading played in your learning this topic?

What are you concentrating on studying at the moment? Can you tell how you are going about that?

Students tend to generalise and talk about other students if you let them. Force them to be specific and to talk about their *own* experiences. For example:

What you say about how some of your friends go about studying in this course is interesting, but can you rather describe how you went about learning topic x?

It is advisable to transcribe the **entire interview** or at least those key features of it that capture the distinctiveness of what a student has said. Do not summarise or interpret the student's words (or the interview questions) – write them down verbatim.

Brief review of conceptions of learning[10]

In order to categorise the students' responses and present them as cases, you need to be alert to what they think 'learning' in topic x means, or how they think their learning in topic x will be assessed, or how they know when they have learned something in the whole or part of topic x. So when a student says: 'I think that you get more knowledge when you memorise what you read' there is an immediate alertness to the possibility that an accumulative conception of learning is present in the particular response context.

Accumulative conceptions. Learning is conceived of as (a) an increase in knowledge, (b) storing information for immediate or future use, or (c) applying what has been thus accumulated. There is no internal 'rearrangement' or transformation of what has been 'learned' in terms of these three conceptions. Learning is essentially conceived of as the

---

[9]Substitute tutorial, laboratory session, small group activity, and so on, as need be for 'lecture' here and elsewhere

[10]Conceptions of learning have been researched using a qualitative (phenomenographic) methodology and the classic work is by Säljö (1979), followed by Marton, Dall'Alba & Beaty (1993). Findings from these two studies posit a hierarchical model comprising, respectively, five and six conceptions that traverse an accumulative – transformative emphasis.

acquisition of information (facts, formulae, definitions, procedures) which are retained for relatively short term immediate or future use. Because the information is stored and retrieved without any internal transformation the process by which material is 'learned' may simply be that of mechanical memorising[11].

> *Learning is getting down what the lecturer says. You've got to try to remember it. You've learned something when you can remember how to do it. The teacher tells you and then you've got to be able to do it the same later all on your own.*

Transformative conceptions. Learning is conceived of as (d) the construction or derivation of personal meaning (understanding, comprehension), (e) thus (possibly as a consequence of understanding something) seeing things differently, or (f) changing as a person. Learning is conceived of as a process of making sense of things – comprehending the meaning of something, being able to reinterpret something in your own words, or explain it to somebody else, developing new insights and, as consequence, changing as a person. You know you have understood something when it makes sense to you, can form an argument for or against it, when you can explain it to somebody else, and so on. Students with a transformative conception often contrast it with accumulative conceptions. For the student who views learning in a transformative sense, the acquisition of information may be mentioned, but it will be further elaborated as perhaps the starting point from which learning as understanding develops.

> *I see learning as an ongoing process. It is a change in the way I see things, change of worldview, change of understanding. It involves experience and reflection ... I know that I often alter my opinion about something after I have been exposed to another perspective*

In interviewing students about their conceptions of learning, bear in mind the following points:

- If you come straight out and ask 'What is your conception of learning?' then you are likely to get mixed or confusing responses! This question should be asked obliquely in response to cues like 'memorising', 'cramming', 'learning', 'understanding', and so on:

    When you used the word 'learning' in that example, what exactly do you mean? How did you know you had learned it?

    When you say you want to get more knowledge about this subject what do you mean?

- Do not present students with a range of alternative 'conceptions' of learning and ask them to choose one! If you do, some will strive to talk themselves into the most sophisticated level, regardless of their own level of understanding.

---

[11]One form of 'unthinking memorising' that is usually interpreted in terms of a surface approach process. There are, however, contrasting forms of memorising (some involving repetition and/or rehearsal), some of which are interpreted as deep approach processes. For operationalised examples of these contrasting forms see Meyer (2000).

■ Just because people use the word 'understanding' doesn't mean they have a sophisticated conception of learning. Probe a bit deeper. Ask questions like this:

What counts as understanding in this course/subject/topic? How do you think we go about assessing understanding?

Is all learning the same for you?

What does the term 'understanding' mean for you in relation to memorising?

Brief review of approaches to studying[12]

In thus exploring 'approaches' to learning bear in mind that:

■ An 'approach' is mainly characterised by an *intention*, but the intention is usually coupled with a *process*. The intention and the process are, furthermore, usually conceptually consonant but need not be in terms of the theoretically important phenomenon of *dissonance*[13]. It isn't therefore always easy, for example, to identify an approach in a neat sense, and especially so in terms of, say, note taking, reading, performing experiments, or rehearsal. You need to be specific:

You mentioned that you wrote some things down during the lecture(s) on topic x. Can you explain why you chose to write those particular things down? You said that you wrote down things that are important. How did you decide at the time what was important?

■ A student's approach may vary between different subjects, or even between different topics within a subject[14]. Fully exploring how consistent a student is in terms of approach across a range of topics can be very interesting but lies outside the scope of this assignment. To reiterate: concentrate on how a particular subject topic engaged in learning terms, or how the 'understanding' of a particular concept is arrived at.

■ Given that processes are 'the mechanisms of production' of learning outcomes, it is important to pin down what students mean when they use terms like 'understand', 'learn', and 'memorise' in the context of learning topic x. Different students may assign contrary meanings to these commonly used terms. So, whenever these terms are mentioned by students you should attempt to explore what the students think they mean. For example:

When you said you were trying to understand topic x, what did you mean by 'understand'? Can you give an example? Can you explain how you might experience not understanding something?

---

[12]The classic work is by Marton & Säljö (1976a,b) who introduced the deep – surface metaphor into the discourse of student learning based on qualitative (phenomenographic) studies of students' readings of academic texts.

[13]Dissonance refers, for example, to an intention that is not attainable in terms of an associated learning process.

[14]Cf earliest empirical studies by Meyer and Watson (1991).

You mention both memorising and trying to understand as things you often try to do together. Do these terms mean the same thing to you?

What criteria, internal to yourself, do you use as a basis for saying that you 'understand' something? So, how would these apply then in terms of topic x?

Your next task is to broadly *categorise* the content of what the three students have reported – please note we are *not* categorising students, or in any sense labelling them as individuals – we are *categorising how students describe their approaches to learning in some given context.* The point here is that such approaches may vary across different contexts. Use the following two category definitions as guides:

Surface Approach: An intentional focus on the superficial aspects of what is being learned, the 'surface' features of the message (text, lecture), a concentration on memorising facts, information, and details. In terms of the classic definition (arising from students' experiences of reading academic texts), a focus on the textual 'sign' rather than what is 'signified'.

I just concentrated on memorising the definitions without paying too much attention to what they really meant.

If an exam requires proofs I will have to learn them by heart.

I make sure I have a complete set of legible, fully annotated lecture notes then make revision notes from these, leaving out ideas I know already... then I learn my revision notes by reading through and rewriting parts until they are known off by heart.

Deep Approach: An intentional focus on what is 'signified', what the message is about, what things mean, and what the point of the message is. This approach actively involves establishing relationships between ideas, between past experience and the message, between the message and the real world.

I was thinking what did it really mean, what was it really about and how did it relate to what I knew.

If you understand something you're able to explain it to other people in a way that they'll be able to understand. You understand the actual meaning rather than the words themselves.

Factors affecting approach

Finally, in exploring what has influenced students to adopt a particular approach to learning, bear in mind that many such factors are likely to arise from students' perceptions of the teaching and learning environment; particularly their perceptions of workload and assessment procedures. Some useful ideas for interview questions on workload and assessment may be found in Lizzio, Wilson & Simons (2002) (Cf appendices 2 and 3 on pages 51 and 52).

The main issues to explore here are:

- how students perceive or experience the workload

- how well (or how poorly) they expect to do in the course

- what they think assessments actually require in terms of learning or expenditure of effort, what assessments reward in terms of marks

- how much freedom of choice they feel they have in terms of what to study

- the quality of the teaching and of the learning environment generally

- prior knowledge about the subjects/topics being studied

Interpreting your data: some examples

Student A says, eg, 'The workload is enormous'. From the student's perspective how does a perception of a 'heavy workload' arise? How is it experienced and what are the possible explanations? From a theoretical perspective how do models of student learning help us explain what such a perception may be associated with and what the *likely* consequences of this perception are therefore likely to be?

Student B says, 'The only thing I get concerned about is exactly what you need to know and what you don't need to know... really what is on the exam. It's not so much reading and understanding but actually reading and understanding the bits you need to know. It's like focusing on the bits that are going to help you get by.' Ask yourself: what is being described here in terms of intention, motivation and process? What does the research literature have to say about this type of response? And again, what factors can influence or predispose a student to approach learning in this manner?

Student C says, 'Then I began to read [the book] and I didn't understand a word of it... So I set myself the task of reading and rereading the book until I could distil it into a number of sentences... So I reread the book a number of times, took notes, and where I found I was just reading a page and thinking I just don't understand a word of this I would draw pictures and try to turn the ideas into sort of stick people and lines... Just to find another way into it.' There are some powerful insights here into how a student with an *intention* to understand material that is clearly initially difficult is adopting a congruent learning *process*.

Student D says: 'In some topics [provides a specific example]... you have to know the names of [provides examples] so you have to memorise. For other topics [provides example] you have to understand it and then you can link it on to other things. This excerpt immediately opens up the possibility of exploring how this particular student may be using different learning processes in different contexts.

Presenting your cases

You are asked to view your interviews as *case*, as composite wholes. You should aim to interpret each case as an integrated picture of how and why that particular student went about studying in a particular way in a particular context. You furthermore need to substantiate your descriptions and categorisations[15] of what students said with appropriate verbatim quotes from your interviews. But note again that you only have about 500 words (*excluding* interview excerpts) for each case. There are good examples of case studies in: Marton, F. et al (1984) The Experience of Learning. pp 178186. Scottish Academic Press.

Acknowledgements: This research-based assignment has evolved in terms of emphasis, rigour, and theoretical underpinning as reflected in the substantial addition of new material and the accompanying 'nested model' paper (Meyer, 2004), from a collegial exercise first proposed by: Gibbs, G. (1989). Certificate in Teaching in Higher Education by Open Learning. Module 9: Improving Student Learning. Oxford Centre for Staff Development, Oxford Polytechnic. Subsequent insights arising from an independent adaptation of the original Gibbs exercise by Michael Prosser at the University of Sydney have also been incorporated into the Durham assignment. Tribute is finally paid to the many enthusiastic colleagues at Durham who, in undertaking this assignment, have been an inspiration for its continual development and to whom this chapter is dedicated.

References

Lizzio, A, Wilson, K and Simons, R (2002). University students' perceptions of the learning environment and academic outcomes: implications for theory and practice. *Studies in Higher Education*, 27, 27-52.

Säljö, R (1979). *Learning in the learner's perspective. I. Some common-sense conceptions*. Reports from the Department of Education, University of Göteborg, No. 76.

Marton, F, Dall'Alba, G and Beaty, E (1993). Conceptions of learning. *International Journal of Educational Research*, 19, 277-300.

Marton, F and Säljö, R (1976a). On qualitative differences in learning. I – outcome and process. *British Journal of Educational Psychology*, 46, 4-11.

Marton, F and Säljö, R (1976b). On qualitative differences in learning. II – outcome as a function of the learner's conception of the task. *British Journal of Educational Psychology*, 46, 115-127.

Meyer, JHF (2000). Embryonic 'memorising' models of student learning. *Educational Research Journal*, 15, 203-221.

Meyer, JHF (1991). Study Orchestration: the manifestation, interpretation and consequences of contextualised approaches to studying. *Higher Education*, 22, 297-316.

Meyer, JHF and Watson, RM (1991). Evaluating the Quality of Student Learning. II - study orchestration and the curriculum. *Studies in Higher Education*, 16, 251-275

[15]Please note again that you are NOT categorising or labelling students. What you are attempting to do is categorise what they said in the interview in a particular context (recognising that they may have said something entirely different to the same question(s) in another response context).

Towards a reconciliation of phenomenographic and critical pedagogy perspectives in higher education through a focus on academic engagement

Paul Ashwin, Lancaster University and Monica McLean, University of Oxford

Key words: phenomenography, critical pedagogy, academic engagement, teaching and learning

Abstract

In this paper, we outline how the literature on phenomenography, specifically Marton and Booth (1997), and the literature that adopts a 'critical approach', specifically Friere (1996), can be brought together to help us to understand the barriers that face students and teachers in engaging in learning and teaching in higher education. Our attempt is motivated by a wish to relate the different foci of each perspective. We argue that the phenomenographic literature has been successful in suggesting theoretically informed and research-based ways in which learning environments might be structured to improve the quality of students' learning. However, it is largely silent on the extent to which barriers to learning can be due to structural inequalities outside of the learning environment. More critical approaches foreground these structural inequalities but their suggestions for teaching and learning practices are often weak. In bringing these two perspectives together, we develop a model of academic engagement that takes into account both experiential and structural influences on the quality of teaching and learning in higher education.

Introduction

This paper is exploratory and experimental. It arises from an interest in understanding university pedagogy by integrating insights about the micro level, that is, the level of teaching and learning practices, with insights about the factors that affect such interactions at the meso (departmental and disciplinary) and macro (national policy and wider social and political) levels. Our research question is: in the context of UK higher education can we reconcile to good effect the ideas of 'critical pedagogy', which casts teaching as moral, cultural, political practice, with the ideas that underpin phenomenographic research in higher education, which explores student experience and perceptions? It is important to be clear about our starting position in attempting the reconciliation of these two perspectives. We see ourselves as starting from within the phenomenographic perspective and trying to expand it to take account of work from a critical perspective because we are uneasy about the phenomenographic literature's severance from disciplinary, economic, social, political and historical contexts.

The first part of this paper outlines our version of a 'critical' project. It sets out the values and beliefs that underpin our work and our understanding of the context in which we are working. We then examine how we might reconcile the two perspectives through a close reading of two key texts, one from each perspective. Finally, we examine the implications of this reconciliation in terms of future research.

A 'critical' project

Our theoretical ambition, then, is to connect research findings that claim to explain and identify ways of improving learning with the polemic and commitment of what can be broadly termed 'critical pedagogy'. The beliefs that direct this ambition are about the nature of formal systems of education as social action and about the purposes and nature of higher education. For us, the education system is inevitably political; that is, it is bound up in the interplay between the state and civil society shaping who we are, what we do, how we think and speak, and what we receive from and give to society.

'Critical pedagogy' derives from the 'critical theory' of the Frankfurt School of philosophers that is characterised by critique of contemporary society and by suggesting action that might create the conditions for a more just society (Bernstein, 1995; How, 2003). Our position and interest in what 'critical pedagogy' might offer can be clarified by a critique of contemporary educational purposes and values. We start with the argument that education systems in democracies have three benign purposes: for personal growth, for an educated citizenry, and for a producing wealth and services. At different historical junctures different policies appear to emphasise different purposes. We are at a moment when the economic purposes are being promoted above other purposes and an adjunct to this is that education is being portrayed by state policy and is enacted in many practices as 'technical-rational'. The meaning and effects of technical rationalism have been widely debated in educational literature (see, for example, Carr, 1989; Dale, 1989; Kemmis 1994; Soucek, 1994). Broadly, in its current configuration, technical-rationalism is associated with education as a system, taking on the values of 'the market', with the rise of 'new managerialism' and with an emphasis on the value of education for the economy. At the heart of a technical-rational approach to education is what Seddon (1997) describes as 'the inherent limitations of intellectual resources based on rational actor theory, a preoccupation with utility' (p178). A concrete example of the tendency, apt for us, is the standardised, technique-focused type of programme for university teachers that Cameron (2003) rails against; another is the promotion of a narrow 'what works' approach to educational research that strips investigation of a consideration of purpose and values.

'Critical pedagogy' enjoins us to identify what social purposes higher education should serve. Our discussions about what a university education is for led us to identify two major phenomena with which we believe higher education ought to engage:

- the persistence of the connection between social origin and destiny (wealth, choice, contentment, health, resources, well-being); and,

- serious, global social problems (conflict, poverty, environment)

An interest in addressing these phenomena amounts to what Jurgen Habermas and other critical theorists refer to as 'emancipatory' purposes for education. Such an interest implies reconfiguring higher education's aims to redress the balance between ethical considerations and consumer interests. Quite different questions might arise than those prevailing at present. For example: 'Are universities reproducing inequalities in society or challenging them?' or 'What forms of interpersonal behaviour are capable of resolving social problems?' or 'Is the 'hedonism of self-interest' (Ball, 1994, p30) encouraged by the "market values" of individual performance, differentiation and competition having deleterious effects on our society?'

There are a number of stances with which we do not want to identify. We do not subscribe to 'narratives of decline' or any form of 'golden ageism'; we welcome the shift from 'elite' to a 'mass' higher education viewing it as potentially democratising, even though stratification within the system is continuing and, perhaps, worsening. Nor do we want to embroil teachers in the old accusation of being agents of inequitable social reproduction (Bowles and Gintis, 1976; Sharp and Green, 1975), but we do suggest a responsibility for teachers and researchers to deliberate on the connections between the ends of education and curriculum design and teaching as intentional activities. We regard the current circumstances as complicated and contradictory, containing both options and constraints. Practically, our position is aligned with those interested in the options presented by educational endeavour in all sectors and guises that envision or enact alternative, better futures (Seddon, 1997, Cooper, 2001). Theoretically, we are searching for explanations which connect broader social trends with how students learn and experience their learning environment and which suggest convincing possibilities for the future yet avoid what Offe (1996) refers to as 'heroic idealism' (p43).

This outline of our interests, commitments and ambitions is the backdrop to our attempt to bring together 'critical pedagogy' and phenomenography.

The phenomenographic perspective and critiques

Phenomenography is one of a range of approaches that underpin the 'approaches to learning' tradition in higher education. In this article we focus on the phenomenographic tradition within the approaches to learning perspective and recognise that some of our arguments might not apply to the more psychologically informed research that is part of the 'approaches to learning' perspective (for example, Entwistle and Ramsden 1983, and Biggs 1993). In their seminal article, using an approach that would later become known as phenomenography, Marton and Säljö (1976) asked students to describe how they went about a reading task and found they could categorise the descriptions into two qualitatively different ways in which students approach learning. They used the terms 'deep' and 'surface' to describe the key features of the variation. Prosser and Trigwell (1999) define the two approaches like this:

> *'The motivation associated with a deep approach to learning is to understand ideas and seek meanings. [Students adopting a surface approach] are instrumentally or pragmatically motivated and seek to meet the demands of the task with minimum effort.' (p91)*

Since then there has been a substantial amount of phenomenographic research focusing on this fundamental difference and the accounts of university learning that are the result of this research are, if nothing else, empirically well-grounded and coherent. It has established a relation between how students perceive aspects of their learning environment and which approach they take. The theory is popular in educational development units responsible for assisting teachers; it offers the possibility of creating an environment that might induce students to seek meaning and understanding (Prosser and Trigwell, 1999).

Recently, criticisms of the 'approaches to learning' literature, which can also be applied to phenomenography, have become more numerous (Haggis, 2003, 2004; Malcolm and Zukas, 2001; Webb, 1997). They tend to fall into two main inter-related categories. The first, is that, as a theory influencing practice, 'approaches to learning' is an under-challenged orthodoxy. Webb (1997) describes the theory as 'foundational' and attacks educational developers for using it uncritically because they have been seduced by its messages that over-simplify the complexities of the educational endeavour. Similarly, in order to express her concern that the ubiquity of 'approaches to learning' leaves important matters unexplored, Haggis (2004) uses Rowland's (1993) idea of how any one theory throws light on some aspects of human experience but always leaves other aspects in shadow.

Another category of criticism identifies the important unexplored matters as issues of power, purposes and broader contextual influences. This criticism incorporates two ideas. The first is that 'approaches to learning' is elitist because, unreflectively, it promotes a version of 'good' learning which has been constructed by the Western enlightenment tradition, which excludes certain types of students. We challenge this, believing that it is as productive to think about the commonality among learners as it is to ponder difference. Nevertheless, it is the case within phenomenography that, beyond references to 'biography' (Marton and Booth, 1997), the reasons for why students perceive similar learning environments differently are under-developed. The second part of the criticism about 'approaches to learning' is that it is a 'meta-narrative' in that it 'appears to have no particular view of humanity and the social consequences of education' (Webb, 1997, p198). We shall show below that phenomenography *does* have a view of humanity, but, at the same time, its distance from 'the urgencies of our society' (Bruner, 1974, p115) is a problem. Phenomenography as an approach to conceptualising university pedagogy is limited by its abstraction from educational purposes and values and from political and social realities[1].

We begin our attempt to reconcile the two perspectives by identifying some similarities. We should note here that our attempt to bring together insights from the two traditions is not unique: see, for example, Mann's (1999, 2001) work on alienation and engagement of university students and the 'academic literacies' literature that emphasises the difficulties that some students more than others encounter in formal education settings because of the ways dominant discourses and power operate (Lea and Street 1989 and Jones at al 1999).

Examining the similarities between the 'critical pedagogy' and phenomenographic perspectives

In general, the critiques cited that posit alternatives to a phenomenographic perspective tend towards a version of 'critical pedagogy', in which the interest is in power relations, emancipatory purposes and equitable treatment of individual students who, in one way or another, can be described as 'non-traditional'. A wide range of theoretical perspectives constitute 'critical pedagogy' but the common features are critique of current conditions and a focus on future possibilities for the transformation of individuals or society. The work emphasises the value-laden and political nature of education and attends to culture, identity and subjectivity. But it often treats the pedagogy of the classroom cursorily or unrealistically: Buckingham (1996), for example, says of two of the most prolific contemporary critical pedagogues, Henry Giroux and Peter McLaren, that they have 'increasingly refused to address questions about the empirical realities of schooling, or about teaching strategies' (p632). Nevertheless, as a tradition, critical pedagogy does suggest principles of practice that centre on the teacher/student relationship, specifically, demonstrating respect for students and their knowledge; and, related to this, using participatory methods which draw on the students' experience.

In our attempt to broaden the phenomenographic perspective to take account of the insights of 'critical pedagogy' we draw on two main sources. From the phenomenographic perspective our source is Marton and Booth's (1997) *Learning and Awareness* whose work in this area began with the reading task research described earlier

---

[1]It is important to know that phenomenography in particular makes this choice consciously – the focus on the learning of 'phenomena' abstracted from 'situation' is deliberate. Marton and Booth (1997) state: 'The thematic field that surrounds the [phenomena being studied] is made up of aspects of a wider, more general global world, with roots in the current culture and branches that reach out to the learners' future world' (p142). They are not critical pedagogues so do not engage with critiques of society or alternative futures.

which was undertaken with Swedish university students during the 1970s. From 'critical pedagogy' perspective we have chosen Paulo Friere's *Pedagogy of the Oppressed* (1996) which has an overt political message and lays out a pedagogic theory for use by teachers in literacy programmes in Brazil, also during the 1970s . The reasons for choosing only two texts is that it would be misleading to claim there is a single version of either perspective and so we wanted specific instances of each to analyse. The reason for choosing the particular texts is partly that they are each key texts within their perspectives, and partly because of the common ground (despite enormous differences) that we can see between them. These commonalities can be seen in the views expressed on the relationship between people and the world, in the relationship that is suggested should exist between students and teachers and in the ultimate aim of education.

No world-person dichotomy

A constant refrain in both books is that the world (reality) and people cannot be understood as separate:

> *[One cannot imagine] abstract man nor the world without people but people in their relations with the world. In these relations consciousness and world are simultaneous (Freire 1996, p62).*

> *There is not a real world "out there" and a subjective world "in here". The world is not constructed by the learner, nor is it imposed upon her, it is* constituted *as an internal relation between them (Marton and Booth, 1997, p12 –13) [emphasis in text].*

The integration of inner and outer is, for both, the heart of understanding how people learn and, for both, the task of education is to transcend person-world dualism so that people understand that the world is simultaneously real and experienced. It is people, therefore, who produce social reality.

Student-teacher relations

In both texts teachers are endowed with a critical role in creating environments in which students are likely to engage in learning that is 'genuine' (Marton and Booth) or 'authentic' (Freire). A condition of this is that teachers identify with their students in order to bring about a meeting of awareness between students and teachers:

> *The essential feature is that the* teacher takes the part of the learner, *sees the experience through the learner's eyes, becomes aware of the experience through the learner's awareness (Marton and Booth 1997 p179) [emphasis in text].*

> *[Educators need to know] both their [students']* objective situation *and their* awareness *of that situation [...] the various levels of perception of themselves and of the world in which and with which they exist (Freire, 1996, p68) [emphasis in text].*

In both cases, the aim is to work *with* students to experience aspects of the world in a new way, as 'co-investigators' (Freire) and as participators in 'the on-going and constantly recurrent constitutions of the object of learning' (Marton and Booth).

Becoming more fully human

For both, being open to change through learning is an essential part of being human. For Freire the human 'vocation' is fulfilled by focusing learning on coming to see the world 'as a reality in process' (p56); Marton and Booth see learning as being open to alternative ways of seeing, the goal of which is to know that reality can be experienced in different ways.

Both books describe the route to such learning as developing the capacity to discern and separate elements of a whole and to integrate the parts back into wholes, and simultaneously to be aware of the process of 'reinventing' (Freire) or 'reconstituting' (Marton and Booth) a world already invented or constituted by others.

On this point, the following two quotations illustrate how close in thinking the two books can become:

> *By learning [...] our experienced world gets more differentiated and more integrated. Our world grows richer, we become more enlightened (Marton and Booth 1997, p158).*

> *When [students] lack a critical understanding of their reality, apprehending it in fragments which they do not perceive as interacting constituent elements of the whole, they cannot truly know that reality (Friere, 1996, p85).*

To summarise: we argue that, in these versions of the two perspectives at least, despite quite remarkable differences in the contexts in which and about which they write, the writers converge on three important issues that concern learning and teaching. The first is that the end of learning is to understand that objective and subjective worlds are or should become one (we expand on this in the next section); the second that, in formal learning situations, teachers must take the part of their students to engage them in developing the capacity to change; the third is that teachers should help students 'reinvent' their experienced world.

Reconciling the differences between the two perspectives

To examine the implications of this 'bridging attempt' (May 1997) we draw, like Haggis (2004), on Rowland's (1993) notion that in any theory some aspects of human experience are highlighted whilst others are cast in shadow. As stated earlier, our attempt started within the phenomenographic perspective and so we shall begin by examining what additional aspects of the educational experience in higher education are illuminated by reconciling the ideas of Marton and Booth with those of Freire.

First, though, there is the question of what exactly needs reconciling. We illustrated above that both Marton and Booth and Freire take non-dualist perspectives on the relation between people and their world. However, what might not be immediately evident is that their non-dualisms are of two different types. Marton and Booth argue for a non-dualist *ontology* – thus all that *exists* is the relation between people and their world. Whereas for Friere, as a Marxist, this 'non-dualism' operates at the level of *epistemology* – thus all that we can *know* about the world is in terms of our experience as humans. This difference is crucial to both of their accounts. For Marton and Booth to argue that there is not a world 'out there', they need to hold a non-dualist ontology, whilst for Freire to be able to talk of teachers knowing about students' objective situation, he needs to be able to argue that there is an objective set of relations that are independent of human perception, regardless of whether we can know these or not.

The problem with Marton and Booth's subjective account is that it obscures structural factors, such as social class, when considering questions of why people experience learning in the way they do. In claiming that the only relevant world is an experienced world, they cannot explain, for example, why university participation amongst young people from the working classes is so much lower than amongst middle-class young people (for a detailed analysis of the differences in participation rates see Gilchrist et al 2003). This is because unless young people *experience* this lack of participation in terms of class then, for Marton and Booth, social class cannot be a key aspect of variation in participation rates. Thus, whilst a phenomenographic approach might constitute variation in the meaning of higher education amongst a group of potential students, the explanations it offers for this variation would be at the level of student perceptions of higher education rather than examining how these perceptions might be structured by different positions within class structures. This problem is expressed well by Michael Apple (1979) in a criticism of phenomenology: 'Phenomenological description… inclines us to forget that there *are* objective institutions and structures 'out there' that have power, that control our lives and our very perception' (p140).

However, if we instead adopt Friere's position that non-dualism operates at the level of epistemology, our position becomes one in which structural issues, as well as experiential issues, or objective as well as subjective factors, become illuminated when we asks questions about students' learning experience. This then starts to give the idea of 'deep and surface approaches to learning' a different meaning. Marton and Booth's focus on how students approach their learning in terms of their intentions and their perceptions of their learning environment is widened to include a focus on how students' perceptions and intentions might be structured by factors that are not necessarily part of their awareness.

To distinguish the richer sense of why students come to take different approaches to learning, we have chosen to focus on the concept of academic engagement which takes the notion of a 'deep approach to learning' further. Building on Friere's argument for problematising the relationship between teachers and learners, we see academic engagement as about problematising the relationships between teachers, students, the discipline, and the institution, as well as the social and political context, in which teaching and learning are taking place.

However, we do not reject all of Marton and Booth's focus on understanding variation in the way a group of people conceive of learning. The evidence that there is identifiable variation in both conceptions of and approaches to learning is powerful when placed in the context of structural issues. Equally, the work of Marton and Booth suggests ways of understanding and potentially overcoming these structural barriers to engagement by focusing on the variation in the ways that people experience these barriers. This is because it is clear that these structural barriers are not all powerful, for example thousands of working class students successfully engage in higher education. Thus it might be possible to examine why these structural barriers impact differently on different students and thus understand what it is that prevents more students from successfully engaging with higher education.

A tentative conclusion: developing a model of academic engagement

We conclude this paper by offering a model (see Figure 1) of the factors that might impact on the quality of academic engagement in higher education. In the model we attempt to illustrate how we have reconciled phenomenography and critical pedagogy through the concept of academic engagement. We are interested in examining the quality of teachers' and students' academic engagement in higher education and what influence different contexts have on the quality of such engagement. These contexts include aspects of the phenomenographic perspective such as course context and disciplinary context but also contexts that play a role in structuring students' and teachers' experiences such as the wider social, political and economic contexts. These contexts are those that are highlighted as important in determining the quality of teaching and learning in the literature from the critical pedagogy, academic literacies, and phenomenographic perspectives that have been referred to so far in this article (Friere 1996, Marton and Booth 1997, Lea and Street 1998, Prosser and Trigwell 1999, Jones et al 1999, Mann 2000, 2001).

In line with the phenomenographic literature, we define 'quality' in terms of forms of engagement that involve students and teachers in developing personal meaning of their disciplines through their interactions with each other rather than forms of engagement that involve students and teachers in exhibiting routinised responses as a way as meeting external requirements.

In the model each segment represents an individual student or teacher within a particular teaching and learning interaction. This could be within a lecture theatre, in a seminar room, in an on-line learning environment, or in any setting in which students and teachers are engaging with a focus on their academic work together. Each circle represents a different context that might, consciously or unconsciously, influence students' and teachers' perceptions of their environment and so affect the quality of their

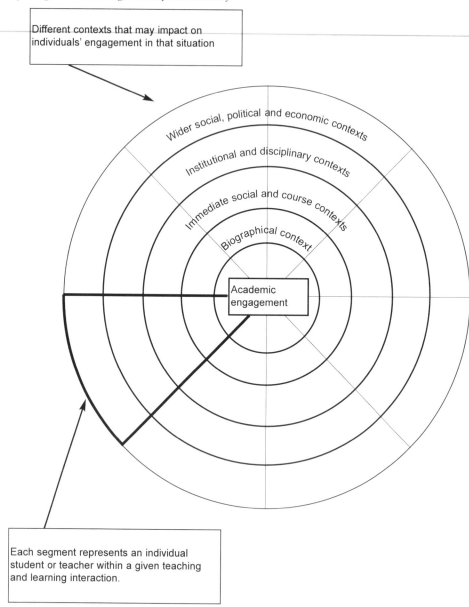

Different contexts that may impact on individuals' engagement in that situation

Wider social, political and economic contexts

Institutional and disciplinary contexts

Immediate social and course contexts

Biographical context

Academic engagement

Each segment represents an individual student or teacher within a given teaching and learning interaction.

Figure 1. Contexts that are hypothesised to influence academic engagement in teaching and learning interactions in higher education

academic engagement within that particular teaching and learning interaction. Thus in line with Marton and Booth, we argue that the structure of students' and teachers' awareness (see Marton and Booth 1997, Chapter 5) affects their understanding of a situation. However, where we depart from Marton and Booth is that the range of factors that we see as impacting on students' and teachers' experiences of higher education go beyond the factors of which students and teachers may be aware. Thus we would argue, in line with Friere, that the categories that students and teachers use to think about the world are partly the result of the impact of social structures such as class, and that they may be unaware of this impact when thinking about teaching and learning. Importantly, also in line with Friere, we are arguing that students and teachers might become aware of the impact of these structures through reflecting on their situation. Further we are suggesting that a key aspect of this reflection would be a consideration of the variation in the ways that these structures impact on the quality of students' and teachers' academic engagement.

In many ways our analysis is similar to the analysis offered by Mann (2000, 2001) and those working from an 'academic literacies' perspective (Lea and Street 1998, Jones at al 1999). However, what we argue is added by our interpretation is a focus on the critical aspects of qualitative variation of the impact of these different contexts. Thus, we are suggesting the use of an adapted phenomenographic research method that attempts to relate variation in the ways in which students and teachers experience teaching and learning situations (ie the quality of their academic engagement) to social structures that impact on the ways in which they think about this experience. We believe that such a project would maintain a focus on the quality of teaching and learning interactions that is characteristic of phenomenography, whilst also taking account of the political nature of the teaching and learning interactions as well as factors at the meso and macro levels that influence such interactions. It is in this way that we would tentatively suggest that we have contributed to a reconciliation of these two powerful ways of thinking about teaching and learning in higher education.

Acknowledgement

We would like to thank members of the BERA (British Education Research Association) Special Interest Group in Higher Education for their helpful comments on an earlier draft of this paper.

References

Apple, MW (1979) *Ideology and Curriculum* (London, Routledge and Kegan Paul)

Ball, SJ (1994) *Education Reform: A critical and post-structural approach* (Buckingham, Open University Press)

Bernstein, JM (1995) *Recovering Ethical Life: Jurgen Habermas and the Future of Critical Theory* (London, Routledge)

Biggs, J (1993) 'What do inventories of student learning processes really measure? A theoretical review and clarification', *British Journal of Educational Psychology*, 63, pp3-19

Bowles, S and Gintis, H (1976) *Schooling in Capitalist America: Educational Reform and the Contradictions of Economic Life*, (New York: Basic Books)

Bruner, JS (1974) *The Relevance of Education* (Harmondsworth, Penguin Books)

Buckingham, D (1996) 'Critical Pedagogy and Media Education: A theory in search of a practice', *Journal of Curriculum Studies*, 28 (6), pp627-650

Cameron, D (2003) 'Doing Exactly What It Says On The Tin: some thoughts on the future of higher education', *Changing English*, 10(2), pp133-141

Carr, W (Ed) (1989) *Quality in Teaching: Arguments for a Reflective Profession*, (London, The Falmer Press)

Cooper, D (2001) 'Against the current: social pathways and the pursuit of enduring change', *Feminist Legal Studies* 9, pp119-148

Dale, R (1989) *The State and Education Policy* (Milton Keynes, Open University Press)

Edwards, M (1998) 'Commodification and Control in Mass Higher Education: A Double-Edged Sword' in Jary, D and Parker, M (Eds) *The New Higher Education: Issues and Directions for the Post-Dearing University* (Stoke-on-Trent, Staffordshire University Press)

Entwistle, NJ and Ramsden, P (1983) *Understanding Student Learning* (London, Croom Helm)

Esland, G (1996) 'Education, Training and Nation-State: Britain's Failing Strategy', in Avis, J, Bloomer, M, Esland, G, Gleeson, D and Hodkinson, P, (Eds), *Knowledge and Nationhood: education, politics and work* (London, Cassell)

Friere, P (1996) *Pedagogy of the Oppressed*. Revised Edition. Translated by MB Ramos. First published in 1970 (London, Penguin Books)

Gilchrist, R, Phillips, D and Ross, A (2003) 'Participation and potential participation in UK higher education' in Archer, L, Hutchings, M and Ross A (2003) *Higher Education and Social Class: Issues of Exclusion and Inclusion* (London, RoutledgeFalmer).

Haggis, T (2003) 'Constructing Images of Ourselves? A Critical Investigation into 'Approaches to Learning' Research in Higher Education', *British Educational Research Journal*, 29 (1), pp89-104

Haggis, T (2004) 'Meaning, identity and 'motivation': expanding what matters in understanding learning in higher education?' *Studies in Higher Education* 29 (3), pp335-352

How, A (2003) *Critical Theory* (New York, Palgrave MacMillan)

Hughes, AG (1956) *Education and the Democratic Ideal*, (London, Longmans, Green and Co)

Jones, C, Turner, J and Street BV (1999) *Students Writing in the University* (Amsterdam/Philadelphia, John Benjamin's Publishing Company)

Jones, K (1989) *Right Turn: The Conservative Revolution in Education* (London, Hutchinson Radius)

Kemmis, S (1994) 'Emancipatory Aspirations in a Postmodern Era', Keynote address to the conference, *Curriculum Changes in Hong Kong: The Needs of the New Era*, The Chinese University of Hong Kong, 29-30 April 1994

Lawson, A (1998) 'Culture and Utility: Phrases in Dispute' in Jary D and Parker, M (Eds) *The New Higher Education: Issues and Directions for the Post-Dearing University* (Stoke-on-Trent, Staffordshire University Press)

Lea, MR and Street, BV (1998) 'Student writing in higher education: an academic literacies approach'. *Studies in Higher Education*, 23, pp157- 172

Malcolm, J and Zukas, M (2001) 'Bridging pedagogic gaps: conceptual discontinuities in higher education', *Teaching in Higher Education*, 6, pp33-42

Mann, S (2000) 'The student's experience of reading'. *Higher Education*, 39, 297 –317.

Mann, S (2001) 'Alternative perspectives on the student experience: alienation and engagement'. *Studies in Higher Education*, 26, 7-19.

Marton, F and Booth, S (1997) *Learning and Awareness* (New Jersey, Lawrence Erlbaum Associates)

Marton, F and Säljö, S (1976) 'On Qualitative Differences in Learning – II Outcome as a function of the learner's conception of the task', *British Journal of Educational Psychology*, 46, pp115-127

May, T (1997) *Social Research: Issues, Methods and Process* (Buckingham, Open University Press)

Offe, C (1996) *Modernity and the State, East West* (Cambridge, Polity Press)

Prosser, M and Trigwell, K (1999) *Understanding Learning and Teaching: The Experience of Higher Education* (Buckingham, Society for Research in Higher Education and Open University Press)

Rowland, S (1993) *The enquiring tutor: exploring the process of learning* (London, Falmer Press)

Seddon, T (1997) 'Education: Deprofessionalised? Or reregulated, reorganised and reauthorised', *Australian Journal of Education*, Vol 41, No 3, pp228-246

Sharp, R and Green, A (1975) *Education and Social Control: A Study in Progressive Primary Education* (London, Routledge)

Soucek, V (1994) 'Flexible education and new standards of communicative competence' in Kenway, J, *Economising Education: The Post-Fordist Directions*, (Geelong, Deakin University)

Webb, G (1997) 'Deconstructing deep and surface: towards a critique of phenomenography', *Higher Education*, 33, pp195-212

Contrasting conceptions of oral assessment

Gordon Joughin

The Hong Kong Institute of Education

Abstract

Although oral assessment has a long history in higher education, is a well established form of assessment in many professional fields, and is a common form of assessment in much vocational education, until recently the literature on oral assessment has not addressed how it is experienced by students. It would be true to say that little is known about oral assessment from the student's perspective.

A phenomenographic study of theology students identified three contrasting conceptions of oral assessment – as 'presentation'; as 'understanding'; and as 'a position to be argued'.

The conception of oral assessment as 'presentation' represents an approach to oral assessment that focuses on reproducing the ideas of others in a one-way presentation. This conception is associated with a limited sense of audience, a failure to perceive interaction as significant, and an absence of anxiety. In this case, oral assessment is seen as either similar to written assignments or as being a more limited form of assessment than assignments. The conception of oral assessment as 'understanding' is associated with students actively seeking to develop their understanding of the subject, making the ideas they encounter their own, being challenged to understand these ideas because of the questioning involved in the assessment process, and seeing oral assessment as having some advantages over written assessment. The conception of oral assessment as 'a position to be argued' is associated with seeing theology in terms of developing one's own point of view, having a strong sense of audience, seeing interaction with that audience as both challenging and demanding understanding, and experiencing a heightened self-awareness. In this case, oral assessment is seen as a significantly richer and more personally engaging form of assessment than written assignments. The structural aspects of these contrasting conceptions can be understood in terms of variation in students' experience of six aspects of oral assessment – the indirect object of learning; the direct object of learning; interaction; audience; affective responses; and comparisons with written assignments.

The conceptions of oral assessment and the aspects of oral assessment identified in this study give rise to a number of important issues regarding oral assessment, including the relationship between students' and lecturers' conceptions of oral assessment and how students might be brought to a more complex understanding of oral assessment.

Introduction

Oral assessment is used to measure at least two quite different kinds of qualities, namely (a) the command of the oral medium itself, typically the skills of communication in general or of language in particular, and (b) the command of content as demonstrated through the oral medium. This paper is concerned with the latter.

Oral assessment is perhaps most often associated with the oral defence of a doctoral thesis. However, oral assessment is now often used in undergraduate education in most disciplines and is a widespread practice in vocational education and schools. Its many forms include debates, group and individual presentations, 'mini vivas', and moots. The particular form of oral assessment which is the subject of the study reported in this paper was an individual presentation to a group of peers within a diploma level adult education programme in theology. This programme articulated into a degree level university programme.

This paper begins by summarising six dimensions of oral assessment identified by literature written from the teacher's perspective. Three conceptions of oral assessment identified through a phenomenographic study of fifteen adult students are then described and delineated in terms of students' experience of underlying aspects of oral assessment. The implications of these conceptions for student learning and for understanding disparities between teacher and student expectations are noted.

Dimensions of oral assessment: from the teacher's perspective

The literature on oral assessment from the student's perspective is limited (Hounsell and McCune, 2000, 2001; Joughin, 1999), while the literature from the teacher's perspective is extensive. A study of the latter literature forms part of the backdrop of the study of students' conceptions of oral assessment reported here since this literature reflects present practice of oral assessment. An analysis of this literature (Joughin, 1998) identified six 'dimensions' of oral assessment: primary content type; interaction; authenticity; structure; examiners; and orality.

Each dimension covers a range of practices. For four of these dimensions ('interaction', 'authenticity', 'structure' and 'orality'), the range has the quality of a continuum. The dimensions of 'primary content type' and 'examiner', however, are not continua but rather consist of more-or-less discrete categories.

Primary content type is concerned with *what* is being assessed. While the objects of oral assessment can be categorised in many ways, the learning which is assessed by oral assessment can be readily classified as one of the following: knowledge and understanding; applied problem solving ability; interpersonal competence; and intra-personal qualities

(Erhaut and Cole, 1993; Glowacki and Steele, 1992; Habeshaw, Gibbs and Habeshaw, 1993; Kaplowitz, Jenkins and Nair, 1996; Levine and McGuire, 1970; Muzzin and Hart, 1985; Raymond and Viswesveran, 1991).

Interaction is concerned with reciprocity between examiner and student, with each acting on, responding to, and being influenced by the other. Interaction can range from a one-way presentation devoid of interaction to a highly interactive form of dialogue.

Authenticity is concerned with the extent to which the assessment replicates the context of professional practice or 'real life' (Wiggins, 1989). Assessment can range from being highly contextualised so that it closely resembles a 'real life' experience, to being decontextualised or remote from the situation of professional practice.

Structure refers to the extent to which oral assessment is based on a pre-determined, organised body of questions or sequence of events. This dimension can range from a tightly structured form of assessment where the questions, the order in which they are asked and the way they are posed follow a given order uninfluenced by the student's responses, to an open structure which is more like a free flowing dialogue.

Examiners concerns who judges the worth of the student's responses. Peer assessment, self-assessment and the use of external professionals, often as members of a panel, are common practices in oral assessment.

Orality refers to the extent to which the assessment is conducted orally, ranging from the exclusively oral format of, for example, the clinical examination in medicine, to assessment in which the oral component is secondary to another component, for example, the oral presentation of a written paper.

The dimensions of oral assessment and their ranges are summarised in table 1.

Dimension	Range		
Primary content type	Knowledge and understanding; applied problem solving ability; interpersonal competence; personal qualities		
2. Interaction	Presentation	vs	dialogue
3. Authenticity	Contextualised	vs	decontextualised
4. Structure	Closed structure	vs	open structure
5. Examiners	Self-assessment; peer assessment; authority-based assessment		
6. Orality	Purely oral	vs	orality as secondary

Table 1: dimensions of oral assessment

Conceptions of oral assessment: from the student's perspective

While the above dimensions of oral assessment were identified through the higher education literature, students' conceptions of oral assessment were identified through interviews with students engaged in the specific programme of study noted previously. The programme was offered in an 'open learning' mode – participants attended an orientation workshop then studied through print materials and self-managed cluster groups that met regularly to discuss the topics they were studying. Participants had access to a group mentor and to the programme tutors.

The programme required students to complete six items of assessment. These alternated between written papers which were submitted to a tutor and oral presentations to the cluster group. The oral presentations were short – five minutes of presentation, five minutes of questioning and discussion, and one minute of personal reflection. At the conclusion of each presentation, students would receive oral feedback from group members, complete a 'feedback sheet', and send the sheet and their notes to their tutor for marking. This programme had two specific advantages in this study: (i) students had an opportunity to become familiar with the oral form of assessment, and (ii) the tasks and criteria for the oral and written formats were identical, with only the mode of presentation changing, so that direct comparisons could be made between the two modes. The specific context of this study should be kept in mind in any consideration of its findings.

Fifteen students in the programme were interviewed using a semi-structured format designed to encourage the description of the experience of oral assessment from the student's perspective.

Within an open structure, the interviews explored what the oral assessment was like for the student, including the student's perception of the context of the assessment, how the student prepared for the assessment, and how the student compared the oral assessment to the written assignment.

Within the assessment format which was the basis of this study, three conceptions of oral assessment were identified. Space does not permit the full illustration of these conceptions by quotations from the interview transcripts – a single illustrative excerpt is included for each category.

A. Oral assessment as presentation

According to this conception, the purpose of the assessment is to produce and deliver a presentation. The focus is on what is being delivered, which is typically seen as a re-presentation of the ideas of others, that is, of the writers whose work has been consulted, rather than as the ideas the student may have developed as a result of his or her reading. The focus on presentation seems to exclude the audience from any active role in the assessment, so that they are seen as passive and not involved in interaction with the student being assessed. This conception is not associated with any a particular affect, and in fact students may volunteer that they do not experience anxiety. When oral assessment is seen as presentation, it is likely to be also seen as less demanding than, or possibly equally demanding as, written assessment. The description of oral assessment in terms of its physical artefacts typifies this conception:

> *"... what are the expectations?*
>
> *To produce a paper that should be 10 minutes ..."*

B. Oral assessment as demonstrating understanding

This conception is associated with the need to develop one's understanding of the topic being studied since the student expects to be subjected to questioning by an audience who will be critically evaluating what they have to say. As with conception A, theology is seen as the ideas of others, though students may make these ideas their own. A heightened self-awareness may be expressed as anxiety or a fear of appearing foolish. Overall, oral assessment is seen as being more challenging than the written assignment.

> *"I think in delivering an oral... you've really got to understand it because if anyone asks you a question and you just go, 'Oh, I really don't know what to say'... You do try to internalise it more because if people really are going to ask you questions about it, you've really got to have some understanding of it, whereas you can write it on paper even if it's your thoughts, you can write it on paper and forget about it because no-one is going to question you."*

C. Oral assessment as arguing a position

This conception is associated with a different conception of theology and with seeing the form of assessment as markedly different to written assessment. Theology is not seen as simply the ideas of others, but as involving the development of a personal perspective. As with conception B, students may experience a heightened sense of themselves, along with a heightened sense of their audience. Whereas in the other conceptions the audience is seen as passive or as judging the student, now the student seeks to act on the audience and persuade them to share the student's position. Oral assessment is seen as a more personal and more engaging form of assessment than the written assignment.

> *"I've really wanted to convince people about these things which I'd taken on board which were very important to me..."*

Aspects of oral assessment

In Learning and Awareness, Marton and Booth note that "a particular way of experiencing something represents a combination of related aspects that are simultaneously present in a person's focal awareness" (Marton and Booth, 1997, p206). In keeping with this, Marton and Pang subsequently depict "a conception or a way of experiencing something in terms of critical aspects of the phenomenon in question discerned and focused upon simultaneously" (Marton and Pang, 1999, p2).

This section focuses on delineating aspects of oral assessment identified through the analysis of the interview transcripts. A consideration of aspects of the students' experience of oral assessment is important for two reasons. Firstly, 'aspects' of oral assessment in a sense parallels the 'dimensions' of the previously noted study in which a foundation for understanding oral assessment in terms of sub-categories was established. What aspects of oral assessment figured in students' awareness and how students experienced those aspects might serve to inform, extend, illuminate, contrast with, or complement the understanding of oral assessment that had emerged through the preceding consideration of its dimensions.

Secondly, the focus on aspects of oral assessment is pertinent in the context of variation theory (Marton and Morris, 2002). Particular ways of experiencing a phenomenon are seen to occur because students attend to different aspects of a phenomenon and experience those aspects in different ways. As Marton and Runnesson summarise this, "we not only discern features, but also discern different qualities... in the relevant dimensions" (Marton and Runesson, 2003, p18). Variation theory applies to the pedagogical level where teachers' use of variation with respect to specific aspects of a phenomenon has come to be seen as perhaps the most critical function of teaching (Lo and Ko, 2002; Marton and Trigwell, 2000; Patrick, 2002; Runesson and Marton, 2002; Tsui, 2002). In the context of the present study, variation theory is pertinent to how students might be helped in coming to see oral assessment in ways that are consistent with teachers' intentions.

Five aspects of oral assessment were identified through the analysis of the interview data: the direct object of learning; interaction; affective factors; audience; and comparisons with written assessment.

(i) The direct object of learning

Four ways in which the direct object of learning, or the nature of theology as seen in the student's specific topic, could be perceived were identified:

(a) Theology as the ideas of others.

> "... well the questions, they were nice explicit questions that said, from memory, 'What were the historical and literary contexts in which Matthew's gospel was written?' So I just went back to the front of the Gospel of Matthew – there's a blurb in the New Catholic Bible."

(b) Theology as making personal meaning from the ideas of others.

> "If I really am going to give you this information, what about it is important to me?"

(c) Theology as making sense of life.

"Theology is such a personal thing and it's your way of trying to define meaning or to interpret the things that are happening around you."

(d) Theology as point of view.

"The course is really spot on as far as tempting you to think and have your own opinions, so it wasn't regurgitating the whole stuff. It was a reinterpretation of stuff, and speaking opinions."

(ii) Interaction

Five ways of experiencing interaction were identified:

(a) Interaction as one-way communication.

"I suppose in some respects they were on the receiving end."

(b) Interaction as questioning leading to elaboration.

"People talked about it and they ask you questions about it and it was nice to elaborate on a few points so that all meant that when you were putting this thing together you didn't just have the bare bones but you had a bit of the padding as well."

(c) Interaction as discussion.

"Well it sort of forced me to do the work in a way, and plus not to let the other members down because we all sort of wanted to talk about things and try and get a bit out of it personally..."

(d) Interaction as questioning requiring understanding.

"I think there is more responsibility to really be clear about that when you know that somebody may in fact ask you a question on the spot."

(e) Interaction as challenge.

"It's gratifying because I like a battle. You see, I had a battle with seven other people. It's really a battle between me and [the audience] because it's you trying to almost impose your viewpoints on someone else."

(iii) Affective factors

Four affective categories were identified:

(a) The absence of anxiety.

"It was never a sort of worry about performing in front of anyone or anything like that. It was a very friendly sort of situation."

(b) A fear of appearing foolish.

"... you try a little bit harder in a way and so you don't come across as being a bit silly and not knowing what you're talking about."

(c) Anxiety.

"I was dreadfully nervous."

(d) A heightened sense of self.

"My adrenalin just goes through... I'm completely fired up and stirred up..."

(iv) Audience

Four different ways in which the audience could be experienced were identified:

(a) Audience as passive recipients.

"I suppose in some respects they were on the receiving end."

(b) Audience as motivators.

"... there's commitment to the group which made me say "You've got to be prepared."

(c) Audience as judges.

"I see the main purpose to show the group what you've studied and what you've learnt and also it's like an evaluation thing. They are checking up on you that you've done it."

(d) Audience as adversaries.

"When it's verbal, people often take it as an attack."

(v) Comparisons of oral and written assessment

The final aspect of students' experience of oral assessment that was identified is concerned with comparisons between oral and written assessment. Four categories of comparison were identified:

(a) The oral assessment as less demanding than the written assignment.

"I find it easier to know what I'm doing with an oral... I make a little bit more sure that I know what I'm talking about in the written piece because I'm sending it to somebody I assume does know what I'm talking about."

(b) The oral assessment and the written assignment as similar.

"Well there's not a great deal of difference."

(c) The oral assessment as having some limited advantages.

"I always reckon there's a little bit more pressure [in the oral]... the real test is when you have to talk about it so I always saw the [oral assessment] as something where you were more open to examination..."

(d) The oral assessment as a richer form than the written assignment.

"I'm a lot better prepared. The assignment I'm a bit, 'Near enough is good enough' because I can just put it on paper and hand it in, whereas with the practicum, because it's a presentation, you're just more conscious of having to justify what you write there and to say it to others. Yeah, I'm a lot better prepared and I learn a lot more from the practicum than I do from the assignments."

Conceptions and aspects of oral assessment

In their discussion of the anatomy of awareness, Marton and Booth state that

The main idea is that the limited number of qualitatively different ways in which something is experienced can be understood in terms of which constituent parts or aspects are discerned and appear simultaneously in people's awareness. A particular way of experiencing something reflects a simultaneous awareness of the particular aspects of the phenomenon. Another way of experiencing it reflects a simultaneous awareness of other aspects or more aspects of the same phenomenon. More advanced ways of experiencing something are, according to this line of reasoning, more complex and more inclusive (or more specific) than less advanced ways of experiencing the same thing, "more inclusive" and "more specific" both implying more simultaneously experienced aspects constituting constraints on how the phenomenon is seen. A certain way of experiencing something can thus be understood in terms of the dimensions of variation that are discerned and are simultaneously focal in awareness, and in terms of the relationships between the different dimensions of variation. As the different ways of experiencing something are different ways of experiencing the same thing, the variation in ways of experiencing it can be described in terms of a set of dimensions of variation. (Marton and Booth, 1997, pp107-108)

Following this understanding of variation, the conceptions of oral assessment identified in this study can be understood in terms of the aspects of oral assessment that "are discerned and appear simultaneously in people's awareness". However, following the terminology and structure applied in this study, it is not simply a matter of certain 'aspects' being discerned, but rather that those aspects are discerned and experienced in particular ways, both separately and in relation to each other. Each conception of oral assessment can therefore be understood in terms of how each aspect of oral assessment is experienced and the relationships between these ways of experiencing the aspects. To put this another way, these aspects can be structured in different ways in a student's awareness, and how a student's awareness of oral assessment is structured is in dynamic relationship with the meaning they give to it. This study has therefore identified structural and referential aspects of the experience of oral assessment that provide insight into the various ways students can experience the phenomenon of oral assessment. These are summarised in table 2 below. (The numbers in brackets refer to the number of students associated with each category.)

	Direct object	Interaction	Affect	Audience	Comparison with written
A. Presentation	Ideas of others (5); Making meaning (2); Making sense of life (1); Point of view (1)	One-way (5); Elaboration (3); Discussion (1)	No anxiety (4)	Passive (6); Motivators (2); Judges (1)	Written as harder (4); Same (3); Limited benefits in oral (2)
B. Understanding	Ideas of others (2); Making meaning (1)	Understanding (2); Discussion (1)	Fear of appearing foolish (2)	Judges (2); Motivators (1)	Oral as richer (3)
C. Arguing a position	Point of view (2); Making meaning (1)	Challenge (2); Understanding (1)	Heightened self-awareness (3)	Adversaries (3)	Oral as richer (3)

Table 2. Conceptions of oral assessment and aspects of oral assessment

Aspects of oral assessment and developing students' conceptions of oral assessment

Students need not only to develop knowledge and understanding but also to learn about the assessment formats that they are required to use to demonstrate their knowledge and understanding. In discussing this dual requirement, Sadler reaches the conclusion that "the same pedagogical devices that I use with respect to the subject matter in the courses I teach make equally good sense with respect to communicating my expectations about the quality of students' work" (Sadler, 2001, p136). The markedly different ways of seeing oral assessment identified in this study supports Sadler's approach – students need to learn about oral assessment in the same way they need to learn about subject matter. Helping students to learn about oral assessment, or develop more complex conceptions of oral assessment, requires firstly a knowledge by the teacher of students' conceptions of oral assessment and secondly an approach to 'teaching' about conceptions that directly addresses the processes involved in effecting conceptual change.

The structure of awareness described by Marton and Booth suggests that learning about oral assessment, and coming to see it in a particular way, involves students in coming to discern certain patterns of variation in the critical aspects of oral assessment. Those aspects of oral assessment need to be opened up for students against a background of the ways in which that variation can be experienced (Marton and Pang, 1999). In other words, students need to become aware of the aspects of oral assessment, and the different ways in which they can be experienced, as the basis for developing more appropriate conceptions of oral assessment in their particular context.

Aspects of oral assessment and dimensions of oral assessment

The dimensions of oral assessment based on teachers' perspectives and the aspects of oral assessment identified from the student's perspective can be juxtaposed to illuminate the former. From this juxtaposition it can be seen that, while a teacher may consider that their assessment can be described 'objectively' in terms of specific points on each dimension, students' experience cannot be described so simply. In the context of the instance of oral assessment considered in this study, we can make the following observations about students' experience in relation to each dimension of oral assessment:

- *Primary content type*. Students' experience of the direct object of learning suggests that they can see the primary content type that is being assessed in markedly different ways.

- *Interaction*. Students' ways of experiencing interaction covered the entire range of the interaction dimension.

- *Authenticity*. In terms of authenticity, students could see oral assessment as a highly authentic and deeply engaging exercise in persuasion, or as a routine, decontextualised 'academic' exercise.

- *Structure*. Some students experienced the structure as predictable and under their control, while others saw the unpredictability of the audiences' questions as a highly significant component of the assessment.

- *Examiners*. Some students showed no awareness of the presence of their peer assessors, while for others this was a critical part of their experience.

- *Orality*. The orality of the experience could be minimal, in which case students were likely to see oral assessment as similar to a written assignment. On the other hand, students who described the oral assessment as a richer form of assessment tended to be acutely aware of the particularly 'oral' aspects of the context, including the presence of an audience, a heightened awareness of themselves, and a strong sense of the oral mode of presentation.

Discrepancies between tutors' and students' perceptions of assessment have been noted in other contexts (see, for example, Hounsell, 1987; Maclellan, 2001). The consideration of dimensions and aspects of oral assessment from the contrasting perspectives of tutors and students provides additional insight into the basis of this divergence.

Conclusion

This study raises a number of issues concerning assessment in general and oral assessment in particular. Firstly, it highlights the potential disparity between tutors' and students' understanding of an assessment task. While tutors may believe a task has been clearly defined, students may view that task in ways that are quite different to what the tutor had in mind. Secondly, students themselves may have markedly differing conceptions of an assessment task, based on variation in their conceptions of the assessment format. Thirdly, conceptions of the assessment format can be understood in terms of how students experience different aspects of the format, and variation in conceptions can be understood in terms of variation in how these aspects are experienced. An understanding of this variation may be an essential basis for bringing students to a more complete awareness of assessment requirements.

References

Eraut, M, and Cole, G (1993). Assessment of competence in higher level occupations. *Competence and Assessment*, 21, 10-14.

Glowacki, ML, and Steele, DJ (1992, November). *A synthesis of the research on alternative assessment methods in teacher education.* Paper presented at the Annual Meeting of the Mid-South Educational Research Association. Knoxville, TN. (ERIC Document Reproduction Service No. ED355257)

Habeshaw, S, Gibbs, G, and Habeshaw, T (1993). *53 Interesting Ways to Assess Your Students.* Bristol: Technical and Educational Services.

Hounsell, D (1997). Contrasting conceptions of essay writing. In F. Marton, D Hounsell, and N. Entwistle (Eds), *The experience of learning* (2nd ed, pp106-125). Edinburgh: Scottish Academic Press.

Hounsell, D, and McCune, V (2000). *A sense of audience in oral presentations by undergraduate students.* Paper presented at the European Association for Research on Learning and Instruction, Special Interest Group on Writing, Writing Conference 2000, 7-9 September. Verona.

Hounsell, D, and McCune, V (2001). *Learning to present: Students' experiences and their implications.* Paper presented at the European Association for Research on Learning and Instruction, Ninth European Conference for Research on Learning and Instruction Biennial Meeting, 28 August – 1 September. Fribourg.

Joughin, G (1998). Dimensions of oral assessment. *Assessment and Evaluation in Higher Education*, 23, 367-378.

Joughin, G (1999). Dimensions of oral assessment and student approaches to learning. In Brown, S and Glasner, A (Eds), *Assessment matters* (pp146-156). Buckingham: The Society for Research into Higher Education and Open University Press.

Kaplowitz, PB, Jenkins, MD, and Nair, P (1997). *The oral examination.* Retrieved September 1998, from http://vh.radiology.uiowa.edu/Providers/Societies/APA/GPCC/oral_Exa 12.96

Levine, HG, and McGuire, CH (1970). The validity and reliability of oral examinations in assessing cognitive skills in medicine. *Journal of Educational Measurement*, 7(2), 63-74.

Lo, ML, and Ko, PY (2002). The 'enacted' object of learning. In Marton, F and Morris, P (Eds), *What matters? Discovering critical conditions of classroom learning* (pp59 – 73). Göteborg: ACTA Universitatis Gothoburgensis.

Maclellan, E (2001). Assessment for learning: the differing perceptions of tutors and students). *Assessment and Evaluation in Higher Education*, 26 (4), 307-318.

Marton, F, and Booth, S (1997). *Learning and awareness.* Mahwah: Lawrence Erlbaum.

Marton, F, and Morris, P (2002). What matters? In Marton, F and Morris, P (Eds), *What matters? Discovering critical conditions of classroom learning* (pp133 – 143). Göteborg: ACTA Universitatis Gothoburgensis.

Marton, F, and Pang, MF (1999). *Two faces of variation.* Paper presented at the 8th European Conference for Learning and Instruction, Göteborg, Sweden.

Marton, F and Runesson, U (2003). *The space of learning.* Paper presented at the European Association for Research on Learning and Instruction, 26–30 August, Padova.

Marton, F, and Trigwell, K (2000). Varatio est mater studiorum. *Higher Education Research and Development*, 19, 3, 381–395.

Muzzin, LJ, and Hart, L (1985). Oral examinations. In Neufeld, VR, and Norman, GR (Eds), *Assessing Clinical Competence* (pp71-93). New York: Springer.

Patrick, K (2002). Doing history. In Marton, F, and Morris, P (Eds), *What matters? Discovering critical conditions of classroom learning* (pp93 – 112). Göteborg: ACTA Universitatis Gothoburgensis.

Raymond, MR, and Viswesvaran, C (1991). *Least-squares models to correct for rater effects in performance assessment.* (ACT Research Report Series 91-8. IA). The American College Testing Program. (ERIC Document Reproduction Service No. ED344947)

Runesson, U, and Marton, F (2002). The object of learning and the space variation. In Marton, F and Morris, P (Eds), *What matters? Discovering critical conditions of classroom learning* (pp19 – 37). Göteborg: ACTA Universitatis Gothoburgensis.

Sadler, R (2002). Ah!… So that's "quality". In Schwartz, P and Webb, G (Eds), *Assessment: Case studies, experience and practice from higher education* (pp130–136). London: Kogan Page.

Tsui, A (2002). The semantic space of learning. In Marton, F and Morris, P (Eds), *What matters? Discovering critical conditions of classroom learning* (pp113 – 132). Göteborg: ACTA Universitatis Gothoburgensis.

Wiggins, G (1989). A true test: toward more authentic and equitable assessment, *Phi Delta Kappan*, May, 703-713.

Assessment: helping diverse students understand the tacit demands of studying in higher education

Overview: Sue Bloxham (Convenor)

The following papers present research from three related projects all funded by a UK Institute for Learning and Teaching in Higher Education 'Making a Difference' Award.

UK national quality initiatives have created a drive towards transparency and consistency in student assessment including robust approaches to marking and moderating student work. This drive has generated a range of institutional and departmental practices including stated learning outcomes and assessment criteria for each assignment and common grade descriptors. However, writing these materials has made more evident the tacit nature of academic discourse which can only develop meaning through use. Furthermore there are often differences in interpretation of language between disciplines, indeed between tutors. Interdisciplinary courses and the diversification of assessment create demands to produce work that conforms to a variety of different academic conventions.

This issue is important because an increasingly diverse student body suggests that we cannot rely on shared cultural understandings amongst those entering university. Haggis and Pouget's (2002) research indicates that the greater heterogeneity of students in contemporary higher education means that we need greater clarity and explicitness about what students need to do in order to deal with their confusion and disorientation in the context of specific disciplines. However, the 'academic literacies' (Lea & Stierer 2000) approach would argue that one cannot transmit clarity in these matters, they can only be understood as a gradual process involving participation in order to absorb and be absorbed into a 'community of practice' (Lave & Wenger, 1999).

The three papers presented in this symposium all explore interventions designed to raise the achievement and aid retention of non-traditional students through active engagement with the demands of assessment. The groups involved are:

- Mature, part-time students on an 'open access' foundation degree
- International students
- Students with low entry qualifications

They are based in the same HEI which has recently developed clear assessment protocols for staff and students including making explicit links between learning outcomes and assessment tasks, assessment criteria and common grade descriptors. The latter is a series of statements, for each credit level, which describe what a student should demonstrate in order to achieve the various grades in the academic marking scale.

Each paper describes and evaluates a planned intervention to assist students in understanding the language and demands of assessment, in particular the interpretation of assessment criteria and grade descriptors. In each case, tutors have actively engaged students in using these statements to assess their own or others' work through the use of exemplars and peer assessment activities. Significant emphasis has also been placed upon students generating and making sense of feedback.

The research methodology has incorporated both quantitative and qualitative methods with the latter experimenting with various tools that combine a resource for learning with a technique for data collection.

Enhancing the academic cultural awareness of international students on an economics programme

Amanda Chapman

St Martin's College, Lancaster

Many universities across the UK are increasing the numbers of international students enrolled, with particular emphasis on students from the People's Republic of China. These international students, 30,000 from China alone, bring in £20bn a year. (Massey, 2004) What happens to these students when they arrive varies from institution to institution and the process of integration into the academic culture is a vital aspect. Research into academic awareness has become more important as the student body becomes increasingly diverse and multicultural. Assimilation into this higher education culture can be a problematic experience for all students. Research (Yorke 2001,Yorke & Thomas 2003) indicates that induction into the requirements of different subjects, curriculum developments and the integration of academic skills can lead to better retention.

This, in turn, has led to more emphasis placed on the need to create explicit and direct criteria for students to improve their understanding of requirements (Haggis & Pouget, 2002). St Martin's College, along with many other higher education institutions has embraced this agenda and produces clear grade descriptors, given to all students in their induction pack. This is a relatively simple step; indeed the explicit side of the debate is easy to address. However, the process is considered to be much more complicated than that for *implicit* criteria. Lea and Steirer's (2000) approach develops the concept of academic literacies and argues that these need to be absorbed over a period of time and cannot be taught. Rust et al (2003) identify the *tacit* nature of assessment criteria and emphasise the difficulty of transferring this tacit knowledge to others.

So where does this leave the international student? The understanding of what is required in higher education is a difficult enough process for home students, especially if they are first generation users of higher education with no obvious academic community to assist them. International students have to deal with a different culture, both academic and social, before they can address the nuances of assessment processes. Biggs (2003, p122) identifies three problems that the international student may encounter:

1. Social-cultural adjustment

2.   Language fluency

3.   Learning/teaching problems due to 'culture'

Chinese students in particular have a very different educational background and different expectations of university life. In terms of assessment, for example, in China exams are the most important components, with little emphasis on course work and group-based activities (Economist, 2003). However, many of the assumptions about Chinese students such as that they are passive and rely on rote learning have been widely researched and disproved (Biggs 2003 and Kember 2000a).

For the economics modules under consideration here, the assignments are worth 60% of the total mark and are individual. However, in class the students are encouraged to participate in many discussions, group-based case studies and worksheets. They mix with the other students and keep communication in English as far as possible. This action-research project is part of a wider cross-college initiative that has a multi-disciplinary approach. The project seeks to enhance the understanding of assessment criteria, using a range of techniques and methods, with the ultimate aim of embedding the use of assessment criteria and grade descriptors into the level one curriculum.

Student group

The student group was a small level one economics group that had contact time twice a week for both semesters. This group was chosen because, although it is only a very small sample, 53.8% of the group were Chinese. The relatively high contact time of four hours a week and the small numbers mean that a good relationship was built up between the lecturing staff and students.

For the total group n = 13

Gender balance   15.3% Female

                    84.7% Male

Nationality   53.8% Chinese

                    46.2% UK

71% of the Chinese group had studied for the St Martin's College International Foundation Certificate the previous year. This certificate was a Level 0 course that had modules in information technology, skills, introduction to business, economics, marketing and human resource management. English as a foreign language was also taught throughout the year.

Assessments

The students studied two level one economics modules, one in each semester: Principles of Microeconomics in semester one and Principles of Macroeconomics in semester two.

For both modules they have a piece of coursework and an unseen examination. The coursework for the first semester module was a series of microeconomic questions together with an article analysis. Semester two coursework was a data analysis question based on performance indicators of the UK economy.

The intervention methods that were used were:

- Tuition with marking criteria and grade descriptors
- Use of exemplars
- Feedback analysis
- Formative peer review analysis

Methodology

The students were given two questionnaires for each assignment, one after the hand-in date but before receiving any feedback and the other after the feedback had been given. Various other smaller questionnaires were handed out with the exercises. These results were then collated to give both quantitative and qualitative data.

Tuition with marking criteria and grade descriptors

St Martin's College has very detailed grade descriptors with precise guidelines regarding what is required by students to get each grade at each level. These were available to students in their student handbook, which they were given in their induction pack when they first come to college. For this exercise the students were required to use the grade descriptors and the marking criteria provided in their module guide to start a discussion based around expectations and achievement. These marking criteria provide a guideline for a successful answer presented in a bullet point format. The discussion was based around the changing requirements for each grade and became a general discussion of degree classifications. Interestingly, and worryingly, the majority of the students admitted that they would not have looked at the grade descriptors at all if we had not done this exercise. This is a danger with all the information that students receive at induction: that this 'information overload' means that vital material will not be found, let alone read and acted upon. This emphasises the need to embed this type of activity within the curriculum for all modules and may be especially important at level one where this is often found within a skills-based module and not reinforced in the academic disciplines. This discussion led to a re-working of the grade descriptors and marking criteria with the students putting them into a language that they could relate to. Talking through the criteria also led to a better understanding of what was required. Again, this emphasises the need to discuss criteria so that the students can understand *exactly* what the words mean.

The first questionnaire was handed in just after the assignment deadline and focused mainly on the process of writing the assignment and a self-assessment offering the students the chance to grade themselves and reflect on their achievement. This self-assessment process appears to be a good way for the students to self-reflect on their learning and self-correct if necessary. Research has shown that direct involvement by students in assessing their own work can be highly effective in enhancing learning and achievement (McDonald and Boyd, 2003).

	Expectation	Actual	Variance
UK students	60–65	52	-8
	60+	64	+4
	60+	71	+11
	60+	50	-10
	50	65	+15
	50–60	61	+1
			Total = +13
Chinese students	55	43	-12
	40	47	+7
	40+	35	-5
	60	55	-5
	60	63	+3
	65	63	-2
	60+	63	+3
			Total = -11

Table 1: Self-assessment for assignment, semester 1

Variance was calculated for these purposes with an underestimation being positive and an overestimation being negative. Obviously this was too small a sample to generate any significant conclusions. However, one interesting point was the percentage of students who had an expectation of 60%. Out of a sample of only 13 students, 8 (61.5%) thought that they should get 60% or higher for their assignment. In reality, 7 students (53.8%) got 60% or higher. However these were not necessarily the ones who thought they should!

The student's perception of the 50–60% grade mark was interesting too. The student who thought he deserved that mark justified it because he had 'only a basic understanding with little essay writing experience'. For the most part the students privileged effort over attainment with many of the justifications for high marks being 'I've done a lot of research' and 'included plenty of references'.

This perception of grading may come from a misunderstanding on the students' part of the 80+ range of marks with economics being marked as a social science rather than an accounting and finance or maths-based course, ie the very high classifications are harder to achieve. Again, this reinforces the 'situated' nature of academic disciplines and the nature of the problem that these interventions sought to address. Indeed the discussion about the grade descriptors in the initial weeks of the project centred on this issue. Despite this, the students in semester one found self assessment exercises very demanding.

For clarification, the level 1 descriptors for 50+ are given at table 2, below.

The students fared no better in semester two. This is clearly a difficult task. After the over-optimistic grade estimations in the first semester, the students were far more cautious this time round. See table 3 overleaf for students' self assessment for assignment, semester 2

The striking thing about the semester 2 assignment was not only how good the majority of the grades were but also how large the variance was. The students were very under-

80–100 AA	Student meets all the requirements to meet an A grade but demonstrates exceptional comprehension of knowledge and understanding. Sophisticated ability to analyse beyond defined classification/principles
70–79 A	Student has met the Learning Outcomes (LOs) of the assessment with thorough knowledge and understanding demonstrating study beyond the core requirements of the subject. The work shows a resourceful and imaginative ability to analyse based on defined classifications, principles, theories or models. Work shows clear evidence that the student has applied given tools/methods accurately to well-defined practical contexts and/or problems
60–69 B	Student has met the LOs of the assessment with evidence of relevant and sound acquisition of knowledge and understanding. The work shows evidence of ability to analyse based on defined classifications, principles, theories or models. Work shows evidence that the student has applied given tools/methods accurately to well-defined practical contexts and/or problems. Although the work recognises inherent complexities in the area of study, some conclusions are reached on the basis of insufficient evidence
50–59 C	Student has met the LOs of the assessment with evidence of acquisition of knowledge of the subject. The work is largely descriptive in nature with evidence of limited reasoning based on defined classifications, principles, theories or models. Work shows some evidence that the student has applied given tools/methods accurately to well-defined practical contexts and/or problems, including limited recognition of the inherent complexities in the area of study.

Table 2: Level 1 grade descriptors

	Expectation	Actual	Variance
UK Students	50–60	66	+6
	40	62	+22
	N/a	66	–
	60 – 70	72	+2
	40 – 50	66	+16
	30	48	+18
			Total = +64
Chinese Students	50	58	+8
	50	63	+13
	N/a	40	–
	55	57	+2
	60	48	-12
	55	61	+6
	60+	60	0
			Total= +17

Table 3: Self assessment for assignment, semester 2

confident for this assignment and this is something that I, as the lecturer, shall learn from. Indeed as Yorke (2003) remarked, 'the act of assessing has an effect on the assessor as well as the student. Assessors learn about the extent to which the students have developed expertise and can tailor their teaching accordingly' (p482).

This was especially true with the UK cohort with some significant underestimation of grades. The most significant underestimation, that of +22, justified his 40% self-assessment with:

'Theory was good I thought but haven't done enough on analysing the figures'

This student admitted that he didn't use the marking criteria at all when preparing the assignment. This was an assignment that involved the collection and analysis of data relating to the UK economy. The students worked extremely hard on this and came up with some excellent analysis. Due to the results above, the marking criteria for this assignment will be looked at again to ensure that students know fully what is expected and how they can achieve good grades. It may be that students need more reassurance that what they are producing is of the right standard. However, these results may be simply down to the passage of time, the students settling into the academic routine and the transition from previous study into higher education.

Use of exemplars

This intervention was to help the student to recognise the standard expected from an essay at higher education level. For this exercise groups of three students were given an assignment from the previous year and using the grade descriptors and marking criteria had to grade them and give feedback.

The semester difference here was a useful indication of the benefits of this type of intervention. In the first semester the students focused on what the assignment looked like, structure, how many graphs, etc. This is what Rust et al (2002) called 'visible' criteria. Despite this, it was still an extremely useful exercise for the majority of the students as it was the first time they had seen a essay at higher education level. The first questionnaire asked the students what they had gained from looking at the exemplars; here are a few of the comments:

'Gave a basic idea of what was expected'

'Knowing how to set the work out and how much work is required'

'I will know some ideas and the format'

'The way they used the information'

Even though the students were only looking at the more obvious criteria and not looking at more complicated concepts such as analysis, I still felt that *all* the students, both UK and Chinese, benefited from this exercise in the first semester. Indeed, the earlier the better, to allay any fears about level and expectations.

In the second semester they were much more discerning and critical, looking at the quality, rather than the number, of references, how the argument was developed and starting to address 'invisible' criteria like analysis. A summary of their marks and feedback together with the actual marks and feedback is given in the table opposite:

As can be seen from the mixed grading above no conclusions could be drawn. One group was exactly right, two were over and one was under. However, for all of them their feedback was comparable with the actual feedback. All the students, both UK and Chinese coped with this intervention well, working in groups analysing the exemplars. The exemplars were kept anonymous to the first years as the authors of the assignments were existing second year students. These authors had given their permission for their work to be utilised in this way, indeed were pleased to have their work seen as exemplars. The anonymous nature of this exercise meant that any comments on the work would not be relayed back to the authors.

As with the first semester, this exercise was extremely valuable for students trying to find their 'academic feet' and establish their own style. With this exercise they saw a variety of top 2ii and solid 2i students' work enabling them to get some new ideas about structure, presentation and form.

	Actual mark	Actual feedback	Student mark	Student feedback
Group 1 All Chinese	67%	Well structured Good statistics Good analysis Plenty of research and reading Some statistics a little odd	67%	Good organisational structure Enough evidence to support opinion Reference information is clear
Group 2 Mixed group	55%	Good content and analysis Good level of research Poor structure and academic style Over use of appendices Unclear referencing	High 60s	Good research and referencing Fairly good structure Could flow better
Group 3 Mixed group	61%	Good structure Extensive analysis Careful observation Clear tables More detail needed on sources Limp conclusion	48%	Basic knowledge Good use of tables Adequate referencing No detailed analysis Doesn't flow
Group 4 All Chinese	58%	Well written Good range of references Wide ranging discussion Key aspects identified More stats needed Poor conclusion	69%	Friendly read Easy to understand Well structured Lacks theory

Table 3: Semester 2 exercise

Feedback analysis

Effective feedback is seen as vital for students to improve their learning experience. Higgins (2000) pointed out that students are often unable to use tutor feedback effectively because they are 'simply unable to understand feedback comments and interpret them correctly' (p2). Sadler (1989) identified three conditions that needed to be met for students to benefit from feedback. The student must:

■ Possess a concept of the goal/standard or reference level being aimed for

■ Compare the actual level of performance with that goal or standard

■ Engage in appropriate action which leads to some closure of the gap

The feedback analysis for this project was two-fold and attempted to address the conditions above. Firstly, in the first semester when the assignment was returned the students were asked to summarise the feedback and develop action points for the future. The idea behind the feedback summary was for students to put the tutor feedback into their own words enhancing their understanding. Also many students had a tendency, when looking at graded work, to just consider the mark and ignore the feedback. By encouraging the students to summarise their feedback they had to both read and rewrite it. The action points were a way to address some of the issues of the final conditions outlined above, eg the closure of the gap between performance and goal. Some of the action points that the students developed were:

'I need to use more examples to prove my points'

'Better English'

'Be more careful with referencing'

'Spend more time proof reading'

'Improve my time management'

'Pay closer attention to the question'

This activity had a number of benefits and gave the students time to reflect on both the process and product of learning. It was carried out in class and coupled with a feedback session with the lecturer to discuss finer details about the assignment and the mark.

The second part of this exercise was a recall feedback analysis carried out in semester two before the coursework was due. This asked students about all the feedback they had had from semester one. The idea behind this was to create *building blocks* between modules and to avoid the situation where students viewed each module as an individual item rather than part of an overall degree. It also asked them how they would use this feedback in order to improve the grade for this assignment. Here are two examples of the students' feedback analysis:

UK student: Feedback has generally been good. Need to look at referencing and keep an eye on my grammar

Chinese student: Excellent article and resources chosen. Good organisation and structure. It is better to use various resources to prove the point.

When asked: 'How are you addressing these issues for this assignment?' The responses were:

UK student: Addressed the referencing by having a one to one tutorial. Getting someone else to read my essay before I hand it in.

Chinese student: Try to read more and more articles to find out various ideas to build an argument in my assignment.

This type of structured reflection can be very beneficial to the student and, as seen in the first example, can encourage students to seek further support if necessary. With different lecturers teaching the different modules available to students throughout their study the onus could fall onto the student to pick up on recurring themes in feedback. The Personal Development Progress Files at St Martin's College had a section on feedback added during the 2003/4 academic year, where a copy of all feedback given to the student was placed. The file is for discussion with the student's Personal Academic Tutor at progress meetings so that any similarity between feedback can be noted and addressed.

This feedback intervention was very useful for the students and follows good academic practice. However, it is very time consuming and works well with small groups such as this economics one. A larger group size would need a more creative approach.

Formative peer review analysis

For this exercise the students brought in a 'work in progress' for their second semester essay. This essay was a data analysis exercise where they had to judge the performance of the UK economy over the previous year using a variety of statistics and targets. They were given the assignment details at the beginning of the semester and we looked at what was required from around week three. These peer review analyses were carried out two weeks before the deadline so that they had done research and had time to make changes. In pairs, they analysed each other's work and offered advice for their partner. Based on the discussions they wrote up a feedback sheet for themselves. No marks were given but the feedback was direct and critical. Here are some of the students' comments about their own essays:

> *'Need to use different statistical sources to help back up and enforce points'*

> *'Done the theory involved, now need to answer the question'*

> *'Need to show I can read statistics accurately'*

> *'Need to build an argument'*

> *'Get recent data and check references'*

As can be seen from the comments above, this was a very useful exercise for the students. The students took this exercise very seriously and spent around 30 minutes reading through each other's essay. The benefits from this intervention were twofold. Firstly the positive effects from formative feedback that gave them plenty of time to address the points raised. The second benefit was the advantages and experience gained from peer review.

The main benefits noted from the peer review were:

- Seeing standards set by peers as well as mistakes of others (and avoiding them in the future)

- Gaining an ability to 'stand back' from own work for assessment purposes (Langan & Wheater, 2003)

The students were grouped by nationality for this exercise as it was considered that the Chinese students would have problems with criticising UK students face to face. This may have been an incorrect assumption on my part but the potential improvement by the students could only be gained by truthful and critical peer analysis. The students had difficulty with the self assessment of this assignment (see above). Yet, with this intervention they could clearly see what was required of them to improve their grade.

Conclusions

Biggs (2003, p139) concludes his research on teaching international students with the following three propositions:

1. Persistent teaching problems lie not in the student but in the teaching.

2. In our teaching, we should focus on the similarities between students rather than on the differences. Differences obviously exist but to focus on them is counterproductive.

3. Accordingly, allowing for the needs of special groups, such as international students, is best done within the whole teaching system.

These propositions form a valid mantra when teaching diverse groups of all kinds.

As far as this project is concerned, from these series of interventions the students gained skills such as self-reflection and the ability to use feedback more effectively. However, as the exemplars exercise and the self-assessment exercise showed, what the majority of students lacked, and future students may also be deficient in, was the ability to grade with any accuracy. In terms of feedback, the exemplars exercise indicated that they could give relatively accurate comments but the translation from this into an appropriate grade was a process that most of them had not reached with any degree of confidence. In terms of their results, the following is a summary table of mean grades for both semesters.

	Mean semester 1 grade	Mean semester 2 grade
All students	54.2	56.2
UK students	59.5	60.7
Chinese students	49.8	52.3
Chinese students with St Martin's College IFC	55.3	55.3
Chinese students without St Martin's College IFC	42.3	48.3

Table 4: Summary of grades for both semesters

As can be seen an improvement was made for all groups across the semesters. The UK students, not surprisingly, had the best results. However the most significant results is with the separation of the Chinese students into those that did the St Martin's College International Foundation certificate the previous year and those that had direct entry into year one of the degree. The Chinese students seem to have benefited from having the extra foundation year at St Martin's College giving them extra time to become acquainted with the 'situated' nature of assessment requirements.

From this first year of these interventions, the following conclusions can be drawn:

- Grade descriptors and marking criteria only become relevant to students if they are embedded within the curriculum

- The use of exemplars is particularly beneficial at level one

- Feedback dissemination must also become embedded if students are to benefit fully.

- International students may benefit from level 0 work at the same institution to become assimilated sufficiently in their academic culture.

References

Anon (2003). 'Western promise', *The Economist*, 29 May 2003

Biggs, J (2003). *Teaching for Quality Learning at University*, 2nd edition, Maidenhead, McGraw Hill

Bloxham, S and West, A (2004). 'Understanding the Rules of the Game: marking peer assessment as a medium for developing students' conceptions of assessment'. *Assessment and Evaluation in Higher Education*, forthcoming

De Vita, G (2003). 'Rethinking the Internationalisation Agenda in UK Higher Education' *Journal of Further and Higher Education*, 27(4) pp383–398

CDLT (2003). *Guidelines for Good Assessment Practice*, St Martin's College, Lancaster

Grey, M (2002). 'Drawing with Difference: challenges faced by international students in an undergraduate business degree', *Teaching in Higher Education*, 7,2, pp153–166

Haggis, T and Pouget, M (2002). 'Trying to be motivated: perspectives on learning from younger students accessing higher education' *Teaching in Higher Education*, 7 (3) pp 323–336

Higgins, R (2000). *"Be more critical!": Rethinking Assessment Feedback* paper presented at the British Educational Research Association Conference, Cardiff University, September 7–10.

Humfrey, C (1999). *Managing International Students* Buckingham, Open University Press

Kember, D (2000a). 'Misconceptions about the Learning Approaches, Motivation and Study Practices of Asian Students' *Higher Education*, 40, pp99–121

Kember, D (2000b). *Action Learning and Action Research: Improving the quality of teaching and learning* London, Kogan Page

Kinnell, M (Ed) (1990). *The Learning Experience of Overseas Students*. Buckingham, Open University Press

Ladd, P and Ruby, R (1999). 'Learning Style and Adjustment Issues of International Students' *Journal of Education for Business*, 74 (6) pp363–368

Langan, AM and Wheater, CP (2003). 'Can students assess students effectively: some insights into peer assessment' *Learning and Teaching in Action*, Winter, MMU
http://www.ltu.mmu.ac.uk/ltia/issue4/langanwheater.shtml (accessed 14.8.04)

Laurillard, D (1993). *Rethinking University Teaching: a framework for the effective use of educational technology*, London, Routledge

Lea, MR and Stierer, B (Eds) (2000). *Student Writing in Higher Education* Buckingham, Open University Press

Massey, K (2004). 'No way to treat a guest' *The Independent*, 22nd July

McNamara, D and Harris, R (Eds) (1997) *Overseas Students in Higher Education: issues in teaching and learning.* London, Routledge

Mullins, G, Quintrell, N and Hancock, L (1995) 'The experiences of International and local students at three Australian Universities' *Higher Education Research and Development*, 14 (2), pp201–231

O'Donovan, B, Price, M and Rust, C (2004). 'Know what I mean? Enhancing student understanding of assessment standing and criteria' *Teaching in Higher Education* 9 (3) pp325–335

Orsmond, P, Merry, S and Reiling, K (2000). 'The Use of Student Derived Marking Criteria in Peer and Self Assessment' *Assessment and Evaluation in Higher Education* 25 (1) pp23–37

Rust, C (2002) 'The Impact of Assessment on Student Learning' *Active Learning in Higher Education* 3(2) pp145–158

Rust, C, Price, M and O'Donovan, B (2003). 'Improving Students' Learning by Developing their Understanding of Assessment Criteria and Processes' *Assessment & Evaluation in Higher Education* 28 (2) pp 147

Ryan, J (2000). *A Guide to Teaching International Students*, Oxford, Oxford Centre for Staff and Learning Development

Sadler, DR (1989). 'Formative assessment and the design of instructional systems', *Instructional Science* 18, pp 119–144

Sander, P (2004). 'How should we research our students'. *ILTHE Scholarship of Teaching Article*, http://www.ilthe.ac.uk/2761.asp (accessed 20/04/04)

Wisker, G (2000). *Good Practice Working with International Students*, SEDA

Yorke, M (2001). 'Formative Assessment and its Relevance to Retention' *Higher Education Research and Development*, 20 (2)

Yorke, M (2003). 'Formative Assessment in Higher Education: Moves towards theory and the enhancement of pedagogic practice' *Higher Education*, 45 (4), pp477–501

Yorke, M and Thomas, L (2003). 'Improving the Retention of Students from Lower Socio-economic Groups' *Journal for Higher Education Policy and Management*, 25 (1), pp.63–74

Helping sport studies students understand the rules of the game: a case study in raising achievement in student writing

Sue Bloxham and Amanda West, St Martins College, Lancaster

Abstract

This paper reports on the second phase of a project designed to improve students' understanding of assessment demands. In the first stage, level one students were involved in a range of activities culminating in peer marking. This peer assessment was, itself, marked by the tutors to encourage students to positively engage with the process. Stage two of the project investigated whether these various intervention activities had any long-term impact on students' approach to writing assignments. Interviews took place with a small group of students who took part in the intervention. For comparison purposes, a matched group of students from another course were also interviewed. The findings suggest that the peer assessment did encourage students to pay attention to assessment information. However, a range of other factors was also shown to impact on student approaches to writing. The paper concludes with a discussion of the practical implications for higher education teaching.

This paper reports on the second phase of an action research project designed to raise the achievement of students with relatively low entry qualifications. Phase one of the project (Bloxham and West, 2004) investigated activities that engaged level one students not just with writing but also in judging and peer assessing writing in relation to assessment criteria. Whilst the immediate outcomes of that project were generally positive, the second phase of the research was designed to explore whether there was any long-term impact of this intervention on the students' approach to written assessments.

Recent research suggests that universities need to actively support students' entry into the academic community (Orsmond, Merry and Reiling, 2002; Rust, Price and O'Donovan, 2003) and this should include both explicit (largely written) knowledge transfer and tacit knowledge transfer (O'Donovan, Price and Rust, 2004). This imperative has generated a range of teaching activities including use of marking exercises, discussion of exemplars together with self and peer assessment.

In addition to the arguments presented by these studies, our work has also been strongly influenced by the 'academic literacies' movement (Lea and Street 2000) with particular reference to the models of student writing that they have identified, namely: *study skills, academic socialisation and academic literacies*. Whilst the emphasis on 'tacit knowledge transfer' extends a view of student writing beyond the notion of 'technical' skills and transparent language, it appears to rest at the stage of *socialisation* where the culture, of which students need to become a part, is established and homogenous. The tacit knowledge which students need to acquire is taken as a given and not contested. In contrast, the third model, *academic literacies*, sees the academic community as heterogeneous where writing is a 'contexualised social practice'. Students enter discourse communities which have their own textual conventions (Bizzell 1992) and thus they must learn to switch their writing practices between the demands of the different subjects, for example learning when and where to use the active or passive voice or adopting interpretive or experimental approaches to report writing.

Whilst we are not able to explore all the implications of the 'academic literacies' approach for the students in this paper, we are concerned to investigate the notion that they are not just struggling to become part of a new community, but that the community itself is seen as shifting and unpredictable. Indeed, Creme and Lea's (2003) advice to students is to recognise that academic writing is not just subject-specific but module-specific depending on the 'orientation of the course and the academic staff who designed it' (p26) and thus assignments need 'unpacking' by students to identify what the 'audience' is looking for.

Furthermore, there is a strong retention element to our research in that we support Creme and Lea's view that writing and learning cannot be separated. Helping students to write is a key element in raising their achievement, and new groups of students may be particularly disadvantaged because they do not bring with them the same tacit knowledge of the system as their privileged peers (Yorke & Longden 2004).

This view is supported by Lillis (2001) who argues that 'essayist literacy is the privileged literacy practice within society' (p53) and that in order to be successful in higher education, students must learn the conventions of this form of literacy. However, some students do not bring with them the linguistic capital that makes the process easy. These researchers are part of a growing group of HE writers who draw on the work of Bourdieu (for example, Thomas 2001) and notions of 'habitus' to explain how traditional students enjoy an unfair advantage in education, firmly rooted in social background and highly resistant to tutor intervention.

> *'Pedagogy based, however subtly, on an 'autonomous' view of educated literacy as an asocial, technological skill... makes teaching and learning an issue of replacing the students' existing repertoire of literacy practices rather than refining and adding to these.' (Pardoe, 2000, p151)*

Nevertheless, there are examples of institutions successfully retaining non-traditional students. Yorke and Longden note that two reasons why students leave courses are failure to cope with the demands of the course and students' experience of the institution and programme generally. Yorke's (1999) research found that inadequate staff support outside the timetable and lack of personal support from staff were related to withdrawal. Thus it is not surprising that his later research (Yorke & Longden 2004) identified that helping students prepare for the academic demands of HE was positively correlated with retention, and needs to focus on helping students adjust to the different expectations of tutors compared with their previous education. Certainly Jones and Abramson's (2001) work showed a strong link between such pre-course activity and improved attrition rates and Braxton and Hirschy (2004) stress the role that institutions can play in facilitating students' sense of social integration.

However, some attention must also be given to the wider circumstances of contemporary students. Yorke and Longden identify 'events that impact on students' lives outside the institution' (p104) as a further general reason why students leave their courses. As they point out, these external factors, such as the demands of employment, the needs of dependents, and financial problems, are less easy for institutions to take action to ameliorate. This does not mean, though, that they are not significant concerns in students' lives which must be managed alongside their studies.

Consequently, writing assignments successfully in higher education can be conceived of as a complex task involving learning of tacit knowledge and new social practices, negotiating the meaning and demands of individual assignments with tutors and peers, and coping with the general demands of higher education in a climate where, for many students, there are considerable external pressures on their time.

Methodology

The aim of the study was to investigate the longer-term impact of activities (practice in using assessment criteria and grade descriptors, peer marking and summarising of feedback) on students' ability to write assignments. This paper describes phase two of this project which commenced one year on from the end of phase one (reported in Bloxham and West, 2004).

Using a qualitative approach, we wanted to examine the way in which students approached written assessments completed approximately one year after phase one. Therefore, a sample of six students who had participated in phase one were invited to participate in in-depth interviews to explore their perspectives on, and experiences of, the assessment process. A similar study took place with six matched students from a Business and Management Studies (BMS) programme who were also in level two but who had not participated in the initial activity. Students from the two programmes were matched in terms of their level one performance with two selected as representative of the best, middle and poorest performing students in their respective cohorts. The sample included four men and eight women aged between 19 and 23 years. The mean age was 20.3 years.

The students were not informed that this project was a follow up to the level one study at the outset of the interview. This enabled the researchers to explore student engagement with the assessment process without reminding them about the level one exercise. The interview schedule commenced with an opportunity for students to describe, in detail, how they had completed a recent written assignment. Follow-up questions investigated, more directly, the sources of information and support that they had used and the impact of the level one intervention. The interviews were conducted by an interviewer who had no link to either programme of study and was unknown to the students. This was done in the belief that students would be more open and honest about their experiences if interviewed by someone unconnected to their programme of studies than if they were interviewed by someone who taught them. A small sample of module booklets and tutor feedback coversheets from level one from both Sport Studies (SS) and BMS were also examined to provide background information.

Transcripts were obtained from the interviews and the data coded by the researchers to reflect the dominant themes reported by the students during the interviews. A number of themes emerged form closer analysis of the data. These were:

- The impact of the intervention activities during their first year
- Informal support
- Preparation and planning activities
- Timing of assignment completion
- Use of feedback on previous assignments
- Students' perceptions of the factors that influence their performance

Discussion

The impact of the intervention activities during their first year

A key purpose of the intervention in year one was to assist students in using and understanding the formal support mechanisms to help them understand the demands of assessment. Such mechanisms include the assignment titles and guidelines for assessment produced in module booklets. These guidelines are presented in bullet point form and constitute the criteria used to mark students' work.

The second formal mechanism is the college grade descriptors. These constitute a written description of the level of work required for a 1st, 2i, 2ii, 3rd or fail assignment at each level of undergraduate study and students receive copies of these on registration.

Eleven students said that they found the assessment guidelines helpful although the extent to which the students were able to articulate what it was they found helpful differed according to their degree programme. BMS students made very general statements such as "I find them helpful" or "I use them". Three mentioned using them to ensure the relevance of their essays. In contrast, all six SS students articulated much more precisely how they used the criteria. They mentioned using them as a checklist, helping them to plan, to make notes, as well as providing a basic outline for their essay, highlighting key areas for inclusion.

This difference can be accounted for in two ways. First, closer examination of BMS and SS module booklets revealed that the former offered more general comments, for example, 'A successful assignment will adopt a formal business report format' or 'A successful assignment will generate material from a variety of sources' and only occasionally more specific guidelines such as 'A successful assignment will generate an understanding of the recruitment and selection process'. By comparison, the guidelines issued in SS module booklets contained much more specific content information such as: 'A successful answer will outline the principles of training' or 'A successful answer will employ structural functionalist theory to explain the relationship between sport and the media'. Additionally, SS module booklets contain a checklist of 'key concepts' which should be included in an essay.

The second factor which might account for the greater clarity of answers from SS students could be because SS students had taken part in a peer assessment exercise which required them to use *the guidelines for a successful answer* to mark work completed by their peers (reported in Bloxham & West, 2004). Unlike other studies, the peer marking was itself tutor-marked as an incentive for the students to engage seriously with the process of writing feedback. Thus, the interviewees were asked whether they remembered peer marking each others' posters and what impact, if any, it had had on the way they approached assignments.

All the respondents could remember what they did the previous year in terms of marking others' posters using a set of grade descriptors. However, none remembered it with enthusiasm and half the group actively disliked the experience for various reasons. Two felt it was not completely anonymous and two were not keen on the group work involved. Four of the six found the exercise difficult because of concerns over how others were marking, having to guess at the boundary criteria and having to mark people down because, although they had put in a lot of effort, they had not done what was required.

Nevertheless, five of the six students, albeit grudgingly in some cases, saw value in the activity including an understanding of how to mark, having the opportunity to see others' work, having to follow a marking scheme and referring to guidelines for a successful answer. Therefore, although the students claimed that the exercise had not influenced their subsequent writing, there is evidence from the data that they were more likely to have paid attention to the *guidelines for a successful answer* in the construction of their assignment. However, the effect of this exercise on students' perception of the value and use of the assessment guidelines warrants further investigation given the difference in module booklets issued by BMS and SS tutors.

Differences were also noted between the two groups of students in relation to the use of grade descriptors. In contrast to the assessment guidelines, it was the BMS students who reported making more use of these. All were aware that such grade descriptors existed and five out of six said that they made use of them. Two mentioned using them when they wanted to improve their grade from a 2ii to a 2i. The reverse situation existed for SS students. None said they used them and only three were aware of them. The greater awareness shown by BMS students of the college grade descriptors is possibly because BMS module booklets contain summaries of the grade descriptors whereas SS booklets do not.

This observation suggests that simply presenting students with information once, for example in a programme handbook, does not mean that they will make use of it. Having a summary of the grade descriptors alongside each assessment rubric appears to encourage students to make use of them. The tendency of SS students to rely solely on the information contained in the module booklet may mean that they are likely to produce only satisfactory levels of work because they meet the requirements for a 'successful answer'. However, a 'successful answer' describes a threshold position and it would be interesting to see whether students understand this phrase to mean 'threshold', 'satisfactory' or better than this. Further research is necessary to explore the meaning that students attach to the phrase 'a successful answer'.

Informal support mechanisms

In addition to the formal support mechanisms students also said that they sought help from informal sources including friends and tutors. Nine students mentioned discussing their assignment with friends, some asking their peers to read their work.

Two thirds of the students also stated that a factor which helped them improve performance was clarification of the assignment by the tutor with half of those specifically mentioning verbal clarification:

> *"I just need someone to say it to me in my sort of, my, I don't know if dialect's the word, the way I can understand, just break it down… only five minutes of my lecturer's time… I'll have it in my head then, I'll just go away and sit down and begin." (SS student)*

This issue of informal clarification appeared important to the students in both groups and is discussed in more detail below.

Stages in completing their assignments: preparation and planning

When asked to describe what they did to complete their assignment, students mentioned planning, researching information from books, the internet and lecture notes as well as friends and tutors. Additionally, they described taking notes, drafting and editing their work. There were no obvious differences in the process by gender or by programme of study, but there were differences related to performance at level one. For example, although only one of the poorest performing students mentioned drafting, all the best performing students talked about drafting. The same was true of note taking. However, all students regardless of their performance in level one undertook planning and editing.

Timing of assignment completion

The most obvious difference in relation to planning and preparation between the best performing and the worst performing students at level one occurred in the way they used their time. All of the poorest performing students talked about completing their assignment in a concentrated period of time. For example, one said "I do a lot at once" and another "I did it on Tuesday, edited it on Wednesday".

The middle band of students reported using similar approaches: "I wrote it without redrafts" and "If I'm really last minute I write for hours at a time". The best performing students, however, adopted a very different approach claiming to draft their work, re-reading it several times and, significantly, to work for shorter periods of time at one go. For example, one said, "I work for 2-3 hours at a time" and another, "I try to write 500 words a day, that takes me about 2 hours". Moreover, whereas the poorer performing students reported that they left things until the last minute, five of the eight middle and best performing students said that they started early. This finding invites further research to ascertain how far students' poor study skills rather than their lack of understanding contributes to the lower marks achieved, and conversely how far good study skills contribute to achieving high marks.

Given that many more students work to support their studies, it could be hypothesised that the time spent in employment and not their poor study skills might compound poor time management skills. To explore this issue students were asked to say how many hours paid employment they undertook in the month preceding the interview. Interestingly, five students who reported writing for long periods of time without a break undertook 80–104 hours paid work in the previous month and one worked 40 hours. This would suggest that external factors such as hours spent in paid employment and not just poor study habits might account for the way students manage their time. Having said this, one student who worked 70 hours in the previous month did not work for concentrated periods of time and was one of the best performing students. Furthermore, two of the poorest performing students did no paid work yet still talked about leaving work until the last minute or doing a lot at one go. If the hours worked in the previous month reflect the general commitment to paid work then paid work on its own does not explain working practices for the preparation and completion of work. Students were not asked to comment on other responsibilities and commitments, such as those to their families, which might have affected the quantity and quality of time spent on their assignments.

Use of feedback on previous assignments

One of the key concerns for tutors is trying to ensure that students use feedback given on assignments in the preparation of subsequent coursework. There are two specific concerns. One is to ensure that students understand the feedback that tutors write and the second is to encourage them to use it. Sampling examples of tutor feedback from a range of SS and BMS assignments revealed that tutors offer 50-125 words written feedback in addition to the grade. Quantitatively more feedback was offered by SS tutors than by BMS tutors possibly because the feedback form for the SS department is twice the size of that for the BMS department.

Nine students reported that feedback was helpful, although two SS students claimed not to use it, and two BMS students indicated that it was of variable quality or quantity. More specifically, students stated that feedback helped them to reference more effectively, improve the structure of their essays, use more sources, answer the question and increased their confidence.

Interestingly, BMS students were better able to articulate the benefits of feedback. This observation is noteworthy because it raises questions about the way that feedback is given and its interpretation by students as the BMS students only receive approximately half the quantity of written feedback as compared with the SS students. Therefore, it is reasonable to hypothesise first, that less feedback helps the students to focus on one or two key areas, second, that BMS feedback is written in simpler language and last, that BMS feedback is providing students with very concrete actions, for example referencing protocols, using more sources of information, and linking paragraphs. This raises further questions about how tutors can provide written feedback which goes beyond the concrete but which is useful to students.

Overall, students placed strong emphasis on the desire for verbal clarification of feedback which raises the question of how far students can digest and act on written feedback. Students' desire for verbal feedback is consistent with Higgins' (2000) view that students struggle to use feedback effectively because they are "simply unable to understand feedback comments and interpret them correctly" (p2). He argues that failure of communication has its roots in, amongst other things, the differing and often tacit discourses of academic disciplines from which students are frequently excluded. Furthermore, Ivanic, Clarke and Rimmershaw (2000) make the point that one tutor's feedback may not apply to another tutor's work and thus students are less likely to pay attention to it.

Two other factors which might be thought to affect students' capacity to comprehend feedback: gender and level one performance, had no impact. And perhaps more surprisingly, those students who performed better in their level one modules did not report making more effective use of feedback than students who had performed less well. This raises questions about the effectiveness of tutor feedback and warrants further attention.

Students' perceptions of the factors that influence their performance

The interviews were designed to elicit information about what the students actually did in writing assignments rather than their general perceptions of the process. Nevertheless we were also interested in giving students an opportunity to outline the factors that they thought helped or hindered their achievement in addition to those about which they were directly questioned. They listed a number of factors that they considered impacted upon their performance in assignments. Those that were mentioned by at least five of the twelve students were:

- General interest, choice over or enjoyment regarding the subject matter of the assignment (9/12)

- Tutor support and clarification regarding the assignment (8/12)

- Approachability of tutor (6/12)

- Having to complete several assignments at the same time (5/12)

The last of the four factors is related to time management and the pressure placed on students via modular programmes of study with the inevitable need to assess the module at its end. For students who study four modules per semester this often means that they have to complete four assessments in a relatively short period of time.

The remaining three factors relate directly to the teaching, learning and assessment process. It would seem that where students enjoy the module and/or have some element of choice this increases their motivation when undertaking the assessment. If this finding can be generalised to all students then offering some element of choice in assessments might enhance students' motivation to complete the work. Tutor support and clarification about the assessment was also considered to be a key factor in enhancing performance. This again speaks to a need to offer students verbal clarification of assessment requirements and tutor expectations. On their, own written criteria – however detailed – do not seem to be sufficient. Finally, five students talked about how the approachability of tutors affected whether they sought additional support. Tutors were not seen as universally unapproachable, but five students mentioned that they would not approach a particular tutor who taught them. This tutor was not the same for all students. Having said that some tutors were unapproachable, eight students talked about tutors in very positive ways as being approachable, available and supportive. Whilst the results are equivocal, tutors should not underestimate the importance of positive inter-personal relationships with students.

Conclusions

This second stage of the project has identified a number of useful findings despite its small, action research approach. There are clearly a number of factors that appear to help students in their writing. Factors that are within the scope of the tutors are:

- Putting all relevant assessment information in the module handbook including assessment criteria and marking scheme so that students can read what is required to achieve both threshold and higher levels of performance

- Engaging students in activities which make them attend to the assessment information (marking criteria and grade descriptors) that is provided in module handbooks

- Providing the opportunity for dialogue about assignments both in the preparation stage and during feedback

Factors which rely on student skills and approach:

- Drafting and redrafting assignments
- Giving themselves enough time
- Writing in shorter periods rather than completing the assignment in one or two long sittings

Whilst the latter list is the responsibility of individual students, tutor-led activities can be used to encourage these successful writing strategies. For example, requiring students to bring drafts of assignments to class for peer assessment against the marking criteria involves them in drafting and redrafting their work and preparing work in advance. It also acts to make students engage with the assessment information in the module handbook such as assessment criteria and marking scheme. Gibbs (1999) gives a good example of this type of practice raising examination performance.

In relation to the impact of our level one intervention that used a range of activities to engage students in assessment of writing, there are mixed results. There is evidence that this process helped students to pay attention to formal assessment information and marking criteria in a way that they would not have done otherwise. Nevertheless the negative reaction to the process suggests that more effort needs to be put into explaining the rationale for the activities to the students. The results also suggest that the work needs extending, possibly into later semesters, to assist students in raising their achievement beyond their initial performance.

The evidence lends support to the notion that assessment language is not seen as transparent by students and further tutor clarification is seen as very important in the process of negotiating just what is expected. This presents a much greater challenge to tutors both in terms of agreeing amongst their subject colleagues what their expectations are (if this is possible) and then expressing them in ways that are understandable to novices in the academic community. Further research is also needed to explore the relative impact of the social capital students bring with them, compared with their writing strategies, in terms of their ability to perform successfully in higher education. Probably the former is far more resistant to tutor intervention.

References

Bizzell, P (1992) *Academic discourse and critical consciousness* Pittsburg: University of Pittsburg Press

Bloxham, S and West, A (2004) 'Understanding the Rules of the Game: marking peer assessment as a medium for developing students' conceptions of assessment'. *Assessment and Evaluation in Higher Education*, 29 (6) pp 721–733

Braxton, JM and Hirschy, AS (2004) 'Reconceptualising antecedents of social integration in student departure'. In Yorke, M and Longden, B (2004) *Retention and Student Success in Higher Education* Maidenhead: SRHE and Open University Press

Creme, P and Lea, MR (2003) *Writing at University, a guide for students* (2nd Edition). Maidenhead: Open University Press

Gibbs, G (1999) 'Using assessment strategically to change the way students learn'. In Brown, S and Glasner, A *Assessment Matters in Higher Education* Buckingham: SHRE and Open University Press

Higgins, R (2000) *"Be more critical!": Rethinking Assessment Feedback* paper presented at the British Educational Research Association Conference, Cardiff University, September 7–10.

Ivanic, R, Clark, R and Rimmershaw, R (2000) 'What am I supposed to make of this? The messages conveyed to students by Tutors' written comments' in Stierer, B (Ed) (2000) *Student Writing in Higher Education* Buckingham: Open University Press

Jones, P and Abramson, M (2001) *Getting Students off to a Flying Start: Improving the Retention of Advanced GNVQ Students Entering Higher Education*. Widening Participation and Lifelong Learning, 3 (2) pp 34–37

Lea, MR and Street. BV (2000) 'Student Writing and Staff feedback in Higher Education: An academic literacies approach', in Stierer, B (Ed) (2000) *Student Writing in Higher Education* Buckingham: Open University Press

Lillis, TM (2001) *Student writing: access, regulation and desire*. London, Routledge.

Norton, L (2004) 'Using Assessment criteria as learning criteria: a case study in psychology'. *Assessment and Evaluation in Higher Education* 29 (6) pp 687–702.

O'Donovan, B, Price, M and Rust, C (2004) 'Know what I mean? Enhancing student understanding of assessment standards and criteria' *Teaching in Higher Education*, 9(3) 325–335

Orsmond, P Merry, S and Reiling, K (2004) 'The Use of Exemplars and Formative Feedback when Using Student Derived Marking Criteria in Peer and Self-assessment' *Assessment and Evaluation in Higher Education* 27 (4) pp309–323.

Pardoe, S (2000) 'Respect and the Pursuit of 'Symmetry'' in Barton, D, Hamilton, M and Ivanic, R *Situated Literacies: Reading & Writing in Context*. London: Routledge

Rust, C, Price, M and O'Donovan, B (2003) 'Improving Students' Learning by developing their Understanding of Assessment Criteria and Processes' *Assessment & Evaluation in Higher Education* 28 (2) pp 147

Thomas, L (2001) *Widening participation in post-compulsory education.* London: Continuum

Yorke, M (1999) *Leaving Early: Undergraduate non-completion in higher education.* London: Taylor and Francis

Yorke, M and Longden, B (2004) *Retention and Student Success in Higher Education* Maidenhead: SRHE and Open University Press

Developing reflective skills: enhancing the use of assessment portfolios in a foundation degree

Peter Boyd, St Martin's College, Carlisle, UK

Abstract

In the UK, the next decade will see a large increase in students enrolling on vocational, employment-based foundation degrees. The intervention into the assessment process reported here involved an open access, part-time foundation degree for teaching assistants in schools; predominantly mature, female students.

The module tutors, in order to develop their shared understanding of the requirements of a professional portfolio assignment and to make the assessment process transparent for students, devised a marking scheme. In addition a formative peer assessment exercise was used to engage students fully with the marking scheme.

Qualitative data analysis of reflective writing and semi-structured interviews identified high emotional investment and the significance of peer relations but that there were potential rewards in terms of promoting reflection on practice and understanding of the assessment process in higher education.

Key words: assessment; portfolio; foundation degree; transparency;

Introduction

The focus of this case study is the socially constructed experience, understandings and interpretations of students and tutors as they engage with Higher Education within the context of accredited professional education on a foundation degree for teaching assistants. Lillis (2001) sets out a challenge by arguing that an institutional practice of 'mystery' is maintained in higher education, which works against those least familiar with the conventions surrounding academic writing, and that institutions fail to teach the conventions of the literacy practices demanded. The case study higher education tutor team in this study aimed to promote transparency, remove at least some of the mystery and so raise student achievement in their written assignments through developing assessment criteria information in an accessible format referred to as the 'marking scheme'. The creation of the marking scheme provided an opportunity for dialogue amongst the tutors regarding the assessment requirements. In addition a formative peer assessment exercise was used to engage students with the marking scheme and to create a dialogue amongst tutors and students. The aim of this dialogue was to allow some discussion and sharing of the tacit assessment expectations that were hidden within and around the marking scheme due to the limitations of written learning outcomes and assessment criteria.

In investigating writing for assessment this case study focuses on a particular assignment consisting of a professional portfolio. This assignment involves selection of work-based evidence and reflective writing to provide a rationale for the evidence provided against a range of professional competence statements and professional development planning. Portfolios are widely used in professional education contexts especially in the health professions (Klenowski 2002). Although characteristically student-centred, the requirements and conventions required in the construction of portfolios are far from transparent for many students and this had proved to be the case for first year students on this course. Previous students found the assignment difficult to understand and operationalise so that many achieved only a mediocre standard with copious but largely descriptive evidence and only a poorly developed rationale.

The student group were mature open access students studying on a vocational foundation degree programme. The increasing diversity of students in HE has highlighted the need for effective induction into the academic community (Haggis and Pouget 2002, Stephani 1998). Other work has identified that, due to the tacit nature of assessment criteria, there is a need for students to fully engage with the assessment process rather than tutors simply making assessment information more explicit (Orsmond et al 2002, Rust et al 2003).

The nature of the programme, the assignment and the student group mean that this case study is embedded in a professional education context, which raises issues concerning the nature of personal, propositional and process knowledge within learning through reflection (Eraut 1994, Schön 1987). The professional and emotional investment of the students in the programme and in the portfolio assessment item is high and the place of affective issues in reflective learning becomes crucial (Brockebank and McGill 2001).

This research project has been influenced by the 'academic literacies' approach (Lea and Stierer 2000, Lillis 2001) in which student writing for assessment is viewed as a social practice within a particular social context. Hoadley-Maidment investigates lecturers' conceptions of successful academic writing in professional education contexts. Key features are the use of academic but also professional language and modes of writing, the continued dominance of argument but also the need for students to link personal experience to theory (2000). These features do generally apply in the case study context and the programme team are able to reasonably claim some shared understanding and agreement over this. However Stierer (2000) identifies the range of academic writing required for a case study professional programme and emphasises the lack of consistent and specific guidance provided for students by lecturers. As so often in professional education within the subject discipline of education the situation is 'layered' so that the tutor team, in trying to make the assessment process more effective, is also attempting to demonstrate good practice to teaching assistants with regard to their work with school pupils.

The tutors, students and the school-based colleagues who act as mentors are viewed as forming a community of practice in terms of subject knowledge development but also in terms of the process of assessment (Elwood and Klenowski 2002). Wenger et al propose an acceptable definition:

> *'Communities of practice are groups of people who share a concern, a set of problems, or a passion about a topic, and who deepen their knowledge and expertise in this area by interacting on a ongoing basis.'(2002 p4)*

The role of tacit knowledge is important to our understanding of how the tutor team assess student assignments and the question of how that knowledge is shared amongst tutors and students is central to this project. The concept of tacit knowledge is used here to include the possibility of partial description, and the importance of non-formal learning in the acquisition of tacit knowledge is also recognised (Eraut 2000).

In searching for understanding of the student experience in relation to assessment the issues of social class and gender must be considered as well as the issue of students' prior educational experiences. McMillan (2000) highlights the different experiences of women in open access higher education contexts. She argues that

> *'the ways in which learner roles are constructed and the contexts in which learning takes place are crucial to understanding success.' (p161)*

The place of this project within the discourse of widening participation raises broader questions regarding the potential lower academic status of vocational programmes, the need to change individuals or to change institutions and above all the role of higher education in the reproduction of existing inequalities (Archer et al 2003).

Key questions which emerged during the project include:

- How does the 'marking scheme' help tutors and students to develop a shared understanding of the assessment requirements?

- How does a peer assessment exercise help to engage tutors and students with the assessment criteria and further develop their understanding of the assessment requirements?

- How do power relationships, including the influence of personal and professional contexts, as well as gender and social class, affect the students' experience of the assessment process and the development of a genuine community of practice?

The case study

The case study is based on a group of students in year one of a part-time foundation degree in Teaching and Learning Support. This is a vocational programme equivalent to the first two years of a traditional degree. The students are all experienced teaching assistants and are employed, mostly paid but a few as volunteers, in schools. A teacher colleague acting as mentor supports each student in their work-based learning. All of the students have successful experience as a teaching assistant prior to admission on to the programme. In terms of prior formal educational experience the overwhelming majority of the student group did not continue with post-compulsory education at the age of sixteen but many have completed vocational qualifications related to education since leaving school. Their teaching assistant role was often taken up as their own children entered nursery or school and most of the student group are in the 30 to 50 age range.

The student cohort includes two separate groups based on two separate sites, the total number of students in the two groups was thirty-one, and the sample size for each element of data varied between 21 and 31. All but one of the students are female, they work in relatively low paid jobs mostly in primary schools which have a dominantly female workforce although men are proportionally over-represented in head teacher posts. The programme tutor team is only 50% female and the three tutors most closely involved in this project are male.

Data gathered at the mid-point of the module included written peer feedback with tutor moderation plus a reflective writing task completed by students after the peer assessment exercise. Data gathered at the end of the module included student self assessments, tutor assessments and feedback and semi-structured interviews with a sample of eleven of the students. In addition semi-structured interviews with the two key tutors involved were completed at the end of the module; these focused on the particular module and portfolio assignment and used the marking scheme as an artefact to frame discussion of the assessment process.

This study is a pragmatic piece of collaborative action research which aims to contribute to the development of the particular programme in terms of the ways by which it supports the students in succeeding in their assessments and in gaining confidence within the academic community. The main focus is to critically consider the experience, power and perspective of a group of mature, open access primary school teaching assistants (TAs) taking part in a foundation degree in teaching and learning support as they are inducted into the academic discourse and community of practice. The study adopts a reflexive methodology (Alvesson and Skoldberg 2000) which views interpretation as central to the research process and acknowledges the importance of the researcher's construction of the data within this process. The reflective writing and interview tape data was transcribed and analysed using a constant comparative method within a grounded theory approach (Strauss and Corbin 1990). The importance of gender, social class and power in understanding the responses of students was recognised but not explicitly analysed due to the limitations of the data gathered.

The marking scheme

There is a current emphasis on explicit expression of assessment requirements through the use of learning outcomes and constructive alignment (Rust 2002). O'Donovan et al

(2004) propose a spectrum of processes supporting the transfer or construction of assessment requirements, standards and criteria which sets out a variety of strategies on a line between explicit knowledge transfer and tacit knowledge transfer. There is a danger of placing too much emphasis on construction of knowledge of assessment requirements *by students* and perhaps more emphasis on the processes by which *tutors* develop this understanding would be appropriate. Rust et al (2003) do emphasise the importance of opportunities for discussion and debate in order for a common view on standards and level to emerge even within a close-knit academic department and this need for tutor team dialogue around the assessment requirements is a key aspect of this case study.

In order to fully understand and complete assignments students need to refer to the institution's generic grade descriptor. The case study institution uses the concept of constructive alignment (Biggs 2003) in the design and validation of programme and module specifications. The planned assessment must address the specified learning outcomes and allow students to demonstrate their knowledge, understanding and skills in relation to these learning outcomes. Therefore students also need to consult the learning outcomes for a particular module which are provided in the module booklet together with guidance and criteria for the assessment.

In wishing to provide clear, coherent and agreed criteria for the students the approach selected by the module team is one that is recommended as good practice within the case study institution and it involves the creation of a 'marking scheme'. The 'marking scheme' is an attempt to agree criteria amongst the tutor team and to provide clear and specific criteria to students for a particular assignment. Module learning outcomes, the generic grade descriptor and the particular assessment criteria for the assignment are all expressed within a one or two page table. The learning outcomes are set out in the left hand column and the criteria for achieving each grade in respect of each learning outcome is set out in the table.

The creation of the marking scheme is a useful exercise in developing tutor agreement over the assessment requirements but it is a compromise document and is not an attempt to completely express the tacit knowledge held by the tutor team. Explicit limits on this, even if it were possible, are imposed by the available time for discussion and by the limitations on size of producing a one-page document. In addition the warning given by Polyani (1967) is acknowledged, that it is possible to distort or damage tacit knowledge during attempts to express it through detailed writing; O'Donovan et al (2004) support this view in the context of assessment criteria.

Having attempted to communicate the assessment requirements through creation of the marking scheme the module tutor team now considered the evidence (Lea and Stierer 2000, Lillis 2001, Rust et al 2003) that merely providing written criteria and expecting students to be able to engage with them is not sufficient. A formative peer assessment workshop was introduced in order to more fully engage the students with the marking scheme.

The peer assessment workshop

In a half-day structured workshop students provided formative written assessment and feedback on sections of their peers' portfolio assignments at a mid-point in the module which is completed over an eight-month period. It is important to make clear that although the peer assessment exercise was four months into the part-time programme the students had only spent twelve days together in face-to-face sessions. Students used the marking scheme as a tool in the marking process.

The peer assessment exercise was intended by tutors to be a relatively informal activity but in practice some students interpreted the event as fairly formal and their writing and later interview responses indicated that they had found it to be a fairly stressful experience. This may have been partly due to the involvement on the day of the researcher as programme leader and on the need to divide the group into separate rooms in order to preserve anonymity of peer markers. A variety of mundane practical circumstances led to one student group not having been as thoroughly prepared as the other for the workshop. A tutor was on hand in each room to offer support in terms of interpreting the marking scheme. This was followed by a plenary session and then an independent reflective writing task designed to translate peer feedback and exposure to other students' work into an action plan for effective completion of the portfolio.

Findings

The findings are set out here generally in the order in which they were collected. First the reflective writing task completed after the peer assessment exercise is discussed and then the end of module self-assessments are introduced. The findings from the end of module semi-structured interviews are then presented and finally the end-of-module interviews with tutors are considered.

The written feedback produced by students during the peer assessment workshop provides some potential insight into the understanding and application of the marking scheme by students. This was checked by the inclusion of a tutor in the peer assessment workshop who second marked a sample of the work that had been marked by students. Comparison of the feedback from tutor and students confirmed that the peer assessment and feedback was closely matched to that from the tutor. Students were able to apply the criteria and complete the assessment task competently; this was not surprising given that their professional context includes assessment processes.

Students did use phrases and words from the marking scheme within their feedback and used the marking scheme to identify both strengths and targets. In comparing the tutor feedback to that from the students one difference was that students appeared to make fewer suggestions for improvement strategies. This perhaps suggests some reluctance by student markers or that they may have found the identification of strategies for improvement to be difficult. The tutor markers may have resorted to tacit knowledge and been able to go beyond the marking scheme in order to identify improvement strategies.

It may however reflect on the marking scheme and might suggest a need for its amendment. In an end of module tutor interview concerning the marking scheme the lack of progression from grade C to B was identified as a problem.

The reflective writing task and action plan completed by students following the peer assessment workshop provides some potential insight into the understanding and application of the marking scheme. It also provides insight into the wider questions relating to the experience of the students with regard to assessment. A theme emerging from this data was student apprehension in assessing the work of their peers and also an apprehension by some of their work being assessed by their peers. This apprehension was expressed by some students as an initial anxiety which was soon over as the reality of the formative exercise became clear. Some students claimed to have enjoyed being assessed whilst for other individual students strong apprehension was expressed.

The wide range of emotional response to the peer assessment was a key feature and was revealed by explicit comments on the stress felt by some students during and around the peer assessment exercise. The data and tutor observations on the day identified that the students' emotional investment was very high and this may have been related to the fact that the portfolios include evidence gathered from the school-based practice of students. The ethical issues and power relations involving tutors and students appeared to be a critical aspect of the process; for one or two students the experience clearly had a strong impact. Students expressed concerns about peer relationships and interaction rather than those more explicitly related to the tutors and their status. Many students commented on their preference for assessment and feedback from a tutor rather than a peer, they did not question the professional expertise or knowledge of the tutors or their right to make assessments. This is not surprising given the higher education context and the position of the tutors as assessors.

Many students claimed to have gained confidence through the peer assessment exercise and felt reassured that they were 'on the right track' in terms of the requirements of the portfolio assignment. The language within the marking scheme was used but was sometimes questioned by students. The terms 'reflection', 'evaluation' and 'critical' were used within students' targets and were the key words raised by students for discussion in the plenary.

End of module self-assessments of their portfolios by students were compared to the final tutor assessments and feedback. The students and tutors all used the marking scheme together with a structured feedback proforma. The purpose of the self-assessment was further development of students' understanding of the assessment process rather than as a contribution to the summative assessment of the portfolio assignment and students were reassured that the tutor marking the assignment would not see the self-assessment. The self-assessments were completed in a fairly informal session and they were presented as a formative exercise rather than as having any significance for the marking process.

The written feedback comments in the self-assessments demonstrated engagement with the marking scheme by students as they included the use of paraphrasing and/or key words from the scheme. There was considerable congruence between the student and tutor feedback and no evidence of direct contradictions between the student and tutor assessments in terms of written feedback.

The self-assessments suggested a failure of the marking scheme to help students to assess the indicative grade of their portfolio compared to the tutor assessments. Twenty-one students completed and submitted the self-assessment; in none of these cases did the student award themselves a higher percentage mark than the tutor and only six awarded themselves the same grade band as the tutor. In eight cases the students awarded themselves a grade lower than the tutor and in seven cases the students were two grades lower than the tutor. These seven students clearly expressed a far lower assessment of the quality of their portfolio than the tutor, which raises doubts about the efficacy of the marking scheme and of the peer assessment exercise. These very low self-assessed grades also raise issues about the modesty or low self-confidence of some of the students in the higher education assessment context.

A contrasting theme arising from the end of module interviews was that students felt that participation in the programme had greatly increased their self-confidence. However they mostly expressed this in terms of their professional performance in the workplace rather than their academic work. They felt that their improving ability to use appropriate 'educational' language and their improved grasp of key educational issues enabled them to make more of a contribution to professional discussion and development of new strategies and that their improved contribution was recognised by colleagues in the workplace. These student perceptions are supported by direct feedback from mentors and head teachers that has been gathered as part of normal programme evaluation methods.

A second key theme arising from the end of module interviews was the continuing 'struggle' to come to terms with assignments and the assessment process. It is important to realise that students were still at an early stage in the programme. They report a gradually increasing but tentative confidence in completing assignments but identified issues including use of appropriate language, varied expectations between tutors, varied levels of guidance between modules, effective reading strategies and delays in receiving feedback. In particular students identified a wide variation in the support that they have experienced in completing their assignments. A wide variety of informal sources of support for completing assignments were used, including using school-based colleagues, relatives and friends. Some students felt that there was a lack of peer support within the group and some students revealed feelings of isolation due to a lack of peer or other support for their assignments. On the other hand some students felt that peer support was good and that it became a key element of their experience as the year progressed.

With regard to the peer assessment, the end of module interviews indicated that some of the critical views of students had moderated with time and the purpose of the exercise within the context of the module and the programme was recognised by a majority of students. However the interviews confirmed the findings from the reflective writing task that high levels of anxiety were experienced by some students and that effective peer relationships were not fully developed prior to the event.

The portfolios themselves were of a good standard with many gaining a high grade and all were well above the pass mark which was an improvement from previous groups. This high standard of work produced is not surprising given the focus on the new marking scheme, the peer assessment exercise and the collaborative research project itself. Many students, when reviewing the draft of this paper in a focus group, felt that the quality and high expectations of the tutors was the most important effect. It is perhaps possible to tentatively claim at least that the developments have helped to avoid confusion amongst those students who previously struggled to gain a pass.

Discussion

There does appear to be a need for more explicit and pro-active support by the programme team for the development of peer relationships, trust and networks in the early part of the course. In addition more explicit focus on prior educational experiences, which is already a feature of the programme, together perhaps with discussion on gender and professional issues, may be an appropriate development.

The varied response to the peer assessment exercise needs to be addressed. There appears to be a need at least to improve the preparation of students for the exercise and perhaps paired 'critical friend' reviews of the portfolio in a previous face-to-face session might be useful in achieving this. Some students in the end of project focus groups felt the peer assessment was simply too early on in the programme.

The varied individualised experience and responses of the students to the assessment process is another key finding and Haggis warns us of the dangers of applying adult learning theory in a simplistic way (2002). A pro-active approach to support of part-time adult learners, which would be relevant to the case study programme, is proposed by Castles (2004). This might involve student questionnaires and pro-active contacting of students in order to monitor their progress through the completion of assessments that are early on in the programme.

Another key finding was that students under-value their own professional experience and knowledge especially in relation to tutors but also in relation to their peers. This need to raise the self-esteem of students in relation to their professional knowledge is important. Lillis argues that opening up disciplinary content to 'external' interests and influences is one key strategy to encourage a more open approach to what counts as relevant knowledge within and across academic disciplines (2003 p205). In the case study context the external interests would include the school employers; the question for the case study programme appears to be to what extent the students and schools are allowed to make a contribution to deciding what knowledge is valid. To what extent do they view knowledge required for the assignments, even the workplace and professionally focused portfolio assignment, as being held by tutors? An action here is that the value of the personal knowledge of the students needs to be discussed within the programme tutor team and made more explicit within the marking scheme. In addition, and consistent with the dual approach adopted, a formative reflective writing exercise perhaps with self-assessment against the marking scheme would promote the dialogue needed to share the tacit knowledge associated with this element of the assessment requirements.

Conclusions

The presentation of assessment information as a 'marking scheme' in a concise format but one which has been specifically aimed at the particular assignment appears to have been reasonably successful in facilitating a shared understanding amongst tutors and students. The further development of this through a formative peer assessment exercise proved to be a highly charged but effective method for engaging the students with the assessment process. This combined approach provided opportunities for tutor-tutor and tutor-student discussion and a growing and shared tentative awareness of the assessment requirements and process within the subject knowledge and professional contexts. The contested nature of the assessment process, assessment as an 'art' rather than a 'science', needs to be acknowledged. The need for dialogue between tutors needs to be made more explicit so that events such as module planning meetings and second-marking of assignments are prioritised and used fully as crucial professional development opportunities.

The power relationships existing within the academic and professional contexts of the students suggest that a more explicit handling of these issues within the programme might at least be an appropriate start to enabling students to raise their self-esteem and participate more confidently in the learning and assessment process especially with regard to the recognition that they already have valid personal, experiential, knowledge to contribute.

Above all there appears to be a need for the programme team to cultivate a community of practice to include students, tutors and mentors and to include the assessment process within the body of knowledge to be shared.

The nature of the professional context appears to have a strong influence over the experience of students in terms of assessment and the location of the case study within professional education in the subject of education appears to have a critical bearing. The strong overlap between study and assessment in professional education, and the subject knowledge of education itself lend themselves to layered learning and teaching. The attitudes held by tutors towards valid subject knowledge and towards relationships with students and employer partners appear to deserve further research because of the influence this has on the sharing of tacit knowledge and the formation of a genuine community of practice.

References

Alvesson M and Skoldberg K (2000) *Reflexive Methodology: New Vistas for Qualitative Research*. London: Sage.

Archer L, Hutchings M and Ross A (2003) *Higher Education and Social Class*. London: Routledge Falmer.

Biggs J (2003) (2nd Edition) *Teaching for Quality Learning at University* Buckingham: SRHE/Open University Press.

Brockebank A and McGill I (2001) *Action Learning: a guide for professional, management and educational development.* London: Kogan Page.

Castles J (2004) 'Persistence and the adult learner: factors affecting persistence in Open University students'. *Active Learning in Higher Education*, Vol 5, No 2, pp166–179.

Elwood, J and Klenowski, V. (2002) 'Creating Communities of Shared Practice: the challenges of assessment use in learning and teaching' in *Assessment and Evaluation in Higher Education* 27 (3) pp 243–256.

Eraut M (1994) *Developing professional knowledge and competence* London: Falmer.

Eraut M. (2000) Non-formal learning and tacit knowledge in professional work. *British Journal of Educational Psychology*, Vol 70, pp113–136.

Haggis T (2002) 'Exploring the 'Black Box' of Process: a comparison of theoretical notions of the 'adult learner' with accounts of postgraduate learning experience'. *Studies in Higher Education*, Vol. 27, No. 2, pp207–220.

Haggis, T and Pouget, M (2002) 'Trying to be motivated: perspectives on learning from younger students accessing higher education'. *Teaching in Higher Education* 7 (3) pp323–336.

Hoadley-Maidment E (2000) 'From Personal Experience to Reflective Practitioner: Academic Literacies and Professional Education' in Lea MR and Stierer B (Eds) *Student Writing in Higher Education*. Buckingham: SHRE/OUP.

Klenowski V (2002) *Developing Portfolios for Learning and Assessment: processes and principles*. London: Routledge.

Lea MR and Stierer B (Eds) (2000) *Student Writing in Higher Education*. Buckingham: SHRE/OUP.

Lea MR and Street BV (2000) 'Student Writing and Staff Feedback in Higher Education: An Academic Literacies Approach' in Lea MR and Stierer B (Eds) *Student Writing in Higher Education*. Buckingham: SHRE/OUP.

Lillis TM (2001) *Student Writing: Access, Regulation, Desire*. London: Routledge.

Lillis TM (2003) 'Student Writing as 'Academic Literacies': Drawing on Bakhtin to Move from Critique to Design'. *Language and Education*, Vol 17, No 3 pp192–207.

McMillan J (2000) 'Writing for Success in Higher Education' in Lea MR and Stierer B (Eds) *Student Writing in Higher Education*. Buckingham: SHRE/OUP.

O'Donovan B, Price M and Rust C (2004) 'Know what I mean? Enhancing student understanding of assessment standards and criteria'. *Teaching in Higher Education*, Vol 9, No 3, pp325–335.

Orsmond, P, Merry, S and Reiling, K (2002) 'The Use of Exemplars and Formative Feedback when Using Student Derived Marking Criteria in Peer and Self Assessment'. *Assessment and Evaluation in Higher Education* 27 (4) pp309–322.

Polyani M (1967) 'The Tacit Dimension' in Prusak L (1997) *Knowledge in Organizations*. Newton: Butterworth-Heinemann.

Rust C (2002) 'The impact of assessment on student learning'. *Active Learning in Higher Education*, Vol 3, No 2, pp145–157.

Rust C, Price M and O'Donavon B (2003) 'Improving Students Learning by developing their understanding of assessment criteria and processes'. *Assessment and Evaluation in Higher Education*, Vol 28, No 2, pp147–164.

Schön DA (1987) *Educating the Reflective Practitioner*. San Francisco: Jossey Bass.

Stephani LAJ (1998) 'Assessment in the Partnership with Learners' *Assessment & Evaluation in Higher Education* Vol 23, No 4, pp339–350.

Stierer B (2000) 'Schoolteachers as Students: Academic Literacy and the Construction of Professional Knowledge within Master's Courses in Education' in Lea MR and Stierer B (Eds) *Student Writing in Higher Education*. Buckingham: SHRE/OUP.

Strauss A and Corbin J (1990) *Basics of Qualitative Research: Grounded Theory Procedures and Techniques*. London: Sage.

Wenger E, McDermott R and Snyder W (2002) *Cultivating Communities of Practice*. Boston: Harvard Business School Press.

Changing the student experience: retention and inclusivity – translating strategy into success

Convenor: Michelle Haynes, Middlesex University

Middlesex University, in common with most institutions of higher education in England, has been attempting to meet the challenges set by the government in respect of widening participation and increasing diversity among the student body. At the same time we have also recognised the need to investigate and improve our rate of retention. We have done this in different ways and at different levels in the university. The ISLER project (The Impact of the Student Learning Experience on Retention) explores the student pathway through the first year to identify issues which prove troublesome and to identify issues which contribute to student departure. School-based research on a much more localised level has also been undertaken with a view to exploring students' expectations as a clue to why they leave early in their course. The first paper in this symposium will report on university-wide research looking at the first year experience, motivations for entering HE and attitudes concerning learning and teaching. The paper by Jenny Jacobs et al reinforces these findings emphasising the crucial nature of the first semester and the need for academics to be aware of the culture shock with which students are faced. The last paper reports on ongoing research in the School of Computing Science which is looking at the expectations of students as they approach different years of their studies and how these change over the years.

All three papers highlight the need to listen to our students and encourage academics to be more sympathetic to student needs. We need to be prepared to listen to our students, and probably more importantly, to adjust our expectations of them in the early stages of their academic careers.

Building success for all our students: enhancing the first year student experience

Deeba Parmar, Middlesex University

Keywords: First year experience, retention, diversity, academic experience

Abstract

This paper focuses upon Middlesex University's response to growing concerns regarding the implication of the widening participation agenda on retention. Ongoing institutional research in the form of the ISLER project (Impact of the Sstudent Llearning Experience on Retention) has been instigated, to better understand the issues that affect our first year students, in particular *academic* related factors that contribute to student departure and/or persistence. Findings illustrated reasons for non-completion often consisted of a mixture of academic related factors coupled with factors external to academic issues. Factors influential to student departure included academic preparedness, the tutor/student relationship and the transition to learning in a higher education environment (ie level and depth of learning, autonomous learning, grading criteria, assessments). Persistence required a degree of dual influences from both the institution and individual. Institutional aspects fostering persistence included active learning techniques, staff members, strategies creating a sense of achievement and belonging to the course/institution, tied with personal traits of investment, self efficacy beliefs and motivation.

Introduction

The massification of higher education coupled with the widening participation agenda has changed the landscape of HE today. Universities have ceased to be the preserve of the elite, resulting in a proliferation of student backgrounds and needs with implications for the retention and progression of students sector-wide and particularly at institutional level due to the considerable differences in student make up within HEIs (Cole, 1997) and the institutional habitus of the institution (Thomas, 2002). This research (ISLER Project) derives from national concerns to 'maintain standards', and 'bear down on rates of non-completion' (NAO, 2002) coupled with internal objectives and concerns to enhance 'the quality of the student experience of learning, teaching and assessment, with a particular view to the needs of an increasingly diverse student body' with the aim to gain a 'better understanding of the effects of the student learning experience on retention and progression', as stated in the Learning, Teaching and Assessment Strategy 2002-05.

The intention of the ISLER project is that it will to generatel institutional research concerning issues of student non-completion, progression and success. The primary aim is to build a body of knowledge regarding the first year experience and the influences on retention and progression in order to make feasible recommendations on enhancing the student experience. While a considerable number of students depart from university in other years, the first year of undergraduate level is considered the period when most students withdraw and is therefore the focus of the research (Yorke, 2002).

Context

Possible contributing factors to non-completion

Considerable UK retention research has built up during the last two decades with a variety of institutions conducting local level research.

A key focus of much of the research concentrates on factors contributing to non-completion with agreement to the influences of withdrawal, although the degrees of influence vary (Yorke, 2000, Mackie, 1998). The factors contributing to student withdrawal highlighted in much of the UK retention research are (Hall, 2001):

■ Academic preparedness

■ Wrong choice of programme

■ Financial difficulties

■ Quality of the student experience

■ Inadequate study skills and advice

■ Academic failure

■ Relationship(s) with peers and staff

Much of the retention research has focused upon transitional issues or issues of student support (Thomas et al, 2002). Although the importance of these issues is recognised, the ISLER project is primarily concerned with the type and range of academic factors that influence student withdrawal and therefore focuses upon the academic experiences.

Methods

A qualitative approach adopting semi structured interviews was adopted since the interest and focus of the research is on the experiences and perceptions of the students. It is of an exploratory nature, building an understanding of students' views within the setting of the focus, the institution. The choice of interviews as the research tool was influenced by the positioning of this research, attempting to understand the students' realities, construction and interpretation about their experiences (Creswell, 2003).

These findings are based upon 76 interviews; 42 with students who withdrew within their first academic year (during 2002/3) and 34 with students who had progressed onto level

2 and were still enrolled within the university. Although we are aware that the subject of study is influential in withdrawal factors (LTSN briefing paper, Foster et al, 2002) this research invited students to participate who were shown to have nondescript withdrawal reasons ('other', 'other-personal', 'unknown', 'written off after lapse of time') from a combination of subject areas that were of interest within the institution. Although the sample is not considerably large, this work is in progress and aims to continue in order to build internal knowledge.

As the research is of a particularly sensitive nature, in that it could be seen to be asking students to justify their withdrawal, it was stressed to all participants that they would be anonymous and the data would be used to inform the institution, and possibly the wider sector, of students' perceptions of reasons for departing or remaining. There maybe some hesitancy with research based upon students reporting their reasons for withdrawal particularly after a period of reflection as withdrawal may also lead to resentment and blame. The participants were also put at ease as much as possible during interviews as I adopted an informal approach, adopting the persona of a peer student, dressing causally and sympathising with their experiences rather than defending the institution. Acceptance was also facilitated by the fact that I am not a teacher so the students would be unlikely to have contact with me again and appeared to give honest accounts of their experiences.

Findings

It became apparent that the academic experiences were often intertwined with factors external to the academic setting. It is noted that as previous research has also found (LTSN briefing note) it was rarely a singular reason that resulted in withdrawal. For the majority of the participants that departed, issues or problems constructed an interrelating web of reasons for withdrawal, which often included both academic and non-academic influences. Non-academic factors of particular influence in this research included the financial concerns, the fear of getting into debt, incurring too much debt to continue studying, paid work interfering with studies and finding living in London too expensive. Commuting issues were also high coupled with the scheduling of their timetable a key influence. Administrative issues and level of helpfulness and approachability of staff members were also as important in student withdrawal as academic issues.

Academic influences on withdrawal

Relationships

The student/tutor relationship was also found to be a strong influence in withdrawal or persistence in that it was a key concern of the students that a tutor/academic would be there to guide and direct their learning or overlook their progress. The one-stop shop approach over the personal tutor system was a concern for some students primarily due to the autonomous learning, or 'cutting the apron strings' as one student described it, particularly at these early stages where they felt they were negotiating 'the rules' of higher education.

Some of the participants attributed this to be a key influential factor to their withdrawal as going to support services was viewed as explicitly 'asking for help', whereas an informal chat with a tutor was viewed as an implicit pathway to the help. Particularly for those students who were concerned about their progress, personal tutors were seen to be a way of contacting someone concerned about their progress and learning in order to 'note if I'm on the right track' and to see if 'I'm I learning what I'm supposed to be learning'.

Learning and teaching experience

A number of participants clearly blamed dissatisfaction with aspects of teaching and learning for their withdrawal. Adapting to new teaching methods, learning environment, the emphasis on autonomous learning and different ways of thinking were cited as influential factors.

Curriculum design was an area which appeared to cause concerns and problems to those new to higher education. Undertaking three modules within a twelve-week period with assessments much within the same phase appeared to be a considerable adjustment to many of the students, particularly in terms of using the time effectively to learn and reflect:

> *I thought higher education was about your development, intellectually, to construct arguments, have peers challenge your ideas, debate, discuss... with this set-up there is no time for reflection and for me a lot of the learning is in the reflection... How the modules, teaching time and assessments are split it feels as if you're on a factory conveyor belt.*
>
> *Alan, student who withdrew*

This participant expressed other common feelings associated with 'conveyor belt learning'. Discontent with the learning experience included learning driven primarily by assessments/grades and learning in isolation with little transferability from module to module.

Workload and timetabled lessons were also seen as a factor in withdrawal. This was an issue that would cause a knock-on effect to other influential factors which could lead to withdrawal, for example workload or time management interfering with paid employment, social experience, therefore fall behind, etc. Workload was also seen to be a problem when it was considered too little in terms of the academic rigour of the course and therefore affecting their opinion of the institution:

> *I've looked at the course I'm doing at another institution [names institution] and that had far more hours per week and the work we'd have had to do was far more. It just seems better, preparing you for more by teaching you more. I'm starting there next September.*
>
> *Sophie, student who withdrew*

Assessment and feedback were also topics that had a considerable degree of influence on student departure (LTSN Newsletter, September 2003). Concerns were expressed regarding a lack of clarity of the level of expectation of 'higher education standard', what the assessments were actually asking for and clarity of the grading criteria. Views on feedback centred around the complaint of lack of useful feedback, the timeliness of feedback and the merger of verbal and written feedback. These comments illustrate the depth and range of concerns within a similar sphere of assessment, grading and feedback:

> *I'm still not sure at this stage [end of first year] what it is I need to do to get the kind of marks I want to achieve. I feel I have passed the assessments and got average grades for the work in semester 1, but I don't know how to move myself up to the next level*

> *John, student who withdrew*

> *I don't even know what the difference between a 6 and a 9 is! [Internal grading classification]... I need to see good work to know how to achieve it.*

> *Katie, student who withdrew*

> *Why are we assessed by presentation? How is that going to help us learn? We just get the talk over with as soon as possible. It's not taken very seriously.*

> *Sam, student who withdrew*

Learning from persisters

As mentioned earlier we are becoming more aware of the influences of withdrawal (Yorke, 2000, Bennett, 2003) but what can we learn from persisters? The clearest thing that emerged from interviews with this group is that those who persist do not do so purely due to the experience they have – students who persist are just as likely to have encountered great difficulties and have more than likely thought about quitting. If many of these persisters have also experienced the same or similar problems as those who have withdrawn, what influences helped these students to remain? These findings have been divided into the following sub-headings: commitment/motivation and learning/teaching.

Commitment and motivation

Commitment and motivation to a course or institution is a strong reason for persistence (Mackie, 1998, Bennett, 2003). This research supports this view and further suggests that a clearer direction of goals, particularly career orientation, appears to be a key motivator in persistence. Many of those who have successfully progressed onto level two had strong motivations for gaining their intended degree; for some it included career goals, others felt a degree would better equip them for a career but were less focused on the field:

> *I'm not entirely sure what career path I want to follow when I finish here but I'm sure having a degree will widen my horizons in a number of ways.*

> *Tessa, student who persisted*

Thus the value placed upon a degree has justified commitment from the participant due to the assumption of its future merit, deferring gratification for future-orientated goals.

This ties in with thoughts of investment, whereby those who persisted are encouraged to remain and overcome difficulties due to their personal, social, financial, emotional and mental investment in applying, accepting and undertaking a place within HE.

> *I feel as like I've got this far so I've got to carry on. I got in didn't I? Course I'm gonna stay.*
>
> *Tom, student who persisted*
>
> *My family are so proud of me I wouldn't want to let them down. I've thought about it but everyone does.*
>
> *Ali, student who persisted*

These 'persisters' also appeared to exhibit a more realistic, balanced view of student life, admitting 'it's not all it's cracked up to be'. However, for some this was seen as 'just life' and the attitude was to 'soldier on'. Concerns and fears were also more likely to be voiced in this group through seeking support from the institution's support services, peers and family members.

Learning and teaching

At the centre of this research aspects of learning and teaching have featured strongly throughout and continue to do so. These findings, in agreement with Tinto's (2003) suggest that students have a greater likelihood of persisting if they are in an environment that fosters learning. This would seem likely as we would expect the majority of students to be in higher education to develop their education to a 'higher level' and therefore 'students who learn are students who stay' (2003:3). It was also clear that those who had remained were on programmes that actively encouraged and employed techniques, persuading students to remain through learning. These programmes often utilised active teaching techniques, balancing traditional lectures with smaller teaching classes and incorporated more formative assessments.

These students appeared to view themselves at the centre of their learning rather than viewing the tutor to be at the centre or 'in charge' of their learning. These participants took far more responsibility for their learning, understanding the importance of autonomous learning:

> *I understand that this [university] isn't like college. You've got to want to do the work and motivate yourself. You don't have people nagging you here so you've got to motivate yourself to work… to prove to yourself you can do it.*
>
> *R3*

The persisters also appeared to have a more realistic understanding of why they had the grades they had attained. The locus of control appeared to be embedded within, with students taking responsibility for their learning outcomes. Typical comments on the grades they had received included:

> *I deserved that mark because I studied for weeks and weeks. I went to the library on my own and actually did the work. I think part of it was to do with planning and actually concentrating and getting on with it rather than putting it off.*

> *I've only got myself to blame for failing [module name]. Now I've learnt that you really do have to work all the way through not just at the end!*

Persisters also felt that either a tutor, member of staff or peers had helped them in creating a sense of belonging and security to the university. Many spoke of 'wonderful' tutors who had taken the time to make them feel part of the university. Others spoke of a sense of achievement tutors had placed upon them, praising them on achieving getting into higher education. These types of activities helped to boost the students' efficacy beliefs into realising that they have made it here and can succeed.

Concluding remarks

Although this research intended to focus purely upon the academic issues influencing student withdrawal, early on it became evident that other factors had to be acknowledged. Although academic related factors are an important factor within first year withdrawal these are often coupled with institutional, social, emotional and personal factors, creating a complex, intricate web.

Some of these factors have been previously identified as possibly contributing to student withdrawal (Mackie, 1998, Ozga, & Sukhnandan, 1997). To some extent we would have expected to have some overlap in findings but other influences appeared to be particular to Middlesex University, and possibly to other modern city-based universities of similar size and socio-geodemographics. These include commuting and self-efficacy beliefs. A significant proportion of our students commute across London and cite the frustration and expense, which, coupled with the timetable issues can often snowball into a major influence for withdrawal. A lack of academic belief or, as Dweck (1999) describes, self-efficacy beliefs, also appeared to be a large influence of our students. This could possibly be due to the students' perception of themselves and/or the institution, with the value of them gaining entry into HE and the institution itself undervalued.

It was clear from the findings that the extent of academic factors is masked within the institutional statistics of withdrawal. Although students expressed academic concerns within the interviews they were less likely to cite academic reasons officially as their primary reason for withdrawal. It appeared that this was due partly to embarrassment at the thought of 'not coping' and partly due to only being able to select one reason for withdrawal, hence the majority of students pulled together their reasons under the umbrella of 'other'. This does little to inform the institution whilst further masking the academic difficulties the students experience.

Issues of support were also heavy influences on departure. The word 'support' was used frequently by students in various contexts but the meanings associated with support tended to range from guidance to mentoring to one to one support. The level of support expected by students and provided by the institution is something that needs to be explicit in order for both parties to be clear about what is expected and required. Coupled with this is the stigma attached to asking for 'support'; some students perceived themselves to be inadequate in coping with the demands of higher education and therefore resisted falling into this category, deferred asking for help and consequently withdrew. This implies that the routes of support need to be more in built so that the perception of 'asking for help' is eliminated.

Some of the issues commented upon by the students, that affected their withdrawal, can be argued to be embedded within the workings of the institution. Widening participation naturally means a considerable increase in difference among the student body but it does not necessarily have to mean a drop in retention. The institutional habitus of the university is therefore a influence in this matter as the ex-Secretary of State for Education indicates: "There is evidence to show that there are unacceptable variations in the rate of 'drop-out' which appear to be linked more to the culture and workings of the institution than to the background or nature of the students recruited" (cited in Thomas, 2002). However, the culture and ethos of Middlesex University has centred on the inclusion of diversity and has embedding this into the institutional culture. Although this institution can clearly be seen to be building a habitus based upon the wider student body, it can be argued the ties and traditions of the higher education sector are within the middle class values and therefore institutions are bound, to some degree, within a larger setting.

This research enforces the notion that retention is not simplistic, or the fault of institution or student alone but is rather a 'reflection of the conditions in which the students find themselves' (Tinto, 2003). Challenges for institutions are therefore to promote university-wide retention thinking, embedded into university culture and curricular without increasing staff workload. Also ensuring internal research is disseminated among university-wide staff members rather than to particular departments to promote a joined up, inter-linking approach to enhancing the student experience. Possibly the greatest action an institution can take is to continue to build on the body of research. As Johnston says, improve retention by design, not by accident (2002).

References

Ballantyne, C (2000) First year students' views of their university experience: Are they glad they came? Presented at *Teaching and Learning Forum 2000*. Available online at http://lsn.curtin.edu.au/tlf/tlf2000/ballantyne.html (Accessed 6 January 2003)

Bennett, R (2003) Determinants of undergraduate student drop out rates in a university Business Studies Department. *Journal of Further and Higher Education*, 27 (2), 123-139.

Cole, M (1997) *Equity and Quality: Improving the Student Learning Experience*. Selected Conference Papers, Denver, Co.

Creswell, JD (2003) *Research Design* (2nd ed). London : Sage

Dweck, CS (1999) *Self-Theories: Their role in motivation, personality and development.* Philadelphia: Psychology Press.

Foster, C et al (2002) Surviving First Year: Access retention and value added. Report on the 2000-01 Pilot. Lifelong Learning Research Group, *Occasional Paper Series*, 1 July 2002.

Johnston, V (2002) Improving student retention – by accident or design. *Exchange* 1, 9-11.

LTSN Briefing Paper, Student Retention. Available online at www.ltsneng.ac.uk/downloads/pdfs/Retention.pdf (Accessed 18 March 2004).

Mackie, S (1998) Jumping The Hurdles. Paper presented at *Higher Education Close Up* Conference, Lancaster University; Department of Education Studies, University of Central Lancashire, 6-8 July 1998.

National Audit Office (NAO) (2002), *Improving student achievement in English higher education.* London: The Stationery Office.

Noble, J and Thomas, L (2004), Leaving Early: Working class students' experience of higher education, presented at *Staying Power* Conference, Teesside University, 6-7 July 2004.

Ozga, J and Sukhnandan, L Undergraduate non-completion. In *Undergraduate non-completion in higher education in England* (Research report 97/29). Bristol, Higher Education Funding Council for England. (1997).

Tinto, V (2003) Promoting Student Retention Through Classroom Practice presented at the *International Student Retention Conference, Enhancing Student retention: Using international research to improve policy and practice*, Amsterdam, 5–7 November 2003.

Thomas, L et al. (2002). *Student Services: Effective Approaches to Retaining Students in Higher Education. Full Research Report.* Institute for Access Studies, Staffordshire University.

Thomas, L (2002) Student retention in higher education: The role of institutional habitus, *Journal of Education Policy*, 17 (4), 423–442.

Walker, L (1999) Longitudinal study of drop-out and continuing students who attended the Pre-University Summer School at the University of Glasgow, *International Journal of Lifelong Education*, 18 (3), 217–233.

Wight, G and Simpson, E (2003) Student Retention and Reasons for Withdrawal presented at the *SHERF Conference* (Scottish Higher Education Retention Forum), 21 March 2003.

Yorke, M (1999) *Leaving Early: Undergraduate non-completion in higher education.* London: Falmer Press.

Yorke, M (2000) The Quality of the Student Experience: what can institutions learn from data relating to non-completion?, *Quality in Higher Education*, 6 (1), 61–75.

Yorke, M (2002) Formative assessment – the key to a richer learning experience in semester one. *Exchange* 1, 12–13.

An investigation of factors which influence the retention and success of undergraduate students in computing science

Pirkko Harvey, Carl Reynolds and Ray Adams

Middlesex University

Abstract

Students reported their perceptions about the issues which influence student retention and success by means of a structured questionnaire which was administered to three cohorts of students. These data have given us some dramatic insights into how our students perceive their critical success factors and suggest new ways in which we can empower our students to achieve success.

Introduction

To better understand the issues which impact on student retention and success, it is vital to consult the students. The strength of this approach is that it allows the participants to have their say without fear or censure. The weaknesses include a dependency upon participants' insight and honesty, and on questionnaire design. Such weaknesses can be ameliorated by follow-on work and use of other methods. The current work is part of an ongoing research project using a variety of methods.

Review

Understanding issues surrounding student retention is becoming increasingly important. According to HEFCE study in 2002, the computing science subject has one of the highest UK dropout rates. Some suggested causes are misconception of what a computing degree entails and poor maths and problem solving skills. Widening participation has increased the pressure to recruit students to popular courses like computing in recent years. Many students come through clearing and do not have a clear idea what to expect of university study or their chosen degree programme. Existing research in retention generally falls into three different categories:

- Taxonomy approach
- Institutional approach
- Single issue approach

Taxonomy approach

The first is classification of withdrawal and this looks to developing taxonomies of "withdrawers". These approaches have identified for example that some withdrawal may be positive and that withdrawal statistics may be misleading. An example of this from Smith and Beggs (2003) challenges retention target setting methods by proposing a new, academically centred paradigm of 'optimum retention' rather than maximum retention. They argue that we should not try to retain students who might be better off elsewhere. The paper also identifies 'low priority of course choice' and work commitments as some of the most likely risk factors for withdrawal.

Institutional approach

Much of the research considers institutional approaches to retention and looks to pastoral care and better information to ensure fewer mismatches between student expectations and the reality of university life. This has been identified as particularly important in the case of computing science (HEFCE 2002). Strategies such as teaching study skills modules have been developed at Middlesex University to assist students in developing required skills. The importance of induction process and the early weeks of student life are acknowledged widely through research.

A holistic approach to student retention is seen as a necessity for the situation to improve (eg Johnston, LTSN). Student retention should not been seen only as the institution's responsibility, but new approaches may be needed in teaching, learning and assessment strategies (Johnston 2002). This is supported by Parmar and Trotter's (2004) project findings, which indicated that teaching was not one of the prime reasons for leaving the university, but was identified as 'an underlying influence'.

Some of the factors Johnston (2003) lists as influencing retention and progression include mode of attendance, hours of employment, hours spent on academic work and the subject of academic study. Johnston also states that "perception of the effect of factors on retention differs from the reality of their effect."

Single issue approach

Some research takes a single possible retention issue and explores it – Johnson's (2002) study highlights the benefits of innovative teaching methods and how these can make a difference in student retention. Students in this study listed 'boredom with the course' and 'failing assessment' as some of the key reasons for leaving. Davies (1999) in a FE study found that students who withdrew were less satisfied with 'teaching quality and support'. Financial and personal problems were often given as reasons for withdrawal but the incidence of problems was no greater in the students who withdrew than in those who were retained.

Our work adopts a different approach as we try to understand factors that enable students to succeed from a lecturer's perspective. Identification of good practices used by successful students might then be propagated. Our concerns focused on issues that we felt were important such as workloads and motivation. This has some parallels with an ongoing study by Roberts et al (2003) that found financial pressures, general discontent and personal reasons as main factors for wanting to leave and career reasons and determination as main factors for staying.

Methods

A questionnaire was designed by the research team and consisted of twenty three questions. Students were informed that the questionnaires were for research purposes only and to improve the student experience. The first questions asked for basic profiling information, including age, gender, year of study, home or international and full or part time. Questions then asked if the student undertook paid work and, if so, the average number of hours worked per week. They were asked to rate the importance of getting a good degree.

Further questions focused upon what, in their view, constituted a good student, actions required for student success, measures of student success, what they needed from the university to be successful, what they would do after graduation and the time they expect to spend on specific activities plus their intended levels of attendance.

The questionnaires were completed by three samples of students: from a first year module (n = 54), a second year module (n=17) and a third year module (n=36), giving an overall sample of 107. The first and third year questionnaires were administered in semester one, and second year questionnaires were administered in semester two. In each case, a lecture was chosen on a quasi-random basis and students present were invited to complete and hand in the questionnaire.

Results

The data were recorded for each group of students on a spreadsheet for cohort-specific analyses and consolidated onto a summary spreadsheet for overall analyses. Cohort One (year one) consisted of 54 students, of which 45 were male, 46 were home students, eight international students and all but one were full time. Their average age was 21.21 years. Cohort Two (year two) comprised 17 students, all but one were second year students (one was a third year student). Cohort Three (year three) included 36 students of which 24 were male, 23 were home students, 13 were international students and 34 were full time.

Reported incidence of paid work

Fifty seven students out of the 107 total reported that they undertook paid work; an overall proportion of just over 53%. Two students did not give an estimate of weekly hours worked; the remaining 55 reported a total of 983 hours per week, giving an average of 17.87 hours per week. Cohort One reported 44% working, Cohort Two reported 53% working and Cohort Three 67% reported working. The observed difference between Cohorts One and Two did not reach statistical significance (t=1.52 on 69 df), whilst the comparison between Cohorts Two and Three did (t=3.60 on 51 df, p<0.01 two tailed). These results are consistent with the view that the proportion of working students increases over their time spent at university. Even when each cohort is considered individually, this overall level contrasts with the figure of 27% of working students as reported by Hill in the *Times Higher* August 6, 2004. However, this latter figure was based upon panel data from both new and old universities.

Within our averages, there is a considerable range of hours reported. Overall, the minimum reported was two hours, whilst the maximum was 50 hours. For Cohort One, the minimum was eight and the maximum was 36. For this group, 44% worked an average of 16.65 hours per week. For Cohort Two, the minimum was nine and the maximum was 50. For this group, 53% worked an average of 23.27 hours per week. For Cohort Three, the minimum was two and the maximum was 40. For this group, 67% worked an average of 17.00 hours per week. Whilst the hours worked seemed relatively stable across groups (Cohort Two had a smaller sample size, which may have produced a slightly noisier, higher estimate), they are higher than we would have expected. Clearly, some students are working unrealistically high hours.

Perceived critical success factors: a good student?

Each of the following analyses relies on student self-report. To avoid repetition, the word "reported" has been omitted from each of the following titles, though it should be assumed unless stated otherwise. This next question asked our students to say what constituted a good student, voting for one or more options from a supplied list of eight items. The observed voting levels differed significantly from each other, as measured by a chi-squared test (X^2 (7 df) = 16.21, p < 0.05, two tailed). They selected "well motivated" as their first choice (78 votes), followed by "active in team work" (66 votes), "shows initiative" (65 votes) and prepares well for class (63 votes). Less popular options were "proactive in class" (41 votes), "disciplined" (55 votes), "honest" (52 votes) and "has an excellent attendance record" (49 votes).

Perceived critical success factors: important to achieve the desired degree?

The next question (Q13) asked how students would rate a list of nine actions, in terms of their importance for them to achieve their desired degree. Students rated their agreement with each factor on a four point scale. To encourage careful attention, one of the items was phrased in the negative voice. The ratings were converted to points as a basis for analysis, the lower the points the better the agreement. Chi-squared analysis showed a very highly significant differentiation between the nine options to be rated, with $X^2 =$ 138.12, df=8, p $\leq$0.001 two tailed.

"Revising well in advance for examinations" (133 points) received best levels of agreement, followed by "managing your time" (137 points), "working very hard on all assignments" (148 points) and "preparing well for all classes" (169 points).

The following were rated as less important: "making good use of computing facilities" (182 points), "good attendance" (189 points), "getting to know fellow students on my course" (191 points) and "making good use of library facilities in the University" (196 points). Whilst all of the above items provoked general agreement, "never to go out socialising during the semester" (322 points) produced disagreement. This suggests that the options were read carefully.

Perceived critical success factors: measuring your success?

The next question (Q14) asked how students would measure their success by selecting one or more measures from a set of five. Few students selected more than two measures. The number of votes per measure differed very significantly from each other, such that $X^2 = 22.44$, df = 4, p < 0.01 two tailed. The most popular measure was "gaining new knowledge and skills" (41 votes), followed by "passing all assessment tasks with excellent grades" (25 votes), "obtaining a job" (19 votes), "passing most assessment tasks" (15 votes and finally "developing new friendships and contacts" (13 votes).

Perceived critical success factors: importance of types of student support?

The next question (Q15) asked how students felt about the importance of the different types of support received from the university. As for question thirteen, student ratings of agreement were converted into points, fewer points again indicating more agreement. The points distinguished between the options very significantly $X^2 =24.87$, df = 8, p<0.005, though the degree of discrimination seemed to be less than for question thirteen. Good quality teaching was agreed to be the most important, even though good attendance was not seen as a top priority in previous questions. The next most important was "having access to academic advice" followed by "good quality computing and library resources are important". As in question thirteen, library and computing resources are said to be less important whilst preparation and time management are rated higher. Other support services are rated less important.

Perceived critical success factors: what do you hope to do after graduation?

The next question (Q15) asked how students about their post graduation ambitions. The votes cast did discriminate significantly between the six options, giving $X^2 = 96.01$, df = 5, p < 0.005. Finding a job was the number one hope (66 votes), though it is not necessarily seen as the main measure of student success in question fourteen. However, an appreciable number of votes were cast for "continue studying to Master's level", 46 (votes). The remaining options, "continue studying to PhD level", "take some time off", "travel" and "do voluntary work" received only a few votes.

Intended effort and attendance

The remaining questions enquired about the hours of work that they intended to put in, as well as the intended levels of attendance. Self study came first (10.87 hours minimum), with the university computing centre next (5.47 minimum), university library (3.57 minimum) and group work (3.44 hours). Expected attendance levels were over 90%.

Discussion

The findings are supported by statistically significant differences in the data based upon chi-squared and t-test (for proportions) procedures. Students took care to notice the direction of the rating scales, responding appropriately when a scale was expressed negatively. It was also clear that this was a subject that was important to them, since they described the importance of gaining a good degree to be near to the maximum (4.62) on a five point scale. On the negative side, intentions about attendance seemed unrealistically high (93% to 96%) and should be born in mind when interpreting these data.

The high levels of paid work reported above were surprising, as was the trend for the number of working students to increase from year one to year three. It was also clear that a minority of students were taking on very long hours of paid work. Figures of 36, 40 and even 50 hours per week were cited by the students themselves; there is no reason to suspect exaggeration. Whilst some students are working unrealistically high hours, others were more restrained. If we cannot expect students to give up paid work, then the solution may be to foster better time management skills. Some students seem to do well despite their work commitments; others seem to do worse than average

Exploration of the students' perceived critical success factors reveals some interesting findings. They recognise the value of personal qualities like good motivation, preparation and initiative. The item "prepares well for class" seems less likely given that they do not expect to spend much of their time in group work (approximately three and a half hours minimum). However, other personal qualities like; "proactive in class", "disciplined" and "honest" were less popular.

In terms of what was important for them to do to achieve their desired degree "revising well in advance for examinations" and good time management were rated most highly, followed by "working very hard on all assignments" and "preparing well for all classes". Curiously, making use of computing and library facilities were seen as of lesser importance. "Good attendance" and "getting to know fellow students on my course" were also rated low. Though our students disagreed with the view that they should "never to go out socialising during the semester", there is no indication that they would socialise with fellow students.

In today's work oriented society, we might have expected our students to place getting a job ahead of other measures of success, we found that the two most popular measures were "gaining new knowledge and skills", and "passing all assessment tasks with excellent grades". "Obtaining a job" came third. Again socialising with peers was rated highly if the relatively low votes for "developing new friendships and contacts" is any indicator. Perhaps this lack of emphasis upon socialising at university reflects the growing tendency for students to be drawn from the London area, where they already have an established social life.

Turning to the question of the importance of the different types of support received from the university, the students focused strongly on good quality teaching and having access to academic advice. This was so even though attendance at lectures was not rated highest. Library and computing resources are said to be less important, though we would have expected them to be seen as crucial to success. Academic support services and counselling services were rated lower. It may be that such services are seen as important only when a student recognises a personal need for them. If so, then there may be some work to be done to raise student awareness without raising stress levels.

Building upon the points that our students see as important – self-motivation, time management and quality of teaching – each of these salient features suggests new strategies with which to facilitate student performance within the context of paid working. Conversely, students gave only modest support for good attendance and socialisation at university. Here, too, new strategies might help them achieve more. Despite the students' awareness of the importance of self-motivation and time management, it is vital to note that they still feel that the quality of the teaching is number one!

References

Davies, P (1999) Student retention in further education: a problem of quality or of student finance? Paper presented at the British Educational Research Association Annual Conference, University of Sussex at Brighton.

HEFCE Circular 2002/52 – Performance Indicators in Higher Education www.hefce.ac.uk/Learning/perfind/2002/

Hill, P The Times Higher Education Supplement, *A Post-Blair generation*, 06/08/04

Johnson, J (2002) Coventry University , Student retention in higher education, 4th Annual LILI Conference, Coventry TechnoCentre, 11 January www.ukcle.ac.uk/lili//2002/johnson.html

Johnston, V (2002) Improving Student Retention – by accident or by design? *Exchange* Issue 1 Spring

Johnston, V (2003) The First Ten Years, The Napier University Student Retention Project

LTSN Student Retention, Briefing Paper (from Information and Computer Sciences) www.ics.ltsn.ac.uk/resources/student_retention/#government (02/08/04)

Parmar, D and Trotter, E, Keeping our Students: Identifying factors that influence student withdrawal and strategies to enhance the first year experience and retention (paper in print)

Roberts, C, Watkin, M, Oakey, D, Fox, R (2003) Supporting Student 'Success': What can we Learn from the Persisters? Briefing paper available from www.ltsn.ac.uk

Smith, E and Beggs, B (2003) A new paradigm for maximising student retention in higher education, IEE Engineering Education Conference, Southampton

Academic needs and academic support for students on sub-degree programmes

Alan Page, Jenny Jacobs and Charles Seechurn,

Middlesex University, London

Abstract

The topic of student attrition and low progression rates is a continuing subject of debate. This paper reports an evaluation of student needs and perceptions on entering the early stages of study on sub-degree programmes. The research was carried out through the operation of a focus group with students and one to one interviews with programme leaders. Interestingly, the students were able to indicate the first semester as crucial to success and highlighted the importance of gaining confidence through success. Tutors identified that methods of previous learning, particularly for those students exiting from FE institutions, discourage deep learning and university-level writing skills. In response, the team have introduced a range of support mechanisms such as reflective formative assessment, comprehensive module readers, increased use of problem based learning and home groups.

Purpose of study

This paper explores the changes in practice that have occurred within the Public Health, Risk and Safety Curriculum Group, at Middlesex University over the past three years to support students on sub-degree programmes. The group offer a range of exit awards: Certificate of Higher Education, professional awards at sub-degree level, BScs and masters awards.

At the commencement of the 2000/1 academic year the team operated a part-time HNC and HND in Environmental Health and a full-time Foundation Certificate in Biological and Environmental Sciences. Evidence suggested that there was a significant attrition rate within the first semester, when compared to similar degree programmes running in parallel, and that completion and progression rates to further studies were poor. In 2000/1, the progression rate on the HNC and HND at the end of year one was 50% and 80% respectively. Completion rate on the Foundation Certificate was just 60%. The teaching team therefore sought to review student feeling towards their programme and to evidence what further support could be offered to such students on commencement and during their programme to encourage a greater degree of success.

Background

Student retention and attrition has been widely researched both in further and higher education in the UK (McSherry and Marland, 1999; Maguire 2001; Smith and Naylor, 2001) and internationally, with significant levels of research conducted in the United States and Canada (Chaney et al, 1998; Mohr, Eiche and Sedlacek, 1998). Many have tried to establish models for persistence and attrition on programmes, most notably Tinto, whose model has been used in subsequent studies (Napoli and Wortman, 1998).

Experience suggests that there is a divide in learner expectation and that of an education establishment's provision. Many higher education institutions encourage student centred learning, with the implicit skills in self-management and independence. It does however have to be recognised that many students entering higher education have been educated under a very different educational paradigm. Thus for many there is an expectation of a learning continuum with a desire for similar educational delivery.

Taylor (2000) does suggest that the transition from secondary to tertiary education, and through it an alteration in learning process, involves a considerable risk of alienation and withdrawal from the university. Many universities have implemented induction programmes to ease the transition to tertiary education (Edward and Middleton 2002).

Previous research has highlighted the importance of intrinsic and extrinsic learning needs (Ramsden 1992, Taylor and Bedford 2004), preconceptions of the programme of study and the practice associated with it (Spouse 2000), views on future career prospects (Sandler 2000) and organisation of the programme and inter-relationship with academic staff (Tinto 1997, 1998; Mohr, Eiche and Sedlacek, 1998; Taylor and Bedford 2004) as major influences on retention to programmes of study. As such, these factors were explored within this study along with past educational experiences.

Methodology

Focus groups were conducted with eight students from five cohorts on three programmes – HNC and HND in Environmental Health and a Foundation Certificate in Biological and Environmental Sciences – during the 2001/2 academic year. The Foundation Certificate and first year of HND share modules whilst the HNC and HND have three modules in common in year two.

A series of framework questions were utilised for the focus group participants. In order to establish the suitability of the questions, a pilot study had been conducted during the previous semester using one to one cognitive interviews with students on the programmes. In addition a post interview was conducted with the respondents to elicit views on the content and conduct of the interview (Czaja and Blair 1996).

The first two questions aimed to establish the students' past educational experiences and in particular the potential impact this may have had on the student's perception on entry and motivation to succeed. Questions 3-5 sought information about the students' reasons for studying the programme (own choice, employer, peer or family pressure) and success of gaining the programme of choice. A further three questions sought to determine the students' perceptions of the programme, organisation, content, delivery and support mechanisms. The final question was open to enable students to discuss any other points that had not been pursued. Students' comments were recorded verbatim. Confidentiality was emphasised through all stages.

One to one non-structured interviews were conducted with the two tutors who managed the programmes to elicit their views on issues that prevent successful student completion. Themes raised in the student focus groups were also explored with the programme leaders to ensure continuity of the study.

Results

The group were heterogeneous in make up with an equal gender split, a wide age profile and part time and full time student participants. Past educational attainment ranged from one A-level to first degree.

A number of themes developed through the discussions including anxiety on entry, expectation levels, volume and pace of work and support offered to students.

Past educational experiences and expectations of university level studies

Past performance raised personal concerns regarding the student's belief in their ability to undertake university level study. All but one student reported that their past educational experience had not been a great success and there were some worries on entering university about the level of study required and what would be expected of them in terms of study:

> *"I was really worried about coming to university from college. I knew it would be a big jump and when the assignments were set I was overwhelmed. There was a fear factor... am I doing it right?"*

> *"I have been out of education for 10 years and all things I learnt to do in the past were rusty."*

> *"I never saw myself coming to university as I never did well at school. It is just that my employer wanted me to come to do this course."*

> *"It really is important to know what is expected of you. I didn't do well at school because I did not know what was expected and university is an even higher standard."*

Pace, volume and assessment

It emerged that students are overwhelmed particularly in the early weeks of semester one with respect to the volume and pace of work:

"BIO 1014 (Introductory Science for HNC students) was set at a very high level… it was a bit frightening and I think a lot of people left because this was our first module and was so packed with information"

"I felt that there is a lot crammed into 12 weeks. Sometimes it is difficult to take it all in and if you have three modules to do it is just too much. Afterwards I feel that I have not remembered anything and then you move onto more modules."

"With three modules to read up on, it is often difficult to read for them all. You just try to keep up and cope."

There was some debate on the practice of providing assignments at the beginning of the semester:

"Having the essay at the beginning is good. You might not look at it but you know it is there."

"At least having the assignment in week one means that you have the whole semester to do it."

"But you don't know anything until week four. I have tried to read around the subject but you just don't know what is important and how up to date it is and if this is what the lecturer wants."

"Having all the assessment at the end does not tell us if we are doing all right… I panicked at the end of the semester and almost did not bother to turn up as I thought I would not do well."

"The topic in the assignment should be covered early. Sometimes you start the essay and then in week eight or nine, you find that they cover the topic and you got it all wrong… You just feel that you might as well wait till the end to see the stuff is covered."

Levels of support

Students felt fully supported by the programme team in terms of general and specific guidance offered, availability and responsiveness.

However, three key issues relating to support were identified. The students requested a range of additional material to support them with their assignments, including graded essays, (good and bad), and copies of past examinations papers with model answers. Second, the students reported that there was a lack of communication between the employer and the university. Finally, the students on the HND programme pointed to the need for more environmental health examples within the teaching and more frequent field visits.

The mechanism and timing of support for assessment was also identified as crucial.

"Provide a graded essay in handbook, and someone to talk through it. Essays create a fear factor... am I doing it right, particularly in the first semester. I think this is why people left because they were frightened off."

"The how to do assignments is done inside the lectures when bombarded with knowledge matter."

"If they went through a graded essay, then we would know what is expected of us."

"Same for exams, sometimes you just don't know much stuff to write and it is really stressful."

Programme leaders' responses

Comments from programme leaders clearly highlight that there is a difference in expectation level between the students and the university. Tutors recognised the difficulties encountered for many of the students undertaking assessment at the university but having entered with different prior assessment experiences:

"In general some of the students are really good, but most have just scraped through in the past and do not have all of skills to get into a subject in depth. Also the speed at which we work in modules often overwhelms these students and in the first semester they get discouraged."

"Their expectation levels are also different to what we require at HE level. Very often they have been doing short answer, breadth of topic type questions, rather than doing any essays in depth and so struggle when it comes to our assignments and the examinations. They often hand in a couple of pages and then challenge us when they don't pass. Even when we go through it they don't seem to understand the issues around depth of argument and this is probably a result of the way in which they have come through the education system."

"Assessment is also an issue. Most of these students have come from modular awards with lots of in-course assessment, so they know how well they are doing almost from the start. Most of the university modules have end of module assessment so these students look at all of the material they need to know and panic. Additionally they often feel that a one page examination answer is adequate."

Staff did not perceive it to be beneficial to provide a range of graded essays/examinations – an issue raised in the focus group. It was felt that this would not facilitate the development of generic skills required at different levels.

There was final comment about the lack of uptake of tutorial support and other feedback mechanisms:

"Despite the tutorial support offered for students to go through their work, few take the opportunity. Students do not use their feedback forms and are more concerned with passing than learning."

Discussion

There remains for many of our students a significant fear factor involved in attending university in the first semester, and students felt that this influenced the students who left the programmes. Many students were overwhelmed by the initial weeks of the programme. The pace and volume of work together with having the assignments handed to them in week one compounded their fears.

It is clear that many of these students lacked confidence on entering university and that they need significant encouragement in order to remain on the programmes. One particular module, Orientation Studies, enables the students to obtain certificates, externally verified and useful in the outside world. The students on the Foundation Certificate and HND programmes highlighted the importance of gaining confidence through success and reported very favourably with regard to Orientation Studies. The students commented strongly on the need for feedback during the semester on all modules rather than an emphasis on end assessment.

The students perceived the inter-relationship between employers and the university as weak. Programme leaders reinforced this view. There is a need to ensure that curricula relate the content to practice to ground the theory – whilst this is common practice it is clear that this must continue throughout the programme and within each module.

The tutors felt that with students on these programmes, dedicated time for tutorials was a beneficial input that significantly assisted the inter-relationship between the tutors and the students. The team operated a tutorial system in which the content of the tutorial is recorded and placed on the student file. This system creates an empowering environment, where the students feel that they are valued and can express personal concerns and difficulties on a one to one basis.

In response to the findings a number of initiatives have been implemented at programme level. These together with initiatives implemented at university level are changing the first year experience for students on these and similar programmes. The outcome of this change in practice is that performance of all the students has increased significantly with improved rates of retention and progression. The developments are summarised below:

- University-wide introduction of a reality check during week four to enable students to reflect on their learning.

- University-wide introduction of OASIS (WebCT) an online learning support for students. This has improved communications and support at programme level especially for part-time day release students through the use of discussion boards, information postings and establishment of home groups.

- Increased use of formative assessment at level one where students have two pieces of work returned within one week of submission date. This does however put additional loading on programme teams.

- Utilisation of OASIS for formative assessment in form of feedback quizzes and assessments.

- Improved communication between employers and the programme team is being sought. Employers are invited annually to the university to consider issues with programme teams about placement, mentoring, workload for students and outcomes.

- Module schedule now shows when assignment and examination papers will be reviewed.

- Organisation of seminars within some modules such as study skills by cohort.

- Review of teaching and learning strategies to include comprehensive readers available both in hard and electronic copy and problem based learning exercises.

References

Chaney, B, Muraskin, LD, Cahalan, MW and Goodwin, D (1998). Helping The Progress Of Disadvantaged Students In Higher Education: The Federal Student Support Services Program. *Educational Evaluation And Policy Analysis* 20 (3) pp197-215

Czaja, R and Blair, J (1996), *Designing Surveys: A Guide to Decisions and Procedures*, Thousand Oaks, CA: Pine Forge Press.

Edward, N and Middleton, J (2002). The Challenge Of Induction! Introducing Engineering Students To Higher Education: A Task-Oriented Approach. Innovations. *Education And Training International* 39 (1) pp46-53

McSherry, W and Marland, GR (1999). Student Discontinuations: Is The System Failing? Nurse *Education Today* 19 (7) pp578-585

Maguire, S (2001). Teaching Geography To Non-Traditional Students: Inducting, Nurturing And Retaining Them. *Journal of Geography in Higher Education* 25 (2) pp233-240

Mohr, JJ, Eiche, KD and Sedlacek, WE (1998). So Close, Yet So Far: Predictors Of Attrition In College Seniors. *Journal Of College Student Development* 39 (4) pp343-354

Napoli, AR and Wortman, PM (1998). Psychosocial Factors Related To Retention And Early Departure Of Two-Year Community College Students. *Research In Higher Education* 39 (4) pp419-455

Sandler, M.E. (2000). Career Decision-Making Self-Efficacy, Perceived Stress, And An Integrated Model Of Student Persistence: A Structural Model Of Finances, Attitudes, Behaviour, And Career Development. *Research In Higher Education* 41 (5) pp537-580

Smith, JP and Naylor, RA (2001) Dropping Out Of University: A Statistical Analysis of the Probability of Withdrawal for UK University Students. *Journal Of The Royal Statistical Society Series A (Statistics In Society)* 164 (2) pp389-405

Spouse, J, (2000) An Impossible Dream? Images Of Nursing Held By Pre-Registration Students And Their Effect On Sustaining Motivation To Become Nurses. *Journal Of Advanced Nursing* 32 (3) pp730-739

Tinto, V, (1997). Classrooms As Communities – Exploring The Educational Character Of Student Persistence. *Journal Of Higher Education* 68 (6) p599-623

Tinto, V, (1998). Colleges As Communities: Taking Research On Student Persistence Seriously. *Review Of Higher Education* 21 (2) pp167-177

Taylor, JA and Bedford, T (2004) Staff perceptions of factors related to non-completion in higher education. *Studies in Higher Education* 29 (3) pp375-394.

Studying the impact of assessment on student learning in physical science and bioscience courses.

Overview: Stephen Swithenby (Convenor)

Universities that seek to improve the inclusivity of their programmes and to increase the diversity of their student body are often faced with increased challenges in the retention of students. Although some of the factors influencing retention are out of the control of the teacher, performance and achievement are highly relevant. There are abundant examples of the relevance of assessment and feedback on the way that people learn and achieve (eg Black and Wiliam 1998, Hattie 1987).

These papers analyse experiences in the development of assessment that supports student learning. They rely on a conceptual framework presented by Gibbs and Simpson at the 2003 ISL symposium concerning eleven conditions under which assessment supports learning. The studies were carried out at the Open University and Sheffield Hallam University, both of which have highly diverse student populations, within the context of the 'Formative Assessment for Science Teaching' project supported by the Fund for the Development of Teaching and Learning.

The Gibbs and Simpson framework, which is compatible with both constructivist and transmission perspectives of learning, is based on the impact of assessment on:

- the quantity and distribution of student effort
- the quality and level of student effort
- the quantity and timing of feedback
- the quality of feedback
- the student's response to feedback.

These could be further summarised within the key themes of engagement and feedback as highlighted by Black and Wiliam and Hattie respectively. The individual conditions are discussed extensively in Gibbs and Simpson (2004).

The diagnosis of potential learning problems with assessment on a range of science courses in the two universities has involved three stages; exploratory open ended interviews, the use of an Assessment Experience Questionnaire (Gibbs et al 2003), and diagnostic follow-up of issues linked to elements of the framework using more specialised tools. Diagnosis feeds into a quality enhancement cycle of change to the teaching strategy and evaluation using the same tools. The overall methodology involves two cycles of evaluation and change in a total of 15 science courses at the two universities.

Initial analysis and findings revealed several issues, three of which are developed in the symposium papers. The first involves a mismatch between staff and student perceptions of feedback and the use to which it is put. The second again deals with perceptions but this time of written feedback on assignments. The third study relates to both the rapidity of feedback and engagement with it, in this case within the context of online assignments. In each case the framework provides a means of sharpening practitioner analysis as a prelude to the optimisation of the applied teaching strategies.

Acknowledgements

The authors would like to thank Graham Gibbs, Laura Hills, and Claire Simpson for many useful discussions.

References

Black, P and Wiliam, D (1998) Assessment and classroom learning. *Assessment in Education*, 5(1), pp7-74.

Gibbs, G and Simpson, C (2004) Does your assessment support your students' learning? *Journal of Teaching and Learning in Higher Education*, 1 (1) In Press

Gibbs, G, Simpson, C and Macdonald, R "Improving student learning through changing assessment – a conceptual and practical framework" *European Association for Research into Learning and Instruction, 2003, Padua, Italy*. Available on http://www.open.ac.uk/science/fdtl/documents/earli-2003.pdf

Hattie, JA (1987) Identifying the salient facets of a model of student learning: a synthesis of meta-analyses. *International Journal of Educational Research*, 11, pp187-212.

Evaluating the effectiveness of written feedback as an element of formative assessment in science

Evelyn Brown, Chris Glover*, Stuart Freake and Valda Stevens

Open University (*Sheffield Hallam University)

Abstract

A study at the Open University and Sheffield Hallam University has investigated the timeliness, quantity and quality of the written feedback that students receive on their assignments and the subsequent use they make of that feedback, within a framework of conditions under which assessment is believed to support students' learning. Students' general views of feedback were elicited through an Assessment Experience Questionnaire (AEQ). A smaller cohort of students was interviewed by telephone to explore their perceptions of the written feedback they had received and the formative use they made of it. The feedback was analysed using a coding system. This analysis is used to suggest explanations of students' responses to the feedback and to shed light on some discrepancies between students' general perceptions of the timeliness and value of the feedback and the specific uses they make of it.

Introduction

This paper reports on work carried out mainly at the Open University (OU) as part of the 'Formative Assessment in Science Teaching' (FAST) project at the OU and Sheffield Hallam University (SHU), The paper focuses on how OU distance-learning science students' perceptions and formative uses of the written feedback they receive on their coursework assessment may be explained by analysing this feedback.

OU assignments are assessed by a team of part-time tutors. Each tutor works with a group of about 20 students and is guided by a common mark scheme and accompanying notes to ensure parity of grading. Written feedback on assignments is the only source of feedback most students receive on their performance and progress and so tutors are expected to spend, on average, one hour per script grading the work and giving feedback. The feedback is provided as detailed comments within the students' scripts and as summaries of performance and marks lost on the accompanying cover sheets. In some instances tutors also provide students with specimen answers that have been produced by the assignment authors. The tutors are expected to return the assessed assignments within three weeks of receiving them.

The work has been undertaken in relation to the conditions under which feedback on assessment is believed to support students' learning (Gibbs and Simpson, 2004).

Quantity and timing of feedback

- Sufficient feedback is provided, both often enough and in enough detail
- The feedback is provided quickly enough to be useful to students

Quality of feedback

- Feedback focuses on learning rather than marks or students themselves
- Feedback is linked to the purpose of the assignment and to criteria
- Feedback is understandable to students, given their sophistication

Student response to feedback

- Feedback is received by students and attended to
- Feedback is acted upon by students to improve their work or learning.

Methodology

An initial evaluation of the extent to which the students' written feedback satisfies the conditions described above was effected at the end of the 2002 OU academic year using an Assessment Experience Questionnaire (AEQ) (Gibbs et al, 2003), administered to 1,050 students across six modules spanning physics, astronomy, chemistry and bioscience at UK higher education levels one to three. The questions elicited students' general perceptions of the quantity, quality and timeliness of the written feedback they received, and the use they made of it. A total of 498 responses were received and areas of less effective aspects of feedback were identified.

Subsequently a further 112 students from the 2003 student cohort studying on the same modules were interviewed by telephone to probe these areas further in relation to the feedback on a specific assignment that had been returned to them. The interviews were conducted by tutors who had tutored each of them. Prior to the interviews the tutors also analysed the feedback on copies of the students' returned assignment using a code for types of feedback that relates to the framework conditions described above (Brown et al, 2003).

Hyland (2001) appears to have made the only previous attempt to quantitatively analyse or code the *written* feedback that tutors provide on distance learners' assignments . The categories of feedback devised by Hyland were designed specifically for language learning. Although there are some similarities with the learning experience of science students, the categorisation is insufficiently focused on the content of students' work to discriminate between the different types of feedback on science modules. It also fails to distinguish between the feed *forward* and feed *back* aspect of tutors' comments, and the distinction between justifying a grade given and explaining the misunderstandings/errors and omissions that led to this grade. These aspects are crucial to the learning process.

Bales (1950) devised a system of interaction process analysis to classify the acts that take place in small face-to-face groups. Although the system is potentially transferable to written feedback, the weaknesses with respect to use with science students are similar to those in the system used by Hyland.

In the current study the degree of explanation afforded by feedback (in its general sense) was also analysed. Three levels of explanation were distinguished. These correspond broadly to the three levels of marking identified by Jarvis (1978). Our level one involves an acknowledgement in some way that an error/weakness has been demonstrated (Jarvis – marking as a means of assessment). Level two illustrates a correct or appropriate expected answer (Jarvis – marking as a means of communicating knowledge). Level three explains either why the student's own answer was incorrect or inappropriate or why the preferred/specimen answer was (more) appropriate (Jarvis – marking as a way of facilitating learning).

Table one opposite shows the categories of feedback used in the coding system of the current study, the degrees of explanation that each involved, and the relationship of these categories to the feedback conditions of Gibbs and Simpson (2004). Note that any one feedback statement by a tutor may contain more than one type of intervention and thus be assigned more than one code. For example, a tutor may acknowledge and correct a factual error (E2) using negative words or phrases (An). Similarly a tutor may comment on irrelevant material (I) included in an answer, that is also erroneous (E).

Results of the evaluation

The Assessment Experience Questionnaire

The responses to the AEQ suggested that, in general, the students were satisfied with the quantity and timing of the feedback they received and felt that it aided their understanding of both their marks and the material that was being assessed. There was no evidence to suggest that the provision of more feedback would enhance learning for most of the students. Most students claimed to read their tutor's feedback (ie the feedback was attended to) but, while satisfied with the feed *back* aspects, they were less satisfied with the feed *forward* potential of their tutors' comments, ie its ability to help them with subsequent assessment tasks. The feedback did not appear to encourage further learning to any large extent for most students, eg by prompting them to re-visit material covered earlier in the module. Some students appeared not to understand the feedback and others were ambivalent about their understanding.

Code	Type of comment	Level of explanation	Feed back/ feed forward	Feedback conditions of Gibbs & Simpson, 2004
Content of student's response				
E	Error/misconception	1, 2, 3	Feed back	Feedback is timely, understandable, linked to purpose of assignment, received by students and attended to, and used to improve their work/learning (where relevant)
O	Omission of relevant material		Feed forward (if relevant to future assessment tasks)	
I	Inclusion of irrelevant material	1, 3		
C	Clarification – of a point made by student			
Comments designed to develop students' skills				
Sm	Mathematical	1, 2, 3	Feed forward	Feedback is acted upon by students to improve work
Sc	Communication			
Se	Use of English			
Sd	Graphs/use of diagrams			
Qualitative assessment of student's achievement				
Ap	Praise for achievement	1, 3	Feed back	Feedback is received by students, attended to and acted upon to improve work/learning
Ae	Encouragement about performance			
An	Use of negative words/phrases (eg 'not', 'never')	Not applicable		Feedback may result in students not attending to or using it
Ac	Negative criticism of student's performance (eg 'careless')			
Am	Marks set in peer group context	Not applicable	Feed back	
Comments that encourage further learning				
R	Refers student to source materials	1, 2, 3*	Feed back or feed forward	Feedback is acted upon to improve work/learning
D	Encourages reflective dialogue with student through questions			
F	Refers student to a future assessment task	1, 2, 3*	Feed forward	

Table 1 The categories of written feedback and their relationship to the framework feedback conditions

*Level of detail is relevant in these categories, rather than level of explanation.

Student interviews

The student interviews confirmed the findings of earlier workers that students tend to be mark focused (eg Brown et al, 1996, Elton and Laurillard, 1979). Nearly all stated that their first priority was to look at the mark and their next priority was to read the summary of their performance on the cover sheet. Most also claimed to read the detailed comments on their scripts at some time but their priority in this activity was to determine where they had 'gone wrong' and then where they had lost marks. Marks are a means of identifying areas of weakness, rather than strength, ie students have a negative view of their learning and achievement. For many students the identification of a weakness was a signal to avoid the weak area in the end-of-course examination, rather than using the feedback to improve their understanding and learning. Most of the students felt that they had been given sufficient feedback to help them understand their mark losses.

Praise, encouragement, a summary of strengths and weaknesses and pointers to where the weaknesses had occurred were deemed the most useful feedback on the cover sheets. However, on their assignment scripts students found detailed comments that identified specific mark loss, distinguishing between error, omission and clarification, and that provided constructive correction, to be the most helpful, consistent with the findings of Roberts (1996). The need to link these comments to improving or expanding on previous understanding, explaining what would have been an appropriate answer or showing why a student's answer was wrong, was evident from the interviews across all modules.

Specimen answers, where provided, were valued least, mainly because they do not relate specifically to a student's own answer. Self-esteem generated by praise, encouragement and a positive tone to the comments were judged important motivators by about a third of the students. For many of the remaining students good marks were more important. Few students deemed skills feedback to be more helpful than feedback on the science content, with the exception of the level one students where there was a 50:50 split.

The majority of the students felt that the feedback they received on one assignment was of little or no use in helping them with the next assignment because the topics assessed had changed. However, many recognised that skills feedback was helpful to subsequent assignments.

Feedback analysis

In total, 4,428 interventions were recorded on the 112 OU science students' assignments, 844 on the cover sheets and 3,584 on the scripts, an average of 40 interventions per script. A random selection of 35 assignments from SHU students studying a comparable range of science courses was also analysed, primarily to test the applicability of the coding system. In contrast to the OU assignments, 577 interventions were recorded, an average of 16 interventions per script. This difference is to be expected as SHU students are exposed to a wide variety of other forms of feedback (see Glover et al, this volume). So far we have found no evidence at either the OU or SHU to support the notion that poorer work receives a greater amount and better quality of feedback than good work (see eg Mutch, 2003). However, the analysis of feedback from OU students' scripts revealed wide variation in the amount of feedback provided by different tutors for scripts receiving similar scores.

Over half the script interventions by both OU and SHU tutors were concerned with the science content, with far smaller proportions devoted to skills development and praise or encouragement (figure one). Interventions designed to encourage further learning were

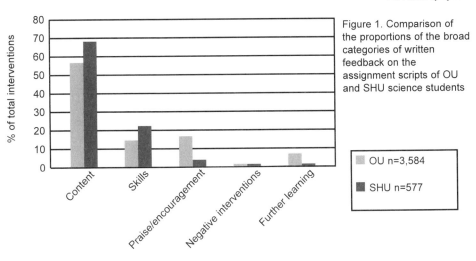

Figure 1. Comparison of the proportions of the broad categories of written feedback on the assignment scripts of OU and SHU science students

comparatively rare, as were the use of negative words and phrases and negative criticism. On the assignment cover sheets, there were higher proportions of interventions relating to praise and encouragement, and to further learning, and a smaller proportion relating to science content (figure two). Many of the cover-sheet comments were marks-focused with phrases such as 'you lost marks because…' being fairly universal but the number of instances where a student's marks were set in the context of the peer group was negligible. The proportion of interventions relating to skills development was similar for assignments and cover sheets.

A more detailed analysis of the interventions relating to science content revealed some differences between the tutors at the two institutions (figure three). The proportion of interventions relating to clarification of students' answers was much higher for SHU students (40%) than for OU students (14%). Over 60% of these interventions from SHU tutors asked students to clarify their answers, rather than providing the clarification,

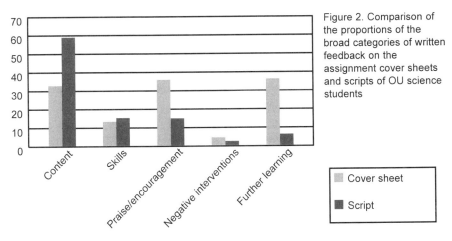

Figure 2. Comparison of the proportions of the broad categories of written feedback on the assignment cover sheets and scripts of OU science students

mostly as rhetorical questions and it was unclear to students how they should act on the feedback. This form of request was rarely used by OU tutors, perhaps because of the more limited opportunities for tutor contact should students have difficulty in complying.

Content feedback was omissions-focused with a similar overall ratio of content omission interventions to error interventions at both institutions (2.4 for the OU, 2.3 for SHU). However there was considerable variation in these ratios among the types of assignments that were set, as high as 5.0 or 6.0 for assignments dominated by discursive questions. The lowest ratio (0.4) occurred in a physics assignment in which there were several calculations.

Analysis of the degree of explanation provided by feedback to OU science students (figure three) revealed that relatively little is at level three, ie explanation of either why the student's own answer was incorrect or inappropriate or why the preferred/specimen answer was (more) appropriate, so the bridge of understanding was rarely built. A similar picture is beginning to emerge from the type of written feedback provided to SHU students. However, exceptionally, level three feedback dominated the feedback on an assignment from one of the OU bioscience modules. The questions in this assignment contained a high proportion of tasks involving explanation or data interpretation, which prompted tutors to provide additional explanation in their feedback.

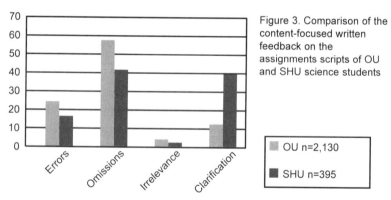

Figure 3. Comparison of the content-focused written feedback on the assignments scripts of OU and SHU science students

Specimen answers were provided by the assignment authors for five of the six OU modules. Seventy-three students out of a potential 97 (75%) received all or part (at need) of the specimen answers. Of these, only eight contained major annotations (explanatory comment) by the tutor with a further 16 containing minor annotations (underlining, sidelining or use of highlighter pen).

Discussion

Although the discussion in this paper focuses mainly on the evaluation of the written feedback provided to the distance-learning OU students, ongoing work at SHU suggests that it is likely to be equally relevant to the written feedback provided to campus-based students.

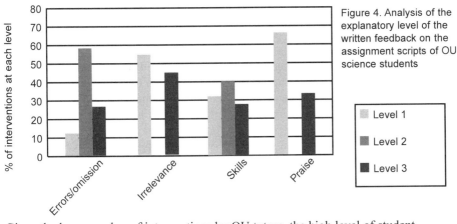

Figure 4. Analysis of the explanatory level of the written feedback on the assignment scripts of OU science students

Given the large number of interventions by OU tutors, the high level of student satisfaction with feedback quantity is easily understood. The strong content focus of assignments influences tutor feedback and make it easy for students to understand the marks they are given. The predominance of level two feedback (knowledge communication through the provision of correct or appropriate answers) appears to lead students to feel that they receive plenty of guidance about their errors and misunderstandings. However, there is a discrepancy between their general perception, revealed through the AEQ responses, that feedback aids their understanding and the analysis of feedback on specific assignments which shows that most of it does not bridge the understanding gap (figure four). This may be why many students are ambivalent in their response to the notion that increasing the quantity of written feedback would increase their learning further. It may also explain why some students have difficulty in understanding some of the feedback. The lack of linkage with the expected achievement demonstrated in the specimen answers may also explain why students do not place a high value on specimen answers.

The positive correlation between the omissions to errors ratio of content-related tutor interventions and the weighting of discursive questions within an assignment is due largely to the lack of criteria-referenced assessment of students' answers. OU science mark schemes usually award most marks for the author's expectations of content and it is difficult for students to know what is expected, Therefore, omission of material deemed relevant by the author is common. A student on the OU module with the highest omissions to errors feedback ratio commented that whether or not the right material to gain the marks was included in an assignment was a lottery. Some students on two other modules with high ratios reported difficulties in understanding what was required by questions. Nicol and Macfarlane-Dick (2004) claim that descriptive information about performance in relation to defined criteria is better received by students and more likely to be acted upon, provided the criteria can be understood (Higgins et al, 2001) and they are viewed holistically by tutors and students and are not regarded as a 'tick-list'.

Given the encouragement OU science tutors are given to highlight areas of mark loss within the assignment coversheet feedback summaries, it is not surprising that students measure their achievement by mark loss and have a negative view of learning.

Ding (1998) provides evidence that even if students read the feedback they receive, they do little with it. SHU students claim that they act on feedback when they think it is offering help. However, the predominance of content-focused interventions by both OU and SHU science tutors, coupled with topic-focused assignments means that very little of the feedback feeds forward to future assessment tasks. Students may have a general perception that they receive feedback quickly enough to be of use to them but, in practice, the feedback cannot be used to enhance future work. They attend to it, by reading it, but they cannot respond to it effectively and so its formative aspects are significantly diminished.

Conclusions

The analysis of written feedback revealed that a high quantity of feedback does not necessarily imply that the feedback is of high value and it may not meet the conditions described in the framework of Gibbs et al (2003).

It is clear that OU science students generally receive a great deal of feedback but it may not be sufficiently precise about future learning. The lack of explanation may also make the feedback difficult for some students to understand.

Although the feedback is returned within three weeks, its value is limited because it is content-dominated, and no longer relevant to the topic being studied. Comparatively little of it feeds forward to future assessment tasks. The strong content focus to feedback reflects the emphasis within tutor mark schemes but the absence of clear criteria for students against which their work will be assessed leads to the feedback also being omissions-dominated and to dissatisfaction among students.

The overall conclusion from this study is stark. If feedback does not aid learning and understanding and does not feed forward, it has limited value, even if crafted carefully and provided quickly.

Written feedback is resource-intensive and must be provided in the most effective ways to maximise students' learning. The form of feedback is dependent on the design of assessment, which should include progressive skills development so that feedback can feed forward effectively. Persuading students to value the skills aspects of feedback at least as highly as the feedback on content may be difficult.

Acknowledgements

The authors are grateful to Graham Gibbs and Claire Simpson, the former for his literature search of methods used to analyse feedback to students and the latter for analysing the AEQ responses. We also thank Pamela Budd, Hilary Denny, Jane Essex,

Christine Harris, Claire Rothwell and Gerry Spalton, the OU tutors who conducted the OU student interviews and the preliminary feedback analyses.

References

Bales, RF (1950) A set of categories for the analysis of small group interactions. *American Sociological Review* 15 (2), pp257-263.

Brown, E, Gibbs, G and Glover, C (2003) Evaluating tools for investigating the impact of assessment regimes on student learning. *BEE-j* Volume 2 (November). Available online at http://bio.ltsn.ac.uk/journal/vol2/beej-2-5.htm

Brown, S, Race, P and Smith, B (1996) *500 Tips on Assessment*, London, Kogan Page.

Ding, L (1998) Revisiting assessment and learning: implications of students' perspectives on assessment feedback. Paper presented to the *Scottish Educational Research Association Annual Conference*, University of Dundee, 25-26 September.

Elton, LRB. and Laurillard, D (1979) Trends in research on student learning. *Studies in Higher Education*, 4 (1), pp87-102.

Gibbs, G, Simpson, C and Macdonald, R (2003) Improving student learning through changing assessment – a conceptual and practical framework. *European Association for Research into Learning and Instruction, 2003, Padua, Italy*. Available on http://www.open.ac.uk/science/fdtl/documents/earli-2003.pdf

Gibbs, G and Simpson, C (2004) Does your assessment support your students' learning? *Journal of Teaching and Learning in Higher Education*, 1 (1) In Press.

Higgins, R, Hartley, P and Skelton, A (2001) Getting the message across: the problem of communicating assessment feedback. *Teaching in Higher Education*, 6 (2), pp269-274.

Hyland, F (2001) Providing effective support: investigating feedback to distance learners. *Open Learning* 16 (3), pp233-247.

Jarvis, P (1978) Students' learning and tutors' marking. *Teaching at a Distance*, 13, pp13-17.

Mutch, A (2003) Exploring the practice of feedback to students. *Active Learning in Higher Education*, 4 (1), pp24-38.

Nicol, D and Macfarlane-Dick, D (2004) Rethinking formative assessment in HE: a theoretical model and seven principles of good feedback practice. in: Juwah, C, Macfarlane-Dick, D, Matthew, R, Nicol, D, Ross, D and Smith, B, Enhancing Student Learning through Effective Feedback, Higher Education Academy Generic Centre, June 2004. Available at http://www.heacademy.ac.uk/senlef.htm

Roberts, D (1996) Feedback on assignments. Distance Education, 17 (1), pp95-116.

Online summative assessment with feedback as an aid to effective learning at a distance

Sally Jordan and Stephen Swithenby, Open University

Abstract

This paper describes the development and evaluation of an online assessment strategy for distance-taught students within the analytical context of the 11 conditions for effective formative assessment described by Gibbs and Simpson (2004). The assessment accompanies a course of short duration with attendant issues in providing effective feedback. A single summative assignment, supported by a practice assignment, awards marks that decrease with the degree of assistance required, and combines summative with formative capability. Feedback is instantaneous, detailed and targeted in response to the answer given by the student, thus prompting student action that promotes learning. Data on student perceptions, performance and study pattern have identified ways of optimising the assessment strategy to increase learning and, in so doing, to meet more closely the 11 conditions of the framework. Feedback from students has identified weaknesses in the distribution of student effort that are being addressed.

Background and module design

The study is based at the Open University (OU) in the UK, whose adult students are studying at a distance via supported open learning. Support is most commonly provided by detailed correspondence tuition, limited face-to-face tutorials and, increasingly, electronic means such as the telephone, computer conferences etc. The tutor is the agent for such support.

A new module *Maths for Science* was presented for the first time in September 2002, with the purpose of giving students confidence and practice in basic mathematical skills. It is a level one module of 10 CATS points, that is presented at three monthly intervals and leads to a simple pass/fail result. The module's assessment and support strategies were influenced strongly by (i) the length of the module and its skills focus and (ii) the desire to provide students with prompt and useful feedback. Of the eleven conditions proposed by Gibbs et al (2003) as a framework for understanding the ways in which assessment can drive effective learning, four of the conditions relating to feedback were particularly relevant:

- Sufficient feedback is provided, both often enough and in enough detail.

■ The feedback is provided quickly enough to be useful to students.

■ Feedback is received by students and attended to.

■ Feedback is acted upon by students to improve their work or their learning.

For such a short course, it is not practical to provide personal tutors as there is little time to establish an informed teacher-student relationship. Written feedback would introduce delays that are comparable with the study period and would militate against effective feedback. Summative assessment should be limited and lead to a clear understanding of the student's acquisition of basic skills.

The initial strategy adopted was to provide a single, summative, online end-of-course assignment ECA that was computer marked. The computer gave feedback that was instantaneous, detailed and targeted to the student's own misunderstandings. In addition, by allowing students three attempts at each question, with increasing feedback at each attempt, the ECA had an active teaching function, by enabling students to act immediately on the feedback provided. Finally, by awarding a mark for each question that decreased with the number of attempts and thus with the amount of feedback given, we could recognise partial achievement, albeit in a rather different way from the 'partial credit' used by others (Beevers et al 1999; McGuire et al 2002).

The introduction of an online ECA for a course of this type was seen as economically desirable. Teacher marking was eliminated. Templates and question types could be re-used and, when appropriate, questions could be generated randomly with minimal effort. In addition to developing an online ECA, the decision was made to develop a practice assessment PA in order to give students an opportunity to familiarise themselves with the technology and the question types and to reduce student anxiety (Sly 1999).

Interactive questions with formative feedback have been in use within the OU since the 1990s. A wide range of different question types have been developed. Usually delivered via CD-ROM they have been well received by students (Whitelock 1998), The question types used in *Maths for Science* are varied with only about one third of the multiple choice variety. The majority required data input, including the entering of mathematical expressions. A way of doing this simply has been recognised by Beevers and Paterson (2002) as one of the major challenges facing computer-assisted assessment in numerate disciplines. In *Maths for Science*, a 'superscript' button is the only departure from the standard alpha-numeric keyboard. All equivalent expressions are recognised as being of equal validity and, in some numerical questions, all values within a defined range are accepted as correct.

Feedback is provided at two levels. An incorrect response generates at the first attempt a simple notification of error 'Your answer is incorrect'. After a second incorrect response the feedback is explanatory and, where possible, is targeted on the error that has been made. For example the feedback shown in figure one (overleaf) recognises that the student's answer is numerically correct but that too many significant figures have been included and the units have been incorrectly stated. After a third attempt at a question, the student is told whether their answer is correct and a detailed explanation is provided.

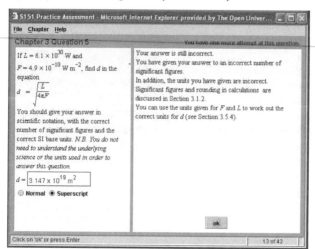

Figure 1. A question from the Maths for Science Practice Assessment

In addition to teaching feedback of the type discussed above, which is provided to students as they answer each question, they are also given a summary sheet at the end, This summary shows students which questions they answered correctly, and at which attempt, but it does not give an overall score. Weighting is applied to different sections of the course and borderline scripts are inspected in detail prior to the meeting of the Examination and Assessment Board and the release of the pass/fail result to students.

In order to limit opportunities for plagiarism, each student receives a randomly chosen set of questions drawn from a question bank. The questions are downloaded in a single download taking 2-3 minutes with a modem of the minimum specification. Delivering online assessments to students' home PCs has the risk of generating software or hardware incompatibilities and students are encouraged to attempt the practice assessment early in their studies. They are also encouraged to complete the ECA well before the deadline. Students are supported by the university's computing helpdesk with, by referral, software developers. Although over 80% of the students were only 'slightly' or 'not at all' familiar with technical internet issues, very few problems were reported and all of these proved tractable.

The assessments were designed to be delivered and submitted online but students may choose to close down the computer at any time. On resumption, the assessment restarts where it was abandoned. The Practice Assessment is available to students for the whole time they are studying and each ECA is made available to students for a limited time at the end of each presentation of the module. Within that time, students can spend as long as they like on the assessment and log on and off as often as they want to.

Evaluation

Maths for Science students have been surveyed by postal questionnaire. One survey, returned by 270 students, focused explicitly on students' use and perceptions of the ECA.

Another used the Assessment Experience Questionnaire, as described by Brown et al (2003) and identified potential issues for *Maths for Science* relating not only to the effectiveness of the feedback, but also to the distribution of the student effort. As a follow up, 50 students were telephoned or emailed in an attempt to gain greater insight into students' study patterns. In addition, there has been extensive data analysis of student use of the assessments and a question by question analysis of students' ECA answers.

There is a high level of engagement with both the End of Course and Practice Assessment though the distribution of effort is highly skewed. Students spend an average of about three and a half hours on the ECA. However, this average conceals a huge variation, from those who spend less than one hour to one student who spent over ten hours online. There is a corresponding variation in the number of separate online sessions spent on the ECA (1 to 22, with a median of 4) and in the total elapsed time from a student starting the ECA to pressing 'submit' (48 minutes to 18 days, with a median of 1.3 days). There is no obvious correlation between the amount of time spent on the ECA and the student's success (correlation coefficient = 0.23).

Around 90% of those who attempt the ECA have used the PA first, but the way in which they use it varies considerably. Most students spend a relatively small amount of the time on the PA just prior to starting the ECA (median < 1 hour). Others make extensive use of it, working through each question many times. One student spent nearly 24 hours active time on the PA. The mean is 2.6 hours. Students who have used the PA are very much more likely to submit an ECA although this is not necessarily a causal relationship

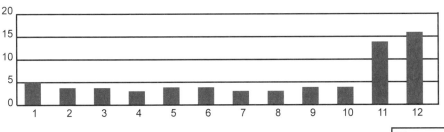

Figure 2. An example of a student estimate of their weekly study effort. ■ Hours

The distribution of effort generated by self report from students is shown in figure two. The driving influence of summative assessment just prior to submission deadlines is clear, particularly when this is combined with records of online activity.

The data on patterns of usage (Practice Assignment uptake, use of second and third attempts at questions in the ECA, etc) demonstrate that feedback is both being provided and being used. In some questions, students made excellent use of the teaching feedback provided. For example, in a question which asked for an answer to a specified number of significant figures, the targeted feedback resulted in *all* of the responses which contained a significant figures error being corrected by the next attempt.

Student views on the usefulness of feedback are superficially contradictory. 89% of the students agreed or strongly agreed with the statement 'the interactive feedback associated with the ECA questions helped me to learn' and 79% of the students agreed or strongly agreed that 'there were occasions when the detailed feedback enabled me to amend my answer and so to provide the correct answer at the second or third attempt.' Moreover, when asked 'What, for you, was the most positive aspect of [the module's] ECA?' many students commented on the instantaneous feedback. However, survey scores for 'timeliness of feedback' were low and the students' comments included several items such as 'As yet I have not had any feedback concerning this course'. This was initially disappointing, given that the primary reason for developing this online assessment system was to give instantaneous, detailed and targeted feedback. However, this result, combined with other findings reported in this symposium (Glover etc al 2004) suggests that this may reflect simply a difference in the use of the word 'feedback' by students and lecturers. For students, 'feedback' is about getting marks. The 'feedback' of pedagogical debate is considered by students to be teaching.

The overall views of students on this form of online assessment were favourable. 79% of the students would like more online assessments of this type in the future. The survey returns contained many positive comments, eg 'I found submitting the ECA on the web very convenient'; 'Perfect for distance learning'. However not all students find it an appropriate means of assessment; eg 'I do not feel comfortable taking an ECA online' and it is disappointing that 10% of students who did not submit an ECA gave as their reason the fact that they did not wish to submit the ECA electronically. Some of these were people with no computer access but some, often those who make extensive use of computers in their jobs, did not want to use a computer in their 'leisure' time, or did not consider it to be an appropriate assessment method.

Discussion and conclusions

The methodology for improvement using the framework of 11 conditions through which assessment supports effective learning includes stages of diagnosis, targeted reform of practice and further evaluation. In this case, the module design stage incorporated reflections on practice and the data reported above indicate that the strategy resulting from these reflections has been broadly successful. It is clear that the assessment strategy has secured student engagement with learning and that the feedback mechanisms have influenced student behaviour, ie they have fed forward into productive learning activity.

However, the distribution of effort data has indicated that learning might be improved further, with consequences for retention, if students made greater use of the Practice Assignment. A number of measures have been introduced to that end. Proactive contact is being made with students encouraging them to make greater use of both assignments. The PA itself has been redesigned to include greater flexibility in the order in which questions are attempted. In addition, mindful of the driving role of marks and the pattern of linkage between the ECA and the PA, the End of Course Assessment is being made available for a longer period so that students are able to engage with the ECA and thus be motivated to make heavier use of the PA over a longer period. In so doing, it is expected that the first two of the 11 conditions will be better fulfilled.

- Assessed tasks capture sufficient student time and effort.
- The tasks distribute student effort evenly across topics and weeks.

Acknowledgements

The authors gratefully acknowledge the module's software development team, led by Philip Butcher, and other members of the Course Team, especially Shelagh Ross, for their help in question writing and analysis. The authors have benefited from many helpful discussions with colleagues involved in the Formative Assessment in Science Teaching project, notably Graham Gibbs.

References

Beevers CE and Paterson JS (2002) Assessment in mathematics. In Khan, P and Kyle, J (eds). *Effective teaching and learning in mathematics and its applications.* Kogan Page, London

Beevers CE, Wild DG, McGuire GR, Fiddes DJ and Youngon MA (1999) Issues of partial credit in mathematical assessment by computer. *Alt-J*, Vol 7, 26-32.

Brown E, Gibbs G and Glover C. Evaluation tools for investigating the impact of assessment regimes on student learning. *BEE-j*, Volume 2 (November). Available online at http://bio/ltsn.ac.uk/journal/vol2/beej-2-5.htm

Gibbs G and Simpson C (2004) Does your assessment support your students' learning? *Journal of Teaching and Learning in Higher Education.* 1, (1), In press

Gibbs G, Simpson C and Macdonald R (2003). Improving student learning through changing assessment – a conceptual and practical framework. *European Association for Research into Learning and Instruction, 2003, Padua, Italy.* Available on http://www.open.ac.uk/science/fdtl/documents/earli-2003/pdf

McGuire GR, Youngson MA, Korabinski AA and McMillan D Partial credit in mathematics exams: a comparison of traditional and CAA exams, Proceedings of the 6th Computer Assisted Assessment Conference, Loughborough 2002, 223-230.

Sly L (1999) Practice tests as formative assessment improves students' performance on computer-managed learning assessments. *Assessment and Evaluation in Higher Education*, 24, No 3, 339-343

Whitelock, D (1998) S103 Students' response to the Block 2 CD-ROM materials: Findings of a postal survey. PLUM report 109 (Internal report), Institute of Educational technology, The Open University, Milton Keynes.

Perceptions of the value of different modes of tutor feedback

Chris Glover, Ranald Macdonald, John Mills and Stephen Swithenby*

Sheffield Hallam University, *Open University

Introduction

This paper reports on research carried out at Sheffield Hallam University as part of a study examining the potential for improving student learning by making changes to the way formative assessment and feedback is presented. The paper focuses on a part of the overall study, the perceptions of the quantity and usefulness of feedback in some biosciences and physical sciences subjects at the university. It will report quantitative survey data gathered from questionnaires administered to groups of between 15 and 100 students (depending on enrolment) on each of seven science courses at the university. In order to follow up student responses, and tutors' perception of these, 13 students were interviewed, and staff focus groups and individual interviews (seven) were held to illuminate and develop issues identified within the initial survey. Written feedback provided on tutor marked assignments was also analysed to further illuminate emerging issues.

The overarching framework within which the study is being carried out is a set of eleven conditions under which assessment best supports learning. These conditions are based on theory and empirical evidence from studies of strategic changes in assessment (Gibbs, 1999; Gibbs, 2002; Gibbs and Simpson, 2004b). The conditions suggest that assessment is most likely to support students' learning if it:

- captures sufficient study time and effort
- distributes student effort evenly across topics and weeks
- engages students in productive learning activity
- communicates clear and high expectations to students

Feedback should:

- be provided both often enough and in enough detail
- be provided quickly enough to be useful to students
- focus on learning rather than on marks or students themselves
- be linked to the purpose of the assignment and to criteria

- be understandable to students, given their sophistication

- be received by students and attended to

- be acted upon by students to improve their work or their learning

The extent to which these conditions have been fulfilled has been investigated using the Assessment Experience Questionnaire (AEQ); a questionnaire (SHUQ) which identified many possible sources of feedback and evaluated the prevalence and perceived value of each; and interviews with both staff and students. The following describes the main concerns of the 11 conditions, and a brief summary of the main findings.

Early findings from the two questionnaires and staff and student interviews

1. The quantity and distribution of student effort

Students distinguished between two different kinds of distribution of effort: being selective about what to study in relation to assessment demands, and studying different amounts in different weeks in relation to the timing of assessment demands. They did not distinguish consistently between different characteristics of the feedback itself (its quantity and qualities), but did distinguish between the feedback itself and what they did with it.

2. The quality and level of student effort

Students worked in spurts, tending to concentrate on material that is going to be assessed. Most felt they needed to learn the material provided, or directed to, by the tutor, but did not read around their subject. Gibbs and Simpson (2004) reported that diary studies (eg Innis, 1996) showed how students in the UK:

> *allocate their time largely to assessed tasks and that this becomes a more narrow focus over time as they become more experienced students, allocating as little as 5% of their time to unassessed study tasks by year three. (p10)*

Whilst evidence suggests that the ideal would be to encourage students to distribute student effort evenly across topics and weeks, and to spread out assessments to enable this, such strategies are often prevented by issues such as module structure and class sizes.

3. The quality of feedback

Students perceived that feedback did not necessarily indicate how to improve subsequent pieces of work. Overall levels of understanding were not clear. Whilst feedback helped to explain the summative element of the assessment, there was a need to make the feedback more understandable, particularly as a formative tool.

4. The quantity and timing of feedback

It was clear that students recognise the potential of feedback as both a formative and important element of their course. However, the amount of feedback they received, and the timing of the feedback was variable.

These initial studies set an agenda for the next phase of the research – a better understanding of students' perceptions of the levels of feedback provided, and the relative effectiveness of the many different sources of that feedback. In order to explore these issues, the second questionnaire (the SHUQ) was devised. It was administered to a group of 147 year two and year four science students.

The questionnaire covered 20 types of feedback believed to be used in the surveyed science courses, broadly grouped under written and oral.

Analysis of data from this questionnaire indicated that students perceived that feedback was most helpful in understanding what they were doing wrong, and what needed to be addressed in order to improve. Where students were not helped, however, was on the practical application of the knowledge of *how* to improve – the development of the skills needed to help improve their work. A frequently occurring example through the student responses has been that of referencing, where they had been told that they were referencing inappropriately, but were confused about how to correct this mistake.

What appears to be the underlying problem here is not one of quantity of feedback, but one of quality. Giving a lot of feedback does not necessarily mean that good feedback has been given. Feedback may be linked to assessment criteria, which may give students a clear picture of what is needed and where they have gone wrong. It may not necessarily indicate what is wrong in relation to these criteria, or more importantly, what students need to do to put it right.

Feedback often consisted of unhelpful comments which they did not understand. There was a general lack of detailed explanation of what students had done wrong, and sometimes tutors provided no explanation. Purely negative, or non-constructive remarks (eg poor, lazy), were not helpful to students at all.

Where staff felt that any of the above concerns were particularly applicable to their own modules, or where they believed they had specific issues which needed to be addressed, they devised strategies to improve assessment and feedback practices for their specific modules or courses. It is important to note that no one strategy was appropriate for all modules – each had different issues, and needed a tailored approach which addressed those specific requirements. The strategies staff devised included:

1. regular in-lecture tests with instant feedback

2. increased amount and timing of feedback on VLE

3. specific feedforward sessions to introduce coursework

4. improved turnaround time

5.   questions provided at end of lectures – discussed at beginning of the next lecture

6.   increased peer assessment

Two sample groups of students were surveyed to ascertain if any improvements in their experience could be identified. One group was given the SHUQ for a second time (cycle two), the results being compared to those from the first SHUQ data set (cycle one).

The other group was asked to state briefly whether they were in favour of the tutor's intervention – strategy one in the list above – and if so, why (or, indeed why not). Comments were written on post-its, and were collected and collated.

From analysis of the data provided by both sample groups it was possible to identify the following trends:

1) Oral feedback was still perceived to be of lesser value than written, but perceptions were changing. Compared with the first cycle, most levels of individual face-to-face feedback (six out of nine categories) showed evidence of improvement in students' perceptions, the remaining three categories showing no change. For example, 35% of students claimed to have received no oral feedback from support staff in the first cycle. In the second cycle, only 28% of students claimed to have received no oral feedback from support staff, an improvement of 7% overall. (See table one for all details.)

What was perhaps most surprising was the large percentage of students who claimed to have received no feedback in support sessions and laboratories, activities where tutor contact was high. In order to attempt to identify possible causes for this, a small group of students involved in laboratory work were asked whether tutors came to them and offered help whilst they were working on their laboratory projects. All students concurred, which

Type of oral feedback	Percentage of students who claimed to have received none in cycle one	Change observed in cycle two
to all students in lectures	14%	no change
From support staff	35%	7% improvement
by visiting the tutor's office	46%	26% improvement
personal from lecturers in labs etc	57%	15% improvement
from other students' in group assignments	44%	no change
from lecturer in corridor	72%	27% improvement
peer feedback on my assignment	44%	no change
during telephone call to lecturer	70%	24% improvement

Table 1 Levels of oral feedback

seemed to contradict the questionnaire findings. However, when questioned further, the explanation became clear: tutor interventions in practical sessions, and face to face feedback in lectures etc was not feedback at all – it was 'just good teaching'. Here was clear evidence of a further mismatch between tutor and student perceptions of the nature of feedback.

2) Changes in perceptions about written feedback were similar to those of oral feedback. Compared with the first cycle, eight out of the 12 categories showed some improvement, the other four remaining the same (see table two).

Here the most noticeable improvements were in the use of the VLE for feedback purposes (20% improvement rate), and the use of email as a means of communication (27%). Whilst all students now claimed to have had marks or grades on assignments, and all had received some written feedback, it is unclear how, in the first cycle, 6% and 8% of students respectively claimed to never have received any.

In summary, early signs are that certain of the strategies are having positive effects, particularly the in-lecture tests, where students have already indicated the positive

Type of written feedback	Percentage of students who claimed to have received none in cycle one	Change observed in cycle two
marks or grades on assignments	6%	6% improvement
on assignments	8%	8% improvement
results of classroom tests	15%	6% improvement
MCQ in-class test scores	16%	no change
model answers	27%	no change
posted on notice boards	36%	no change
on drafts of assignments	42%	5% improvement
automated MCQ feedback on Blackboard (VLE)	42%	no change
by email	57%	27% improvement
other students' feedback	56%	8% improvement
on Blackboard	73%	20% improvement
on exams	31%	7% improvement

Table 2 Levels of written feedback

benefits on their learning of attending these tests. There is also a strong suggestion, however, that some practices have improved very little, and in some cases, not at all.

3) Feedback still offers little help with skills development.

Table three indicates that, whilst certain of the categories have assumed different levels of relevance to the students, it is clear that, over the research period so far, there has been little improvement, particularly in the area of skills development.

The staff perception is clear: even if students do read comments they do little with them. Content is often seen as discrete and subject-specific. If the feedback they receive does not help students to improve generic skills, but is instead focused solely on subject-specific aspects of assignments, then feedback may be irrelevant for subsequent work on other units (see Ding 1998). This notion is reinforced by the SHUQ cycle one finding that "feedback helped me understand specific course content" was only ranked 9th most helpful category out of 12. This response raises questions about the value of course-

Change in ranking from cycle one	2004 position	How the feedback helped
Improvement by three places	1	Made it clear what I need to do to improve
No change	2	Helped me appreciate how well I am getting on
No change	3	Motivated me to keep going and try harder
Down three places	4	Helped me to understand where I went wrong
Up one place	5	Helped me with subsequent assignments
Down one place	6	Helped towards exams
No change	7	Engaged me in further study
Up one place	8	Helped me understand specific course content
Down one place	9	Helped me understand why I got my grade or mark
No change	10	Helped me develop my intellectual skills
Up one place	11	Helped me develop my academic skills
Down one place	12	Helped me develop my learning skills

Table 3 Helpfulness of feedback

content specific feedback at two levels – the degree to which it helps with that particular piece of work, and the degree to which it can, or should, feed forward to the next.

4) Whilst feedback included more emphasis on ways the student could improve, turnaround time was still problematic, although there was improvement in some subjects. End-loading of assessments because of timetabling of modules means that any feedback can become summative rather than formative. Timetabling is thought by some to prevent the implementation of strategies designed to overcome many of these problems.

Mutch (2003) suggests that:

> *Advice literature needs to focus not only on improvements in individual practice, but also on issues such as programme design... which places reflection on feedback at its heart. (p36)*

Although staff have argued that logistical issues such as timetabling larger numbers of students, the effects of modularisation, etc, are perhaps problems beyond the remit of individual tutors, one specific issue which both staff and students feel needs to be addressed is the timing of the *return* of feedback to students. This has emerged as, perhaps, one of the most crucial issues, and one which underpins all 11 conditions of learning. In essence, as Gibbs and Simpson (2004a) maintain:

> *If students do not receive feedback fast enough then they will have moved on to new content and the feedback is irrelevant to their ongoing studies and is extremely unlikely to result in additional appropriate learning activity, directed by the feedback. (p16)*

However much it is argued that feedback should be formative rather than summative, when assignments are not returned in time, students cannot use feedback formatively. Tutors have argued that feeding forward is less important, as students are mark-focused anyhow. This contention is echoed by Higgins et al (2001), who report:

> *We have heard this argument from many academics over the last few years: students are indifferent to tutors' feedback comments and care only about the grade. At best, they will read a response to their work only when it provides 'correct answers' for the exam. (p270)*

Evidence from the research at Sheffield Hallam University does not support this contention, however. Students there maintain that, where help is offered, the feedback is read. 74% of students responded that they do read the feedback carefully and try to understand, with as few as 6% only reading the marks. However, there is still uncertainty about how well it is attended to. It may be read carefully but may not acted upon. Here only 34% of students responding claim to use the feedback to go over what they have done (compare Ding 1998).

If feedback is to influence future learning successfully, it is self-evident that assessed work must be returned in time for the student to engage with the feedback. Hornby (2004) observes: "As the old adage goes, 'Feedback is like fish it goes off after a week'".

There are debates about what can be considered 'timely' – suggestions include: immediate; within minutes/hours rather than days. For tutors at Sheffield Hallam, timely is couched in terms of a three week turnaround for most types of work, a particular exception being laboratory reports which, because of the need to stagger the practical work, groups of students would be starting their assignment after others had received theirs back – a clear opportunity for plagiarism which needed to be prevented.

For many students, timely is at least getting work back in time for revision, if not to feed forward to the next piece of work. Overall, students were dissatisfied with the speed in which work is returned. When asked about their satisfaction, more students felt that the feedback they receive was too late to be useful than those who felt they got it back in plenty of time. Responses can be seen in table four below.

	Always	Most of the time	Some of the time	It always comes back quickly
Whatever feedback I get comes back too late to be useful	3%	43%	51%	3%

Table 4 Timeliness of feedback

In general, students argued that the timely return of work would depend on the nature of the assignment, but overall were dissatisfied with some of their modules.

Conclusion

In this study it has become evident that, if feedback is to successfully influence future learning:

■ assessed work must be returned in time for the student to engage with the feedback

■ feedback on content is only useful if it changes understanding

■ feedback on process becomes feedforward if it can be used in subsequent work

The research so far has produced clear evidence that there is a need for improved and speedier feedback. It has also been shown that improvements to assessment practice devised by tutors only have lead to relatively small changes in student perception and satisfaction.

However, the research is still in a developmental stage, and it is as yet unclear what enduring effects these changes may have had. Similarly there is an emergent belief that such strategies are merely 'tinkering' with assessment practices, and there is a growing perception of a need for more radical changes to assessment which incorporate more feedback, eg peer assessment; larger, high stake assignments split into staged, lower stake assignments with feedback on each stage. To place the research into a broader context, it is argued that changes in assessment and feedback practices should not be just at the level of individual practice, important though these may be. Assessment should be an integral part of the students' learning, and constructively aligned (Biggs, 1999) with a strategy which is seen as an important part of course design and planning. Unless this can be achieved, then it is unlikely that the findings from the research, summarised in the paragraph above, will be realised, and individual initiatives, however well intentioned, will only act as stop gap solutions.

References

Biggs, J (1999) *Teaching for quality learning at university.* Buckingham: The Society for Research into Higher Education and The Open University Press

Ding, L (1998) Revisiting assessment and learning: implications of students' perspectives on assessment feedback. Paper presented to *Scottish Educational Research Association Annual Conference*, University of Dundee, 25-26 September

Gibbs, G (1999) Using assessment strategically to change the way students learn. In Brown, S and Glasner, A (eds), *Assessment Matters in Higher Education: Choosing and Using Diverse Approaches*. Buckingham: SRHE/Open University Press

Gibbs, G (2002) Evaluating the impact of formative assessment on student learning behaviour. *European Conference for Research into Learning and Instruction Assessment Conference*, Newcastle.

Gibbs, G and Simpson, C (2004a) Measuring the response of students to assessment: the Assessment Experience Questionnaire in Rust, C (ed) *Improving Student Learning Theory Research and Scholarship*. Oxford: OCSLD.

Gibbs, G and Simpson, C (2004b) Does your assessment support your students' learning? *Journal of Teaching and Learning in Higher Education*, 1 (1) (forthcoming)

Higgins, R, Hartley, P and Skelton, A (2001) Getting the message across. *Teaching in Higher Education* 6 (2) pp 269-274

Hornby, W (2004) Dogs, Stars, Rolls Royces and Old Double Decker Buses: Efficiency And Effectiveness In Assessment. Draft paper presented at one of a series of eight workshops on various assessment sub-topics were run for the Scottish higher education sector between January and June 2004. http://www.enhancementthemes.ac.uk/defaultpage131cd0BlueSub.aspx?pageID=139 Accessed 10th October, 2004

Mutch, A (2003) Exploring the practice of feedback to students. *Active Learning in Higher Education* 4(1) pp 24-38